AF332992

THE WORLD ECONOMIC ORDER
PAST AND PROSPECTS

THE WORLD ECONOMIC ORDER

Past and Prospects

Edited by
Sven Grassman
and
Erik Lundberg

First edition 1981
Reprinted 1983

Published by
THE MACMILLAN PRESS LTD
London and Basingstoke
Companies and representatives
throughout the world

Printed in Hong Kong

British Library Cataloguing in Publication Data

The world economic order
  1. International economic relations – Congresses
I. Grassman, Sven II. Lundberg, Erik
382.1   HF1410

ISBN 0–333–26999–3

Contents

Preface

The Institute for International Economic Studies at the University of Stockholm has during the past few years been engaged on a research project concerning the international economic order with particular emphasis on the relations between the developed and the less developed countries. One result of these efforts was a conference, in commemoration of the University of Stockholm's Centenary Jubilee, attended by international scholars in the field of development economics which was held in Saltsjöbaden, Stockholm, in August 1978. The papers presented at the conference as well as part of the discussions are published in this volume.

We are grateful to the SAREC organisation in Stockholm for financing the conference, which was arranged by a committee consisting of Sven Grassman, Erik Lundberg, and myself. The volume has been edited by Grassman and Lundberg who have also written the introduction. The success of the conference is largely due to the efficient research assistance and organising work carried out by Birgitta Eliason, Refik Erzan, and Edda Liljenroth.

The conference was a great stimulus for the researchers at our Institute, and I hope that this volume will be of similar interest to all scholars in the field of economic development and international economic relations.

The editors and publishers wish to thank the following who have kindly given permission for the use of copyright material: the International Monetary Fund, for the data from *International Financial Statistics*; North-Holland Publishing Company, for the table from 'An International Comparison of Industrial Efficiency: Peru and the U.S.A.' by C. Clague, in *Review of Economics and Statistics*, vol. 49 (1967); the Organisation for Economic Co-operation and Development, Paris, for the table from the report *Trade by Commodities, Market Summaries: Imports*, vol. 1 (1975); the United Nations Publications Board, for the tables from the *UN Yearbook of International Trade Statistics, 1977*, the *Handbook of International Trade and Development Statistics* and the *UN*

Yearbook of Industrial Statistics; and the World Bank, for the tables from *World Development Report 1978*.

Institute for International Economic Studies   **ASSAR LINDBECK**
University of Stockholm
December 1978

List of Participants

Dr Mohiuddin Alamgir (Bangladesh), Bangladesh Institute of Development Studies, Dacca

Professor Samir Amin (Senegal), African Institute for Economic Development and Planning, Dakar

Professor Jagdish Bhagwati (USA), Massachusetts Institute of Technology, Cambridge

Professor William Branson (USA), Princeton University, Princeton

Professor Michael Bruno (Israel), The Hebrew University, Jerusalem

Professor Hollis Chenery (USA), World Bank, Washington, DC

Professor Kemal Dervis (USA), World Bank, Washington, DC

Professor Carlos Díaz-Alejandro (USA), Yale University, New Haven

Dr Rolf Eidem (Sweden), Institute for International Economic Studies, Stockholm

Professor Ronald Findlay (USA), Columbia University, New York

Professor Herbert Giersch (West Germany), Institut für Weltwirtschaft, Kiel

Dr Sven Grassman (Sweden), Institute for International Economic Studies, Stockholm

Dr Carl Hamilton (Sweden), Institute for International Economic Studies, Stockholm

Dr Gary Hufbauer (USA), US Treasury, Washington, DC

Professor Richard Jolly (United Kingdom), University of Sussex, Brighton

Dr Donald Keesing (USA), World Bank, Washington, DC

Professor Ryutaro Komiya (Japan), University of Tokyo, Tokyo

Professor János Kornai (Hungary), Hungarian Academy of Sciences, Budapest

Professor Arthur Lewis (USA), Princeton University, Princeton

Professor Assar Lindbeck (Sweden), Institute for International Economic Studies, Stockholm

Professor Erik Lundberg (Sweden), Stockholm School of Economics, Stockholm

Professor Ronald McKinnon (USA), Stanford University, Stanford

Professor Michael Michaely (Israel), The Hebrew University, Jerusalem

Professor Gunnar Myrdal (Sweden), Institute for International Economic Studies, Stockholm

Professor Louka Katseli-Papaefstratiou (USA), Yale University, New Haven

Professor Richard Portes (United Kingdom), Birkbeck College, London

Dr Marian Radetzki (Sweden), Institute for International Economic Studies, Stockholm

Professor Carlos Rodriguez (USA), Columbia University, New York

Mr Maurice Scott (United Kingdom), Nuffield College, Oxford

Professor Amartya Sen (United Kingdom), Nuffield College, Oxford

Dr Peter Svedberg (Sweden), Institute for International Economic Studies, Stockholm

Professor Bo Södersten (Sweden), University of Lund, Lund

Dr Hans Tson Söderström (Sweden), Institute for International Economic Studies, Stockholm

Professor Jean Waelbroeck (Belgium), Université Libre de Bruxelles, Brussels

Professor Stanislaw Wellisz (USA), Columbia University, New York

Dr Alexander J. Yeats (Switzerland), UNCTAD, Geneva

Introduction
On the Nature of the International Economic Disorder

Sven Grassman
and
Erik Lundberg (Sweden)

During the last decade resignation and desperation with the slow rate of progress in reducing famine, disease and inadequate living standards for large portions of world population has prompted increasingly urgent and impatient all-out formulations and policies for change in the international economic system—culminating in the United Nations' proposal for a New International Economic Order. When the stagnation of the 1970s, unprecedented in postwar history, was superimposed on the persistent problems of inequity and economic disorganisation in the less developed countries, this further weakened the potential of substantial income transfers.

The fact that attempts to create satisfactory economic growth in the poorest countries have proved so difficult, and the fact that the wealthy industrialised economy could also fail so blatantly, prompted questions as to whether there are deficiencies in the total international economic system as such. The Stockholm University Centenary Symposium on the *Past and Prospects of the World Economic Order*, giving rise to the present conference volume, is one of many attempts to sort out, define and give some partial answers to such staggering questions concerning the very functioning of the world economy.

It is an interesting question how and why there is such a general dissatisfaction with the international economic order, especially from

the point of view of representatives of the less-developed countries (LDCs). First, it must be noted, of course, that there is no operational definition of the concept 'world economic order', and nobody at this symposium tried to present anything approaching a definition. Perhaps a kind of loose definition may be discovered just by looking closely at all the different problems that the papers contained, as well as at all the ramifications of the intensive discussions pursued during the symposium. But to this type of 'definition in terms of operation' should be added problems that we had not time to include but clearly belong to the functioning of the world economic order.

Whatever the present economic order means it must be borne in mind that nobody, no national or international authority, has *chosen* the present order. And there will be very little of conscious choice as to a future order. To be able to understand the nature of the present international system—whatever it means—it must be looked at from the point of view of a complex historical development process with roots back into the colonial conditions of the eighteenth and nineteenth centuries. Further, we cannot understand the malfunctioning of the present system without also looking into the disintegration processes during the interwar period. Of particular importance is the explosive rise of new nations after the war, as well as the unique development experiences in the 1950s and 1960s.

It is natural for economists to start the analysis from a critical attitude as to the performance of economic systems. The exposure of the failures of the system is a necessary condition for finding ways of reform or persuasive arguments as to a radical change in the system. But a reader of this volume will find that an effort has been made to give a balanced account of the working of the world economic system, even if much emphasis is put on the failures. In fact, a most surprising part of the postwar experience is the success as to rapid growth and development of international trade and finance. This was a big surprise from the point of view of the general pessimistic expectations prevailing at the beginning of the postwar period and even in comparison with the rather more optimistic outlook at the beginning of the 1960s. In comparison with the industrialisation and growth of underdeveloped European countries during the nineteenth century, the performance during the postwar period of present LDCs has been much superior, both as to growth and development of trade. As to the development of income distribution, the experiences have varied a lot, but they can hardly have been worse than in Europe during the nineteenth century.

In a way it is something of a paradox that the *average*, surprisingly

good performance of the LDCs during the postwar period is now being considered as rather frustating. Much emphasis is placed on the widening income gaps—both as between LDCs and developing countries (DCs), as between the LDC economies themselves, and also inside these countries. Performance is regarded as good or bad depending on what the reference is—having earlier superior or inferior experiences in mind, or expectations that are moving with changing conditions. For instance, when considering the performance of the international financial system, we may compare its relative stability during the 1974–76 years of great disturbances with the nearly complete breakdown of the financial system after 1929 and its subsequent very serious repercussions on the LDC world. This time the tremendous balance-of-payments disturbances following the oil price shock had hardly any contractive effects on most LDCs, largely thanks to the resilience of the international financial system. But the expectations tend to shift upwards with the experiences. Therefore most observers are rather inclined to neglect the surprisingly good performance of the system and instead concentrate attention on the rising instability due to the rapid accumulation of debts of many LDCs.

There is a bad habit of putting all the LDCs into one category and working with only one dichotomy: the LDC world versus the industrialised world. Such simplifying categories may be useful for some types of problems. But in this volume we are continuously reminded of the dangers of working with such extremely heterogeneous groupings. The complexity of the world order and its performance very much refers to the big *dispersion* in achievement of the LDCs; we are not even quite sure where to draw the boundary line to the 'rich' countries in a continuum—at Israel, Spain, or at Brazil? The gaps (in GNP per head) are wider inside the category of LDCs than between the richest LDCs and the average of the industrialised countries. The symposium group of economists were well aware of the consequent difficulties involved in generalisations about conditions in LDCs. And yet—with tongue in cheek—the participants often had to use the simple categories of rich and poor countries. Also obviously there was a clear awareness that the world economy does not only consist of LDCs (in the usual sense) and Western industrialised countries, including Japan. Attention was also paid to the Eastern socialist third of the world.

When deliberately assigning rather specific subjects to our contributors, the organisers have endeavoured to obtain analytical treatments of some different aspects of the functioning of the international economy.

The problems range from trade and technology to international finance and price formation on world markets. Our aim has been to sort out a number of aspects that we think are particularly relevant for the discussion of the gross inequities and malfunctioning of the world economy.

In Figure 1 we have depicted some of the most pertinent aspects of the international economic system, topics that are treated from different angles in the essays collected in this book. With the setup of problems presented in this volume the overwhelming impression from the analysis is that the poor performance, compared with expectations and hopes, and the inequities of the world today are only to a limited extent due to deficiencies in the international exchange itself—as manifest in the rules of the game, trade policies, access to markets, transfer of technology and the formation of prices on world markets.

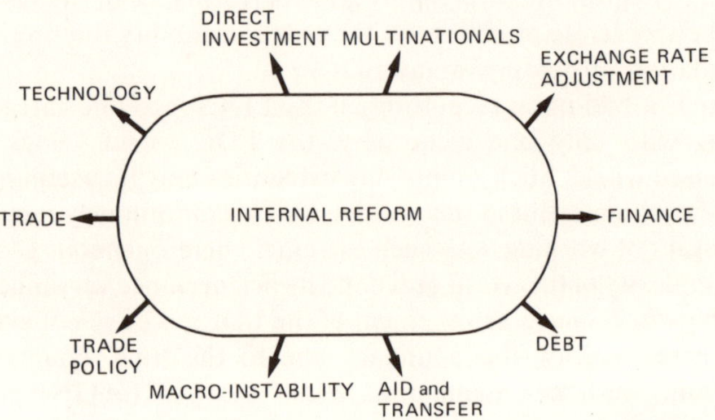

Fig. 1

If one wants to take the world economic order concept in an extremely broad sense it is of course true that any system that allows famine, instability and grossly unjust income distribution between nations is a bad and a deficient system. Such a sweeping and non-economic interpretation of the international economic system concept is, however, not very helpful. Taking a more concrete attitude, and accepting present realities as to geographical split-up, differences in

natural wealth, social history and present educational levels, one arrives at the conclusion that the functioning of the international part of the economic system, in the particular respects indicated in Figure 1, could not be a major obstacle for growth and prosperity in the world.

The trade income ratio for the whole world was 13 per cent in 1975, measured as world exports divided by world GNP.[1] Already from this single ratio it should be evident that trade, interaction and communication between nations cannot possibly be the major reason for, source of, or obstacle to, world output and prosperity. International division of labour can no doubt bring substantial gains and increased efficiency for individual nations, as could denial of such participation represent corresponding losses of potential increased income. But given the fact that nations vary so much in size, and the fact that most small economies are very open and rely more heavily on trade with other nations, while larger countries are inward-looking with small trade–income ratios, it makes little sense to regard the functioning and the terms of economic interaction between nations as the general cause of poverty and inequity.

In a sense, it would be less misleading to attribute much of the inequity and inefficiency in the international economic system to the fact that the size of nations and their population and natural endowments are so unevenly distributed over the world. If the interaction between nations as such were to be the major source of wealth and, conversely, non-participation in this interchange would be a major reason for explaining the poverty of some countries, one would expect wealth to be proportional to the smallness and openness of nations – that is, if the international trading system is a good and efficient one. On the other hand, if the system is inefficient and non-conducive to growth and wealth one would rather expect that great, inward-looking nations would be more wealthy. When looking at the development experience of different nations, we find that in the rich world there is no correlation whatsoever between openness and reliance on trade on the one hand and income level on the other hand—the United States is at least as well off as the North European countries. In the poor world we find that the biggest and rather closed economies suffer from the worst poverty, while some of the small, open and trade-reliant nations have experienced the quickest economic development.

In general, the evidence of today's wealth distribution and the past development experience suggests that the functioning of international markets and the reliance of national economies on trade cannot be the major source of or obstacle to wealth in the world economy. Trying to

explain poverty, inequity and inefficiency in terms of deficiencies in international exchange does not seem to be consistent with economic realities in the present and past. The issue seems to be rather a *projection* of problems of individual economies on an abstract and allegedly deficient international economic system. The search for scapegoats is common in all political and economic intercourse, and it is understandable in the context of desperate hopes and frustration in a world of famine and despair. Internal evils have always been projected onto foreign enemies by princes and presidents throughout history. In the case of the poor world's demand for a New International Economic Order the projection of internal evils onto international markets and institutions is quite natural. It should rather be viewed as a political motto in the rally for increased real transfers and help to bring about necessary internal reforms.

No doubt the unevenness in national endowments combined with deficiencies in international markets strongly discriminate against certain types of nations and producers. This is a major subject of some of the present contributions. What one may object to is the attempt to view the major part of world economic disorder today in terms of deficient international exchange. That might be true to a limited extent, as is clearly brought out by the intense attempts to cope with the terms-of-trade problem—both the ethics and the economic mechanics of it—that are to be found in many places in this volume. When scrutinising the various aspects of the system treated in this volume, however, we rather find that the present system, with necessary amendments, is of some help for certain nations, that it is a tremendous source of wealth and growth for certain other nations and that it has very little to offer a few nations of today such as, say, Bangladesh. However, it is difficult to see that any conceivable new or alternative international economic system as to trade, technology, finance and price formation in the world markets would help some of the poorest countries, because it is not deficiencies in the international system that are the reason for their poverty. The solutions for these countries must mainly be sought in massive internal reforms and unrequited real transfers on a scale that *no* international economic system whatsoever would bring about. On the other hand such transfers are feasible in *all* international economic systems, including the present one, if the political will to, and economic conditions for, such a change are fulfilled.

As mentioned above, we are not able to define the world economic order in any precise terms, but that does not prevent us from discussing

various aspects that clearly belong to it. As economists we have an urge to give precision to the analysis of these various aspects by presenting and using economic statistics and by theoretical analysis or model-building. There are a lot of time-series statistics and comparative country statistics in this volume. At the same time there exists a general awareness of the serious deficiencies in these statistics, especially referring to many of the LDCs. The critical attitude to the sources of statistics as well as to the manipulation of the primary data in order to obtain averages and time-series of aggregate nature does not prevent us from using these statistics—even those of very doubtful character—for reaching approximate and tentative conclusions and grand generalisations.

The defence of this acceptance of often bad statistics is on the lines that these statistics are better than no statistical information at all, that they are the best available, and anyhow statistics are an indispensable part of our language. An awareness of the deficiencies of available statistical information is always at the back of our minds, but it does not prevent us from drawing interesting although preliminary conclusions about the size of gaps, trends in development, etc. Our hope or belief is that challenging inferences, although based on statistical information of doubtful value, will mean progress in the understanding of the system. The results will—in the progress of scientific research—be scrutinised and ultimately replaced by new research with improved statistics and better methods of analysis.

In the division of work among economists in this field there is an important group of theorists and model-builders. They are raising relevant questions, bringing theoretical order into the analysis, and ultimately having their theories tested by means of available statistics. Some few model-builders—they were represented at this symposium— have their analytical exercises based on such high levels of abstraction that demands of testing by means of existing statistics would be regarded as a misunderstanding or even an insult. And yet such theories might be useful and needed for long-run systematic thinking. Other models are closer to reality—for example, those referring to economic growth and the formation of terms of trade—and are needed for interpreting strategic bits of the international economic order. In the volume the reader will find in every chapter more or less sophisticated theories, on varying levels of abstraction, of how different parts of the international system may be related. And certainly all these bits of statistical information and analysis can only give partial aspects of how the international system works.

It is natural that the main emphasis is on *the past* of the system, how it seems to have worked, especially during the postwar period. An understanding of the past development is of course a necessary condition for knowledge about its way of operating at present and of making plausible forecasts about the future.

Among the group of economists participating there was a great variety of political creeds, concealed or open. Economists nowadays are very aware of valuation issues; they are even sometimes conscious of the risk that their choice of model or even of statistics is determined by some kind of valuation of aims, feeling of injustice, hopes for a future better world, etc. Different views within our group came out quite clearly in the way we emphasised and weighed failures and successes in the development of the system. That was probably also the case with our fears and hopes about future trends.

Behind these hopes and fears there were, or should have been, some kind of *ethical valuations* and principles. In the papers and discussions, stress was sometimes laid on mutual interests of people in the world in rich and poor countries. More rapid growth in LDCs would, according to this view, stimulate the economies in the industrialised countries and vice versa. On the other hand, strong views, but with evidence, are represented among the essays, according to which there are inevitable conflicts between poor and rich countries. Expansion in rich countries to an indeterminable extent is going on at the cost of development in poor countries.

Conflicting views on such fundamental questions can partly be related to conflicts over ethical principles. There are relationships between ethical principles and norms for international income distribution. But these principles are conflicting and—as the present essays show—they cannot easily be clearly stated and isolated. The stated ethical principles are in practice not at all the same as those that can be revealed from actual policies. There is no ethical consensus as to norms of income distribution among countries and people—not even among enlightened economists. Compromises on unclear ethical grounds are being made all the time, and they are necessarily unclear. One reason for this is that we never know well enough the consequences of alternative policies as to efficiency and income distribution.

ENDNOTE

1. Sources for these figures are the *International Financial Statistics* and the *World Bank Atlas* (1977).

Part I

Trade Structure

1 The Rate of Growth of World Trade, 1830–1973

Arthur Lewis (USA)

I

Why did world trade grow so rapidly after the Second World War, up at least to the recession commencing in 1974? The growth rate from say 1953 to 1973 averaged 8.0 per cent per year.[1] The period immediately preceding the war was disastrous; 1913 to 1939 averaged only 0.9 per cent per year. But even in the so-called golden age of capitalism, say 1873 to 1913, the rate of growth of world trade averaged only 3.3 per cent per year.

The jump to 8 per cent per year caught us by surprise. Economists had adjusted themselves to the idea that international trade could no longer serve as an 'engine of growth', to use a phrase of Dennis Robertson's. A whole subset of development themes was invented to cope with a world where trade was stagnant—balanced growth, import substitution, structural inflation, the two-gap model, regional integration—all these are vital if world trade is growing at 1 per cent per year, but are trivial for countries with some flexibility, if it is growing at 8 per cent. It took some time to realise that world trade was growing at unprecedented speed; now we are in danger of assuming that it will always grow at this speed, and if it does not, we may again take some time to catch up.

This paper originated in the desire to discover whether this fast postwar speed was indeed unprecedented, by pushing our data of world trade further back into the nineteenth century; and if there were earlier periods of fast growth, whether we could identify their causes and make useful comparisons with our own experiences. The paper has turned out differently from its original plan. It was to have been a long analytical exercise accompanied by a brief statistical appendix. Instead, preparing the statistical appendixes has taken all the time available; they have become almost a separate paper.

The trouble is that hard data (customs returns based on current values) get scarcer as one pushes backwards, to the extent that it does not seem worthwhile to attempt a guess for all countries before 1850. Already in that year about half of our total of world trade is based on estimates of varying quality, compared with 20 per cent in 1872. Hitherto all quantitative discussion of world trade before 1870 has derived from a small table in Mulhall's *Dictionary of Statistics*, which contains figures for the sum of imports and exports at 20-year intervals starting in 1830. Simultaneously with testing his results, I offer an annual series.

II

The sum of the exports of the USA, UK, France and Germany[2] grew at 4.8 per cent per annum (constant prices) between 1830 and 1860, comparing with 3.4 per cent per annum between 1883 and 1913. The UK was in the lead, averaging 5.6 per cent to 1860, followed by the US and France, each with 5.0 per cent; Germany had not yet got into its stride.

The rest of the world may already have been growing at the rate it achieved between 1853 and 1872, which was 4.0 per cent per annum. If so, then the growth rate for world trade as a whole from 1830 to 1860 was 4.4 per cent per annum. This rate is not approached again until the period 1899 to 1913, which averaged 3.8 per cent.

Figure 1 obscures the earlier turning point, because the Civil War cut US exports (of which cotton had been the largest item) most severely.[3] If one excludes the USA, the turning-point is then clearly at 1872. World trade as a whole apart from the USA grows at 4.3 per cent from 1853 to 1872, at 2.7 from 1872 to 1899 and at 4.1 per cent from 1899 to 1913.

Exports of manufactures and of primary products grew at roughly the same fast rates between 1853 and 1872 and more slowly between 1872 and 1899. But after 1899 exports of manufactures grew rapidly, while exports of primary products maintained their previous pace. This absence of a Kondratiev upturn in primary products is also borne out by the League of Nations figures in *Industrialisation and Foreign Trade*.[4] Changes in the relative rates of growth of exports of manufactures and of primary products before 1914 are explored in Appendix IV.

III

In order to arrive at causes, we use a model in which the main driving

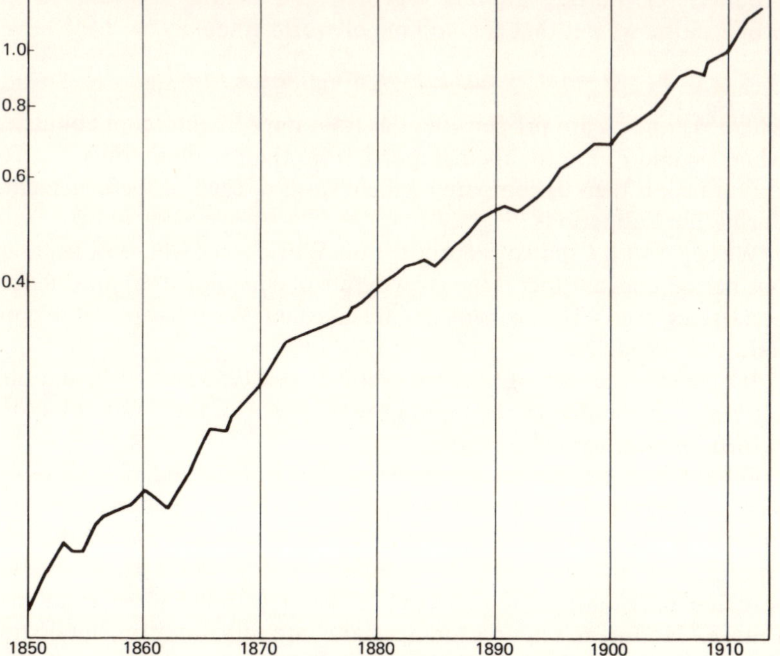

Fig. 1   World exports at 1913 prices, 1850–1913

force is the rate of growth of manufacturing in the leading industrial countries. Their growth causes them to import more, and they pay for their imports with exports. This model is part of the family that sees the development of 'peripheral' countries as a response to the industrialisation of the 'core' countries. However, the model is only a device for arranging our data; it does not yield any results on its own.

We are going to translate world trade into a function of industrial production (I) in the core countries. World trade equals the imports of core countries plus the imports of peripheral countries. The imports of peripheral countries divide into imports from core countries and imports from each other (h). Imports into peripheral from core countries are in payment for imports into core from peripheral countries—subject to capital transfers (k) and to service earnings (s); subject also, if we are comparing different dates, to changes in the terms of trade. One final element is to divide imported goods into manufactures (m) and primary

products (c). Putting all this together, and taking m and c to be propensities, we get that the volume of world trade

$$Q = (m_0 + c_0)I + p(m_1 + c_1)I + k - ps + h$$

where m_0 and c_0 are propensities for total imports into core countries while m_1 and c_1 are for their imports from the periphery only.[5]

Our task is then to compare the behaviour of each of these elements during our subperiods.

We begin with I, industrial production. World trade will grow faster in one period than another if the growth rate of core industrial production accelerates, even if the propensities are constant. What happened to core industrial production?

Its growth rate was higher than ever between 1953 and 1973, and this certainly contributed to the rapid growth of world trade. Other factors helped, to which we shall return.

What about the comparison between 1830 to 1860 and 1872 to 1899? The growth rate of core countries was almost certainly reduced in the last quarter of the nineteenth century. Hoffmann's index[6] shows this for Britain, and my revision[7] of his index confirms his results, though reaching back only as far as 1854. Crouzet gets the same result for France.[8] Hoffmann's figures for Germany[9] are very doubtful, but do not show retardation. Germany may even have been growing faster in the last quarter than over 1830 to 1860. The USA was not a core country in our sense in the nineteenth century, but in comparison with the 1850s it too shows no retardation, if one is not trapped by the wide swings of its Kuznets cycle.[10]

British and French retardation should make a difference of about 0.3 points to the growth rate of industry. Bairoch[11] indeed gets 2.6 for all Europe between 1830 and 1860, and 2.2 between 1872 and 1900. The golden age of capitalism was really a silver age. This deceleration goes some way towards explaining why the growth rates for world trade over these same periods were say 4.2 and 3.0, but it does not go all the way.

What happened to industrial production after 1899 is still controversial. Bairoch finds acceleration for Europe as a whole, and this accords with Schumpeter's Kondratiev thesis. My study for the aggregate of the USA, Britain, France and Germany shows however a constant rate of growth from 1872 to 1913, allowing for periods of severe Kuznets depression.[12] This accords with the steady growth rate of world trade in primary products shown above. Peripheral Europe was industrialising more rapidly after about 1890 (Russia, Austria, Italy and others), but these countries were still exporters of primary products, and

their industrialisation would not have added greatly to imports of primary products. Even if the world was industrialising more rapidly this would not be inconsistent with the steady growth rate of the core and of world trade.

IV

Next we come to the propensity to import primary products. This is the big difference between 1830 to 1860 and subsequent periods. The contrast is especially marked with 1953 to 1973, since the driving force in the latter period is an increased propensity to import manufactures.

The driving force of 1830 to 1860 was the propensity to import raw materials, not food or manufactures. Imports of manufactures into the core countries were rather small. Food and raw materials rose from 93 per cent of French imports in 1830 to 97 per cent in 1860. According to Bondi's calculations, between 1828 and 1864 German imports of primary products rose from 79 to 89 per cent of imports.[13] In the British case imports of manufactures rose as fast as imports of primaries, but the contribution of British imports of manufactures to the rate of growth of world trade was negligible, since in 1860 manufactures were only 7 per cent of British imports.

The driving force was raw materials, not food. The elasticity of French imports of raw materials with respect to industrial production was about 2 for 1830 to 1860, and about 1.4 for 1872 to 1899. The British raw material elasticity fell from about 1.5 to about 0.84. Food imports became important only after 1870, when American wheat flooded European markets. The dynamic force was cotton, which was on the fast-growing segment of its logistic curve in the first half of the nineteenth century. UK domestic consumption of cotton[14] rose by 4.0 per cent per annum between 1828–32 and 1856–60, but only by 1.6 per cent per annum between 1880–84 and 1905–09. Neither was this phenomenon confined to Britain. According to Sundbärg[15] cotton consumption in the rest of the world rose by 6.0 per cent per annum between 1826–30 and 1856–60, but by 3.3 per cent per annum between the latter date and 1896–1900.

The other side of this coin is the foreign trade of the USA, where in 1860 manufactures were 60 per cent of imports but only 11 per cent of exports. US imports of manufactures and of primary products were both growing at over 6 per cent per annum. Exports were growing at 5 per cent per annum, the difference being accounted for mainly by improving terms of trade and to a minor extent by capital import. Our model treats US foreign trade as a dependent variable rather than a prime mover over this period, since we assume that the USA grew cotton because the UK was willing to buy it, and would not have grown it but for the pull of demand.

The fact that the driving force was in raw materials discounts the proposition that world trade decelerated after 1872 because of the return to high tariff barriers, after the liberalising trends of the preceding half-century. These new tariffs were on food and manufactures, but not on raw materials; and the decline in the growth rate of raw material imports was particularly marked in the UK (1830–60 3.5 per cent[16] per annum, 1872–99 1.8 per cent per annum) which had no tariffs. Tariffs are relevant to the elasticities of food and manufactures, but not of raw materials.

Apart from the logistic principle, there is another reason why the propensity to import raw materials should vary with stages of in-dustrialisation. In the early stages a country may be self-sufficient in a wide range of raw materials, which it then outgrows. For example, Japan had all the coal it needed until the First World War. Britain used to be self-sufficient in iron ore, copper and tin. These are minerals, but a country's demand may also outgrow its supply of agricultural requirements, either due to geographical factors, or comparative costs. We could then get the kinds of growth paths shown in Figure 2, where industrial production grows at a constant rate (the diagram is semi-logarithmic); import of raw materials begins later, and then rises asymptotically; and finally reduces its elasticity. The final stage is due to economy in the use of raw materials, and to the constant rise of value added in manufacturing relative to raw materials used. It is not easy to

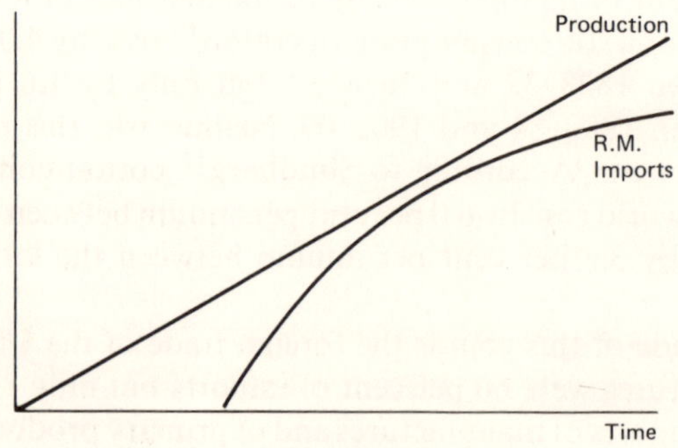

Fig. 2

quantify these trends but they are generally recognised, and give reason to expect that our c will fall as our I rises over time.[17]

The rate of growth of raw material imports slowed down after 1860; cotton did not resume its dominance over the growth of world trade. Despite the emergence of wheat, trade in primary products settled down to a steady rate of growth a little smaller than that of industrial production. To quote an earlier study:

> World manufacturing seems to have grown at about 3.6 per cent per annum between 1883 and 1913, and world trade in primary products at about 3.1 per cent per annum, giving an elasticity of about 0.86. Between 1950–52 and 1969–71 world manufacturing grew at 5.9 per cent per annum and world trade in primary products at 5.1 per cent per annum, yielding an elasticity of 0.87. So here is one coefficient which has remained constant over nearly a century.[18]

The rate of growth of world trade in primary products was unexpectedly and unprecedentedly high after the Second World War. This was the effect of rapid industrialisation on an unchanged propensity to import.[19]

V

The driving force of world trade after the Second World War was the imports of manufactures by the core countries. The demand thus generated was not confined to the core countries themselves, but spread over to the LDCs as well. Table 1 shows aspects of this. In current prices world trade in manufactures multiplied by 10.5 between 1953 and 1973, compared with 2.2 for world trade in beverages and sugar. The share of manufactures in world trade, which had been more or less constant (in current prices) since the last quarter of the nineteenth century, suddenly rose from 46 to 61 per cent. Strangely, with the exception of fuel, manufactures are the only group in which the LDCs maintained their share of world trade, growing as fast as the industriial countries. Manufactures thus rose to 21 per cent of LDC exports, or more than the exports of beverages, sugar and agricultural raw materials added together. Already manufactures constitute more than 20 per cent of the exports of some 20 LDCs, and there are more than 50 LDCs whose exports of manufactures exceed $25 million.

What accounts for this reversal? The share of imports of manufac-

TABLE 1
WORLD TRADE 1953–73

	Total 1973 $ billion	Multiple 1973 1953	LDC shares 1953	LDC shares 1973
Beverages and sugar	10.6	2.2	0.88	0.82
Agricultural raw materials	34.7	3.5	0.39	0.28
Food	75.4	6.6	0.35	0.19
Minerals and metals	32.4	6.6	0.50	0.29
Fuel	65.0	8.7	0.61	0.69
Manufactures	346.7	10.5	0.067	0.069
Total	564.8	7.9	0.30	0.20

tures in the industrial countries' consumption of manufactures had fallen steadily over several decades. According to Maizels's figures the ratio for Western Europe fell from 20 per cent in 1899 to 19 per cent in 1913 and less than 10 per cent in 1937.[20] That the ratio of imports to production would fall with industrialisation acquired the status of a law. That the 1937 ratio was abnormally low could be seen from the fact that it implied a negative elasticity. So it was no surprise when the ratio rose to 11 per cent in 1955. Even the return to the 1899 level by 1965 was surprising only for the speed with which it occurred. The explosion however continued; by 1973 the ratio of imports to consumption of manufactures in Western Europe was about 30 per cent. Tariffs are much lower than in 1899 or 1913, so a higher ratio is appropriate. But will the ratio continue to rise? It cannot rise indefinitely, since this would ultimately mean that European countries consumed only what they imported, and exported all that they produced—an outcome inconsistent with the fact that a significant part of industrial production is tied locationally to the domestic consumer market. Ultimately therefore this ratio must stabilise or fall. If it stabilises, imports will rise no faster than production, and the growth rate of trade in manufactures will drop back from the 11 per cent per annum level of 1953–73 to more like 5 per cent per annum. How soon this will happen we cannot of course predict. As far as we can tell, the ratio could continue to rise beyond say 40 or 50 per cent before altering direction.

It is tempting to connect changes in this ratio primarily with changes in tariff levels, but the direction of initial causality is not established (that tariffs reduce imports is not disputed). World trade in manufactures[21] rose at 4.1 per cent per annum between 1853 and 1872, at 3.1 per cent per annum between 1872 and 1899 and at 4.3 per cent between 1899 and 1913. The fast pace of 1899 to 1913 is irrelevant to the argument; it was connected with capital export and the terms of trade. But the slowdown after 1872 is at the core of the argument. This preceded the raising of tariff levels; tariffs were raised because trade was slack, and not the other way round. The propensity m is not a constant, but a variable which moves in the same direction as the rate of growth of industrial production. A fast pace of production increases imports of primary products and exports of manufactures (via the primary producers' increased purchasing power). Bottlenecks in manufacturing increase and order books lengthen, so imports of manufactures increase, beyond what would occur if production were growing less rapidly. Economies of scale are more fully exploited, good trade also weakens the protectionist forces, and tariff barriers are reduced. When industry slackens all this is reversed, and imports of manufactures decline faster than production.

Thus the explosive growth rate of world trade in manufactures after the Second World War was a natural product of the faster pace of industrialisation. Industrial production of OECD countries was rising at about 3.3 per cent per annum in the last quarter of the nineteenth century, with world trade in manufactures rising at about 3 per cent, giving an elasticity of about 0.9. The elasticity for 1953–73 is about 2.0. About half the growth rate of imports (about 5 per cent per annum) could be explained by a constant propensity; some part results from the greater import propensity of rapidly expanding markets, and the rest is due to other causes.

VI

The most important of these other causes in the nineteenth century was changes in the terms of trade. This played a major role in the trade explosion of 1830–60. Thus over this period UK imports grew at 4.1 per cent per annum, and UK exports at 5.6 per cent per annum, the change in the terms of trade adding 1.5 percentage points to the growth rate of British exports (capital exports were still small).

The terms of trade of Western Europe continued to deteriorate until the beginning of the 1880s, when they turned around and improved for nearly two decades. The fact that they were improving is one of the reasons why world trade in manufactures grew so slowly over the two decades that British historians call 'the Great Depression'. After 1895 the terms of trade again deteriorated, adding half a percentage point per year to the growth rate of European exports.[22]

These are the direct income effects. It is also possible that p is related both to c and to the rate of growth of I. A change in the terms of trade making primary products cheaper might increase the volume of imports, either via the price elasticity of demand, or via driving domestic producers out of business. The price elasticity of demand for food and raw materials is low enough within the revelant price ranges to be ignored. But competition with domestic producers is very real, as with the entry of US wheat into European markets. One can only assume that the value of c would have fallen even more after 1880 but for the terms of trade (the competition of US wheat).

The effect of the terms of trade on the rate of growth of industry is more controversial. The argument is that the reduced purchasing power of the farmers restricts the market for industry. The theoretical answer is that the purchasing power of the farmers falls only to the extent that the purchasing power of the industrial sector increases. I have examined the problem elsewhere, especially in relation to France, and remain sceptical.[23]

These changes in the terms of trade derive from changes in the relative growth rates of industrial and agricultural production.[24] The decisive change can be either industrial or agricultural. After 1872 the growth rate of industrial production slowed, but at the same time the opening up of the Middle West flooded Europe with agricultural products, and the terms of trade moved sharply in favour of industry. The growth rate of industry does not seem to have changed between 1872 and 1913, but the US agricultural frontier closed after 1890, and the terms of trade reversed themselves in favour of agriculture. Between 1913 and 1939 the deficiency was in industrial demand, so the terms of trade again reversed themselves, this time to favour industry. The period 1953–73 is interesting because it is the first in which we have rapid industrialisation with the terms of trade moving against agriculture. Agricultural potential increased enormously after the Second World War, partly because of a worldwide green revolution (hybrids, pesticides, fertilisèrs—still predominantly a temperate phenomenon), and partly because of the opening up of Asia, Africa and Latin America by roads and trucks. The increased rate of industrialisation was therefore more than matched by the increase in agricultural potential, and the terms of trade moved against agriculture. Therefore the terms of trade do not help in explaining the fast growth of world trade after 1953 (as they do for after 1830 or after 1899). On the contrary, exports would have grown even faster but for the change in the terms of trade.

The period 1953–73 is also anomalous in another sense. In the past industrial and agricultural prices have moved in the same directions (both upwards or downwards), the changes in the terms of trade resulting from faster movement of one group or the other. But in this period industrial prices were moving upwards although agricultural prices were moving downwards. This was due primarily to a change in the magnitude of money wage rate changes in the industrial countries. At the end of the nineteenth century industrial wage rates changed typically by 1 to $1\frac{1}{2}$ per cent per annum, just about keeping pace with the change in productivity. Now the forces which kept money wage changes close to changes in productivity have ceased to operate, and the gap grows wider in each decade. The economic system has mutated, and market economies may now expect ever-rising prices no matter what happens to the terms of trade.

VII

Capital export rose steadily over the thirty years before the First World War, subject to wide fluctuations. We do not know whether it was larger in 1873 than in 1883; it probably was. In 1883 it was equivalent to 4.7 per cent of world exports[25]; in 1890 to 7.9 per cent, in 1899 to 8.3 per cent and in 1913 to 9.1 per cent. Appendix IV shows that capital export accounts for about one-third of the increased growth rate of exports of manufactures after 1899.

When we turn to 1953–73 the orders of magnitude are much lower than in 1913. The amount of capital exported in 1973 is not known precisely. The transfer of resources to developing countries in that year[26] was equal to about 4.7 per cent of world exports; the unknown element is the extent of transfers between developed countries. For that year only seven members of OECD reported a net inflow of long-term capital, amounting to another 1.8 per cent of world exports.[27] Clearly capital export is relatively smaller now than it was before the First World War. However, for its contribution to the rate of growth from 1953–73 we must compare 1973 with 1953 and not with 1913. The situation in 1953 is not known precisely. We may guess that capital export made a significant but not large contribution to the rate of growth of exports between 1953–73.

VIII

Exports of services have probably diminished relatively to exports of goods, making it necessary for the core countries to export more goods in payment for their imports.

The cost of transport seems not to have risen as much as the cost of goods. This is reflected in the difference between the value of world exports f.o.b. and of world imports c.i.f. which used to be 8 per cent, and has been running only at about 4 per cent. However most of this change occurred before the 1950s, and some of it may be due to the larger proportion of manufactures in world trade, since the difference was always wider in primary products.

Apart from this, developing countries now provide more services for themselves, own relatively more ships, run their own insurance business, and do more domestic banking. They have also built up a tourist industry, of some $8 to $10 billion a year. (One may also mention here the remittances of migrant workers, which are almost as large as the tourist expenditures.)

These trends require the core countries to export more commodities in payment for their imports.

IX

We come finally to the trade of the peripheral countries with each other. This has always been small. We have a count showing that in 1883 the four leading countries UK, USA, France and Germany imported from the tropical countries and East Asia goods valued at $1,086 million c.i.f., or say $978 million f.o.b.[28]. Exports from these countries totalled $1,235 million in that year, so 21 per cent went other than to the leading four. We would probably exaggerate if we put their exports to each other at 10 per cent, which would make them less than 2 per cent of world trade.

In 1953 exports of LDCs to each other were 25 per cent of their trade; by 1973 this was down to 20 per cent, despite two decades of efforts at regional integration. These figures were equivalent to about 7 per cent of world trade in 1953 and 4 per cent in 1973. They are so small that changes in them make no significant contribution to understanding changes in the rate of growth of world trade. Presumably if the leading countries slow down, larger and more successful efforts will be made to effect regional integration; a period of booming world trade is not propitious for efforts in this direction.

X

We can now answer the question with which we began: what caused the explosion of world trade? The basic underlying cause was the faster pace of growth in the industrial countries, but there were other positive and negative elements. The terms of trade were a negative factor; trade between developing countries was too small to have much effect; the propensity to import raw materials and food was neutral; capital export was neutral or insignificant; and the relative decline of service income was positive if not large. The biggest factor, the propensity to import manufactures, would have been raised by faster industrial growth even if tariff levels had remained unchanged, but it was also bolstered by declining tariffs.

We seek to understand the past in order to chart the future. Can this fast pace be resumed after we get out of the current recession? This becomes two separate questions: can industry resume its fast pace, and can the propensity to import manufactures continue to increase.

I cannot answer first question easily. People who think that fast growth has ended advance one or other of five reasons.

(1) The mature industrial countries (excluding the USA) have exhausted their reservoirs of low-paid labour and, without immigration, can no longer grow fast through internal transfers or expansion of labour participation.

(2) Fast growth in Europe was due to catching up on a backlog of innovations which had been accumulating since 1900, and whose economic feasibility the USA had already demonstrated.

(3) There are no great innovations in sight, of Schumpeterian quality.

(4) Consumer demand has shifted at the margin from manufactures to services, whose crawling productivity will keep down the rate of growth.

(5) The ratio of profits to national income has been declining for some time in leading industrial countries.

I cite these beliefs neither to endorse them nor to controvert them, but I note that every major downturn (1847, 1872, 1893, 1907, 1929, 1974) has brought forth predictions that the market economy will never again grow so rapidly, and that these predictions have always been wrong. This does not imply that such a prediction will *always* be wrong.

The second question is easier. Currently Western European countries import about a third of the manufactures that they consume. This proportion can continue to rise, but not indefinitely, and when it stops rising the rate of growth of their imports of manufactures will drop to or below the 5 per cent per annum rate which now appears to be their maximum 'natural' rate of industrial growth. Whether that date is set for the 1980s or the 1990s I do not know.

ENDNOTES

1. I have chosen 1953 because we have a detailed breakdown for that year in Paul Lamartine Yates's, *Fifty Years of Foreign Trade* (London: Allen & Unwin, 1959).
2. Germany is a difficult case. There are no customs values before 1872, and those from 1872 to 1879 have to be rejected (see Appendix I).
3. Actual exports fell less than recorded exports because of cotton exports from the South evading the Federal records.
4. See Chart 7.1 and accompanying text in my book, *Growth and Fluctuations 1870–1913* (London: Allen & Unwin 1958).
5. If we use m_2 snd c_2 for imports of core countries from each other, this reduces to

$$\{(m_2 + c_2) + (1 + p)(m_1 + c_1)\}I + k - ps + h.$$

A further elaboration would recognise that the terms of trade for commodities and for services may diverge. In this paper we do not investigate the differences between the various compartments of m and c.
6. Walter G. Hoffmann, *British Industry* 1700–1950 (Oxford: Blackwell, 1955).
7. Op. cit., Appendix I.
8. Francois Crouzet, 'Un Indice annual de l'Industrie Francaise', *Annales, Economies, Société, Civilisations* (1970)
9. Walter G. Hoffmann, *Das Wachstum Der deutschen Wirtschaft seit der Mitte des 19. Jahrhunderts* (Berlin: Springer-Verlag, 1965).
10. Gallman's figures for manufacturing yield a growth rate of 6.0 per cent between 1874 and 1894, which are comparable dates. This is slightly higher than his rate for 1849 to 1859, but below his rate for 1839 to 1849 (9.9 per cent). Lebergott's data also show the labour force in manufacturing growing faster from 1870 to 1900 (at just under 3 per cent) than from 1850 to 1860; and it also shows explosive growth during the 1840s. Robert E. Gallman, 'Commodity Output 1839–1899', in Conference on Research in Income and Wealth, *Trends in The American Economy in the Nineteenth Century*, Studies in Income and Wealth, Vol. 24 (Princeton, 1960). Also Stanley Lebergott, *Manpower in Economic Growth* (New York: McGraw-Hill, 1964).

11. Paul Bairoch, *Commerce Extérieur et développement économique de l'Europe au XIXe siècle* (Paris: Mouton, 1976).
12. The result depends very much on what figures one uses for German production in the 1870s. Hoffman used the customs returns to get raw material usage, but the customs returns were defective, and the methods then used were abandoned in 1879. This problem is discussed in Appendix I, in the context of deriving a series for German exports. Its relevance to industrial production is discussed in Appendix II of *Growth and Fluctuations*, op. cit. If one uses more realistic figures for German production, then core industrial production grows at a constant secular rate from 1872 to 1913.
13. Gerhard Bondi, *Deutschlands Aussenhandel 1815–1870* (Berlin: Akadamie-Verlag, 1958) page 146.
14. This is the sum of net imports of cotton plus changes in stocks minus exports of yarn and cloth. Calculated from data in Robert Robson, *The Cotton Industry in Britain* (London: Macmillan, 1957). Robson incorporates the earlier work of Ellison.
15. Gustav Sundbarg, *Aperçus Statistiques Internationaux* (New York: Gordon & Breach, 1968). Our figure is mill absorption of cotton minus UK domestic consumption as defined above.
16. Actually 1829–31 to 1859–61 and 1871–73 to 1898–1900.
17. On economy in the use of raw materials see C. T. Saunders, 'The Consumption of Raw Materials in the UK, 1851–1950', *Journal of Royal Statistical Society*, cxv, Part III (1952).
18. W. A. Lewis, op. cit., page 175. Appendix IV yields a higher growth rate for primary products between 1883 and 1913, 3.36 in fact.
19. Incidentally, those who believe that the outburst of imperialism in the last quarter of the nineteenth century was mainly due to a search for raw materials must take into account that the propensity to import raw materials was lower in the second half of the nineteenth century than in the first half, but of course politics lags behind economic events.
20. Calculated from Alfred Maizels, *Industrial Growth and World Trade* (Cambridge: Cambridge University Press, 1969). But the ratio of trade in manufactures to industrial production grew over this period. See Appendix IV for further discussion of the situation before 1914.
21. Source: Appendix IV.
22. These terms of trade are calculated from data in Appendix IV.
23. *Growth and Fluctuations, 1890–1913*, op. cit., pp. 44 to 50.
24. If we were working with a model in which the dynamic force was the growth of primary production in the peripheral countries, this is the point where we would start: by studying changes in the relative growth rates of production of industry and agriculture and the effects of these changes on the terms of trade. We would arrange our data differently, but would end up considering the same phenomena—the propensities to import, price elasticty, capital export, etc. Choice of models depends to some extent on how wide a range of influence one attributes to changes in the terms of trade.
25. Relying on Arthur I. Bloomfield, *Patterns of Fluctuations in International Investment Before 1914* (Princeton Studies in International Finance No. 21, 1968). This is the sum of outflows from the UK, France and Germany,

minus inflow into the USA.

26. As reported by the Development Assistance Committee of OECD: *Development Cooperation* (annual).
27. Derived by aggregating item 77b d in the country pages of IMF's monthly *International Financial Statistics*. The definitions may not be watertight, since nearly half of this capital flow went to Germany, which reported borrowing $4.6 billion in 1972 and $4.5 billion in 1973.
28. W. A. Lewis, op. cit., pp. 167–8.

Appendix I
Exports from Germany, 1836–89

The German trade statistics for this period cannot be used at all without some doctoring, for the following three reasons.

(1) Prior to 1872 the customs authorities published quantities but no values. Three statisticians have sought to make good this deficiency. In 1848 Junghanns calculated the value of trade from 1834 to 1846, but he used constant prices, so this is really a volume series. Then, Hubner, over the course of a number of years (1850–63), calculated values at current prices. These earlier results were reprinted by Bondi (1958) who added the missing years 1851 and 1864 to 1871 at current prices.[1]

(2) When the Empire was formed the customs authorities began by mixing up special trade and transit trade, so the 1870s trade seemed to explode; however, this was corrected in 1880. The result is that the official volume is much larger in 1879 than in 1888, whereas in fact exports were much larger in 1880 than in 1879.

(3) The customs area changed several times, as new territories were added. Specifically there are notable breaks in the series in 1838, 1842, 1854, 1867, 1872 and 1888, for this reason, in addition to the break already noted at 1879. The series is grossly misleading unless some effort is made to adjust for these breaks, but most users of German trade statistics have simply ignored this problem. A notable exception is Bodo von Borries[2] who tries to separate out internal trade from the external trade of the area which was Germany in 1913. His work however covers only the first twenty years of our period and contains not annual data but three-year averages.

Walter Hoffman[3] used the statistics as they came, in spite of these difficulties. He used the statistics of imports to derive raw material usage, and therefore industrial production, upon which he then erected trade and transport for his national income series. But unfortunately this invalidates his pre-1880 results, in so far as they derive from trade figures.

However, it is to Hoffmann that we have turned for our own enterprise. He produced index numbers of exports (total and by commodity categories) from 1836 onwards. We have assumed that these figures are a correct statement of volume between the breaks (except in 1858 and over 1874–79). Our main problem then is how to join Hoffmann's series at the seven points where it is fractured. One should note that the use of the volume series between the fractures assumes that the new territories added in were growing at the same rates as the rest.

To join the fractures we have used the following tools.

(1) We went to the import statistics of other European countries and the United States, and added together their imports from Germany and territories not yet incorporated. The value of German exports was then adjusted to show the same rate of change, and the same percentage change was also applied to the volume index (that is, the price index remained unchanged). This was done at 1887–89, 1878–80, 1871–72 and 1867–68. Unfortunately there are not enough import data by the time one gets to 1853.

(2) So at 1852–54, 1841–42 and 1836–39 we assume the volume growth rate between the terminal dates to be the same as for the UK. This checks out with Borries's data (page 186, special trade) which when converted to volume by his price index (page 88) grows at a rate of 2.8 per cent per annum between 1836–39 and 1854–56, compared with our index which grows at 3.0 per cent per annum. Both rates seem low, and ours therefore seems slightly more plausible than his.

(3) The price index implicit in comparing Hoffmann's volume data with the value series included in Bondi looks very strange at 1879–80, 1871–72 and 1867–68. At those dates we have assumed that the German export prices changed to the same extent as British export prices.

The period 1872–80 was the most difficult to adjust. Comparison with other countries suggested that the volume figures were all right for 1872 and 1880. The figures were racing up to a peak in 1878. One could link values for 1878 to those for 1880 by using other countries' import statistics, and transform this to volume by assuming that the export price movement over 1878 to 1880 was the same as for Britain. Old 1874 and new 1878 volumes were then linked by dividing the old series by one rising steadily at the appropriate rate of growth.

Hoffmann's quantity for 1858, when compared with Hubner's value, implies a sudden price increase of 29 per cent, in a year when prices on the contrary were slipping. A more appropriate figure is interpolated.

Apart from making a new series for total exports, we have also made a new series for exports of manufactures, whose problems are slightly easier because the confusion of the 1870s did not much affect manufactures; so Hoffmann's index for 1872–80 can be accepted as it stands. For the rest we have generally assumed that the volume change at the breaks was the same in manufactures as in the new series for total exports.

The results are shown in Table 2 and Figure 3. Our total and Hoffmann's are close at the terminals; but his figures are too high in the 1870s because of the confusion with the transit trade (by as much as 30 per cent), and much too low in the 1840s (as much as 35 per cent) because of ignoring the changes in the customs area.

TABLE 2
EXPORTS FROM GERMANY, 1836–89*

| | Current prices Total trade | | 1913 Prices | |
	Old value	Revised value	Total Trade	Manufactures
	1	2	3	4
1836			449	227
1837			397	196
1838			499	227
1839			512	253
1840			468	232
1841			523	244
1842			523	244
1843			472	253
1844			523	276
1845			535	270
1846			523	287
1847	518	804	548	322
1848	483	750	573	288
1849	514	798	663	316
1850	522	811	752	355
1851	535	831	689	371
1852	555	862	714	410
1853	754	1032	821	471
1854	1002	1064	802	461
1855	926	983	767	422
1856	956	1015	732	440
1857	1059	1124	836	464

TABLE 2
EXPORTS FROM GERMANY, 1836–89* (*continued*)

	Current prices Total trade		1913 Prices	
	Old value	Revised value	Trade Trade	Manufactures
	1	2	3	4
1858	1052	1116	843	421
1859	922	996	749	484
1860	1060	1125	854	504
1861	1062	1127	941	493
1862	1112	1180	871	512
1863	1106	1174	941	569
1864	1131	1200	1020	639
1865	1155	1226	993	600
1866	1514	1607	1202	639
1867	1622	1722	1316	750
1868	2257	1766	1446	823
1869	2275	1781	1406	801
1870	1967	1754	1398	857
1871	2564	2006	1603	940
1872	2317	2353	1699	984
1873	2277	2313	1608	900
1874	2343	2279	1653	929
1875	2492	2321	1733	998
1876	2546	2272	1692	1049
1877	2760	2359	1827	1115
1878	2885	2361	1911	1223
1879	2775	2301	1847	1178
1880	2923	2630	2036	1260
1881	3029	2726	2089	1355
1882	3224	2901	2174	1403
1883	3259	2920	2267	1447
1884	3190	2871	2399	1522
1885	2854	2569	2363	1470
1886	2974	2676	2553	1645
1887	3137	2823	2672	1749
1888	3207	2985	2783	1823
1889	3165	3165	2858	1914

---

* For 1890–1913, see W. G. Hoffmann, op. cit.

The big question is why total exports increased so little between 1854 and 1860. This is not affected by anything we have done, since it falls between the breaks, and is in the Hoffmann series. Between those years

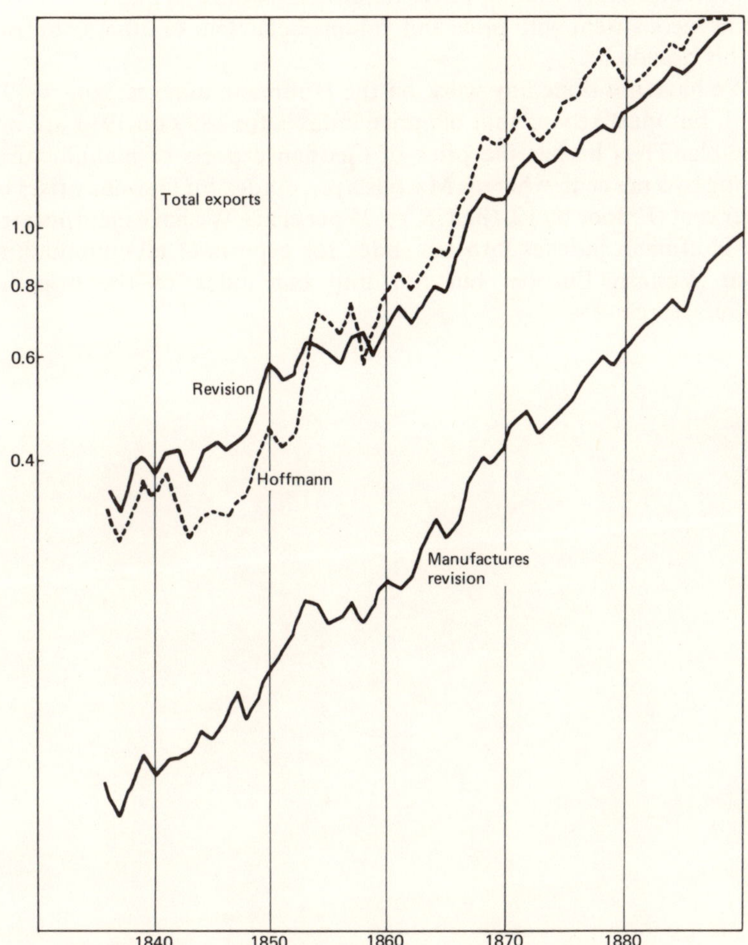

Fig. 3   Germany's exports at 1913 prices, 1836–89

British exports increased by 37 per cent, French exports by 66 per cent, and German exports only by 6 per cent (in constant prices). The same retardation appears in the series for exports of manufactures.

Finally we should mention that the price index we are using for the 1870s is the one implied on the original customs values and Hoffmann's volumes. This is very different from the index offered by Desai[1], which shows a much faster fall of prices (and therefore rise of quantities), and seems inconsistent with price and volume behaviour of other countries in this decade.

We have not done any work on the Hoffmann indexes from 1889–1913, but must record that his price indexes for 1899 on 1913 are not credible. Thus he has the price of German exports of manufactures falling by 5 per cent, whereas Maizels's price index for Germany rises by 8 per cent (France by 12, the UK by 25 per cent). We have incorporated the Hoffmann indexes into our index for exports of all commodities from Western Europe, but not into our index of the price of manufactures.

Appendix II
World Exports at Current Prices
1850–1913

The principal source is a US Government publication (Department of Commerce and Labour, Bureau of Statistics, *Statistical Abstract of Foreign Countries*, Washington, 1909) which has the advantage over all other sources that careful enquiry was made into current exchange rates of all the countries included, and these are incorporated in the annual conversions into US dollars. Supplementary data after 1906 can be obtained from the UK Government *Statistical Abstracts* for foreign countries and for colonies. This includes exchange rates but these are frequently par rates instead of market rates. Figures for 1913 are available in the League of Nations annual trade surveys published in the 1920s. Data for Europe are given in B. R. Mitchell, *European Historical Statistics* (New York: Columbia University Press, 1975), unfortunately in domestic currencies, without conversion ratios.

Given these aids it is relatively easy to assemble the data from say 1883–1913. The principal reason for reproducing it here is that the majority of Third World scholars do not have access to statistical abstracts published before the First World War.

The main problem is what to do when data are missing. Sometimes a search of consular reports yields fruit; *The Statesman's Year Book* also helps, from about 1860 onwards, and so do some of the commercial dictionaries published in the middle of the nineteenth century, such as J. R. McCulloch's *A Dictionary; Geographical, Statistical and Historical*, published at various dates from 1841–66. Ransacking these sources is very time-consuming, and very frustrating; and it is hardly worth while to spend a day in the library discovering that a particular country's exports were valued at $5 million in 1855 (0.2 per cent of the world total). One must abandon from the start any idea of getting exact trade figures for each of over one hundred countries and colonies in the middle of the nineteenth century.

Apart from the UK and USA, all countries are grouped geographically as: Northwest Europe, Other Europe, Temperate Settlements, Tropics and East Asia. This facilitates dealing with missing data, and also the conversion from current to constant prices.

Missing data are treated in three ways. If we have exports in constant but not in current prices (Norway 1850–65, for example) we multiply by the group's price index number (see Appendix III). But we could not do this for special cases referred to below.

If there is a blank space in a country's row between two dates for which we have more or less reliable figures we interpolate, assuming that this country has the same fluctuations as another of similar structure (such as Venezuela 1898–1902 modelled on Colombia); or also the same fluctuations as the total of its group's reliable data. Interpolated numbers are shown in italics in Table 3. Such numbers should be used only for their original purpose, which is to help get a reasonable figure for the total of world trade.

The number of tropical countries is very large. In an earlier publication we listed seventy-five, and produced an export figure for each for 1883, 1899, and 1913. We have selected the larger countries from this list for separate treatment, but have classified as 'Other' a great number of small countries whose exports were 11 per cent of tropical trade (1.7 per cent of world trade) in 1913. The ratios of these 'Other' to total tropical trade are slighly different in these years; we assume that the change of ratios from 1883–99 and from 1899–1913 occurs gradually. We also extend the series back to 1874 by assuming that this ratio is constant between 1874–83.[5]

Where there are blank spaces at the beginning of a country's series, it is placed in the category 'Other' of its group. We have made a special effort to get reliable estimates for 'Other' for the benchmark years 1850, 1861, 1872, 1883, 1899 and 1913 (except that to maximise usable data the tropical group substitutes 1870 and 1874 for 1872). The number of countries included in 'Other' therefore changes at each benchmark date; this is emphasised by placing an asterisk on the year before the change.

Working backward from 1872 (or 1874) to 1850 we have divided the 'Other' group into two subsets, one which grows at the same pace as the sum of the group (is a constant proportion of each year), and the other which grows only half as fast as the rest of the group. 'Other' in Northwest Europe grows at the same pace as its group (including UK); so does 'Other' in Temperate Settlements. In Other Europe Italy grows as fast as the rest of the group, but the remaining countries grow only half as fast. In the Tropical Countries all 'Other' grow as fast as the group between 1874–83. Before 1874 only Indonesia, Straits

Settlements, Peru and Venezuela grow at the same pace as the group.

Data are supposed to be for special trade, but in some cases only general trade is available. Where the original series begins as general and changes to special, general trade is reduced proportionately for our series. Gold and silver bullion are excluded unless mined in the country.

Some special problems follow.

NETHERLANDS

The existing series is useless. In the first place it is necessary to exclude re-exports of colonial produce, which varied between a quarter and a third. However, even after such produce and wheat are excluded the series grows too rapidly between 1883–1913 (at 5.5 per cent per annum compared with 3.0 per cent for Western Europe). This means that an increasing amount of re-export of industrial goods was entering into the statistics.

Secondly the series is at constant prices, presumably those of 1846, when it starts; by 1913 these prices are much too high. However, one cannot simply omit the Netherlands; it is too large. We proceed as follows.

Exports per head in 1913 were recorded as Netherlands $198, Belgium $95, Switzerland $69, Denmark $61. Actually Netherlands should be less than Belgium, not more than twice as much. After the war the other three countries caught up on Belgium, which had been set back by the war, and the figures for 1929 read Belgium $112, Netherlands $106, Switzerland $101.

We therefore assume that the correct figure for Netherlands in 1913 is about $75 per head, or $466 million. This was 5.6 per cent of the total for Western Europe, including the UK. It is assumed that Netherlands was 5.0 per cent of the total from 1872–90, and then rose by steps to 5.6 per cent in 1913.

SWITZERLAND

Before 1885 Swiss exports are given only in quantities. A rough comparison of 1872 and 1885 suggests that volume grew by about a quarter, or slightly less than the total for Western Europe (including UK) which grew by 28 per cent. A series is therefore calculated in which Switzerland's proportion of Western Europe's exports falls over these dates from 4.17 to 4.07 per cent.

CANADA

Statistics for the Federation, excluding interprovincial trade, commence only in 1867. Earlier figures shown here are 78.6 per cent of general exports (the ratio of special to general exports over 1868–70).

CUBA

Before 1898 trade statistics were published only sporadically. We know annual production of sugar in tonnes, and the free market price of sugar, so we can calculate the value of sugar production. However, other exports were significant. Alternatively the USA was the largest customer, and we have annual imports from Cuba in the US trade statistics.[6] The US was said to be taking about 60 per cent of Cuba's trade in the 1890s, so we have divided this latter series by 0.6. Compared with the sugar series, this result seems to give too little trade in the 1850s and 1860s.

PERU

Customs returns start in 1890. Before that we have the volume index prepared by Shane J. Hung in *Price and Quantum Estimates of Peruvian Exports 1830–1962*, Research Program in Economic Development, Princeton University, Discussion Paper No. 33 (1973). Unfortunately the price series do not extend back before 1890. For lack of data, we have simply joined the volume series to the value series.

CHINA

We have used the revision by Hsiao Liang-Lin, in *China's Foreign Trade Statistics, 1864–1949*, (Cambridge, Mass.: Harvard University Press, 1974). This increases the value of exports, while leaving the quantity unchanged.

COMPARISONS

Mulhall's figures for world trade in 1850 and in 1880 come to $3630 and $13,063 million. These figures are for imports plus exports. If there is a 10 per cent gap between exports and imports, exports are 47.6 per cent of those totals, namely $1728 and $6217 million. Our figures for these dates are \$1755 and \$6499 million.[7] The fit is remarkably close, considering the softness of our data for 1850.

In the League of Nations monograph *Industrialisation and Foreign Trade* Hilgerdt offered figures for world exports from 1881. In a slightly revised unpublished version he put 1883 at \$7040 and 1913 at \$19,200 million. Our figures are \$6867 and \$18,697. A large part of the difference will be due to our different treatments of Netherlands trade.

John Hanson has an unpublished thesis in the Library of the University of Pennsylvania entitled: *The Nineteenth Century Exports of Less Developed Countries*. He offers figures for world exports in 1840, 1860, 1880 and 1900. His total for these last three years are \$3136, \$6462 and \$9628 million. Our totals are \$3327, \$6499 and \$9596. So our totals seem to be trustworthy.

TABLE 3
WORLD EXPORTS AT CURRENT PRICES ($MILLION)

	1850	*1851*	*1852*	*1853*	*1854*	*1855*
USA	135	179	155	190	214	193
UK	347	362	380	481	472	465
			Northwest Europe			
France	208	225	244	294	275	303
Germany	197	202	209	251	258	239
Belgium	40.5	38.6	44.4	56.8	75.1	66.4
Sweden	*8.0*	9.3	9.1	12.9	17.8	20.6
Norway	*11.0*	*11.6*	*11.5*	*13.7*	*12.7*	*12.3*
Denmark						
Switzerland						
Netherlands						
Other	94	99	105	129	130	129
	557	586	624	758	769	771
			Other Europe			
Russia	76.3	73.6	87.5	113	47.5	28.4
Austria	51.7	64.2	68.6	92.1	108	116
Italy	*51.1*	*54.6*	*61.5*	*81.9*	*96.0*	*109*
Spain	22.8	23.2	26.6	39.1	46.4	58.9
Finland	1.9	2.0	2.0	2.1	*2.5*	*2.8*
Greece	*2.4*	2.4	1.8	1.5	1.2	1.9
Portugal						
Romania						
Turkey						
Bulgaria						
Serbia						
Other	57	59	65	84	98	112
	264	279	313	414	399	429
			Temperate Settlements			
Canada	15.5	16.0	18.5	27.4	27.7	31.5
Australia	13.1	13.2	52.9	70.2	67.7	73.5
New Zealand	*0.4*	0.4	0.7	1.5	1.5	1.6
South Africa	3.1	3.2	3.8	5.2	3.7	5.2
Chile	12.4	12.1	14.1	12.1	14.5	19.2
Newfoundland	*4.7*	4.7	4.7	5.7	5.0	5.6
Argentina						
Uruguay						
Other	14	14	16	14	16	22
	63	63	111	136	136	158

TABLE 3
WORLD EXPORTS AT CURRENT PRICES ($MILLION)
(*Continued*)

	1856	*1857*	*1858*	*1859*	*1860*	*1861*
USA	266	279	251	278	316	205
UK	563	593	567	634	660	608
France	368	363	367	441	443	374
Germany	*247*	*273*	*271*	*242*	*273*	*274*
Belgium	71.4	80.0	73.6	79.8	90.8	87.6
Sweden	17.9	17.4	14.9	19.1	20.8	19.5
Norway	*14.9*	*14.2*	12.5	14.9	14.6	14.4
Denmark						
Switzerland						
Netherlands						
Other	150	156	153	167	176	161
	869	903	893	964	1019	932
Russia	122	126	110	107	132	121
Austria	124	113	112	106	129	141
Italy	*100*	*99.4*	*90.6*	*88.4*	*106*	*109*
Spain	49.7	54.6	45.4	48.1	51.3	56.4
Finland	2.8	3.2	2.6	2.9	4.4	6.2
Greece	4.5	4.2	4.3	4.2	4.6	4.8
Portugual						12.9
Romania						
Turkey						
Bulgaria						
Serbia						
Other	93	89	78	73	85*	71
	496	490	443	430	512	523
Canada	35.0	30.6	26.9	29.6	36.6	37.5
Australia	78.9	78.3	71.1	82.2	78.1	84.6
New Zealand	1.4	1.6	2.0	2.5	2.8	3.0
South Africa	6.5	9.7	8.8	9.8	10.8	10.3
Chile	18.2	19.8	18.3	19.6	25.4	20.4
Newfoundland	6.5	8.0	6.4	6.6	6.2	5.3
Argentina						13.8
Uruguay						9.0
Other	20	22	21	22	28*	
	167	170	153	172	188	184

TABLE 3
WORLD EXPORTS AT CURRENT PRICES ($MILLION)
(*Continued*)

	1862	*1863*	*1864*	*1865*	*1866*	*1867*
USA	180	186	144	137	338	280
UK	603	712	780	806	918	880
France	436	508	568	600	618	549
Germany	*287*	*285*	*292*	*297*	*391*	*419*
Belgium	96.9	103	115	116	124	115
Sweden	21.2	21.6	20.1	26.6	24.2	29.7
Norway	17.1	19.5	*16.5*	*17.4*	18.3	18.4
Denmark						
Switzerland						
Netherlands						
Other	171	192	209	218	245	235
	1030	1130	1221	1275	1420	1366
Russia	119	117	111	132	117	171
Austria	143	142	157	168	160	198
Italy	111	122	111	108	118	141
Spain	51.2	55.8	58.4	54.8	50.4	54.5
Finland	6.4	7.4	7.2	7.8	6.0	8.2
Greece	4.8	4.0	4.3	7.1	7.1	8.4
Portugal	*12.8*	*13.2*	*13.2*	17.5	18.5	16.9
Romania						
Turkey						
Bulgaria						
Serbia						
Other	69	70	69	72	68	84
	517	531	531	566	545	683
Canada	34.4	42.8	45.5	46.7	56.2	38.6
Australia	87.8	94.0	92.2	95.8	92.2	89.3
New Zealand	4.0	4.7	6.4	6.9	7.8	9.3
South Africa	10.2	11.4	13.6	11.8	13.6	13.2
Chile	22.0	20.1	27.2	25.7	26.7	30.7
Newfoundland	5.7	6.0	5.4	5.6	5.8	5.1
Argentina	18.5	20.8	21.6	25.2	25.8	32.0
Uruguay	9.1	*10.0*	6.6	*10.5*	11.0	12.5
Other						
	192	210	219	228	239	228

TABLE 3
WORLD EXPORTS AT CURRENT PRICES ($MILLION)
(*Continued*)

	1868	*1869*	*1870*	*1871*	*1872*	*1873*
USA	269	324	383	446	452	550
UK	873	923	970	1084	1246	1240
France	542	598	545	558	731	736
Germany	*429*	*433*	*424*	*488*	*572*	*562*
Belgium	127	133	133	172	203	224
Sweden	28.6	31.1	38.1	43.5	54.5	60.2
Norway	18.2	20.7	21.4	21.3	27.5	31.7
Denmark					*41.5*	*40.5*
Switzerland					*132*	*126*
Netherlands					*158*	*160*
Other	236	250	249	277		
	1381	1466	1410	1559	1920	1940
Russia	150	156	216	243	215	238
Austria	209	213	192	228	189	198
Italy	152	153	146	207	224	218
Spain	50.9	50.1	75.8	84.2	98.0	112
Finland	9.1	9.5	8.5	8.8	9.8	14.4
Greece	7.0	8.0	6.5	10.9	9.7	11.1
Portugual	17.3	18.7	21.6	23.0	25.0	25.4
Romania					32.1	30.4
Turkey					49.2	53.5
Bulgaria					*4.9*	*5.3*
Serbia					6.2	6.8
Other	82	83	89	106*		
	677	691	755	912	863	913
Canada	48.5	52.4	59.0	57.6	65.8	76.5
Australia	105	97.5	87.5	106	109	128
New Zealand	9.3	9.2	12.4	12.0	16.8	17.5
South Africa	12.5	12.6	14.4	19.9	32.5	30.1
Chile	29.5	27.7	27.0	32.0	37.1	38.3
Newfoundland	4.3	6.2	6.3	6.4	5.8	6.6
Argentina	28.7	31.3	29.2	26.0	45.6	45.7
Uruguay	12.6	14.4	13.2	13.8	16.0	16.9
Other						
	251	251	249	273	329	360

TABLE 3
WORLD EXPORTS AT CURRENT PRICES ($MILLION)
(*Continued*)

	1874	*1875*	*1876*	*1877*	*1878*	*1879*
USA	554	497	576	608	723	755
UK	1164	1086	975	967	937	931
France	719	753	695	668	618	628
Germany	*555*	*564*	*552*	*573*	*574*	*559*
Belgium	215	213	205	209	215	230
Sweden	62.1	56.4	61.8	59.4	50.0	50.2
Norway	31.5	27.0	30.9	28.6	24.0	23.4
Denmark	41.9	41.2	42.9	38.6	36.8	37.8
Switzerland	*127*	*125*	*117*	*115*	*111*	*110*
Netherlands	*153*	*150*	*141*	*140*	*135*	*136*
Other						
	1905	1929	1846	1832	1764	1774
Russia	289	254	249	273	308	306
Austria	228	250	254	284	279	283
Italy	189	197	233	180	193	207
Spain	88.8	86.4	85.1	99.2	92.2	101
Finland	18.0	16.5	19.0	20.2	17.1	18.2
Greece	11.2	13.0	10.3	10.1	11.0	10.7
Portugual	24.7	26.2	22.7	24.9	19.7	19.3
Romania	26.0	28.0	45.4	27.2	41.9	46.1
Turkey	51.7	41.6	46.5	48.2	49.2	36.9
Bulgaria	*4.5*	*4.6*	*4.9*	*4.8*	*4.9*	3.9
Serbia	5.4	*5.8*	*6.2*	*6.1*	*6.2*	7.5
Other						
	937	923	976	978	1022	1041
Canada	76.7	69.7	72.5	68.0	68.0	62.4
Australia	125	121	114	112	116	103
New Zealand	18.2	20.4	21.1	22.8	22.9	22.0
South Africa	30.7	31.9	27.4	29.4	30.7	33.9
Chile	36.5	35.9	37.8	29.7	31.7	42.7
Newfoundland	7.4	6.5	6.7	6.9	5.7	6.0
Argentina	43.0	50.2	46.4	43.2	36.2	47.6
Uruguay	15.8	13.1	14.2	16.4	18.1	17.2
Other						
	353	349	341	329	329	335

TABLE 3
WORLD EXPORTS AT CURRENT PRICES ($MILLION)
(*Continued*)

	1880	*1881*	*1882*	*1883*	*1884*	*1885*
USA	876	814	750	778	734	674
UK	1084	1137	1174	1165	1132	1036
France	674	692	695	671	628	600
Germany	*639*	*662*	*705*	*710*	*698*	*624*
Belgium	235	251	256	259	258	231
Sweden	64.5	60.8	68.9	69.9	64.5	66.2
Norway	28.3	31.9	32.1	30.3	29.4	26.2
Denmark	47.4	43.5	43.0	44.6	40.2	35.6
Switzerland	*125*	*129*	*133*	*132*	*122*	*122*
Netherlands	*152*	*159*	*164*	*162*	*156*	*144*
Other						
	1965	2030	2097	2079	1996	1849
Russia	248	257	310	306	289	263
Austria	275	297	314	298	272	249
Italy	213	225	222	228	206	183
Spain	123	128	146	138	119	133
Finland	23.8	20.7	23.1	22.8	21.7	17.3
Greece	11.6	13.5	14.7	16.0	14.2	14.7
Portugal	26.6	22.3	24.4	24.6	24.5	24.5
Romania	42.3	39.9	47.2	42.6	35.5	47.9
Turkey	38.0	37.4	49.7	48.2	54.5	56.3
Bulgaria	7.6	6.1	6.6	8.9	6.8	8.7
Serbia	6.8	7.8	7.8	7.8	7.7	7.3
Other						
	1015	1055	1166	1140	1051	1005
Canada	72.9	83.9	94.1	87.7	79.8	79.1
Australia	133	134	133	146	140	130
New Zealand	24.4	23.8	26.6	29.8	29.7	28.4
South Africa	41.8	44.6	44.9	38.7	38.4	34.3
Chile	51.6	60.5	71.2	76.0	68.1	38.4
Newfoundland	5.7	7.9	7.1	7.2	6.7	4.7
Argentina	56.4	55.9	58.3	58.1	65.6	80.9
Uruguay	20.4	20.9	22.8	26.1	25.6	26.1
Other						
	406	431	458	470	454	422

TABLE 3
WORLD EXPORTS AT CURRENT PRICES ($MILLION)
(*Continued*)

	1886	*1887*	*1888*	*1889*	*1890*	*1891*
USA	700	703	680	814	846	957
UK	1034	1078	1140	1210	1281	1201
France	632	631	631	720	730	694
Germany	*650*	*686*	*726*	769	808	772
Belgium	228	239	240	281	277	293
Sweden	60.8	65.1	73.7	78.3	77.5	82.9
Norway	26.5	27.3	31.3	33.7	33.3	33.3
Denmark	37.4	41.2	42.1	46.4	52.3	55.9
Switzerland	121	125	126	135	135	129
Netherlands	*147*	*152*	*159*	*173*	*179*	*173*
Other						
	1903	1996	2029	2237	2292	2233
Russia	227	266	360	383	389	378
Austria	251	232	245	264	309	325
Italy	197	193	171	183	1773	168
Spain	140	139	147	157	167	150
Finland	14.9	14.9	17.5	19.8	17.8	20.1
Greece	15.3	19.8	18.5	20.8	18.5	20.7
Portugual	28.2	22.9	25.3	25.2	23.3	23.1
Romania	49.3	51.3	49.5	52.9	53.3	53.0
Turkey	53.1	55.9	49.7	59.6	66.8	56.5
Bulgaria	9.7	8.8	12.4	15.6	13.7	13.7
Serbia	7.9	7.0	7.5	7.5	8.8	10.1
Other						
	994	1010	1103	1189	1239	1218
Canada	77.8	81.0	81.4	80.3	85.3	88.7
Australia	106	114	140	144	143	175
New Zealand	27.2	28.9	31.6	40.9	42.9	41.6
South Africa	39.7	42.9	48.6	51.1	53.5	59.4
Chile	38.4	44.7	54.8	49.5	50.8	49.3
Newfoundland	4.9	5.3	6.7	6.1	6.2	7.5
Argentina	67.4	81.5	96.6	87.0	97.3	99.6
Uruguay	24.6	19.3	29.0	26.8	30.1	27.9
Other						
	386	418	489	486	509	542

TABLE 3
WORLD EXPORTS AT CURRENT PRICES ($MILLION)
(*Continued*)

	1892	*1893*	*1894*	*1895*	*1896*	*1897*
USA	923	855	807	808	987	1080
UK	1104	1060	1049	1098	1167	1138
France	673	629	598	656	661	699
Germany	718	751	720	806	857	883
Belgium	264	262	252	267	283	314
Sweden	81.0	85.1	84.5	88.6	96.7	102
Norway	31.8	34.0	33.2	34.4	36.9	42.8
Denmark	55.8	53.1	59.4	58.1	58.6	65.2
Switzerland	126	124	119	127	132	133
Netherlands	*163*	*164*	*157*	*170*	*179*	*185*
Other						
	2113	2102	2022	2207	2305	2424
Russia	232	303	350	360	356	374
Austria	291	311	307	294	314	311
Italy	183	185	195	199	203	211
Spain	111	105	101	119	132	128
Finland	18.1	22.2	26.2	27.6	30.7	32.6
Greece	15.9	17.0	14.3	13.9	14.0	15.8
Portugual	26.6	25.3	25.8	29.1	28.2	29.5
Romania	55.1	71.5	56.8	51.2	62.5	43.3
Turkey	67.6	68.5	58.4	60.5	68.2	67.9
Bulgaria	14.4	17.7	14.1	15.0	21.0	11.5
Serbia	9.0	9.4	8.9	8.4	10.3	10.8
Other						
	1024	1135	1158	1178	1240	1236
Canada	99.0	106	104	103	110	124
Australia	162	162	156	164	160	184
New Zealand	41.5	37.7	40.5	35.7	40.1	42.5
South Africa	64.2	69.1	71.8	87.7	88.8	113
Chile	48.2	54.2	54.0	54.7	56.5	49.3
Newfoundland	7.5	6.4	5.9	6.2	6.6	4.9
Argentina	109	90.8	98.1	116	113	97.6
Uruguay	26.8	28.6	34.6	33.7	31.4	30.3
Other						
	559	554	565	601	606	645

TABLE 3
WORLD EXPORTS AT CURRENT PRICES ($MILLION)
(Continued)

	1898	*1899*	*1900*	*1901*	*1902*	*1903*
USA	1234	1253	1453	1438	1333	1458
UK	1134	1285	1416	1361	1378	1413
France	683	807	799	780	827	827
Germany	913	1022	1120	1077	1134	1219
Belgium	345	376	371	353	372	407
Sweden	97.2	101	110	99.1	106	119
Norway	40.6	40.2	43.6	41.5	45.7	46.5
Denmark	63.9	72.4	75.6	78.3	85.7	94.4
Switzerland	139	155	163	163	170	173
Netherlands	*192*	*214*	*228*	*215*	*232*	*243*
Other						
	2474	2787	2911	2807	2973	3129
Russia	377	323	369	392	443	516
Austria	328	378	394	383	389	432
Italy	232	276	258	265	284	293
Spain	106	124	115	102	113	126
Finland	34.7	35.7	38.2	36.1	39.1	41.3
Greece	17.0	18.1	19.8	18.1	15.4	16.6
Portugual	33.6	31.1	33.4	30.5	30.7	33.0
Romania	54.7	28.8	54.0	68.3	72.3	68.6
Turkey	64.9	59.1	68.8	69.8	70.4	80.2
Bulgaria	12.8	10.3	10.4	16.0	20.0	20.9
Serbia	11.0	12.7	12.8	12.7	13.9	11.6
Other						
	1273	1296	1373	1394	1491	1639
Canada	145	143	169	177	196	214
Australia	195	236	223	242	214	235
New Zealand	45.4	50.5	57.2	53.8	56.5	62.5
South Africa	129	124	45.1	62.9	101	140
Chile	60.7	58.9	60.7	62.7	67.8	70.9
Newfoundland	5.2	6.8	8.6	8.3	9.5	9.9
Argentina	129	178	149	162	173	213
Uruguay	31.3	37.8	13.4	28.7	34.8	38.6
Other						
	740	836	726	797	852	985

TABLE 3
WORLD EXPORTS AT CURRENT PRICES ($MILLION)
(*Continued*)

	1904	*1905*	*1906*	*1907*	*1908*	*1909*
USA	1426	1599	1773	1895	1729	1701
UK	1461	1603	1825	2070	1833	1838
France	865	946	1024	1088	982	1112
Germany	1269	1393	1545	1664	1555	1602
Belgium	421	478	543	554	488	546
Sweden	112	122	136	141	130	127
Norway	45.8	50.6	57.6	59.0	57.1	63.4
Denmark	96.1	105	106	113	119	120
Switzerland	173	188	209	224	202	213
Netherlands	*253*	*279*	*313*	*342*	*312*	*328*
Other						
	3235	3562	3934	4185	3845	4111
Russia	518	555	564	542	514	735
Austria	424	456	484	498	456	470
Italy	308	334	372	379	334	361
Spain	131	139	153	160	152	157
Finland	41.6	47.8	54.3	52.0	47.6	50.0
Greece	17.5	16.2	23.8	22.9	21.5	19.8
Portugal	33.2	31.3	33.0	33.2	31.1	33.8
Romania	50.5	88.2	94.8	108	73.8	90.4
Turkey	77.2	*84.0*	86.6	*87.0*	73.3	80.7
Bulgaria	30.4	28.6	22.1	24.4	21.8	21.7
Serbia	12.0	13.9	13.8	15.8	15.1	18.1
Other						
	1643	1794	1901	1923	1739	2036
Canada	198	191	236	181	247	243
Australia	279	276	339	354	313	318
New Zealand	61.5	65.3	75.8	97.5	79.3	95.5
South Africa	151	174	213	235	223	249
Chile	78.8	98.8	99.5	102	116	109
Newfoundland	10.4	10.7	12.1	12.1	11.8	10.8
Argentina	255	312	282	286	356	386
Uruguay	39.8	31.9	34.5	35.3	40.8	45.7
Other						
	1073	1159	1292	1303	1387	1458

TABLE 3
WORLD EXPORTS AT CURRENT PRICES ($MILLION)
(*Continued*)

	1910	*1911*	*1912*	*1913*
USA	1829	2058	2363	2448
UK	2092	2207	2368	2553
France	1213	1181	1305	1337
Germany	1816	1970	2177	2454
Belgium	662	696	768	722
Sweden	160	178	201	215
Norway	72.3	78.0	87.7	103
Denmark	131	145	161	172
Switzerland	233	244	264	267
Netherlands	*375*	*395*	*426*	*466*
Other				
	4662	4887	5390	5736
Russia	746	819	782	783
Austria	490	487	554	561
Italy	401	426	463	485
Spain	165	166	178	183
Finland	56.4	62.1	66.1	78
Greece	28.1	27.4	28.2	23
Portugal	39.1	37.3	37.5	38
Rumania	120	134	125	130
Turkey	79.7	*85.0*	*87.0*	94
Bulgaria	25.1	35.9	*30.0*	18
Serbia	19.1	22.7	16.4	15
Other				
	2169	2302	2365	2408
Canada	279	274	290	356
Australia	362	386	384	382
New Zealand	108	92.5	106	112
South Africa	277	294	333	342
Chila	116	121	137	149
Newfoundland	11.8	12.0	13.9	15
Argentina	362	316	467	515
Uruguay	41.4	43.0	49.4	72
Other				
	1557	1538	1780	1943

TABLE 3
WORLD EXPORTS AT CURRENT PRICES ($MILLION)
(*Continued*)

	1850	1851	1852	1853	1854	1855
			Tropical Countries			
India	84.3	88.4	96.7	99.6	93.9	92.1
Brazil	28.9	39.5	39.4	41.0	44.4	50.8
Colombia	5.1	6.0	6.5	4.8	7.1	5.6
Ceylon	4.7	5.2	5.6	7.0	7.6	8.9
Philippines	4.0	4.1	4.9	5.8	6.9	8.2
British West Indies	15.1	15.6	15.6	14.6	14.4	15.3
Br Guyana	4.0	4.2	4.8	4.9	6.8	6.5
Cuba	22.6	27.8	29.3	30.9	28.3	30.7
Straits Settlements						
Indonesia						
Algeria						
Siam						
Nigeria						
Gold Coast						
Egypt						
Mexico						
Peru						
Venezuela						
Indochina						
Costa Rica						
Madagascar						
Other, fast	37	42	44	46	46	48
Other, slow	132	145	150	150	147	148
	338	378	397	405	402	414
			East Asia			
Japan						
China	50	52	54	57	59	62
	50	52	54	57	59	62
World total	1755	1899	2034	2441	2451	2492

TABLE 3
WORLD EXPORTS AT CURRENT PRICES ($MILLION)
(*Continued*)

	1856	*1857*	*1858*	*1859*	*1860*	*1861*
India	112	123	134	145	136	161
Brazil	52.7	64.0	52	55	57	65
Colombia	7.2	9.0	9.8	9.3	11.8	11.9
Ceylon	7.4	11.0	9.4	10.5	10.9	11.1
Philippines	9.7	*9.4*	*9.2*	*8.9*	*8.6*	*8.4*
British West Indies	17.9	24.9	23.2	20.8	20.4	20.4
Br Guyana	*8.0*	*11.2*	*10.4*	6.0	7.4	7.7
Cuba	*40.7*	*74.3*	*37.9*	*54.5*	*54.0*	*51.1*
Straits Settlements						30.0
Indonesia						
Algeria						
Siam						
Nigeria						
Gold Coast						
Egypt						
Mexico						
Peru						
Venezuela						
Indochina						
Costa Rica						
Madagascar						
Other, fast	56	72	63	68	67*	42
Other, slow	169	209	177	186	178	186
	481	608	525	565	552	596
Japan	*1*	*1*	*2*	*3*	4	3
China	*64*	*67*	*70*	73	76	*63*
	65	68	72	76	80	66
World total	2907	3111	2905	3119	3327	3113

TABLE 3
WORLD EXPORTS AT CURRENT PRICES ($MILLION)
(*Continued*)

	1862	*1863*	*1864*	*1865*	*1866*	*1867*
India	177	233	319	331	319	204
Brazil	63	65	72.5	78.2	76.6	76.8
Colombia	11.5	10.4	24.7	18.1	16.5	12.6
Ceylon	10.7	15.5	13.0	14.9	14.9	16.2
Philippines	*11.7*	*15.4*	*21.1*	22.0	*36.7*	*23.5*
British West Indies	24.0	30.0	41.3	28.9	23.7	22.2
Br Guyana	6.6	8.2	9.0	10.2	10.6	11.5
Cuba	*40.0*	*40.1*	*61.7*	*50.0*	*62.6*	*64.0*
Straits Settlements	35.1	40.4	40.5	47.2	48.3	30.1
Indonesia						
Algeria						
Siam						
Nigeria						
Gold Coast						
Egypt						
Mexico						
Peru						
Venezuela						
Indochina						
Costa Rica						
Madagascar						
Other, fast	43	52	68	68	69	52
Other, slow	188	222	236	278	275	203
	610	732	957	946	953	716
Japan	6	13	*14*	*14*	*15*	*15*
China	*84*	*99*	91	100	94	96
	90	112	105	114	109	111
World total	3222	3613	3957	4072	4522	4264

TABLE 3
WORLD EXPORTS AT CURRENT PRICES ($MILLION)
(*Continued*)

	1868	*1869*	*1870*	*1871*	*1872*	*1873*
India	248	258	255	269	308	269
Brazil	84.3	71.6	76.4	74.5	92.9	109
Colombia	17.1	20.3	17.6	17.9	21.5	18.0
Ceylon	16.9	16.2	18.3	17.3	15.0	26.2
Philippines	*28.5*	*29.7*	29.2	*20.4*	*17.1*	17.1
British West Indies	23.1	22.6	23.7	26.7	24.8	24.7
Br Guyana	10.9	10.5	11.6	13.4	11.9	10.8
Cuba	*68.0*	*95.0*	*89.6*	*95.9*	112	129
Straits Settlements	34.5	36.5	42.4	45.8	55.0	55.0
Indonesia			31.0	45.3	65.2	53.3
Algeria			24.2	*25.4*	31.9	29.6
Siam			6.8	7.5	6.3	6.8
Nigeria			3.6	3.8	3.1	3.0
Gold Coast			*1.9*	*2.0*	*1.6*	*1.6*
Egypt						
Mexico						
Peru						
Venezuela						
Indochina						
Costa Rica						
Madagascar						
Other, fast	60	63*	33	34	40.0	39*
Other, slow	229	235*	195	204	227	218*
	820	859	858	904	1033	1010
Japan	16.0	13.3	15.0	18.5	17.6	21.9
China	114	111	102	124	139	125
	130	124	117	143	157	147
World total	4401	4638	4747	5321	6000	6160

TABLE 3
WORLD EXPORTS AT CURRENT PRICES ($MILLION)
(*Continued*)

	1874	*1875*	*1876*	*1877*	*1878*	*1879*
India	268	252	255	254	275	244
Brazil	101	109	102	100	93.3	98.0
Colombia	23.5	32.1	17.8	14.5	19.9	21.9
Ceylon	20.5	25.7	19.6	25.9	18.7	16.2
Philippines	17.4	17.8	14.6	*17.7*	*16.7*	*19.4*
British West Indies	23.9	27.1	24.2	26.5	24.1	27.7
Br Guyana	13.4	11.4	14.8	14.8	12.2	13.2
Cuba	142	108	93.3	110	94.8	106
Straits Settlements	53.2	56.0	53.6	59.4	61.4	61.5
Indonesia	58.2	*72.0*	85.8	88.6	72.3	70.6
Algeria	*28.0*	*30.3*	*30.4*	*32.2*	*31.7*	*32.9*
Siam	5.9	8.2	7.6	8.7	8.2	9.5
Nigeria	3.4	3.5	4.0	4.5	3.8	4.1
Gold Coast	*1.8*	*1.8*	*2.1*	*2.3*	*2.0*	*2.1*
Egypt	66.4	65.9	67.0	63.0	40.0	70.4
Mexico	28.0	27.7	*27.7*	31.3	29.7	29.9
Peru	24.5	18.5	21.0	22.2	23.1	11.3
Venezuela	14.8	17.3	16.1	11.3	*16.8*	*18.6*
Indochina						
Costa Rica						
Madagascar						
Other, fast	119	124	121	123	118	120
Other, slow						
	1013	1008	978	1010	962	978
Japan	19.3	18.0	25.2	21.9	23.4	24.7
China	120	120	130	114	109	114
	139	138	155	136	132	139
World total	6065	5930	5847	5860	5869	5953

TABLE 3
WORLD EXPORTS AT CURRENT PRICES ($MILLION)
(*Continued*)

	1880	*1881*	*1882*	*1883*	*1884*	*1885*
India	272	302	331	331	349	326
Brazil	96.2	101	93.2	84.5	94.9	94.9
Colombia	22.4	23.8	21.2	17.8	13.4	10.2
Ceylon	20.5	14.8	14.7	13.9	13.2	12.4
Philippines	21.1	21.9	18.4	23.0	19.8	20.6
British West Indies	27.2	24.2	28.9	27.5	26.4	23.6
Br Guyana	12.7	12.6	15.6	15.4	11.3	8.7
Cuba	*109*	*105*	*117*	*109*	95.3	70.5
Straits Settlements	63.0	62.9	71.6	83.8	84.0	79.5
Indonesia	70.2	71.2	80.3	80.2	76.3	75.6
Algeria	34.8	28.2	33.4	31.6	30.1	37.6
Siam	8.7	8.8	8.6	8.0	9.8	7.9
Nigeria	3.8	3.3	3.8	3.8	4.2	4.2
Gold Coast	*2.0*	*1.7*	1.7	1.7	2.3	2.4
Egypt	68.7	65.1	54.3	60.8	62.7	56.5
Mexico	29.7	26.8	26.0	36.9	41.9	40.4
Peru	5.6	4.9	5.6	6.1	6.8	7.0
Venezuela	11.0	*20.2*	14.0	19.7	19.5	18.0
Indochina				15.4	14.6	17.0
Costa Rica				*2.1*	3.5	2.5
Madagascar				0.6	0.6	0.8
Other, fast	124	130	133*	120	122	115
Other, slow						
	1003	1029	1073	1093	1101	1032
Japan	23.4	27.6	33.5	31.8	29.4	31.9
China	125	115	108	110	105	98.0
	150	143	142	142	134	130
World total	6499	6639	6860	6867	6602	6148

TABLE 3
WORLD EXPORTS AT CURRENT PRICES ($MILLION)
(*Continued*)

	1886	*1887*	*1888*	*1889*	*1890*	*1891*
India	310	314	312	321	347	366
Brazil	72.1	99.8	109	116	125	126
Colombia	12.1	15.1	14.1	13.0	16.2	23.0
Ceylon	12.3	13.2	13.5	15.4	18.3	20.7
Philippines	20.1	19.4	19.5	25.4	20.7	20.2
British West Indies	21.0	24.9	28.1	27.9	29.4	25.5
Br Guyana	8.8	10.4	9.5	11.4	9.4	10.3
Cuba	*85.2*	*82.5*	*82.2*	*86.8*	*106*	*103*
Straits Settlements	76.1	86.6	90.1	90.1	104	97.6
Indonesia	74.9	75.2	74.1	79.5	71.0	90.1
Algeria	34.8	35.1	37.2	44.6	48.3	43.6
Siam	7.8	12.0	12.0	11.1	15.6	8.4
Nigeria	3.9	3.5	3.6	3.5	4.3	5.2
Gold Coast	2.0	1.8	1.9	2.0	2.9	3.3
Egypt	50.1	53.8	51.5	59.1	58.7	68.6
Mexico	35.7	38.9	37.3	44.6	47.5	53.3
Peru	8.3	6.5	8.8	8.3	6.9	8.1
Venezuela	16.5	17.2	17.2	19.9	23.7	26.1
Indochina	15.9	14.8	13.8	11.2	11.0	12.9
Costa Rica	2.3	4.7	4.0	4.6	6.6	6.1
Madagascar	0.7	0.5	121	129	140	148
Other, fast	111	119				
Other, slow						
	981	1049	1061	1125	1213	1266
Japan	39.6	41.1	49.5	51.4	49.5	61.8
China	108	112	120	125	126	137
	148	153	170	176	176	199
World total	6146	6377	6672	7237	7556	7623

TABLE 3
WORLD EXPORTS AT CURRENT PRICES ($MILLION)
(*Continued*)

	1892	*1893*	*1894*	*1895*	*1896*	*1897*
India	368	324	313	288	371	337
Brazil	105	142	123	140	128	130
Colombia	14.4	16.0	14.9	13.4	16.7	16.0
Ceylon	19.2	20.4	19.1	20.8	22.5	23.3
Philippines	19.2	22.2	16.5	*14.3*	*17.7*	*17.0*
British West Indies	28.7	31.7	27.3	24.1	23.9	23.5
Br Guyana	9.4	9.0	7.4	6.3	6.9	6.4
Cuba	*130*	*131*	*126*	*88.2*	*66.7*	*30.7*
Straits Settlements	92.8	89.0	88.2	89.4	92.2	91.2
Indonesia	86.4	77.4	80.4	90.5	80.2	84.5
Algeria	45.0	34.0	47.9	56.3	45.9	55.0
Siam	6.9	21.2	11.9	12.2	15.1	14.5
Nigeria	4.8	8.2	8.9	8.8	8.8	7.8
Gold Coast	3.2	3.5	4.1	4.3	3.8	4.2
Egypt	65.9	63.2	58.8	62.4	65.4	60.9
Mexico	56.1	58.1	42.9	47.7	58.7	59.8
Peru	9.7	9.3	7.2	*6.5*	10.7	15.1
Venezuela	21.0	16.7	21.5	22.3	21.5	18.6
Indochina	20.3	18.0	19.9	18.6	17.1	22.6
Costa Rica	4.7	4.3	5.1	5.2	5.6	5.5
Madagascar	148	148	149	140	0.7	0.8
Other, fast					149	143
Other, slow						
	1260	1249	1187	1160	1228	1168
Japan	62.4	54.7	56.0	69.8	62.1	81.2
China	123	105	111	127	119	132
	185	160	167	197	181	213
World total	7168	7115	6955	7249	7714	7904

TABLE 3
WORLD EXPORTS AT CURRENT PRICES ($MILLION)
(*Continued*)

	1898	*1899*	*1900*	*1901*	*1902*	*1903*
India	381	370	367	424	427	515
Brazil	92.8	86.9	182	194	175	177
Colombia	16.9	15.2	10.5	10.7	9.3	12.1
Ceylon	27.1	32.8	29.9	28.3	31.9	33.2
Philippines	*14.8*	14.8	23.0	24.5	28.7	32.4
British West Indies	26.3	29.2	30.0	29.8	30.3	25.7
Br Guyana	8.6	9.4	9.6	8.3	8.5	8.5
Cuba	*25.4*	*42.3*	45.2	63.1	51.1	77.8
Straits Settlements	99.0	113	128	124	125	138
Indonesia	87.5	101	104	103	107	110
Algeria	52.7	64.4	44.3	50.5	57.7	55.5
Siam	16.1	15.2	15.2	21.2	21.8	19.1
Nigeria	7.9	8.2	8.7	9.9	12.6	12.5
Gold Coast	4.8	5.4	4.3	2.7	3.8	4.8
Egypt	58.4	75.9	82.9	79.8	89.2	96.6
Mexico	62.1	69.4	74.6	77.3	75.6	83.1
Peru	14.7	16.4	21.8	23.0	18.0	18.8
Venezuela	14.9	*13.4*	*9.3*	*9.4*	8.2	7.7
Indochina	24.6	26.6	30.0	31.0	35.8	23.2
Costa Rica	5.7	4.9	6.3	5.8	5.7	7.3
Madagascar	1.0	1.6	2.1	1.7	2.5	3.1
Other, fast	148	160	174	186	184	201
Other, slow						
	1190	1276	1403	1508	1509	1663
Japan	82.5	107	102	126	129	144
China	126	157	132	135	150	156
	209	264	234	261	279	300
World total	8218	8997	9516	9566	9815	10587

TABLE 3
WORLD EXPORTS AT CURRENT PRICES ($MILLION)
(*Continued*)

	1904	*1905*	*1906*	*1907*	*1908*	*1909*
India	531	546	594	599	516	628
Brazil	189	215	255	263	215	310
Colombia	19.2	14.6	16.5	16.1	15.7	17.2
Ceylon	32.8	33.2	35.6	42.0	42.2	47.6
Philippines	29.2	33.5	32.6	33.1	33.2	31.4
British West Indies	27.5	32.3	31.2	37.8	32.7	34.1
Br Guyana	9.4	9.3	8.7	8.0	9.9	9.3
Cuba	93.1	99.2	105	111	98.6	117
Straits Settlements	143	138	177	173	155	159
Indonesia	119	124	133	147	190	184
Algeria	52.5	44.2	54.1	65.3	76.6	76.1
Siam	25.4	27.3	32.5	35.9	36.8	37.7
Nigeria	14.2	13.9	15.3	20.4	16.6	20.3
Gold Coast	6.5	8.0	9.7	12.8	12.3	12.9
Egypt	103	101	123	140	106	130
Mexico	94.5	97.1	135	124	120	115
Peru	19.8	28.0	27.7	27.9	26.6	34.4
Venezuela	15.6	14.0	15.6	15.8	15.2	16.2
Indochina	30.2	32.6	34.1	42.4	40.5	46.9
Costa Rica	6.8	8.1	8.8	9.4	7.8	8.2
Madagascar	3.7	4.4	5.4	5.6	4.5	6.5
Other, fast	213	218	246	254	230	262
Other, slow						
	1778	1842	2096	2183	2002	2304
Japan	159	160	211	215	188	206
China	170	170	195	214	181	216
	329	330	406	429	369	422
World total	10,945	11,889	13,227	13,988	12,904	13,870

TABLE 3
WORLD EXPORTS AT CURRENT PRICES ($MILLION)
(*Continued*)

	1910	*1911*	*1912*	*1913*
India	701	764	828	834
Brazil	307	325	363	317
Colombia	17.8	22.4	32.3	34
Ceylon	54.0	59.0	64.5	76
Philippines	40.4	40.3	50.9	48
British West Indies	36.8	37.4	36.4	38
Br. Guyana	8.4	10.1	8.4	10
Cuba	145	130	148	164
Straits Settlements	184	194	213	221
Indonesia	180	211	241	270
Algeria	114	107	115	97
Siam	40.5	31.1	30.0	43
Nigeria	25.8	26.2	29.6	36
Gold Coast	13.1	18.4	20.9	26
Egypt	144	143	172	156
Mexico	129	146	148	150
Peru	36.0	45.9	45.8	43
Venezuela	16.8	18.8	25.9	29
Indochina	48.5	40.6	42.4	59
Costa Rica	8.4	8.9	10.0	10
Madagascar	8.8	9.2	12.6	11
Other, fast	287	300	322	323
Other, slow				
	2546	2687	2958	2995
Japan	228	223	262	315
China	252	249	279	299
	480	472	542	614
World total	15335	16151	17766	18697

Appendix III
World Exports at 1913 Prices

This part of the exercise is the most hazardous, because of the paucity of price indexes.

USA

Douglas North has price and quantity data up to 1860, and Lipsey[8] from 1879. We have made an index for the intervening years, using those unit values of exports that were available in the *Statistical Abstract* an agricultural series from 1869 implicit in Lipsey, and the so-called Aldrich report which is the basis of most US wholesale price indexes. The index is in two segments, one running from 1860–69, which is calculated on both 1860 and 1869 bases, which are then averaged geometrically, and the second segment based on 1869 and 1879 and treated in the same way. The period is tricky to handle because the dollar was floating, and exports are printed sometimes in currency and sometimes in specie without warning, while prices are in currency. Here is the resulting price index in specie (1913 = 100)

1860	108	1867	158	1874	110
61	110	68	123	75	103
62	171	69	140	76	98
63	241	1870	115	77	99
64	291	71	122	78	90
65	231	72	120	79	93
66	213	73	115		

Note that the standard sources show US trade for years ending 30 June, while Lipsey's figures, used here to 1869, are for calendar years.

NORTHWEST EUROPE

We have price indexes going back to the 1870s for the UK, France, Germany (implicit in Appendix I) Belgium, Sweden, and Denmark, and have averaged Sweden and Denmark for Norway.[9] The year-by-year volumes yielded by these indexes are summed and divided into the year-by-year sum of values to give a price index for Western Europe, which is then applied to Switzerland and the Netherlands. For the periods before 1872 Belgium and Denmark drop out and the index for Western Europe is based on the other four countries.

OTHER EUROPE

The exports of this group were primarily agricultural and so require a different price index. There is an index for Italy[10] which we have not used because of doubt as to the foreign exchange value of the lira in the late 1870s. We have used for this group Levy-Leboyer's index of prices of imports into France.

TEMPERATE SETTLEMENTS

There are indexes for Canada and Australia and part of an index for Argentina which we have completed.[11] These produce an index for the group, excluding South Africa gold, which is added separately. These indexes do not extend back before 1872. Before that year we have used the Sauerbeck index of wholesale prices in the UK.[12]

TROPICAL COUNTRIES

The heart of this is the price index of tropical export crops that we introduced in our Wicksell Lectures, and have reproduced in our recent book.[13] This has been modified by adding over 1890–1913 special indexes of prices of minerals and of manufactures, with weights of 8:1:1, which make little difference to the result. We have also subtracted 10 per cent of an index of ocean freights, to correct from c.i.f. to f.o.b. prices. This crop index has been extended back to 1850, with a new set of weights at 1871; but freights are not deducted from this part.

EAST ASIA

We have volume indexes[14] for Japan from 1873 and for China from

1867. Prior to this we have made an index of the prices of tea and silk with weights of 3:2.

COMPARISON

We are not aware of any other study of world trade at constant prices, apart from Hilgerdt, applying British price indexes to his totals. Bairoch however, has published an index for Europe.[15] Our total values are surprisingly close, considering that our methodologies for handling missing items are quite different. Thus the figures run, in million dollars

	Bairoch	*This text*
1859–61	2160	2094
1869–71	3260	3257
1913	10,590	10,697

Our price indexes are close around 1870, but are 3 per cent apart around 1860.

	Bairoch	*This text*
1859–61	127.6	123.7
1869–71	119.1	118.3
1913	100	100

Table 4 summarises our results at 1913 prices.

TABLE 4
WORLD EXPORTS AT 1913 PRICES ($ MILLION)

	1850	*1851*	*1852*	*1853*	*1854*
USA	124	160	179	225	205
UK	334	354	375	431	421
Northwest Europe	484	494	506	573	570
Other Europe	258	282	313	379	355
Temperate Settlements	88	90	150	153	142
Tropics	402	485	509	445	423
East Asia	57	59	60	61	62
	1747	1924	2092	2267	2178

TABLE 4
WORLD EXPORTS AT 1913 PRICES ($ MILLION)
(*Continued*)

	1855	*1856*	*1857*	*1858*	*1859*
USA	180	238	218	217	244
UK	425	503	515	504	551
Northwest Europe	586	615	655	672	699
Other Europe	365	378	376	383	365
Temperate Settlements	167	176	168	179	195
Tropics	422	463	507	510	512
East Asia	64	66	68	70	74
	2209	2439	2507	2535	2640

	1860	*1861*	*1862*	*1863*	*1864*
USA	293	186	105	77	49
UK	579	530	500	536	535
Northwest Europe	759	741	776	862	932
Other Europe	424	429	414	410	411
Temperate Settlements	203	201	201	207	221
Tropics	484	532	492	567	725
East Asia	75	69	97	109	100
	2817	2688	2585	2768	2973

	1865	*1866*	*1867*	*1868*	*1869*
USA	59	159	177	219	232
UK	580	640	652	693	737
Northwest Europe	982	1092	1099	1161	1229
Other Europe	461	463	596	613	638
Temperate Settlements	241	250	242	268	274
Tropics	802	829	663	745	774
East Asia	97	92	110	115	118
	3222	3525	3539	3814	4002

	1870	*1871*	*1872*	*1873*	*1874*
USA	337	366	376	477	503
UK	794	890	924	889	884
Northwest Europe	1206	1324	1557	1568	1598
Other Europe	671	768	708	756	826
Temperate Settlements	275	292	320	346	335
Tropics	802	819	868	878	873
East Asia	114	118	146	134	137
	4199	4577	4899	5048	5156

TABLE 4
WORLD EXPORTS AT 1913 PRICES ($MILLION)
(*Continued*)

	1875	*1876*	*1877*	*1878*	*1879*
USA	484	587	613	805	810
UK	878	856	882	888	936
Northwest Europe	1673	1627	1662	1673	1698
Other Europe	844	884	903	1001	1041
Temperate Settlements	322	326	336	338	349
Tropics	908	923	902	875	923
East Asia	143	152	147	151	155
	5252	5355	5445	5731	5912

	1880	*1881*	*1882*	*1883*	*1884*
USA	857	778	695	761	747
UK	1051	1150	1165	1197	1207
Nortwest Europe	1817	1886	1936	1977	1994
Other Eruope	974	1023	1154	1190	1173
Temperate Settlements	416	443	471	475	462
Tropics	912	1009	1042	1051	1135
East Asia	166	157	173	178	185
	6193	6446	6636	6829	6903

	1885	*1886*	*1887*	*1888*	*1889*
USA	734	810	818	752	940
UK	1148	1198	1253	1333	1386
Northwest Europe	1955	2087	2164	2197	2349
Other Europe	1149	1149	1212	1372	1359
Temperate Settlements	495	469	507	588	584
Tropics	1134	1141	1206	1220	1250
East Asia	178	206	169	194	197
	6793	7060	7329	7656	8065

	1890	*1891*	*1892*	*1893*	*1894*
USA	989	1082	1121	1060	1138
UK	1406	1331	1280	1231	1284
Northwest Europe	2409	2404	2350	2342	2382
Other Europe	1416	1482	1328	1493	1659
Temperate Settlements	607	702	735	766	837
Tropics	1304	1361	1355	1343	1380
East Asia	173	215	221	236	259
	8304	8577	8400	8471	8939

TABLE 4
WORLD EXPORTS AT 1913 PRICES ($MILLION)
(Continued)

	1895	*1896*	*1897*	*1898*	*1899*
USA	1119	1381	1552	1792	1721
UK	1396	1472	1452	1443	1561
Northwest Europe	2630	2720	2821	2838	3066
Other Europe	1712	1832	1826	1798	1705
Temperate Settlements	907	881	916	1013	1093
Tropics	1398	1445	1407	1506	1575
East Asia	284	245	284	285	305
	9446	9976	10,258	10,675	11,026

	1900	*1901*	*1902*	*1903*	*1904*
USA	1782	1812	1638	1684	1640
UK	1496	1510	1609	1646	1682
Northwest Europe	3093	3095	3309	3454	3560
Other Europe	1668	1834	1934	2069	2021
Temperate Settlements	936	1040	1032	1195	1286
Tropics	1670	1774	1910	2028	2067
East Asia	264	319	337	335	359
	10,909	11,384	11,769	12,411	12,615

	1905	*1906*	*1907*	*1908*	*1909*
USA	1909	1971	1990	1919	1804
UK	1849	1987	2148	1977	2060
Northern Europe	3847	4155	4279	4082	4371
Other Europe	2154	2073	2050	2036	2301
Temperate Settlements	1329	1388	1351	1504	1504
Tropics	2142	2329	2322	2249	2560
East Asia	340	374	370	387	481
	13,570	14,277	14,510	14,154	15,081

	1910	*1911*	*1912*	*1913*
USA	1789	2203	2475	2448
UK	2247	2329	2457	2553
Northwest Europe	4850	5047	5461	5736
Other Europe	2238	2376	2389	2408
Temperate Settlement	1569	1614	1808	1943
Tropics	2472	2687	2929	2995
East Asia	550	529	579	614
	15,715	16,785	18,098	18,697

Appendix IV
World Trade in Manufactures

DATA

We have constructed an annual series of world exports of manufactures, based on individual series for the UK, France, the USA, and Germany, and on group data for other countries.

UK values at current prices are taken from Schlote. However, Schlote's quantities at 1913 prices cannot be used, since for total UK exports we have used Imlah's quantities, and this series rises faster than Schlote's. The solution adopted is to calculate the ratio of manufactures to total trade in constant prices, as given by Schlote, and apply this ratio to Imlah's totals. Alternatively one could assume that Schlote's imports of primary products at constant prices were correct, and subtract from Imlah's totals to get exports of manufactures at constant prices. This series would be more volatile, but would not on average differ greatly.

French values at current prices are as given in the trade returns from 1846 onwards. The trade returns also give quantities at constant prices from 1826–63. Values before 1846 and quantities after 1863 are found by applying Levy-Leboyer's price index.

US series from 1879 are based on Lipsey's 'Finished Manufactures', from which one must subtract refined petroleum, and to which one must add certain semimanufactures (leather, metals and chemicals). The same adjustments are made to official data back to 1860 and to Douglas North's data for earlier years. Both Lipsey and North provide price indexes for the periods they cover. The gap in between is filled partly from export unit values and partly from wholesale prices.

German values in current prices are available in the trade returns from 1872 onwards, except that they have to be adjusted downwards from 1880–88 for the break at 1888, and upwards from 1872–79 for the break at 1879. For reasons given in Appendix I, we have not used Hoffmann's quantities or his prices before 1872, but have used his quantity index, in association with our price index (see below) to arrive at German exports of manufactures in current prices from 1850–72. Here manufactures is the sum of semifinished and finished products.

The results for these four countries are not very different from Maizels' figures for 1913 ($m).

	UK	France	US	Germany
Maizels	1960	787	846	1726
This text	1928	813	869	1824

We differ significantly on exports from the rest of Europe, of which Maizels offers only a sample. Here we have relied on Lamartine Yates, whose coverage is much wider. And have further assumed that Netherlands exports of manufactures were 50 per cent of domestic exports in 1913. This gives exports from other Western Europe as $773 million and exports from 'Other Europe' as $671 million in 1913, respectively 39.7 and 27.9 per cent of total exports. Finally, we create two annual series, by assuming these proportions to be constant all the way back to 1850. This is a large assumption, but we cannot be certain whether these proportions rose or fell, and reasonable changes do not seem to make much difference to total exports of manufactures, which in the earlier years are dominated by Britain, France and Germany.

We also add a series for Canada, Japan and India, using Maizels for 1899 and 1913, and guesstimating the other years. This comes to $349 million in 1913, making total exports in manufactures $7227 million.

Our $7227 million compares with Yates' $6928, which is probably the most comprehensive and careful estimate for 1913. We could easily adjust our figure downward for 1913, but to take this adjustment back year by year to 1850 would require detailed sorting of export statistics of many countries for strict conformity with the Brussels classification, and the yield would not be worth the effort.

Our price index is derived by summing exports from the UK, France and the USA in both current and constant prices. A reliable German price index would be a great help.

The final result is given in Table 6, which shows world exports of manufactures in current and in 1913 prices.

A similar table can be derived for world exports of primary products by subtracting from total world exports in current prices in Table 3 and in 1913 prices in Table 4.

This process also yields an implicit price index of primary products. Surprisingly, but comfortingly, this index is not very far from the Sauerbeck index.[16] We give the data here in five-year averages around peak years (except that 1911 was not a peak year). We also include the terms of trade (primary products divided by manufactures), which we shall be using in a moment. All series are on the base of 1913 = 100.

Prices of primary products	*1853*	*1872*	*1899*	*1911*
This paper	98.9	113.9	80.2	97.5
Sauerbeck (less freights)	97.8	112.0	79.0	95.7
Terms of trade	83.4	89.9	95.8	101.4

Our weakest spot is in primary product prices for the second half of the 1850s (not shown here). Our index for 1857–61 averages 114.3 as against Sauerbeck's 105.5. One can see the effect of this in Figure 4, which displays exports of primary products and of manufactures at constant prices. A too-high price index explains why the primary products points from 1855–61 lie so far below the straight line running from 1853–72, in contrast with similar points for exports of manufactures. We need more price indexes for primary producing countries in the 1850s and 1860s. (The large gap in the 1860s was due to the effects of the Civil War on exports of raw cotton and of cotton manufactures).

The terms of trade move against manufactures all the time in the figures shown above, but this is because dates important to these terms have not beeen shown. Our results follow the usual pattern. The terms of trade for primary products reach a peak in the early 1880s, averaging 104.0 over 1881–85, slide down to 95.8 over 1897–1901, and then rise again up to the First World War.

The share of manufactures in world trade declined only slightly in constant prices from 1853–72, but because of adverse terms of trade there was a marked decline of the share in current prices.

	1853	*1872*	*1899*	*1911*
Ratio in constant prices	0.364	0.360	0.358	0.382
Ratio in current prices	0.406	0.385	0.368	0.378

The reversal of this decline after 1899 is a challenging problem.

ANALYSIS

This material can be used to investigate the changes in the rate of growth of world trade in manufactures.

Figure 4 shows that both manufactures and primary products

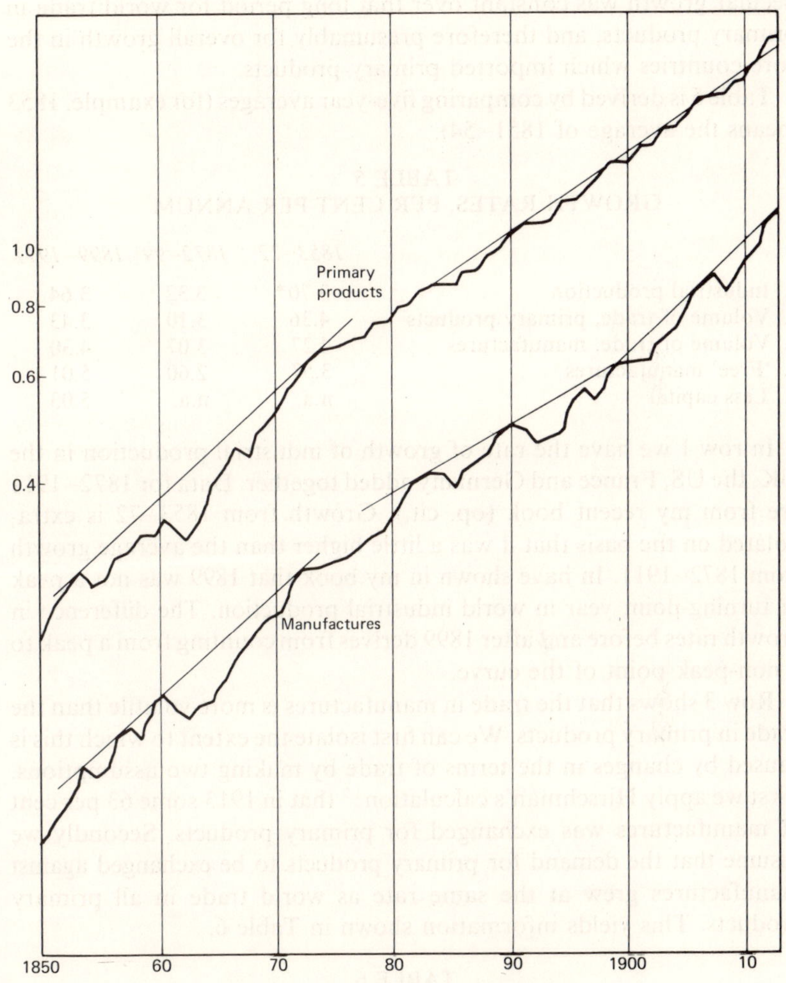

Fig. 4   World trade in 1913 prices

decelerated after 1872; however, in manufactures there was a new
acceleration after 1899. One could make a similar acceleration for
primary products by counting from the peak of 1872 to a trough in 1887
and a peak in 1913, but this would not be legitimate. If one counts only
from peak to peak, the primary product peaks lie more or less on a

straight line from 1883 onwards (except that 1913 is a little too high). Secular growth was constant over that long period for world trade in primary products, and therefore presumably for overall growth in the core countries which imported primary products.

Table 5 is derived by comparing five-year averages (for example, 1853 means the average of 1851–54).

TABLE 5
GROWTH RATES, PER CENT PER ANNUM

	1853–72	1872–99	1899–1911
1. Industrial production	3.70*	3.32	3.64
2. Volume of trade, primary products	4.36	3.10	3.43
3. Volume of trade, manufactures	4.27	3.07	4.30
4. 'Free' manufactures	3.57	2.60	5.01
5. Less capital	n.a.	n.a.	5.03

In row 1 we have the rate of growth of industrial production in the UK, the US, France and Germany added together. Data for 1872–1911 are from my recent book (op. cit.). Growth from 1853–72 is extrapolated on the basis that it was a little higher than the average growth from 1872–1911. In have shown in my book that 1899 was not a peak or turning-point year in world industrial production. The difference in growth rates before and after 1899 derives from counting from a peak to a non-peak point of the curve.

Row 3 shows that the trade in manufactures is more volatile than the trade in primary products. We can first isolate the extent to which this is caused by changes in the terms of trade by making two assumptions. First we apply Hirschman's calculation[17] that in 1913 some 63 per cent of manufactures was exchanged for primary products. Secondly we assume that the demand for primary products to be exchanged against manufactures grew at the same rate as world trade in all primary products. This yields information shown in Table 6.

TABLE 6
1913 PRICES ($MILLION)

	1899	1911
1. World trade in primaries	6967	10,437
2. World trade in manufactures	3883	6438
3. Primary products for manufactures	2672	4002
4. Manufactures for primaries	2559	4056
5. 'Free' manufactures	1324	2382
6. Capital export	799	1436
7. Other uses of manufactures	525	946

TABLE 7
WORLD EXPORTS OF MANUFACTURES ($MILLION)

	Current values	At 1913 prices		Current values	At 1913 prices
1850	731	636	*1882*	2545	2500
1851	766	677	*1883*	2540	2571
1852	819	719	*1884*	2483	2592
1853	1026	829	*1885*	2260	2465
1854	990	819	*1886*	2317	2600
1855	993	832	*1887*	2399	2720
1856	1156	936	*1888*	2518	2855
1857	1212	957	*1889*	2708	3070
1858	1130	926	*1890*	2806	3114
1859	1278	1020	*1891*	2718	3040
1860	1345	1090	*1892*	2525	2922
1861	1230	1021	*1893*	2539	2952
1862	1272	1004	*1894*	2484	3067
1863	1465	1046	*1895*	2703	3448
1864	1617	1076	*1896*	2892	3615
1865	1633	1142	*1897*	2884	3632
1866	1767	1231	*1898*	2986	3785
1867	1721	1303	*1899*	3345	4020
1868	1745	1393	*1900*	3561	3983
1869	1826	1468	*1901*	3485	3997
1870	1855	1508	*1902*	3657	4307
1871	2077	1678	*1903*	3812	4448
1872	2345	1791	*1904*	4050	4682
1873	2331	1790	*1905*	4487	5146
1874	2272	1819	*1906*	4960	5421
1875	2226	1853	*1907*	5370	5659
1876	2119	1884	*1908*	4824	5226
1877	2110	1943	*1909*	5064	5559
1878	2121	2034	*1910*	5708	6040
1879	2106	2098	*1911*	6186	6410
1880	2327	2244	*1912*	6778	6952
1881	2443	2450	*1913*	7227	7227

This is derived as follows: Rows 1 and 2 are calculated from Table 4 and Table 7. In row 4 $4056 is 63 per cent of $6438 in row 2. The equivalent in primary products is found by dividing by the terms of trade (in current prices rows 3 and 4 are the same). From row 1 we get that trade in primaries multiplied by 1.498. So the 1899 figure for row 3 is $2672. Multiplying by the terms of trade gives $2559 for row 4. The cost of adverse terms of trade is (4056 − 2559 × 1.498), which is $222. If this is excluded, trade in manufactures grew at 4.00 per cent per annum.

If the terms of trade had been constant and if the exchange of manufactures against other than primary products had grown only at 3 per cent per annum, exports of manufactures would have been smaller by $722 million. So the loss on the terms of trade explains about one-third of the 'abnormality' of 1911.

Continuing, we then subtract row 4 from row 2 to arrive at 'free' manufactures, that is, those not used to pay for imports of primary products. 'Free' manufactures are exchanged against other manufactures, or used for capital export, or exchanged against services. This is the growth rate shown in row 4 of Table 5.

Next we subtract capital export.[18] This grew at 5.0 per cent per annum. If it had grown at say 3.3 per cent it would have been smaller by $256 million. So capital export explains about the same as the loss on the terms of trade.

The residual in row 7 is growing rather fast—at about 5.1 per cent per annum. This may mean that the exchange of manufactures for manufactures is increased. But if this were so, imports of manufactures into the industrial countries would have risen relatively to consumption, and this is denied by Maizels' data.

A plausible alternative explanation is that the proportion of primary products paid for with manufactures increased between 1899 and 1913. In particular the USA was in a state of sharp transition. Manufactures rose over this twelve-year period from 21 to 34 per cent of US exports in current values. This means that the USA switched to some extent from paying for imports of primary products with primaries to paying with manufactures. If we put the extent of the switch at only 7 per cent of US trade (about $140 million) row 7 grows only at 3.0 per cent per annum, and this is perfectly consistent with a decline in the ratio of imports to consumption in the industrial countries.

The chief ingredients in the relatively high growth rate of exports of manufactures between 1899 and 1911 would then be the terms of trade, rapid growth of capital export, and increased use of manufactures to pay for imports of primary products.

Using the same technique we can work back through 1872 and 1853, except that we do not have data for capital exports. The results shown in Table 5 bring out the relative prosperity of 1853–72, and also what British historians call the great depression of 1872–99. The figures in the second vertical column of Table 5 exaggerate the depression because 1899 was not a turning point. Still it is clear that trade grew more slowly than production in the middle period, just as trade grew faster than production in the periods on either side.

Since capital export grew rapidly between 1853 and 1872 it is not impossible that the prosperity of the industrial countries to import manufactures was already declining in this period, especially as the USA, France and Germany freed themselves from dependence on British iron and textiles. It seems quite plausible that the share of manufactures exchanged against manufactures was declining continually from 1853–1913, and that this was why the share of manufactures in world trade declined down to 1899. An alternative explanation would be the rise of invisible income throughout the century (especially dividends, interest, commissions and insurance) which reduced the need to export manufactures to pay for imports of primary products. One should however note that the decline of this share to 1899 could be partly due to the assumption we have made to arrive at a series for Europe other than the UK, France and Germany (in other words, that manufactures were a constant proportion of the exports of this group). The decline would disappear if we assumed that in this group of countries the share of manufactures in total trade doubled over this period. Such an extreme assumption is however less plausible than the alternative assumptions that import substitution of manufactures was already well under way in continental Europe and the USA, at the expense of the UK; and that invisible income reduced the relative share of manufactures in world trade.

ENDNOTES

1. Gerhard Bondi, op. cit.
2. Bodo von Borries, *Deutschlands Aussenhandel, 1836 bis 1856* (Stuttgart: Gustav Fischer Verlag, 1970).
3. Op. cit.
4. A. V. Desai, *Real Wages in Germany 1871–1913* (Oxford: Oxford University Press, 1968).
5. W. A. Lewis, ed., *Tropical Development 1880–1913*, (London: Allen and Unwin, 1970), pages 47–9. For Colombia we have used this series presented by W. P. McGreevey, *An Economic History of Colombia 1845–1930* (Cambrige: Cambridge University Press, 1971).
6. A continuous series from 1851 is given in *US Monthly Summary of Commerce and Finance* (1904) vol. 11, no. 10, p. 3723.
7. Mulhall published several revisions of his figures in different books. The latest *Dictionary* version shows exports separately, but only in ten-year averages. His averages for 1861–70 and 1871–80 are $4034 and $5908 million, comparing with our $4055 and $5939 million.
8. Douglas North, *The Economic Growth of the United States 1790–1860* (Englewood Cliffs, N. J.: Prentice-Hall, 1961). R. E. Lipsey, *Price and*

Quantity Trends in the Foreign Trade of the United States (Princeton, N. J.: Princeton University Press, 1963).

9. A. H. Imlah, *Economic Elements in the Pax Brittanica*. (Cambridge, Mass.: Harvard University Press, 1958). Maurice Levy-Leboyer, 'L'Heritage de Simiand; Prix, Profits et termes d'échange au XIX^{e}Siècle', *Revue Historique* (January–March 1970). Charles P. Kindleberger, 'Les Termes d'échange de la Belgique entre 1870 et 1952', in Banque Nationale de Beligique, *Bulletin d'Information et de Documentation* (September 1954). G. Fridlizius, 'Sweden's Exports 1850–1960', *Economy and History*, vol. VI (1963). A. Ølgaard, *Growth, Productivity and Relative Prices* (Amsterdam, 1968).

10. P. Ercolani, 'Documentazione Statistica di Base', in G. Fua, ed., *Sviloppo Economico in Italia*, vol. III (Milan: Angeli, 1969).

11. M. C. Urquhart and K. A. H. Buckley, *Historical Statistics of Canada* (Cambridge: Cambridge University Press, 1965). Roland Wilson, *Capital Imports and the Terms of Trade* (Melbourne: Melbourne University Press, 1931). A. G. Ford, 'Export Prices for the Argentine Republic', *Inter-American Economic Affairs*, vol. 9 (1955). The indexes for Australia and Argentina are added together to provide a price index for the sum of New Zealand, Chile, Uruguay and South Africa (excluding gold).

12. 'On Prices of Commodities and the Precious Metals', *Journal of the Royal Statistical Society* (September 1886).

13. Op. cit., pp. 280–1.

14. The Oriental Economist, *The Foreign Trade of Japan: A Statistical Review* (Tokyo, 1935). Hsiao Liang-Lin, op. cit., p. 274–5.

15. Paul Bairoch, 'European Trade in the XIX Century', *Journal of European Economic History*, vol. 2, no. 1 (1973).

16. Raw materials and food indexes combined in the ratio 4:3; 10 per cent of ocean freight index subtracted between 1870 and 1913, but not in earlier comparison.

17. A. O. Hirschman, 'The Commodity Structure of World Trade', *Quarterly Journal of Economics* (1943).

18. Data consists of annual capital export from the UK, France and Germany minus annual capital import into the USA, divided by our index number of the prices of manufactures. Annual series from Arthur I. Bloomfield, *Patterns of Fluctuation in International Investment before 1914* (Princeton University: Princeton Studies in International Finance No. 21).

Comments

Alexander Yeats (Switzerland)

Without doubt, the impressive body of empirical evidence Professor Lewis assembles in this paper has important implications for development policy in general, and the choice of a trade-development policy in particular. If the future prognosis is for a resumption of the 8 per cent growth rate in world trade which occurred over 1953–73 (11 per cent for manufactures) this seemingly favours outward-oriented growth strategies. However, if world trade expands more slowly, it may be necessary to re-examine alternative growth strategies which are essentially inward-looking in nature. Unfortunately, as Professor Lewis so clearly indicates, little in the historical record suggests that 1953–73 growth rates constitute a 'norm' or have been sustained over other periods during the last 150 years. This is perhaps the single most important message conveyed to us in the paper.

While Professor Lewis's data will undoubtedly be a valuable input into empirical analyses of the trade-growth relationship, my comments are largely devoted to observations on the curious period 1953–73 and its implications for developing countries. In particular, three questions are posed concerning the study's findings: (1) To what extent was the high growth rate due to special factors such as the formation of customs unions from which the LDCs did not receive direct benefit? (2) Were there important differences in the trade patterns of *individual* developed countries, particularly with regard to developing nations? (3) How important are variations in the rate of growth in world trade for LDCs as opposed to other factors such as the industrial nations' commercial policy measures. A further *crucial* consideration concerns the extent to which the rate of growth of trade is an endogenous factor which can be influenced by policy measures, institutional reforms, or supply factors in the developed and developing countries.[1]

Concerning the first question on the influence of customs unions, Professor Lewis notes that one explanation for the rapid rate of growth in manufactures centres on the important role of the European import-consumption ratio which rose from about 11 per cent in 1955 to 30 per cent in 1973. While the unprecedented rise in this coefficient was a key factor maintaining the growth rate for manufactures, analysis of changes in the ratio for different groups of exporters shows that the benefits were very unevenly distributed.

As an illustration, Table 1 compares changes in the EEC(6), Japan and US import-consumption ratio for manufactures over the period 1959–60 to 1975. The table shows the sharp increase in this coefficient for the European countries was due primarily to intratrade, with the external trade ratio rising *less than* 3 percentage points from 7.56 to 10.45. Had the ratio for the EEC changed in line with that for external trade, I estimate that the growth rate for world trade in manufactures would have been about 8 or 9 per cent as opposed to 11 per cent. A further reduction would be required to account for the full EEC(9) integration and the effects of EFTA. Such data suggest that European integration was an important factor in the recent growth in manufactures and needs to be accounted for in any analysis of the 1953–73 period. Table 1 also shows that the import-consumption ratio for LDC products in these three markets is small, reaching a maximum of 2 per cent in the United States. The important point which emerges, however, is that a stabilisation of the import-consumption ratio should have a relatively minor effect on LDC trade since they did not directly participate in its expansion in the first place.[2]

Aside from the effect of customs unions and European integration, it appears important to inquire why the *individual* country parameters for Professor Lewis' trade model (page 14) have developed so differently. These differences are of sufficient magnitude to have serious repercussions on the trade position of developing countries.

As an illustration, Figure 1 shows the performance of nineteen developed countries as markets for the LDCs in 1976. The vertical axis measures imports of manufactures per capita from LDCs, while the horizontal axis shows the LDCs' percentage of each countries' manufactured imports. The figure thus indicates the *level* and *share* of each developed country as a market for LDC exports of manufactures. The cross-bars in the figure show averages for these variables. Industrial countries in the upper right quadrant (like the USA) are above average in *both* the level and share of imports from LDCs, while those in the lower left are below average in both measures. The differences depicted in the diagram have important implications for the developing countries. For example, if France brought its per capita imports up to the group

TABLE 1

IMPORTS OF MANUFACTURES FROM SELECTED COUNTRY GROUPS AS A PERCENTAGE OF APPARENT CONSUMPTION IN THE EUROPEAN ECONOMIC COMMUNITY (6), JAPAN AND THE UNITED STATES

Manufactures	EEC(6)			USA			Japan		
	1959–60	1975	change	1959–60	1975	change	1959–60	1975	change
Apparent Consumption ($m)	107,861	586,877	479,016	275,779	831,669	555,890	25,096	290,466	265,370
Trade as a percentage of consumption									
External imports	7.56	10.45	2.89	3.28	7.13	3.85	6.02	5.97	−0.05
Imports from:									
Developing countries	1.46	1.78	0.27	0.73	2.01	1.28	1.16	1.80	0.64
Socialist countries	0.51	1.01	0.50	0.02	0.09	0.07	0.12	0.30	0.18
Developed Market Economies of which:	12.16	24.06	11.90	2.53	5.03	2.50	4.74	3.86	−0.88
United States	1.81	2.11	0.30	—	—	—	3.08	1.78	−1.30
EEC(6)	6.62	16.40	9.78	0.74	1.42	0.68	0.72	0.79	0.07
United Kingdom	1.02	1.53	0.51	0.33	0.41	0.08	0.31	0.26	−0.05
Japan	0.09	0.68	0.59	0.36	1.34	0.98	—	—	—
Other	2.62	3.34	0.72	1.11	1.85	0.74	0.64	1.02	0.38

Source: Adapted from United Nations Conference on Trade and Development, *Handbook of International Trade and Development Statistics, Supplement 1977* (New York, 1978), p. 286.

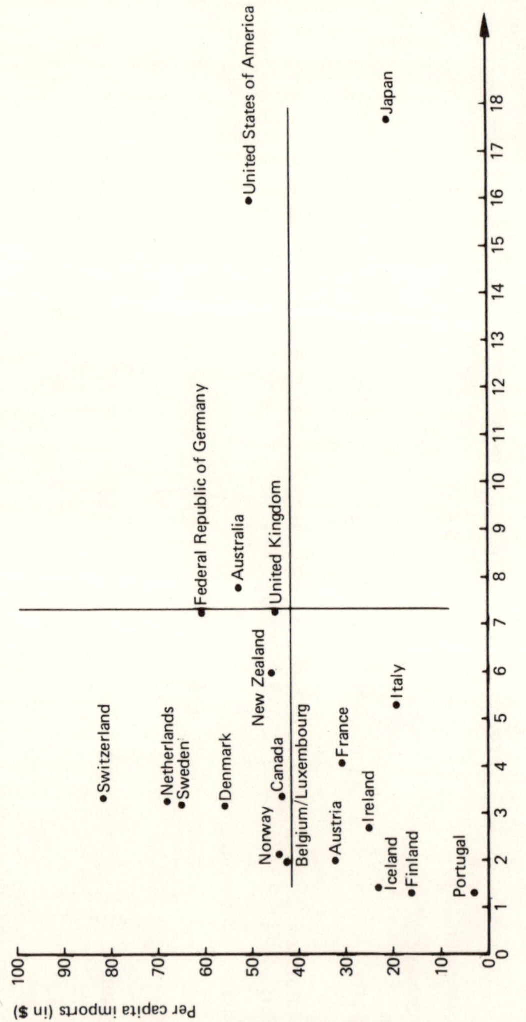

Fig. 1   Per capita of manufactures from developing countries in 1976 by individual developed countries and the share of such imports in total (LDC market share).

average, LDC trade in manufactures with this country would increase by 87 per cent. Further analysis of Professor Lewis' historical record to account for these differences deserves a high priority, but a partial explanation might again focus on the role of customs unions. For example, protocols between EFTA and the EEC now permit duty-free trade in many manufactures so a common external tariff applies to the USA, Japan, several other developed nations, and *the LDCs*. Future expansion of the EEC also threatens to extend trade barriers facing LDC products in European markets.

While much of the analysis in Professor Lewis's paper deals with trade in manufactures, the importance of this exchange relative to traditional LDC exports should be noted. In 1973, almost 80 per cent of developing country export earnings came from commodities (66 per cent excluding petroleum). Furthermore, eight developing countries accounted for about 80 per cent of manufactures exports, and these seem to have been little affected by the 1973–77 slowdown in world trade. As such, commodity trade is of major importance to most LDCs even though their recent activities in shipbuilding, steel, textiles, clothing, footwear and several other sectors have been the subject of much discussion. As such, success of such UN sponsored programmes as the *Integrated Programme for Commodities*, an expanded *Generalised System of Preferences*, liberalisation of export restraints and other NTBs, or even a halt to the new protectionism could offset lower world trade growth rates. I offer no quantitative evidence on the magnitude of these tradeoffs, but empirical analyses of the extent to which these types of policy actions could offset lower rates of growth in world trade deserve a high priority. My own personal belief is that such enlightened international programmes could provide considerable flexibility in this respect. Professor Lewis also shows (Table 1) considerable erosion of LDC commodity trade shares. The tie between these market share losses and the commercial policies of industrial nations (such as the Common Agricultural Policy) is of major importance to developing countries and needs further analysis.

Two final points I would like to mention concern the impact of changes in transport costs on world trade as well as the influence of other factors affecting supply. Studies by the National Bureau of Economic Research show that sizeable reductions in shipping costs were made over the period 1830–1913 with the American Export Freight Rate Index falling by about 70 per cent.[3] Without doubt, the influence of these declining transport costs on the growth of world trade must be accounted for.[4] On a more general level, if I have one possible reservation about Professor Lewis' analysis of factors contributing to trade expansion, it relates to what may be a lack of sufficient weight given to the influence of supply in both the current and historical prospective. The potential importance of supply factors in the current period can be appreciated by noting that the export performance of such countries as Korea, Taiwan, Singapore, Hong Kong and other fast growing exporters of manufactures have been little affected by the post-1973 slowdown in world trade. If supply factors continue to be favourable LDCs have the potential to operate above any depressed future rate of growth in world trade. Studies such as that conducted by Irving Kravis (op. cit., footnote 1, page 75) also suggest that supply factors provided a major trade stimulus for many countries over earlier parts of this century, while the adoption of new technologies and opening of new lands was undoubtedly an important factor influencing nineteenth-century trade growth rates.

ENDNOTES

1. Irving Kravis analysed changes in LDC trade in terms of a 'world market factor' which showed what exports would have been if variations in demand were the only source of change, and a 'competitive factor index' which showed the effect of changes in market shares. The fact that the largest differences in LDC export earnings are due to the competitiveness factor suggests that *internal* policies pursued by these countries may be more important than exogenous factors such as variations in world demand. See Irving Kravis, 'Trade as a Handmaiden of Growth: Similarities Between the Nineteenth and Twentieth Centuries', *Economic Journal* (December 1970), pp. 850–72.
2. One important ratio which changed over the recent period relates to energy. In Western Europe, the share of petroleum (virtually all imported) in total energy consumption increased from 18 per cent in 1955 to 59 per cent in 1973. These imports of petroleum were paid for in manufactured exports, the two flows boosting the growth in world trade.
3. See Douglas North, 'Ocean Freight Rates and Economic Development 1750–1913', *Journal of Economic History* (December 1958), pp. 537–79. It is not clear if these dramatic reductions in freight costs invalidate some of the estimates of import-industrial production elasticities reported by Professor Lewis (p. 15) since they produced rightward shifts in import supply curves. In contrast, the elasticity concept implies fixed demand and supply schedules.
4. Transport costs are also worthy of study in the current period since United Nations investigations have shown LDC *ad valorem* freight rates have risen over the last decade, and that these charges may now range from two to three times MFN tariffs facing many developing country exports. For examples of two such studies which give detailed calculations of freight costs for

Indonesian and Indian exports see Alexander J. Yeats, 'An Analysis of the Incidence of Transport Costs and Tariffs on Indonesia's Exports to the United States', *Bulletin of Indonesian Economic Studies* (November 1976), pp. 61–76 or 'A Comparative Analysis of the Incidence of Tariffs and Transportation Costs on India's Exports', *Journal of Development Studies* (October 1977) pp. 97–107.

2 The Changing Composition of Developing Country Exports

Hollis Chenery and Donald Keesing (USA)

The role of exports from developing countries has been at the centre of postwar discussions of the world economic order. Until the mid-1960s the developing countries (LDCs) had a steadily declining share of world exports, and manufactured goods provided only about 10 per cent of their export earnings. Slow export growth was correctly perceived as a major obstacle to accelerated development.

This picture has changed dramatically over the past fifteen years without any drastic change in the policies of industrialised countries toward the LDCs. The sustained growth of the world economy up to 1974 and the shift toward more export-oriented strategies by a large number of developing countries have accelerated the growth of LDC exports, primarily from those countries in a position to export manufactures. For developing countries as a group, the export lag appears to have been overcome, and nearly half of the increase in earnings now derives from manufactures.[1]

When we take a less aggregated view of recent performance, major features of the earlier picture re-emerge. Export expansion has been a major contributor to the growth of a number of countries, whose incomes have risen substantially over the past twenty years. However, both export expansion and GNP growth have been concentrated in countries containing only a third of the population of the developing countries. The poorer LDCs, concentrated in South Asia and sub-Saharan Africa, supply only 10 per cent of LDC exports and still have most of the features that characterised the Third World in the 1950s.

The purpose of this paper is to assess the main factors causing this transformation of LDC exports and to consider the contribution that they may make to the future growth of different groups of countries.[2] Since the bulk of export growth is expected to take place in manufactured goods, we focus mainly on this category. The first section of this chapter examines the changing composition of exports since 1960 and its association with the emergence of a small number of successful LDC exporters of manufactures. The second section relates this performance to the development strategies and changing comparative advantage of different groups of countries. The final section takes up growth prospects and some of the policy issues raised.[3]

I EXPORT TRENDS IN DEVELOPING COUNTRIES

Since at least the 1950s, LDC exports have grown in volume more slowly than those of industrialised countries (MDCs) and those of the world as a whole, largely because they have been concentrated in primary products, where the growth of demand and world trade has been relatively slow. This situation is now changing rapidly as increasing numbers of LDCs shift toward manufactures. The share of manufactures in exports has risen rapidly, and they will soon comprise over half of LDC merchandise exports other than oil.[4] If this expansion continues as expected, it will lead over the next few years to an export growth rate roughly equal to that of the rest of the world. These trends for major commodity groups are summarised in Table 1.[5]

EXPORT TRENDS BY REGION

Growth of exports and output has been generally fastest in regions, such as East Asia, that have been most successful in exporting manufactures, while low growth performance has been especially characteristic in low-income countries (those with GNP at or below $250 in 1976). If Indonesia is excluded, the low-income countries have experienced very little growth in their exports since 1965. GNP increased in the low-income countries at only 3.1 per cent per annum from 1960–75 compared to 6 per cent in the other ('middle-income') LDCs. Exports per head are twelve times higher in this second group. Broad differences in the composition of exports between these and other groups of countries are summarised in Table 2.[6]

In coming years, much as in the recent past, export growth is expected to be fastest in regions with a high proportion of manufactures in their

TABLE 1
PAST AND PROJECTED RATES OF EXPORT GROWTH BY BROAD PRODUCT GROUPS
(in constant 1975 prices)

	World 1960–75	LDCs 1960–75	World 1975–85	LDCs 1975–85	Per cent of LDC Exports 1960	1975	1985	Per cent share of Increase 1960–75	1975–85
Fuel and energy	6.3	6.2	3.6	3.4	39	40	30	42	18
Agricultural products	4.2	2.6	4.4	3.1	43	27	20	16	12
Non-fuel minerals	3.9	4.8	4.2	5.8	7	7	7	6	6
Manufactures	8.9	12.3	7.8	12.2	11	26	43	36	64
Total merchandise	7.1	5.9	6.4	6.4	100	100	100	100	100

Sources: World Bank, *World Development Report, 1978*, Tables 13 and 25 and unpublished projections for WDR

TABLE 2
WORLD EXPORTS BY MAJOR GROUPS OF COUNTRIES, 1975

	Low income Africa and Asia	Other developing	Industrialised	Centrally planned	Capital surplus oil exporters	World
Value of exports (US$ billion)	18	162	551	82	52	865
Per cent share of:						
World population	30	22	17	30	0.3	100
World exports	2	19	64	9	6	100
Export composition (per cent)						
Fuel and energy	33	41	3	18	100	19
Agricultural products	36	26	16	16	—	17
Non-fuel minerals	9	7	5	6	—	5
Manufactures	23	26	76	60	—	59
Total	100	100	100	100	100	100

Sources: World Bank background data for *World Development Report* 1978 based on UN trade statistics; populations from *World Bank Atlas* (1977)

TABLE 3
PROJECTED GROWTH RATES OF DEVELOPING COUNTRIES'
EXPORTS BY REGION, 1980–85, COMPARED TO ACTUAL RATES
FOR 1965–76
(Per cent per annum)

Region	*1965–76*	*1980–85*
Sub-Saharan Africa	4.3[a]	3.4
Low-income Asia	3.8[b]	5.7
Middle-income Asia and Pacific	12.2	10.0
North Africa and Middle East	12.8[c]	4.1
Latin America and Caribbean	4.7	5.6
Southern Europe	9.2	8.4
All developing countries	8.3[c]	6.6

[a] With Nigeria and Gabon excluded this becomes 2.6
[b] With Indonesia excluded this becomes 1.1
[c] This is biased upward by the deflators used (see note below), as a result of rising oil prices

Note: 1965–76 rates are not in constant prices but are deflated by unit value indexes taken from UN *Yearbook of International Trade Statistics* (1976) vol. I, p. 81, and UN *Monthly Bulletin of Statistics* (July 1978), p. xx. These show unit value of LDC exports for all LDCs (1970 = 100) increasing from 93 in 1965 to 331 in 1976, and for importers of petroleum, from 89 in 1965 to 196 in 1976. Oil exporters' nominal export growth was deflated by the first and that of other LDCs by the second index.

Sources: 1965–76 estimated based on export statistics from IMF *International Financial Statistics* and *Direction of Trade*, UNCTAD *Handbook of International Trade and Development* Statistics (June 1978); 1980–85 projections based on projections based on background studies for WDR

exports. This is illustrated by Table 3, which shows projected growth rates of LDC exports by region in 1980–85 (a choice of years which allows us to exclude complications associated with the post-1975 recovery) compared to 1965–76. Export growth is expected to be fastest in the middle-income countries of East Asia and the Pacific followed by Southern Europe; these are the regions most successful (and most specialised) in manufactures. Sub-Saharan Africa is expected to have the slowest export growth followed by North Africa and the Middle East; these are the regions most dependent on primary commodities.

TRENDS IN PRIMARY EXPORTS

Fuel
In contrast to the slow growth in most other primary exports, there has been a bonanza in LDC oil exports, thanks to the fourfold rise in price in 1973–74, following a sustained growth of volume at rates of 6 to 7 per cent per annum. As a result, even with capital-surplus oil exporters excluded, fuel has come to outweigh all other primary exports combined.

Benefits from this windfall have been concentrated in a small set of oil-exporting countries. It includes two large, poor countries—Indonesia and Nigeria—whose growth has been substantially accelerated in the past five years. The other OPEC members have benefited even more, but their total population is less than 100 million people.

Prior to the oil price rise, world demand for fuel exports rose faster than world income, but since then it has been expanding more slowly. The greatly increased incentives to expand domestic fuel supplies and to economise on energy use are helping to turn up new sources in LDCs while slowing the growth of world trade and consumption. On balance, the prospect seems to be for growth in export volumes at rates of 3 to 4 per cent per annum with a possibility of future price increases in real terms.

Agricultural products
Table 1 shows that agriculture, livestock, forestry, fishing and food processing together supplied 43 per cent of LDC exports in 1960,[7] but this share fell to 27 per cent in 1975 and is trending downward. World demand for exports of agricultural products nearly keeps pace with world income, growing at rates over 4 per cent per annum. Expansion of export demand reflects not only rising incomes but also growing food deficits in many centrally planned economies (CPEs) and LDCs. While the LDCs as a group were virtually self-sufficient in food in the 1950s, by 1975 their net imports exceeded 30 million tonnes. Present estimates point to a food deficit of some 45 million tonnes by 1985.

The LDC share of world exports of agricultural products has fallen over time; their growth rate of 2.6 per cent from 1960–75 was less than half that achieved in MDCs. This weak performance has been due, first, to an initial concentration in tropical products such as coffee, cocoa, tea and bananas, in which world demand has expanded only slowly. Second, trade and tax regimes in many LDCs have discouraged agricultural production and exports in favour of other activities, notably manufacturing for the home market. Third, world efforts to raise farm output through agricultural research and extension, investments and improved inputs are largely concentrated in temperate zones and richer countries, where LDC exports are also held back by MDC protection. However, despite these handicaps, agricultural *output* in LDCs has actually grown faster than in MDCs, but has been offset by rising home demand due to population and income growth.

Increasing the growth rate of agricultural exports from LDCs hinges on accelerating supply in the face of fast-growing domestic demand. In a number of agricultural products (grain, meat, timber, rubber, etc.), the potential export market is favourable, even though food products face widespread protection, particularly from non-tariff barriers in OECD countries designed to give better prices to farmers. Policies toward agriculture have been improving in some of the major developing countries. As a result, both production and export growth are expected to rise, the latter to over 3 per cent per annum up to 1985. Efforts to stabilise prices and earnings in agricultural commodities, to the extent they are successful, could contribute to export expansion by reducing uncertainties that discourage investment. Projected growth rates of LDC exports in leading agricultural products, together with those in leading minerals are shown in Table 4.

Non-fuel minerals
In this category (which includes non-ferrous metals), LDCs have achieved export growth rates close to 5 per cent. While world demand expands more slowly than world income, the LDC share of total supply is growing, thanks to untapped supplies and less exploitation than in more industrialised countries. These resource advantages are partly offset by the reactions of MDC investors to increased taxation and the political uncertainties in LDCs. Here, as in oil, the diffusion of technology has improved the bargaining position of host countries, which increasingly have the options of national ownership or joint ventures as alternatives to foreign-owned mining operations. (Domestic demand beyond the processing stage is usually a negligible influence on export availability.)

Growth of LDC mineral exports is projected to accelerate somewhat and to continue to outpace world demand, with export growth rates approaching 6 per cent per annum. To a somewhat lesser extent than in fuel, these exports come mainly from a small set of LDCs. The mineral exporters rarely have high GNP per capita compared to the general range for middle-income countries, and in sub-Saharan Africa most of

TABLE 4
HISTORICAL AND PROJECTED GROWTH RATES OF LDC EXPORTS BY VOLUME IN LEADING AGRICULTURAL AND MINERAL PRODUCTS

	Value in 1974 (US\$ million)[a]	*Volume growth rate of LDC exports (per cent per annum)*	
		1960–76[b]	*1974/76–1990*
Copper	5320	3.7	3.3
Sugar	5083	2.8	2.7
Coffee	3984	1.7[c]	2.6
Facts and oils	3877	5.7[c]	5.2
Timber logs	2747	8.6[c]	2.2
sawnwood		8.8[c]	8.0
Cotton	2291	−0.2[c]	−0.3
Rubber	2212	3.6	3.6
Iron ore	1693	6.9	3.9
Phosphate rock	1692	5.2	5.1
Cocoa	1555	2.2[d]	2.5
Tin	1256	0.9	1.5
Maize	1153	5.4[e]	3.6[e]
Rice	1094	−0.7	0.0
Tobacco	691	3.9[c]	5.3
Tea	672	1.8[c]	2.3
Beef	609	−1.7[f]	5.4
Bananas	602	3.3	2.1

[a] No one year is entirely representative because of price fluctuations; for example, in 1974 prices were exceptionally high in copper and phosphate rock
[b] Trend growth rates
[c] 1961–76
[d] 1955–76
[e] Growth rates are for all coarse grains
[f] 1961/63–1974/76

Source: Commodities and Export Projections Division, World Bank

these would be classed as low-income or even 'least developed' countries were it not for their mineral exports.

Diversification
A notable trend in primary exports has been product diversification at the country level, outside the oil-exporting countries. Our colleague, Martin Wolf, has compared the concentration of primary commodity

exports in 1960 to that in 1974 for 55 non-OPEC LDCs.[8] The proportion of these countries dependent on one commodity for more than half of their primary export earnings fell from 49 per cent in 1960 to 18 per cent in 1974. The mean share of the leading single primary commodity fell from 47 per cent to 35 per cent, but there was no tendency for the second and third exports to decrease in relative importance. This diversification seems to be largely a result to deliberate efforts by LDCs to escape from dependence on a single commodity by building up exports of other products.

TRENDS IN MANUFACTURED EXPORTS

The most basic change in the pattern of LDC exports has been the spectacular growth in manufactures. From 1960 to 1975 these exports expanded at rates of over 12 per cent per annum. This growth accelerated in the late 1960s and early 1970s and has continued strongly despite the setbacks suffered by the world economy since 1973. During the world recession of 1975 the volume of LDC manufactured exports seems to have risen in volume by at least 6 to 7 per cent even though output and consumption of manufactures fell sharply in MDCs.[9] In the 1976 recovery, LDC manufactured exports leaped forward by over 20 per cent; and in the slow growth conditions of 1977, they appear to have expanded once again in real terms by over 10 per cent, despite a decline in clothing and textiles, although world trade increased by only 4 per cent.[10]

Country concentration
The bulk of manufactured exports come from a small number of industrially relatively advanced LDCs (as shown in Table 7 below). The Republic of Korea, Taiwan (Republic of China), Spain and Hong Kong together supply close to 45 per cent of the total. Next come Yugoslavia, Brazil and Mexico. However, the growth in these exports has been widely shared, as illustrated by Table 5. More than forty LDCs now have exports worth over $100 million, compared to 22 in 1970 and fewer earlier. Although the scale and pace of this growth have varied from one country to another, in many the upsurge has been persistent and powerful.

At a product level, the breadth of this advance is impressive. From almost any year in the 1960s to 1976, real growth rates have been over 10 per cent, not only in clothing and electronic assembly (which have made striking gains), but also in machinery, transport equipment, textile yarn

TABLE 5
INCREASING NUMBERS OF LDCS EXPORTING MANUFACTURES,
1965–75
(Cumulative, at 1975 prices)

Exports of manufactures over:	1965	1970	1975
US$2 billion	0	2	9
US$1 billion	3	6	12
US$500 million	7	11	15
US$200 million	12	15	25
US$100 million	18	22	40
US$50 million	27	37	46

Source: WDR Table 15 and UN trade data; price index from UN *Monthly Bulletin of Statistics*

and fabrics, steel, chemicals, and almost every other major group. Growth of 10 per cent per annum or more seems to be the rule rather than the exception even at the level of individual products.[11] However, most of these strong performances started from a low base in the 1960s, particularly in products that are technically complex, skill-intensive and/or subject to strong economies of scale.

Looked at slightly differently, the steady advance of manufactured exports has been accompanied by an equally persistent diversification, with successful export breakthroughs being widespread. In practically every case the more complex and difficult-to-produce of these products come initially from one or two of the most industrialised LDCs. Among less industrialised LDCs, one finds the same sort of process going on at a smaller scale and in simpler products.

Exports by destination
Strong growth has taken place in manufactured exports in all major markets. Especially rapid expansion has occurred in LDC exports to MDCs, which have outpaced the rest. Those going to other LDCs and to CPEs have also increased in 1960–75 at annual rates above 10 per cent.

Table 6 illustrates the compositional differences between manufactures exported to MDCs and to other LDCs in 1975. In the aggregate, nearly two-thirds of LDC manufactured exports go to MDCs, nearly one-third to other LDCs, and limited amounts to CPEs. There is considerable variation by product; products such as clothing and electronic products go mainly to MDCs, while products such as textiles

TABLE 6
COMPOSITION OF LDC TRADE IN MANUFACTURES BY DESTINATION, 1975
(Per cent)

	Trade among LDCs[a]	LDC Exports to MDCs	LDC Imports from MDCs	Share of inter-LDC Trade in total LDC imports
Machinery and transport equipment	31	18	55	6
Textiles	14	10	4	28
Clothing	5	19	1	39
Chemicals	13	7	12	11
Iron and steel	6	5	10	7
Other manufactures	31	41	19	15
Total	100	100	100	10

[a] Includes significant re-exports, notably in machinery and transport equipment.

Source: UN *Yearbook of International Trade Statistics*, various issues and chemicals are traded more among LDCs. This is also true of some types of machinery and transport equipment. However, trade in capital goods among LDCs is quite limited; nine leading exporters reported only $587 million in exports of non-electrical machinery to other LDCs in 1974.[12]

Table 6 shows the composition of LDC imports from MDCs, which outweighed trade in the opposite direction by $123 billion to $26 billion, or more than 4 to 1, along with the share of trade among LDCs in total LDC imports of manufactures in each broad product group.

Overview

In summary, the rapid growth of manufactured exports appears to have been mainly the result of a supply breakthrough. Demand growth has played only a secondary role, especially since LDC shares of most markets were initially quite small. Substantial growth has taken place even in products in which aggregate demand grew only slowly; in clothing, consumption appears to have grown in MDCs at about 3 per cent per annum while LDC exports to MDCs grew at over 20 per cent per annum.

LDC success in exporting manufactures seems to have four main explanations, all but one of them on the *supply side*:

(1) Rapid overall development has increased the industrial capabilities of the leading exporters of manufactures and contributed to their ability to move into related export products.

(2) There has been a widespread shift in LDC policies away from inward-looking industrialisation around the home market, towards a systematic effort to export industrial products.

(3) Improvements in transport and communications have facilitated growth of trade and an international division of labour even over long distances.

(4) International trade policies of the industrial countries have maintained access to their markets and, at least until recently, continued the postwar trend toward trade liberalisation in industrial products. LDC exports have benefited from Dillon and Kennedy Round tariff cuts, offshore assembly provisions in tariffs, preferences from the European Community, Generalised System of Preferences (GSP) schemes in various MDCs, and resistance to pressures for more restrictive non-tariff barriers.[13]

For the last two reasons, trade in manufactures has grown faster than output in both MDCs and LDCs. The faster export growth in developing countries is attributable to the first two influences—rapid industrial development and a shift toward outward-looking policies.[14]

It is not widely appreciated how many developing countries have been changing their policies to promote manufactured exports. This shift began around 1960 and went further later in Spain, Taiwan (Republic of China), Republic of Korea, Yugoslavia, Greece, Israel and Portugal.[15] In the course of the 1960s, Brazil, Mexico and Singapore and to a lesser extent others (such as Pakistan) shifted policies in the same direction. More recently export promotion measures have become a significant component of industrialisation policies in many other countries, notably Colombia, Argentina, Uruguay, Chile, Sri Lanka, Tunisia, Morocco, Haiti, Dominican Republic, some of the Central American republics, Cyprus, Malta and Mauritius.[16]

II CHANGING COMPARATIVE ADVANTAGE AND LDC GROWTH

A number of studies have shown a strong relationship between export expansion and the growth of GNP.[17] It is fairly well established that countries cannot continue to grow rapidly by steadily reducing the share of imports in GNP and that expanding the share of imports and exports in GNP permits more efficient allocation of resources and more rapid growth. At least over an extended period, export growth seems to be a necessary though not a sufficient condition for rapid GNP growth.[18]

The previous discussion shows that in order to accelerate the growth of exports the developing countries have in recent years changed their export composition substantially, shifting away from the slower-growing primary products toward manufactures, and within manufactures, diversifying into new commodities as skills and experience are acquired. We will now examine this process in somewhat more detail for groups of countries that differ in their initial income levels, resources and trade policies.

Recent empirical studies have had considerable success in explaining the composition of manufactured exports from LDCs in terms of both the Heckscher–Ohlin approach (including skills as a factor of production) and more recent technological explanations based on the product cycle, technical progress and scale economies.[19] There have been fewer explorations of other influences, such as learning processes in marketing and product design, that contribute to success in exporting manufactured goods. These influences appear to be part of a cumulative process that has produced a relatively small number of very successful LDC exporters.

COMPARATIVE ADVANTAGE BY COUNTRY GROUPS

To illuminate the relationships among initial economic structure, trade policies and export performance, we shall use a modified version of the classification of trade and production patterns proposed by Chenery and Syrquin (1975). Table 7 classifies selected developing countries (including all those having more than $150 millions worth of manufactured exports in 1977)[20] into four groups. The first three contain countries with a per capita income (in $1976) of more than $300, which are well advanced in the process of development; the fourth consists of poorer countries.

(1) *Countries that specialised relatively early in exports of manufactures* and have followed generally outwardlooking policies.

(2) *Large semi-industrial countries*, with relatively low export shares in GNP, that have achieved considerable success in industrialisation based mainly on the home market, but in recent years have also tried to promote exports of manufactures.

(3) *Countries now shifting part way from a specialisation in primary exports* in an effort to diversify their exports and accelerate development.

(4) *Large poor countries* with significant exports of manufactures.

These groupings are meant to illustrate the main policies and countries involved, without being exhaustive.[21] Brief comments follow on each group.

Group (1) Early specialisation in manufactures
This group contains four East Asian countries (Hong Kong, Singapore, Taiwan and Korea) and three Mediterranean countries (Israel, Portugal and Greece). Although wage levels were somewhat higher in the Mediterranean group in 1960, they are all characterised by limited natural resources, relatively educated labour, and the need to export manufactures (or services) in order to develop. The composition of their exports generally corresponds to expectations based on trade theories of both factor-proportions and product-cycle types. With local variations, their exports have been built initially around labour-intensive,

TABLE 7

EXPORTS OF MANUFACTURES AND COUNTRY CHARACTERISTICS OF SELECTED LDCs

Country	Population (mils; 1976)	GNP Per Capita (US$ 1976)	Avg. Growth (per cent per annum) 1960–1976	Manufactures as per cent of Goods Exports 1960	Manufactures as per cent of Goods Exports 1975	Total (US$ mils) 1976	Exports of Manufactured Goods Per Capita (US$) 1976	Textiles, clothing, Footwear and Leather Products (per cent of Total)	Real Average Growth (per cent per annum) 1965–75
I. Specialised in Exports of Manufactures									
Israel	3.6	3,920	4.3	61	83	1,850	514	10	11.1
Singapore	2.3	2,700	7.5	26	43	1,790	778	13[a]	15.0[a]
Greece	9.1	2,590	6.1	9	48	1,252	138	45	28.7
Hong Kong	4.5	2,110	6.5	80	97	6,480	1,440	58	11.9[a]
Portugal	9.7	1,690	6.5	55	71	1,198	124	44	7.8
Taiwan (Rep. of China)	16.3	1,070	6.3	14	81	6,921	425	44	28.8
Korea, Rep. of	36.0	670	7.3	14	82	6,675	188	50	36.0
II. Large Semi Industrial Countries									
Spain	35.7	2,920	5.5	12	70	6,025	169	19	22.6
Yugoslavia	21.5	1,680	5.6	44	72	3,383	157	21	9.9
Argentina	25.7	1,550	2.8	4	25	972	38	23	16.7
Brazil	110.0	1,140	4.8	3	27	2,332	21	29	25.4
Mexico	62.0	1,090	3.0	12	52	2,327[b]	38	15[b]	21.2
Turkey	41.2	990	4.2	25	36	446	11	70	32.2
III. Emerging from Primary Specialisation									
Venezuela	12.4	2,570	2.6	0	1	115[c]	8[c]	2[c]	20.1
Iran	34.3	1,930	8.2	3	1	208[c]	6[c]	71[c]	8.9
Chile	10.5	1,050	0.9	4	8	109[d]	11[d]	0	n.a.
Malaysia	12.7	860	3.9	6	18	667[c]	54[c]	14[c]	18.2

Tunisia	5.7	840	4.1	10	20	203	36	49	15.0
Colombia	24.2	630	2.8	2	21	306[c]	13[c]	39[c]	17.3
Ivory Coast	7.0	610	3.4	1	12	117	17	27	17.4
Morocco	17.2	540	2.1	8	13	197[c]	12[c]	61[c]	16.6
Philippines	43.3	410	2.4	7	17	255[c]	6[c]	27[c]	7.8
Thailand	43.0	380	4.5	2	23	305[c]	7[c]	28[c]	30.0

IV.   Large Poor Countries

Egypt	38.1	280	1.9	10	34	386	10	73	7.8
Indonesia	135.2	240	3.4	0	1	119	1	(low)	14.1
Pakistan	71.3	170	3.1	22	55	589[c]	9[c]	79[c]	[e]
India	620.4	150	1.3	44	45	1,961[c]	3[c]	52[c]	2.8
Bangladesh	80.4	110	−0.4	—	63	220	3	97	[e]

[a] Including re-exports
[b] Estimated including border zone, with help of U.S. as well as Mexican data
[c] 1975
[d] 1974
[e] For Pakistan and Bangladesh together, exports of manufactures grew at 8.5 per cent

Sources: First five columns from World Bank, *World Development Report*, statistical annex; other trade from UN *Yearbook of International Trade Statistics* and other UN sources, plus national statistics for Taiwan (Republic of China) and Mexico; populations for 1975 and 1974 from *World Bank Atlas*; real export growth 1965–75 computed using UN unit value index for SITC 5–8 for developing countries as a deflator.

technologically stable ('older') products such as textiles, clothing, footwear, assembled electronic components, toys, etc.[22]

In these footloose industries, the role of policy is substantial in determining the location of particular products. For example, over 90 per cent of LDC clothing exports and almost all the electronic products come from locations where imported inputs are given virtual free-trade treatment by one means or another. The electronics exports come from places with favourable treatment of 'multinational' corporations (MNCs) as well.[23]

More than trade theory has emphasised to date, LDCs' limited capabilities in marketing and related aspects of design appear to restrict their capacity to export even labour-intensive consumer and capital goods.[24] LDCs depend heavily on outsiders to market exports of these products even where production is in local hands (as is typical, for instance, in footwear and clothing). Tailoring production to what the customer needs, and marketing suitably differentiated products, involves experience, skills, information and organisation that are difficult for newcomers to achieve. As a rule LDC firms compete mainly in markets for consumer goods where a cost-cutting strategy can be effective, for example, in selling to wholesalers for distribution to people (in LDCs or MDCs) too poor to be concerned with brand names. They may also furnish production capacity to MDC firms that know how to compete in markets characterised by brands and administered prices. Even marketing consumer goods exports with help from MDC buyers involves a learning process that is not easy. It is striking that a large majority of LDC exports of clothing come from just three countries in this group—Hong Kong, Republic of Korea and Taiwan—perhaps because they have accumulated the necessary information links and experience in getting the product together and delivering reliably on time, even though several of the other LDCs that are trying to export clothing have lower wages, and all have fewer problems with quotas.

Group (2) Large semi-industrial countries

The countries in Group (2) have developed a substantial industrial structure based on import substitution and protection and have gradually dismantled at least some of these policies over the past ten to twenty years. Spain and Yugoslavia were the first to undertake this shift and have reached per capita levels of manufactured exports that are comparable to Group (1). However, the share of exports in GNP for these large countries is considerably below that of most of the smaller, more specialised economies in Group (1).

Most of these countries began to expand manufactured exports when afflicted with shortages of foreign exchange; in some cases the benefits of increasing imports may have outweighed considerations of efficiency in the choice of export sectors. Over time these countries have managed to develop export markets for the capital goods, chemicals and other intermediate goods for which their domestic markets, augmented by exports, provide sufficient economies of scale. As a result, Spain, Yugoslavia and Brazil have become the leading LDC exporters of capital goods.[25] This is a logical direction for the evolution of comparative advantage in large middle-income countries, but success depends to an even greater degree than in consumer goods on design, marketing and technical services.

Although the present diversified export pattern of the Group (2) countries (which is discussed further in the next section) is largely the result of protection and import substitution, it is still a matter of dispute as to whether the earlier, inefficient policy was a precondition for the present degree of success in building up exports based on scale economies. This issue—which is discussed for the Latin American countries by Diaz-Alejandro (1974)—is of mainly historical interest for the present members of this group, and for India, which now has a long history of inefficient import substitution. However, it is central to the future policies of prospective members of Group (2), such as Egypt, Pakistan and Indonesia.

The continued success of the Group (2) countries depends on a set of cumulative processes somewhat different from those in the smaller, more specialised economies of Group (1). The potential advantages of large countries lie in their ability to develop economies of scale based on their home markets, leading over time to production and exports of machinery and transport equipment along with standardised intermediate goods such as chemicals and basic metals. This sequence has been followed most successfully by Spain, Yugoslavia and Brazil.

Another reason for this pattern of specialisation is that several of the Group (2) countries have considerable export earnings from natural resources, contributing to relatively high wage levels.[26] This may mean that like other resource-rich countries before them (the United States, Canada, Sweden, and Australia) they will be forced to build their industrial exports around relatively skill-, capital- and natural-resource-intensive products, where their wage levels will not be a serious handicap.

Group (3) Countries emerging from primary specialisation
The countries shown in Group (3) all exported relatively insignificant amounts of manufactures in 1960 but have achieved significant increases in the past fifteen years. This has helped to diversify their exports and as a rule has improved their prospects for more rapid export growth. The optimal timing of such a shift into manufactured exports depends in part on the prospects of (and effects on) primary exports. To accomplish this shift through the market mechanism has proved difficult for countries rich in natural resources whose current exchange rates are based on this pattern of specialisation. Conversely, countries in this group that still have rather low wage levels by comparative standards, such as Colombia, the Philippines and Thailand, find this shift easier.

Within Group (3), Malaysia, Colombia and Thailand have managed to stimulate the growth of manufactured exports without excessive interference with markets, through subsidies or otherwise. The Philippines and Chile have shifted policies sharply in recent years in pursuit of this goal.

In Iran and Venezuela industrial exports are almost inevitably energy- or capital-intensive, while the poorest Group (3) countries are pushed more in a labour-intensive direction. In between, there is not a compelling need to stress labour-intensive exports.

Group (4) Large poor countries
This group includes the principal countries with income levels below $300 per capita that have achieved a significant volume of manufactured exports or have the industrial base to do so in the near future.[27] They also include 75 per cent of the population of all countries with per capita incomes of $280 or less in 1976, and the possibility of their benefiting more fully from international trade is therefore of great concern to world development; this is a heterogeneous group. At one extreme, India has a long history of industrial development and a diversified production capability; at the other, Bangladesh has little industrial capability beyond processing of jute, and its manufactured exports are almost wholly jute textiles. Limited supplies of foreign exchange have hampered the growth of India, Pakistan and Egypt over most of the past fifteen years, while Bangladesh is heavily dependent on external aid.

The industrial base for exporting a variety of manufactured goods has already been established in India, Egypt and Pakistan, but these countries have only followed policies favouring manufactured exports for brief periods (Pakistan in the late 1960s, India in the last several years). In addition to the comparative advantage deriving from low wages, all three (and particularly India) are in a position to benefit from the economies of scale inherent in a large domestic market. As shown in the next section, the composition of Indian exports shows some changes in this direction in recent years.

CHANGING COMPOSITION OF MANUFACTURED EXPORTS

Compared to manufactured exports from industrial countries, those from LDCs contain a much smaller share of capital goods and consumer engineering products, and a larger share of clothing, footwear and textiles. This is a familiar reflection of differences in skilled versus unskilled labour requirements and the technical complexity of the goods involved. However, only a small number of LDCs in Groups (1) and (2) have been particularly successful in exporting finished consumer goods, including clothing and footwear, let alone capital goods.

Table 8 shows the product composition of manufactures in seven main categories, chosen on the bass of marketing characteristics as well as technological and factor requirements. Only in the principal countries in Group (2)[28]—Spain, Yugoslavia, Brazil and Argentina—do capital goods comprise more than 12 per cent of manufactured exports, compared to the 32 per cent average in MDCs. Capital and consumer goods[29] together comprise over 40 per cent of exports only in Hong Kong, Taiwan, Korea, Spain, Yugoslavia and Brazil, which are also the six largest LDC exporters of manufactures. In almost all leading MDCs, this share is over 40 per cent.

In countries with limited exporting experience—particularly those of Groups (3) and (4)—exports of manufactures consist largely of textile yarn and fabrics and other standardised intermediate goods, such as leather, plywood, cement, steel and assorted chemicals. These products have widely recognised objective standards and descriptions and can be marketed through existing channels of trade not unlike standardised primary commodities. Many resource-rich LDCs export relatively capital-intensive standardised goods. One also finds exports of less standardised intermediate goods—for example, electronic components—and trade in household articles and equipment, building materials, etc., in which transport costs and proximity play an evident role.[30]

Table 9 shows changes in the composition of exports in leading countries from 1965–75, illustrating the rising share of capital goods and consumer goods in almost all cases. This trend helps to confirm that

TABLE 8
PER CENT COMPOSITION OF MANUFACTURES EXPORTED FROM SELECTED LDCS AND DEVELOPED COUNTRIES IN 1975

Country	Capital goods	Consumer engineering	Clothing and footwear	Other clearcut consumer goods	Textiles including rugs	Standardised intermediate excluding textiles	Other and miscellaneous
Developed countries	31.8	9.4	2.7	4.0	4.6	24.1	23.3
Developing countries[a]	12.5	5.8	21.8	9.8	14.9	16.2	19.0
Group (1)							
Israel	8.9	1.7	6.9	4.1	3.2	6.4	68.8
Greece	5.2	1.3	17.8	3.1	17.3	40.1	15.2
Hong Kong	2.8	11.3	45.7	19.7	9.7	0.7	10.0
Portugal	9.0	5.9	18.4	2.5	23.0	15.2	25.9
Taiwan	9.5	9.8	27.8	14.9	15.1	8.5	14.4
Korea	7.0	5.2	32.4	12.3	15.7	14.7	12.7
Group (2)							
Spain	23.5	5.6	11.4	8.4	4.6	22.3	24.2
Yugoslavia	25.4	3.1	13.2	5.5	6.1	21.1	25.5
Argentina	18.0	7.8	2.8	4.3	0.3	24.9	41.9
Brazil	25.4	6.1	12.2	5.0	12.4	21.1	17.8
Turkey	2.8	0.5	25.2	2.0	33.6	22.6	13.4
Group (3)							
Venezuela	0.3	—	—	0.7	2.1	40.3	56.6
Iran	0.7	0.5	10.9	1.0	60.1	6.5	20.3
Malaysia	11.4	4.5	8.5	3.4	5.1	16.6	50.5
Tunisia	1.1	0.4	26.7	1.4	11.5	51.8	7.1
Colombia	6.7	1.2	11.4	12.1	21.9	25.7	20.9
Ivory Coast	20.2	0.9	2.1	—	20.5	26.4	29.9

Morocco	2.4	0.2	26.6	6.4	29.2	20.9	14.4
Philippines	—	0.4	14.1	25.5	8.7	22.2	29.1
Thailand	0.9	2.9	16.2	7.4	24.5	16.5	31.6
Group (4)							
Egypt	1.0	0.3	22.0	6.5	47.7	13.6	8.9
India	9.3	1.2	11.2	4.4	30.6	21.0	22.3
Pakistan	2 0	—	7.2	6.4	66.1	13.1	5.2
Bangladesh	—	0.4	—	0.3	88.2	9.5	1.6

[a] Countries listed only

Sources: Computed from data in UN *Yearbook of International Trade Statistics, 1976*, based on classifications explained in endnote 28.

TABLE 9
EXPORTS OF CAPITAL GOODS AND CLEARCUT CONSUMER GOODS AS A PER CENT OF MANUFACTURES EXPORTED FROM LEADING DEVELOPING COUNTRIES IN 1975 COMPARED TO 1965

Country	Capital goods		Consumer goods		Combined total	
	1965	1975	1965	1975	1965	1975
Group (1)						
Israel	2.0	8.9	8.5	12.7	10.5	21.6
Greece	7.1	5.2	11.5	22.2	16.6	27.4
Hong Kong[a]	1.5	2.8	57.3	76.7	58.8	79.5
Portugal	3.5	9.0	12.8	26.8	16.3	35.8
Taiwan	3.4	9.5	19.4	52.5	22.8	62.0
Korea	2.5	7.0	34.0	49.9	36.5	56.9
Group (2)						
Spain	20.4	23.5	21.2	25.4	41.6	48.9
Yugoslavia[b]	29.9	25.4	19.9	21.8	49.8	47.2
Argentina	14.7	18.0	13.3	14.9	28.0	32.9
Brazil	16.8	25.4	—	23.3	16.8(+)	48.7
Group (3)						
Malaysia	12.9	11.4	15.8	16.4	28.7	27.8
Colombia	5.3	6.7	4.5	24.5	9.8	31.2
Group (4)						
Egypt[b]	0.3	1.0	5.8	28.8	6.1	29.8
India	1.3	9.3	5.5	16.8	6.8	26.1

[a] Re-exports are included in 1965 but not 1975.

[b] Exports to centrally planned economies (where marketing is quite different) were important in Yugoslavia in both years and in Egypt's consumer goods exports in 1975.

Source: Computed from data in UN *Yearbook of Industrial Statistics*

export success has been based in part on learning special skills involved in marketing and producing for customer specifications.[31]

Two other points deserve some comment. First, a few leading Group (1) and (2) countries are now exporting technically complex products, such as supertankers, aircraft and heavy machinery. Second, in regard to the product cycle, there seems to have been, if not a shortening of this cycle, a moving up in it on the part of some LDCs, as reflected in exports by some of the Group (1) countries of such products as 'citizens' band' radios, TV games and pocket calculators, and the latest types of digital watches, as well as 'knockoff' copies of fashion designers' latest popular clothing styles.[32] One may also class colour television sets, steel, petrochemicals and even large ships as 'older products' in which leading LDCs have started to compete successfully; and they have already taken over much of the export market for radios and monochrome television sets. Large-scale exports of passenger cars from Brazil and Korea may soon materialise on the same basis.

III FUTURE PROSPECTS

Although the recent trends in LDC exports have been quite encouraging, the question remains whether world markets for manufactures will support the export needs of the LDCs in the future. This question leads to such matters as economic management and protectionism in MDCs, LDC policies and supply potentials, and the country distribution of increases in exports. We will comment selectively on these issues in the general context of the *World Development Report*.

EFFECTS OF WORLD GROWTH

To illustrate the sensitivity of LDC exports to growth in the advanced countries, the *World Development Report* makes alternative assumptions about the rate of the advanced (MDC) countries' growth varying from 3.7 per cent to 4.7 per cent per annum for the period 1975–85, with the midpoint (4.2 per cent) as the base case. The corresponding variations in world trade and in LDC exports are shown in Table 10. In the aggregate, the latter vary from 5.4 per cent to 7.4 per cent, proportionately more than the variation in world growth.

The breakdown indicated for major categories of exports depends largely on the supply response of producers, which is taken up below. Overall it is assumed that manufactured exports are highly responsive to demand conditions while primary exports are assumed to be limited more by supply conditions over this period.

SUPPLY VS DEMAND CONSTRAINTS

As a result of LDC successes, market penetration and employment effects have reached a sufficient level in many products so that protectionist responses have been triggered in MDCs. MDC demand growth has therefore become a major concern, and demand limitations along with supply will shape LDC performance in the future. The

TABLE 10
IMPLICATIONS OF ALTERNATIVE ECONOMIC GROWTH
ASSUMPTIONS FOR LDC EXPORTS, IMPORTS AND OUTPUT
GROWTH
(Average annual percentage growth rates, 1975–85)

	Base scenario	Low growth scenario	High growth scenario
GDP in MDCs	4.2	3.7	4.7
GDP in LDCs	5.7	5.2	6.1
World trade	6.4	5.7	7.4
LDC Imports	5.6	4.8	6.5
LDC Exports[a]	6.3	5.4	7.4
Fuel	3.4	3.1	3.4
Agricultural products	3.1	2.7	3.2
Nonfuel minerals	5.8	5.3	6.6
Manufactures	12.2	10.2	14.2

[a] Including services.

Source: WDR, Tables 32 and 33 and background projections

seriousness of protective pressures and of MDC demand constraints
will depend to some extent on how many LDCs are highly successful at
the same time. Nevertheless, growth of LDC exports of manufactures
will continue to depend heavily on supply performance almost regardless of the treatment of these exports or the economic situation in
MDCs.

Supply potential
In the long run, policies will be decisive in shaping LDC export
performance; not just trade and exchange rate policies but how well
development is managed on all fronts, how fast industrialisation moves
forward, and whether countries become internationally competitive.
Since it takes time for better policies to produce these effects, there are
only a few candidates to add to the successful manufacturing exporters
in Groups (1) and (2) within the next decade.

   In terms of our previous classification, only one or two Group (3)
countries (notably the Philippines at this moment), and perhaps India in
Group (4), now pursue policies that might increase their manufactured
goods exports to the higher levels of Groups (1) and (2).

   There is also uncertainty in regard to what products LDCs can develop next. The Republic of Korea and Taiwan are making an intensive effort to build up exports of capital goods and other complex products, spurred by restrictions imposed on their simpler exports. As our earlier comments suggest, this will be a difficult shift. Another question is, how fast can Brazil, India, Mexico, Argentina, etc., expand their manufactured exports, if they tilt policies further in this direction, given the domestic orientation of their production capacity, infrastructure, and experience? A third question is, how fast can exporting and marketing knowhow be built up in LDCs that are now only minor exporters?

More generally, LDC exports are no longer expanding from such a low base, so high growth rates may be difficult to maintain in the countries that have already reached relatively high levels.

Market penetration

LDCs now have a substantial share in MDC markets for manufactured imports, as Table 11 illustrates. In relation to MDCs' total consumption of manufactures, the LDC market share remains small except in a few narrow product categories. Nevertheless, at the margin LDCs are making a significant impact on MDC demand for manufactures. Table 12 shows that from 1970–75—partly as a result of the recession at the end of the period—increased imports from LDCs supplied about 7 per cent of the increase in MDC consumption of manufactures. This marginal share is projected to remain over 5 per cent until 1985. The

TABLE 11

IMPORTS FROM LDCS AS A PERCENTAGE OF DEVELOPED COUNTRY IMPORTS IN SELECTED MANUFACTURES, 1975

	US	Japan	EEC (excluding intertrade)	All developed countries (including intertrade)
Clothing	81.0	65.3	74.1	44.6
Footwear	61.5	53.1	61.7	34.5
Textiles	43.3	42.0	50.5	18.9
Electrical machinery	42.4	23.8	15.8	12.0
Nonelectrical machinery	6.5	7.1	7.9	3.0
Transport equipment	1.7	2.4	12.3	2.3
All manufactures	19.9	20.1	21.4	9.4

Source: OCED, *Trade by Commodities, Market Summaries: Imports*, vol. 1 (1975)

TABLE 12
LDC EXPORTS OF MANUFACTURED PRODUCTS AS A SHARE
OF MARKETS IN INDUSTRIALISED COUNTRIES IN SELECTED
YEARS FROM 1960–85
(Per cent)

	1960	1970	1975	1985	*Share in market growth*		
					1960–70	*1970–75*	*1975–85*
In imports	5.9	5.8	8.9	13.6	5.8	18.6	17.5
In consumption	0.4	0.7	1.2	2.7	1.0	7.1	5.4

Source: WDR, Table 26

total share in consumption is projected to rise from 1.2 per cent in 1975 to 2.7 per cent in 1985.

In particular products, market penetration is considerably higher. For example, in textiles and clothing together, by 1975 the share of consumption reached 5 per cent, varying in the largest MDCs from 8 per cent in the Federal Republic of Germany to 2 per cent in France. In the European Community as a whole, imports from LDCs supplied 55 per cent of the market for men's woven shirts and 45 per cent for women's blouses, as well as 22 to 26 per cent in five other major products.[33] In the USA in the same year, imports from all sources (mainly from LDCs) supplied 56 per cent of the market in women's sweaters and over one-fourth in a number of other types of clothing.[34] Imports from LDCs also supplied roughly half the radios and monochrome television sets purchased by US consumers.

Effects of protection

This successful market penetration has contributed to the steady decline of some of the industries most affected, particularly those in which demand is growing slowly (clothing and footwear). Repercussions on prices, profits, and employment have hurt all the more because of depressed business conditions and high unemployment in MDCs. Imports from LDCs (and Japan and CPEs) have become a lightning-rod for feelings caused by other factors—automation, technical progress, competition among MDCs, etc.[35]

One result has been greatly intensified pressure for protection. In some industries—clothing, textiles, footwear, steel—these pressures have succeeded in creating new protective measures across a wide front.

In others the pressures have been generally resisted so far, but scattered inroads have been made. The overall outcome still hangs in the balance, with efforts being made to stem the tide and add new international agreements, as a result of the Tokyo Round.

Alongside protection, subsidies to industry have reached unprecedented proportions in MDCs and are now a major obstacle to LDC exports, especially in Western Europe. Shipbuilding, steel and textiles products are among the sectors most affected.

The direct impact of recent increases in protection on LDC exports of manufactures will be greatest in clothing, textiles and footwear. These products comprised over one-fourth of LDC manufactured exports to MDCs in 1975, and (as Table 7, page 96, shows) they are especially important for the poorer and less industrialised LDCs.

The most severe new restrictions have come in textile products, with the European Community leading the way. Principal suppliers have been forced to accept quotas for 1978 in some products that are below 1976 levels, and most of the new quotas grow through 1982 at low rates in the range from 0.5 to 4 per cent per annum. Not only have all the significant LDC suppliers in each product been hit by quotas but very low 'trigger levels' have been set for adding quotas against other suppliers if they start to be successful.[36] New, more severe import restrictions have also been created in Canada, Australia, Sweden and Norway. The United States, which has had an effective system of quotas up to now, has imposed a one-year standstill in its quotas on Hong Kong, Taiwan and Korea, holding them in 1978 at 1977 levels; their aggregate quotas until 1982 will allow for a combined growth rate of just 4.5 per cent per annum over 1971 levels in their textile product exports to the USA.[37] The combined result will be to slow sharply the growth of LDC textile and clothing exports, which had kept pace with the overall growth of LDC manufactured exports up to 1976.

To determine the net effect of these changes, the *World Development Report* makes illustrative projections of what 1975–85 growth of manufactured exports might be like. This growth pattern is compared to 1970–75 in Table 13. Growth of clothing exports is projected conservatively at 5.5 per cent past 1976 and textiles at 4.5 per cent, as a result of recent increases in protection in MDCs.

Using these projections as a starting point, we get a sense of the quantitative importance of protection, at least in clothing and textiles. If trade barriers in textile products were eased to the point where exports of clothing grew at 15 per cent and those of textiles at 12 per cent from 1975–85, the overall growth rate of LDC exports would increase from

TABLE 13
PROJECTED GROWTH AND CHANGING COMPOSITION OF LDC
EXPORTS OF MANUFACTURES BY BROAD PRODUCT GROUPS,
1975–85

	Average growth rates (per cent per annum in 1975 prices)		*Percentage of total*	
Product group	*1970–75*	*1975–85*	*1975*	*1985*
Clothing	20.3	8.3	13	9
Textiles	17.8	6.2	12	7
Chemicals	16.5	13.0	10	11
Iron and steel	10.7	14.5	6	7
Machinery and transport equipment	20.3	17.3	23	36
Other	10.2	10.0	36	30
All manufactures	14.9	12.2	100	100

Source: WDR, Table 27 and background estimates

6.4 per cent to 6.9 per cent and that for exports of manufactures, from 12.2 per cent to 13.5 per cent.

Prospects for trade among LDCs
The upsurge of protectionist pressures in MDCs intensifies interest in the possibilities for accelerated growth of trade among LDCs.

This trade is already growing at well over 10 per cent per annum, and the politically realistic possibilities for regional common markets, shared industrial plants, etc., are largely being exploited. The only way that countries that are far apart are likely to open their markets to one another further is through reductions of protection in major LDCs on a most-favoured-nation basis. This could come about through unilateral shifts in policies or through reciprocal concessions in future negotiations with MDCs, for example in exchange for reduced NTBs. Moderated protection in major LDCs and reduced NTBs in MDCs both appear highly desirable for LDC growth over the long run, and would help MDCs as well.

Along with trade liberalisation, expansion of trade among LDCs depends also on continuing progress in particular markets, for example in making LDCs more competitive in capital goods. For the latter purpose, better financing of supplier credits and improved information and marketing are examples of matters deserving attention. However, it would be unreasonable to expect a rapid acceleration of the growth of trade among LDCs except as a result of a general liberalisation of their import restrictions.

THE CHANGING ROLE OF MANUFACTURED EXPORTS

In the postwar period the possibility of exporting manufactured goods to the more advanced countries has done much to make possible the emergence of a number of transitional countries that are now approaching the status of mature industrial economies. Although many of them are small, the group also includes several large countries—such as Spain, Yugoslavia, Brazil, Mexico, Korea. Their graduation into the ranks of the MDCs could potentially make a substantial change in the world trade outlook for the remaining LDCs, yet most of them will still have incomes and wages below the MDC average for a long time to come. In this concluding section we will speculate on the likelihood that manufactured exports can facilitate the growth of poor countries and the changes in international policy that may be required if this is to take place.

Success in exporting manufactures—unlike minerals—has come largely from a skilled and hardworking labour force and efficient development policies. There appears to be a strong element of learning by doing, which underlies the concentration of manufactured exports in a small number of countries. Once countries have acquired this ability, it seems to offset rising wages for a considerable period and makes it possible to retain their shares of markets in which they would otherwise be losing their comparative advantage.

This cumulative aspect of export performance and the increasing number of successful competitors may make it increasingly difficult for newcomers to get established in the sectors in which they have a comparative advantage. Even if transitional countries make room, expansion of exports from a few successful LDCs could swallow up most of the opportunities, leaving too little for the rest of the LDCs.

If we assume a second-best world in which the advanced countries are only willing to move away from unprofitable types of manufacturing rather slowly, there is a strong argument for favouring the poorest countries in the limited number of sectors where they are likely to become efficient exporters. Where the export market is already being parcelled out by quotas—which cannot be avoided in textiles and some agricultural products—it may be necessary to redesign quotas to discriminate systematically in favour of the least developed and poorest LDCs, if not others that need exports most.[38]

However, there are also potential dangers for LDCs in a systematic attempt to regulate the pattern of trade:

(1) Competition to export successfully, under the present system, stimulates LDCs to higher standards in their policies and economic management, both at the national level and at the level of the firm. Would a less competitive approach do this and lead to desirable learning effects?

(2) Any change away from a system of buying goods abroad wherever they are most satisfactory seems certain to diminish the benefits from trade and make buyers less satisfied with imports from LDCs. Is this cost worth the gain to poor countries?

Since the existing trading system has managed to accommodate the rapid growth of LDC manufactured exports up to now, it may not be easy to strike a balance of these issues. However, these are questions that should be of great concern to the developing countries in discussing a New International Economic Order.

ENDNOTES

1. Although the rise in the price of oil contributed enormously to the increased export revenues of a few developing countries—notably Iran, Venezuela, Nigeria, Indonesia, Algeria and Iraq—supply as well as demand limitations make a continuation of these increases unlikely. (Throughout this paper, the capital surplus oil countries—Kuwait, Libya, Oman, Qatar, Saudi Arabia and United Arab Emirates—are treated as a separate group so as not to distort the analysis of other developing countries.)
2. For simplicity, only merchandise exports will be considered; henceforth, exports means merchandise exports except where specifically noted.
3. This study is an outgrowth of continuing work in the World Bank on the prospects for developing countries in relation to the future evolution of the world economy. It makes use of two recent reports, *Prospects for Developing Countries, 1978–1985* (World Bank, Development Policy Staff, 1977) and *World Development Report, 1978* (WDR).
4. Even if Southern Europe is excluded, this share is now close to 40 per cent.
5. This is the 'base' or middle case in which GNP in MDCs is projected to grow at 4.2 per cent per annum (cf. Table 10 below).
6. Apparent similarities between low and middle-income LDCs in the composition of exports disappear in a disaggregation by regions.
7. Or 52 per cent in current prices.
8. In unpublished research for *World Development Report*.

9. This export growth was largely masked by a shift in the terms of trade against these exports.

10. These estimates are all preliminary.

11. A detailed analysis of LDC produce performance is given in Donges and Riedel (1977).

12. Based on an unpublished World Bank stuy by Yoriko Kawaguchi; the nine LDC exporters are Brazil, Argentina, India, Yugoslavia, Malaysia, Mexico, Hong Kong, Korea and Colombia. In machinery and transport equipment, UN trade statistics appear to be inflated by re-exports among LDCs and to understate exports to MDCs.

13. However, trade liberalisation has favoured MDC industrial exports over LDC specialties, which tend to be exempted from tariff cuts and GSP schemes.

14. The initial composition of these exports would almost certainly have led to a slower growth rate in LDCs than MDCs, if both groups of countries had maintained their market shares.

15. In Hong Kong export promotion efforts began by the late 1940s, while various industrial countries (and Puerto Rico) set examples in the 1950s.

16. Still others have begun to experiment with export processing zones (for example, Indonesia, Syria), export-oriented investments (for example, Venezuela, Iran) or regional common markets of various kind (in Africa, Latin America and the Caribbean).

17. See, for example, Maizels (1968), Chenery (1971), Balassa (1977a) and Michaely (1977). The last allows for the fact that exports are a component of GNP by relating GNP growth to the increase in the *share* of exports in GNP, with highly significant results.

18. For limited periods, capital inflows can replace exports as a source of foreign exchange, but in cases of successful development this has only deferred the need to expand exports by a decade or so.

19. See, for example, Hufbauer (1970), Hirsch (1974), Stern (1975), Helleiner (1976), and Balassa (1977b). A number of regional applications are given in Giersch (1974).

20. Except Jamaica, whose exports of manufactures consist almost entirely of aluminium oxide, and New Caledonia, which exports ferrous nickel.

21. A classification of all transitional countries is given in Chenery (1977), which also traces the past growth of each of the main groups. In addition to the countries shown in Table 7, there are many smaller exporters of manufactures.

22. Natural resource processing has also played a role in several cases.

23. Although a few products such as radios are largely produced by locally owned firms.

24. Marketing and related aspects of design are defined here to include almost all non-production activities required to adjust a product to the tastes of the customer, to profit from product differentiation, to find buyers and 'sell' them on the product, and to test, package, ship, distribute and service the product so as to meet the special needs of the customer. We would exclude from 'design', and treat as a separate activity, major innovation including the development of new products, as well as technology transfer, adaptation, and research having to do with production.

25. Followed by Taiwan, Republic of Korea, Argentina and India. The role of market size is evident.
26. This is particularly true in Argentina, Spain and Brazil, and is becoming true of Mexico, as a result of new oil discoveries.
27. Haiti, Kenya, Sri Lanka and Vietnam have some potential but their actual exports of manufactures are still very small.
28. Apart from Ivory Coast, which assembles trucks and heavy construction equipment for partners in a regional customs union. In this table, *capital goods* are defined as Standard International Trade Classification (SITC) categories 71 (less 714–9), 722.1, 723.2, 724.9, 726, 731, 732.3, 734.1 and 735; *consumer engineering goods* include SITC 724.1, 724.2, 725, 732.1, 864 and 891; *clothing and footwear*, SITC 84 and 85; *textiles*, SITC 65; *other clearcut consumer goods*, SITC 696, 82, 83 and 89 (less 891); *standardised intermediate goods*, SITC 5 (less 541, 553, 554 and 571), 611, 631, 641, 661, 662, 664 and 67.
29. Consumer goods here are the sum of three categories in Table 8: consumer engineering, clothing and footwear, and other clearcut consumer goods.
30. LDCs close to MDC markets, such as Mexico or Yugoslavia, emphasise labour-intensive products in which transport costs and delivery time afford them an advantage. Transport costs are also important in trade among LDCs.
31. The requisite management, marketing and design capabilities appear to be areas where LDCs are weak compared to MDCs and MNCs, and may be profitable areas for LDC development efforts.
32. Regarding the product cycle as a general phenomenon, see especially Vernon (1966) and Wells (1972).
33. Based on unpublished EEC data.
34. Gloves and mittens, men's woven shirts, and knit blouses, woven shirts and blouses, trousers and slacks, coats, and body support garments for women (based on data from US Department of Commerce).
35. Actual labour displacement by LDC imports appears small compared to that resulting from these other influences, based for example on estimates in Wolter (1977), Frank (1977) and other objective studies.
36. For example, in each of eight 'sensitive' products of Group (1), which account for over 60 per cent of EEC imports from LDCs by weight, a quota will be created against any supplier whose exports come to exceed 0.2 per cent of EEC imports from LDCs and CPEs combined. In group (2) (most other major products) this threshold share is 1.2 per cent to 1.5 per cent.
37. Based on recent agreements and data in US International Trade Commission (1978).
38. To some extent 'textile' quotas already operate in the direction suggested, but they strongly discourage new exporters from getting started, no matter how badly the exports are needed. In the aid field, donor policy has already been moving in this direction, but there has been less evolution of trade criteria appropriate to the transitional status of the middle-income countries.

REFERENCES

Balassa, B., 'Export Incentives and Export Performance in Developing Countries: A Comparative Analysis', *World Bank Staff Working Paper* No. 248 (January 1977a).

Balassa, B., 'A "Stages" Approach to Comparative Advantage', *World Bank Staff Working* No. 256 (May 1977).

Chenery, H., 'Targets for Development', in Barbara Ward (ed.), *The Widening Gap* (New York, 1971) pp. 27–47.

Chenery, H., 'Transitional Growth and World Industrialization', in Bertil Ohlin, Per-Ove Hesselborn and Per Magnus Wijkman (eds.), *The International Allocation of Economic Activity* (London: Macmillan, 1977) pp. 457–90.

Chenery, H. and Syrquin, M., *Patterns of Development, 1950–1970* (London, 1975).

Diaz-Alejandro, C. F., 'Some Characteristics of Recent Export Expansion in Latin America', in Herbert Giersch (ed.), *The International Division of Labour: Problems and Perspectives* (Tübingen, 1974) pp. 215–35.

Donges J. B. and Riedel, J., 'The Expansion of Manufactured Exports in Developing Countries: An Empirical Assessment of Supply and Demand Issues', *Weltwirtschaftliches Archiv* (1977) Band 113, Heft 4, pp. 58–87.

Frank, Jr., C. R., *Foreign Trade and Domestic Aid* (Washington, DC, 1977).

Giersch, H., (ed.), *The International Division of Labour; Problems and Perspectives* (Tübingen, 1974).

Helleiner, G. K., 'Industry Characteristics and the Competitiveness of Manufactures from Less-Developed Countries', *Weltwirtschaftliches Archiv* (1976) Bank 112, Heft 3, pp. 507–24.

Hirsch, S., 'Hypotheses Regarding Trade between Developing and Industrialized Countries', in Herbert Giersch (ed.), *The International Division of Labour: Problems and Perspectives* (Tübingen, 1974).

Hufbauer, G. C., 'The Impact of National Characteristics and Technology on the Commodity Composition of Trade in Manufactured Goods', in Raymond Vernon (ed.), *The Technology Factor in International Trade* (New York and London, 1970), pp. 145–231.

Maizels, A., *Exports and Economic Growth of Development Countries* (Cambridge, 1968).

Michaely, M., 'Exports and Growth: An Empirical Investigation',

Journal of Development Economics (1977) vol. 4, pp. 49–53.

Stern, R. M., 'Testing Trade Theories', in Peter B. Kenen (ed.) *International Trade and Finance: Frontiers for Research* (Cambridge, 1975).

US International Trade Commission, *The History and Current Status of the Multifiber Arrangement* (Washington, DC, 1978).

Vernon, R., 'International Investment and International Trade in the Product Cycle', *Quarterly Journal of Economics* (May 1966) vol. 80, pp. 190–207.

Wells, Jr., L. T., (ed.), *The Product Life Cycle and International Trade* (Boston, 1972).

Wolter, F., 'Adjusting to Imports from Developing Countries', in Herbert Giersch (ed.), *Reshaping the World Economic order* (Tübingen, 1977) pp. 97–130.

Comments

Mohiuddin Alamgir (Bangladesh)

Professors Chenery.and Keesing have made an important contribution
to our understanding of the recent growth pattern and future prospects
of LDC exports. Their findings are different and the suggested future
outlook more optimistic than those presented earlier in the work of
Maizels. The authors suggest that if the present export trend continues,
'it will lead over the next few years to an export growth rate roughly
equal to the rest of the world'.

While the authors' findings are impressive, they conceal a lot of
information. A wide range of countries have been defined as developing
countries which makes it difficult to interpret the aggregative figures. To
give one example, when a country such as Bangladesh is included in the
group of countries with significant manufactured exports, one hardly
realises that the share of one item (jute) is above 90 per cent and that the
item has been facing serious problems on both the supply and demand
side for quite some time. Moreover, the future prospect is not very
good. In general, it can be pointed out that the lumping together of low-
income Asian and African countries with those which have emerged as a
class in themselves (such as the Republic of Korea, Taiwan, Hong
Kong, Singapore) cannot be very rewarding.

It is true, however, that Chenery and Keesing tried to get around the
above problem by using a typology of sample countries, based on what I
call symptomatic criteria. This is actually a derivative of the stage theory
of growth. The authors discuss the policies and natural factors that
explain the status of different countries in their classification schema,
but it is not very clear whether there exists a feasible path for countries
to move from a lower stage of export performance to a high stage and, if
it does, is it worth while? What the authors have missed here is that the
current international division of labour can be explained primarily in
terms of the degree of integration of different countries within the world
capitalistic system. All leading examples of export-oriented industrialis-

ation have followed a capitalist development path. It should be realised that under a non-capitalistic development path which is more self-reliant and somewhat inward looking, 'export expansion at any cost' may not be an admissible strategy.

As for export performance, what is important to the developing countries is the growth of their capacity to import out of own export earnings. To analyse this, one has to correct the nominal export figures for change in terms of trade. According to the *World Development Report*, to which Chenery and Keesing constantly refer, between 1960–75 the terms of trade of low-income countries declined at a rate of −0.2 per cent a year, implying a growth rate of purchasing power of only 0.7 per cent a year. These figures are somewhat misleading because the base year (1960) is different from that used for the analysis of growth of merchandise exports (1950). This asymmetry in the selection of period of analysis is difficult to understand.

To assess the overall export performance of developing countries, the aggregative data on exports should be supplemented by country-by-country data on the growth of purchasing power. Besides, so far in the purchasing power analysis we have been concerned with changes in net barter terms of trade whereas for capturing the implication for welfare changes we should take into account changes in factoral terms of trade, single or double, a task which has so far been avoided as being conceptually and empirically intractable. The theory of unequal exchange has made some conceptual contribution in this respect but I am sure Professor Samir Amin, a participant of this symposium and an advocate of the theory, will agree that more work needs to be done.

The authors' exclusive emphasis on manufactured exports is unfortunate because one is encouraged to overlook the fact that even today, for all the LDCs taken together, export of primary products accounts for more than three-quarters of total exports. More important, Chenery and Keesing did not bring out clearly the fact that the export (manufactured) growth and its diversification was attained by many developing countries at a high social cost, a fact that should have been made explicit in an analysis of trend over time. The experiences of India in the 1970s and Pakistan and Latin America in the 1960s have shown that a wide range of fiscal, monetary and other special concessions were necessary to realise the export growth. In all cases, the net export earnings were probably much lower than those indicated by gross figures. An overview on the basis of cross-country data may be useful at times for identifying broad patterns, but for policy analysis one needs to examine the experiences of individual countries in depth. In this context, it is necessary to carefully assess if the diversification of exports into capital goods and consumer durables through MNCs benefits the countries as much as one is led to believe. Similarly, exploitation of natural resources for export by MNCs should be treated with caution.

In both cases, one should calculate the net export earnings while evaluating export performance. There should be some guidelines for countries to follow so that a country like Bangladesh, when faced with the critical decision regarding external collaboration in the exploitation of its natural resource (gas) can incorporate adequate safeguards to protect national interests. Exports, particularly manufactured export-oriented industrialisation, implicate changes in income distribution both in the medium and long run unless appropriate corrective measures are undertaken. Unfortunately, Chenery and Keesing do not pay much attention to the distribution issues.

Considering export projections, one is struck by the difference between World Bank and UNCTAD figures. This only leads one to conclude that all export projections are only suggestive because, given the uncertainty associated with all parameter estimates, the margin of error is likly to be high. It is somewhat asymmetric that in making projections, the authors have emphasised demand rather than supply factors, whereas in analysing past trends they focused more on supply factors. Even if we tentatively accept their figures as a basis for discussion, it is not clear if it will be possible for developing countries to overcome the internal and external barriers to export expansion. The structural transformation implicit in the strategy for export expansion may be very difficult to realise. The underlying issues are much more involved than those contained under economic management efficiency to which Chenery and Keesing draw our attention. Sufficient in-dications are available that the new wave of protectionism in the developed countries will continue to be a rule rather than an exception for quite some time to come. Only a technological revolution leading to the introduction of a large number of new products may change the situation fundamentally. However, new products in the form of synthetic substitutes for LDCs' natural product exports will only worsen the situation for them. The case of jute provides a prime example. Therefore, future export growth of LDCs will depend partly on whether MDCs can be persuaded to disinvest in synthetic substitute development.

It is important to realise that the relationship between the poor developing and rich developing countries is often a mirror image of that between developing and developed countries. Therefore, while the suggestion by Chenery and Keesing to increase trade among LDCs is basically sound, it should be borne in mind that such an arrangement for increased trade may not always work to the benefit of the weak partners. Such export growth could only be 'tied' exports rather than 'free' exports, thus implying an intrinsically lower real value for exports. More often than not this seems to be precisely the outcome of barter deals that many poor countries enter into with their rich counterparts. I am not pleading here either against barter deals *per se* or against increased trade among LDCs, but I feel that these suggestions require much closer scrutiny than they have received so far in international deliberations.

Chenery and Keesing do not focus upon the important fact that political and institutional considerations sometimes hinder the realisation of export growth to the detriment of potential trading partners. For example, the economic relationship among countries of South Asia is far from normal. A number of interesting proposals involving production and trade of fertiliser and raw jute between India and Bangladesh are yet to be taken up seriously. The volume of trade between India and Pakistan and Bangladesh and Pakistan is far below the potential levels. Political considerations, on the other hand, sometimes force countries to enter into trade relations which are not very remunerative. In the early 1970s, I have heard Bangladesh officials complaining bitterly about certain aspects of trade with some of the countries of the socialist block. Moreover, poor countries who export often become susceptible to blackmail by MDCs. In 1974, famine-stricken Bangladesh faced the threat of its food supply from the USA being cut off because it exported raw jute to Cuba. Finally, Bangladesh was forced to cancel further shipments of jute to Cuba.

The above considerations make me somewhat sceptical of the prospect of LDCs' export growth of a magnitude suggested by Chenery and Keesing. Conceptually, the problem is that despite many important contributions in the field of international trade theory, we still lack a comprehensive framework to explain trade between countries.

3 Income Levels and the Structure of Trade[1]

Michael Michaely (Israel)

Certain goods are naturally expected to be exported by rich nations, and other goods by poor; likewise, some goods are expected to be imported primarily by rich countries, and others by poor. Does a good exported by rich countries tend to be also imported by their likes—or by their poor partners? What are the possible explanations of the income level of exports and imports? And how do these explanations square with *a priori* theories of the determinants of the pattern of international trade?

These, and a few associated questions, is the subject matter of this chapter. In the first section, an appropriate index for the measurement of the income level of trade flows is proposed, and some of the attributes of the findings indicated by this measure pointed out. The second section explores the issue of similarity versus dissimilarity in the structure of exports and imports. In the section following the income levels of exports and imports are examined in the light of, and used as a partial test of, existing theories of the trade pattern. Next, building on the indexes of income level of the traded goods, attention is paid to the income level of trade flows of *countries*. Finally, in the last section the *total* income represented in trade flows, rather than per capita income levels, are measured and explored.

Appendix A considers the effect of taking into account the dispersion in the income levels involved in the trade flow in each good; in Appendix B an alternative measure of the income level of trade flows is discussed.

I

The income level of world exports of good i is defined by the following index, y_i^x:

$$y_i^x = \sum_j y_j \frac{X_{ij}}{X_{i.}}, \text{ where:}$$

$$X_{ij} = \text{exports of good } i \text{ by country } j$$
$$X_{i.} = \text{world exports of good } i$$
$$y_j = \text{index of income of country } j$$

The latter term is, in turn, defined as follows:

$$y_j = 100 \frac{Y_j}{Y_u}, \text{ where:}$$

$$Y_j = \text{per capita GNP of country } j; \text{ and}$$
$$Y_u = \text{US per capita GNP.}$$

The index is defined, thus, as an average, weighted by the share of each country in world exports of the good, of the income levels of the countries exporting the good. A country's 'richness' or 'poorness' is defined by its per capita GNP—still the best possible single measure, despite its various well-known shortcomings (especially in international comparisons). The income level is presented as an index, by showing it as a ratio of the US per capita income—the world's highest at the point (1973) to which the present study is related.[2]

In this way the highest possible level of the index is 1 – or 100, as it is put here for convenience; this would be the income level of exports of a good exported exclusively by the United States. The lowest boundary of the index is, of course, the index of the income level of the poorest country which conducts any trade. In this study this lowest index is 1.0 (for Laos).

The income level of world *imports* of good i, designated by y_i^m, is defined in an exactly parallel way; that is, it is defined by the formulation given above, where X_{ij} and $X_{i.}$ are replaced by, respectively, M_{ij} and $M_{i.}$—country j's imports and world imports of the good.

The indexes of income levels of exports and imports, classified by the three-digit SITC into 174 goods,[3] have been calculated for the year 1973.[4] The results are presented in Table 1 and a few simple characteristics of the findings shown in this table are pointed out below.

TABLE 1
INDEXES OF INCOME LEVELS OF EXPORTS AND IMPORTS, BY COMMODITY

SITC Code	Commodity	Income level of exports (y_i^x)	Income level of exports (y_i^m)
0	*Food and live animals*		
001	Live animals	60.85	49.84
011	Meat—fresh, chilled, frozen	58.56	63.64
012	Meat—dried, salted, smoked	74.86	49.53
013	Meat—canned or prepared	58.29	70.88
022	Milk and cream	70.05	34.91
023	Butter	69.11	51.39
024	Cheese and curd	71.69	64.75
025	Eggs	69.43	60.98
031	Fresh fish	46.80	67.73
032	Canned or prepared fish	52.04	62.17
041	Unmilled wheat	88.30	29.95
042	Rice	53.20	16.80
043	Unmilled barley	78.37	56.37
044	Unmilled maize	81.70	51.32
045	Unmilled cereals, n.e.s.	76.04	54.90
046	Wheatmeal or flour	72.24	12.12
047	Non-wheatmeal or flour	70.50	39.74
048	Cereal preparations	71.08	49.33
051	Fresh fruit and nuts	30.79	66.65
052	Dried fruit	40.13	54.41
053	Preserved or prepared fruit	43.92	67.74
054	Fresh vegetables	47.50	63.26
055	Preserved or prepared vegetables	44.52	68.10
061	Sugar and honey	24.74	52.16
062	Sugar preparations	61.23	62.10
071	Coffee	11.39	76.82
072	Cocoa	16.80	69.25
073	Chocolate	66.69	67.27
074	Tea	10.12	40.31
075	Spices	13.45	45.60
081	Animal feeding stuff	58.51	59.22
091	Margarine, shortening	68.14	44.51
099	Food preparations, n.e.s.	67.28	47.20
1	*Beverages and tobacco*		
111	Non-alcoholic beverages, n.e.s.	65.98	55.86
112	Alcoholic beverages	54.30	68.21
121	Tobacco, unmanufactured	54.85	59.73
122	Tobacco manufactures	71.69	43.19

TABLE 1 (*Continued*)

SITC Code	Commodity	Income level of exports (y_i^x)	Income level of imports (y_i^m)
2	*Crude materials, inedible, except fuel*		
211	Hides and skins	60.74	52.07
212	Fur skins	69.28	70.88
221	Oil seeds, nuts, kernels	73.92	60.52
231	Crude synthetic rubber	29.89	52.99
241	Fuel wood and charcoal	55.73	56.75
242	Rough wood	37.43	53.35
243	Shaped wood	69.56	65.63
244	Raw cork and waste	22.14	53.02
251	Pulp and waste paper	80.83	61.90
261	Silk	19.10	57.45
262	Wool and animal hair	58.31	55.61
263	Cotton	33.64	43.88
264	Jute	9.67	42.84
265	Vegetable fibres, excluding cotton and jute	31.83	55.31
266	Synthetic, regenerated fibre	68.02	46.43
267	Waste of textile fabrics	79.70	38.63
271	Crude fertilisers	32.08	51.65
273	Stone, sand and gravel	63.63	64.61
274	Sulphur	64.36	49.47
275	Natural abrasives	56.60	69.46
276	Other crude minerals	60.18	58.71
281	Iron ore, concentrates	51.46	67.64
282	Iron and steel scrap	84.14	45.62
283	Non-ferrous base metal ore, concentrates	39.55	64.76
284	Non-ferrous metal scrap	75.33	64.77
285	Silver and platinum ores	59.46	71.94
291	Crude animal materials, n.e.s.	50.57	65.49
292	Crude vegetable materials, n.e.s.	53.42	64.66
3	*Mineral fuels, lubricants, related materials*		
321	Coal, coke, briquettes	83.12	60.39
331	Crude petroleum	23.45	55.48
332	Petroleum products	38.49	67.71
341	Natural gas and manufactures	65.66	72.98
4	*Animal and vegetable oils and fasts*		
411	Animal oil and fats	80.46	44.56
421	Fixed vegetable oils, soft	50.53	41.06
422	Fixed vegetable oils, non-soft	24.91	57.92
431	Processed animal and vegetable oils	69.41	53.62

TABLE 1 (*Continued*)

SITC Code	Commodity	Income level of exports (y_i^x)	Income level of imports (y_i^m)
5	*Chemicals*		
512	Organic chemicals	75.00	53.49
513	Inorganic elements, oxides, etc.	69.20	56.18
514	Other inorganic elements	71.81	47.81
515	Radioactive and associated elements	86.44	76.90
521	Coal, petroleum etc. chemicals	56.24	57.47
531	Synthetic organic dyestuffs, etc.	81.06	45.20
532	Dyes n.e.s., tanning products	49.51	32.54
533	Pigments, prints, etc.	71.04	48.22
541	Medical and pharmeaceutical products	71.34	41.90
551	Essential oil, perfumes, etc.	61.97	54.13
553	Cosmetics etc.	66.36	49.97
554	Soaps and cleaning preparations	70.94	48.20
561	Manufactured fertilisers	68.26	37.41
571	Explosive and pyrotechnic products	63.86	46.18
581	Plastic materials, etc.	73.50	54.58
599	Chemicals n.e.s.	72.78	46.31
6	*Manufactured goods classified by material*		
611	Leather	44.72	62.20
612	Leather manufactures	55.53	65.66
613	Fur skins, tanned or dressed	64.30	65.78
621	Rubber materials	71.81	52.54
629	Rubber articles, n.e.s.	65.61	62.14
631	Veneers, plywood, etc.	50.91	67.40
632	Wood manufactures, n.e.s.	64.23	72.76
633	Cork manufactures	30.70	65.67
641	Paper and paperboard	76.57	60.40
642	Paper articles	68.92	53.78
651	Textile yarn and thread	56.54	49.46
652	Woven cotton fabrics	47.08	53.48
653	Woven non-cotton fabrics	56.91	55.22
654	Lace, ribbons, tulle, etc.	65.33	53.07
655	Special textile products	68.49	57.23
656	Textile products n.e.s	40.45	50.04
657	Floor coverings, tapestry, etc.	56.16	72.04
661	Cement building products	46.50	51.40
662	Clay building products	62.20	59.88
663	Other non-metal mineral manufactures	71.41	59.99
664	Glass	70.74	61.78

TABLE 1 (*Continued*)

SITC Code	Commodity	Income level of exports (y_i^x)	Income level of imports (y_i^m)
	Manufactured goods classified by material (contd.)		
665	Glassware	66.12	55.66
666	Pottery	61.51	68.48
667	Pearls, precious and semi-precious stones	50.52	62.62
671	Pig iron	56.53	68.06
672	Ingots of iron and steel	66.74	40.39
673	Iron and steel shapes	71.23	58.01
674	Universals, plates and sheets of iron and steel	68.05	55.32
675	Hoop and strip of iorn and steel	75.18	55.66
676	Rails and other track materials of steel	65.12	28.63
677	Iron and steel wire, excluding rod	71.80	55.61
678	Iron and steel tubes, pipes, etc.	70.18	56.08
679	Iron and steel castings, unworked	75.24	48.89
681	Silver, platinum etc.	62.29	72.03
682	Copper	42.96	63.26
683	Nickel	74.22	80.08
684	Aluminium	69.93	60.51
685	Lead	57.62	55.64
686	Zinc	64.47	62.86
687	Tin	19.07	66.89
689	Non-ferrous base metals, n.e.s.	62.79	71.71
691	Structures and parts n.e.s.	68.79	47.52
692	Metal containers	64.40	45.38
693	Non-electric wire products	65.49	60.81
694	Nails, screws, etc., of iron, steel or copper	71.06	67.75
695	Tools	74.81	54.01
696	Cutlery	61.71	62.28
697	Base-metal household equipment	58.27	57.25
698	Metal manufactures, n.e.s.	69.82	58.60
7	*Machinery and transport equipment*		
711	Non-electric power machinery	76.86	59.32
712	Agricultural machinery	75.94	50.87
714	Office machines	75.53	64.25
715	Metal-working machinery	77.35	49.71
717	Textile and leather machinery	74.53	41.07
718	Machines for special industries	77.71	42.14
719	Non-electric machines, n.e.s.	75.99	49.50

TABLE 1 (*Continued*)

SITC Code	Commodity	Income level of exports (y_i^x)	Income level of imports (y_i^m)
	Machinery and transport equipment (Contd.)		
722	Electric-power machinery, switches	74.64	50.00
723	Equipment for distributing electricity	66.38	46.72
724	Telecommunications equipment	67.54	60.72
725	Domestic electric equipment	67.26	61.56
726	Electromedical, X-ray equipment	80.13	58.89
729	Electric machinery, n.e.s	72.54	57.71
731	Railway vehicles	69.76	29.60
732	Road motor vehicles	76.21	67.81
733	Road non-motor vehicles	66.81	68.86
734	Aircraft	87.17	55.47
735	Ships and boats	66.84	57.38
8	*Miscellaneous manufactured articles*		
812	Plumbing, heating and lighting fixtures	67.83	58.25
821	Furniture	67.94	72.64
831	Travel goods, handbags	46.24	73.96
841	Clothing, except fur	45.33	73.15
842	Fur clothing	57.41	79.05
851	Footwear	41.12	78.84
861	Scientific instruments and apparatus	75.12	60.03
862	Photographic and cinematographic supplies	76.79	57.73
863	Developed cinema film	55.67	43.67
864	Watches and clocks	79.68	54.69
891	Musical instruments, recorders, etc.	66.76	68.18
892	Printed matter	67.62	61.26
893	Plastic articles, n.e.s.	68.72	67.50
894	Toys, sporting goods, etc.	58.40	71.16
895	Office supplies, n.e.s.	72.63	49.43
896	Works of art, etc.	73.21	71.49
897	Gold and silver ware, jewellery	60.71	67.36
899	Other manufactured goods	56.46	62.06

First, the dispersion of the indexes of income levels is much more substantial in exports than in imports. The range of the index in exports is from 9.7 (in good (264) jute) to 88.3 (in good (041) wheat)—the maximum possible range being, we recall, from 1.0 to 100. In imports, the range is from 12.1 (good (046) wheatmeal or flour), to 80.1 (good (683) nickel).[5] The weighted averages of the indexes are 61.8 for exports, and 58.3 for imports. The coefficient of variation—the ratio of the standard deviation to the mean—is 0.29 in exports, and 0.20 in imports.

It might be expected that the extreme cases, both high and low, of income levels of exports would be associated with a high degree of country concentration of these exports, with very few rich countries exporting the high-income good, and similarly very few poor countries exporting the low-income good. This, of course, is immediately evident for the two most extreme cases—wheat being exported primarily by the USA, one of the world's richest countries, and jute being exported predominantly by Bangladesh, one of the world's poorest. But it is also true as a general rule. Thus, if we take the ten goods with the highest income level in exports,[6] the (unweighted) average coefficient of country concentration of these exports[7] is found to be 54.7—in comparison with an average of 37.3 for all exports. The average for the ten goods with the lowest income levels[8] is 46.4; in this group, it is not as high as in the former because some of the goods with the lowest income levels, such as sugar, coffee, or cocoa, are exported by several low-income countries.

It is interesting to note that, as a general rule, a positive association exists between the income level of exports of a good and the degree of country-concentration of these exports. The Spearman rank-correlation coefficient between the two series is 0.38; this should be considered quite high, particularly in view of the fact, noted above, that the extremely low-income goods have a *higher* than average level of country concentration.[9] In imports, the association is even stronger; the rank-correlation coefficient of the income level and the country-concentration of imports is 0.66. We can thus see that the higher the income level of exports and imports of a good, the more these exports and imports tend to be concentrated in a small number of countries.

When goods are aggregated into large categories, the dispersion among the aggregates should naturally be substantially smaller than among individual goods. When the major categories of the SITC are used (nine categories, 0 to 8), the dispersion becomes surprisingly small. This may be seen from columns (1) and (3) of Table 2. It appears that the (unweighted) average income levels for these categories only range from 53.2 (for category 3—mineral fuels) to 73.8 (for category 7—machinery and transport equipment); whereas the range for imports is between 49.3 (category 4—animal and vegetable oils and fats) and 65.0 (category 8—miscellaneous manufactured articles). This low dispersion *among* categories must imply a high degree of dispersion *within* each category;

TABLE 2

LEVELS, DISPERSION AND ASSOCIATION OF EXPORTS AND IMPORTS, BY MAJOR CATEGORIES

Category	y_i^x		y_i^m		Spearman rank correlation coefficient of y_i^x and y_i^m
	Mean	coefficient of variation	Mean	coefficient of variation	
	(1)	(2)	(3)	(4)	(5)
0 Food and live animals	55.4	0.39	53.7	0.28	−0.418
1 Beverages and tobacco	61.7	0.09	56.8	0.18	
2 Crude materials, inedible	53.2	0.38	57.4	0.17	0.151
3 Mineral fuels, lubricants	53.2	0.52	64.1	0.12	
4 Animal and vegetable oils	56.3	0.43	49.3	0.16	
5 Chemicals	64.4	0.29	49.8	0.20	0.159
6 Manufactured goods, by material	61.4	0.19	58.6	0.15	−0.238
7 Machinery and transport equipment	73.8	0.08	54.0	0.19	−0.098
8 Miscellaneous manufactured articles	63.2	0.18	65.0	0.15	−0.534
All goods	59.0	0.29	56.7	0.20	−0.232

this may in fact be seen from columns (2) and (4) for exports and imports, respectively. It appears, indeed, that in the case of exports the degree of dispersion within each group is in the majority of categories *higher* than for the total of individual goods; only two categories—1 and 7—appear to be relatively homogeneous. This indicates, therefore, that the category to which a good belongs is not one of the characteristics which determine the income level of the good's exports or imports—an indication which is not inconsistent with the findings presented later on in the investigation. The only clearcut exception to this rule, for the export trade, is category 7 (machinery and transport equipment). In this category both the average income level is substantially above all the rest, and, the dispersion within the category is particularly low. So this is the only major category of goods which may be clearly designated as a high-income category of exports.

II

Conventional, factor-proportions theory of the determinants of trade patterns would lead us to the following expectation: a country with an abundance of certain factors will *export* goods intensive in these factors, and *import* goods intensive in the other factors. In a world of two factors, labour and capital, the result is obvious. A country with an abundance of capital (relative to labour) is a rich country, and this country will export to its poor partner capital-intensive goods. A country, on the other hand, abundant in labour is a poor country; and it, in turn, will export (to its rich partner) other labour-intensive goods. Hence, the income level of the *exports* of a certain good, and the income level of its *imports*, should be radically different. Even if the factor-proportions theory is viewed less crudely—with more factors admitted, or when factors such as tech-nological innovations, for instance, are introduced—the expected result remains basically unchanged, namely that, in general the higher the income level of the exports of a good, the lower should be the income level of its imports, and vice versa.

A product-differentiation, demand-determined theory, on the other hand, such as that suggested by Linder,[10] would lead to the opposite expectation. By this theory, countries of a similar income level trade mainly among themselves, in a range of goods which are inherently quite similar, although somewhat differentiated. Thus, rich countries export and import (by trade among themselves) one class of goods; whereas poor countries export and import another class of goods. Hence, a good whose income level is high in exports may be expected also to have a high level of income in imports; whereas a low-income level in exports would be associated with a low level in imports.

We thus have clearly conflicting expectations from the two sets of theories; and we may test the expectations against the actual findings, by the use of rank-correlation coefficients. The factor-proportions pattern would lead to a high *negative* rank correlation of the series of income levels of exports and imports; whereas the Linder theory would lead to a high *positive* rank-correlation. The rank-correlation coefficients are presented in column (5) of Table 2.

It appears that when all commodities are included, the rank-correlation coefficient, -0.232, is *negative*, but quite small. The sign would indicate a vindication of the conventional factor-proportions expectation. But the fact that the correlation is weak suggests that *both* forces—the forces indicated by both sets of theories—are working, with varying strength or weight in the case of each good.

It may be worthwhile, therefore, to see whether the rank-correlation coefficients would be different when ranking is done within each *class* of goods separately. This is also shown in column (5), for the major categories (the one-digit) in the SITC classification (categories 1, 3 and 4 are omitted because there are only four goods in each). In a very basic way this classification system orders and ranks classes by the level of fabrication—the value added in manufacturing, and the level of sophistication. It appears that the signs of the rank-correlation coefficients do indeed vary among major classes, but the coefficients themselves are again mostly rather small. In two categories—the first 0 and the last 8—they are quite substantial (-0.418 and -0.534, respectively); and here, they are again *negative* in both cases. That is, within each of these categories it may be stated more strongly that the higher the income level of a good in exports, the lower it tends to be in imports—the result expected by conventional theory.[11]

Since the argument for similarity of exports and imports of a country is intimately associated with the hypothesis that high-income countries tend to both export and import goods of a highly heterogeneous nature, one further test has been conducted. A measure of the degree of product differentiation—which will be mentioned later—is available for 120 out of the total of 174 goods. These have been divided into three groups of 40 goods each, according to the degree of product differentiation—group 1 including the goods with the highest measure of differentiation, and group 3—those with the lowest differentiation. According to the hypothesis tested—Linder's—it is mainly in group 1 that a positive association of the income level of exports and imports should be expected. In fact, the rank-correlation coefficients within each of these three groups are as follows: -0.222 in group 1; -0.392 in group 2; and -0.317 in group 3 (for the 120 goods as a whole, it is -0.234). Thus, although the negative association of the income levels of exports and imports is somewhat weaker for goods in group 1 than for the rest, it is *negative*—in contrast to the hypothesis postulated, and in accordance with the predictions of 'conventional' theory.

It has been noted earlier that the *average* income levels do not differ radically among the major categories. In addition, it should be pointed out now that inasmuch as such differences do exist, they do not reveal any clearcut order. It might have been expected, intuitively, that the higher the level of fabrication, the higher will be the share of high-income countries in exports of the good; and of low-income countries in its imports. That is, that the income level of exports should increase as one moves from category 0 to category 8, and the income level of imports should fall. In fact, if such an order appears at all, it would seem to be a very weak one. A simple explanation of the determination of the income levels by degree of fabrication would thus seem to be rejected outright; but we can now attempt to explain the determination of income levels.

III

A high-income export good is, by definition, exported by high-income countries. What would a highly developed, high-income country be expected to export?

One such expectation—the most obvious—has already been noted. A high-income country is, almost invariably, a country with an abundance of physical capital; hence, it may be expected to export capital-intensive goods. A rich country is—again, almost invariably—abundant in human capital as well; hence, it may be expected that such countries will export goods intensive in human capital. These two factors, physical and human capital, may be considered as two components of one aggregate—the total size of an economy's capital—with attention given only to the total. Recent evidence suggests, however, that the two are not close substitutes, and should therefore be better treated as separate factors.[12]

A closely related attribute is the abundance of human skills, which may be expected in highly developed countries. The correlation of an 'average' level of skills in a country and the size of its human capital will undoubtedly be very high. Yet, the two are not entirely identical by definition; separate hypotheses are found in the literature with regard to the effect of a 'skill ratio'.[13] Hence, if data are available, the 'skill' factor may be better treated separately from human capital.

Another explanation of the nature of the exports of a highly developed country, popular in various versions in recent years, lies in technological aspects—the 'technology gap' or 'product cycle' explanations of trade patterns. The rich country is expected, by these hypotheses, to export primarily goods in which the embodied technology is the result of new, recent innovations. A corollary—in the 'product cycle' version—is that each such 'good' would be highly heterogeneous, whereas standardised goods would be exported by lower-income countries. The heterogeneity (or diversification) attribute is stressed by the Linder theory: this expects both exports and imports of a rich country to be of highly heterogeneous goods, as a result of the greater variations in demand introduced by high income.

The testing of such hypotheses has now become readily feasible, due to the well-known work of Hufbauer,[14] where the attributes of each good are quantified. Beside estimates relating to the possible determinants of trade mentioned above (excluding human capital, which is not incorporated in Hufbauer's study), Hufbauer also provides estimates of the wage level in the production of each good. This might be regarded as a proxy estimate of human capital, or of the level of skills; but it is designed to test directly Kravis' hypothesis,[15] that the export industries of rich countries are high wage-level industries. In addition, Hufbauer introduces a measure of scale economies; since a rich country tends, due to its very richness, to also be a *large* economy in the relevant sense (that is, in terms of total income, or total demand), it may be expected to have an advantage in industries where scale economies are positive and large (in the relevant range of production). This assumes, of course, less than perfect mobility of goods (in the full sense—including, for instance, perfect information) in world trade. Still another characteristic estimated by Hufbauer is the degree to which a good is sold to final consumers—rather than being an intermediary in the production of other goods. This is intended to test the contention that less developed economies tend to export intermediary goods; whereas highly developed economies tend to produce and export goods which are required mainly by final consumers, the production of which presumably tends to be more sophisticated.

We shall, therefore, test the following attributes of goods as possible explanatory variables of the income level of exports of the good; unless otherwise specified, the estimates of the variables are taken from the Hufbauer study:[16]

X_1 = physical-capital/labour ratio
X_2 = human-capital/labour ratio[17]
X_3 = a measure of skill ratio
X_4 = wage level
X_5 = a measure of economies of scale
X_6 = ratio of scales to final consumers
X_7 = a 'first-trade date', as a measure of recentness of technological innovation (in this study, the *later* the date, the higher the index);
X_8 = degree of dispersion of unit prices of the good, as a measure of product differentiation.[18]

The discussion thus far has referred to exports. For imports we have, again, two alternative hypotheses. 'Conventional' theories would lead to the expectation that a variable which contributes to a high-income level of the exports of the good should make the opposite contribution—to a low-income level—in imports. The Linder hypothesis, on the other hand, of exchange of basically similar goods, should lead to the expectation that a contribution of a variable to a high-income level of exports should do the same for the income level of imports.

Of the total of 174 goods altogether, Hufbauer's study provides data for 120: a sample of nineteen goods[19] (out of a total of 73) which belong to the SITC major (one-digit) categories 0–4 (where most of the value added is derived from natural resources or from non-manufacturing activity); and all (101) goods which belong to categories 5–8—roughly, the semi-manufactured and manufactured goods. Human-capital data (from the Branson–Monoyios study) are available only for the latter group (of 101 goods). I have therefore run three multiple regressions: (1) A regression for all (120) goods for which Hufbauer's data are available, where the explanatory variables exclude X_2 (human capital); (2) the same regression, with same data, but only for the (101) goods in categories 5–8; and (3) a regression covering again only the latter group (of 101 goods), but in which human capital is added to the explanatory variables.[20] Regressions (4) to (6) perform, similarly, the respective tests for imports. The results are summarised in Table 3.

The performed tests seem, from Table 3, to yield the following findings:

(1) When all (120) goods are tested, all variables together provide a modest part of the explanation of the determination of the income level of exports; and none at all for imports. The adjusted R^2 is 0.382 for exports, and nil (and, of course, insignificant) for imports.

(2) As might be expected, the performance improves substantially when only the (101) goods in the categories 5–8 are included: the adjusted R^2 rises then to 0.462 in exports, and to 0.178 in imports (the latter being this time significant at the 5 per cent level). The fact that the exclusion of only nineteen goods improves the explanation to this extent suggests that if these goods are an approximately representative sample of all goods in the categories 0–4, inclusion of these (had the data been available) would probably have reduced the explanation to nil, for exports as well as for imports. It also suggests, on the other hand, that had the removal of the effect of natural resources been done more thoroughly than by just excluding goods in the categories 0–4 (that is,

TABLE 3.
EXPLANATORY VARIABLES OF INCOME LEVELS: CORRELATION COEFFICIENTS

Equation no.	Adjusted R^2	Partial correlation coefficient (r) of							
		X_1	X_2	X_3	X_4	X_5	X_6	X_7	X_8
Exports									
1.	*0.382*	−0.096		0.084	*0.349*	−0.108	*0.128*	*0.328*	*0.169*
2.	*0.462*	−0.093		*0.311*	*0.204*	0.363	*−0.313*	*0.199*	*0.374*
3.	*0.392*	−0.061	0.093	*0.236*	*0.289*	0.024	−0.085	*0.217*	*0.306*
Imports									
4.	0.048	−0.001		−0.130	−0.079	−0.151	0.036	0.014	0.012
5.	*0.178*	0.063		*−0.318*	0.036	*−0.193*	*0.201*	−0.024	0.060
6.	*0.193*	*−0.175*	0.065	*−0.320*	−0.051	*−0.168*	*0.219*	−0.064	−0.001

Italicised figures are significant at the 5 per cent level.

primarily, if a finer classification and selection of goods for coverage had been made), the variables under consideration would have yielded together a substantially better explanation of the income level of trade.

(3) Partial correlation coefficients show that, in general, each variable separately performs better in explaining exports than in explaining imports — as has been seen before to be true for all explanatory variables together. This applies (again — as it was for the aggregate) particularly when all 120 goods — including, that is, those of the 0–4 group — are tested.

(4) The most surprising finding, from the partial correlation coefficients, is the poor showing of X_1 — the physical-capital/labour ratio. Intuitively, again, this variable might have been expected to provide the most obvious explanation: rich countries might first and foremost be expected to export capital-intensive goods. In fact this characteristic of the good — its capital intensity — contributes practically nothing to the determination of the income level of trade.[21]

(5) The human-capital variable (X_2) also appears — again, quite surprisingly — to contribute little: its partial correlation coefficient in exports is significant, and is of the 'right' sign; but it is rather low. In imports it is not significant (at the 5 per cent level). Its addition to the list of explanatory variables *lowers* somewhat the R^2 of the regression as a whole (from 0.462 to 0.392) in exports; and leaves it practically unchanged for imports.[22]

(6) Five variables, out of those tested, seem to contribute to the determination of the income level of exports (and — less clearly, as is implied by our former observations — of imports): the level of skill (X_3); the wage level (X_4); the ratio of sales to final consumers (X_6); the 'newness' of the good — as measured by 'first-trade date' (X_7); the degree of heterogeneity of the good (X_8); and, somewhat less clearly, the degree of economies of scale (X_5). Of these, all but one — X_6 — influence the income level of exports in the hypothesised direction; in other words, they contribute to its increase. The degree to which the good is destined to final consumers (X_6) operates, on the other hand, in the opposite direction: the higher this degree, the *lower* the income level of exports, and the higher the income level of imports.

(7) Whenever the significant (at the 5 per cent level) pairs of coefficients for exports and imports are matched (that is, the partial-correlation coefficients of X_i in regression 1 and 4, 2 and 5, 3 and 6 — eight such pairs altogether), their signs are in *opposite* directions. That is: when a variable contributes to a high-income level of exports, it also contributes to a low income level of imports. This agrees with the

expectations of 'conventional' theory, in contrast to those of Linder's theory. It also agrees with the results of the rank correlations that have been observed in Table 1. There again it may be noticed that among the categories 5 to 8, in three (6, 7, 8) the rank correlation coefficients of the income levels of exports and imports are negative, within each category; and only in one category, 5 (containing 16 goods, out of the total of 101 in categories 5–8) is the rank correlation positive.

In this connection, the degree of heterogeneity of a good — variable X_8 — deserves special attention, since the contention of the Linder theory is intimately connected with this measure: it is contended that high-income countries will trade with each other in the same range of goods, each 'good' being more heterogeneous than in trade of lower-income countries. Hence, a positive correlation of the income levels of exports and imports should be expected particularly when goods are highly heterogeneous.

Table 3 shows positive signs (and relatively substantial levels) of the partial correlation coefficients for this variable, X_8, in the export regressions 2 and 3, which are the relevant ones for the present purpose; and insignificant results in imports. No conclusion can thus be drawn from the matching of the export and import coefficients for this variable (except, perhaps, that the absence of significant correlation coefficients in imports with opposite signs to exports, whereas such opposite coefficients are found for some other variables, may give some slight support to the Linder contention). This finding is in agreement, thus, with the conclusions indicated earlier by the rank-correlation analysis of the income levels of exports and imports.

IV

Having at our disposal the index of income level of trade of each *good*, we may now move back to the trade of a *country*, and inquire about the income level of the goods traded by the country: does the country trade in high income level goods, or in low-level goods? We shall confine this inquiry to the export side, and conduct it by using an index of the income level of the country's exports.[23] This index, y_j^x, is defined as:

$$y_j^x = \sum_i \frac{X_{ij}}{X_{\cdot j}} y_i^x, \text{ where}$$

$$X_{ij} = \text{exports of good } i \text{ by country } j;$$
$$X_{.j} = \text{total exports of country } j; \text{ and}$$
$$y_i^x = \text{index of income level of exports of good } i.$$

The index of income level of exports is presented, for 108 countries, in column (2) of Table 4.

TABLE 4
THE INCOME LEVEL OF EXPORTS OF COUNTRIES

Country	Per capita GNP (in percentage of US) (y_j) (1)	Index of Income level of exports Actual (y_j^x) (2)	Expected (y_j^x) (3)
Afghanistan	1.5	49.6	38.5
Algeria	9.2	32.2	40.7
Angola	7.9	31.5	40.4
Argentina	26.5	60.0	45.7
Australia	70.2	54.9	58.2
Austria	56.6	68.9	54.4
Belgium–Luxembourg	73.5	58.9	59.2
Bolivia	3.7	36.8	39.2
Brazil	12.3	37.7	41.6
Bulgaria	25.6	32.3	45.5
Burma	1.3	47.6	38.5
Cambodia	1.1	41.3	38.4
Cameroon	4.0	27.7	39.3
Canada	87.9	60.3	63.3
Central African Republic	2.6	37.0	38.8
Chad	1.3	39.0	38.5
Chile	11.6	45.2	41.4
Colombia	7.1	26.0	40.1
Congo	5.5	42.8	39.7
Costa Rica	11.5	32.6	41.4
Cuba	8.7	28.8	40.6
Czechoslovakia	46.3	63.0	51.4
Denmark	84.0	60.9	62.2
Dominican Republic	8.4	29.4	40.5
Ecuador	6.1	31.6	39.9
Egypt	4.0	39.0	39.3
El Salvador	5.6	30.0	39.7
Ethiopia	1.5	34.6	38.5
Finland	58.1	64.5	54.8
France	73.2	60.3	59.1
French Guiana	1.8	48.9	38.6
German Federal Republic	85.8	63.9	62.7

TABLE 4 (*continued*)

Country	Per capita GNP (in percentage of US) (y_j) (1)	Index of income level of exports	
		Actual (y_j^x) (2)	Expected ($\hat{y}_j^x$) (3)
German Democratic Republic	48.4	39.1	52.0
Ghana	4.8	29.1	39.5
Greece	30.2	48.2	46.8
Guatemala	8.1	34.7	40.4
Haiti	2.1	32.5	38.7
Honduras	5.2	38.4	39.6
Hong Kong	23.1	50.7	44.7
Hungary	29.8	10.5	46.7
India	1.9	42.7	38.7
Indonesia	2.1	29.2	38.7
Iran	14.0	27.3	42.1
Iraq	13.7	50.7	42.0
Ireland	34.7	53.6	48.1
Israel	48.5	47.1	52.0
Italy	39.5	58.0	49.4
Ivory Coast	6.1	24.5	39.9
Jamaica	16.0	35.8	42.7
Japan	58.5	63.3	54.9
Jordan	5.5	48.9	39.7
Kenya	2.7	32.3	38.9
Laos	1.0	58.6	38.4
Lebanon	15.2	57.5	42.5
Liberia	5.0	46.8	39.5
Libya	56.9	24.2	54.4
Malawi	1.8	44.5	38.6
Malaysia	9.2	30.7	40.7
Mali	1.1	51.9	38.4
Mauritania	3.2	49.1	39.0
Mexico	14.4	47.9	42.2
Morocco	5.2	39.6	39.6
Mozambique	6.1	41.1	39.9
Netherlands	69.8	56.9	58.1
New Zealand	59.4	57.8	55.1
Nicaragua	8.7	40.4	40.6
Niger	1.6	56.4	38.6
Nigeria	3.4	32.2	39.1
Norway	75.2	60.7	59.7
Pakistan	1.9	48.6	38.7
Panama	14.8	34.6	42.3
Papua–New Guinea	6.6	24.2	40.0

TABLE 4 (*continued*)

Country	Per capita GNP (in percentage of US) (y_j) (1)	Index of Income level of exports	
		Actual (y_j^x) (2)	Expected (y_j^x) (3)
Paraguay	6.6	51.2	40.0
Peru	10.0	47.0	41.0
Philippines	4.5	38.2	39.4
Poland	33.7	54.1	47.8
Portugal	22.7	51.5	44.6
Rwanda	1.1	20.9	38.4
Saudi Arabia	26.0	21.2	45.6
Senegal	4.5	49.6	39.4
Sierra Leone	3.6	45.5	38.8
Singapore	29.5	45.8	46.6
Somalia	1.3	51.5	38.5
South Africa	16.9	45.9	43.0
South Korea	6.5	51.6	40.0
Spain	27.6	51.6	46.0
Sri Lanka	1.9	18.1	38.7
Sudan	2.1	46.4	38.7
Sweden	95.3	65.0	65.5
Switzerland	98.4	65.7	66.3
Syria	6.5	38.8	40.0
Thailand	4.4	41.9	39.4
Tanzania	2.1	30.8	38.7
Togo	2.9	28.5	38.9
Trinidad and Tobago	21.1	36.6	44.2
Tunisia	7.4	42.1	40.2
Turkey	9.7	42.4	40.9
Uganda	2.4	18.9	38.8
United Kingdom	49.4	59.6	52.3
United States	100	63.9	66.8
Upper Volta	1.1	54.6	38.4
Uruguay	15.3	52.8	42.5
Venezuela	26.3	29.6	45.7
Yemen	1.6	38.6	38.6
Yemen Democratic Republic	1.8	34.3	38.6
Yugoslavia	16.3	53.8	42.8
Zaire	2.3	41.8	38.8
Zambia	6.9	43.7	40.1

The income level of exports of a country must by definition be, *on average* for all countries, simply the country's level of per capita income. For individual countries, however, there is no need for this equality to hold; some countries may be expected to export 'above' their income level, that is, to have an index of the income level of exports higher than their per capita income levels, whereas other countries may be expected to export 'below' their income levels.

Column (1) of Table 4 presents the per capita income level of each country. A comparison of these levels with those presented in column (2) shows immediately that almost all countries export 'above' their income levels. The exceptions are partly a few oddities such as oil-exporting and Soviet *bloc* countries, to which further reference is made below. Mainly, however, the group of countries which export 'below' their income levels consists of the top high-income countries (whose shares in total exports, it should be recalled, are very high). These are (in alphabetical order): Australia, Belgium-Luxembourg, Canada, Denmark, France, Germany, Netherlands, Norway, Sweden, Switzerland, and the United States. The income level at which a country turns from exporting 'above' to exporting 'below' appears to be around 60 as percentage of US per capita income).

Upon reflection, however, it would appear that this finding of 'above' and 'below' exporting countries represents merely a technical attribute, rather than any phenomenon of substance in world exports. A rich country shares its exports with other countries, which on average may be expected to be poorer than the country involved. The index of income level of the goods which the country exports may therefore be expected to be lower than the country's own income level; and the opposite must hold for a relatively poor country. This may easily be visualised by considering the two extreme cases. Take, on the one hand, the USA—the highest-income country. Assuming that each of the goods exported by the USA is also exported, to some extent at least, by other countries (which are, by definition of the case, poorer than the USA), each of the goods exported by the USA will have an index of income level of exports lower than 100; and so inevitably will be the index of income level of the US exports, which is the weighted average of the indexes of individual goods. And the opposite must be true, in the same way, for countries such as Laos, Cambodia, Mali, Rwanda, or Upper Volta — which appear to have the lowest per capita income levels (just 1 per cent of the US level).

To overcome this technical difficulty, and arrive at comparisons which may reveal any substance, a (linear) regression of the index of income level of exports of countries on the countries' level of per capita income was run. The inference of this procedure is that a country may be said to export at its income level if the index of income level of its exports is similar to what would be expected from this regression. Likewise, a country would be judged to be exporting 'above' or 'below' its income if its index of income level of exports is, respectively, higher or lower than the expected value. The regression fitted is:

$$y_j^{-x} = 38.11 + 0.287\, y_j, \text{ where}$$
$$y_j^{-x} = \text{expected income level of country } j\text{'s exports; and}$$
$$y_j = \text{per capita income level of country } j \text{ (in percentage of US income)}$$

R^2 is 0.368, and the result is significant at practically any desired level. The values of the income level of exports expected from this regression are presented in column (3) of Table 4.

A comparison of columns (2) and (3) of this table would show, naturally, that the actual and expected indexes of income level are never precisely equal; and the decision as to what is a 'large' or a 'small' deviation of the two from each other is a rather arbitrary matter. I have selected one standard deviation of the distribution as a dividing line, and termed a country as one which trades 'above' if its actual income level of exports is higher than its expected value by more than one standard deviation, or as trading 'below' if its actual income index is lower than its expected value by more than the standard deviation. These countries are listed in Table 5.

It appears that the large majority of the countries listed in Table 5 share one common attribute—whether they trade 'above' or 'below'—they are mostly relatively poor countries. Such countries tend, by and large, to be relatively specialised in their exports — to have, that is, a high measure of commodity concentration of their exports. In such instances chance plays a heavier role. If the few goods in which the country specialises happen to be high-income goods, the country will have a relatively high index of income level of its exports and will hence appear to be trading 'above'; and the opposite would be true if the very limited list of the country's exports happens to consist of goods exported largely by relatively low-income countries.

Two groups of countries seem, from Table 5, to share other specific attributes. One consists of the oil-exporting countries: all oil countries covered in the data — Iran, Libya, Saudi Arabia and Venezuela — appear on the list of countries which export 'below'. This phenomenon is explained rather simply. Oil appears to be a good exported primarily by

TABLE 5
COUNTRIES WITH DEVIATING INDEXES OF INCOME LEVEL OF EXPORTS

Exporting 'above' income

Exporting 'below' income

Country	Per capita income (in percentage of US)	$y_j^x - y_j^{-x}$ standard deviation	Country	Per capita income (in percentage of US)	$y_j^x - y_j^{-x}$ standard deviation
Afghanistan	1.5	1.11	Bulgaria	25.6	− 1.33
Argentina	26.5	1.44	Cameroon	4.0	− 1.17
Austria	56.6	1.46	Colombia	7.1	− 1.43
Czechoslovakia	46.3	1.18	Cuba	8.7	− 1.19
French Guiana	1.8	1.03	Dominican Republic	8.4	− 1.13
Korea	6.5	1.18	German Democratic Republic	48.4	− 1.30
Laos	1.0	2.04	Ghana	4.8	− 1.05
Lebanon	15.2	1.52	Hungary	29.8	− 3.65
Mali	1.1	1.36	Iran	14.0	− 1.50
Mauritania	3.2	1.02	Ivory Coast	6.1	− 1.55
Niger	1.6	1.80	Libya	56.9	− 3.05
Pakistan	1.9	1.00	Malaysia	9.2	− 1.01
Paraguay	6.6	1.13	Papua-New Guinea	6.6	− 1.59
Senegal	4.5	1.03	Rwanda	1.1	− 1.77
Somalia	1.3	1.32	Saudi Arabia	26.0	− 2.46
Upper Volta	1.1	1.63	Sri Lanka	1.9	− 2.08
Uruguay	15.3	1.04	Togo	2.9	− 1.05
Yugoslavia	16.3	1.11	Uganda	2.4	− 2.01
			Venezuela	26.3	− 1.62

low-income countries. At the same time, *some* of the oil-exporting countries are made relatively rich, in per capita income terms, by the very export of oil: Libya and Saudi Arabia are most obvious examples, beside other countries and territories which are not included in the study. This leads to the appearance of such countries as exporting 'below' their income level.[24] Also, the exporting of oil is done primarily by rather similar countries, having roughly the same (low) range of per capita income (with the exception of the small-population exporters of oil). Since in each of these countries oil is the major export good, total exports of such countries tend to have a low-income index, and thus to deviate from the values expected from a regression whose results were determined by the fact that low-income countries mostly share their exports with higher-income countries.

The other group which may be distinguished is that of Soviet bloc countries. Of the six countries in the bloc covered in this study, five appear in the list in Table 5 (the sixth, Poland, has an index of income level exceeding its expected value by 0.64 standard deviations). Of these five, Czechoslovakia appears to be trading 'above'; whereas the four others — Bulgaria, Cuba, East Germany, and Hungary, the latter by a very wide margin — seem to be trading 'below'. The number of observations here is small, and the appearance they give may be a result of accident. Yet, the assertion often made that the trade structure in the Soviet bloc leads its peripheral countries to specialise in goods normally exported by low-income countries may find some support in these observations.

Is there a consistent difference between exporters 'above' and 'below' their income levels in the success of their export performance? This question seems to be of some significance. Assertions are often made that a high rate of increase of exports of a country, particularly a less developed one, requires, *inter alia*, specialisation in 'advanced' goods; and this would imply an export structure which yields a relatively high index of income level.

A casual look at Table 5 does not seem to disclose any systematic difference, in export performance, between the countries exporting 'above' and those exporting 'below' their income level. On the other hand, some positive indication is yielded by observation of the group of countries whose average export growth in the last two decades has been most rapid. This group would include Greece, Hong Kong, Israel, Japan, Jordan, South Korea, Portugal, and Yugoslavia (data for Taiwan, a country with another remarkable export performance, are not available in this study). It appears, from Table 4, that countries in this group predominantly export 'above'—Israel being the only exception and Greece being a borderline case. Thus, some support may be claimed for the above-mentioned assertion, of the benefit in export performance derived from specialisation in relatively high-income goods; but the evidence is too sporadic to yield, on this issue, more than a suggestive indication.

V

So far this chapter has dealt with the per capita income level of the structure of trade; but now the *total* income of exporters and importers can also be observed. Similarly to the per capita index, the index of total income of exports of a good, Y_j^x, is defined as:

$$Y_i^x = \sum_j Y_j \frac{X_{ij}}{X_{i.}}$$

where Y_j stands for country j's total GNP (relative to the US GNP), and X_{ij} and $X_{i.}$, as before, are country j's and the world's exports of good i. Similarly, Y_i^m will be a measure of the total income level of imports of good i. The values of these indexes are presented in Table 6. Averages for the major categories are shown in columns (1) and (2) of Table 7.

TABLE 6

INDEXES OF TOTAL INCOME LEVEL OF TRADE

SITC Code	*Exports*	*Imports*	*SITC Code*	*Exports*	*Imports*
001	17.2	16.6	044	69.7	13.4
011	10.4	27.1	045	59.0	17.4
012	9.5	13.2	046	30.6	1.3
013	6.0	44.3	047	37.9	3.0
022	12.0	11.4	048	23.6	15.9
023	7.8	13.8	051	14.3	21.5
024	9.7	24.0	052	22.0	14.0
025	11.5	16.5	053	18.7	21.6
031	12.5	42.2	054	14.9	19.8
032	17.7	24.2	055	11.6	26.5
041	61.6	9.0	061	5.0	32.2
042	43.5	2.6	062	14.4	21.5
043	27.7	14.6	071	4.9	44.3

TABLE 6 (*Continued*)

SITC Code	Exports	Imports	SITC Code	Exports	Imports
072	3.3	31.9	411	54.7	13.6
073	11.5	19.4	421	25.5	10.4
074	3.5	16.0	422	9.3	26.4
075	4.9	23.0	431	18.9	11.6
081	33.2	13.0			
091	24.1	9.5	512	31.2	17.0
099	23.9	12.1	513	24.2	23.7
			514	28.5	13.4
111	15.4	10.7	515	64.1	41.8
112	12.9	33.9	521	33.6	15.0
121	45.6	21.3	531	20.5	14.4
122	32.4	9.9	532	14.9	12.7
			533	22.6	9.4
211	27.0	17.6	541	23.9	11.0
212	21.5	23.6	551	21.9	22.6
221	64.3	18.1	553	21.4	12.6
231	10.3	23.4	554	26.0	9.6
241	16.6	12.7	561	26.4	16.9
242	28.3	21.6	571	24.5	17.1
243	14.9	33.5	581	26.6	11.8
244	2.5	21.1	599	29.5	12.5
251	19.2	29.4			
261	6.8	27.3	611	15.9	21.0
262	7.9	19.6	612	15.9	24.7
263	28.6	13.4	613	21.0	16.2
264	2.2	12.1	621	28.1	8.1
265	6.1	15.4	629	22.3	25.6
266	26.3	11.3	631	16.8	31.1
267	47.8	9.4	632	17.1	33.9
271	26.7	10.6	633	5.9	19.4
273	15.2	16.3	641	18.2	27.1
274	27.3	14.2	642	22.4	12.2
275	24.3	30.6	651	16.7	12.7
276	19.0	22.9	652	17.6	18.2
281	6.4	32.1	653	18.4	17.8
282	54.5	15.0	654	16.9	15.9
283	7.6	28.1	655	21.9	16.6
284	31.8	20.2	656	16.7	14.7
285	12.5	45.8	657	14.4	19.4
291	13.4	24.5	661	11.0	19.6
291	13.2	21.4	662	20.9	15.9
			663	23.0	15.5
321	44.8	17.4	664	24.4	20.7
331	1.1	24.0	665	20.9	18.5
332	8.9	31.0	666	20.8	36.6
341	11.7	41.5	667	15.6	24.7

TABLE 6 (*Continued*)

SITC Code	Exports	Imports	*SITC* Code	Exports	Imports
671	11.9	28.5	718	36.3	11.6
672	20.2	9.4	719	32.1	13.8
673	14.3	21.9	722	31.1	14.2
674	21.4	23.3	723	23.9	15.9
675	22.4	14.9	724	27.3	29.9
676	22.0	6.8	725	22.1	17.9
677	17.2	27.0	726	31.0	23.3
678	26.0	18.2	729	35.1	22.1
679	38.1	13.8	731	32.7	7.5
681	20.5	40.5	732	30.7	32.1
682	11.1	22.1	733	23.4	30.1
683	14.3	47.9	734	69.7	19.4
684	19.7	20.2	735	19.9	7.8
685	12.6	21.7	812	19.7	15.6
686	10.8	36.5	821	15.3	23.9
687	5.2	39.1	831	14.7	38.2
689	22.9	28.6	841	11.0	29.8
691	25.0	9.2	842	13.1	21.4
692	19.6	9.2	851	10.0	43.5
693	17.5	31.0	861	35.0	20.3
694	25.9	34.3	862	38.1	18.0
695	28.5	16.8	863	30.9	16.3
696	21.1	29.8	864	13.6	24.7
697	19.1	21.6	891	29.3	35.1
698	25.4	19.8	892	25.6	16.2
			893	23.0	23.6
711	38.3	24.5	894	24.8	35.3
712	36.6	18.9	895	31.2	13.6
714	41.6	23.6	896	40.3	39.0
715	28.9	14.2	897	22.4	26.0
717	24.2	19.9	899	18.3	28.9

By and large, the indexes of total-income level reveal the same pattern as those of per capita income levels—as witnessed, for instance, by comparisons of the appropriate columns in Table 7 and Table 2. Some of the results seem to be indicated even more strongly by the total-income indexes, in particular, the high-income level of exports of commodities in category 7 (machinery and transport equipment). Column (3) of Table 7 presents the correlation coefficients of export and import income levels, within each category and for all goods. These coefficients appear to be negative, by and large—again, an indication which comes out stronger than that which follows from column (5) of Table 2—in other words,

TABLE 7
TOTAL-INCOME LEVELS AND ASSOCIATION OF EXPORTS AND
IMPORTS, BY MAJOR CATEGORIES

| Category | Average for category | | Spearman rank correlation coefficients of |
| | Y_i^x | Y_i^m | Y_i^x and Y_i^m |
	(1)	(2)	(3)
0 Food and live animals	20.2	19.3	−0.658
1 Beverages and tobacco	24.1	19.0	
2 Crude materials, inedible	20.8	20.9	−0.353
3 Mineral fuels, lubricants	16.6	28.5	
4 Animal and vegetable oils	27.1	15.5	
5 Chemicals	27.5	16.2	0.241
6 Manufactured goods, by material	19.1	22.0	−0.402
7 Machinery and transport equipment	31.9	19.3	−0.310
8 Miscellaneous manufactured articles	23.1	25.5	−0.426
All goods			−0.361

goods tend to be traded more between large (by total-income yardstick) and small countries than among similar countries.

The similarity of indications yielded by total-income and per capita income measures is of course not surprising. A country's level of total income is the result, by definition, of its level of per capita income and its size, in terms of population. The measures of total income of the trade structure may thus be expected to reflect, first, the effect of the level of per capita income. But they should also reflect, in comparison with the measures of per capita income level, the added impact of the size of the economy. A small-sized economy may be expected to manifest a different production pattern and to specialise, partly at least, in a different range of goods than would a large country with a similar level of per capita income. In particular, it is usually expected that large economies have the advantage, and will tend to specialise, in industries in which economies of scale are particularly pronounced—the aircraft industry, or railroad equipment, are obvious examples.[25]

The particularly high total-income level of the exports of machinery and transport equipment may be an indication, indeed, of the added impact of scale economies on the pattern of specialisation. A simple regression of the index of total income level of exports on Hufbauer's measure of scale economies which has been used in the earlier analysis, for the commodities for which this measure is available, yields a correlation coefficient (r) of 0.257; in imports, the correlation coefficient is -0.300. Both coefficients are significant and of the expected sign. This might conceivably be, however, due to the positive correlation which exists between scale economies and the level of per capita income level of exports, and the negative correlation in imports. A multiple regression of the total-income measure on the per capita measure of the income level and on the measure of economies of scale yields the following partial-correlation coefficients: In exports, the coefficient of the two income measures is 0.650, and the coefficient of correlation with economies of scale is 0.146 (not significant at the 5 per cent level; $R^2 = 0.425$); in imports the two coefficients are, respectively, 0.787 and -0.210 ($R^2 = 0.797$). The expected relationship of the total-income level of trade flows to economies of scale is thus still borne out, particularly in the pattern of imports.

Appendix I
Dispersion of the Income Level Indexes of Individual Goods

The index of the income level of a trade flow which has been used in this study all along is, of course, a weighted mean of the income levels of the (geographic) components of such flow — where, for instance in exports, the X_{ij}/X_i. is the weight assigned to the exports of each country j. It may be asked, however, what the *dispersion* of this series (of X_{ij}/X_i.) is around its mean. The lower this dispersion — the more, that is, exports are concentrated in countries whose income level is close to the weighted mean — the more can the latter be said to be an indication of the income level of the 'typical' country which exports that good; the higher this dispersion, the less meaningful it becomes to conceive of such 'typical' country.

The levels of dispersion of the export and import series of each individual good are presented in Table 10. It would be completely arbitrary to suggest a cut-off point, in which the weighted average becomes non-representative, and I shall not attempt it here. Instead, a few generalisations will be offered.

It would be noticed that most measures of dispersion are quite close to each other — particularly in imports, but by and large also in exports. Thus, the degree of 'representativeness' of the index of income level used here is rather similar for most goods.

Inasmuch as differences in the levels of dispersion do exist, it is difficult to distinguish any common attributes of the goods in which dispersion levels are particularly high or particularly low. Specifically, average dispersion levels for the major categories of commodities (not shown here) do not reveal any substantial differences among these categories. It may be mentioned, though, that the lowest dispersion level in exports is found in category 7 (machinery and transport equipment). This is consistent with the finding, mentioned earlier in the study, that the variation *among* goods, in their indexes of income levels, is particularly low in this category.

If we consider that indexes of income levels are more meaningful, in some way, when the dispersion around the average is small, it may be worth-while to try and see whether just the 'more meaningful' indexes give the same indications and yield the same inferences as the rest. In attempting to test this, commodities have been ranked according to their levels of dispersion in exports and imports, separately (starting with the *lowest* dispersion measure), and the top half (60 out of 120 goods for which the relevant data are available) have been selected to consist of a new population of observations. For this group, the effect on income levels of exports and imports of the various attributes with which these levels are presumed to be connected has been tested by a multiple regression, in the same way which has been done before for all (120) goods. The results, which should be compared with those of Table 3, are presented in Table 8. The test has been carried out only through the regressions equivalent to those which are represented in lines (1) and (4) of Table 3.

TABLE 8

EXPLANATORY VARIABLES OF INCOME LEVELS: CORRELATION COEFFICIENTS FOR A SUBGROUP

Dependent variable: index of per capita income level in	*Adjusted R^2*	*Partial correlation coefficients (r) of*						
		X_1	X_3	X_4	X_5	X_6	X_7	X_8
Exports (y_i^x)	0.455	−0.057	0.180	0.661	0.134	0.044	0.277	0.151
Imports (y_i^m)	0.074	0.129	−0.028	−0.196	−0.266	0.035	0.199	0.116

Italicised figures are significant at the 5 per cent level.

On the whole, Table 8 would lead to roughly the same conclusions as Table 3. The R^2s are somewhat higher—but not by any substantial margin. The showing of variable X_4 (the wage level) in exports and of X_5 (the measure of scale economies) in imports are of the same sign as in Table 3 but more impressive. In particular, one of the major inferences made earlier is supported again: the physical-capital variable fails to assert itself as influencing the pattern of specialisation and trade; it appears again with the 'wrong' signs, but its correlation coefficients are not significant.

Appendix II
An Alternative Measure of the Income Level of Trade

The analysis of this study has been conducted all along through the use of a specific index of the income level of exports and imports, namely a weighted average of the income levels of the trading countries — with some regard being paid, in the previous Appendix, to the dispersion around this average. Alternative indexes of the income level are conceivable; one such alternative will be presented and discussed in this Appendix.[26]

The measure used in this study, we recall, is (say, for exports):

$$y_i^x = \sum_j y_j \frac{X_{ij}}{X_{i.}}, \text{ where:}$$

X_{ij} = exports of good i by country j;
$X_{i.}$ = world exports of good i; and
y_j = country j's per capita income (as proportion of US income).

However, instead of multiplying $X_{ij}/X_{i.}$ (country j's share in world exports of good i) by y_j (country j's income level), one could draw a *regression* of the two, showing their relationship to each other. In such a regression, where y_j is the independent and $X_{ij}/X_{i.}$ the dependent variable, the slope will indicate the tendency of the country's share in exports to change with the country's income level; the larger (algebraically) this slope, the more this good tends to be exported by high-income countries. This could be, then, another measure of the income level of exports; similarly, the slope of a regression of import shares on countries' income levels will indicate the income levels of imports of the various goods.

Such linear regressions have been run for all 173 goods. They have the general form:

$$\frac{X_{ij}}{X_{i.}} = a + by_j,$$

where the b's yield the measure under consideration (and similarly for imports). The results are presented in Table 9.

TABLE 9
AN ALTERNATIVE MEASURE OF INCOME LEVELS

(*indicates values which are not significant at the 5 per cent level)

SITC	Exports	Imports	SITC	Exports	Imports
321	0.087	0.050	642	0.067	0.052
331	0.009*	0.051	651	0.051	0.045
332	0.032	0.068	652	0.040	0.050
341	0.062	0.071	653	0.051	0.052
			654	0.061	0.049
411	0.082	0.037	655	0.066	0.055
421	0.043	0.034	656	0.035	0.047
422	0.010*	0.054	657	0.043	0.071
431	0.067	0.050	661	0.040	0.048
			662	0.057	0.058
512	0.074	0.049	663	0.069	0.058
513	0.068	0.054	664	0.068	0.060
514	0.070	0.045	665	0.063	0.053
515	0.089	0.076	666	0.056	0.068
521	0.055	0.054	667	0.042	0.057
531	0.081	0.040	671	0.051	0.066
532	0.041	0.025	672	0.063	0.032
533	0.069	0.045	673	0.057	0.056
541	0.070	0.038	674	0.065	0.053
551	0.059	0.051	675	0.074	0.052
553	0.064	0.047	676	0.061	0.018
554	0.069	0.045	677	0.070	0.054
561	0.066	0.030	678	0.068	0.054
571	0.060	0.044	679	0.074	0.044
581	0.072	0.052	681	0.058	0.070
599	0.072	0.042	682	0.033	0.060
			683	0.072	0.080
611	0.036	0.058	684	0.069	0.058
612	0.050	0.064	685	0.051	0.050
613	0.061	0.062	686	0.060	0.060
621	0.070	0.050	687		0.064
629	0.062	0.061	689	0.059	0.070
631	0.045	0.065	691	0.066	0.044
632	0.061	0.073	692	0.062	0.042
633	0.015*	0.064	693	0.062	0.060
			694	0.069	0.068
641	0.076	0.059	695	0.074	0.052

TABLE 9 (*Continued*)

SITC	Exports	Imports	SITC	Exports	Imports
696	0.057	0.061	735	0.063	0.053
697	0.054	0.055			
698	0.068	0.058	812	0.065	0.056
			821	0.065	0.072
711	0.076	0.057	831	0.038	0.074
712	0.075	0.048	841	0.039	0.073
714	0.075	0.062	842	0.052	0.079
715	0.077	0.044	851	0.032	0.080
717	0.073	0.035	861	0.074	0.058
718	0.078	0.838	862	0.076	0.055
719	0.075	0.046	863	0.049	0.039
722	0.074	0.047	864	0.080	0.051
723	0.063	0.044	891	0.063	0.067
724	0.064	0.059	892	0.065	0.059
725	0.064	0.060	893	0.666	0.067
726	0.080	0.056	894	0.053	0.071
729	0.071	0.055	895	−0.054*	0.046
731	0.067	0.022	896	0.071	0.069
732	0.075	0.068	897	0.056	0.067
733	0.063	0.069	899	0.050	0.060
734	0.090	0.052			

A glance at this table will show immediately that the slope measures for practically all goods are positive; in the few cases where they are negative, they are mostly not significantly different from zero.[27] This should come, of course, as no surprise; as a rule, the higher the country's per capita income, the higher its total income and, in an even stronger way, its share in world exports and imports; and this should be reflected, as a rule, in each of the goods in which the country trades. The measures of slope presented in Table 9 do not therefore tell us, by themselves, whether the exports (imports) of a good tend to be concentrated in high-income countries. They could be made, however, to give such indication when compared with an 'average' tendency. This average is yielded by a regression of the shares of countries in *all* goods on the countries' income levels, similar to the regressions for each individual good. The outcome of this procedure is as follows:

$$\frac{X_{.j}}{X_{..}} = -0.135 + 0.049 \; y_j \quad (R^2 = 0.396, \text{ and significant at practically}$$

any level);

and

$$\frac{M_{\cdot j}}{M_{\cdot \cdot}} = -0.0138 + 0.046\, y_j \quad (R^2 = 0.391, \text{ and significant at practically}$$

any level);

where

$X_{\cdot j}$, $M_{\cdot j}$ are country j's total exports and imports of goods;

and

$X_{\cdot \cdot}$, $M_{\cdot \cdot}$ are total world exports and imports of goods.

Whether a given slope for an individual good indicates that the good tends to be exported by high-income countries may thus be inferred by comparing this slope with the magnitude 0.049; in imports, it would be compared with 0.046.

TABLE 10

MEASURE OF DISPERSION (σ) OF INCOME LEVELS OF EXPORTS AND IMPORTS

SITC	Exports	Imports	SITC	Exports	Imports
001	26.47	24.37	062	20.82	25.08
011	24.24	23.05	071	18.27	22.32
012	20.12	15.01	072	24.74	22.67
013	26.43	25.97	073	20.09	19.08
022	14.80	27.89	074	19.69	28.37
023	13.37	22.14	075	22.50	33.61
024	15.50	23.39	081	34.73	22.09
025	16.51	25.77	091	23.85	22.30
031	32.27	25.66	099	22.97	26.23
032	29.35	24.07	111	16.69	27.28
041	18.96	26.15	112	23.60	23.32
042	42.34	22.05	121	42.20	24.78
043	18.08	27.34	122	25.95	26.12
044	30.49	20.92	211	27.92	23.14
045	31.97	18.73	212	25.27	21.06
046	22.98	21.83	221	37.33	19.10
047	33.97	29.21	231	31.31	28.03
048	18.66	27.58	241	36.54	23.06
051	29.77	22.04	242	43.32	18.07
052	35.14	24.30	243	28.91	23.44
053	29.99	19.96	244	11.96	29.64
054	31.31	23.24	251	20.82	25.45
055	26.53	22.65	261	25.16	13.03
061	27.63	31.51	262	20.49	19.74

TABLE 10 (*Continued*)

SITC	Exports	Imports	SITC	Exports	Imports
263	41.09	26.60	629	20.92	24.94
264	18.67	27.45	631	32.26	21.35
265	33.23	22.29	632	27.48	21.06
266	20.07	27.98	633	20.11	22.35
267	22.31	26.89	641	18.23	24.85
271	41.84	22.76	642	20.67	24.63
273	23.34	20.39	651	27.09	27.35
274	35.43	27.25	652	33.32	24.24
275	36.61	23.97	653	25.27	25.55
276	30.21	23.60	654	25.08	25.53
281	36.61	18.98	655	21.71	24.63
282	18.62	23.39	656	34.96	27.09
283	37.87	21.93	657	27.62	18.15
284	21.56	23.30	661	27.18	30.03
285	36.78	24.08	662	22.32	23.83
291	28.87	22.15	663	20.27	22.57
292	27.08	22.54	664	19.62	24.00
321	14.86	17.95	665	22.09	26.15
331	22.64	26.28	666	18.37	25.46
332	29.47	24.36	667	26.64	23.40
341	26.86	24.73	671	29.83	22.57
411	24.76	27.66	672	16.02	28.22
421	35.62	27.73	673	19.64	26.05
422	31.01	27.20	674	17.80	29.37
431	21.93	23.58	675	15.58	26.95
512	20.19	26.95	676	27.43	31.62
513	21.10	26.19	677	16.94	29.43
514	21.25	27.14	678	20.23	26.63
515	20.30	19.81	679	25.65	31.28
521	38.59	24.56	681	27.61	23.37
531	19.66	27.75	682	35.56	22.90
532	31.94	28.40	683	20.74	25.21
533	19.16	26.84	684	23.94	22.61
541	23.14	27.07	685	29.54	24.65
551	29.55	26.12	686	27.59	30.28
553	20.96	27.02	687	24.38	25.21
554	23.07	24.79	689	30.81	21.44
561	25.05	33.63	691	21.18	28.86
571	26.59	29.07	692	20.38	26.82
581	18.25	23.29	693	18.78	27.10
599	20.58	26.67	694	21.00	24.22
611	31.60	24.55	695	22.02	25.99
612	24.36	23.48	696	22.98	25.37
613	25.57	23.28	697	24.54	25.54
621	21.04	24.00	698	21.52	24.15

TABLE 10 (*Continued*)

SITC	Exports	Imports	SITC	Exports	Imports
711	21.53	25.97	812	23.24	23.06
712	21.61	29.49	821	22.76	17.78
714	23.21	23.06	831	26.91	21.91
715	20.03	28.79	841	27.15	19.71
717	20.72	31.99	842	29.90	18.41
718	20.09	28.50	851	22.11	18.42
719	20.57	27.04	861	20.35	24.62
722	20.89	26.95	862	19.83	25.07
723	23.30	28.76	863	32.07	31.27
724	22.27	27.18	864	24.39	30.07
725	22.25	22.53	891	20.14	24.89
726	16.56	26.93	892	23.47	22.36
729	24.39	26.46	893	22.80	20.47
731	24.96	29.89	894	27.42	22.37
732	18.81	23.58	895	69.74	25.39
733	21.61	23.59	896	26.59	22.31
734	20.34	26.66	897	27.94	25.79
735	17.74	22.58	899	27.19	25.07

The sign of such comparisons — that is, the determination of whether a good tends or not to be exported (imported) by high-income countries — seems less important than the size of the slope. Here, one would be inclined to repeat, with this measure, the various experiments, comparisons and tests conducted in the main study by the use of the weighted average as the index of income levels of exports and imports. Such re-experimentation seems, however, to be redundant in view of the very large proximity of the indications yielded by the two alternative measures. The rank correlation coefficient of the slope measure and the weighted-average measure is, in exports, 0.952; and the simple (Pearson) correlation coefficient is 0.829. In imports, the rank correlation coefficient is 0.972; and the simple correlation coefficient is 0.939. It thus appears that tests conducted by the use of the slope measure of income level would have yielded roughly the same results and inferences as those that have been presented in the main body of this study.

ENDNOTES

1. This study was undertaken partly during my tenure as Fellow of the Leonard Davies Institute of International Relations at the Hebrew University of Jerusalem. It was completed while I was at the Institute for International Economic Studies, University of Stockholm in 1977 and 1978.

I wish to express my gratitude to both organisations as well as to members of the latter Institute for helpful comments in a seminar discussion of the paper. I particularly wish to acknowledge my indebtedness to Alexander J. Yeats for much constructive advice. Skilful research assistance has been contributed by Matti Gutraich in Jerusalem and Mary Berg in Stockholm.

2. The division of each country's income level by that of the USA serves for convenience of presentation, and is of course entirely immaterial in the present context; each country's income could instead be represented by its absolute level (dollars per year), or divided by any other *common* number. But the principle of dividing each country's income level by that of the richest country does become significant in a *time-series* study. Such a study is planned as a sequence to the present one.

3. The SITC contains 175 goods. But for commodity no. 688—uranium and thorium—the required data are not available. The omission of a single good is immaterial for the following analysis.

4. To shift from the index as it is presented here to an expression of the income level in absolute terms (in US dollars), the index shown (taken as a fraction of 100) should be multiplied by 6200 which is the level of US per capita GNP in 1973.

5. Interestingly enough, practically the same good (wheat, or wheat flour) which is exported by the richest countries, is imported by the poorest—and this is a purely agricultural product. As we shall see later, this polarisation of income levels in exports and imports is not clearly evident in general.

6. These are, in a descending order of income level: (041) wheat; (734) aircraft; (515) radioactive materials; (321) coal; (282) iron and steel scrap; (044) maize; (531) synthetic dyes; (251) pulp and waste paper; (411) animal oils and fats; and (726) electric-medical equipment:

7. This is the Gini–Hirschman coefficient of concentration (for 1973), defined for any good i as

$$\sqrt{\overline{\sum_j \left(\frac{X_{ij}}{X_{i.}}\right)^2}}$$

where X_{ij} are exports of good i by country j, and $X_{i.}$ are total world exports of the good.

8. These are, in an ascending order of income level: (264) jute; (074) tea; (071) coffee; (075) spices; (072) cocoa; (687) tin; (261) silk; (244) cork; (331) crude petroleum; and (061) sugar.

9. Excluding the above-mentioned group of the ten goods with the lowest income level of exports, the rank correlation rises to 0.49.

10. S. B. Linder (1961).

11. This is also true for categories 7 and 8 together—these two sharing among them most highly fabricated goods. The export–import rank correlation for this combined group is -0.490.

12. See W. H. Branson and N. Monoyios (1977).

13. The main reference here is, of course, the series of studies by D. B. Keesing—such as (1965) or (1971).

14. G. Hufbauer (1970).

15. I. B. Kravis (1956).
16. The data appear in Hufbauer (1970), Table A-2, pp. 212–20, and their construction is explained in the following notes to the tables (pp. 221–3), as well as in a few places in Hufbauer's text.

    Despite the great amount of work and great ingenuity invested in the construction of these data, they are obviously imperfect, and occasionally based, inevitably, on assumptions of an arbitrary nature. Yet I believe that it is, by and large, a body of data sufficiently accurate for a purpose such as the present one—the test of general hypotheses—especially when the number of observations (that is, goods) is as large as in the present case.

    One specific argument that has been levelled against Hufbauer's series is that they are based on data of the US alone (except in one instance, in which they draw on Japanese data). This, of course, might be a serious problem for some purposes. But, again, for a purpose such as the present one reliance on US data would not be damaging, as Hufbauer himself pointed out, unless factor-intensity reversals are common; and most available studies suggest that they are not.
17. Estimates of the human-capital/labour ratio have been provided by W. Branson, from the worksheets to Branson and Monoyios, op. cit. These estimates refer to 1967; Hufbauer's estimates are based on data for various years in the 1960s.
18. Although explanations and details are provided in the source, and will not be repeated here, one point concerning this measure should probably be indicated: Hufbauer's estimates, like those of the present study, are provided for 'goods' classified by the three-digit SITC; but the measures of price dispersion for each such 'good' are *averages* of measures of dispersion of 'goods' classified by the *seven-digit* SITC. This, of course, lends these measures greater credibility.
19. These goods are: (013) canned, prepared meat; (032) canned, prepared fish; (046) wheatmeal or flour; (047) non-wheatmeal or flour; (048) cereal preparations; (053) preserved fruits; (055) preserved vegetables; (061) sugar; (062) sugar preparations; (091) margarine, shortening; (111) non-alcoholic beverages; (112) alcoholic beverages; (122) tobacco manufactures; (231) crude synthetic rubber; (242) rough wood; (251) pulp and waste paper; (266) regenerated synthetic fibres; (332) petroleum products; and (421) fixed vegetable oils, soft.
20. In this regression, the data for physical-capital/labour ratio were also taken from the Branson–Monoyios study.
21. Moreover, most of the coefficients for X_1 appear with the 'wrong' sign. But this should probably be disregarded in view of the fact that the coefficients are not significant at the 5 per cent level.
22. The relevance of these comparisons may be somewhat impaired, though, by the fact that in regressions 3 and 6 the physical-capital/labour ratio is estimated by a different set of data than in 2 and 5.

    It might be thought that the poor showing of the human-capital variable may be due to it (probably) being highly correlated with other explanatory variables, which 'get the credit'; this might be true particularly in relation to the variable of skills. To test this possibility, I have eliminated the latter variable X_3 (this is not shown in Table 3). This leaves the multiple-correlation coefficient for exports practically unchanged, and lowers somewhat this coefficient for imports. More important, however: the partial correlation coefficients of the human-capital variable are still very low—for exports, the coefficient is even *lower* (0.041) than when the skill variable is included!

23. An attempt to analyse similarly the imports of countries has proved to be rather fruitless, due to the fact that the indexes of income level of imports are remarkably similar among countries.

24. It should be recalled that the study's data refer to the year 1973, only at the end of which has the oil price risen dramatically. At present-day prices, oil-exporting countries would appear, as a whole, to be relatively richer: and the income level of exports of oil would not be nearly as low as the level recorded in 1973.

25. Analyses of this issue may be found in various contributions in E. A. G. Robinson (1960), particularly that of Simon Kuznets. See also Chenery and Taylor (1968).

26. This measure has been suggested to me by Alexander Yeats.

27. The significance levels of the negative-sign slopes are as follows: In exports: good 071–0.534; 072–0.892; 074–0.453; 075–0.851; 264–0.582; 895–0.116. In imports: 046–0.880.

REFERENCES

Branson, W. H. and Monoyios, N., 'Factor Inputs in US Trade', *Journal of International Economics*, vol. 7 (1977) 111–31.

Chenery, H. B. and Taylor, L., 'Development Patterns: Among Countries and Over Time', *Review of Economics and Statistics*, vol. L (1968) 391–416.

Hufbauer, G. C., 'The Impact of National Characteristics and Technology on the Commodity Composition of Trade in Manufactured Goods', in R. Vernon (ed.), *The Technology Factor in International Trade* (New York: Columbia University Press for the National Bureau of Economic Research) (1970) 145–231.

Keesing, D. B., 'Labour Skills and International Trade: Evaluating Many Trade Flows with a Single Measuring Device', *Review of Economics and Statistics*, vol. 47 (1965) 287–94.

Keesing, D. B., 'Different Countries' Labor Skill Coefficient and the Skill Intensity of International Trade Flows', *Journal of International Economics*, vol. 1 (1971) 443–52.

Kravis, I. B., 'Wages and Foreign Trade', *Review of Economics and Statistics*, vol. 38 (1956) 14–30.

Linder, S. B., *An Essay on Trade and Transformation*, (Stockholm: Almqvist & Wiksell, 1961).

Robinson, E. A. G., (ed.), *Economic Consequences of the Size of Nations* (London: Macmillan, 1960).
Trade data are drawn from issues of the UN *Yearbook of International Trade Statistics*; income data, from issues of the World Bank *Atlas*.

Comments

Gary Hufbauer (USA)

Michael Michaely has developed an ingenious yardstick to assess the structure of trade. Each three-digit SITC product is associated with a weighted average of the per capita incomes (vintage 1973) of, respectively, the exporting countries and the importing countries. This exercise enables each three-digit SITC product to be characterised by 'representative' per capita income levels, both as an export and as an import.

Michaely performs a number of interesting measurements with his yardstick. For example:

(1) Michaely regresses the yardstick figures against familiar underlying characteristics of goods: physical-capital/labour ratios, wage levels, economies of scale, first trade dates, and so forth. The underlying characteristics explain, in expected fashion as to sign, about 40 per cent of the variation in the per capita income level of three-digit exports, but only about 10 per cent of the variation in the per capita income level of three-digit imports. Like previous empirical studies, Michaely's work indicates a comforting rationality in the pattern of exports, but a discomforting irrationality in the pattern of imports.

(2) The results broadly support conventional factor proportions analysis; imports and exports embody dissimilar characteristics, and there is a general negative correlation between the per capita income level of a good as an export and the same good as an import. Likewise, there is a negative correlation between the total income levels (per capita income times population) of three-digit goods as exports and as imports. But as with similar studies in the past, the findings are not robust.

(3) Michaely finds a strong correlation between the per capita income level of exported goods and the coutry concentration of exporting nations. This finding could be read to suggest that poor

nations are exploited by rich. But interestingly, the parallel correlation is even stronger on the import side. If such correlations reveal 'exploitation', it is primarily of one rich nation by another.

(4) Michaely calculates a weighted value for the per capita income level of each country's export composition. The weighted value is compared with that country's 'expected value' based on a regression analysis. Michaely finds that rich industrial countries are usually near their expected values, while some poor countries and certain Eastern European countries display weighted values significantly above or below their expected values. In addition, some (by no means all) countries with a successful history of export led growth show an export composition with weighted per capita income values above expected values.

As we have learned to expect from Michaely, his analysis is crisp and insightful. The ingenious yardstick he has devised contains at least two desirable features: it enables ready calculations across a range of goods and countries; and it appears to capture the essentials of the factor proportions analysis. The Michaely yardstick also points the way to future analytical and normative work. For example: How does the per capita income level of a particular category of goods behave over time (does it display product cycle characteristics)? And what is the time-series experience of 'success' countries like Japan, Korea, Taiwan, and Brazil?

Observers sometimes remark that the farflung activities of international banks and multinational enterprises have 'repealed' the law of comparative advantage. This remark contains a good deal of truth for the locational decisiveness of physical capital, an increasingly mobile factor. There is no compelling reason why nations with a general abundance of capital—most of which is tied up in housing, office buildings, transportation, and various utility services – should specialise in capital-intensive manufactured goods. But the locational impact of less mobile factors (for example, labour skills and technology attributes) still show up on the pattern of export trade. On the other hand, even these less mobile factors display a weak locational impact on the pattern of import trade.

Like Travis, I ascribe this weakness on the import side to the pervasive influence of commercial policy, so often deployed, as it is, to slow down the workings of comparative advantage. This supposition has not been subjected to extensive empirical examination. It would be most interesting to combine an analysis of the trade impact of a liberalised commercial regime with Michaely's yardstick. In a hypothetical more free trade world, would, import patterns better reflect the characteristics of immobile factors?

Part II

Technology and Trade

4 The Technology Transfer Issue

Carlos Rodriguez (USA)

Technology has always been an important issue in international trade theory. Ricardo based his theory of comparative advantage on the existence of 'relative' technological differences among trading partners. The neoclassical model, with its taxonomy of goods, factors and production functions provides the analytical basis for the modern version of the Heckscher–Ohlin theory of comparative advantage and also a convenient framework with which to analyse the effects of exogenous technical change on trade patterns, terms of trade and functional distribution of income, a task which mostly preoccupied trade theorists during the 1950s and 1960s. In spite of the early recognition given to technological differences and technological change, it is fair to say that the main focus of theoretical analysis has been the study of trade in either goods or factors of production. Only in recent years have theoretical models been developed which study 'technology transfer', which is the process through which the 'superior' technological knowledge of one trading partner is 'moved' to the geographical location of the other partners. The term 'transfer' as applied to the above process is probably misleading since it is consistently being used, both in the popular and scientific literature, in reference to such diverse situations as the receiving country purchasing the technology, renting it through royalty payments, receiving it free, imitating it or simply allowing foreign firms to produce within its borders with the superior technology. In connection with the last interpretation, too many authors have identified 'technology transfer' with the issue of direct foreign investment and, in particular, with the popular issue of the multinational corporations.

In spite of all its ambiguities, the issue of technology transfer is a dominant one in world policy forums both in relation to West–East transfers (should the US sell computer technology to Russia?) and to North–South transfers (or Centre and Periphery, DCs and LDCs). Fuelled by the political recognition obtained as a consequence of the developments associated with the New International Economic Order, the LDCs have pressed for action both in terms of increased access to northern technology and opening of the northern markets for the goods they could therefore manufacture. Contrary to the earlier optimistic views of the 1950s and 1960s there seems to be now a growing recognition of the fact that neither income transfers nor capital accumulation are feasible ways of closing the ever-increasing income gaps between the rich and poor countries. 'Technologically advanced country' has become a synonym for a rich country and there is a general feeling that a sustainable improvement in the relative standard of living of the poor countries cannot be achieved without a transfer of the technical knowledge which constitutes perhaps the most fundamental source of wealth in the developed world. Unfortunately, recognising the problem does not seem to be of great help in this particular issue. The object of the transfer, in other words, technological knowledge, is an evasive one.

I   WHAT IS TECHNOLOGY AND HOW IS IT TRANSFERRED?

According to Jones (1970) 'Technology refers to the way in which resources are converted into commodities'. Such definition is easily understood in the case of 'disembodied' technology where conventional factors of production are combined according to a set of blueprints in order to produce commodities; technology here is the set of blueprints and is usually associated with the shape of the production function. Technology is of the 'embodied' type if at least some of the conventional factors utilised must have followed a prior process of specific adaptation before being combined with other conventional factors and blueprints in the production of the final commodities. In this case some of the 'total' technology input for producing the final commodity is already imbedded in the specific factors used at that stage. Theoretical models of international trade in disembodied and embodied technology have been developed in Rodriguez (1975) and Berglas and Jones (1977); these papers, however, describe the transfer of existing technology without specification of the process through which such technical knowledge was created. In both cases the authors analyse the optimal amount of technology transfer from the point of view of the country which owns it;

noticing that making technology available to foreign trade partners may reinforce their trade competitiveness it is not surprising that in both cases the authors find that the optimal rate of technology transfer (and its price) is the one which allows for the maximum exploitation of any monopolistic position in the foreign markets for goods and factors by the owner of the technology.

In Rodriguez (1975) the object of the transfer is the production function itself, while in Berglas and Jones (1977) the transfer is effected through the relocation of the existing stock of machines in which the technology is embodied. Both papers only offer a partial view of the technology transfer process. In general, transfer of embodied technology can proceed at two levels:

(1) Transfer of the specific factors in which the technology is embodied.

(2) Transfer of the blueprints and any other specific capabilities required to produce those factors.

Transfer of disembodied technology only seems to require giving accessibility to the set of blueprints; notice, however, that the capability for generating new or comparable blueprints may require the use of specific factors and additional blueprints which may not be readily transferable. As an example of the latter notice that most of the technological output produced in the field of, say, social sciences by the Northern countries is readily available to the South in the form of journal articles (the blueprints); such blueprints, however, may not be readily applicable for the specific problems of the South before some adaptation requiring the input of specific human capital and physical research facilities which may not be readily transferable.

II   CREATION OF TECHNOLOGICAL KNOWLEDGE

It follows from the previous discussion that the process of technology transfer in its several dimensions is not one which is amenable to a relatively simple analytical characterisation. It is clear, however, that an essential ingredient for the understanding of the problem required a grasp of the process through which new technological knowledge is generated. Two main polar views can be discerned here with respect to the fundamental characterisation of the process of technical change:

(1) Technical change as a process which is unresponsive to economic incentives.

(2) Technical change being determined by economic incentives.

The first view can be illustrated by means of Schumpeter's characterisation of the process of technological change being the result of innovations done by naturally gifted individuals (the 'entrepreneurs'). Taking this view to the extreme its implication would be that the rate of creation of innovations is fully determined by the existing stock of 'entrepreneurs' and therefore not affected by economic incentives. Notice, however, that even in this extreme case, the geographical distribution of the world output of innovations may be endogeneously determined by the locational preferences of the entrepreneurs. Due to the social externalities associated with the process of technical change we can thus conceive countries competing for the fixed stock of entrepreneurs through a variety of incentives ranging from better salaries, research facilities, relaxed immigration requirements, intellectual freedom, etc. The 'brain drain' of professional and trained personnel from LDCs towards DCs during the last few decades is, of course, a well-documented fact and may have played an important part in a process of 'reverse' transfer of technology. There is little doubt that the brain drain process has worked towards increasing the relative technological advantage of immigration to the developed countries. In addition, due to international patent and tax laws and the existence of direct locational externalities, the economic benefits derived from the new technology created are likely to accrue mostly to those within the country of immigration (being distributed to the migrant through his salary or royalties, the government through taxes in excess of cost of public services provided and to whoever is the recipient of any net positive externalities). The technology transfer effects of the brain drain are likely, therefore, to have contributed to a more unequal distribution of world income among countries. While some may view this last conclusion as indicative of the need to stop the brain drain process, there are other important issues involved. If, instead of looking at countries as the object of the analysis we concentrate on individuals, we find there are three main agents in the brain drain process: the original residents of the DC of immigration, those 'left behind' in the LDC and, finally, the migrant himself. In the absence of externalities or taxes the following distribution of welfare changes is most likely to take place as a consequence of the migration:

(1) Original residents of the DC *gain*.
(2) Those left behind with LDC *lose*.
(3) The migrant *gains*.

If the migrant is still considered as an element of the social welfare function of the LDC his gain is likely to more than compensate the loss to those left behind and welfare of the LDC may be actually higher; since original residents of the DC also gain, both DC and LDC are better off although income distribution within the LDC nationals has changed. If, however, the gain to the migrant is incorporated with the gain to the DC, then the likely result is that the DC gains and the LDC loses. To which country the welfare gain of the migrant should be added is an unsettled issue. Furthermore, the existence of externalities and redistributive taxation will affect the distribution of gains and losses described above, probably in the direction of worsening the loss to those left behind in the LDC of emigration. As a way to compensate those left behind Bhagwati (1972) has proposed the use of an income surtax on professional and trained personnel who migrate from LDCs to DCs, the proceeds to be distributed back to the LDCs. While Bhagwati's surtax would work towards mitigating the losses to those left behind it should be noticed that it imposes the burden of compensation exclusively on the migrant and that other more egalitarian compensation mechanisms, where *all* residents of the DCs share in the North—South redistribution could be devised. Unfortunately, lack of space does not permit a more detailed elaboration here on the issue of the brain drain; the reader is referred to the recent collection of essays edited by Bhagwati and Pantington (1976) for an in-depth analysis of the legal and theoretical aspects of the brain drain.

The second view of the process of technical change postulates that technological advances are responsive to economic incentives; as a consequence the rate of technical progress becomes an endogenous variable subject to direct or indirect policy control. Most prevalent within this view is the assumption that the output of new technology is positively related to the amount of research and development (R and D) input, a relationship which in itself may be subject to increasing returns to scale. Schumpeter, in his latter writings (1945), advocated the possibility of increasing returns to scale of R and D output with respect to both R and D input and firm's size giving rise to what has later been called the Schumpeterian Hypothesis (see, for example, Fisher and Temin, 1973): an increase in industrial concentration will result in larger aggregate industry output of new technology. The policy prescription derived from this view is clear: policy measures which promote industrial concentration would result in a higher rate of technical growth and therefore lower production costs; the cost-reduction effect may even outweigh the price distortion associated with monopolistic pricing such that higher industrial concentration may result in a net social gain. While the above policy prescription may have some degree of intuitive appeal its logic is somehow faulty. Arrow (1962a) showed that the pecuniary incentives to develop new cost-saving techniques vary inversely with the degree of monopoly power; the incentive for cost-reducing investments is likely to be higher for a competitive firm which, if successful, would benefit not only from the cost reduction but also from the additional monopoly power due to its now larger market share. The fact is that increasing returns to scale of R and D output with respect to R and D input and firm's size may not be a generalised phenomenon and also that in those industries where it happens to exist we will most likely *already* observe a high degree of concentration. Promoting concentration in an existing competitive industry may prove to be a costly mistake to the extent that the industry was competitive because of the absence of increasing returns to scale in R and D.

III THEORETICAL MODELS WITH ENDOGENOUS TECHNOLOGY

Granted that new technical advances are not totally random but may be responsive to economic incentives invites the question of what those incentives are and, of particular interest to us here, to what extent is this process affected by the degree of openness of the economy. We shall now discuss three of these possible channels.

(1) The R and D approach
(2) The 'learning-by-doing' approach
(3) The 'learning-by-seeing' approach

THE R AND D APPROACH

The most obvious link between invention and economic incentives comes from assuming the existence of a well-defined relationship between conventional R and D inputs and R and D output. This approach has received much attention in the growth literature (see, for example Arrow (1962b), Phelps (1966) and Nordhaus (1969)) and was applied to the open economy by Chipman (1970). Chipman is, however, concerned with the effects of optimal induced technical change on trade patterns. Trade takes place only in goods (final or intermediate) and *not* in technology *per se*; the issue of technology transfer is therefore not dealt with in the paper. As pointed out by Chipman, if all of the R and D costs and benefits were internalised by the firms there would be no fundamental difference between the operations of the market for innovations and those of conventional markets. Much of R and D output, however, has the characteristics of a 'public good', requiring either direct government control over its creation or the establishment of patent agreements aimed at 'privatising' the invention during some specified time-period in order to allow for some positive rent to the inventor since without such rent there would not be any private incentive to R and D investment at all. To the extent that a market-oriented allocation of R and D resources is considered desirable, international adherence to patent agreements is a necessary requirement for the global sustenance of the system. Unfortunately, most LDCs which are not at the present big producers nor consumers of advanced technology benefit relatively little from the existence of such patent agreements. Depending on how strongly patent laws are enforced in international disputes, there could be, however, some room for 'benign' violation of patent agreements by LDCs through the development of slightly modified techniques which would never have been done without the knowledge of the new patented invention.

While global efficiency considerations do call for universal enforcement of patent laws, distributional considerations could be invoked (in the absence of an established income 'transfer' mechanism) towards favouring a lesser strict enforcement of such laws for LDCs. In this regard, allowing for a shorter expiration of patents in the case that the new competitive production is located in an LDC would seem to be a direct and simple way to influence at least some amount of 'technology transfer'.

The public good nature of some types of technical knowledge implies that the use of knowledge by one user does not deprive the amount available of it for others. It follows then that the costs associated with the development of such technical knowledge must not be related to the rate at which the knowledge will be utilised and therefore that they will be independent from the size of the market for the good whose production benefits from the new knowledge. Since the benefits from a cost-reducing innovation depend on the volume of output, it follows that the rate of return to this type of innovation is fundamentally determined by the market size for the product. Under free international trade all countries, small or large, share in the world market (so far the largest possible!) and thus, the incentive to R and D investment is independent from the size of the country where the investment originates. If, however, there is the possibility of increased trade barriers applying to new products or to those existing products benefiting from the cost-reducing innovations, the expected profitability of the foreign trade component of total sales will be reduced. Clearly, the larger the likelihood of trade barriers being imposed on the new or improved products, the larger the importance of the size of the domestic market in determining the rate of return to the innovation. It is therefore possible that the expected rate of return for the same innovation be lower if the investment is done in a smaller country than if it is done in a larger country. Trade barriers, therefore, can impose a misallocation of the world's R and D expenditures by creating a bias towards relocating R and D expenditures in those countries with the larger internal markets.

THE 'LEARNING-BY-DOING' APPROACH

The learning-by-doing hypothesis originally presented in Arrow (1962a) assumes that the rate of technical innovation is positively related to the accumulated experience of the firm in the production process, in particular with investment experience. Other measures of experience often used to describe this process range from accumulated output to accumulated labour input.

The possibility of technical improvements (lower costs) due to production experience has often been used to provide a theoretical basis to the 'infant industry argument' for protection. According to the argument, since protection from foreign competition allows for greater domestic output, learning is higher and so is technical growth. Notice, however, that technical growth should not be a rigid target *per se* independently of the costs required for its achievement. If, in the absence of protection, the owner of the firm where the learning possibilities exist does not want to undertake the short-run losses due to higher output in order to obtain the long-run benefits due to lower costs, it must be because such investment (in learning) is not profitable compared with other alternatives. Clearly, the fact that short-run losses may result in long-run benefits is not a sufficient argument for undertaking a project or for the government to subsidise it. Only if there are positive social externalities or if there are distortions in the goods' or factors' markets is it possible for the private and social evaluation of the net present value of an investment project to differ. Such would be the case if the market rate of interest (used to discount the future benefits due to lower costs) exceeds the social discount rate; in this case, however, the proper intervention, which must be aimed at the distortion, is not to protect the output of the 'infant industry' but to extend credit to it at the social discount rate.

Arrow's seminal work on learning by doing, describing a one-sector aggregative model of a closed economy, was extended to a two-sector open economy by Bardhan (1970). Bardhan's work describes a neoclassical two-sector economy producing a consumption and an investment good, both also being traded at a fixed international relative price. There is the possibility of Hicks neutral technical change in the investment sector through learning by doing—the rate of technical change in the investment sector therefore increases with the rate of output of the sector—but there is no learning possibility in the consumption goods sector.

Notice that while in Arrow's one-sector economy the benefits from learning derived from investment apply to the whole economy, in Bardhan such benefits are restricted to the investment sector. Bardhan, like Arrow, assumes that private firms do not internalise the benefits from learning and he therefore proceeds to determine the optimal rate of subsidy to investment output which maximises the present discounted value of the utility derived from consumption. Given world prices (fixed terms of trade) the subsidy is positive along the optimal path in order to allow for a difference between the marginal cost of investment goods and the market price equal to the shadow value of the extra learning induced by a marginal unit of output. While in Arrow's closed economy there is no difference between output of investment goods and investment, such difference takes place in Bardhan's open economy where the learning is derived from *producing* investment goods and not from investment *per se*; it is therefore possible for learning to take place in the investment sector even though the sector is actually disinvesting (in other words, if the investment sector is labour-intensive, as the capital stock grows the investment sector contracts at constant prices). Another distinct feature of Bardhan's model is the assumption of a positive rate of 'forgetting' as applied to the accumulated stock of learning; such assumption is necessary for the economy to have a steady-state since otherwise the efficiency of the investment sector would continue increasing without bounds to the extent that there is no production at all. This last assumption raises the question of whether 'learning by doing' can really be a source of creation of new technical knowledge or rather a mechanism through which *existing* technical knowledge is *adapted* into the production process through experience. In this latter view we can, in very broad terms, distinguish between the stock of existing technical knowledge (T) and the stock of adapted technology $(A < T)$; for production purposes it is A and not T which is relevant and learning by doing would be the way through which existing technology is adapted for production. Algebraically, such learning process could be described by:

$$\frac{dA}{dt} = \alpha L(T - A)$$

where L is the actual rate of employment (or output, or investment) and $(T - A)$ is the 'adaptability gap' (or 'learning gap'). This view of the learning-by-doing process may be more realistic than the one previously described where experience alone could be, abstaining from 'forgetting,' a source of creation of unlimited technical knowledge. In this view, for example, the discovery of a new superior wheat variety becomes an instantaneous addition to the stock of technology the moment the first seed is processed. It becomes 'adapted' technology only when farmers have learnt about its existence and have acquired enough experience with it to actually obtain the theoretically hypothesised yields. I will elaborate further on this view in the last section of the paper where an aggregate model of technology creation, adaptation and transfer will be developed.

THE 'LEARNING-BY-SEEING' APPROACH

It is widely accepted in the literature that direct foreign investment is associated with the process of transfer of technology. However, to the extent that foreign investors get paid the higher marginal return of their more advanced technology (which *they* own) it is not clear what is being transferred there. Of course, as with any type of international factor movement, domestic residents get to gain the well-known 'triangle' due to the higher marginal productivity of the inframarginal units of foreign investment and all those additional gains derived from taxation (see MacDougall, 1960) but there is nothing specific regarding technology transfer there. Only to the extent that there are some direct technological spillovers from the superior foreign technology to the domestic technology can we say that technology transfer takes place. Such spillover may take the form of direct 'learning' of advanced methods by workers engaged in production in the foreign controlled sector which may be transferred to the rest of the domestic productive sectors. The wage policy of foreign-controlled firms will be in this case a crucial variable in determining the turnover rate of their workers and therefore the magnitude of this type of technology transfer.

In more general terms, the rate of transfer may not be so strictly associated with labour use and its turnover rate, but more with any type of interaction between the advanced technology sector and the rest of the economy. In this interpretation, the mere fact that the advanced technology is present in the economy is enough to guarantee a slow process of transfer to the backward sector. Such interpretation is made in Findlay (1978) who assumes that the rate of technology transfer between the advanced-foreign and backward-domestic sectors increases both with the amount of penetration of the domestic economy by the foreign technology (measured by the ratio of foreign capital to domestic capital) and also with the current level of the 'technology gap'. Denoting by T^F and T^D to the levels of foreign and domestic technologies and by K^D and K^F to the levels of domestic and foreign capital (due to accumulated foreign investment), Findlay's technology transfer function is:

$$\frac{dT^D}{dt} = \Phi\left(\frac{K^F}{K^D}\right)(T^F - T^D)$$

Foreign technology is assumed by Findlay to grow at a constant rate, λ, and there is no source of domestic creation of technology other than the learning process described above. The level of domestic technology is therefore bounded by $T^F(t)$ and its steady-state growth rate by λ. The relevant endogenous variable in Findlay's model is therefore not the level of T^D but the level of the technology gap, $\dfrac{T^F - T^D}{T^D}$. To the extent that a steady-state equilibrium exists, domestic technology is bound to grow at the same rate, λ, as the foreign technology; from the learning function we therefore obtain the following steady-state relationship between the technology gap and the ratio of foreign to domestic capital:

$$\lambda = \Phi\left(\frac{K^F}{K^D}\right)\left(\frac{T^F - T^D}{T^D}\right)$$

Since $\Phi' > 0$, the steady-state relationship between $\dfrac{K^F}{K^D}$ and $\dfrac{T^F - T^D}{T^D}$ is negative, as shown in Figure 1 by the $\lambda\lambda$ curve.

Given the learning function, domestic policies aimed at closing the technology gap are constrained to do so at the expense of a higher relative amount of foreign to domestic capital. Policies which improve

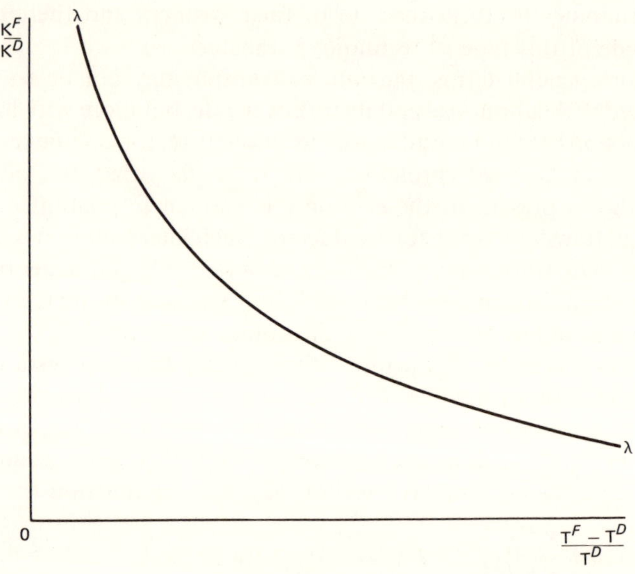

Fig. 1

on the learning function will, however, shift $\lambda\lambda$ to the left and allow for a more favourable tradeoff; such would be the case if the educational level of the labour force is increased and this facilitates the learning process or if patent laws applying to foreign firms operating at home are relaxed. Notice that a leftward shift in $\lambda\lambda$ does not necessarily imply a reduction in the equilibrium technology gap since K^F/K^D is also an endogenous variable. Thus, if the improvement in the learning function is done at the expense of profits to foreign investment, K^F/K^D may fall and this would work towards a larger technology gap which may even outweigh the favourable effect of the improvement in the learning tradeoff.

Koizumi and Kopecky (1973) also analyse the technology transfer implications of direct foreign investment in a dynamic model with endogenous domestic and foreign capital stocks. Contrary to Findlay where the technology transfer takes place through a 'slow' learning process, Koizumi and Kopecky assume such a process to be instantaneous and their technology transfer function is directly imbedded in the receiving country's production function.

$$Q = \Phi(K^F/L)F(K^D + K^F, L)$$

where Q is domestic output and the term (K^F/L) captures the technological spillovers due to the presence of foreign capital; such spillover is assumed to take the form of an externality and is not therefore internalised by foreign investors who perceive the marginal product of this capital as $\Phi \cdot \partial F/\partial K^F$ (same as that of domestic capital) rather than the 'social' marginal product,

$$\Phi \cdot \frac{\partial F}{\partial K^F} + F \cdot \frac{\partial \Phi}{\partial K^F}.$$

An important assumption in Koizumi and Kopecky is that if the country is net creditor, or $K^F < 0$, the efficiency of home production is diminished since $\Phi(K^F/L) \gtrless 1$ as $K^F/L \gtrless 0$. Such assumption is justified on the plausible grounds that a creditor looses the externalities derived from the managerial and technical talent needed to operate the foreign investment projects.

IV   A DYNAMIC MODEL OF TECHNOLOGY TRANSFER

INTRODUCTION AND DESCRIPTION OF THE MODEL

I will now develop a highly aggregative dynamic model with the purpose of illustrating some of the main features of the process through which technology is created, transferred and adapted. In the conclusion to his paper, Findlay (1978, pp. 14–15) states: 'What is also beyond the scope of our model is any explanation of the forces that determine the ability to create new technology as opposed to borrowing it. Historically, regions that have been borrowers of technology have frequently themselves eventually taken the lead, while the impetus of the original leaders has flagged.' The model to be described here makes an attempt to fill in the gap mentioned by Findlay by allowing both for international technology transfer (borrowing) and domestic creation of technology through R and D investment. Emphasis will be put on finding conditions under which, through R and D investment, the steady-state level of domestic technology may overtake that of foreign technology such that the country reaches a state of 'technology autarchy' as opposed to a state of 'technological dependency' in which the growth rate of domestic technology is constrained by the growth rate of foreign technology.

One of the key building-blocks of our model will be the distinction between the stock of technology (T) and the stock of 'adapted' technology (A). Such distinction is made by Nelson and Phelps (1966) who refer to A as the 'best practice level of technology' and to T as the 'theoretical level of technology'; in their model T grows at an exogenous exponential rate, while investment in human capital is the crucial variable explaining the transformation of T into A. In the model described here, R and D investment will, at least temporarily, affect the growth rate of T while learning by doing will explain part of the transformation of T into A.

In order to abstain from issues related to capital accumulation I will assume that a single composite good (Q) is produced by labour (L_1) in conjunction with the stock of adapted technology according to the following relationship:

$$Q = \sigma A L_1 \tag{1}$$

I therefore identify the stock of adapted technology with the 'efficiency' level of the average worker; the parameter σ is then the average productivity of efficient labour input and, since it will serve no useful purpose in the analysis that follows, it will be assumed to equal unity. The total labour force is also assumed to be constant and equal to unity; at every instant the labour force is allocated between production of the final good (L_1) and R and D activities $(L_2 \equiv 1 - L_1)$. Gross output (Q) is either consumed (C) or used as an input in R and D (R); per capita consumption is therefore:

$$C = AL_1 - R \tag{2}$$

At every moment there is a stock of available domestic technology (T_D) which exceeds or at most equals the stock of adapted technology $(T_D > A)$. The 'adaptability gap' will be alternatively referred to by $T_D - A > 0$ or $T_D/A > 1$. Following the learning-by-doing hypothesis I assume that the rate of adaptation of existing technology is proportional to the experience gained by labour in final production (and therefore to L_1) and to the level of the adaptability gap. In addition, the stock of available domestic technology (T_D) grows through time and, depending on its degree of 'appropriateness', a certain fraction (β) of the *new* technology created can be adapted immediately into the final production process without the intermediate learning stage. The stock of adapted technology therefore grows through time according to:

$$\dot{A} = \alpha L_1 (T_D - A) + \beta \dot{T}_D \tag{3}$$

where α captures the learning-by-doing effect and β captures the appropriateness of new technology; I make the reasonable assumption β is restricted between zero and one.

Domestic technology increases through time due to both domestic R and D output and to transfer from foreign technology (T_W) when $T_W > T_D$; the transfer component equals a constant number, γ, times the 'technology gap', $T_W - T_D$. Since I abstain from modelling the capital accumulation process I cannot incorporate Findlay's interesting assumption about the speed of technology transfer (γ) depending on the degree of penetration of the domestic economy by foreign investment; in a very loose way, however, exogenous increases in the degree of openness of the economy could be expected to be associated with higher values of γ in the present model. I assume domestic output of R and D can be represented by a constant returns to scale production function increasing in the input of physical output, R, and efficient labour input, $A(1 - L_1)$. Hence, the change in the stock of domestic technology is:

$$\dot{T}_D = F[R, A(1 - L_1)] + \gamma(T_W - T_D) \tag{4}$$

The stock of foreign technology is assumed to grow exponentially at the constant rate λ_w. As indicated before, the transfer of foreign technology is conceived as being operative only when there is a positive technology gap; if, through R and D output the stock of domestic technology overtakes T_W, the transfer mechanism ceases and $\gamma = 0$ in equation (4) above. (If the transfer mechanism operates in reverse, the growth rate of foreign technology would then adapt to the endogenously determined domestic growth rate as the home country makes the technological leadership.)

Equations (1) to (4) describe the dynamic behaviour of the economy given the allocation of R and D inputs, $A(1 - L_1)$ and R. A complete characterisation of the market structure for technological activities from which an equilibrium allocation of R and D resources could be obtained will not be attempted here. Rather, the allocation of R and D resources is taken as given and from there implications for the dynamic behaviour of the economy are derived. The externalities associated with the technology process and the (resulting) high degree of government interference in the allocation of R and D resources in most modern societies do, however, give a certain degree of realism to the above assumption.

Transforming (3) and (4) into growth rates and using the linear homogeneity property of $F[R, A(1 - L_1)]$ we derive:

$$\frac{\dot{A}}{A} = \hat{A} = \alpha L_1(\tau_D - 1) + \beta \tau_D \hat{T}_D \tag{3'}$$

$$\frac{\dot{T}_D}{T_D} = \hat{T}_D = \frac{(1-L_1)}{\tau_D} f(x) + \gamma(\tau_W - 1) \tag{4$'$}$$

where $\tau_D = T_D/A \geq 1$ is the domestic adaptability gap,

$\tau_W = T_W/T_D$ is the technology gap,

$x = \dfrac{R}{A(1-L_1)}$ is the R and D physical input per unit of efficient R

and D labour input, assumed to be a policy-determined variable together with L_1.

Noting that $\hat{\tau}_D = \hat{T}_D - \hat{A}$ and $\hat{\tau}_W = \lambda_W - \hat{T}_D$, (3$'$) and (4$'$) can be transformed into:

$$\hat{\tau}_D = -\alpha L_1(\tau_D - 1) + (1 - \beta\tau_D)\left[\frac{(1-L_1)}{\tau_D}f(x) + \gamma(\tau_W - 1)\right] \tag{5}$$

$$\hat{\tau}_W = \lambda_W - \left[\frac{(1-L_1)}{\tau_D}f(x) + \gamma(\tau_W - 1)\right] \tag{6}$$

Equations (5) and (6) completely describe the time-path of the adaptability (τ_D) and technology (τ_W) gaps given the values of the exogenous parameters L_1, x, λ_W and those describing the learning process (α), the appropriateness of new technology (β) and the transfer process (γ).[1]

Notice in equation (6) that in the absence of any domestic R and D activities, that is, $(1 - L_1) f(x) = 0$, the rate of change in the technology gap would be determined exclusively by the foreign rate of growth and the level of the gap itself. Such a differential equation would be unambiguously stable and the steady-state solution would yield $\tau_W = 1 + \lambda_W/\gamma$; this value of τ_W exceeds unity, indicating that when the only source of growth in domestic technology is the transfer process it will never overtake foreign technology. With positive domestic R and D activities, however, it may be possible for domestic technology to overtake foreign technology such that τ_W would become less than unity. In this situation, which we denote by technological autarchy, the transfer mechanism ceases to operate and equations (5) and (6) no longer can describe the behaviour of the system. For $\tau_W < 1$ we should set $\gamma = 0$ in equations (3$'$) and (4$'$) and the relevant dynamic variables become the adaptatibility gap (τ_D) and the growth rate in domestic technology ($\lambda = \hat{T}_D$). Substituting $\gamma = 0$ into equations (3$'$) and (4$'$) and using $\hat{\tau}_D = \lambda - \hat{A}$ we obtain the following expressions describing the motion of the economy under technological autarchy:

$$\hat{\tau}_D = \lambda(1 - \beta\tau_D) - \alpha L_1 \tau_D \tag{7}$$

$$\lambda = \frac{(1 - L_1)}{\tau_D} f(x) \tag{8}$$

Notice that in the steady-state solution to the autarchy system, equations (7) and (8), the growth rate of domestic technology (λ) is an endogenous variable which can be affected by changes in parameter values while in the steady-state solution of the dependent system, equations (5) and (6), the constancy of τ_W requires T_D to grow at the same rate as T_W.

In comparing the steady-state solutions to the dependent and autarchy systems it is easy to verify that the set of parameter values which yields $\lambda = \lambda_W$ in equation (8) is exactly the same which yields $\tau_W = 1$ in equation (6). Such a set of parameter values, therefore, defines the boundary between the autarchy and dependent systems and its precise properties will be discussed later in detail.

STEADY-STATE AND COMPARATIVE STATISTICS FOR THE DEPENDENT SYSTEM

Assuming the set of parameter values is such that a steady-state solution to equations (5) and (6) with $\tau_W > 1$ exists, the associated growth rate of the economy will be given by the growth rate in world technology (λ_W). The allocation of R and D inputs (L_2 and x) will determine which fraction of the growth rate in domestic technology will come from domestic R and D and which one from transfer without affecting the growth rate itself. The long-run levels of the technology and adaptability gaps are, however, endogeneously determined by R and D inputs and other exogenous parameters. Equating (5) and (6) to zero and solving for the steady-state values $\bar{\tau}_D$ and $\bar{\tau}_F$ we obtain

$$\bar{\tau}_D = \frac{\lambda_W + \alpha L_1}{\beta\lambda_W + \alpha L_1} > 1 \qquad \text{as} \quad 0 < \beta < 1 \tag{9}$$

$$\bar{\tau}_W = 1 + \frac{1}{\gamma}[\lambda_W - (1 - L_1) \equiv (x)/\bar{\tau}_D] > 1 \qquad \text{(by assumption)} \tag{10}$$

It follows from equation (9) that the smaller the adaptability gap, the larger the learning parameter (α), or the larger the fraction of population engaged in final production (and therefore in learning); τ_D will also be higher, the higher the growth rate of world technology. Notice that τ_D is independent from the R and D production function or the transfer parameter γ.

Increasing the scale of R and D operations (higher $(1 - L_1)$, same x) has an ambiguous effect on the technology gap; this is so because even though R and D output tends to be larger as L_2 rises, the lower L_1 implies less learning and therefore each worker in R and D will be relatively less efficient than before; the assumption that only learning by labour engaged in final production is useful for the adaptation process is crucial to the latter effect; the implications of assuming that there is adaptation by all employed labour are straightforward and will be discussed later. The technology gap is, however, unambiguously reduced by increases in either R and D expenditures per efficient worker (x) or in the transfer parameter (γ).

Since the path of world technology is exogeneously given we can normalise per capita consumption in equation (2) by T_W to obtain:

$$C/T_W = \frac{A}{T_W}L_1 - \frac{R}{T_W} \qquad \text{and since} \quad R = xA(1 - L_1) \tag{2'}$$

$$C/T_W = \frac{A}{T_W}[L_1 - x(1 - L_1)] = \frac{[L_1 - x(1 - L_1)]}{\tau_D \tau_W} \tag{11}$$

In the steady-state C/T_W will be constant and therefore the growth rate of per capita consumption will be λ_W. Given the exogenity of T_W, however, the height of the steady-state time path of per capita consumption will vary directly with the steady-state level of C/T_W. We can see from equation (11) that, for given levels of R and D inputs, the height of the consumption path is inversely related to the levels of the technology and adaptability gaps. As shown before, increases in α, β or γ will reduce the steady-state value of either or both gaps; therefore, the higher the steady-state consumption path, the larger are the values of the learning, appropriateness and transfer parameters. Changes in the allocation of R and D inputs, $(1 - L_1)$ and x, will affect both the numerator and denominator in equation (11) and have an ambiguous effect on C/T_W; the reason for the ambiguity is that as R and D expands any gain in consumption due to a lower τ_W comes at the expense of smaller output (due to lower L_1), larger τ_D (due to lower L_1) or a smaller fraction of output available for consumption (due to higher R and D). In interpreting the above results it should be borne in mind that comparison of different steady-state consumption paths do not have any precise welfare meaning unless due account is taken of the transitional adjustment period; therefore, the desirability of a policy change leading

to a higher steady-state consumption path can only be judged in the light
of the short-run costs involved.

CONDITIONS FOR TECHNOLOGICAL AUTARCHY

It is possible to obtain the configuration of values of R and D inputs, x
and $(1 - L_1)$, which determine whether the steady-state equilibrium will
be under technological dependency or autarchy. To do so we set $\bar{\tau}_W = 1$
in equation (10)—or $\lambda = \lambda_W$ in equation (8)—and obtain the condition:

$$f(x) = \frac{\lambda_W(\lambda_W + \alpha L_1)}{(1 - L_1)(\beta\lambda_W + \alpha L_1)} \tag{12}$$

which describes the boundary in the (x, L_1) space between technological
dependency and autarchy. The slope of such relationship is given by:

$$\left.\frac{dx}{dL_1}\right|_{\tau_W = 1} = \frac{f(x)}{f'(x)}\left[\frac{\alpha}{(\lambda_W + \alpha L_1)} - \frac{\alpha}{(\beta\lambda_W + \alpha L_1)} + \frac{1}{1 - L_1}\right] \tag{13}$$

For $L_1 = 0$ the above slope will be positive or negative depending on $\alpha\beta$
$+ \beta\lambda_W - \alpha \gtrless 0$ while as L_1 approaches unity the slope must be positive
(as L_1 tends to unity x must tend to infinity in order to satisfy equation
(12)). It follows that the 'boundary' relation between x and L_1 may be a
decreasing one for low L_1, while eventually must be increasing as L_1
approaches unity; equation (12) is shown in Figure 2 as the curve $\bar{\tau}_W = 1$,
under the assumption that for a low L_1 its slope is negative. Since a
higher x unambiguously reduces $\bar{\tau}_W$ it follows that the area below the $\bar{\tau}_W$
$= 1$ curve (area I) corresponds to $\bar{\tau}_W > 1$ (technological dependency)
while the area above $\bar{\tau}_W = 1$ shows the values of x and L_1 yielding
technological autarchy (area II).

An additional restriction comes from the fact that in a feasible
allocation R and D resources cannot exceed the value of the final output,
in other words, consumption must be non-negative. From equation (11),
$C \geq 0$ requires equation (13) $x \leq \dfrac{L_1}{1 - L_1}$, a restriction incorporated in
Figure 2 as the $C = 0$ curve indicating that only allocations of x and L_1
below it are feasible. The feasible area of technological autarchy is
therefore limited to area IIa and that of technological dependency to
area Ia.

It is clear from the case depicted in Figure 2 that increases in $(1 - L_1)$
and x together can take the system into the feasible autarchy region IIa.
Changes in $(1 - L_1)$ or x alone, however, may not be able to do so as the

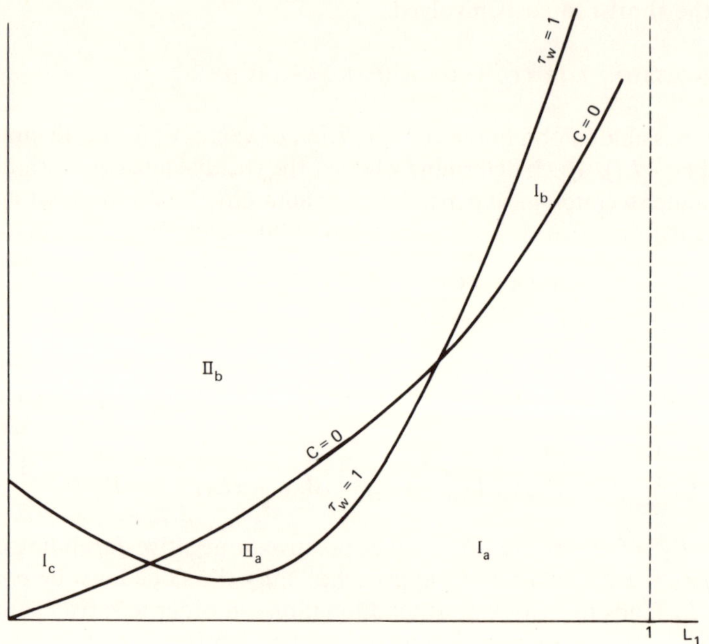

Fig. 2

system may hit the $C = 0$ boundary in regions Ib or Ic. There is also a minimum amount of R and D expenditure per efficient worker below which technological autarchy cannot be reached no matter how many R and D workers are assigned; such value corresponds to the minimum value of the $\bar{\tau}_W = 1$ curve.

So far it has been assumed there is an intersection between the $\bar{\tau}_W = 1$ and $C = 0$ schedules such that a feasible region with technological autarchy exists; this is not, however, necessarily the case. Notice, from equation (12) that the $\bar{\tau}_W = 1$ schedule will be shifted upwards with increases in λ_W or decreases in α or β. A combination of high λ_W and low learning and appropriateness parameters may therefore yield a configuration such as the one shown in Figure 3 where there is no feasible autarchy region.

The likelihood of existence (and dimensions) of an area of technological autarchy is independent from the technology transfer parameter γ;

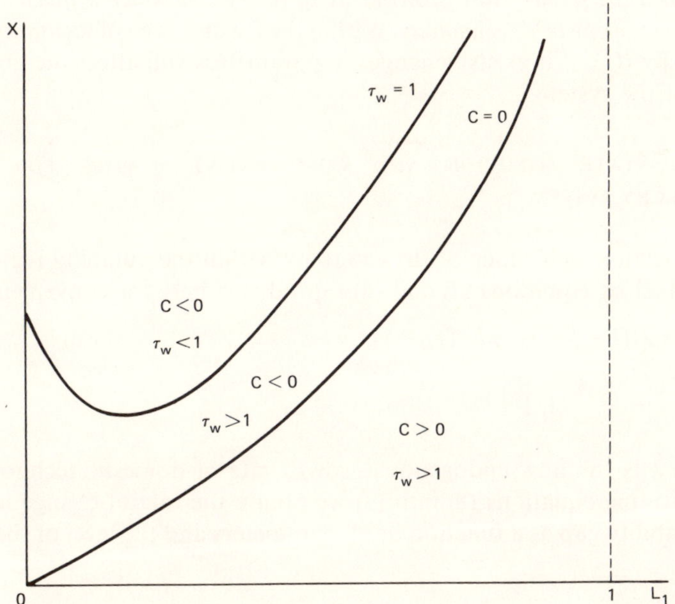

Fig. 3

this follows readily from equations (12) and (13) which delimit such an area since γ is not included in either equations. The intuitive reason is that technology transfer according to the mechanism postulated in equation (4) can contribute to *reducing* the technology gap but *never* to closing it (unless γ is infinity) since for the transfer to operate a positive gap is necessary. Thus, the boundary in equation (12) just shows the pairs of x and L_1 for which, through domestic R and D output, domestic technology grows precisely at the rate λ_W; the consumption restriction in equation (13) is, of course, independent from γ since it just stipulates that R cannot exceed gross output.

To summarise some of our results so far we can mention that as the possibility of attaining technological autarchy (or leadership) increases, the higher the values of the learning parameters (α) or the appropriateness parameter (β) while it is independent from the transfer parameter (γ). Within the area of technological dependence (area Ia) changes in parameters (α, β, γ, L_1 x) will affect the height of the steady-state consumption path and the adaptability and technological gaps but *will not affect the steady-state growth rate of the system which is given by the growth rate of world technology*. Within the feasible area of technological autarchy (IIa, if it exists), changes in parameters will affect the growth rate of the system.

STEADY-STATE SOLUTION AND COMPARATIVE STATICS FOR THE AUTARCHY SYSTEM

The dynamic behaviour of the economy within the autarchy region is described by equations (7) and (8) reproduced here for convenience:

$$\hat{\tau}_D = \lambda((1 - \beta\tau_D) - \alpha L_1(\tau_D - 1) \tag{7}$$

$$\lambda = \frac{(1 - L_1)}{\tau_D} f(x) \tag{8}$$

where λ is the now endogenous growth rate of domestic technology. Substituting equations (8) into (7) we obtain the rate of change in the adaptability gap as a function of all parameters and the level of the gap itself:

$$\hat{\tau}_D = \frac{(1 - L_1) f(x)}{\tau_D} (1 - \beta\tau_D) - \alpha L_1(\tau_D - 1) \tag{14}$$

Local stability requires $\dfrac{\partial \hat{\tau}_D}{\partial \tau_D}$ evaluated around the steady state to be negative; such a condition is satisfied since such a derivative equals:

$$\frac{\partial \hat{\tau}_D}{\partial \tau_D} = -\alpha L_1 \frac{(\tau_D - 1)}{\tau_D} - \beta f(x) \frac{(1 - L_1)}{\tau_D} - \alpha L_1 < 0 \tag{15}$$

provided $\bar{\tau}_D > 1$ (which we will prove in a moment).

Equating equation (7) to zero and solving for the steady-state λ we obtain:

$$\bar{\lambda} = \frac{\alpha L_1(\bar{\tau}_D - 1)}{(1 - \beta\bar{\tau}_D)} = \Psi(\bar{\tau}_D) \tag{7'}$$

Equations (7') and (8) can be solved simultaneously for the steady-state value $\bar{\lambda}$ and $\bar{\tau}_D$. I now show graphically the nature of the steady-state solution. From (7') we get $\bar{\lambda} = \Psi(\bar{\tau}_D)$ satisfying

$$\Psi(1) = 0$$
$$\Psi(1/\beta) = \infty$$
$$\Psi(\tau_D) < 0 \qquad \text{for } 1 > \tau_D > 1/\beta$$
$$\Psi(\tau_D) > 0 \qquad \text{for } 1 < \tau_D < 1/\beta$$
$$\Psi'(\tau_D) > 0 \qquad \text{for all } \tau_D$$

The equation has two branches, one defined for $\tau_D < 1/\beta$ and the other for $\tau_D > 1/\beta$ and is represented in Figure 4. The other steady-state equation (8) describes a rectangular hyperbola, both branches being also shown in Figure 4. It is clear from Figure 4 that there are two sets of values of $(\bar{\lambda}, \bar{\tau}_D)$ satisfying equations (7′) and (8), corresponding to the two intersections at points a_1 and a_2. Of course, the configuration at a_2, with negative $\bar{\lambda}$ and $\bar{\tau}_D$ does not make economic sense (and is also unstable). The steady-state solution of the autarchy system is therefore at a point a_1 in the positive quadrant. Notice that the equilibrium $\bar{\tau}_D$ is larger than unity, which guarantees, from equation (15), the local stability of the system.

A higher learning (α) or appropriateness (β) parameter will shift the $\bar{\lambda}$ = $\Psi(\tau_D)$ schedule in Figure 4 upwards therefore yielding a new steady-

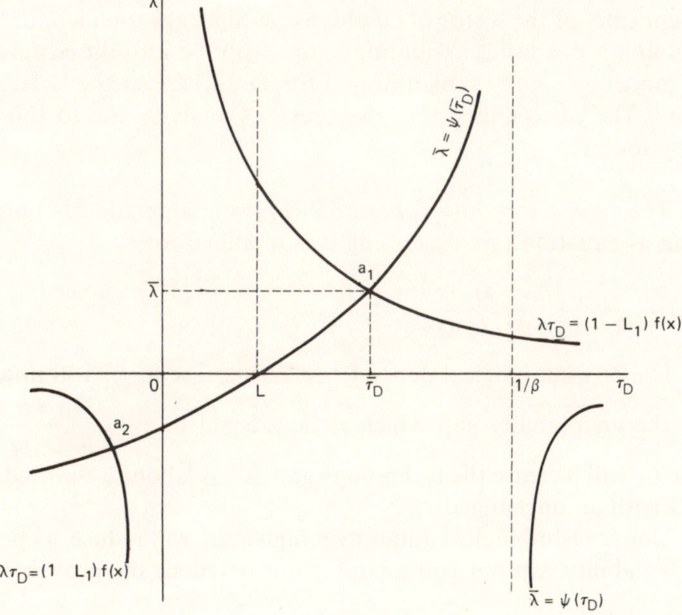

Fig. 4

state with a higher growth rate and lower adaptability gap. An increase in R and D expenditure per efficient worker (x) will shift the $\lambda\tau_D = (1 - L_1)f(x)$ schedule rightwards such that the growth rate is raised but at the expense of a larger adaptability gap. Devoting more workers to R and D (less L_1) will shift both schedules in Figure 4 to the right such that the net effect on the growth rate is ambiguous but the adaptability gap is increased.

A *CAVEAT* ON THE LEARNING PROCESS

In the previous analysis we found ambiguous comparative statics results for changes in the fraction of the labour force assigned to R and D activities. These ambiguities result from the assumption that only labour engaged in final production 'learns' to adapt existing technology. Putting more labour into R and D works towards more output of new technology but at the expense of a lower rate of adaptation; since R and D *uses* adapted technology as an input (the term $A(1 - L_1)$) it is therefore possible that this latter negative effect outweighs the positive effect of more labour input such that total R and D output falls. An alternative assumption would be that *all* employed labour engages in learning independently of the sector of employment. Since the total labour force equals unity, this latter assumption can easily be introduced into the prior model by simply substituting α for αL_1 wherever the latter term appears. The main changes in the previous analysis due to this new assumption are:

(1) The $\bar{\tau}_W = 1$ schedule in Figure 2 is now unambiguously upward-sloping as equation (10) describing it is modified to:

$$f(x) = \frac{\lambda_W(\lambda_W + \alpha)}{(1 - L_1)(\beta\lambda_W + \alpha)}$$

(2) Under technological dependence an increase in L_1 will now not affect the adaptability gap which is now equal to $\tau_D = \dfrac{\lambda_W + \alpha}{\beta\lambda_W + \alpha}$; the higher L_1 will increase the technology gap as less labour is devoted to R and D with an unchanged τ_D.

(3) Under technological autarchy a higher L_1 will reduce, as before, the adaptability gap but will unambiguously reduce the growth rate.

V CONCLUSIONS

In the previous section an attempt was made to incorporate domestic creation of technology into the process of technology transfer. One of the implications of the model described is the possible existence of two well-defined regions for parameter values within which the economy would reach either technological dependency or autarchy. Under technological dependence the growth rate of the economy is given by the growth rate of world technology and therefore domestic R and D activities will only determine which fraction of technology output comes out of domestic sources and which from transfer from abroad. Under technological autarchy the growth rate of the economy is fully determined by domestic R and D activities and, although not specifically modelled here, the growth rate of the rest of the world would adapt to that of the domestic economy.

The model attempted to incorporate in as simple a manner as possible several processes which are mostly discussed in the context of the technology issue, that is, learning by doing, appropriateness and transfer. This was done at the cost of assuming the constancy of the relevant parameters describing those processes and an exogenous allocation of R and D inputs. While I do not see a simple way of endogenising the appropriateness parameter, the transfer parameter could be made endogeneous along the lines of Findlay (1978) and the learning parameter could be explained by a human capital approach as in Nelson and Phelps (1966). Although these modifications would improve the realism of the model they would require a great deal of additional analytical complexity which should not surprise us since the technology issue is a complex one.

ENDNOTE

1. The linear approximation to equations (5) and (6) around the steady state $\bar{\tau}_D$, $\bar{\tau}_W > 1$ is described by the matrix of partial derivatives (evaluated at $\bar{\tau}_D, \bar{\tau}_W$):

$$K = \left[\frac{\partial \hat{\tau}_i}{\partial \tau_j} \right] \qquad i, j = D, W$$

The system in equations (5) and (6) will be locally stable if the matrix K is negative definite, a condition which is satisfied since

$$\text{Trace } K = -[\alpha L_1 + \beta\gamma(\bar{\tau}_W - 1) + \beta f(x)(1 - L_1)/\tau_D^2] - \gamma < 0$$

$$\text{Det } K = \gamma[\alpha L_1 + \beta\gamma(\bar{\tau}_W - 1) + f(x)(1 - L_1)/\tau_D] > 0$$

(given $\tau_W > 1$)

REFERENCES

Arrow, K. J., 'The Economic Implications of Learning by Doing', *Review of Economic Studies* (June 1962).

Arrow, K. J., 'Economic Welfare and the Allocation of Resources for Invention', in *The Rate and Direction of Inventive Activity* (Princeton University Press, 1962).

Berglas, E. and Jones, R., 'The Export of Technology', in *Carnegie-Rochester Conference Series on Public Policy*, Volume 7, Supplement to the *Journal of Monetary Economics* (1977).

Bhagwati, J., 'United States in the Nixon Era: The End of Innocence', *Daedalus* 101 (1972).

Bhagwati, J., and Pantington, M., *Taxing the Brain Drain,* Volumes I and II, (North-Holland, 1976).

Chipman, J., 'Induced Technical Change and Patterns of International Trade', in *The Technology Factor in International Trade* (NBER, 1970).

Findlay, R. W., 'Relative Backwardness, Direct Foreign Investment and the Transfer of Technology: A Simple Dynamic Model', *Quarterly Journal of Economics* (February 1978).

Fisher, F., and Tenin, P., 'Returns to Scale in Research and Development: What Does the Schumpeterian Hypothesis Imply?', *Journal of Political Economy* (January/February 1973).

Jones, R. W., 'The Role of Technology in the Theory of International Trade', in *The Technology Factor in International Trade* (NBER, 1970).

Koizumi, T. and Kopecky, K., 'Economic Growth, Capital Movements and the International Transfer of Technical Knowledge', *Journal of International Economics* (February 1973).

MacDougall, G. D. A., 'The Benefits and Costs of Private Investment from Abroad: A Theoretical Approach', *Economic Record*, 36 (1960).

Nelson, R. and Phelps, E., 'Investment in Humans, Technological Diffusion and Economic Growth', *American Economic Review* (May 1966).

Nordhaus, W., *Invention, Growth and Welfare: A Theoretical Treatment of Technological Change* (MIT Press, 1969).

Phelps, E., 'Models of Technical Progress and the Golden Rule of Research', *Review of Economic Studies* (April 1966).

Rodriguez, C. A., 'Trade in Technological Knowledge and the National Advantage', *Journal of Political Economy* (February 1975).

Schumpeter, J., *The Theory of Economic Development* (Cambridge, Mass., 1934).
Schumpeter, J., *Capitalism, Socialism, and Democracy* (1942).

Comments

Jean Waelbroeck (Belgium)

The international transfer of technology is one of the hot potatoes which have been thrust on the conference table by proponents of the New Economic Order. On this topic, Professor Rodriguez has produced a rather mathematical paper. There is nothing wrong in this—as Professor Lundberg stressed in opening the symposium, this is a conference on the research aspects of the New Economic Order proposals. We are a dispassionate group, and are certainly willing to look at problems in the dispassionate language of mathematics.

Let us look at the thinking tool which Professor Rodriguez has constructed for us. This is a simple growth model, focused on three basic aspects of technical change:

(1) The international transfer of technology
(2) R and D as an instrument to raise productivity
(3) The natural growth of productivity through the process of learning-by-doing.

The model is basically descriptive. There is no attempt to derive optimal paths or to derive the characteristics of optimal policies. The model is also non-quantifiable; a number of variables cannot be measured.

The time available does not allow me to cover fully a rather long paper. There is little point in summarising the excellent summary overview of the literature provided in the first part. So I shall concentrate on Professor Rodriguez' latest contribution to this literature, the model of the second part. Its equations are (slightly rearranged; the notation is from Rodriguez):

$$Q = AL, \tag{1}$$

Supply demand balances for goods and labour

$$C + R = Q \tag{2}$$

$$L_1 + L_2 = 1 \tag{3}$$

Production function R and D sector

$$\dot{T}_D = F(AL_2, R) + \gamma(T_W - T_D) \tag{4}$$

$$\dot{T}_D = \sigma AL_2 + \gamma(T_W - T_D) \tag{4'}$$

Transformation process of technical knowhow into productivity

$$\dot{A} = \alpha L_1 (T_D - A) + \beta \dot{T}_D \tag{5}$$

where equation (4') is a simplified version of equation (4). The latter equation allows for richer policy choices, but as AL_2/R is assumed to be fixed except in the discussion of Figure 2, little is lost by this simplification.

The model has a number of noteworthy characteristics.

(a) Equation (4) implies that a country gets a kind of free windfall from being backward (if $T_W > T_D$, so that available domestic technology lags behind the best achieved elsewhere).

(b) This term vanishes when T_D overtakes T_W, or when the country's technology becomes the most advanced in the world. The model has thus two distinct operating 'regimes', and is akin from this point of view to the two-gaps model, or the Barro Grossman version of Keynesian theory.

(c) 'Learning' takes place only in the goods sector—the L_2 term in equation (4). The author does not appear to regard this feature of the model as essential.

I will not go through the paper's extensive analysis of the model's properties. It may be more useful to point out the isomorphism between this and the Harrod Domar model of growth. The analogy with the latter's well-known properties can help to understand how the present model functions.

Setting $Q^* = Q + AL._2$, $R = 0$, $\sigma K_D^* = T_D$, $\sigma K_W^* = T_W$, $K = A$, $AL_2 = I$ produces the mathematically equivalent model.

$$Q^* = \sigma K \tag{1}$$

$$C = \sigma K_1 \tag{1'}$$

$$C + I = Q^* \tag{2}$$

$$K_1 + K_2 = K \tag{3}$$

$$\Delta K^* = I + \gamma(K_W^* - K_D^*) \tag{4}$$

$$\dot{K} = \alpha \; \frac{K_1}{} \; (K_D^* - K) + \beta \dot{K}_D^* \tag{5}$$

when equation (1) is the production function, (1′) defines the resources used in producing consumer goods, (2) is the production expenditures identity, (3) defines the total capital stock; (4) is a capital accumulation equation which states that the increase in the stock of capital equals domestic investment plus an amount of aid proportionate to the difference between the world and the country's capital stocks; (5) is a pretty classical gestation lags equation defining the process through which the capital created becomes productive.

This discussion shows that the only mathematical difference between Professor Rodriguez' model and the Harrod Domar scheme is the K_1/K term in equation (5). This is the term which accounts for the model's intricacies, and which Professor Rodriguez suggests should perhaps be dropped.

Returning to the paper, Professor Rodriguez uses his model for three purposes:

(a) To analyse its steady-state properties in the two possible regimes: $T_W > T_D$ (technological dependence); and $T_D = T_W$ (technological autarchy).

(b) To trace out in (R, L_1) space the maximum feasible growth frontier, attained when all resources are allocated to the two components of R and D expenditures.

I conclude by stating my criticisms of the paper. For this purpose, I suggest that we transport ourselves again to the imaginary North–South conference evoked at the beginning of my remarks. Let us think that a suitably simplified version of the paper was one of the conference's background papers, and let us imagine the reactions of the practical people around the conference table.

I think that the northern participants would be mainly bothered by the concept of technological autarchy. They would feel that there is no such thing as a country so advanced that it does not learn from what others are finding; the 'autarchy regime' of the model does not correspond to anything in the real world. They would wonder how some variables are to be measured.

The southern participants would react more sharply. They would have two basic objections. The first is that what is treated as fixed coefficients in the model is what they want changed by the new economic order negotiations; the model, they would feel, is not focused on the real issues in the debate. The second criticism would be that the focus on steady-state properties is also unfortunate; what they want to achieve at all costs is to grow faster than developed countries.

Listening to these criticisms, I would defend the paper by saying that it was not meant to be immediately useful. Its usefulness should be judged in terms of the research which it will inspire, rather than of its policy implications.

5 Technology and International Trade: a Heckscher–Ohlin Approach[1]

Carl Hamilton and
Hans Tson Söderström (Sweden)

I INTRODUCTION

The step from Ricardo to Heckscher–Ohlin in international trade theory carried with it some optimistic overtones with respect to the international distribution of income. The factor price equalisation theorem reduced the problem of rich and poor nations to a question of trade, capital accumulation and functional distribution of income. The promotion of free trade would in the long run be sufficient to equalise between countries the rewards of labour and capital. Reality's failure to comply with this theoretical prediction has produced a variety of suggestions as to which simplifying assumptions of the Heckscher–Ohlin model are not fulfilled in the real world.

The problem of non-identical production functions between countries seems to be generally accepted as one of the—if not *the*—major obstacles for the empirical applicability of the Heckscher–Ohlin model. At a theoretical level we have Jones' (1970) result that major theorems derived from the Heckscher–Ohlin approach, including the factor price equalisation theorem, disappear if technologies are allowed to differ between countries. At an empirical level we have a host of studies (a sample is quoted below) demonstrating that technologies applied in similar industries do indeed differ significantly between countries. The combined effect of these two observations has seemingly been a major blow to the factor proportions approach to the international allocation of resources and distribution of income. The answer to Harry Johnson's (1970) 'fundamental question . . . whether orthodox international trade theory has once again reached a position of commitment to an antiquated and misleading model of the production process, which has to be rejected to further the progress of economic science' has thus appeared to be 'yes'. It has even been argued that '. . . the Heckscher–Ohlin model represents a step backward from the earlier Ricardian tradition' (Jones, 1970, p. 78), because of its disregard of technology differentials between countries. As a consequence we have witnessed an upsurge of 'neo-Ricardian' or 'neotechnology' models of international trade, which—alas—do not possess the simplicity, clarity and intuitive appeal of the Heckscher–Ohlin model.

In the view of the present authors this is a sad and unnecessary development. It is sad because the Heckscher–Ohlin approach constitutes a major building block in the theory of allocation of resources and distribution of income, with properties familiar to all economists. It is also an unnecessary development, because there is no *a priori* reason why production technology should be regarded as a *deus ex machina* rather than a phenomenon to be explained by economic theory. And there is no reason why the factor proportions approach should not be applied to the explanation of international differences in technology. Thus, to discard this approach because one of its assumptions is 'unrealistic' would be like throwing away not only the baby and bathwater but even the bathtub itself—a bathtub in which we were all quite comfortable.

The idea of explaining international differences in technology by reference to international differences in factor endowments is not new, of course. But for some reason it appears that this possibility has only been *mentioned* in the literature, never actually *analysed*. It seems to us that an answer to Harry Johnson's 'fundamental question' requires a thorough investigation of the explanatory power of the allegedly antiquated model with respect to new empirical observations. We shall therefore undertake an analysis of the standard two-by-two-by-two model, with the only modification that our model contains only one final output, the other product being an intermediate input—'technology'. Comparative advantage in technology production is determined only by factor endowments in the standard Heckscher–Ohlin tradition.

The present paper, then, attempts to investigate the usefulness of the standard factor proportions approach in the explanation of international differences in technology. The plan for our investigation should be clear from the organisation of the remainder of the paper, which is as follows: in Section II below the concepts of 'technology' and 'technology differentials' are discussed. We introduce a number of constraints on the technology concept, which will permit us to treat technology as a regular commodity in our analysis.

We then proceed to study the allocation of resources in an economy characterised by a production system where technology is endogenously determined. This is done first for a closed economy, Section III, and then for an open economy, Section IV, where the focus of the analysis will be on the dependence of production technology on international trade. In Sections V, VI and VII we shall attempt to substantiate the assumptions made in Section II by reference to empirical studies of technology differentials, technology transfer, etc. We hope to demonstrate that a much larger subset than is commonly believed of what goes under the label of 'technology' can be sorted into the technology concept used in our analysis. Even so, it is quite clear that only a subset of technology can be handled by so restrictive a model. The explanatory power of the factor proportions approach in situations with observed significant technology differentials between countries will therefore be subjected to renewed discussion in the final section, when we attempt to summarise our findings and evaluate our results by returning to Harry Johnson's 'fundamental question'.

II   THE TECHNOLOGY CONCEPT

The starting point for our analysis is the empirical observation that in production of a certain amount of a well-defined homogeneous final output, Q, primary factor requirements differ between countries, even at the same relative factor prices. The simplest way of analytically representing this observation is to apply the notion of internationally differing production functions, that is,

$$Q = f_i(K_V, L_V), \tag{1}$$

where f_i thus denotes the particular production function of country i, and K_V and L_V represent the input of capital and labour at the 'shopfloor level', where the measurement is undertaken.

The statement that such intercountry differences in production functions render the Heckscher–Ohlin model invalid is not in general correct. As has been pointed out (Haberler, 1961, p. 19; Ohlin, 1977, p. 101; Findlay, 1977b, p. 65), it is always possible to attribute differences in output resulting from equal inputs of conventional labour and capital, *either* to the existence of some (several) additional factor(s) of production, *or* to differences in the *quality* of labour and/or capital, and hence to maintain identical specifications of production functions between countries. The Heckscher–Ohlin model can in principle accommodate situations with more than two primary factors of production or with conventional factors weighted by quality.

It is assumed in this paper that observed intercountry differences in production functions can be represented by internationally differing factor weights, that is:

$$Q = f(b_i K_V, a_i L_V), \tag{2}$$

where $f(\ )$ applies to all countries, and b_i and a_i are the factor weights specific to country i. It is furthermore assumed that these factor weights are uniquely determined by a scalar measure of *technology input*, T_i, that is, $a_i = a(T_i)$ and $b'_i = b(T_i)$. In addition, it is assumed that the effect of technology input on factor weights is Hicks neutral, so that $a(T_i) = b(T_i)$. Consequently,

$$Q = f[a(T_i)K_V, a(T_i)L_V], \tag{3}$$

where T_i is technology input in country i. The Hicks neutrality assumption implies that the production function is (weakly) separable[2] in K_V and L_V on the one hand and T on the other. It can therefore be written

$$Q = Q[V(K_V, L_V); T_i] \tag{4}$$

where the technology-contingent production function $V(\ \ )$ will henceforth be referred to as a 'shopfloor production function'. Varying rates of technology input have the effect of changing the final output resulting from a given level of shopfloor input without affecting the marginal rate of substitution between K_V and L_V.

It is assumed that production function $Q[\ \ ]$ is linear homogeneous in V *and* T.[3] Consequently, we can write

$$Q = V(K_V, L_V)Q[1; \tau] = V(K_V, L_V)q(\tau) \tag{5}$$

where *technology intensity*, $\tau = T/V$, denotes technology input per unit of shopfloor production, and $q(\ \ )$ is a non-decreasing concave function of τ. Varying intensities of technology input can now be represented by a family of isomorphic unit isoquants in the $K_V - L_V$ space. In Figure 1, $\overline{Q}$ stands for one unit of Q and $0 < \tau_0 < \tau_1 < \tau_2 < \tau^*$.

We can now let τ_0, τ_1, and τ_2 represent the prevailing intensity of technology in production at different points in time, or in different

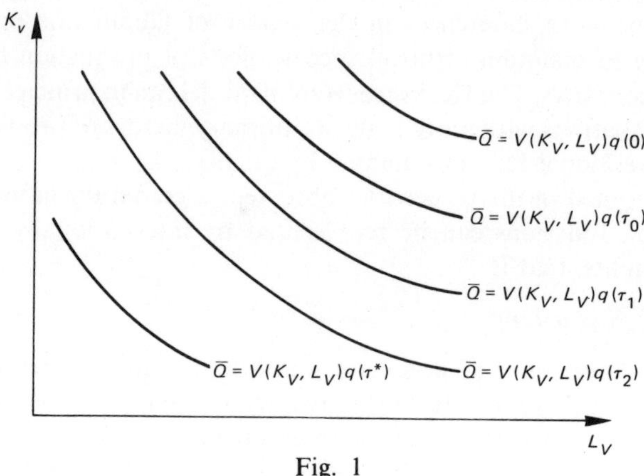

Fig. 1

locations at the same point in time. In particular, the literature on technology differentials in international trade usually seems to take as a point of departure that an exogenously given τ is identical for all producers within each country, but that τ differs between countries. This may be a valid approach to the extent that technology can be regarded as a free public good, like hours of sunshine, which affects agricultural output.

In this paper, in contrast, it is assumed that a *free access technology*, consisting of the application of the most elementary production principles, and defined by $Q = V(K_V, L_V)q(0)$, is available at zero resource cost worldwide. It is then assumed that producers in any country can allocate resources to an increase of technology input over and above the free access level; in other words technology takes the status of *a produced intermediate input in production*. The production function for technology, $T = T(K_T, L_T)$, is assumed to be linear homogeneous and identical between countries.

By production of technology is meant the resource-consuming activity of identifying production problems, searching over existing technological knowledge for a solution, adapting the solution to the specific situation, adapting other inputs in the production process to the new technical solution, and continuously supervising and maintaining the smooth running of the production process under varying technical conditions. It is evident that production of technology input, as understood here, is not just an R and D activity in the traditional sense.

In fact, it may involve no R and D element at all. Our concept of technological input is closer to the coordinating activities of management in general, required to carry on an enterprise where 'not all markets are well established or clearly defined and/or in which the relevant parts of the production function are not completely known' (Leibenstein, 1968). Consequently, technology input is not assumed to accumulate into a capital asset over time, but to fulfil the same role in production as a lubricant which increases the productivity of labour and capital.

The application of the most advanced principles of production, as given by the general state of knowledge at a certain point in time ('the book of blueprints') defines the *technology frontier*, τ^*. Beyond this limit further increases in technology intensity will have no factor augmenting effects on shopfloor production. The book of blueprints, and therefore τ^*, is assumed to be identical between countries at any point in time. Returning to equation (1), observed international differences in production functions can now (by assumption) be entirely attributed to differences in technology intensity, τ. This variable will be endogenously determined for closed and open economies in the ensuing analysis.

The assumptions made so far can be summaried as follows:

(1) The production function for final output is separable in (technology-contingent) shopfloor production, V, and technology input, T:

$$Q = Q[V(K_V, L_V); T],$$

where Q and V are twice continuously differentiable linear homogeneous functions of their respective arguments.

(2) There exists a well-defined scalar-valued technology production function, $T(K_T, L_T)$, which is also twice continuously differentiable, and linear homogeneous in K_T and L_T.

In addition, we shall derive our analytical results under the assumption of an efficient market allocation of technology. This requires two additional constraints on the technology concept.

(3) Technology is a private good, that is, it does not possess the public good character of knowledge and information in general. Technology input is consumed in the production process, and is not freely available to other users as well.

(4) Technology is appropriable and traded under full information.

Assumptions (3) and (4) are brought out explicitly at this point, because it is important to bear in mind what is implied when an efficient market allocation of technology is postulated in the analytical sections. What has bothered earlier writers in the area of trade and technology is of course the *non-fulfilment* of some or all of assumptions (1) to (4). As we shall argue more elaborately in Section VI below, we think there is good reason to believe that a substantial part of observed differentials in production technology can be attributed to a technology concept which reasonably well fulfils our assumptions. Furthermore, we find it convenient from an analytical point of view to start out with the simplest possible representation of technology, which makes our model completely analogous to the textbook version of the Heckscher–Ohlin model. We shall return to the complications caused by the non-fulfilment of various assumptions in the concluding section.

III RESOURCE ALLOCATION WITH ENDOGENOUS TECHNOLOGY IN A CLOSED ECONOMY

Resource allocation under competitive equilibrium in the closed economy is determined by maximisation of aggregate output, Q, subject to the production function

$$Q = Q[V(K_V, L_V); T(K_T, L_T)] \tag{4}$$

and to the resource constraints

$$K_V + K_T = \overline{K} \text{ and } L_V + L_T = \overline{L}.$$

The normal way to solve this problem is of course to 'maximise out' V and T on the assumption that they are always optimally selected. This would leave us with the integrated production function $Q = g(\overline{K}, \overline{L})$. It will prove fruitful for our purposes, however, to keep the production process disintegrated and to focus precisely on the optimal input selection. Output is maximised when the marginal value products of the two factors are equalised between shopfloor production and production of technology. This is illustrated in a familiar way in Figure 2 below. Factor intensities are assumed to differ between the two production activities $V(\ )$ and $T(\ )$, so the transformation set is strictly convex. The point of tangency between the transformation curve, $\overline{V} - \overline{T}$, and the highest attainable Q isoquant determines the allocation of resources between V and T, and thereby the *optimal technology intensity*, $\tau_1 = T_1/V_1$, that is, the optimal input of technology per unit of shopfloor value added. The optimal technology intensity is indicated in Figure 2 by

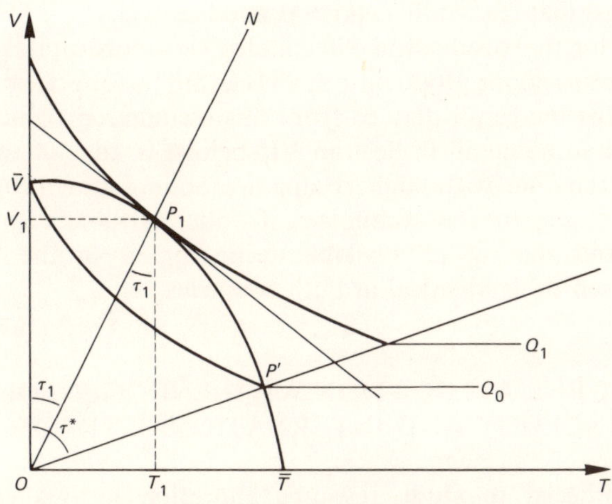

Fig. 2

the slope of the bisector ON. As Figure 2 demonstrates it will not normally be optimal to employ all factors in shopfloor production, thereby applying only the free access technology. That would have resulted in a final output of

$$Q[V(\bar{K}, \bar{L}); 0] = Q_0 < Q_1$$

As factors are withdrawn from shopfloor production, V, and applied to production of technology, T, total output increases up to the point where technology intensity reaches τ_1. If even more factors are used for approaching the technology frontier, total output will decline. It is therefore clear that—given limited resources and increasing opportunity cost of technology input—the optimal technology is not necessarily *on* the technology frontier as determined by τ^*, where the Q isoquants have a kink. An attempt by the economy in Figure 2 to produce on the technology frontier would reduce final output to Q_0 (production point P').

The marginal rate of transformation at the production point, P_1, determines the price of shopfloor production relative to the price of technology input, $\Omega = P_V/P_T$.[4] For the closed economy it is now possible to derive relative prices, $P_V/P_T = \Omega$, relative factor rewards, $\omega = w/r$ and technology intensity, $\tau = (T/V)$, as functions of the capital–labour ratio ($k = \overline{K}/\overline{L}$) alone (see Söderström, 1977). It can be demonstrated that $\Omega'(k) > 0$, $\omega'(k) > 0$, and finally that $\tau'(k) > 0$, under the assumption that production of technology is a more capital-intensive process than shopfloor production at all relevant factor price ratios. The implication of the result derived from this assumption (which will be discussed in some detail in Section VII below) is, that of two closed economies the one with higher capital–labour endowment will be producing closer to the technology frontier, although production functions and the set of available technologies—in the 'book of blueprints' sense—is identical in both countries.

IV   RESOURCE ALLOCATION WITH ENDOGENEOUS TECHNOLOGY AND INTERNATIONAL TRADE

We now proceed to study resource allocation in two economies characterised by a production system as described in the previous section, when trade in technology input and the composite final output is opened up. It is assumed that the two countries differ in capital–labour endowments, but that the technology frontier, free access technology, and the three production functions $Q[\ \ ]$, $V(\ \ )$, and $T(\ \ )$ are all identical between the two countries. It is also assumed that technology input can be exchanged for the composite final output in international trade.

In the open economy context it is important to recall the flow and private good character of technology. Under our assumptions, technology can be *either* used as an input in domestic production, *or* traded internationally in exchange for final output. We shall therefore need to distinguish between domestically produced technology, T, technology used as an input in domestic production, T_Q, and internationally traded technology, T_N:

$$T = T_Q + T_N.$$

It should be noted that T_N can take on negative values, and it is therefore possible to have $T_Q > T$.

In the trade analysis we shall need a transformation curve between the two tradeables, Q and T_N. To construct such a curve we make use of the transformation curve in Figure 2, reproduced as production block $0_1 V_1 T_1$ in Figure 3. Varying amounts of technology trade can be represented by sliding this production block horizontally in the co-ordinate system which determines the isoquants, and measuring tech-

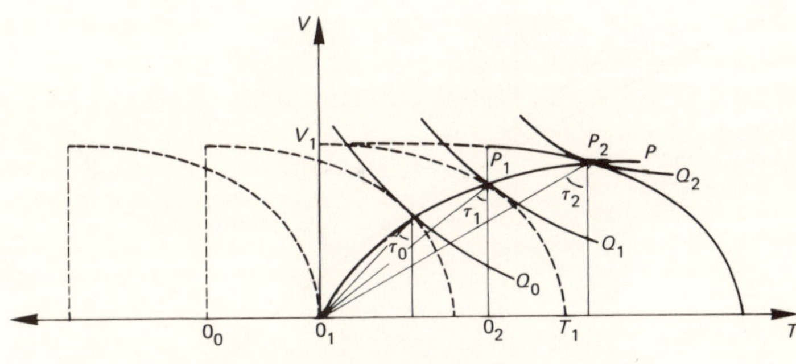

Fig. 3

nology exports by the distance from the origin of the production block to the origin of the co-ordinate system. This permits us to determine—for each level of technology exports—the optimal input combination of the remaining factors in domestic production.

When the two origins coincide we are back in Figure 2; the production point is P_1, volume of final output is Q_1, and trade does not take place. This provides us with a point of reference on the $Q - T_N$ transformation curve: point P_1 in Figure 4.

Export of technology is illustrated by sliding the production block to the left in the co-ordinate system (Figure 3). With the origin of the production block at 0_0, technology export amounts to $0_0 0_1$ and production of final output is reduced to Q_0. At the new production point P_0 technology intensity is $\tau_0 < \tau_1$, that is, domestic shopfloor production of final output takes place further away from the technology frontier (cf. Figure 1). P_0 is given in Figure 4 by co-ordinates Q_0 and T_{N0}.

Technology import is represented by shifting the production block to the right in the co-ordinate system in Figure 3. With the origin at 0_2 technology imports amount to $0_1 0_2$ and production of final output can be increased to Q_2. Technology intensity at the new production point P_2 will have increased to τ_2, which moves the unit isoquant in shopfloor production closer to the technology frontier (cf. Figure 1); P_2 is also reproduced in Figure 4.

A complete transformation curve between Q and T_N as depicted in Figure 4 can thus be constructed by sliding the production block back and forth in Figure 3 and checking off the corresponding production

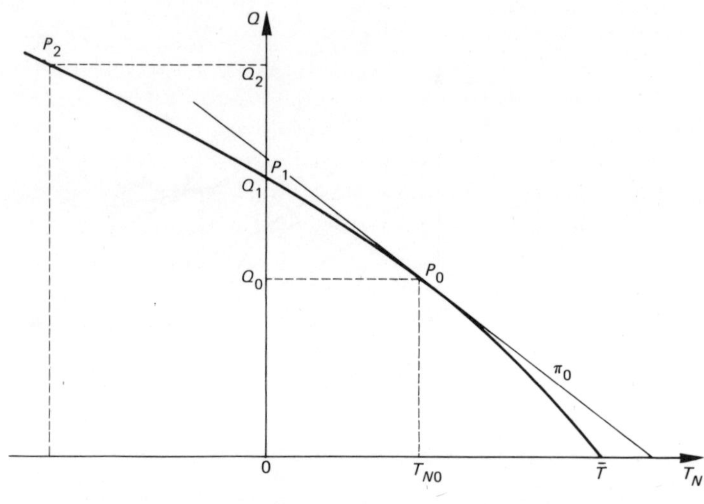

Fig. 4

points in Figure 4. This provides us with all the tools necessary to determine technology in shopfloor production as a function of prices in international trade. Consider any relative price, say $\pi_0 = (P_Q/P_T)$ established on world markets. This relative price determines uniquely production point P_0 on the $Q - T_N$ transformation curve. To this production point corresponds a unique position of the production block in Figure 3 with a corresponding production point P_0. At this point technology intensity τ_0 is uniquely determined, and τ_0 in turn determines the position of the unit Q isoquant in the $K_V - L_V$ space, as depicted in Figure 1. This process can be used to derive technology intensity in production of final output as a function of world market prices alone.

Under autarchy the relative price of final output in terms of technology is—as noted above—determined solely by factor endowments. In a free trade equilibrium without transport or transfer costs this relative price will be equalised between countries. It can be demonstrated that all the celebrated theorems of international trade theory that are derived from a model with two final outputs and no intermediates continue to hold in this model with one final output and one intermediate input under the assumptions made (Söderström, 1977). On top of these theorems we can therefore add a corollary on 'technology equalisation', stating that—within the framework of the present model—technology intensity in shopfloor production will be equalised between countries in a free trade equilibrium with incomplete specialisation, irrespective of differences in primary factor endowments.[5]

Returning to our original problem, we have seen how the view of technology as a produced intermediate input in production can throw some light on questions concerning international technology differentials. If technology cannot be traded between countries, comparative advantage in technology production—which can in turn be attributed to relative factor endowments—will determine shopfloor production technology. In particular—under the factor intensity assumptions made—a capital-rich country will be producing closer to the technology frontier than will a capital-poor country. Given the non-tradeability of technology this will be an optimal state of affairs. It should be noted that any attempt to make the capital-poor economy apply more 'advanced' methods of production (in order to save on shopfloor factor input) will disturb the optimal allocation of resources and bring about a decline in real income.

If, on the other hand, technology can be internationally traded, we should observe capital-rich economies as exporters of technology in exchange for final output. As a consequence we should observe a long-run tendency toward international technology equalisation. This conjecture, however, rests entirely on the assumptions made in Section II above. Some of these assumptions will be subjected to empirical investigation in the next three sections. Section V presents empirical evidence on the existence and nature of technology differentials between countries. Section VI presents the case for technology as a private good and Section VII discusses the relative factor intensities in shopfloor production and technology production. Even so, a number of assumptions used are left unsubstantiated. To these assumptions we shall return for a brief discussion in the concluding section of the paper.

V TECHNOLOGY DIFFERENTIALS—EMPIRICAL EVIDENCE

Technology differentials are not easy to ascertain empirically. Ideally one would like to have access to studies in which points like 2 and 3 in Figure 5 were compared, that is, where exactly the same factor intensity is used in both a developed and a developing country.[6] The difference in shopfloor labour ($L_{V2} - L_{V3}$) and shopfloor capital ($K_{V2} - K_{V3}$) require-

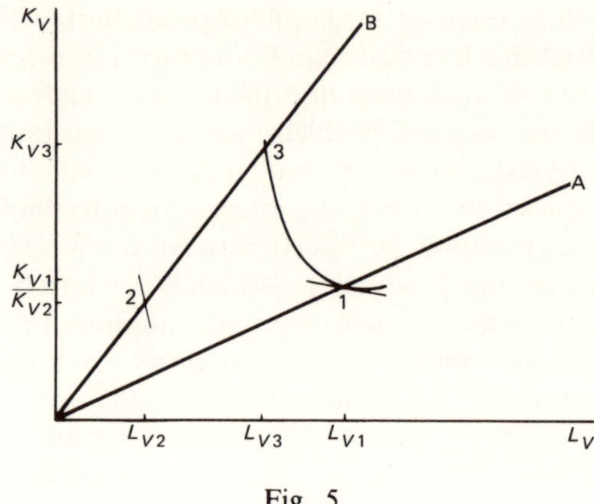

Fig. 5

ment per unit of final output would then provide a measure of technology differentials to be matched against technology input.

Comparisons of this kind between developed and developing countries are few and far between. Clague (1967) and (1970) compared industrial efficiency at the shopfloor level[7] between Peru and the United States. He tried to model a 'laboratory' situation of the kind described above and defined a difference in efficiency in two industries in the following way:

> To say that in a particular industry, country A's efficiency is only half that of country B is to say that, if A's workers were endowed with as much capital per man as B's workers, and if the factories in A were expanded or contracted until their average size was equal to that of B's factories, then output per worker would be half as large in A as in B.

In his empirical work Clague could observe (see Figure 5) three things: (a) lines A and B representing the capital-labour ratios of Peru and the USA respectively, (b) points 1 and 2 showing the amounts of capital and labour needed in Peru and the USA to produce one unit of output and (c) the factor price lines of the two countries. Specifying a CES production function for each industry[8] it was possible to draw a Peruvian isoquant to point 3 in the diagram, that is, point 3 shows what the capital and labour requirements would be in Peru if in the Peruvian factories the capital–labour ratio were the same as in the US factories.

The author then also adjusted for differences in scale between factories in the two countries and, finally, arrived at a measure of 'Peruvian relative efficiency' in different industries. The result is reproduced in Table 1 below; for example, for shirts Clague's result is interpreted as the US input of labour (having normalised for input of capital) is only 40.70 per cent of the Peruvian input of labour.

TABLE 1
PERUVIAN RELATIVE EFFICIENCY

Shirts	40.70
Shoes	54.41
Hosiery	29.63
Leather tanning	33.10
Cotton textiles	27.66
Glass containers	34.36
Tyres	56.90
Raw sugar	80.52
Chemicals	97.92
Wheat flour	73.78
Cement	85.52

Source: Clague (1967), p. 489

A second study using a different approach from Clague's to measure the extra labour and capital is Doyle (1965). Doyle compared the costs of two cement plants, one located in Indonesia and the other in California. Both plants were of the same US design (the same 'wet' process) and manufacture; both plants started in the first half of 1957. The study covered 1957–60. The Indonesian plant—although in scale about two-thirds of the US plant—used more shopfloor labour to carry out the same tasks as in the US plant. In total, about four times as many employees (at all levels) were used in the Indonesian plant.[9] 'Depreciation cost' and 'interest cost' per tonne was about 4.6 times higher in the Indonesian plant. Looking at the overall production cost per tonne, it was found to be about 1.5 times higher in the Indonesian plant.[10]

The conclusion from these two empirical studies is that it seems likely that international technology differentials of a significant magnitude do in fact exist at the shopfloor level.

VI   TECHNOLOGY—A PRIVATE GOOD

One of the standard assumptions of international trade theory is that knowledge about the set of technologies once produced is available without cost to all producers and that the use of this knowledge by one producer does not reduce its availability to others—in short, that technology is a public good.

In our model we have abandoned this view of technology as it seems disturbingly unrealistic to us for the following two reasons.

(1) It ignores the search cost involved in finding the right blueprint to use. It also ignores the fact that, as a rule, firm-specific and product-specific (and perhaps also country-specific) adaptations have to be undertaken every time a blueprint is going to be put into practice. Such adaptations are not costless, of course, and lend to technology a private rather than a public good character.

In the literature there is qualitative empirical information on these costs of technology. The information is contained in studies on choice of techniques in developing countries and is concerned with both the investment decision and ascertaining actual choices *ex post*.[11]

When discussing the empirical literature on the resource cost of technology, it is useful to keep Figure 5 in mind. *We* would like to have measures of the resource cost of going from point 1 to point 3, but we realise that the authors mentioned below discuss the cost of technology in less narrowly depicted situations than ours. However, the resource costs involved are of the same kind in all the cases.

(2) 'The book of blueprints' itself—even though *intrinsically* a public good—is often subjected to monopolistic restrictions in order to turn the knowledge into an appropriable private good. Such restrictions are often supported by the legal and institutional framework of economies, in order to protect incentives to production of new knowledge. For example, new (foreign) technology is often available only in the form of patents, licences, and trademarks against royalty payments. With regard to developing countries such technology costs have been looked into in several studies (see Helleiner, 1975, p. 163, for references). Sometimes also the technology producer can appropriate blueprint knowledge without support of the legal system. It is well known that there is a cost of new technology when it can only be acquired embodied in physical capital (machinery or complete production plants) in human capital (instruction courses, consulting services), or in intermediate products (IBM punching cards, Coca Cola extract).

In an empirical study of factor intensities in Kenya, Pack (1976, p. 53) noted:

> The neoclassical textbook view assumes there is a *deus ex machina* at work, translating factor prices into correct choice of technique, whereas such translation depends critically on the abilities and perception of a set of talented managers who may not exist in various factories . . . Technical adaptation is only part of the role of 'good' managers. Typically they are also responsible for searching the international market for appropriate equipment, whether used or not. This involves the ability to evaluate specifications in the listings of used machinery dealers as well as the catalogues of new equipment producers. We would argue that in the absence of technical expertise, appropriate relative factor prices may be of limited efficacy in achieving socially appropriate factor proportions.[12]

Pack goes on to infer (p. 55) that '[it] is quite clear in the Kenyan context that substantial productivity growth has taken place simply as a matter of reorganization of production and better training and supervision.'

In a comparative study of choice of techniques for can-making in Kenya, Tanzania and Thailand, Cooper, *et al.* (1975 p. 107, italics added) draw attention to the concept of availability of techniques

> The [comparative study of can-making] also shows that the concept of availability of different techniques needs to be more clearly formulated. What does 'availability' mean—in particular, what does it mean as far as the private decision-maker is concerned? In the first place, it seems clear that there are costs involved in establishing what is available. *The curious notion that what is available is in some way immediately known to everyone in the industry, or can be discovered at no cost, is not valid.*

Magee (1977, p. 11) takes up the same point: 'While economists frequently assume that engineers or technicians provide [production] functions, there are actually large and costly investments in information which must be made to create the most efficient methods of production'.

In several studies is also stressed the cost of adapting to local conditions (given that developing country factor prices are non-distorted). Thus Pickett, Forsyth and McBain (1974) in a study of two industries (sugar and footwear) in Ghana and Ethiopia as well as Wells (1972) in a study of fifty plants in Indonesia stress very much the role of an engineer in deciding the technology employed. The authors' argument is that the engineer, having been trained to handle modern, capital-intensive equipment, is always looking for 'engineering efficiency' (as opposed to economic efficiency) and is more at home with the modern capital-intensive techniques of the developed countries than with possible local alternatives. As the possibility of factor price distortions is given little weight by these authors, an alternative formulation is that the cost of locally adapted/identified techniques seems to be significant.

Several authors have also noted differences in the cost of search, adaptation and 'trial-and-error' between local firms in developing countries and subsidiaries of multinational firms.

In a paper by Hal Mason (1973) fourteen US subsidiaries and fourteen 'closely matched local counterparts' in Mexico and the Philippines were compared. It was found that the US firms used their resources differently from the local ones, and the reason given was that the US firms had already made an investment in learning by doing in the form of longer experience of industrial production (p. 353):

One inference we might draw from the skills data is as follows: United States firms have a long experience in the production of technically refined products and have developed well-defined producers for their production. Because of this, they can employ lower level skills in the production process. At the same time, however, to see that the procedures are being properly followed and implemented, a larger input of supervisory talent is required. Also, quality control is highly important and calls for a relatively large input of technical talent. Local firms on average are not as well endowed with information systems and well-defined production procedures. As a consequence they must use more accountants and rely on skilled workers more heavily.

What about search and adaptation costs within multinational firms? One would expect the resource cost to be lower within these firms compared with interfirm trade, as it seems that the problems of appropriability and other barriers to trade in technology would disappear or lose much of their importance. However, from a study by Teech (1977) of the cost of transmitting technical knowhow within multinational firms it seems that even within these firms the cost of technology can take on a significant magnitude. Thus Teech estimated that for his sample (p. 247), 'transfer costs' averaged 19 per cent of total project cost of the recipient and 'clearly, the data do not support the notion that technology is a stock of blueprints usable at nominal cost to all'.

So far we have been discussing industrial production only. It should be pointed out, however, that the cost of search, adaptation, and trial-and-error is at least as relevant in agricultural production. It is, for example, well known that in order to overcome the search cost for small, decentralised and independent production units like farms, governments in developed as well as developing countries have for a long time worked with demonstration farms, extension service, intensive agricultural district programmes, etc. That a new seed technology has to be adapted to local conditions is also common in agriculture. For instance, a necessary condition for spreading new high yielding varieties (the 'green revolution' for example) among cultivators, is continuous research on adaptation to specific local conditions. Just to quote one author—Myint (1972, pp. 8–9):

Firstly, research is needed to adapt the new high-yielding varieties to the divergent local conditions of different Southeast Asian countries. For instance, the Green Revolution has not spread to the Central Plain of Thailand, both because of the difficulties of water control and the unsuitability of the dwarf varieties to flood conditions. Secondly, more research is needed to make the new varieties of rice more appealing to the consumers' tastes. Otherwise the market for them will remain limited. Thirdly, in order to obtain the full benefits from the Green Revolution, a more intensive use of land and multiple cropping is necessary. It has been suggested that in order to recover the overhead costs of the elaborate irrigation facilities when required, four or five crops may have to be grown annually on a given piece of land. This makes it especially important to diversify the crops, since the market for rice will be saturated soon. So far, of the new high-yielding varieties only rice has made its impact on Southeast Asia. Research to widen the range of the Green Revolution to other crops is an important condition for maintaining its momentum.

A pertinent example of a gradual increase in the private good nature of search and adaptation has been provided by Solo (1966, p. 483):

Take the hypothetical need to control insects on a tropical plantation. There might be equipment in use elsewhere which can be used for spraying insecticides, but it would have to be adapted on the spot to climate and terrain, to the shape of the infested plant, and to the locus of its infestation or to the skill of indigenous labor . . . It might then be necessary to compound and produce an appropriate insecticide which would require a knowledge of the chemistry of pesticides and of the habits and vulnerabilities of the insect to be controlled . . . And if, as is frequently the case, not enough is yet known about the habits and vulnerabilities of the pest or the pesticidal efficacy of locally available materials or the possibilities of control through the use of the pest's own parasites, then a conceptual and analytical apparatus of science must be turned to search for the new information which is required.

Our conclusion from this empirical section is that technology input definitely appears to be resource-consuming, not transmitted without cost among producers and that it very often seems to be firm and/or product specific. Our review of empirical studies has also enhanced the importance of distinguishing clearly between 'applied technology' and 'basic technological knowledge', as only the latter, perhaps, is non-firm (or non-product) specific and should correctly be described as a public good.

VII   PRODUCTION OF TECHNOLOGY—THE RELATIVELY CAPITAL-INTENSIVE ACTIVITY

The analysis in Sections III and IV raise the question of the relationship between factor endowments and technology. Considering two closed economies, can differences in factor endowments between those economies explain differences in the technology employed? The answer is yes, provided that production of technology and shopfloor production do not have the same factor intensity. For the empirical applicability of our model we need a stronger assumption to be fulfilled—that production of technology is the relatively capital-intensive activity. If human capital and physical capital are permitted to be aggregated into one single capital concept (discussed below), the assumption about production of technology being the relatively capital-intensive activity seems, judging from the empirical literature, to be a harmless one.[13]

The argument in favour of aggregation is that at any point in time one can either invest in physical capital or human skills. Both choices involve a reduction of today's consumption to achieve a higher future consumption; human and physical capital are two different kinds of jelly—but both still jelly.

In his evaluation of trade theories Hufbauer (1970)—discussing the factor proportions theory—takes up precisely the question of aggregation of physical and human capital in the theory of international trade (p. 176):

> Since skill-intensive commodities overlap with capital-intensive commodities, while the acquisition of human skills and physical capital both involve acts of saving, there is no reason not to join forces by combining human skills and physical capital into a single measure of man-made resources. Indeed, Bhagwati and Kenen have advocated this approach on a theoretical plane, some of the earlier cited authors have used it in their empirical work, and Lary has put it to fruitful use in examining the export prospects of developing countries. [Bhagwati (1965), Kenen (1965), Lary (1968).] [In a footnote:] Kenen and Yudin (1965), Bharadwaj and Bhagwati (1967) and Roskamp and McMeekin (1968) where, generally speaking, human capital has been superimposed on physical capital.

Lary's (1968) well-known study of *Imports of Manufactures from Less Developed Countries* is of particular interest. Lary used as a guide to total factor intensities in different manufacturing industries value added per employee which 'permits an integrated treatment of the flows of services rendered by capital and labor in manufacturing. This contrasts with most previous studies in which the contribution of capital is measured as a stock rather than as a flow of services, and that of labor merely by total man hours or man years without regard to differences in skills (p. 19).'[14]

Branson and Monoyios (1977), however, are critical towards aggregation of human and physical capital in explaining US trade. Their view is based on an empirical study showing a significantly positive correlation between human capital and US net exports across commodities, and a negative, but only 'marginally significant', correlation between physical capital and US net exports across commodities. Branson and Monoyios provide (p. 113) three arguments why, in their view, aggregation of human and physical capital is questionable:

> First, it eliminates the possibility of detection of positive correlation of net exports with human capital inputs and negative correlation

with physical capital inputs, if such exists in the data. Second, it seems unlikely that the two types of capital are close substitutes in production, which is the condition for such aggregation in production models. Finally, economists who investigate the role of human capital in production more frequently combine it with the labor input as an 'effective labor' adjustment.

On the last point they refer to Griliches (1970) who 'presents a tentative test of the hypothesis that human capital and physical capital are, in fact, *complements* in production. His results are not clear, but they certainly do not suggest that the two factors are perfect substitutes. See Griliches (1970, pp. 106–9).'

What can be said about these arguments? The first one seems to us to be an argument against aggregation not only in the present context but a warning against aggregation in general, the reason being that in aggregation one loses pieces of information which are available in an analysis at a more disaggregated level. However, whether aggregation is acceptable or not depends on the specific question posed by the investigators. Branson and Monoyios are worried about losing information on the behaviour of components of the aggregate, that is, human and physical capital. But if one is primarily interested in the *total* flow of services from both kinds of capital, and not the composition of the capital concept, the authors' objection to aggregation seems unwarranted.

The second argument, that 'it seems unlikely that the two types of capital are close substitutes in production', appears to us to depend entirely upon the time perspective chosen. In the short run Branson and Monoyios may in some instances be right but surely it must be the long run or the very long run which are of interest when discussing, for example, the question of determinants of international trade flows, and in such a discussion the crucial question must be the overall level of consumption foregone rather than the composition of investment (given that resources are efficiently allocated).[15] In the time-perspective of this paper it seems very reasonable to us to assume that capital is malleable into human or physical capital.

Branson and Monoyios' third argument against aggregation is really just an observation that others, for example Griliches (1970), have chosen a different approach from the human capital one when they have investigated education and skills. Branson and Monoyios do not, however, explain why that approach is inherently superior to the human capital one. For example, Griliches, posing a different question from ours, may have attained at least as good results had he used a different approach from the one he actually used.[16]

The conclusion of this section is that objections raised against aggregating human and physical capital seems unwarranted, and therefore that our assumption about technical progress being the more capital-intensive activity is a reasonable one.

VIII CONCLUSIONS

The aim of the present paper has not been to present another specific model of 'technology transfer' or 'diffusion of technology'. Our ambition has been of a more methodological nature, in other words, to demonstrate that at least part of the technology issue can be usefully handled within the framework of conventional trade theory in the Heckscher–Ohlin tradition. Technology can be regarded as a produced intermediate good. Comparative advantage in technology production can be determined by reference to factor endowments. Under autarchy we will observe some countries (under our assumptions: the capital-rich ones) producing closer to the technology frontier than other countries. This should surprise us no more than to observe Portugal under autarchy consume more wine relative to cloth than England even under the assumption of identical community indifference curves. Trade in technology, on the other hand, will tend to equalise technology *input* between countries, even though technology *output* will be more unequally distributed over countries than under autarchy.[17] Technology differentials between countries, according to this view, must be attributed to impediments to international trade in technology. Also, from an efficiency point of view, technology differentials should not be regarded as a problem of 'X-efficiency' or 'free lunches', but rather as a problem of *allocative inefficiency*, provided the impediments to technology trade could be eliminated without costs in terms of factor use or market distortions.

We hope to have demonstrated in this paper that if only technology can be regarded as a compeitively produced intermediate input, it poses no methodological problems to apply the standard Heckscher–Ohlin model to the 'technology issue', and that all the basic results of pure trade theory will easily carry over. The principal remaining doubt about the applicability of the standard model in the present context must therefore refer to the validity of our technology concept. A few remarks on this problem will conclude the paper.

It is advisable in this matter, we believe, to distinguish between *basic technological knowledge* on the one hand and *applied production technology* on the other. The expansion of basic knowledge, more or less by definition, resists analytical explanation, and it seems reasonable therefore to let the prevailing state of knowledge at each moment of time be exogenous to economic models. Basic knowledge, however, is a true public good, and it seems hard to make a case for international differences in its availability. Applied production technology, on the other hand, is something entirely different. It is the result of continuous observations on the state of the world and of the translation of these observations into different factor allocations. The outcome of this process will be dependent on (exogenous) available basic knowledge and the amount of resources which are allocated to the process.

These propositions seem to be fairly uncontroversial. But there are a number of points where our specification of technology production and the role of technology in the production process differs significantly from established standards and can be subjected to serious doubt.

(1) Technology production can be a function of things other than the instantaneous rate of input of capital and labour allotted to this purpose. First, it can be a function of *past* inputs of labour and capital for technology production, so that technology accumulates to a capital *stock* over time.[18] Secondly, technology can be a *joint output* resulting from the production of final output or from the accumulation of physical capital; what is commonly labelled 'learning by doing' (Arrow, 1962).

(2) Production of final output may not be *separable* in shopfloor production on the one hand and technology production on the other. Even weak separability is a fairly strong condition which is easily violated. There is a very relevant possibility of biased substitution effects, implying for instance that an increase in technology input has more capital-augmenting than labour-augmenting effects on shopfloor production. Such non-neutralities may cause a reversal of the factor intensity ranking with well-known consequences for the celebrated theorems.[19] A special case of such bias is the possibility that the factor-augmenting effects of a given technology input vary between different factor intensities—'localized technical progress' (Atkinson and Stiglitz, 1969). The value of technology will then differ between countries, depending on factor intensity, and render the preceding analysis invalid. Other special cases of non-neutralities, violating the separability condition, can also be envisaged.

(3) Even though the separability condition may hold, the *linear*

homogeneity assumption can be violated. In particular, if the final output function demonstrates constant returns to scale in shopfloor production alone, it will demonstrate increasing returns to scale in shopfloor production *and* technology input. This would preclude a competitive allocation of resources and destroy the celebrated theorems (see Kemp, 1969, Chapter 8).

(4) Even disregarding the possibility of increasing returns to scale, there are a number of questions with respect to the efficiency of a market allocation of resources in an economy where one of the produced goods is technology. First, there are the public goods and appropriability problems already discussed. To the extent that there are any *public good* elements in our technology concept, a market allocation of technology under full appropriability will be clearly inefficient because of the restrictions on technology use (see, however, Demsetz, 1969). If, on the other hand, technology is *inappropriable*, underproduction of technology will be a consequence of pure market allocation. Second, technology production has been described as a continuous search over technological knowledge for solution to new specific production problems. The outcome of any search process is by its very nature *uncertain*, and so the production of technology should appropriately be modelled as a problem of allocation under risk. Third, fully appropriate information is marketed under *monopolistic* conditions, which violates our assumption of perfectly competitive markets. The optimal trade policy of a technology exporting country entails full exploitation of its monopoly power in the foreign market (Rodriguez, 1975). However, if there exists a genuine threat of entry from successful imitators, it can be demonstrated that the optimal long-run monopoly price will always be below the short-run profit maximising price (Magee, 1977). Fourth, it is possible that technology can only be appropriated in conjunction with physical commodities into which it is 'embodied'. If technology is only marketed in embodied form it cannot be allocated independently of these commodities, and consequently only a constrained optimum can be reached. In the literature on direct foreign investment it is often assumed that technology can only be marketed embodied into machinery—'capital'—see for example, Berglas and Jones (1977).

We end at this stage our enumeration of complications in a Heckscher–Ohlin framework that may be caused by varying technology concepts, even though it could no doubt be possible to keep going for another few pages. It may be clarifying, however, to tabulate some of the dimensions of the technology concept, which are crucial for the selection of an appropriate model of 'technology and trade'. In

Table 2 below we have indicated nine dimensions, which are pertinent to our analysis, and for each dimension we have given a 'range'. It goes without saying that there are strong interdependences and considerable overlapping between several of these dimensions.

TABLE 2
DIMENSIONS OF THE TECHNOLOGY CONCEPT

1. Stock	——————— *	Flow
2. Public	——————— *	Private
3. Non-appropriable	——————— *	Appropriable
4. Embodied	——————— *	Disembodied
5. Non-tradeable	——————— *	Tradeable
6. Monopolistic market	——————— *	Competitive market
7. Learned (without resource cost)	——————— *	Produced
8. Labour-intensive production of technology	——————— *	Capital-intensive production of technology
9. Biased substitution effects	——————— *	Unbiased (Hick's neutral)

Going through the 'technology and trade' literature one might usefully try to nail down different authors' technology concepts with respect to these dimensions as a first step in identifying the reasons for the application of different models and the origin of conflicting results. The technology concept employed in the present paper is indicated by stars in Table 2. All these restrictions on the technology concept are necessary to squeeze it into the simple Heckscher–Ohlin framework and to reproduce the standard equalisation results.

As our references indicate, it is possible to incorporate other technology concepts into modified Heckscher–Ohlin models, and in some cases to retain the basic conclusions, although in revised or reinterpreted form. Harry Johnson's fundamental question is therefore passed on to the reader as a matter of judgement. If 'the technology factor' turns out to be a major determinant of trade flows, the international allocation of resources, and the international distribution of income, how should we go about modelling this phenomenon? Should we regard technology as just a sample commodity in the Heckscher–Ohlin framework and keep working with the standard model, adjusted for intermediate inputs, joint outputs, public goods, increasing returns to scale, monopolistic markets, risk and accumulation? Or should all these complications lead us to abandon the familiar paradigm? Should we thus set out for new models of international trade, where technology with all its specific characteristics is already from the beginning at the center of the stage, and where the traditional determinants of trade patterns are subordinated to this factor? Our ambition has not been to suggest a definite answer to this question, only to indicate that the former alternative may in many instances be a good starting point.

ENDNOTES

1. We have benefited from the comments and suggestions of M. Bruno, G. Calvo, R. Findlay, R. Jones, B. Ohlin and other participants in the Institute's workshop on trade theory, 11–23 August 1978.
2. The necessary and sufficient Leontief condition for weak separability is

$$\frac{\delta}{\delta T}\left(\frac{\delta Q/\delta K_V}{\delta Q/\delta L_V}\right) \equiv 0.$$

See, for example, (1975), p. XXXII.
3. This of course implies that Q demonstrates decreasing returns to scale in K_V and L_V alone.
4. To the extent that technology is traded on competitive markets this price ratio will be manifested in market prices. In the absence of markets for technology the (now implicit) price ratio will still be relevant in determining the allocation of resources within each firm.
5. For a formal proof of technology equalization in the present model, see Söderström (1977).
6. Figure 5 is based on Clague (1967), p. 488.
7. Note that administration and management efficiency were not measured in either of these two studies. 'Labor productivity was calculated using data for production workers only. Managerial personnel were excluded' (Clague, 1970, p. 190).
8. Clague applied a CES production function for intercountry comparisons in the way developed by Arrow *et al.* (1961).
9. Computed from Table 6.5 in Doyle (1965).
10. Computed from Table 6.1 in Doyle (1965). We have used an average shadow foreign exchange rate of 35:1. This rate is an approximation arrived at on the basis of Doyle's figures in Chapter 2. The figure of 1.5 times higher unit cost in Indonesia is an average over four periods. All computations above exclude investments in 'social overhead' which occurred in Indonesia but not in the USA.
11. If the investment cost is found to be higher in developing countries than in developed countries (for example, due to an initially higher cost of technology) this can be looked upon as a cost incurred in every period—the cost of interest and amortisation of a loan needed to cover the extra initial cost of technical progress.

12. A similar point is made by Helleiner (1975) and reported in Riedel (1975), p. 513:

> Moreover, because foreign firms in LDCs, particularly those engaged in the two types of activities just mentioned [that is extracting natural resources and supplying LDC markets which would otherwise have been precluded by trade barriers], often face little competition in LDC markets, the impact of input prices (and hence relative input availabilities) on the choice technique is rather weak.

13. Compare, for example, figures in Mansfield (1968) over research and development expenditure by industry with, for instance, value added by industry in Keesing (1965), Appendix, or various measures in Lary (1968), Appendix A.

14. It was pointed out to us that in an unpublished paper Bela Balassa (1977) has experimented with an aggregated measure of capital as well as with separate variables for physical and human capital in an empirical development stages approach to comparative advantage. In a similar kind of investigation, S. Hirsch (1975) has applied an aggregated capital concept. On the specific question of complementarity of physical and human capital, see Fallon and Layard (1975).

15. Cf. Findlay's (1977a) model of international trade which explicitly incorporates a time element.

16. This possibility is also discussed by Griliches (1970, p. 80):

> [N]ote that I have not elaborated on the alternative of using the growth in 'human capital' to construct [Divisia index of input quality labour]. For productivity measurement purposes, we want indexes based on 'rental' rather than 'stock' values as weights. It can be shown (see Selowsky, 1967), that if similar data are used consistently, there is no operational difference between the quality index described [on pp. 72–75 in Griliches' text] and a 'human capital times rate of return' approach, provided the capital valuation is made at 'market prices' (i.e., based on observed rentals) rather than at production costs. For my purposes, the construction of 'human capital' series would only add to the 'roundaboutness' of the calculations. Such calculations (or at least the calculation of the rates of return associated with them) are, of course required for discussions of optimal investment in education programs.

Note also that Griliches is very careful indeed in interpreting his results (pp. 108–9):

> A preliminary and crude foray into data for twenty-eight 'two-digit' industries in the United States in 1949 and 1963 yielded some not very strong support for the hypothesis outlined here. There is a positive relation between *capital* per unskilled worker and *skilled worker* per unskilled worker across these industries. The simple weighted correlation coefficient between the logarithms of these variables is 0.48 in 1949, 0.50 in 1963, and 0.47 for the change in these variables between these two years.

While such correlation coefficients are 'significant' at conventional levels, the over-all fit is quite poor and there are a number of notable outliers. The chemical industry has a high capital–labor and a high skill ratio, but the electric machinery industry has a high skill ratio and a relatively low capital–labor ratio, while the utility industries have very high capital–labor ratios but only average skill ratios. Similarly, the highest rates of growth in capital-per-man occurred in this period in mining and construction. Mining had also probably the highest rate of growth in the relative number of highly skilled workers, while construction had one of the lowest. There are no easy answers.

17. In the spirit of the Heckscher–Ohlin tradition it is also possible to demonstrate how the use of technology, even when technology is non-tradeable, can be equalised between countries by way of trade in two final outputs which differ in technology intensity. Complete technology equalisation will result in the absence of complete specialisation in the two final outputs. A formal demonstration of this point is deferred to a later paper.

18. The number of models of 'dynamic comparative advantage' with capital accumulation endogenously determined is too large to call for any specific reference (see for example, Kemp (1969), Chapter 10). Findlay (1977a) with exogenous factors reduced to labour and rate of time preference is perhaps more 'basic' than others.

19. The robustness of the celebrated trade theorems under biased substitution effects in the general context of intermediate inputs is investigated in a number of papers expanding on a pioneering article by Vanek (1963). Some of the more recent contributions are discussed in Riedel (1976). A model with induced substitution bias is analysed in Chipman (1970).

REFERENCES

Arrow, K. J., 'The Economic Implications of Learning by Doing', *Review of Economic Studies* (June 1962).

Arrow, K. J., Chenery, H. B., Minhas, B. S., and Solow, R. M. (1961), 'Capital–Labour Substitution and Economic Efficiency', *The Review of Economics and Statistics*, vol. XLIII, no. 3 (1961).

Atkinson, A. B. and Stiglitz, J., 'A New View of Technological Change', *Economic Journal* (September 1969).

Balassa, B., (1977), 'A "Stages Approach" to Comparative Advantage', paper presented at the 5th World Congress of the International Economic Association, Tokyo (August 29–September 3 1977).

Berglas, E. and Jones, R. W., 'The Export of Technology', in *Carnegie-Rochester Conference Series on Public Policy*, vol. 7 (1977).

Bhagwati, J., 'The Pure Theory of International Trade: A Survey', reprinted in *Surveys of Economic Development*, vol. II (Cambridge, 1965).

Bhalla, A., (ed.), *Technology and Employment in Industry* (Geneva: ILO, 1975).

Bharadwaj, R. and Bhagwati, J., 'Human Capital and the Pattern of Foreign Trade: The Indian Case', *Indian Economic Journal* (October 1967).

Branson, W. H. and Monoyios, N., 'Factor Inputs in US Trade', *Journal of International Economics* (May 1977) (IIES reprint no. 71).

Caves, R. and Jones, R., *World Trade and Payments*, 2nd edn (Boston, Toronto: Little, Brown, 1973).

Chipman, J. S., (1970), 'Induced Technical Change and Patterns of International Trade', in R. Vernon (ed.), *The Technology Factor in International Trade* (NBER, Columbia University Press, 1970).

Clague, C., 'An International Comparison of Industrial Efficiency: Peru and The United States', *Review of Economics and Statistics*, vol. 49 (1967).

Clague, C., 'The Determinants of Efficiency in Manufacturing Industries in an Underdeveloped Country', *Economic Development and Cultural Change*, vol. 18 (1970) pp. 188–205.

Cooper, C., Kaplinsky, R., Bell, R., and Satyarakwit, W. 'Choice of Techniques for Can-making in Kenya, Tanzania and Thailand', in Bhalla, A. (ed.), *Technology and Employment in Industry* (Geneva: ILO, 1975).

Demsetz, H., 'Information and Efficiency: Another Viewpoint', *Journal of Law and Economics*, vol. 12 (1969). Reproduced in D. M. Lamberton (ed.), *Economics of Information and Knowledge* (Penguin, 1971).

Doyle, L. A., *Inter-economy Comparisons. A Case Study* (Berkeley, CA.: University of California Press, 1965).

Fallon, P. R. and Layard, P. R. G., 'Capital-Skill Complementarity, Income Distribution and Output Accounting', *Journal of Political Economy*, vol. 83 (April 1975).

Findlay, R., 'An "Austrian" Model of International Trade and Interest Rate Equalization', Institute for International Economic Studies, Seminar Paper No. 86 (1977a).

Findlay, R., 'Comment on Ohlin (1977)' in B. Ohlin, P-O Hesselborn and P. M. Wijkman (eds) *The International Allocation of Economic Activity* (London: Macmillan 1977b)

Griliches, Z., 'Notes on the Role of Education in Production Functions and Growth Accounting', in Hansen, W. L. (ed.), *Education, Income and Human Capital* (New York: NBER/Columbia University Press, 1970).

Haberler, G., *A Survey of International Trade Theory* (Princeton, 1961).

Helleiner, G. K., 'The Role of Multinational Corporations in the Less Developed Countries' Trade in Technology', *World Development*, vol. 3, no. 4 (April 1975) pp. 161–89.

Hirsch, S. 'The Product Cycle Model of International Trade—A Multi-Country Cross Section Analysis', *Oxford Bulletin of Economics and Statistics*, vol. 27 (November 1975).

Hufbauer, G., 'The Impact of National Characteristics and Technology on the Commodity Composition of Trade in Manufactured Goods', in R. Vernon (ed.), *The Technology Factor in International Trade*, National Bureau of Economic Research (Columbia University Press, 1970).

Johnson, H. G., *Comparative Cost and Commercial Policy Theory for a Developing World Economy*, Wicksell Lectures (Stockholm: Almqvist and Wiksell, 1968).

Johnson, H. G., 'The State of Theory in Relation to the Empirical Analysis', in R. Vernon (ed.), *The Technology Factor in International Trade* (New York: NBER, Columbia University Press, 1970).

Jones, R. W., 'The Role of Technology in the Theory of International Trade', in R. Vernon (ed.), *The Technology Factor in International Trade*, National Bureau of Economic Research (Columbia University Press, 1970).

Keesing, D., 'Labour Skills and International Trade: Evaluating Many Trade Flows with a Single Measuring Device', *Review of Economics and Statistics* (August 1965) pp. 287–94.

Kemp, M. C., *The Pure Theory of International Trade and Investment* (Englewood Cliffs, N.J.: Prentice-Hall, 1969).

Kenen, P. B., 'Towards a More General Theory of Capital', Columbia University International Economics Workshop (December 1965), mimeographed (1965).

Kenen, P. B., 'Nature, Capital and Trade', *Journal of Political Economy*, vol. LXXIII, no. 5 (1965).

Kenen, P. B. and Yudin, E., 'Skills, Human Capital and US Foreign Trade', Columbia University International Economic Workshop, (December 1965) mimeographed.

Lary, H. B., *Imports of Manufactures from Less Developed Countries*, (New York: NBER, 1968).

Leibenstein, H., (1968), 'Entrepreneurship and Economic Development', *American Economic Review* (May 1968).

Magee, S., 'Multinational Corporations, the Industry Technology

Cycle and Development', *Journal World Trade Law*, vol. 11, no. 4 (1977).

Magee, S., 'Application of the Dynamic Limit Pricing Model to the Price of Technology and International Technology Transfer', in *Carnegie-Rochester Conference Series on Public Policy*, vol. 7 (1977).

Manfield, E., *Industrial Research and Technological Innovation* (New York: Norton, 1968).

Mason, H. R., 'Some Observations on the Choice of Technology by Multinational Firms in Developing Countries', *Review of Economics and Statistics*, no. 3 (August 1973).

Myint, H., *Southeast Asia's Economy* (Harmondsworth: Penguin, 1972).

Ohlin, B., 'Some Aspects of the Relations between International Movements of Commodities, Factors of Production, and Technology', in B. Ohlin, P-O Hesselborn and P. M. Wijkman (eds.), *The International Allocation of Economic Activity*, (London: Macmillan 1977).

Pack, H., 'The Substitution of Labour for Capital in Kenyan Manufacturing', *Economics Journal, 86* (341) (1976) pp. 45–58.

Pickett, J., Forsyth, D., and McBain, N., 'The Choice of Technology, Economic Efficiency and Employment in Developing Countries', *World Development*, vol. 2 (March 1974).

Riedel, J., 'The Nature and Determinants of Export-Oriented Direct Foreign Investment in a Developing Country: A Case Study of Taiwan', *Weltwirtschaftliches Archiv*, Heft 3 (1975).

Riedel, J., 'Intermediate Products and the Theory of International Trade: A Generalization of the Pure Intermediate Good Case', *American Economic Review*, vol. 66, no. 3 (June 1976).

Rodriguez C. A., 'Trade in Technological Knowledge and the National Advantage', *Journal of Political Economy*, vol. 83, no. 1 (February 1975).

Roskamp, K. W. and McMeekin, G. C., 'Factor Proportions, Human Capital and Foreign Trade: the Case of West Germany Reconsidered', *Quarterly Journal Economics* (February 1968).

Sato, K., *Production Functions and Aggregation* (North-Holland/American Elsevier, 1975).

Selowsky, M., 'Education and Economic Growth: Some International Comparisons', (University of Chicago Ph.D. Dissertation, 1967).

Solo, R., 'The Capacity to Assimilate an Advanced Technology', *American Economics Review, Papers and Proceedings*, May 1966, pp. 91–7. Reproduced in N. Rosenberg (ed.), *The Economics of*

Technological Change (Harmondsworth, Penguin, 1971).

Söderström, H. Tson, 'Roundabout Production and the International Pattern of Specialization', Stanford University Centre for Research in Economic Growth, Research Memoranda Series, No. 209 (February 1977).

Teech, D. J., 1977, 'Technology Transfer by Multinational Firms: The Resource Cost of Transferring Technological Know-How', *Economic Journal*, vol. 87 (June 1977).

Vanek, J., 'Variable Factor Proportions and Interindustry Flows in the Theory of International Trade', *Quarterly Journal of Economics*, vol. 77 (February 1963).

Wells, Louis T., (ed.), *The Product Life Cycle and International Trade* (Boston, 1972).

Comments

Kemal Dervis (USA)

The paper by Carl Hamilton and Hans T. Söderström starts by noting that the Heckscher–Ohlin theory carries very optimistic overtones with respect to the international distribution of income. This optimism stems from the factor price equalisation theorem, itself based on the assumption of identical production functions or an identical set of blueprints across countries. It is true that interpreted in standard textbook fashion, the Heckscher–Ohlin approach pushes into the background technology and 'technological gaps' as determinants of trade and distribution.

The Hamilton–Söderström paper proposes to remain faithful to the Heckscher–Ohlin approach while letting technology play a crucial role. There are many ways of endogenising technology. The present paper chooses a very special one using the factor proportions approach to *explain* international differences in technology. This is achieved by treating technology as a produced non-durable, intermediate good characterised by a relatively capital-intensive production process. Technology and shopfloor input jointly produce 'output'. The simple neoclassical production model where primary factors directly produce one or more commodities is thus transformed into a two-stage production model where primary factors produce shopfloor input and technology and these intermediate inputs then produce final output. As is well known from production theory of the activity analysis type, the introduction of intermediate goods does not affect the basic structure of neoclassical production models. The results of the paper are therefore not surprising: factor price equalisation still holds under the usual assumptions regarding specialisation, factor-intensity reversals and the number of factors and goods. For factor price equalisation the number of factors must not exceed the number of goods. If technology is tradeable and there is a world price of technology in terms of output, all relative prices are equalised and the 'book of blueprints'—including the book of blueprints to produce technology—being the same across countries, production techniques will also be the same. We therefore arrive at a 'technology equalisation' theorem: total factor productivity will be equalised between countries in free trade equalibrium with incomplete specialisation, irrespective of factor endowments. If technology is not tradeable, a model with a single tradeable output does not yield technology equalisation because the factor price equalisation theorem does not hold. But the introduction of a second output re-establishes technology equalisation.

What we get is a contradictory message: on the one hand Hamilton and Söderström stress that the Heckscher–Ohlin theory is defective because of its reliance on identical technologies and cite much empirical evidence in support of their criticism; on the other hand they appear to propose a theoretical framework which tends to lead to the very 'technology equalisation' result that they started by criticising. But in a sense this contradiction may constitute the strength of the paper. It shows what one obtains by treating technology as a standard good within a static neoclassical model. It can therefore be interpreted as underlining the limitations of such a treatment.

The problem is inherent in two of the basic assumptions made. Technology is treated as an ordinary private good on the argument that augmenting the technological intensity of production costs real resources. That is quite true. But it does not follow that the seller of technology loses what he sells, as is the case for ordinary capital or consumption goods. It may be the case that by selling technology the owner loses monopoly profits associated with restricted ownership, but this does not establish technology as a private good in the ordinary sense. Technology is neither a pure public good—it costs resources for anyone to acquire even if it already exists—nor a pure private good— once acquired it is not easily lost.

Second, Hamilton and Söderström treat technology as a good that depreciates fully within one production period. It cannot be accumulated. In fact technology is durable not only in the sense that one does not lose it by selling it but also in the usual sense that it depreciates very slowly and can be accumulated.

When we put these two characteristics of technology together, first that the owner does not lose it by selling it and second that it is very durable, we can get much closer to an evaluation of international inequality that stresses the importance of large differences in total 'shopfloor' productivity. These differences reflect the weight of history with some allowance for natural resources and geography. History has resulted in unequal accumulation of physical capital and human skills and knowledge. The latter may be more important than the former. International inequality cannot be eradicated overnight, therefore, either by a process of static resource reallocation and free trade or by the South delinking itself and putting an end to 'unequal exchange'. What is required is a dynamic historical process in which the South accumulates human and physical resources more rapidly than the North. I do not think that the fact that commodities are traded is in itself an important equalising or unequalising factor. But indirectly trade may induce more equality if the greater surpluses and temporary monopolistic profits it allows in the technologically advanced economies are more than counterbalanced by a more rapid spread of technological knowledge and a process of technological diffusion that may be linked to the volume and structure of trade.

From the point of view of the South an activist trade and investment policy that seeks to maximise technological diffusion may be superior to both a neoclassical policy of *laissez-faire* and an autarchic policy aimed at self-sufficiency. The Heckscher–Ohlin apparatus is in need of fundamental extensions if it is to be useful in analysing these questions.

6 The Less-Developed Countries and Transnational Enterprises[1]

Carlos Díaz-Alejandro (USA)

This essay ranges over many issues, but it does not survey exhaustibly the topic of interactions between the less-developed countries (LDCs) and transnational enterprises (TNEs). The vastness of such a topic imposes certain selectivity. Both TNEs and LDCs are heterogeneous, and even the area of their interaction contains great variety.

TNEs from industrialised countries are interested mainly in the markets of, and supplies from, industrialised countries. Substantial TNE interest in the Third World is limited to a handful of LDCs (which nevertheless contain a non-trivial share of LDC population); more than one-fifth of the foreign direct investment stock in LDCs in 1975 was held by oil-producing countries and a further two-fifths by ten other countries.[2] Only LDCs with large internal markets or significant natural resources receive sustained attention from TNEs. Fundamental issues raised by TNE activities in the world economy should therefore concern industrial countries as well as LDCs, and the fate of TNEs will depend more on what happens in industrialised countries than on LDC policies. However, LDC–TNE relations are often asymmetrical; a small and very poor LDC is likely to be of marginal interest to TNEs, but LDC policy-makers may attach great importance to TNE decisions regarding their country.

Both the special assets sustaining the market power of TNEs, and their motivations for going into LDCs are diverse. The special asset may be knowledge of advanced technology or a popular trademark built up by many years of advertising. Indeed, under contemporary conditions it seems that even the simplest products (or processes) upon close inspection turn out to have specialised wrinkles, often of doubtful social benefit, giving firms special assets. The variety is such that the concept of special assets of firms may become empty without a careful typology. Motivations for producing within LDCs, rather than exporting to them either goods or services embodying the special asset, are also variegated, ranging from jumping import restrictions to preparing for export cheap LDC resources, such as primary commodities or semiskilled labour. Given the diversity of special assets and of the stimuli triggering foreign investment, one may doubt *a priori* claims regarding unambiguous welfare implication of TNE activities.

The ambiguity of the welfare implications of TNE activities is reinforced by noting the heterogeneity of LDCs, not just in domestic market size and natural resource endowment, but also in the responsiveness of their government officials to different domestic social groups and in the bargaining ability of those officials. LDC government officials may or may not bargain cleverly and firmly with TNEs; may or may not focus their bargaining on substantive issues; and may or may not distribute equitably the fruits of their bargaining efforts among their fellow-countrymen.

The agnostic approach of this essay is in the spirit of that line of economic thought teaching that private profit-seeking behaviour may lead to socially desirable results but only if certain conditions are met, conditions which involve both economic and political variables, and whose presence cannot be taken for granted, particularly in LDCs. If there is a simple formula to understand the nature and consequences of TNEs, this essay has not found it.

Before tackling some specific types of LDC–TNE interaction, Section I of this essay reviews some of the theorising and controversies about international firms. Section II discusses TNE activities involving LDC exports, with examples of both the old and the new. Section III covers TNE participation in LDC import-substituting industrialisation. Both Sections II and III may be viewed as polar cases of LDC–TNE interaction; there are, of course, many other types of TNE involvement in LDCs which are left out, such as those in services and in activities producing simultaneously for domestic and foreign markets. Section IV makes a few additional observations on technological transfer and international rules.

I THE INTERNATIONAL FIRM

Social science has difficulty coming to grips with TNEs. Traditional economic theory, whether neoclassical or Marxist, is uneasy in the presence of imperfect competition and the modern corporation. Furthermore the sources and diffusion of technical change are typically incorporated into economic models in a mechanistic fashion. Finally, standard democratic theory has little room for 'corporate citizens'. Yet much of the practical debate about TNEs, or large corporations in general, revolves around their market power, their contribution to innovation and its diffusion, and their political consequences. Mainstream theory provides little guidance in these debates, either in the North or in the South.

Indeed the *positive* theory of the capitalist, corporate firm used by many LDC economists, such as Norman Girvan, or by radical economists, such as the late Stephen Hymer, is close to that advanced by heterodox Northern economists such as Raymond Vernon and John Kenneth Galbraith. Such a theory views the modern corporation as an institution which in its search for a satisfactory and secure return to its special asset substitutes reliance on imperfect external markets for internal planning. The more the firm expands and the larger its investments become (each new investment often having a longer maturation period), the greater will be the perceived need to control its economic environment so as to reduce business and other risks. Whether the firm commits large funds to develop a mine or a new product, it will feel the urge to strengthen a marketing network yielding loyal customers. Only a lunatic will let auction (spot) markets decide the fate of multibillion dollar investment projects.

The corporate commitment to private planning involves reliance on hierarchical, bureaucratic organisations internalising informational networks and encouraging 'team spirit'. The right balance between centralisation and decentralisation will be a major preoccupation of top management. Investment decisions, including those in R and D, with horizons well into the future, will tend to be centralised.

TNEs are viewed as simply the contemporary culmination of the tendency for capitalist firms to expand and control their environment. Dramatic advances in transport and communication over the last hundred years facilitated first the expansion of local firms from regional to national dimensions, and more recently from national to international dimensions.

The regional–national–transnational expansion path applies in principle to any capitalist firm, regardless of historical origins or home country. The analytical focus is on the firm, not on countries, nor on an aggregated, homogeneous capital in contrast with some versions of theories of imperialism and dependency, and with standard non-classical theory. The characteristics of firms at each point in the expansion path will, of course, differ; TNEs will be fewer and larger than regional corporations. There is constant movement along the path, both upward and downward, fuelled by technological innovations, oliogopolistic rivalries and by political events. TNEs sit on top of this swarming pyramid, but uneasily. Oligopoly remains, but oligopolists may die. In a changing world, they must continuously reproduce the barriers to entry protecting their leading position.

It is important to emphasise that both oligopoly and innovation are ingredients in this view of capitalist firms and TNEs. One could conceptualise the oligopoly with given production functions for an un-changing number of products. Equilibrium solutions to oligopolistic interdependence may then vary according to other specific assumptions, but they will be inferior to either the classic competitive solution or to state ownership with marginal cost pricing. Yet it appears unrealistic to contemplate oligopoly lasting very long without innovation, gene-rated by private firms searching for quasi-rents. The oligopoly-cum-innovation combination is not easily comparable to the classic com-petitive solution nor to public ownership, hence the recurring debate over antitrust and patents. It could also be argued that, while in the long run it is difficult to imagine oligopoly without innovation, under contemporary conditions it is even harder to imagine innovation without oligopoly for some sectors of the economy. The process of innovation and its diffusion need neither be predictable, nor orderly nor efficient.

Focusing on the firm and on the regional–national–transnational expansion path does not mean that national boundaries are irrelevant for understanding TNE activities. It does remind us that within countries, particularly large ones like the USA, there are corporations with plants scattered geographically to take advantage of transport economies, proximity to customers and domestic market imperfections. Market imperfections, of course, are more severe once national boundaries are taken into consideration; actual or threatened import restrictions, factor price inequalities and information gaps are some of the most obvious ones.

The vision of a contemporary TNE sketched above differs from the atomistic, price-taking version of the competitive firm found in introductory (but not industrial organisation) textbooks. It is different, but is it better or worse from a *normative* viewpoint? On this question opinions differ sharply, particularly between Northern and Southern observers.

John Kenneth Galbraith has put forth perhaps the best case for large corporations in general and TNEs in particular.[3] The thesis is that TNEs naturally arise when international trade consists of modern technical, specialised, or uniquely styled manufactured products. Auction markets may be feasible for wheat or sugar, but electric generators will involve customer markets and TNEs.[4] When advanced technology is involved, it is argued that multinational operations realise the economies of scale. TNEs are credited with favouring a more free trade, with a reduction in economic conflicts among countries where they operate, and even with the creation of the world's first truly effective international civil service (which will be news in the Vatican).

Stephen P. Magee has expressed related notions arguing that TNEs are specialists in the production of information that is less efficient to transmit through markets than within firms.[5] TNEs are said to produce sophisticated technologies because appropriability is higher for these than for simple technologies. The appropriability of the returns from information and complementarities among different types of information dictate large firm size. Magee concludes that private market generation of new information and new techniques may require concentrated industry structures and large firm size, so that any policy proposal aimed at increasing private market technology transfer through reducing the market power of the TNEs via increased intraindustry competition is close to a contradiction in terms.

Neither Galbraith nor Magee is blind to the dangers posed by the concentration of power in the large corporation. Galbraith notes several danger zones and emphasises that the large corporation has power both in markets and states, giving it the capacity for antisocial action. Magee notes that:

The rational firm will create artificial and sophisticated masking devices, artificial product differentiation, and expend resources to appropriate the returns on earlier investments . . . A rational monopolist or collusive oligopoly will prevent or delay the introduction of a randomly discovered new unskilled-labor-intensive technology with *low* appropriability, if it is highly substitutable for an existing technology that has a higher *private* present value because of its *higher* appropriability.[6]

The contradiction between private and social rationality could not be expressed any clearer by a radical economist.

Yet, when all is said, Galbraith and Magee, as well as Kindleberger and Vernon, end up with relatively complacent views of TNEs. Compared with most LDC observers, their evaluation of the evidence will differ in two crucial areas: degree of competition in world markets, and the political power of corporations.

Measures of industrial concentration and market power are notoriously tricky. For a given country, the share in all manufacturing value added (or assets) of the largest hundred firms could point toward greater concentration, while measures of concentration in particular product markets could show no clear trend. Furthermore, Vernon argues that conventional measures of industrial concentration for a national market have become increasingly inadequate, primarily because such measures have not captured the buyers' perception of a larger number of substitutable sources for the products in which the buyers are interested. For the world production of eight standardised products, he shows declining concentration indices between 1950 and 1975, if one takes the TNE output of each product as a single unit irrespective of where its production takes place. This dispersion of industrial leadership could mean that while the aggregate position of TNEs in a given LDC may be growing, the market power of each TNE may have declined.[7]

Some would argue that rivalry between, say, Japanese and US TNEs is only a temporary stage, which will eventually lead to a *modus vivendi* involving market sharing or even the formation of even larger (and more truly multinational) units of capital. Experience so far indicates that the variety of nationalities of TNEs is one of the most robust structural bases for the maintenance of competitive pressures in world markets. One can also foresee that the most advanced semi-industrialised LDCs will enter their own TNEs into these oligopolistic rivalries. It has also been noted that besides the rivalry among TNEs of different nationality the alternatives faced by LDCs in recent years have been expanded by the entry into the international arena of many new and relatively small firms from industrialised countries.[8]

The precise nature of the interaction between private TNE planning and the performance of markets remains murky and paradoxical. In some cases, TNE private planning results in thin and residual open markets for transactions falling outside the TNE closed planning network. Such remaining open markets tend to behave erratically; LDCs unwilling to hook into TNE networks may have no choice but to go there. LDC goods exported via residual markets are particularly vulnerable to the protectionism of industrialised countries, as they have no TNE friend in court. For all international trade, intrafirm trade is already more important than that carried out among different firms at arm's length. While there are difficult problems in defining and measuring intrafirm trade, not to mention in establishing departures of intrafirm pricing from ideal competitive pricing, in a pioneering paper Gerald K. Helleiner concludes that a very high proportion of US imports from developing countries originates with 'related parties'.[9] On the other hand, the scanning TNE central planning boards may pick up opportunities and economic signals more quickly than atomistic agents in auction markets could. Indeed, large corporations are resented by the abrupt fashion in which they transfer their activities from, say, high-wage to low-wage areas, presumably a stimulus which would also have triggered resource reallocation under purely competitive conditions, but perhaps more gradually. Put another way, up to a point TNE private planning may make for fiercer oligopolistic competition in customers' markets.

Charges that international markets are characterised by oligopoly are sometimes dismissed by Northern observers with the remark that imperfect markets bear no necessary link to profits, and that profit rates registered by TNEs do not seem abnormal over the long run, especially when all research and development expenses are taken into account. Even if published reports were reasonably accurate, the remark overlooks the debate over the 'perks' enjoyed by the corporate technostructure, which are of course registered as expenses, as well as other expenses of doubtful social justification, such as advertising for building up the image of the corporation. Within broad limits, the corporate technostructure seems to have considerable leeway to reward ingroup employees; threats from stockholders or takeovers by outsiders represent weak checks on executive discretion. While some argue that debatable 'perks' add up to small sums, or represent normal returns to investment in human capital, others regard them as key motivations for setting up barriers to entry. It may be conjectured that the demonstration effect of such 'perks' motivates some LDC public and private technocrats in their struggle for a New International Economic Order and their own bureaucratic hierarchies; the joys of travelling in a Concorde, and of the three-martini lunch have universal appeal.

Be that as it may, it remains true that while industrialised countries have legislation curbing abuses of economic power and restraint of trade, at the international level such regulations are weaker. National legislation may exempt international operations from antitrust action, or lead to conflicts with other nations leading to sporadic, ineffectual or inefficient control of monopolistic practices. The balance between collusion and competition in international operations is tilted in the direction of collusion and/or inefficiency by the lack of clear international antitrust agreements.

Although it has been noted that the large private corporation does not fit easily into democratic theory,[10] and there is general recognition of significant corporate political power in capitalist societies, Northern observers derive comfort from the countervailing forces at work in pluralistic industrial nations. Historical abuses of corporate power are viewed as aberrations rather than as examples of the norm. Northern academic observers frequently rub shoulders with corporate executives in pleasant surroundings, induced feelings of good fellowship and, in the part of the academic, a conviction that the limited vision and intellectual range of executives must check their potential for really serious mischief.

While Northern observers prefer looking at the future belittling the past, history lies heavily on Southern perceptions of the present. The political and economic abuses of colonialism and hegemonism, the close and open co-operation between foreign governments and foreign companies, are viewed not as phenomena which suddenly ended in 1945 or 1955, but which evolved into subtler manipulations and interactions which are with us today. ITT-type scandals, which in the North are typically viewed as aberrations, are regarded in the South as merely the tip of the iceberg.

Southern observers can argue that the TNE–home government link is crucial for sustaining a pillar of TNE power, that is, their technological advantage. The major industrialised countries have heavily subsidised research and development, often under the rubric of defence expenditures, which later on has provided the basis for corporate prosperity. A recent example of such government-corporate alliance is provided by deep-sea mining, an area in which US private corporations are now benefiting from defence research carried out earlier by the US government. Kennecott Copper Corporation, International Nickel Company, Deepsea Ventures Incorporated, and Lockheed Aircraft Corporation, the four leaders of the seabed mining consortiums, now loudly complain how bureaucratic red tape, in the form of a proposed international 'law of the sea', hampers their private enterprise, yet it is unlikely that they will proceed very far without double-checking their plans with Washington civilian and military bureaucrats.

TNE corporate power, which in the North is countervailed by trade unions, consumer organisations and other private and public actors, meets weaker institutions in LDCs. Typically, the public sector will have the role of *interlocutor*, not always *valable*. The energy generated by defensive nationalism may be the most robust countervailing force offsetting TNE political and social influence in LDCs.

The political and social consequences of TNE presence in LDCs may be regarded, from the viewpoint of the corporation, as secondary repercussions of the drive for satisfactory and secure profits. Furthermore, the repercussions are likely to be contradictory, difficult to foresee and certainly variable among different types of LDCs. But on balance, a case can be made that corporate business needs will produce an attitude favouring authoritarian LDC regimes which repress trade union activity and consumers organisations. While right-wing authoritarian regimes will be most congenial, it should not be surprising if left-wing authoritarian regimes also become favoured, once messy revolutionary transitions are out of the way and such regimes become interested in dealing with TNEs. Business publications show little enthusiasm for democratic struggles in the Third World, nor for President Carter's campaign for human rights. Business reasons can induce IBM to pull out of India while maintaining operations in South Africa; business reasons operating within a peculiar European political framework led I. G. Farben to set up a branch plant at Auschwitz.

Historical background will make Northern and Southern observers react differently to corporate organisation charts. To the Northerner such charts simply embody commonsense principles of organisation, subject to tinkering in detail, but whose basic pyramidal structure is rooted in the wisdom or at least the practice of the ages.[11] Southerners view the pyramid from the base noting that the apex is typically located in New York or London. An author like Norman Girvan will reproduce in his book corporate organisation charts which were blandly presented in standard industrial organisation books, but surrounding them with sadomasochistic overtones, relating hierarchies to dominance/dependency relationships and to subjugation.[12] Independent traders meeting in an open, competitive market can exchange goods and services in an impersonal and standoffish fashion, but doing business with a TNE will involve becoming enmeshed into a system of hierarchies and personalised alliances. Such alliances will have effects spilling beyond the economic life of LDC agents, influencing their social, cultural and political life. The 'team-spirit' of the TNE may come to dominate other allegiances of those enmeshed in the organisation, regardless of their national origins.[13]

This section started by noting that social science theory has difficult-ies handling TNEs. Robust empirical work on international firms, not surprisingly, has been sketchy and inconclusive, particularly regarding their operations in LDCs. Among other difficulties, a clear comparison between international and LDC firms, controlling for such variables as economic activity and size, is seldom possible. Thus, whether in general TNEs cause higher levels of economic concentration in LDCs, or whether they earn higher profit rates than local firms, remain debated issues. Such generalisations may never be possible outside some kind of typology, to which the rest of the paper turns. Even with typology, however, extant empirical work warrants few strong generalisations on the economic (not to mention political) consequences of TNEs in LDCs.[14]

II   TNEs AND LDC EXPORTS

This section will touch on some issues arising from two types of LDC activities primarily oriented toward foreign markets and involving TNEs. For minerals the involvement is old and has been declining, at least in relative terms; for non-traditional LDC exports the involvement is fairly recent and shows great dynamism.

The interaction between TNEs and LDCs in minerals presents in their purest form some of the themes developed earlier: the sources of potential conflicts are many and substantial, and so is the potential surplus to be generated and shared. The rents generated by mineral production can be divided into three categories: those arising from the exhaustible nature of the resource (Hotelling–Solow rents); those arising from differential qualities of mines, either because of location or of mineral content of the ores (Ricardian rents); and those arising from oligopolistic control of production, processing, and marketing.[15]

Throughout history international trade in minerals has been as-sociated with violence and conflict, and few open and competitive auction markets. TNEs, mainly based in countries of substantial power, arose to replace 'market anarchy' for minerals. For commodities with high fixed and low variable costs, and where information is imperfect, badly diffused or asymmetrically located, it is reasonable to expect a non-market institution to replace open markets. Incentives for vertical integration become large when uncertainty regarding the supply price of the upstream good pressures the informational needs of downstream firms. Once they came into existence, TNEs routinely erected barriers to entry, including hoarding mineral deposits, limiting technological diffusion and establishing exclusive processing and marketing networks.[16] TNEs participating in the international trade and investment in minerals engaged not only in oligopolistic rivalry of a purely commercial nature, but were also part of international political rivalry. The symbiotic relationship between many TNEs and home governments has been clearest perhaps in the case of oil especially in the years around the First World War and the decade and a half following the outbreak of the Second World War.

Since the Second World War, there has been a trend of growing LDC participation in mineral rents. This seems best explained, in spite of the vagueness of the phrase, by an increase in LDC bargaining power. Decolonisation, superpower political rivalry, economic rivalry among TNEs of different nationalities, and the expansion of LDC expertise, knowledge and political awareness have contributed to this trend. In retrospect, it could be argued that the characteristics of mineral industries made the rise of LDC bargaining power almost inevitable. The concentration of mines, in contrast with the diffusion in the production of most tropical crops, made taxable surplus highly visible even to a 'soft state' and, eventually, also vulnerable to the exchequer.

LDCs, and countries such as Australia and Canada, have not only increased their shares in mineral rents, but by creating their own state enterprises have also threatened what may be called the commodity stabilisation regimes of the TNEs. The greater number of actors in world markets for exhaustible resources promises greater competition and more choices for consumers. An expanded role for auction markets, especially the London Metal Exchange, has been reported in recent years for copper, aluminium, and nickel. Those changes to a large extent can be attributed to LDC assertiveness in the production and marketing of those minerals. In spite of rhetorical commitment to free markets, nickel and aluminium TNE executives appear unhappy over the expanding role of the London Metal Exchange.[17] The presence of LDC firms, whether private or public, in the marketing of exports, and in services ancillary to LDC foreign trade (banking, shipping, insurance) represents an important break with the pattern of foreign domination of such activities which historically have been important sources of quasi-rents.[18]

So one possibility for the near future is that with the TNE commodity stabilisation regime in decadence, and no alternative regime firmly in place, world markets for exhaustible resources would become more competitive but also more unstable and unpredictable. Under these circumstances, prices observed in markets will be poor guides for fresh investments. During a transition period which could be long, the LDC share in world investment and exploration expenditures in mining would decline, as indeed has happened recently.[19] Eventually the world market would once again become fragmented, as users of raw materials seeking predictability in prices and in the flow of supplies would seek special 'consumer relationships' with producers. This could occur in geographical patterns of the 'spheres of influence' type. For minerals with substantial production within industrialised countries, such as copper in the US, charges of 'dumping' against LDC state enterprises will encourage protectionism, even as the same countries express anxiety about access to LDC supplies for other minerals and fuels.

An alternative scenario would feature the emergence of a *modus vivendi* between LDC national enterprises, including paper organisations, and the TNEs. This collusion between LDCs and TNEs to share in oligopoly profits is what some observers see as a key feature of OPEC, and what some see as desirable in the copper case. The stability of this new partnership will depend on other changes in world markets, particularly those where management, technology and capital can be hired separately, as well as the will of LDCs to expand their ability to combine all of these inputs. Note that the discovery and exploitation of new deposits appears to be increasingly complicated and expensive, and the technological and organisational skills of TNEs may be helpful for such tasks. Even Vietnam, which has amply demonstrated its vocation for national autonomy, will deal with TNEs in its search for oil deposits, for example.

There are many other possible futures for international trade and investment in minerals and fuels. In an unlikely fit of rationality and farsightedness the various actors could agree to Keynes–ITO stabilisation agreements. Mongrel proposals, such as the peculiar International Resources Bank launched in the 1976 UNCTAD Nairobi meeting by Henry Kissinger, could be revised and adopted, perhaps under the supervision of the World Bank and regional development banks.

The search for a new order in minerals and fuels is likely to be a messy and complicated process. LDC–TNE relations in the area of minerals and fuels will remain tense and conflicting, even if history were to be totally forgotten. As noted by Raymond Vernon, for each particular deal in minerals or fuels there is an inexorable cycle in the bargaining strength of TNEs and LDCs. Lamentations and exhortations are unlikely to change the dynamics of this cycle, which is based on a sharp break from a situation of great uncertainty, asymmetries and little TNE commitment, to a situation of much more information, symmetry as well as large TNE investments *in situ*. The 1974–75 recession and the slow recovery since then have postponed pressures for that search, but not for long. Some Northern voices warn that the search could involve military action; they may sound archaic but they are not without influence.[20]

We now turn to LDC–TNE interaction in the area of non-traditional exports. Since the mid-1960s a growing number of LDCs have given greater incentives to their new exports. The results have been impressive, even after the world economy turned sluggish during the mid-1970s, particularly for about ten semi-industrialised LDCs. Non-traditional exports are made up of a broad range of goods, including traditional primary products now exported with more domestic value added, but manufacturers form its most dynamic component. Most of these goods are produced by locally owned firms, but an important part originate in TNE subsidiaries and a good share of the marketing of all non-traditional exports is carried out by foreign firms. For all LDCs, exports of manufactured products produced by TNEs may not exceed 20 per cent, with a higher percentage for Latin America and lower one for East Asia. Contrary to general impressions, this share has apparently not registered any significant increase since 1966.[21]

It is likely that either as producers or merchandisers TNEs will remain important actors in LDC export drives, thanks *inter alia* to their special information and marketing networks, as well as to their greater ability to resist protectionist pressures within their home countries. Commodities using labour-intensive techniques of production are natural candidates for exporting, but the drive could include an increasing share of other goods as well. A clear and dynamic example of TNE association with LDC manufactured exports involves subcontracting and assembly activities, often located in free trade or special border zones.

There are a number of intriguing similarities as well as contrasts between TNE–LDC old-fashioned interactions in minerals and plantations, and those recent ones involving labour-intensive exports generated in free-trade or border zones. In both cases the operations have 'enclave' characteristics, with heavy import dependence and limited linkages into the domestic economy. In both cases TNEs control information and marketing networks to such an extent that host governments have little idea of prices, costs, and other accounting details. Under the Cuban *ancien regime*, US sugar corporations producing within the island provided some insurance protectionist excesses emanting from the US Congress; a similar role as friend-in-court is now played by Northern TNEs producing or selling LDC labour-intensive goods. LDC vulnerability may be even greater in the case of new exports; for minerals and plantations the presumption is that the LDC has some natural asset not easily found elsewhere, while cheap unskilled labour is in plentiful supply. Yet, plantations, mines, and labour-intensive activities all vent abroad an LDC surplus which under autarchy would have a low opportunity cost at home. So these activities generate rents or quasi-rents which could be captured partly or totally by private or public host country actors. Under the right political and geographical circumstances, a host-country government can also control undesirable social and cultural spillovers of such enclave activities. Enclaves, in fact, may be very suitable for such vigilance.

While there is a presumption that export-oriented TNE activities in LDCs will yield net economic benefits to host countries, the magnitude of benefits could be eroded by overly generous subsidisation of social overhead capital and other inputs, such as credit. It is not inconceivable that there may be projects for which the host country gains less from taxing mineral rents or from returns to labour above opportunity cost, than what it gives away in subsidised capital.

III   TNEs AND LDC IMPORT SUBSTITUTION

As early as the 1920s some Latin American observers began to differentiate between two types of inflowing direct foreign investment: that associated with exports of minerals and other primary products, and that going into the nascent import-substituting manufacturing sector. The latter was more popular than the former. Since then, particularly since the Second World War, much LDC industrialisation has been associated with direct foreign investment and TNEs, and an increasing share of all direct foreign investment flowing into LDCs has been for manufacturing activities selling primarily in the protected domestic market. But early enthusiasm for foreign investment in manufacturing has waned.

International corporations deciding to set up plants in LDCs typically took that step after their exports to those countries were threatened by LDC import barriers of one type or another; in other words, in contrast with the case of minerals, most direct investment in manufacturing became a substitute for trade. Once an international corporation took the investment decision, it was not unusual to observe similar moves, rational from their private viewpoints, by its oligopolistic rivals. As the nineteenth century witnessed railroad manias in country after country, semi-industrialised LDCs have gone through waves of automobile manias, petrochemical manias, etc. LDCs have learned little from each other in this area; Kenya, for example, seems to have repeated Argentine excesses regarding TNE-related import substitution.

While during the 1930s and 1940s the combination of import restrictions and inflows of direct investment into manufacturing had a number of redeeming features, the more prosperous world conditions of later years highlighted its negative aspects. Foreign-owned plants benefited from exhorbitant effective rates of protection in many cases, shielding both excess costs and profits. Even without excess profits, it is not difficult to show in a simple neoclassical model that a small tariff-imposing country importing a capital-intensive good will see its welfare reduced by an inflow of foreign capital. While the presence of foreign capital increases claims on exportable goods, required for the real transfer of (normal) profits abroad, the combination of tariffs and capital inflow will distort the productive structure in the direction of importable goods.[22]

In a more realistic model which recognises that the small country deals with a foreign firm with monopolistic power, perhaps due to the firm's special asset, it can be shown that an import tariff which does *not* induce a decision by the foreign firm to produce locally could lead to the small country being better off than either having a zero tariff, or one so high that it triggers a capital inflow for import substitution. If the 'switchover' tariff is less than the optimal tariff when only imports are contemplated, the small country could maximise its welfare by prohibiting subsidiary production ('switchover') and imposing the optimal tariff on imports.[23]

The venerable infant industry argument was sometimes used to defend protection and other subsidisation of the local activities of TNEs. Common sense soon began to question whether the learning-by-doing of infants bearing names such as General Motors and Ford should be subsidised by local consumers. A related debate involved the desirability of regulating the sale to TNEs of matured locally owned enterprises, which had been nurtured through infancy and adolescence by direct and indirect public subsidies.

While many investments by TNEs in the import-substituting sector of LDCs could pass an *ex post* social cost-benefit test, a large number could not. Major blame for this situation, of course, rests with host-country policies, but TNEs and their home governments were not passive spectators to LDC policy-making on import restrictions and the number of TNEs permitted in a given industry. TNEs lobbied for greater protection, as firms would, but perhaps with greater-than-average persuasive powers. When in their attempt to limit entrants in a new field LDCs left out TNEs of some nations, home-country embassies often would express their unhappiness, sometimes making references to limitations being placed on competition. Once the TNEs settle behind protective walls, they will resist changes in the *status quo*.

I would conjecture that the inefficiency of much TNE investment in the import-competing sector of LDCs lies behind many complaints and criticisms of TNE practices in the Third World. Much of the discussion on transfer pricing, for example, arises in the context of industries which receive significant and reliable protection thanks to tariffs and import controls, yet feel hampered by exchange controls from freely remitting their profits abroad. The latter restrictions are justified by the former privileges, yet inevitably the combination induces cat-and-mouse games besides providing rich possibilities for imaginative though socially unproductive practices. The real surplus generated by TNEs in the import substituting activity is insufficient to satisfy both the company's profit aspirations, expressed in convertible foreign exchange, as well as host-country expectations in areas such as taxation, employment and externalities. Similar remarks can be made about the inconclusive debate on whether or not TNEs use appropriate technology in their plants, or about the balance-of-payments effects of TNEs. Surely debates over appropriate technology or balance-of-payments effects are more muted, say in TNE activities in oil rather than in manufacturing.

TNE involvement in the local production of some of the most sophisticated or novel lines of LDC consumption has also raised the appropriate product issue. Since at least last century, some economists have viewed the introduction in LDCs of new consumer goods, either via imports or local production, as a spur to development. This view stresses the incentive effects as well as the linkages of the new consumption habits. In recent years a critical interpretation portraying TNEs as purveyors of consumerism has gained prominence. The new gadgets are said to be limited to consuming élites, as in the case of automobiles, but in other cases are charged with distorting mass consumption toward products of dubious nutritional or aesthetic worth, such as soda pop, corn flakes, filtered cigarettes, and plastic bags, to the detriment of goods rooted in local tradition and sound habits, such as mother's milk, cigars and handicrafts. TNEs and their retinue of public relations firms blitz local culture until the old ways are seen to be backward and shameful, while consumption of TNE goods becomes a sign of modernity and sophistication. Local production of the new goods promotes their use by swelling local pride at being at the frontier of progress, and by the knowledge that employment is being generated. Attempts by some TNEs to adapt their products to LDC circumstances and needs, as in the case of nutritious soft drinks or smaller and simpler autos and hotels, are regarded as exceptions proving the rule. The commercial success of such exceptions has been mixed.

The economic and political complexities found in TNE involvement in LDC import-substituting industrialisation become even more acute when LDCs attempt to expand the size of the protected market by the creation of customs unions.[24] It is recognised that TNEs could be powerful instruments of integration, indeed so powerful that they may lead the process to their great gain, and with repercussions the host countries regard as undesirable. When a group of these countries had been following, each on their own, policies of import substitution, a common market could bring about significant gains by rationalising existing activities (such as trade creation). If existing plants are owned by TNEs, they may oppose the process, but some may go along with it expecting to cut costs and increase profits. Such long-run real productivity gains may be shared between TNEs and host countries, and among host countries, in various and not easily predictable ways. When the customs union aims at creating new activities (such as trade diversion), the host countries will naturally hope to retain as much of the perceived benefits from the enlarged market as possible, squeezing the maximum concessions from new TNE entrants. Hence the establishment of such regulations as the Andean investment code. But the less efficient the new investment plans the more likely it is that the bargaining between LDCs and TNEs, and among the partner countries, will be time-consuming and mystifying.

IV   TECHNOLOGY AND RULES

In this last section I will say a few more words on the subject of TNEs and technological transfer to LDCs, raising the question whether the bargaining between TNEs and LDCs can be aided by international rules.

Reliable empirical evidence on the different channels of technological diffusion and on the varying costs of each channel to receiving countries is not plentiful. What seems clear is that TNEs are neither the only nor necessarily the cheapest (for LDCs) mechanism for technological diffusion. Producers of machinery, consultants, students, and specialised publications are some of the other conduits of technological diffusion, which under some circumstances become attractive alternatives to parts of the TNE package.

One should note that a TNE presence in LDC manufacturing, by itself, is no evidence of technological diffusion to LDC residents; it is only a geographical fact. At one extreme the TNE may keep to itself all relevant knowledge, leaving local residents as ignorant of the technology as if they were importing the product. At the other extreme, the TNE presence could lead to a costless copying of its technological advantage by competing local entrepreneurs, although it is difficult to see why the TNE would actively promote such a process. TNEs could, however, promote technical improvement among local producers supplying inputs to the TNE. A low-cost and rapid diffusion, involuntary and undesirable from the viewpoint of most TNEs, is most likely to occur in large semi-industrialised LDCs than in small and very poor LDCs.

The peculiarities of technological knowledge as a commodity make *both* LDCs and industrialised countries perceive that they are cheated by the somewhat metaphysical international technology market. Anxious OECD countries have been flirting with technological protectionism, discovering suddenly all sorts of imperfections and externalities. Fortunately, the various channels of technological diffusion provide some defence against this type of protectionism, which at least since the Industrial Revolution has not been successful for long.

Granting these caveats, TNEs remain one of the important participants in the international technological market, reluctant to share their special technological assets with outsiders, but less secretive regarding technologies not fundamental to their quasi-rents. They are also important forces in the generation of fresh innovations. Their dual role will keep them in a delicate position in the struggle between Southern forces promoting low-cost technological diffusion, and Northern efforts to maintain and extend technological leadership, whose quasi-rents make up part of the higher Northern *per capita* income.[25] This struggle is unlikely to yield orderly patterns. Already in 1960 Albert O. Hirschman was noting a secular trend toward a continuous shortening of the time needed for a new industry to become footloose, comparing the historical spread of textiles, chemicals, automobiles, antibiotics and transistors.[26] He challenged the view that the 'imitators' would follow the 'talented innovators' only at a respectful distance and with well-adjusted speed, and only to occupy positions of comparative advantage which the innovators were more or less ready to yield. It is interesting that the notion of a neat and orderly separation of the world between talented innovators and timid followers, which some regard as the implicit ideology of US foreign economic policy during the period after the Second World War, reappears in some of the dependency literature which takes for granted LDC technological serfdom, barring profound socio-economic structural changes.

One can note in passing the emergence and rapid growth of a new source of technology for LDCs: *other* LDCs.[27] Significant adaptive technological efforts have been carried out in several semi-industrialised LDCs, leading to new wrinkles in manufacturing production processes making them more suitable to smaller markets, or taking advantage of secondhand machinery, or adapting to lower quality raw materials and intermediate products. There are also examples of product changes. Such technological niches were often carved out by LDC firms engaged in import-substitution which are now in the position to exploit their special asset either by exporting, licensing or investing in other LDCs.

Bargaining between LDCs and TNEs, whether over Hotelling–Solow and Ricardian rents, or over technological marketing quasi-rents or over rents generated by protection, is likely to remain rough and bitter. The normal rate of return to capital found in theoretical constructs is not easily definable in concrete, everchanging circumstances. Policies of individual LDC governments toward TNEs will no doubt continue to fluctuate, sometimes erratically, depending on whether a given LDC has been most recently impressed by TNE excesses, or by the difficulties and frustrations of effectively running the apparatus of control over foreign investors. But the secular trend is unlikely to be away from growing LDC assertiveness, with public sectors continuing to be the host-country major counterparts to TNEs in the bargaining game. Under these circumstances, rhetoric and debate will also remain apocalyptic. LDCs will continue to be lectured on the dangers of killing the celebrated goose. Yet despite occasional confiscations (in most cases amply covered by *ex ante* risk premia) and despite threats to let LDCs stew in their own juice, a substantial number of TNEs will keep knocking at some LDC doors.

Unless one wishes to see the contradictions between LDCs and TNEs (or, more generally, between TNEs and governments) ending up in a drastic systemic change in the world economy, it is natural to imagine reforms in the international economic order which would reduce the deadweight losses, irrationalities, and abuses existing in this area. The modest proposals put forth by OECD and UNCTAD attempt to bring into the international jungle some of the rules and regulations on corporations which have been common in advanced industrialised countries for many years. These include standards of disclosure and accounting, regulation of restrictive business practices, codes on corrupt practices, and co-operation among tax authorities of different countries. More ambitious proposals would culminate in a GATT-type of organisation to regulate and oversee TNE activity. It is remarkable that weak proposals on disclosure of information, even when coming from OECD, have met with hostility from TNEs and some of their home countries.[28] In the context of the North–South dialogue it could also be useful to review Northern legislation regarding access to national capital markets and patents to see whether it unnecessarily tends to limit open-market alternatives to TNEs.

In this as in other arenas of international economic interaction we are still witnessing the consequences of the paradox Lionel Robbins identified in classical liberal thought. He noted that the famous liberal harmony of individual actions was only a harmony because legal restraints and institutions created at the national level an arena in which it might emerge. The *laissez-faire* of English classical thought demanded a strong national state. But when dealing with international problems, liberalism adopted a different attitude; when relations between different states were concerned, its attitude became that of philosophical anarchism, or tacit reliance on an imperial or hegemonic power for policing the international economy.[29]

The outlook for the emergence of generally accepted rules and regulations for international firms is not promising. Even among highly industrialised nations there are growing mutual recriminations regarding unfair behaviour; witness especially criticisms of Japanese firms and their trade practices. As 'two, three, more Japans' emerge, each with its own cultural style, these problems are likely to multiply. Established old oligopolists are unlikely to accommodate smoothly to the rise of lean and 'ill-mannered' new oligopolists. Rather than universal rules of the game, new political and economic subsystems of bewildering variety could emerge.

To most LDC policy-makers these systemic preoccupations are likely to appear premature. Their key preoccupation must remain the exact role, if any, TNEs can play in accelerating development in their countries. Governments of LDCs with both political will and local expertise will naturally be in a better position to guide and control TNE specific contributions to their country's development than those of LDCs lacking both or either. The latter will be unable to look too carefully into the package TNEs bring in. The depackaging of the TNE bundle is not an easy task, and the governments of the poorest LDCs may for many years be satisfied in obtaining just tax revenues and employment from TNE operations. Even the more advanced LDCs which are quite able to, say, run on their own existing new mines, may choose to call on TNEs to help them in opening up new mines. For some projects depending on continuous access to new technology LDC negotiators may prefer some TNE equity participation over a simple licencing agreement, so as to obtain a longer-range TNE commitment to the venture.

On the whole, the arguments presented in this paper imply that, suitably directed by responsible host-country planning and channelled selectively, TNEs can contribute to achieving *specific* developmental targets by supplying clearly defined services and expertise. The international economy of the 1970s, with all its problems, has allowed greater flexibility to many LDCs in choosing between TNE packages and alternative ways of reaching economic goals, in contrast with the international economy of the 1950s or those of earlier decades. LDC selectivity regarding TNEs should become as expected and acceptable in the international community as the selectivity industrialised countries apply to immigrant labour.

END NOTES

1. I gratefully acknowledge comments from Jagdish Bhagwati, Benjamin I. Cohen, Wesley Cohen, Charles P. Kindleberger, Paul Krugman, Richard Levin, Louka Papaefstratiou, Gustav Ranis, Peter Svedberg, Simon Teitel and Raymond Vernon.
2. United Nations Economic and Social Council, *Transnational Corporations in World Development: A Re-examination* (New York: E/C. 10/38, 20 March 1978) p. 8.
3. John Kenneth Galbraith, 'The Defense of the Multinational Company; How Management Puts its Worse Foot Forward and in its Mouth', *Harvard Business Review* (March–April 1978) pp. 83–93. See also his 'A Hard Case', in *The New York Review of Books* (20 April 1978) pp. 6–9.
4. On auction and customer markets see Arthur M. Okun, 'Inflation: Its Mechanisms and Welfare Costs', *Brookings Papers on Economic Activity*, vol. 2 (Washington DC, 1975).
5. Stephen P. Magee, 'Information and the Multinational Corporation: An

Appropriability Theory of Direct Foreign Investment', Chapter 13 in Jagdish N. Bhagwati (ed.), *The New International Economic Order: The North–South Debate* (Cambridge, Mass.: MIT Press, 1977) pp. 317–40.

6. Stephen Magee, op. cit., pp. 327–8. The italics are Magee's.

7. Raymond Vernon, *Storm Over the Multinationals: The Real Issues* (Cambridge, Mass.: Harvard University Press, 1977) pp. 77–82.

8. United Nations Economic and Social Council, *Transnational Corporations in World Development: A Re-examination* (New York: E.C.10.38, 20 March 1978) p. 7.

9. Gerald K. Helleiner, 'Intrafirm Trade and the Developing Countries: Patterns, Trends, and Data Problems' (processed, University of Toronto, September 1977).

10. Charles E. Lindblom, Politics and Markets; *The World's Political–Economic Systems* (New York: Basic Books, 1977) pp. 5 and 356.

11. As noted by Fernand Braudel: 'Capitalism does not invent hierarchies, any more than it invented the market . . . ; it merely uses them'. See his *Afterthoughts on Material Civilization and Capitalism* (Baltimore, MD: The Johns Hopkins University Press, 1977) p. 75. He adds in the same page: 'For this is indubitably the key problem, the problem of problems. Must the hierarchy, the dependence of one man upon another, be destroyed?'

12. Norman Girvan, *Corporate Imperialism: Conflict and Expropriation. Transnational Corporations and Economic Nationalism in the Third World.* (White Plains, N.Y.: M. E. Sharpe, 1978). See especially his figure 1, p. 21, adapted from a book by Alfred D. Chandler, Jr.

13. In earlier and more candid years orthodox northern authors openly noted the conflicting loyalties generated by TNEs operating in LDCs. Discussing during the 1930s whether US subsidiaries in Latin America should hire Latin Americans as executives, Dudley Maynard Phelps wrote:

> For such major positions very few nationals with the requisite training and experience are available, and, even if they are available, it might not be good policy to place them in a position to know all the affairs of the concern or to instruct them with intimate details of the company's policies. Moreover, it is necessary, at times, for a concern operating in a foreign country to have relationships with the government representatives of its own country . . . Obviously, in cases of this type, members of the legation could not talk freely before the executives if the latter were nationals. In general, it seems questionable whether a concern should risk the chance of divided loyalty and consequent biased decisions by hiring nationals for major executive positions.

Dudley Maynard Phelps, *Migration of Industry to South America* (New York: McGraw-Hill, 1936) p. 262.

14. This echoes the conclusion of Sanjaya Lall in his review of empirical work: 'Transnationals, Domestic Enterprises, and Industrial Structure in Host LDCs: A Survey,' *Oxford Economic Papers,* volume 2, No. 2 (July 1978) pp. 217–48.

15. For a more detailed discussion of these concepts and other issues relating to mineral TNEs see my 'International Markets for Exhaustible Resources,

Less Developed Countries, and Transnational Corporations,' Yale Economic Growth Center Paper No. 256 (December 1976).

16. Examples of 'virtual monopoly positions' for several minerals are given in Rex Bosson and Bension Varon, *The Mining Industry and the Developing Countries* (Oxford University Press, published for the World Bank, 1977) pp. 40–2. Links between mining TNEs and large financial groups are also noted.

17. See 'Big Aluminum Firms Don't Like Plans for Trading on London Metal Exchange,' *The Wall Street Journal* (19 December 1977) p. 20. In its issue of 15 May 1978, p. 38, *Business Week* reports that despite strong opposition from Britain's Aluminium Federation, the LME seems likely to go ahead as early as next fall with aluminum trading. The item adds: 'Producers fear a more open market would open the door to producers from developing countries with lower energy costs'.

18. See W. Arthur Lewis, *The Evolution of the International Economic Order* (Princeton, NJ: Princeton University Press, 1977) pp. 22–3.

19. United Nations, *Transnational Corporations in World Development: A Re-examination*, op. cit., p. 67. The percentage of mining exploration expenditures carried out in LDCs has declined from 30 per cent during 1966–70 to 14 per cent during 1971–75.

20. Tensions in Africa have been related by some to that region's mineral wealth. See 'The Mineral Connection', *The Economist* (9 July 1977), p. 82. That article quotes Sir Neil Cameron, the chief of the British Defence Staff, saying that in the future NATO might be obliged to wage peripheral wars to keep its share of the world's resources.

21. See the useful article by Deepak Nayyar, 'Transnational Corporations and Manufactured Exports from Poor Countries', *The Economic Journal*, Vol. 88, No. 349 (March 1978) pp. 59–84. Further empirical work is needed to establish more precisely the role of TNEs in new LDC exports, separating TNE presence in production and merchandising, and according to importers (TNE home country, other OECD countries, other LDCs, etc.).

22. The proposition involving a simple two-good, two-factor neoclassical model is presented in a paper by Richard A. Brecher and myself, 'Tariffs, Foreign Capital and Immiserizing Growth', *Journal of International Economics*, 7 (1977) pp. 317–22.

23. The results of a partial-equilibrium model for a small country dealing with a monopolistic firm are presented by Peter Svedberg, 'Optimal Tariff Policy on Imports from Multinationals', processed University of Stockholm (1978), (forthcoming, *Economic Record*). While the tariff reduces consumer's surplus in the small country, the tariff revenue captures part of the foreign firm's monopolistic profits.

24. The costs and benefits from economic integration when there are foreign firms affected by the process have been analysed by Ernesto Tironi, 'Economic Integration and Foreign Direct Investment Policies: The Andean Case', unpublished PhD thesis, Department of Economics, MIT, (Cambridge, Mass., August 1976). See also Constantine V. Vaitsos, 'Regional Integration cum/versus Corporate Integration,' mimeo, The Institute of Development Studies, Sussex, England (January 1978).

25. For a model in which developed countries must continually innovate not

just to grow but even to maintain their real income in the presence of technological borrowing by LDCs, see Paul R. Krugman, 'A Model of Innovation, Technology Transfer, and the World Distribution of Income,' (processed, Yale University, March 1978).

26. Albert O. Hirschman, 'Invitation to Theorizing about the Dollar Glut', *The Review of Economics and Statistics*, Vol. XLII, No. 1 (February 1960), pp. 100–2. This note not only pioneers in product-cycle theorising, but to a 1978 reader it also has a remarkably prophetic ring about the US balance of payments.

27. For a discussion of budding LDC TNEs see Louis T. Wells, Jr., "The Internationalization of Firms from Developing Countries," and C. F. Díaz-Alejandro "Foreign Direct Investment by Latin Americans", both in T. Agmon and C. P. Kindleberger, eds. *Multinationals from Small Countries* (Cambridge, Mass.: MIT Press, 1977) pp. 133–195.

28. See reports in *The Economist* (5 November, p. 102 and 17 December, p. 108) both 1977.

29. Lord Robbins, *Money, Trade and International Relations* (London: Macmillan, 1971) pp. 253–4.

Comments

Peter Svedberg (Sweden)

In certain respects, this survey paper by Professor Díaz-Alejandro resembles the famous Swedish *smörgåsbord*: it is extremely rich in variety, covering most aspects of the interrelationship between rich and poor countries through the TNE; it also offers some exquisite dishes— sections, paragraphs; but, as with most *smörgåsbords*, it also includes dishes that have been on the table many times before, and some that I think would have been better served *à la carte*.

In trying to cover everything, one runs the risk of covering nothing. Professor Díaz-Alejandro has not stumbled into this pitfall, but comprehensive and important areas of research, such as the appropriate technology and product issues, the diffusion of technology, and others, have been dealt with in one or two pages. Of course, with such limited space, one cannot do much more than state the standard arguments pro and con and give reference to recent contributions. However, although Professor Díaz-Alejandro has tried to cover too much, I enjoyed the main thrust of the paper. In my opinion, many a liberal economist has bent over backwards in attempts to denounce the LDCs' claims for new rules concerning conduct, restrictive business practices, and national- isations, and for cheaper access to technology, etc. Professor Díaz- Alejandro's account in the section on 'LDC minerals and TNEs' of the many inherent 'imperfect' characteristics of the TNE *per se*, of the markets in which they operate, and the many rents and quasi-rents there are to bargain for, places the 'Southern' view in a more benevolent light. This, however, is not to say that I see exactly how the new regulations and rules for TNE activities demanded by the LDCs, and looked upon with great sympathy in the concluding section of the paper, are to be formulated, or what they should, and can, actually accomplish. After these general remarks, let me proceed by discussing more specifically a few points raised in the paper.

I THE QUESTION OF ALTERNATIVES TO THE TNE

In discussing the normative aspects of the TNE in LDCs, Professor Díaz-Alejandro asks (p. 236): 'Is it [the TNE] better or worse from a normative, welfare viewpoint. . . . [than] the atomistic, price-taking version of the competitive firm found in introductory text-books?'

I think this question is somewhat wrongly posed. We cannot easily conceive—except in wishful thinking—that the differentiated goods produced today by TNEs, at declining costs, embodying firm-specific technology, and sold on highly concentrated markets, could equally well be produced by atomistic, price-taking firms of the neoclassical type. Therefore, if the prevalent demand pattern is taken as given, we have to recognise that the alternative to having TNEs is not having atomistic firms, but to let the present transnational firms supply their products in alternative ways (to the extent that such exist). This could be done either through the export of finished products from the home-country production sites, or the export (licensing) of the firm-specific knowledge to firms in other countries and let them produce the goods in question.

A change in what we consider as the alternative to the TNE has implications for the welfare analysis of specific issues. Let us take the issue to which Professor Díaz-Alejandro pays most attention, that is the notion put forward by Stephen Magee (1978) in his 'appropriability theory' of foreign direct investment. The point of departure here is that the existence of the TNE is due to its ability to erect barriers to entry through production of technology and product characteristics, the quasi-rents to which they can appropriate (firm-specific technology). For their survival, the TNEs thus tend to overinvest in technology with a high degree of appropriability, thereby inducing a wedge between private and social efficiency. It seems to me that the elimination of the TNE would not do away with this inefficiency, but only change its nature. Instead of concentrating on producing technology with a high degree of appropriability when transferred through direct investment, the firm would shift to producing technology with a high degree of appropriability when transferred by the alternative means, in other words, either through licences or embodied in exported finished goods. There is no *a priori* reason why the distortion thus induced would be smaller than those induced at present with TNE direct invest-ments.

II TNE AND PRIMARY-COMMODITY PRICE STABILITY AND LEVELS

My second comment is on what I consider to be one of the exquisite 'dishes' on Professor Díaz-Alejandro's *smörgåsbord*. That is the section (pp. 242-6) where he puts forward the notion that the dominance of TNE over the LDCs' production and trade in some commodity markets may have had a favourable impact on the stability and levels[1] of prices. If so, and to the extent that the LDCs have shared the possible gains from more stable and higher commodity prices, this would be a benefit accruing from foreign direct investment, which I think has been very much overlooked in the literature. Professor Díaz-Alejandro advances as an example the International Nickel Company. By posting prices on a take-it-or-leave-it basis, the company may have brought substantial stability to the nickel market. Another market in which it is possible that the domination of a few, large TNEs has brought, not only more stable, but also higher prices is the banana market. But whether the producing LDCs have shared in these potential benefits is, of course, not thereby ascertained. In my opinion study of these markets from this perspective is a very interesting field for future research. If the hypotheses advanced by Professor Díaz-Alejandro have some substance in them, the possibility exists that 'with the TNE in decadence', world markets for primary commodities will become even more unstable in the future.

III THE REGIONAL–NATIONAL–TRANSNATIONAL EXPANSION PATH

My third comment is on Professor Díaz-Alejandro's notion in the section dealing with the positive theory of the TNE that 'the Regional–National–Transnational expansion path applies in principle to all capitalistic firms . . .'. I only want to remind us that there is also sometimes the Regional–National–Transnational–*National* path, or at least the transnational property of firms in some industries tends to diminish at times. This is perhaps at present most pronounced in the petroleum industry, where the insurmountable patents and knowledge once held by a handful of truly transnational oil companies have disseminated into public domain during the last decade (as put by Vernon). Going back into history, one would probably find that the same has happened several times before, for instance, in sectors like public utilities, plantation agriculture, mining, etc., once important fields for foreign direct investment, But there are, of course, also developments in the opposite direction. One example is the plate-glass industry which for decades has been dominated by domestic firms in most countries. All of a sudden, patented new production techniques (the float process) have made it possible for a few firms in this industry to go transnational.

However, the notion of an irrevocable Regional–National–Transnational expansion path may give the false impression of inevitably growing involvement by TNEs in world trade and production. In the Third World at least, this is probably not so. According to my own preliminary findings, the ratio of the stock of foreign direct investment by TNEs in the LDCs to GDP has fallen drastically and steadily since the early days of this century.[2] In other words, in quantitative terms, direct-investment involvement by TNEs is becoming increasingly less important in the LDCs–while it is possible, but not ascertained, that TNE involvement through alternative channels tends to grow (cf. UN (1978), pp. 68–70).

ENDNOTES

1. The notion of the TNEs acting as a cartel on behalf of the LDCs has been presented in a mimeographed paper by R. Cooper (1974). The idea that the dominance of a few TNEs over certain primary-commodity markets has brought price stability has some support in Marian Radetzki's (1978) findings.
2. Indexed, the ratio has fallen from 100 in 1913 to about 16 in 1976. To the extent these figures are biased due to data limitations, it is probably mostly in the direction of understating the stock of investments in 1913 (cf. Svedberg, 1978).

REFERENCES

Cooper, R., 'Nationalization vs. Vertical Integration in Extractive Industries', mimeo (New Haven, Conn.: Yale University Press, 1974).

Magee, S., 'Information and Multinational Corporation: An Appropriability Theory of Direct Foreign Investment', in Bhagwati, J. (ed.), *The New International Economic Order: The North–South Debate* (Cambridge, Mass.: MIT Press, 1978).

Radetzki, M., 'Market Structure and Bargaining Power', *Resources Policy* (June 1978).

Svedberg, P., 'The Portfolio-Direct Composition of Foreign Direct Investment in 1914 Revisited', *Economic Journal*, vol. 88 (December 1978).
United Nations (UN), *Transnational Corporations in World Development: A Re-examination* (New York: E/C, 10/38, 20 March 1978).

Part III

Adjustments in Production and Trade

7 Problems of Adjustment to Imports from Less-Developed Countries[1]

Herbert Giersch (West Germany)

I INTRODUCTION

The group of less-developed countries (LDCs) has set as its target an increase of its share in world manufacturing production from around 7 to 8 per cent now to 25 per cent in the year 2000. Although the figure is probably too high to be realistic, it can be taken as a symbol of the LDCs' efforts to improve their position in world production and international trade. Advanced countries are called upon to support these efforts by freeing imports from LDCs.

The West German Government, in 1971, under Willy Brandt and in matters of economic policy dominated by a professional economist (Karl Schiller), gave a fairly unambiguous anticipatory response:

> Structural changes which are triggered by the increasing integration of the developing countries into the international division of labor must not be hampered; they must rather be supported, if necessary by adequate measures of structural policy. Especially the exodus of labor and capital from the industries where an adjustment of the changed market conditions becomes necessary, must not be obviated by preservation subsidies. (*Bundesregierung*, 1971).

The response would have been less positive,

— had the country suffered from unemployment
— had trade associations and labour unions had a hearing, and
— had weak rather than strong growth prevailed in the decades before,

so that it had not become popular to be optimistic in the liberal tradition of Anglo-Saxon political economy.

II   FREE TRADE AND REAL WAGES

Neo-classical economics contains the message of the Stolper–Samuelson theorem: Labour in advanced countries will suffer a decline of real wages in terms of each and every commodity if free imports are permitted from countries where labour is not the scarce factor.[2] In a similar vein, the Lerner–Samuelson theorem implies that free trade will—under certain conditions—lead to an international factor price equalisation even if no factor movements take place. To become equal through trade, real wages must rise where they are low, and fall where they are high, in the absence of free trade. Neoclassical economics thus shows free trade to be an issue of conflict between labour in capital-rich and in capital-poor countries.

Neo-Marxian economics attempts to re-establish the presumption in favour of a worldwide class conflict between capital and labour. The notion of 'unequal exchanges' (Emmanuel, 1972) is introduced to demonstrate that the rich in the North benefit by exploiting the poor workers in the South. Although Samuelson has shown that the argument is wrong (Samuelson, 1976), it nevertheless has strong emotional appeal. Those who use it fail to ask themselves whether it would really be better for the workers in the South if the capitalist countries refused to employ them (Lerner, 1976).

A similar reasoning starts from the proposition that advanced countries are so powerful that they can determine which international transactions and markets are to be free or restricted. They will opt for freeing the capital market and those segments of commerce which increase the demand for capital and reduce the demand for labour. This raises two points:

(1) The first is an observation: In the 1960s European investors were not so much interested in free access to foreign countries but attempted—with the consent of domestic labour—to promote immigration from the South. Why was there no class conflict over this issue in the European North? The answer will be approached in more detail below (page 269).

(2) The second point is a presumption: If the present relationship between freedom and protection is biased against labour and the LDCs,

a removal of the remaining restrictions, upheld by capitalists in the advanced countries, should lead to higher real wages and/or employment in the world at large. However, we observe that moves towards freer imports from LDCs into advanced countries are not only resisted by capitalists but also by labour. This is in line with the Stolper—Samuelson theorem. It may, however, apply only to specific labour-intensive industries which have no chance for survival without protection. Here, labour and capital are—so to speak—complementarily locked in. Nevertheless, labour in general may feel that it is at least indirectly affected and that there is a depressing effect which free imports from labour-rich countries will have on the full employment level of real wages.

The conflict between labour here and labour in the LDCs seems to be bridged by a newly emerging ideology. It recommends protection for more growth in the advanced countries—along the lines of the Cambridge (England) New Economic Policy Group. The LDCs are advised to concentrate on 'basic needs' and on integration among themselves so that they need not rely so much on outward-looking policies and free access to the product markets of advanced countries. This type of thinking—implying a two-factor model and a worldwide class conflict between labour and capital—thus supports ideas of disintegration, delinking or what ever the current terminology is. The fear of exploitation overshadows the hope that there are gains from trade to be exploited which could make everybody better off.

Such pessimism is perhaps warranted for some countries which are comparable to those weak persons, both young and old, who find the competitive struggle and the resulting division of labour anything but attractive. Lord Kaldor (1978) seems to hint at that with regard to an advanced country. A national economy may indeed have become so incapable of adjusting its internal structure to exogenous changes that it needs to be inward-looking in order to survive, just as age persons tend to become more inward-looking. Without protection of even the least competitive industries and firms there would not be enough profits to maintain capital intact or to generate some modest growth. Economists and political leaders in such countries (1) tend to stress the demand rather than the supply aspects of growth, (2) tend to call upon other countries to generate demand—rather than stimulate domestic private investment ahead of demand, (3) tend to complain about the country's commodity terms of trade as a bad fate—rather than stress the simple rule that improvement requires a change in the country's product mix in compliance with (or anticipation of) chaning income elasticities of demand and prices, (4) tend to favour government policies—rather than emphasise the problem-solving capacity of private decision-makers, or (5) tend to be sensitive to a strong popular quest for individual security and interpersonal equality. There are, of course, elements of a positive feedback mechanism in this. Economists, by giving advice which is sound only in the short run, can play an accelerating role. If this is the case one may call the country a 'Keynesian economy' in view of Keynes' emphasis on the short run and his contribution to the stagnation thesis for the medium run.

As the problem of LDCs is not the subject of this paper, there is no place to dwell upon the distinction between inward and outward-looking economies in the Third World. It is sufficient to note that both types do exist and that outward-looking economies are growing more rapidly—or that rapidly growing economies tend to be more outward-looking. The only inference to be drawn here is that inward-looking LDCs are more stagnant compared to fast-growing outward-looking countries which are in a process of catching-up and which are likely to be the major beneficiaries of outward-looking policies in the West.

The counterpart of a Keynesian advanced country may be called a 'Schumpeterian country'. The model of such an economy may be conceived to have the following properties:

(1) Firms and families have a high adaptive capacity; they consider exogenous disturbances to be challenges which have to be met with a forward-oriented response.

(2) Their emphasis on a forward-oriented response corresponds with a high capacity to learn (research), to innovate, to experiment, and to imitate.

(3) Institutional arrangements are not so tight and inflexible as to become a brake on forward-oriented responses.

(4) Incomes (after taxes and transfers) contain high compensation for risk-bearing (profits), learning (human capital), and successful response to changes (relative factor prices sufficiently flexible interregionally and interindustrially). Rewards for pure (unskilled) labour and capital are correspondingly less important. So is the fear that free imports from capital-poor and labour-rich countries might significantly worsen the distribution of income.

(5) Most people's time horizons are long enough to transform the 'Big Tradeoff' between equity and efficiency (Okun, 1975) into a tradeoff between equality and growth, where prospects for high growth de-emphasise the natural feelings of envy. The time horizon may be

related to the age structure of the population.

(6) Supply (and supply policy) is considered to be more important than demand (and demand management). Demand is taken for granted or is created in a process of innovation guided by the search for outlets with a high income elasticity of demand. The terms of trade are rarely of concern as they tend to improve (on a Paasche basis) or quickly recover from exogenous shocks under the impact of adjustments in the product mix or the export basket.

(7) Because of its high (actual or expected) human capital content domestic labour is complementary (rather than competitive) to both domestic capital and with immigrant labour. Domestic labour can specialise for job opportunities higher up in the hierarchy, which are less accessible to foreigners on account of the language barriers. This makes for a low resistance against foreign workers.[3]

(8) Economists and other intellectuals still praise the virtues of openness *vis à vis* the future (indeterminacy) and the rest of the world; they consider competition not only as an allocative mechanism but also as a social instrument of discovery (Hayek) and believe that competition, in additional homeopathic doses, will strengthen rather than weaken the vitality of the socio-economic system (which is seen as a catallaxy rather than a hierarchically co-ordinated entity). As long as economists entertain ideas akin to eighteenth century Anglo-Saxon philosophy, the country can be assumed to be fairly young (as England during the Industrial Revolution).[4]

Keynesian and Schumpeterian countries can well coexist if the former do not insist on more than occasional help so that the latter remain free to render their best service to the rest of the world by making use of their relatively high capacity to adjust. This makes the outward-looking countries in the Third World the natural partners of advanced Schumpeterian countries.

If economic policies are to express people's preference and behavioural patterns, there is no good reason for the West to speak with one voice or to form a trade policy convoy. Those who are able to make greater progress in freeing imports from LDCs should be at liberty to do so. This raises the question as to whether the conditional MFN clause should not be substituted for the unconditional clause. It would allow for progress at the expense of perfection. Once experiments of partnership between young developing countries have proved beneficial, they will be imitated or joined by others.

An important success condition is certainty about the inevitability of adjustment. Enterpreneurs tempted to look backward and to engage in defensive activities should not be given hope for political support, as such activities would entail costs for the domestic economy and the Third World.

III   BEYOND THE POINT OF NO RETURN

At this juncture a pause is necessary in order to survey some questions that need to be discussed subsequently.

Experience from European integration suggests that adjustment is facilitated if the decision to remove import barriers is irreversible and preannounced. Would this apply also to the present case?

If an irreversible decision is advantageous, one would like to know something about the size and the nature of the adjustment problem. What does past and current research tell us?

In European integration the free trade commitment was made in combination with decisions opening the prospects for a common labour market, and firms seemed to like that. Do we have a similar complementarity here?

If intraindustry adjustment is unimportant in trade between countries with different levels of development and income, what does interindustry adjustment involve?

Interindustry adjustment might still be intrafirm adjustment, if the firm covers various industries. By the same token intrafirm adjustment can also be interregional and even international if the firm is a multiplant enterprise. Is intrafirm adjustment easier than interfirm (or market) adjustment?

To cope with the adjustment problem, where are governments better than markets and where are markets better than governments? What is the possible role of information and economic research in this field?

Policy certainty reduces information costs. If it is true that alternatives are not given but must be searched for, then even the elimination of one or several possible options must reduce the cost of decision-making. This speaks in favour of making the free import commitment definite and irreversible. But any policy change, the more so if it is irreversible, ought to be preannounced, so that decision-makers in the private sector know what they have to (or need not) take into account in farreaching decisions. This is not in order to please the business sector, but to avoid inefficient decisions which involve a waste of resources, eventually at the expense of real wages. Moreover, an irreversible commitment must be creditable, and in order to be so it must appear to be feasible and reasonable *ex ante*. A host of questions will be raised in the legislature during the ratification process. This is why we must assess, at least, the order of magnitude of the adjustment problem. Before doing so, it may be useful to ask who—on the political scene—is likely to challenge the estimates. Experience suggests that major opposition will not originate from firms and other profit maximisers. They may already anticipate the adjustment called for although they will testify against it if asked in official hearings. Strong opposition is rather certain to come from various trade associations, labour unions and similar non-profit institutions which pursue goals like membership maximisation, growth for growth's sake or mere survival. As will be seen later, sensitive industries are often regionally concentrated. Regional representatives in political decision-making bodies will, therefore, be amongst the hardest opponents.

IV   THE SIZE OF THE ADJUSTMENT PROBLEM

At the time when the West German government made the policy declaration quoted at the beginning of this chapter, the Kiel Institute started empirical work on the long-term problems of the economy, including its structure of protection, its structural anomalies, and its actual and potential problems of adjustment to imports from LDCs. It is on this work that this section most heavily draws. Figures and estimates relate to West Germany, but some findings are likely to have a wider application. The sector which will have to bear the brunt of the burden of adjustment to imports from LDCs is manufacturing. As a matter of qualification we should note at the outset that its share in the country's GDP and employment is so much beyond any norm derived from international cross-section analyses (related to per capita income) that there is reason to believe in a backlog adjustment process; this holds to the extent that the anomaly can be imputed to the long-lasting undervaluation of the currency which clearly benefited the international sector, mainly manufacturing.[5] The backlog hypothesis does not, of course, apply to that part of the anomaly which is due to permanent factors such as the raw material deposits and cheap river transportation in the Ruhr district and the waste disposal system of the Rhine. Less of the structural anomaly needs to be corrected, if the country should play a greater role as a capital exporter and hence also as an exporter of capital goods to LDCs.

With regard to the starting position and past trends we note:

(1) The division of labour in manufacturing with the LDCs is explainable by human capital and raw material intensity: German industries tend to be the more competitive in trade with LDCs the more human-capital intensive and the less raw-material intensive they are (Fels, 1974; Wolter, 1977a).

(2) The system of protection discriminates more against LDCs than against industrial countries (Fels, 1974). Nevertheless, persistent protection could not reverse the declining industries' weak position, nor could it prevent the developing countries from capturing additional shares of domestic consumption (Wolter, 1977b).

(3) In 1975, in most German industries, imports from developing countries accounted for less than 5 per cent of domestic consumption. Exceptions are musical instruments, toys and sporting goods (9.9 per cent), clothing (9 per cent), leather and leather manufactures (8 per cent), non-ferrous metals (6.6 per cent) and textiles (5.4 per cent). Nevertheless, low-wage countries exerted considerable adjustment pressure on a number of domestic industries. First, imports from these countries have increased at an unprecedented rate since 1970. Second, in several sub-branches of manufacturing developing countries gained considerably larger market shares than is evident from overall industry figures. And third, due to their low wage level and concomitant price competitiveness in certain industries the supply from developing countries induced strong price competition on domestic markets (Wolter, 1977b).

(4) In recent years imports of manufactures from LDCs grew annually between 30 per cent and 100 per cent—albeit starting from low levels—in goods such as plastic products, glass, electrical engineering, office machinery, light metal products, road vehicles, precision and optical goods, clocks and watches, fine ceramics, and ships and boats.[6]

(5) The brunt of the adjustment burden is borne by economically weak groups, since it is the industries with a high share of low-skill (especially female) employment and the industries concentrated in backward regions which are under particularly strong adjustment pressure (Fels. 174; Wolter, 1977b).

(6) The industries so far most severely affected by adjustment pressure are characterised by a relatively large number of small and medium-sized firms. Nevertheless, within these industries, the medium-sized firms (100 to 1000 employs) tended to cope with the adjustment

problem better than the larger and the small ones (Fels, and Horn, 1976).

(7) Even in those industries of manufacturing which are characterised by relatively high R and D expenditures and above average human-capital intensity such as chemicals and engineering, there continue to exist firms which (still) have standardised and labour-intensive products in their output mix (Dicke and Weiss, 1978).

(8) In general, it can be said that firms which spend much on research and development, planning and organisation, and industrial designing, and firms which produce in small lots to customer specification have proved to be resistant to competition from LDCs.

Studies of the West German engineering industry which go further into detail lead to the following conclusions:[7]

(1) Adequately defined skill variables—such as the relative importance of craft persons, operators and managerial personnel—go far to explain why some subsectors are more competitive *vis à vis* LDCs than others, but surprisingly enough certain proxies for the technology factor, like R and D intensity, did not yield significant results.

(2) Standardised engineering products do not enjoy a comparative advantage in West Germany.

(3) If the output is motor vehicles or metal products, competitiveness greatly depends upon proximity to competitive suppliers of component parts or other inputs from industrial sources.

(4) The range of products under severe competition from LDCs is wider than was initially expected.[8]

(5) The adjustment process in labour-intensive industries seems to have been aggravated by relatively sharp increases in wages for unskilled labour since 1970. A test of substitutability of craft persons and physical capital for unskilled labour revealed a relatively high elasticity (Dicke and Weiss, 1978). This finding is consistent with the recent relative increase in the rate of unemployment of unskilled workers.

A rather detailed study of the steel industry shows that producers in the United States and Western Europe are about to lose their international competitiveness in mass steel. Adjustment pressure is less strong in rolling mill operations where skill requirements are high and proximity to customers is important. The highly advanced countries remain competitive in new steel technology, in speciality steel products and their application, in new capital goods for the steel industry, and in the supply of whole steel plants. Mass steel production, which is too costly in advanced countries and for which there is not enough demand in poor countries is moving towards semi-industrialised countries (Wolter, 1977c).

As to the static effects of policy changes in favour of free imports, relevant studies for West Germany do not lead to dramatic results.

(1) Eliminating MFN tariffs only would raise the welfare level in the Federal Republic of Germany by not more than DM 700 million per year (per capita: DM 12) (Glisman, 1977).

(2) If non-tariff barriers to imports of textiles and apparel were abolished, real income would rise by about DM 1500 million per year (per capita: around DM 25). These are the most highly protected products in the Federal Republic of Germany outside agriculture and coal mining (Glisman, 1977).

(3) Tariff liberalisation would reduce employment in West Germany's manufacturing sector by about 1.2 per cent, a figure which would become even lower if additional employment opportunities for increased exports were taken into account (Fels and Glisman, 1975).

The overall static effects of trade liberalisation on real income and employment were also estimated as of minor importance by other authors for other countries (for example, Magee (1972); Cline *et al.*, (1976)).[9]

This is not incompatible with more dramatic results for those branches of industry which were thought to be particularly sensitive to free imports from LDCs (Dicke *et al.*, 1976).[10] The main conclusions, which refer to the extreme case that both tariff and non-tariff barriers would be abolished, indicate that the leather and clothing industries would almost lose their bases of existence, unless they can succeed in concentrating on high income elasticity products subject to the vagaries of fashion—a possibility open to firms producing close to leading consumer markets.

On the assumption that the export potential of LDCs and their imports from Germany will increase more than in the past so that a 20 per cent upward shift in the trend of imports from and exports to LDCs takes place, a research group of the Kiel Institute arrives at the following conclusions (Hiemenz and Schatz, 1977):

(1) Full liberalisation of imports from LDCs will reduce the number

of jobs in German manufacturing by another 0.8 million. This would be more than 11 per cent of present employment in manufacturing (in 1976: 7.4 million).

(2) Foreign *gastarbeiten* (guestworkers) will be more than proportionately affected since they are highly concentrated in lines of production and jobs where skill requirements are low. The effect will be particularly strong where foreigners compete with domestic female workers; it will be less so where foreign workers are—or have made themselves—complementary to domestic workers by accepting work which requires heavy physical effort or otherwise has high disutility.

(3) Should foreign workers be discriminated against in the sense that they would not be offered a new job whenever they lost one in this process,[11] they would still bear not more than 20 per cent of the job losses.[12] Even under such discrimination, therefore, employment of domestic workers in manufacturing would still decline by 0.7 million or 9 per cent of present employment in manufacturing (1976) (Hiemenz and Schatz 1977).

Foreign workers are presumably more mobile than their domestic competitors. This is why, in the first place, their influx contributed to the industrial agglomeration tendencies and to the growth of urban centres in the 1960s. Their return home in the adjustment process under the assumed discrimination strategy would minimise the employment problems in these regions. This applies to North Rhine–Westphalia and Baden–Württemberg where more than a quarter of all employees in manufacturing were foreigners in 1974. In all peripheral regions, however, the job losses due to increased imports from LDCs would far outweigh the present employment of guestworkers (Hiemenz and Schatz 1977, p. 55 and Table 3*). A strategy to ensure that all employment effects would fall on guestworkers would, therefore, require either the migration of German workers from the periphery to the central areas (plus a change in industrial occupation) or some relocation of the unaffected branches of manufacturing into those peripheral areas that most resemble the LDCs in their industrial structure. The relocation would be preferable to migration for reasons of regional balance. It would prevent an overcongestion in central areas, should the decline of employment in manufacturing be compensated by a growth of the service sector which—in some respects—seems to have locational advantages in those central areas where the employment impact of more import competition would be small.

To form a general judgement on the size of the adjustment problem the following points relating to West Germany stand out:

(1) If free imports from LDCs would not destroy more than 0.8 million jobs until 1985, as has been estimated, the task appears manageable as it affects only about 11 per cent of employees in manufacturing over ten or more years, and hence not much more than 1 per cent per annum.

(2) These displacement effects are small if compared to past technological displacement.

(3) Compared to the displacement effects of past imports from LDCs they are large.[13] The burden will be felt more than in the past when it was eased by high employment growth and the selective import of guestworkers, and when its impact was less concentrated in individual industries and regions.

Any general judgement at this stage can only be of a tentative nature and will therefore be coloured by personal predilections. The author's feeling is that an advanced country of the Schumpeterian type could well consider adjustment to free imports from LDCs as a 'salutary jolt' toward growth in new directions. A trade challenge may well compensate for the apparent weakening of the technological growth stimulus. But there is an unfortunate coincidence of a labour-saving bias in both trade and technological development, which is likely to require new and early responses if it is not to overstrain the labour market's capacity to adjust. This appears to be the sensitive point at a time when an increased desire for job security is raising the social costs of economic growth (as we measure it) to levels which make growth look less and less attractive.

V   TOWARD A FORWARD-LOOKING ADJUSTMENT POLICY

If the advanced Schumpeterian countries dared to make an irrevocable promise to LDCs to remove all import barriers but to stretch adjustment over a period of, say, ten years, they need not, in the author's opinion, resort to industry-specific government assistance programmes. The conversion potential of established firms in an advanced country should actually be large enough to cope with the adjustment problem without specific help.[14]

General, as opposed to industry-specific, measures to increase the conversion potential[15] would include:

(1) Supply-oriented policies to promote economic growth, notably tax incentives for job creation, for making relative wages more responsive to market conditions, and for promoting product innovation—including product innovation in the investment goods sector, which will become process innovation once the new equipment is installed. (As a complement to supply-oriented policies, the society must be prepared to tolerate high after-tax incomes from innovative and entrepreneurial activities, not only because of the incentives they provide, but also because of their contribution to a growing test market for new high-income elasticity products.)

(2) Investment grants for returning foreign workers if it is reasonably assured that they will take their job with them, perhaps under the guidance and with the knowhow and market information of their previous employers.

(3) Free information from independent competing research institutions to firms in sensitive industries about structural trends and available adjustment opportunities, including locational innovation, in other words, the transfer of production to low wage areas within the country and low wage countries in the world at large.

(4) Removal of barriers to intranational and international locational innovation, including an offer to LDCs for forming a 'free investment club' that would serve to protect against expropriation without due compensation and thus promote the flow of direct foreign investment.[16]

These propositions assume that markets, if well supplied with low-cost (or even free) information have the capacity of doing better than governments, which often ignore or distort information. The often-made suggestion of creating in West Germany or elsewhere a government agency to control the structure of industrial investment has little appeal, except in an economy which is so backward that a good investment plan could be drawn up by imitating more advanced countries, which must and do rely on decentralised entrepreneurial search processes. There is, however, a side issue bearing directly on the adjustment problem: Should governments in advanced countries veto investment which raises the capital–labour ratio in defence against job destruction from LDCs (defensive investment)? A positive case can be based upon the argument that such investment means 'job abortion' in LDCs if the latter lose in the ensuing 'investment war', and a waste of resources if the latter win. It can also be argued that such defensive investments lead to an excessive capital-intensity of world production and hence to a capital-shortage type of world unemployment. The tendency for such defensive investment must be expected to be great in ageing economies notably among businessmen, who have narrow technological knowledge, so that incapability of product innovation adds to a natural aversion to locational innovation. Labour unions, who also in any case dislike international locational innovation, will reluctantly support defensive investment. However, even here the case for a government body to veto specific investment is weak, since it requires a high degree of certainty about the lack of medium-run prospects for product innovation or even technological breakthroughs. In any case, government would be well advised to rule out positive acts, such as delaying the removal of import barriers or subsidising the (defensive) investment under the heading of adjustment assistance. A principle for government behaviour that takes this consideration into account would be: no adjustment assistance without product innovation or locational innovation.

While the market is superior to government in future-oriented decision requiring information which has to be searched for, firms may be superior to markets when it comes to adjustment. If firms are large and decentralised, they may be tantamount to integrated labour markets and integrated capital markets. As multiproduct, multiplant, multiregional, or multinational firms, they should be more efficient in coping with the adjustment problem than a polypolistic group of firms adding up to the same size. Otherwise, their survival in competition with smaller firms would merely rest on monopoly power. In this case, however, they would invite antitrust action. This could be suspended as long as the monopoly gains are used for an intrafirm transfer system designed to reduce the hardship of adjustment. If their existence is due to superior efficiency they should be able to handle the adjustment task without government assistance. Hence, no adjustment assistance to firms above a certain size. An exception may be made when they perceive a new diversification potential, the exploitation of which, however, will often require a new management.

The multinational firm has undiscovered virtues in an international adjustment process.[17] It can gradually shift production to LDCs when import barriers are lowered and it can serve its old market from the new source of supply. Job destruction here, and job creation there are synchronised by central decisions. The market could hardly do better because of subjective uncertainty, that is imperfect information on what the competitors do: Someone has to start, either a producer in an LDC, who seizes the opportunity of more free entry into an advanced country and acts in the expectation that he can crowd out some competitor there; or a producer in the advanced country gives up in an act of anticipatory adjustment, thus making room for more imports and production in an LDC. Thus, the market essentially copes with the international adjustment problem by *ex post* co-ordination only.

The best alternative to international intrafirm adjustment is anticipatory adjustment. Outcompeting is worse from a cosmopolitan point of view, since it absorbs entrepreneurial resources in LDCs where they are particularly scarce. Advocates of anticipatory adjustment have heard all of the more or less respectable arguments for import protection and a few new points relating to uncertainty about the future (see, for example, Scheid, 1974). The uncertainty arguments are not dissimilar to the popular belief that it is advisable not to engage in speculation and hence to refrain from portfolio adjustment. However, non-action constitutes action when the system is changing, and perhaps the most fatal action when the government has decided about the direction. All the uncertainty arguments against anticipatory adjustment are, therefore, based on the assumption that the point of no return will not be reached.[18] This is why preannouncement and irreversibility are so important. LDCs have good reasons to press for them.

Seen in this context, anticipatory adjustment might deserve assistance out of taxpayers' money.[19] Funds for this purpose could be diverted from foreign aid or from maintenance subsidies, which must be phased out if adjustment is the prime objective. Recipients could be:

(a) workers, if the purpose is retraining, migration, or self-employment;

(b) firms, if they perform the task of retraining and job relocation;

(c) regional authorities, if they can show that adjustment in the region's industry mix is vital, that it requires the replacement of economically obsolete parts of the infrastructure by the new industry-specific investments, and that the new industries or firms are at the doorstep.

As process innovation is excluded, being a defensive action, and as product innovation is a continuous process and can easily be financed by bank loans and bond or stock issues, the adjustment assistance could concentrate on locational innovation, interregional and international.

The domestic locational restructuring of the viable part of manufacturing must be expected to meet with the following difficulties:

(1) To the extent that the firms are based on raw material deposits and cheap access to waterways, they will have to incur higher transportation costs or switch to other inputs or other sources of supply.

(2) To the extent that skilled labour is industry-specific, labour will have to move together with the locus of production from the central areas to the periphery. But where shall the incentive come from, if the periphery has absolute locational disadvantages which are not compensated in the form of lower real wages?

(3) The political process favours policies to keep costs from rising in the central areas, either in the form of rent control or in the form of public infrastructure investments in the transportation system. Both respond to strong short-run pressures in constituencies which are thought to be decisive in general elections.[20]

Far sighted regional policies, which seem to be wasteful in the short run, could be a way out of the dilema.[21] Other solutions would be a sharp decline of rents in peripheral areas and the introduction of labour-saving innovations to raise labour productivity when firms move their production sites to the periphery of the domestic economy. The latter case requires an elaboration of the principle established above: process innovation should not be subsidised unless it is part of a locational innovation programme.

Subsidies to locational innovation can be tied to the condition that the recipient firm offers an undiminished—or increasing—number of jobs to domestic workers at prevailing wage rates. In this case a product innovation or a change in the product mix would be a prerequisite. A clearcut government announcement to grant such adjustment assistance could induce hesitant firms to leave the protectionist camp and to join the free trade league. Such adjustment assistance, indirectly linked to product innovation and scaled to job creation for new products, could be viewed as a general form of structural policy in support of the growth sector.

Apart from anticipatory adjustment assistance, there may be a case for compensating the owners of specific resources for the losses they suffer in the adjustment process. The case may be based upon equity considerations: nobody should suffer from policies which were introduced after specific resources were acquired. Political considerations may suggest that such compensation is the easiest way of removing resistance to change. While compensation would thus encourage change on the one hand, it will also be a burden—in the form of higher taxation on those who happen to earn transitory high incomes as rewards for (successful) innovative activities. This negative effect on spontaneous economic growth, which by itself is a factor facilitating adjustment, calls for qualifications of the compensation principle. Possible forms of qualification, in addition to those already mentioned, could be:

(1) No compensation to capital owners, since they should have started speculating about changes in government policies in the continuous learning process going on in financial markets.

(2) No compensation for the loss of human capital, unless the owner has a low conversion potential due to his old age.

(3) No compensation to immobile skilled workers, unless they are prepared to accept part of the adjustment burden by moderating wage claims as a possible means of slowing down the adjustment process.

Instead, means and efforts to raise the professional and locational conversion potential of the labour force at large are called for. As hope for specific compensation impairs interest in raising the conversion potential, false hopes should be destroyed as early as possible by making the compensation rules known together with the irreversible decision to move towards free imports from LDCs and whatever principles of adjustment assistance society deems to be the acceptable compromise between equity and efficiency.

ENDNOTES

1. The author is grateful to Hugo Dicke, Gerhard Fels, Frank Weiss and Frank Wolter for helpful comments on an earlier version.
2. This sentence disregards the qualification which the authors make with reference to the multifactor case. However, the purpose of the theorem is to show 'that there is a grain of truth in the pauper labor type of argument for protection' (Stolper and Samuelson, 1941, p. 356).
3. Domestic capital benefits from a selective immigration because the labour makes it easier for the firms to invest where they are. Selective immigration reduces the otherwise existing pressure to invest in peripheral areas or in the places where the foreign workers come from (see also page 275).
4. It appears tempting to make these conjectures operational, so that the relative economic age of countries or regions could be identified, but this would require a fairly comprehensive research programme. A guess may, however, be appropriate with regard to West Germany on the basis of the

author's personal observation and intuitive interpolation: that country still has some features of a Schumpeterian economy despite definite signs of ageing not yet visible from a distance.

5. See Fels, Schatz and Wolter (1970); Fels-Schatz (1977/1); Dicke and Heitger (1977).

6. In nominal terms; the Statistical Office does not publish price indices for regional trade flows.

7. See Dick (1978), Dicke (1978), Heitger (1978), Weiss (1978).

8. It includes: most metal products; in electrical engineering: switchgear, wiring devices, household appliances, lighting fixtures, and radio and television sets and their components; among road vehicles: the bicycle; in mechanical engineering: mountings and fittings, sewing machines and standardised tools.

9. It has to be noted that these studies and those mentioned before in this paragraph do not quantify dynamic effects of liberalisation.

10. The study referred to assumes *inter alia* that the removal of import barriers will not affect the real exchange rate. The reason given (p. 106, footnote) is that the study is limited to the impact effects of liberalising imports from LDCs only and that so far these imports had little weight in the import bill.

11. Such discrimination against guestworkers if conveived as a policy would of course have to be accompanied by fair compensation payments. It could be supplemented by a grant or a loan that allows the recipient to take the job with him when he returns, perhaps also temporarily assisted by his firm. It should not be impossible to find adequate institutional forms.

12. This compares to 80 per cent for a discrimination strategy applied to a total trade development in conformity with past trends. The difference is due to the fact that the assumed 20 per cent shift in trend would more severely affect industries in which guest workers are not so heavily concentrated or have already been laid off.

13. Roughly eight times as large according to Wolter (1977b, pp. 120, 128).

14. A firms' or a country's conversion potential can be defined as its potential capacity to change the product mix. It is related (a) to size, since size is a proxy for the diversity of resources, and (b) to the availability of non-specific factors which can be turned to alternative uses.

Old vintages in the stock of physical capital and human capital permanently employed indicate a high conversion potential at the time of replacement. The postulate of raising a firm's conversion potential includes the recommendation

(a) to drop low income elasticity products from the product mix at an early stage;

(b) to add new products (Schumpeter-goods) to the output mix, even if this lowers profits, as a safeguard against the dangerous situation that would arise if old products were to be dropped under competition from LDCs without having discovered the high-income elastic goods which could fill the gap and without having acquired the experience to produce them in line with traditional quality standards;

(c) to hire workers with a great learning capacity as a form of investment;

(d) to replace management when it turns out to suffer from product fetishism ('We are steel makers, not profit maximisers');

(e) to start joint ventures and even merger negotiations as measures of a last resort to import new technology or an imaginative management.

A country's conversion potential depends upon: (a) the conversion potential of its firms in the international sector; (b) the information and transaction costs of interfirm adjustment; and (c) the costs of regional and professional adjustment in the labour market.

15. Apart from benefiting the country itself, such measures help LDCs because (a) they lead to higher real wages in advanced countries, thus making it easier for LDCs to compete; and (b) they promise a quick withdrawal of advanced countries from the supply of standardised products with a high content of unskilled labour and hence raise the income elasticity of world demand for the same products from LDCs. That is what matters most to prevent the LDCs from adopting costly strategies of unbalanced growth and delinking, and from wasteful efforts to develop a growth pole of their own—with emphasis on heavy industries, which are very capital-intensive and create dangerous dual economy problems.

16. Such an arrangement would have to go beyond existing bilateral agreements. It should include a set of rules for the behaviour of large multinational firms and a negative list of what governments would refrain from regulating and controlling. The negative list is necessary to reduce uncertainties emanating from the general fear that governments might interfere with markets in various ways that would destroy confidence and start a vicious circle that might either end with the emigration of the form and its capital or the expropriation of the reduced capital value left at a token compensation. The major point, however, would be the creation of a common fund for paying compensation, in the case of outright expropriation, according to international rather than national law. Claims to future allocations of Special Drawing Rights would be the capital-poor countries' contribution in the form of collateral. If we assume that an advanced country and a semi-developed country made such an arrangement as an open club to which others could accede if they were prepared to accept the rules of the game, the enterprise—if successful at the start—might grow due to the promises it holds out (a) to those capital owners and entrepreneurs in advanced countries who have to resort to international locational innovation; and (b) to all factors complementary to foreign investment in the participating LDCs.

For both countries—or groups of countries—it would raise allocative efficiency and smooth the adjustment process to the extent that trade and factor movements are complementary in a Schumpeterian growth scenario.

17. As a conglomerate it can cope with structural change and adjustment within its own confines: importing from foreign subsidiaries, improving the quality of the imported products so that they better fit the tastes of the domestic market, supporting R and D, changing the emphasis in its product mix towards new goods, retraining the employees, pensioning off workers with obsolete skills, utilising plant sites and retrainable workers in domestic problem areas for new lines of production, and coping with the resistance of labour unions and local communities against import-induced structural change. Being usually more powerful than a small firm under severe competition, the large conglomerate with its wider profit margins is less

under the exigencies of shortrun survival. It can be less averse to short-run risk and take a longer view in its decision-making process. While it will respond more slowly to short-run changes in the incentive structure (as all big animals) it can afford to devise and maintain intrafirm transfer payments which help to mitigate the impact of change on individuals. In this respect it is—in its extreme form—a substitute for the social functions of both the family and the state. Public pressure is certainly strong for large firms to pursue intrafirm redistribution policies. Representative in this respect is the large Japanese firm.

Note that it is the conglomerate rather than the textbook big one-product firm that can internalise the adjustment costs; and it must be a conglomerate sufficiently decentralised in its decision-making process so as to offer scope for Schumpeterian managers. Needless to add, it must be active as an innovator and subject to competition from LDCs. These pressures seem to have been a strong factor making large enterprise more multifarious, 'as they often must develop into conglomerates in their search for survival opportunities' (Namiki, 1973, p. 252).

18. Anticipatory adjustment is criticised by means of familiar protectionist arguments and statements to the effect that
    (a) it is too difficult to identify the sensitive products and industries well in advance by conventional methods (time-series, market share analyses, country-by-country cross-section analyses);
    (b) the factor-proportions theorem on which predictions could be based disregards the productivity of human skill and ingenuity, notably in circumstances where need is likely to be the mother of invention;
    (c) neither product innovations nor process innovations can be ruled out as legitimate means to rescue the status quo (although defensive process innovations may enhance the labour-augmenting bias in the techniques adopted and may exacerbate the world job gap and capital deficiency);
    (d) surveys conducted among engineers give reason to believe that a technological breakthrough for an industry subject to competition from LDCs is just around the corner and that, therefore, the correct policy is temporary protection or maintenance assistance rather than accepting the burden of adjustment;
    (e) domestic production offers positive external effects, such as support for peripheral regions, marginal male workers, and married female workers, or renders non-pecuniary benefits to customers, like the military system, or to the whole population in case of war or periods of trade disruption.

To these points one can reply (in reverse order):

    (f) external economies of the permanent and reversible type are a matter for permanent direct subsidies and have nothing to do with the adjustment problem;
    (g) defence consideration can often be better met by stockpiling than by protection; they should, therefore, be kept out of consideration when non-weapons are at stake;
    (h) income tranfers to peripheral regions, old workers, females and other

disadvantaged groups can be divorced from the production of sensitive goods. The transfers may then be granted only under the condition that product protection is being phased out. The amount could be made dependent upon the recipient's active participation in anticipatory adjustment;

(i) it is up to the individual recipient firm to decide whether support for anticipatory adjustment is needed or whether it is advantageous to wait for a technological breakthrough or to embark on defensive investment for process innovation;

(j) it is the firms themselves rather than any research institution or government, which has to identify sensitive products. How sensitive a product is to competition from LDCs will be discovered in the market while import protection is being phased out under the preannounced plan.

19. Assisting anticipatory adjustment can be justified along the following lines:
  (1) Above average effective protection is prima facie evidence for a lag in the adjustment process. Unless it has already become redundant, it merits replacement by adjustment assistance.
  (2) However, assistance for anticipatory adjustment in exchange for above average protection is not justified if the recipient uses it either for simply maintaining capital intact, or for defensive process innovation, or even for product innovation. Hopes for survival based on product innovation are a suitable subject of communication with commercial lenders and investors rather than with government authorities. Hence, practically only inter or intranational locational innovation are left as possible bases for anticipatory adjustment assistance.

20. In these circumstances there is reason to fear that some of the peripheral regions of West Germany are bound to suffer a decline in manufacturing production and employment. The decline may, where possible, be compensated by promoting tourist activities and by concentrating the allocation of federal funds for research in these areas in the hope that a centre for the production of knowledge may attract people who are capable and venturesome enough to make use of new knowledge in the production of commodities which are likely to find a market.

21. It can be presumed that the advanced countries in Europe are similarly structured and face similar regional adjustment problems. In the framework of its regional policy the EEC may experiment with the creation of three or four new growth poles in areas which (a) have severely suffered in the past from the existence of national economic frontiers; (b) have gained a higher development potential from the removal of former national economic frontiers; and (c) suffer from a severe decline in manufacturing employment due to increased competition from LDCs.

The argument for support rests on the assumption that the decline in economic activity is temporary in view of the lift in the region's development potential. For a similar proposal see Cairncross *et al.* (1977), Chapter 3, notably p. 88, recommendation 17.

REFERENCES

Bundesregierung, Presse- und Informationsamt der, 'Entwicklungs-politische Konzeption der Bundesrepublik Deutschland für die Zweite Entwicklungdekade', Bulletin (Bonn, 1971). Translated in R. Scheid, 'The Export Needs of Developing Countries and the Need for Adjustment in Industrial Countries', in H. Giersch (ed.), *The International Division of Labor—Problems and Perspectives* (Tübingen, 1977).

Cairncross, A., Giersch, H., Lamfalussy, A., Petrilli, G. and Uri, P., *Economic Policy for the European Community* (London 1977).

Cline, W. R., Kawanabe, N., Kronsjo, T. O. M. and Williams, T., *Trade, Welfare and Employment Effects of Multilateral Trade Negotiation in the Tokyo Round* (The Brookings Institution, 1976, unpublished).

Dick, R., *Der Einfluss der Industrialisierung der Entwicklungsländer auf den Maschinenbau der Bundesrepublik Deutschland und anderer Industrieländer* (Kiel, 1978 (ms)).

Dicke, H., *Aussenhandels- und nachfragebestimmter Strukturwandel des westdeutschen Strassenfahrzeugbaus,* Kieler Studien 152 (Tübingen, 1978).

Dicke, H., Glisman, H. H., Horn, E.-J. and Neu, A. D., *Beschäftigungswirkungen einer verstärkten Arbeitsteilung mit den Entwicklungsländern,* Kieler Studien 137 (Tübingen, 1976).

Dicke, H. and Heitger, B., 'Der Zusammenhang swischen Aussen- und Binnenwirtschaftssektor im Entwicklungsprozess', *Die Weltwirtschaft* (1977).

Dicke, H. and Weiss, F., 'Angebotsbedingter Strikturwandel in der westdeutschen Investitionsgüterindustrie', *Die Weltwirtschaft*, 1 (1978).

Emmanuel, A., *Unequal Exchange* (London, 1972).

Fels, G., 'The Export Needs of Developing Countries and the Adjustment Process in Industrial Countries', in H. Giersch (ed.), *The International Division of Labor—Problems and Perspectives* (Tübingen, 1974).

Fels, G. and Glisman, H. H., 'Adjustment Policy in the German Manufacturing Sector', in OECD, Adjustment for Trade (Paris, 1975).

Fels, G. and Horn, E.-J., 'Kleine und mittlere Unternehmen im Prozess des weltwirtschaftlichen Strukturwandels', in K. H. Oppenländer (ed.), *Referate und Diskussionsbeiträge der Tagung* vom 8. bis 10.

Oktober 1975, veranstaltet vom Ifo-Institut für Wirtschaftsforschung (Munich, 1976).

Fels, G. and Schatz, K.-W., 'Sektorale Entwicklung und Wachstumsaussichten der westdeutschen Wirtschaft bis 1980', *Die Weltwirtschaft* (1977).

Fels, G., Schatz, K.-W. and Wolter, F., 'Sektoraler Strukturwandel im weltwirtschaftlichen Wachstumsprozess', *Die Weltwirtschaft*, 1 (1970).

Glisman, H. H., Die gesamtwirtschaftlichen Kosten der Protektion, Kielder Diskussionsbeitrag No. 35 (Kiel, 1977).

Heitger, B., Strukturelle Anpassungsprobleme der Metallverarbeitung in den Industrieländern als Folge der Industrialisierung der Entwicklungsländer (Kiel, 1978 (ms)).

Hiemenz, U. and Schatz, K.-W., 'Internationale Arbeitsteilung als Alternative zur Ausländerbeschäftigung', *Die Weltwirtschaft*, 1 (1977).

Kaldor, N., 'Seul le protectionnisme peut sauver l'angleterre', *Le Figaro* (18–19 February 1978).

Lerner, A., Comment on G. Kohlmey 'World Trade and Intraregional Trade, Trends and Structural Changes', in Fritz Machlup (ed.), *Economic Integration Worldwide, Regional, Sectoral* (London, 1976).

Magee, S. P., 'The Welfare Effects of Restrictions on U.S. Trade', Brookings Papers on Economic Activity (Washington, DC, 1972).

Namiki, N., 'The Japanese Economy—An Introduction to its Industrial Adjustment Problems', in K. Kapina (ed.), *Structural Arrangements in Asian-Pacific Trade*, Japan Economic Research Center Paper No. 01 (1973).

Okun, A., *Equality and Efficiency: The Big Tradeoff*, The Brookings Institution (Washington DC, 1975).

Samuelson, P., 'Illogic of Neomarxian Doctrine of Unequal Exchange', in David A. Belsey *et al.* (eds.), *Inflation, Trade, and Taxes* (Columbus, 1976).

Scheid, R., 'The Export Needs of Developing Countries and the Need for Adjustment of Anticipatory Structure Adjustment', in H. Giersch (ed.), *The International Division of Labor—Problems and Perspectives* (Tübingen: J. C. B. Mohr, Paul Siebeck, 1974).

Stolper, W. and Samuelson, P., 'Protection and Real Wages', *The Review of Economics and Statistics* (1941). Reprinted in *American Economic Association, Readings in the Theory of International Trade* (Philadelphia, 1949).

Weiss, F. D., *Electrical Engineering in West Germany—Adjusting to*

Imports from Less Developed Countries, Kieler Studien 155 (Tübingen, 1978).

Wolter, F., 'Factor Proportions, Technology, and West German Industries' International Trade Patterns', *Weltwirtschaftliches Archiv* (1977a).

Wolter, F., 'Adjusting to Imports from Developing Countries', in H. Giersch (ed.), *Reshaping the World Economic Order* (Tübingen, 1977b).

Wolter, F., 'Perspectives for the International Location of the Steel Industry', Kiel Working Paper No. 60 (Kiel, 1977c).

Comments

Erik Lundberg (Sweden)

The introduction to Giersch's paper presents a strong exposition of the fundamental problems that are treated. I can classify them into four groups:

(1) The targets of the LDCs as to share of world manufacturing production and needed expansion of exports to developed countries.

(2) The needs of adjustment in the developed countries to attain increasing integration of the LDCs into the international division of labour.

(3) The constraints to the adjustment process. Many forms are mentioned in the paper. There is general resistance to change on the side of entrepreneurs and trade unions in industrial branches threatened by competition. The strength of this resistance is very much influenced by the type of economy and the general setup of economic policy. Giersch mentions, but does not enter deeply into, actual difficulties in the present state of the Western economies, characterised by slow growth, great unemployment, overcapacity in many fields where also export offensives of progressive LDCs are especially strong.

(4) Conclusions about feasible policies of adjustment follow from the discussion of the above three categories.

Giersch makes a challenging distinction between types of economies, a typology that is strategic both for his analysis and for the policy conclusions. There are, according to Giersch, two opposite extremes: (1) inward- and outward-looking countries that more or less, but not quite, correspond to (2) Keynesian and Schumpeterian types of economies.

According to Giersch, the characteristic properties of *the Keynesian*, inward-looking type of economy are: low capability of adjustment, rather inflexible institutions, propensities to favour government policies rather than relying on the functioning of markets. As to policy, there is a tendency to stress short-term demand variables and to emphasise individual security and equality in income distribution. General attitudes to development are pessimistic, with fear of exploitation over-shadowing hopes of gains from trade. The consequent policy reactions tend to favour protection and disintegration. It is mainly the *Weltanschauung* of Kaldor and the Cambridge New Economic Policy Group as applied to the stagnating UK economy that Giersch apparently has in mind in his rather devastating characterisation.

The opposite Schumpeterian outward-looking type of economy has the following characteristics: rapid growth, high adaptive capacity with forward-oriented responses, flexible institutional arrangements, tolerance for high profits and inequality, competition functioning as a social instrument of discovery and innovations. Policy is supply- and not demand-oriented and with a long-term horizon.

I think that Giersch's dichotomy is useful in some respects, challenging for discussion, and is an excellent opening for both analysis and policy suggestions.

One suggestion is that 'Schumpeterian countries' should lead integration by opening up free trade with corresponding outward-looking LDCs. However, there are risks involved of oversimplification. Even West Germany, maybe Giersch's model economy, surely also contains Keynesian features. There are mixtures in all countries. Giersch is tactful enough not to mention Sweden as an outstanding example of Keynesian attitudes and inward-looking policies of full employment and income equalisation, followed by structural crises. It is in fact easier to select and characterise a doctrine or a Kaldor-type economist corresponding to Giersch's inward-looking characteristics than to find clearcut examples among countries. It is in a way disturbing to Giersch's typology that there are small, open, outward-looking economies like Sweden, carrying on Keynesian policies. I shall return to this question when discussing adaptation policies.

A central issue in Giersch's paper refers to the size and nature of the adjustment problem. The size is one thing, and Giersch presents interesting information pertaining to West Germany. The nature of the problem is determined by the type of economy in question, by the set of adjustment policies, and not least by *how* the liberalisation of trade with LDCs is presented and carried out. In this last respect Giersch has the appealing idea that there should be an irreversible decision and commitment to liberalise trade, making a parallel with the European integration. Such a policy would minimise uncertainty and open up a long-term adjustment process.

The main conclusion from research carried out by the Kiel Institute is that the real size of the burden of adjustment to imports of manufactured goods from the LDCs often tends to be exaggerated and overdramatised in the political debate. Summing up, in macro-terms the size of the adjustment problem seems to be quite limited under realistic conditions. The static effects of tariff and trade liberalisation on employment—at the most according to the calculations referred to, would amount to destroying jobs corresponding to 1 per cent per annum of employment in manufacturing.

But Giersch shows that it is not enough to look at total shares in consumption of industrial goods. There are problems of rising adjustment pressure because: (a) imports have been increasing at an unprecedentedly rapid rate since 1970; (b) market shares are much bigger in many sub-branches than shown in overall industry figures; (c) there is in several fields strong and disturbing price competition due to the relatively low wage costs in LDC industries; (d) the adjustment burden is very much concentrated on economically weak industries and groups of employed persons. These groups embrace low-skill (especially female) employees, often located in backward regions; (e) the adjustment pressure is aggravated because of efforts to raise the relatively low wages of these vulnerable groups of unskilled labour which often have relatively high unemployment.

The calculations of effects on employment as presented by Giersch are, of course, based on a number of assumptions that can be discussed. I shall only take up one issue. The strength of the adjustment pressure must very much depend on the size of the country in question and on the adjustment policy of other industrialised countries. Take the case of Sweden. We have here a tradition of low tariffs and a minimum of other trade barriers. But the competitive pressure on Sweden's textile and clothing industries, as well as on shipyards and iron and steel, is partly a function of the relatively more restrictive policies of other industrialised countries. What Giersch misses is a treatment of the *interdependence effects* of trade policies in the various countries. The destructive effects on employment in small open economies tend to be disproportionately strong as a result of the transmission of protectionist attitudes and policies of bigger countries.

As Giersch's results indicate, the macro-size of the adjustment burden for industrial countries as a whole may be small. But this adjustment problem is additional to other, often much larger, needs of resource reallocation, arising from various sources of structural change. High and rising wage costs imply rationalisation pressure especially on labour-intensive branches that primarily tend to be hurt by low wage competition from LDCs. There are also *indirect* repercussions from intensive Japanese export competition shifting to new fields, partly as a result of LDC export competition in the old Japanese export branches. Certainly in principle—as Giersch argues—increased competition from LDC exports could and should work as a *dynamic stimulus* to the development of Schumpeterian countries. This competition leads to the *destruction* of activity in labour-intensive branches, forcing the economies to withdraw from producing standardised products with a high content of unskilled labour, and thereby giving the opportunity as well as the impetus to the *creation* of new jobs in other activities containing new technology and high human-capital intensity. The import demands of LDCs are increasing more rapidly than their exports, giving the industrialised countries opportunities to expand.

But Giersch admits that there are limits to flexibility and variable degrees of resistance to mobility even in an economy with Schumpeterian attitudes. There are, in all developed countries, new aims of job security; there are lots of restrictions as to mobility of resources and in the incentive structure; there are sensitive branches and regional problems aggravated by LDC competition. Therefore we witness strong protectionist tendencies and resistance to rapidly rising imports from LDCs. And therefore—as Giersch admits—there is a need for a *government adjustment policies*.

Giersch introduces the concept of the *conversion potential* of a country's economy. It depends on a number of variables: conversion potential of the individual firms in the country, information and transaction costs, costs of regional and professional adjustment in the labour market. Giersch's main point is a glorification of well-functioning markets and multinational corporations for keeping up or raising conversion potential. And Giersch warns against specific government assistance programmes and against subsidies of investment in industries exposed to LDC competition. Such subsidies should be allowed only on the condition of product innovation, when temporary protection could be allowed.

Giersch makes an important distinction between protection and adjustment assistance, and warns against the use of such assistance for protection that implies postponement or avoidance of adjustment. Giersch stresses the importance of anticipatory adjustment, presumably following the announcement of irrevocable liberation policies. Giersch adds that rules of compensation being applied to owners and employees hurt by structural disturbances could help in removing resistance to change.

I agree with most of Giersch's arguments about this kind of adjustment policy. I share his view about the great risk of government interference on a large scale. But on the other hand I have doubts as to Giersch's rather complete confidence in the efficient functioning of markets and of multinational corporations. I object to Giersch's too general formulation that 'the market is superior to government in future-oriented decisions' but with the addition that multinational corporations may be superior to the market as regards the adjustment process. I miss some balancing criticism and an analysis of the conditions under which free markets really are effective in regard to longer-term adjustment trends towards the effective division of labor between industrialised countries and LDCs.

Is it not true that markets tend to function badly in response to large disturbances, to big structural changes? Take the experience of the early 1970s, with overinvestment in many branches during the boom—the subsequent overcapacity problems are serious and to some extent aggravated by export competition from progressive LDC industries. Take the situation of shipyards as an example! The price signals in the boom of the 1970s were very misleading as to future market conditions. And the same is probably true of *present* freight rates and ship-prices under severe overcapacity conditions. Giersch is right in saying that uncertainty arguments can easily be misused, but they cannot be neglected, as he seems to do.

I come back to Giersch's stimulating but dangerous dichotomy of Keynesian and Schumpeterian economies. My point is that our Western economies need a lot of Keynesian-demand stabilisation policies in order to function somewhat along Schumpeterian lines. The present conditions in most developed countries with slow growth and severe overcapacity problems just in branches where LDC industries should expand exports, is not a good world for trade expansion or for finding effective division of work between industrialised countries and LDCs.

So my conclusions and potential recommendations are a little different from Giersch's. I cannot agree with the statement that markets *generally* are superior to government policy. There is only a question of alternatives to a limited extent. Markets will function badly when governments' (Keynesian) policies are deficient—then markets will give wrong signals as to long-term allocation of resources and division of work. And governments' policies may become still worse just because markets are not functioning well. The need for selective policies will increase. There are apparent risks that the world economic system is at present becoming very messy because of all kinds of interferences with the market system. But it does not help to dream of a pure Schumpeterian world that does not exist and will never be accepted by most countries. Instead we need international rules of co-ordination of such government policies that are necessary to make market systems work reasonably well or at any rate, better than at present.

8 Short-term Policy Trade-offs under Different Phases of Economic Development

Michael Bruno (Israel)

I INTRODUCTION

The natural emphasis on the long-run structural difficulties of developing countries and the need for a 'New Order' often overshadows the fact that much of the day-to-day involvement of policy-makers in developing countries, as well as of the governments and international institutions called upon to help, centres on problems of short-run economic stabilisation. A country typically runs into balance-of-payments difficulties with (without) considerable domestic inflation, it is in urgent need of outside financial help to keep imports and economic activity going, and it asks for short-term loans from whatever source available.

Usually the agreement to help, whether in the form of a debt consortium by a group of industrial countries or aid from an international agency, is made conditional upon the acceptance of a set of conventional macro-policy principles in the form of a 'stabilisation programme'. Normally, this is of the kind that a developed country would be expected to carry out when facing temporary short-term balance-of-payments difficulties.

The typical policy package is a combination of an across-the-board exchange-rate adjustment and complementary domestic demand restraint measures mostly in the form of formal credit restrictions. In the case of an LDC these are usually coupled with a stipulation that certain distortions be removed from the system. Obvious candidates for removal, in addition to import restrictions, would be subsidies on exports and on domestic food products. There follows any one of several possible outcomes:

(1) If the imposed programme is very stringent and the country in question happens to be democratic in its decision-making process the government may fall before the programme is even carried out (take Portugal as a recent example).

(2) If the programme is accepted the often ensuing rise in the prices of basic food products or the economic recession cause considerable internal unrest, workers' demonstrations, strikes, etc. (take Egypt as a recent example). At times this may reach the point of endangering the whole social fabric of the country. A strong and autocratic government may at this point use brute force and succeed (*vide* Chile, but can that be called a success?).

(3) In a more liberal system the country and its government may survive but the soaring inflation or the renewed upsurge of economic activity may wipe out the initial temporary reduction in the balance-of-payments deficit. The country may then resort to its former methods, using quantitative restrictions, differential subsidies, and the like. If it goes back to ask for more short-term aid and manages to prove that it is in danger of going under, it may get some, usually insufficient, help, this time without such severe strings attached. It will then muddle along until the next crisis.

(4) There are, of course, some cases—and among LDCs there are not many—in which such a stabilisation programme succeeds in the sense that a few years elapse before the next crisis occurs, or else—very rare indeed—it never recurs.

Is this a necessary and inevitable sequence of events? Maybe stabilisation programmes in LDCs are often misconceived and some re-evaluation of basic principles is called for, or at least they have to be modified to fit the particular institutional setup of an LDC. That this is a very serious problem and one requiring special attention in the general framework of a 'New Order' should be clear. It is enough to look at the amount of short-term aid which has in recent years followed upon crises of this kind and consider the general dissatisfaction with the results. The amount of criticism that has been levelled against what is sometimes termed 'IMF practice' may be testimony to the fact that this is a serious matter for objective consideration, even if one does not want to take sides in the debate.[1]

Our discussion here will centre on two major questions arising from this discussion. The first relates to the inadequacy of considering short-run stabilisation problems in an LDC in the same light as an adjustment problem in a highly developed economy. The main point to be made under this heading is that rarely, if at all, can a short-run stabilisation problem in an LDC be divorced from the underlying long-run development issues, and the remedies cannot be independent of the country's structural features. Nor does stabilisation policy have any chance of success unless integrated with a long-run strategy. Macro-tools that may be standard in one context and make sense within a certain well-developed institutional setup may achieve the wrong results in a system whose institutions (such as the financial system) are not fully developed.

The second question, which is not unrelated to the first, pertains to the whole issue of what constitutes distortive measures. For example we have been conditioned to believe that, with the exception of some obvious infant-industry arguments in favour of temporary import restrictions, free trade is always superior to intervention such as export promotion schemes of various distortive kinds; GATT and IMF regulations forbid the use of export subsidies, for example. But one can show, both on theoretical grounds and on the basis of the accumulated experience of some export success stories, that under certain circumstances they are a very effective tool before the system is developed enough to be ripe for full trade and exchange liberalisation. Or consider the question of food subsidies. Modern public-finance theory tells us that except for lump-sum taxes and subsidies no measures of fiscal intervention can be free of distortions. It is a choice of evils. In a country in which a system of family allowances or demogrants is administratively feasible the use of food subsidies as an income-maintenance measure rather than family allowances may be considered relatively inefficient. But where such an alternative is not administratively feasible food subsidies may be justifiable even on efficiency grounds (minimum nutrition levels).

The rest of this paper discusses some of these questions in greater detail. Our observations are mainly centred on the class of countries often termed semi-industrialised economies (SIEs) and may not always be relevant to the predominantly agricultural countries in the very first stages of their development. In Section II we take up the relationship between phases of economic development and alternative policy regimes particularly in the area of foreign trade and the balance of payments. Section III presents a simplified macro-economic framework in which some of the policy tradeoffs will be taken up. Section IV discusses circumstances under which conventional macro-tools may be ineffective. Section V takes up the question of distortive measures.

II DEVELOPMENT PHASES AND ALTERNATIVE POLICY TOOLS

It has long been agreed that the process of industrialisation is one in which a country typically goes through several phases of economic development. These are marked by sharp changes not only in the level of productivity and capital accumulation and the structure of output and trade, but also in the development of economic institutions. The latter in turn affects the kinds of policy tools and regulatory devices that can be employed on a current basis.

The area in which this aspect of development has been studied most is that of balance-of-payments and trade policies. All countries start at some stage to rely very heavily on quantitative import restrictions, almost all go through various forms of trade liberalisation and greater reliance on exchange-rate policy and the price system, and very few eventually end up with full exchange convertibility. There is a world of difference between these various regimes, but no less important is a typology of countries by the pattern of intervention in the fiscal and monetary policy field. A country in which most of the government's revenue comes from import tariffs, and there is no transfer system except for food subsidies, is a world apart from that in which there is a well-developed personal income tax. Likewise, monetary policy in a country with virtually no banking system outside a small modern enclave (where the rest of the economy relies on its own finance or a highly imperfect 'curb' market), has very different implications from one that takes place in a fully monetarised economy with reasonably well-developed financial intermediaries.

A good recent example of a comparative study in the trade policy field is the set of NBER studies edited by Bhagwati (1978) and Krueger (1978).[2] These studies have examined the experience of ten different developing economies within a common analytical framework. This suggests a five-phase division of the evolution of exchange rate and trade regimes. A brief summary of three phases is as follows (see Bhagwati, 1978):

Phase I: Significant imposition of quantitative restrictions (QR) on imports in a rather 'crude' and 'unsophisticated' manner.
Phase II: QR still reign but the control mechanism becomes very complex and differentiated with supplementary price measures, tariffs, export rebates. Even when there are export subsidies the effective exchange rate on exports is always lower than that on imports, which are highly protected.

Phase III: There are tidying up operations, rationalisation of import tariffs, some tariff-subsidies are replaced by formal parity changes. It may take the form of a devaluation-cum-liberalisation package accompanied by external grants to facilitate expansion of (liberalised) imports.
Phase IV: This is a successful culmination of Phase III liberalisation efforts. There is much greater uniformity of incentives. *Inter alia*, the effective exchange rate on exports is equated with that on imports.
Phase V: There is full convertibility on current account, and no quantitative restrictions are employed to regulate the balance of payments—pegged exchange-rate in equilibrium or else flexible rate regime. Monetary and fiscal policy are employed as instruments to achieve payments balance instead of reliance on an exchange control mechanism.

The switch from Phase II to III and in particular the successful movement to Phase IV seem the most difficult steps in the process. Out of the ten countries included in the NBER project only three (Brazil, Israel, and South Korea) have successfully gone through Phases I to IV and stayed there.[3] Five countries (Chile, Colombia, Ghana, Philippines, Turkey) have been cycling through Phases II–III–IV, arriving back at Phase II. Two countries (Egypt and India) have been in Phase II over a long period.

To the extent that one can draw any general conclusions on the success and failure of movements to Phase III and IV it would seem that attempts to liberalise imports and rely only on exchange-rate adjustment may fail for one or more of several reasons: (a) The inflation that follows devaluation sooner or later neutralises the initial boost to exports, in other words, there is no *real* devaluation. (b) The accompanying domestic restraint measures lead to severe recession which is socially and politically unacceptable. (c) While the import substitution bias is reduced, the real devaluation as such does not provide enough of a sustained push to export growth. (d) Import liberalisation and output expansion cause an increase in imports, and the lack of sustained foreign aid over a transition period forces the country into exchange crises and eventually to revert to quantitative restrictions (Phase II).

The success stories such as Brazil, Israel, and South Korea are all cases in which export promotion has been sustained and aggressive, using a whole assortment of measures in addition to the formal exchange-rate system (more on this below). Also these were countries which at critical points managed to receive considerable capital inflows either in the form of aid (Israel, Korea) or in the form of foreign investment (Brazil, Korea).

All these countries suffered from inflation which was fought with varying degrees of success. (In at least one case, Brazil, success was achieved at considerable social cost in terms of unemployment and income maldistribution).

The NBER study does not provide a typology of the monetary, fiscal, and other accompanying policy measures that would apply at each of the phases. Although countries may differ in this respect, it would seem safe to say that Phase II (and certainly Phase I) is usually one in which the fiscal and monetary systems are fairly undeveloped. There would normally be credit rationing and considerable financial activity going on outside the formal banking system in what is a highly segmented and imperfect money market. On the other hand movement to Phase III and IV (let alone Phase V) would be accompanied by rapid development of financial institutions, monetary reform and a gradual liberalisation of the financial system (this has certainly happened in Korea and Israel).

What is important to stress, however, is the fact that all these developments are in the nature of farreaching structural changes, which take time. At any rate they cannot be tackled incidentally within a short-term stabilisation framework of the kind that would normally apply to a balance-of-payments crisis in a highly developed economy. Before analysing the weaknesses of conventional macro-policies in more detail we turn to the choice of a suitable analytical framework.

III   STYLISED MODEL OF MACRO-ECONOMIC TRADEOFFS

Spelling out a fully fledged macro-system for various phases of development is far beyond the scope of this paper; moreover, it would obscure the main issues taken up here. On the other hand, an analysis with no common formal framework would not serve our purpose either. We therefore choose a middle way by using a simple model with one equation for each of the main objects of tradeoff to be discussed here, the current account balance of payments deficit (D), the domestic price level (p) and domestic output (X).[4] We start with a specification of the current account deficit:

$$D = I_n + p_n^* N\left(\frac{w}{p_n}, X\right) - P_e^* E\left(\frac{p_e}{w}, K_e\right), \tag{1}$$

where I_n = exogenous imports (mostly investment goods)

N = intermediate imports

X = domestic (non-exportable) output
E = net exports (value added)
w = nominal wage
p_i = price of tradables, $i = n, e$
    (world price indicated by asterisk)
e = exchange rate
t_i = tariff or subsidy rate on imports or exports, $i = n, e$
$p_i = p_i^* e(l + t_i)$
K_e = non price supply factors (productivity, export-biased
    investment, government marketing effort, etc.)
D = current-account deficit

The above representation of the current account recognises only two kinds of imports, those that are exogenous to the price system (I_n) and in an LDC context mostly consist of investment goods, and all other imports (N). The latter are assumed to be inputs to the one composite domestic production sector (X) in which the variable inputs consist of labour (with wage payment w) and imports (with domestic price p_n); N is therefore a positive function of X and w/p_n. This formulation ignores the possible separate role of final consumption imports but is sufficiently realistic to be useful.[5] Similarly only one composite export good is represented here, in terms of its value added, being a positive function of the export price relative to the domestic wage (short-run supply effect) and of the various long-run supply push factors.[6]

Domestic import and export prices are both viewed as a product of three factors, the world price, the formal exchange rate and the informal parts of the effective exchange rate, import tariffs and export subsidies, respectively.

It is most convenient to decompose the change in the current-account deficit into the rates of change of the underlying variables. We normalise the base-period world prices to equal unity and denote the corresponding trade values by a zero subscript. The resulting components of the change in the deficit ($\dot{D}$) take the following form:

$$
\begin{aligned}
\dot{D} = {} & N(1 - \eta_n)\hat{p}_n^* - E_0(1 + \eta_e)\hat{p}_e^* && \text{(2) international terms of trade (a)} \\
& + \dot{I}_n && \text{exogenous investment imports (b)} \\
& + (N_0\eta_{nx})\hat{X} && \text{intermediate imports (c)} \\
& - (N_0\eta_n + E_0\eta_e)(\hat{e} - \hat{w}) && \text{real (formal) devaluation (d)} \\
& - N_0\eta_n(1 \mp t_n) && \text{import tariffs (e)} \\
& - E_0\eta_e(1 \mp t_e) && \text{export subsidies (f)} \\
& - E_0\eta_{ek}\hat{K}_e && \text{non-price export-push (g)}
\end{aligned}
$$

where η_n and η_e are the price elasticities of imports and exports and their elasticities with respect to the other variables are η_{nx} and η_{ek}. Time changes are denoted by dot ($\dot{X} = X_t - X_{t-1}$); and percentage rates of change by circumflex ($\hat{X} = \dot{X}/X_{t-1}$).

The deficit increases with a deterioration in the (elasticity weighted) international terms of trade [item (a)], with an increase in exogenous imports (b), and with a rise in domestic economic activity (c). A real devaluation defined relative to nominal wage will reduce the deficit (d) and so will an increase in tariffs (e), export subsidies (f),[7] and exogenous export-push efforts (g). Obviously the size of the various effects depends on the changes in the underlying variables and on the corresponding elasticity of response which may differ between the short-run and the long-run as well as along different phases of economic and institutional development. This will be taken up again below.

Next we supplement the external balance with two simplified equations for the price (p) and the output (X) of domestic goods. Consider the nominal wage ($\hat{w}$) and domestic consumer prices ($\hat{p}$) as represented by

$$\hat{w} = \beta_0 + \beta_1 \hat{p}_{-1} \tag{3}$$

$$\hat{p} = -\alpha_0 + \alpha_1 \hat{w} + \alpha_2 \hat{p}_n + \alpha_3 \hat{M}_{-1} + \alpha_4 \hat{t}_x. \tag{4}$$

Equation (3) represents wage adjustment as a function of lagged price changes (with $\beta_1 = 1$ when there is full inflationary adjustment). The additional term (β_0) may represent long-run shifts (due to productivity growth or exogenous wage push), or, alternatively, elements of endogenous labour-market pressure (Phillips curve) which will here be ignored. Equation (4) is a fairly standard price adjustment equation based on markup over variable costs (in the form of wages and import costs), a lagged effect of money (more on this below), and the possible effect of indirect taxes (t_x) with subsidies represented as $\hat{t}_x < 0$. The separate role of price expectations, other than through wages or money, is ignored here.

Equations (3) and (4) can be combined into one reduced-form equation

$$\hat{p} = a_0 + a_1 p_{-1} + a_2 p_n + a_3 \hat{M}_{-1} + a_4 \hat{t}_x, \tag{5}$$

where

$$a_0 = -\alpha_0 + \alpha_1 \beta_0, \; a_1 = \alpha_1 \beta_1 \text{ and } a_3 = \alpha_3, \; a_4 = \alpha_4.$$

The solution of an output supply and demand system can likewise be shown to lead to an approximate equation for output change,[8]

$$\hat{X} = b_0 + b_1 \hat{p}_{-1} - b_2 \hat{p}_n + b_3 \hat{M}_{-1} + b_4 \dot{F}_{-1} + b_5 \dot{I}_{x-1}, \qquad (6)$$

where $F = G - T =$ government deficit and $I_x =$ purchase of domestic investment goods.

This formulation ignores possible repercussions on demand for domestic output of a change in income from exports and of changes in the relative price of domestic and imported final goods. Although this is by no means necessary we have assumed that the effect of the money supply, M, fiscal policy, F, and exogenous investment demand, I_x, is lagged. We note that in both equations (5) and (6) we may substitute $\hat{p}_n = \hat{p}_n^* + \hat{e} + (1 \hat{+} t_n)$.

The elements of the government budget can be spelled out further. Assuming that all of current government expenditure takes the form of payments to employees (L_g), we have $G = L_g w$ and net tax payments (in the base period) can be written as $T_0 = t_n N_0 - t_e E_0 + t_x c X + Ty$, where $c =$ share of X on which t_x is imposed, and $T_y =$ direct taxes (assumed exogenous). Summing up we can write for the government deficit

$$F = L_g w - t_n N_0 + t_e E_0 - t_x c X - T_y. \qquad (7)$$

Similarly we can spell out the components of the money supply. The change in the money base (or high-powered money) can be expressed as the sum of the government deficit $(F)^9$ and the current account balance in domestic currency $(-eD)$. Denoting the money multiplier by μ we can therefore write for the rate of change of money:

$$\hat{M} = M^{-1} \mu (F - eD), \qquad (8)$$

where $F = G - T$ is given by equation (7).

The growth rate of the money supply may thus rise as a result of any one of three effects: (a) An increase in the government deficit, F. (b) A decrease in the domestic value of the current account deficit (eD); note that a devaluation may, *ceteris paribus*, cause a monetary *contraction* even though the deficit in foreign currency (D) falls. We have $(e\dot{D}) = D\dot{e} + e\dot{D} > 0$, if $-\dot{D} < \hat{e}D$, which may be the case for a sufficiently high D (see Díaz-Alejandro, 1963; Krugman and Taylor, 1976). (c) Deliberate expansionary monetary policy expressed through a rise in μ.

Finally we note that total employment (L) in this simplified system has three components, government employment (L_g), employment in the domestic sector (L_x) and employment in the export industry (L_e). Let us denote their shares by $\ell_i = L_i/L$. If we denote the elasticity of substitution between the two factors in the X sector by σ, the demand elasticity for L_e by $\eta_{\hat{\ell}_e}$ (and likewise for the other factor $\eta_{\hat{\ell}_{ek}}$), it can be shown that the rate of growth of total employment will be given by

$$\hat{L} = \ell_g \hat{L}_g + \ell_e \eta_{\hat{\ell}e}[\hat{p}_e^* + (1 \hat{+} t_e)] + \ell_n \sigma[\hat{p}_n^* + (1 \hat{+} t_n)] + \ell_e \eta_{\hat{\ell}ek} \hat{K}_e \quad (9)$$

$$+ (\ell_e \eta_{\hat{\ell}e} + \ell_n \sigma)(\hat{e} - \hat{w}) + \ell_n \hat{X}.$$

This equation is again self-explanatory. An increase in total employment may, *ceteris paribus*, come about as a result of growth in government employment, as a result of an increase in world prices or effective tariff (subsidy in the case of exports), an export-shift effect (K_e), a change in the real exchange rate ($\hat{e} - \hat{w}$), or, finally, and usually the dominant factor, is domestic output growth ($\hat{X}$).

IV   THE SHORTCOMINGS OF CONVENTIONAL MACRO-POLICIES

Let us now consider the effect of some standard macro-policy tools within the above framework. Consider first the current-account balance—equation (2). The most important elements making for a structural increase in the deficit, other than the possible deterioration of the terms of trade[10] [item (a) of equation (2)], are the next two items, the required imports of capital goods (b) and the current imports of intermediate goods (c), which are a function of the level of economic activity. Consider the effect of a devaluation ($\hat{e}$). What matters is not the nominal but the real devaluation ($\hat{e} - \hat{w}$); using equation (3), this can be written as ($\hat{e} - \beta_1 \hat{p}_{-1}$). If wages fully adjust to past prices (that is, $\beta_1 = 1$) and the underlying price (that is, marginal cost) relationship, equation (4), is linearly homogeneous,[11] then the resulting reduced form, equation (5), will be linearly homogeneous in the nominal variables, that is, $a_1 + a_2 + a_3 = 1$. If the coefficient of the money stock in equation (5) is small (or it may even be negative—see below) or else if money is accommodating to price increases, then it is easy to see that the long-run real effect of a devaluation is nil because prices will eventually be increasing at the same rate as the exchange rate. Putting $\hat{p} = \hat{p}_{-1} = \hat{M}_{-1}, a_1 + a_2 + a_3 = 1$ and $\hat{p}_n = \hat{e}$ in equation (5) we find $\hat{p} = (1 - a_1 - a_3)^{-1} a_2 \hat{e} = \hat{e}$, so that $\hat{e} - \hat{w} = 0$. If the degree of homogeneity is greater than one ($a_1 + a_2 + a_3 > 1$) and/or $a_3 \leq 0$ we get a real appreciation ($\hat{e} - \hat{w} < 0$). The speed with which devaluation will spend itself depends on expectation mechanisms (in a rational-expectations world this will, of course, happen immediately), degree of wage indexation, etc. Typically there will be a temporary real devaluation whose duration depends on the country's ability to prevent wages and prices from increasing. This is hard to do if the anti-inflationary tools are not very effective or if there are strong social and political pressures.

Even if there is a real devaluation in the short run the response of $\dot{D}$ may be small. The price elasticity of imports [η_n in equation (2)] is usually quite low and the export supply elasticity (η_e) may be low in the short run, with the real effects taking time to bear fruit. This is very costly in terms of exchange-reserve loss or further short-term indebtedness. If the devaluation is part of a devaluation-cum-liberalisation package, its cost-push price effect will be moderated [note that in equation (5) $\hat{p}_n = \hat{e}$ $+ t_n) < \hat{e}$ in that case]. On the other hand liberalised imports [item (e) in equation (2)] will push up the deficit.

All these factors suggest reasons for the failure of an attempt to move a country through Phase III (let alone IV) more than temporarily, unless inflation is successfully fought or there is sufficient supplementary finance available to tide the country over the difficult and often long transition period during which a trade and payments reform is to take place.

What can one say about the effectiveness of supplementary measures, in particular a monetary squeeze? First of all it should be noted again that a devaluation may itself initially bring about a monetary squeeze, even without deliberate monetary policy. In terms of equation (8) eD may increase (even if D falls) thus depressing money growth unless the government deficit, F, increases in a non-neutral fashion.[12]

Consider the effect of a fall in $\hat{M}$ on prices [equation (5)] and output [equation (6)]. The short-run tradeoff between the price and output changes is given by the ratio of the coefficients b_3/a_3. In an LDC, especially one in Phase II (or III), b_3 is likely to be relatively high while a_3 may be very low or negative. The main reason for that, argued at great length elsewhere (see Bruno, 1978), is imperfections in the financial system where money serves as a factor of production.

Imagine a country in which the money market is underdeveloped and highly segmented with only part of the economy served by the banking system. There exist credit restrictions and official interest rates do not reflect correct opportunity costs. Private firms which may or may not obtain credit rations have to appeal to the 'curb' market, where the supply of loanable funds is characterised by increasing marginal cost of borrowing due to high risk of default. A squeeze on credit rations in such an economy will drive firms up the steep supply curve for loanable funds. The increased real cost of finance will mainly force them to cut output supply and at times may even force them to increase prices (which would show in the fact that in equation (5) the coefficient a_3 may even be negative).[13] Whether or not it takes such an extreme form, the upshot of the argument is that a monetary squeeze is almost certainly going to show primarily through a reduction in domestic output (X) from the supply side and at best only marginally in demand and price restraint. This will have a two-fold effect. There will be a reduction in employment (L_X) which will not be matched by an increase in employment coming from the substitution effect in the X sector and the (sluggish) output expansion effect in the export sector.[14] On the other hand there will be a reduction in import requirements [item (c) in equation (2)]. Thus the main and only bonus of a squeeze will be in terms of the relief of pressure from the current-account deficit. However, the economic and social costs in terms of unemployment may be intolerable. What is more, this will at best be only a *temporary* relief. A resumption of economic activity will bring about a renewed increase in imports with its attendant resumption of foreign-exchange difficulties. This is a syndrome that has again and again been recorded in the history of LDCs precisely at the stage which we have been analysing here. It is a good illustration of a case in which structural problems cannot be cured through conventional short-term stabilisation measures.

Why is this less of a problem in a more developed economy? The more developed the financial system of the country, the more likely is the price-output tradeoff of monetary policy going to work in favour of price-depression rather than output-contraction. In the extreme case of a country in Phase V under a fully flexible rate system money would affect domestic prices directly through the exchange rate and only marginally through output.

Monetary reform may, of course, help to make monetary tools a more effective anti-inflationary device, but this is a long and difficult process. In its absence one may still consider partial substitutes in the form of increases in average interest rates coupled with a relaxation of formal credit rationing which may bring down *marginal* interest rates.[15] This would relieve the upward pressure on prices and the downward pressure on output.

The upshot of the discussion so far is that the conventional macro-medicine cannot be divorced from the particular institutional framework within which it is prescribed and that there are good reasons why in many cases it might fail to achieve its purpose or, even if it does so at first, the resulting social tensions may eventually make it politically un-feasible. It is also important to stress again that in a typical LDC short-term stabilisation problems cannot be treated separately from the long-run structural problems from which they usually arise. In particular a country undergoing transition from Phase II to IV will usually require sustained financial help for which the occasional spurts of first aid are not a good substitute.

V   WHEN SHOULD DISTORTIVE INSTRUMENTS BE USED?

An important lesson to be learnt from experience is that the reform of a system in which there are controls and quantitative restrictions cannot proceed on the basis of the alignment of one market alone. For example, full liberalisation of foreign trade and payments cannot be carried out successfully when the internal financial system remains highly segmented or administratively controlled. Since a full reform of any market requires the development of suitable institutions that will take care of its activities this is by definition a very long process that will usually reach completion only at a rather late stage of economic development. This is one of the reasons why the whole notion of what constitutes a distortive policy measure and what kind of intervention is 'free' of distortions becomes a rather different issue from what it would be in a developed free market system. The relevant question is the following—given certain objectives (in the area of the balance of payments, and of economic activity, inflation, and income distribution) are there strategies that might achieve one (or two) objectives at less cost (that is, lower tradeoff) compared with some of the conventional tools discussed above? Next, what has, in this respect, been the experience of countries that have successfully made the transition? Have they been any less distortionary in their methods of intervention?

Again let us start with the balance-of-payments constraint. The NBER studies suggest very strongly that countries which have made a successful transition to a more liberal trade and payments regime (such as Brazil, Israel, and South Korea) are cases in which the traditional import substitution bias was reduced at a fairly early stage of development in favour of an active export-promoting policy. They also show that it is not enough to equate effective exchange rates at the margin. Sri Lanka and Indonesia, for example, are cited as cases in which trade was substantially liberalised and yet the rapid export-growth stage was not reached. There seems to be need for a strongly interventionist export drive. In the examples cited this has taken a variety of forms, from straight subsidies, cheap short-run and long-run credit, government marketing arrangements, to income tax relief and export-target setting for individual exporters. Some of these measures are obviously distortive however looked at, yet they have been used with a reasonable amount of success judging by the final results. On theoretical grounds one can make out a case for export promotion at an effective rate that is higher than the rate for import substitutes. There is need for a learning process, as in any other infant industry. In addition, in the case of an export there is the problem of market penetration in which any new start provides an externality for other exports. Reliance on the formal exchange rate alone will not suffice, quite apart from the inflationary implications of devaluations which have already been analysed.

Among the various forms of intervention a good theoretical case can be made for the use of a flat-rate export subsidy based on value added, which has been extensively used in most of these countries, particularly in Israel. It is certainly less distortive than, for example, subsidised credit which distorts relative factor prices. Up to a point it is superior to devaluation, especially if financed out of an income tax, because it does not raise import prices directly.[16] As with any other distortive instrument this is a matter of degree. Under a fixed rate regime one possible strategy, which was quite successfully pursued in some countries, is to raise export subsidies gradually, by more than the domestic inflation rate, so as to achieve a continuous increase in the effective real rate ($\hat{p}_e - \hat{w} > 0$). Every few years when the subsidy rate reaches very distortive levels there is a tidying-up operation in which there is a large formal devaluation and subsidies are reduced or removed completely. Then the process can start again. It would seem that this is a method that achieves balance-of-payments objectives at a relatively low cost in terms of inflation and without the need for a severe output squeeze.

Unfortunately the use of export subsidies is not allowed by GATT or by normal IMF procedures, for reasons that cannot really be defended. If temporary tariffs on imports are allowed as an infant industry protection, why not use export subsidies? More glaring is the fact that the international rules of the game seem to tolerate very extreme and often truly distortive investment promotion laws, cheap export credit schemes, and a host of other forms of intervention which interfere with free trade and at the same time do so in ways which cause considerable domestic distortions as well. Why should LDCs not be allowed to have straight subsidies on exported value added as a counterpart to a value-added tax imposed on domestic production in many developed economies, a tax from which their exports are exempt?

I believe that there is a strong case for serious rethinking on this score. A similar, though somewhat less strong, case can be made for the use of differential wage subsidies for export activities. These may help the trade balance and at the same time induce employment, which is a critical issue in many LDCs.[17]

Another instrument which stabilisation policy might use and which for some reason is not considered part of the conventional toolkit is the direct use of government budgetary allocations so as to achieve minimum import use for a given employment objective. Two examples of such measures come to mind. One goes under the name of expenditure-switching policies. When there is a severe foreign-exchange shortage, an expansion of investment in housing activity, for example, at the expense of heavily import-intensive investment projects carried out by the public sector, may be a more effective short-term foreign-exchange saving and employment-inducing device than the imposition of across-the-board credit ceilings which hurt private sector production activity and often leave the public sector agencies unscathed. Likewise it may be legitimate for an international lender to impose on a country the introduction of a separate public-sector foreign-exchange budget, in addition to the regular budget denominated in domestic currency. Separate accounting of all public sector receipts and expenditures in foreign currency has the advantage of imposing foreign exchange discipline by quantity signals where a price signal in form of devaluation may be ineffective.[18] I am not aware that this type of tool is part of the conventional macro-prescriptions.

As a further example of a distortive measure consider food subsidies. The usual case against them rests on the allocational inefficiencies caused by price distortions, the fiscal burden imposed, or their inefficiency as a redistributional device compared with straight income transfers to the target social groups. This argument is quite relevent to a more developed economy with a highly developed fiscal system and which has alternative redistributional devices at its disposal (Israel, for example). It loses most of its weight in a country in which no alternative transfer systems (and only a weak income tax) exist and where the achievement of a minimum real subsistence level for low income groups[19] is a central objective of economic and social policy. In other words, it may be a good second best (where only third bests exist) of keeping the real consumption wage (w/p) high while the product wage (w/p_e) is kept low.[20] Finally there are circumstances in which straight subsidies, even when financed by money creation, may be anti-inflationary, at least in certain critical transition periods in which price expectations have to be damped down.[21]

VI CONCLUDING REMARKS

The analysis of the last two sections should not be wrongly interpreted to suggest that conventional macro-tools are irrelevant in a typical LDC, that there is no such thing as a distortive policy intervention and that therefore anything goes. One must naturally warn very strongly against using such arguments to rationalise what is often nothing more than reluctance to take unpopular, but justified, policy measures or an excuse for wasteful public spending. The fact that auxiliary export promotion measures, such as subsidies, are often called for, is not inconsistent with the claim that greater use be made of exchange rate adjustments as a major tool of balance-of-payments correction, provided it is skilfully done. Likewise the argument on the limitations of the use of 'financial programming' as it is often conceived is not inconsistent with very strict fiscal discipline. Finally the argument that some policy measures are not as distortive as they are sometimes made out to be is not inconsistent with the fact that there are many more practices that should be condemned under any frame of reference, no matter how liberal our interpretation. What has been argued here is that special attention should be paid to aspects of stabilization problems specific to LDCs. The following main points can be restated:

(1) Short-run stabilisation policy in an LDC cannot be divorced from the deeper structural problems which usually determine the nature of the short-run issues. Likewise the remedies cannot be kept independent of the long-run strategy of development and gradual reform. This simple truth may have important implications for the way in which the international community presently organises the long-run and short-run aid relationships between DCs and LDCs. For example, closer co-ordination of activities between the two great neighbours, the IBRD and the IMF, is called for.

(2) An undiscerning application of conventional stabilisation plans may be ineffective or even harmful because the specific institutional setup is ignored or else assumed to adjust very quickly. There is need to review the conventional wisdom on the policies to be applied at various stages of economic and institutional development. Also there is a strong case for reconsidering some measures of intervention whose use could be justified within a broader framework of analysis, in particular the question of export subsidies.

(3) An attempt should be made to make short-run external aid conditional not so much on immediate liberalisation and reform but

rather to judge it by criteria based on long-run performance, such as the country's general commitment to remove an import substitution bias, to expand exports, and to carry out gradual market reform.

(4) There is a strong case to be made for guaranteeing short-run finance in a more sustained manner to tide countries over the difficult and often prolonged transition period from Phase II to Phase IV. Irregular and unexpected spurts of aid will be much less effective than the guarantee of sustained help on condition that a long-run reform strategy is in fact carried out by stages. The social product of international capital flows at such a crtical stage may in fact be very high indeed. After all, when the economy's activity is constrained by the availability of intermediate goods imports the shadow price of foreign exchange is the reciprocal of the marginal import coefficient. This is almost always higher than the market rate of exchange.

ENDNOTES

1. Much of the criticism is in the nature of oral tradition among economists from industrial countries who have visited LDCs; some of it gets into the press (see, for example, Eckaus, 1977). Sometimes the criticism is sheer political propaganda. But the IMF itself seems to be sufficiently concerned to be making some efforts towards such a re-evaluation of its own accord.
2. Among the country studies most relevant to our present discussion are those for Brazil (Fishlow), Israel (Michaely), and South Korea (Frank, Kim, and Westphal).
3. Israel may recently have reached Phase V.
4. A more detailed analysis of parts of this framework can be found in my (1978) discussion paper.
5. Beyond a certain stage of development final consumption imports become less important. Alternatively one can consider even these goods as undergoing some minor processing (packaging and trade) before they reach the final consumer. Also ignored are interest payments. These can be assumed to be included in I_n or else be subtracted from new loan receipts in the capital account.
6. We have ignored the separate role of world demand (other than the price p_e^*) but this could also be incorporated.
7. It should be clear that item (e) [and sometimes also (f)] is a stylised representation of what in the real world usually consists of different tariffs (or subsidy rates) for different goods.
8. This may be obtained from a supply equation in which output is a negative function of real factor prices (of which only changes in the real import price are included here) and a Keynesian output demand equation in which the exogenous elements are the government deficit ($F = G - T$), purchases of domestic investments goods (I_x) and the real money supply ($\hat{M} - \hat{p}$). Finally, substituting from equation (5) one obtains equation (6).

9. We assume that the whole of the deficit is financed by borrowing from the central bank.
10. In the 1970s, and certainly for most LDCs, this is no longer the important issue it once was.
11. Below we make the point that in an LDC the degree of homogeneity may be greater than unity (see note 13).
12. In recent years this has happened in Israel as a result of asymmetrical indexation of government transactions with the public (see Bruno and Sussman, 1978). Another factor that is ignored here is the possibility of capital inflows following upon a devaluation.
13. In the paper just cited it is shown that this may also show itself in the fact that the price equation will not be linearly homogeneous (that is, $a_1 + a_2 > 1$ $a_3 < 0$) while output may exhibit less than zero homogeneity ($b_1 - b_2 + b_3 < 0$). This has been shown empirically for the Argentinian case (see Cavallo, 1977).
14. In terms of equation (9) we get $-\ell_n \hat{X} > (\ell_e \eta_{\hat{\imath}e} + \ell_n \sigma)(\hat{e} - \hat{w})$.
15. For a recent reference to this possibility in Portugal see Lundberg (1978).
16. Consider the above model—a formal devaluation raises prices [see equation (5)] while an export subsidy (t_e) will affect the internal system indirectly and only if there is an increase in F which is financed by money creation. Obviously export subsidies may involve distortions, if not imposed evenly, and may even induce administrative corruption, like any other micro-intervention.
17. The way most investment promotion schemes go, they heavily bias investment programmes in the direction of high capital intensity. A wage subsidy may thus be justified for more than one reason (see Little, Scitovsky, and Scott, 1970).
18. In many countries public agencies make real plans which are unaffected by devaluation (that is, their budgetary allocations are adjusted automatically to increased costs). A foreign-exchange budget is a form of self-imposed rationing of a scarce resource.
19. Food subsidies are sometimes also used as a means of guaranteeing producers' incomes in agriculture. The special structural role of agriculture in the inflationary process of LDCs is an important subject which we are ignoring here.
20. An alternative would be to have a higher nominal wage coupled with higher export subsidies or differential wage subsidies for export industries. In spite of distortions the food subsidy may be preferable from an equity standpoint because its incidence will be more progressive.
21. The argument in terms of our model would be that the price-depressing effect of a negative t_x in equation (5) outweighs the negative effect of the increase of F (and $\hat{M}$) on prices and the trade balance.

REFERENCES

Bhagwati, J. N., *Anatomy and Consequences of Exchange Control Regimes*, National Bureau of Economic Research (1978).

Bruno, M., *Stabilization and Stagflation in a Semi-Industrialized Economy*. (Discussion Paper No. 781.) (Jerusalem: Falk Institute, 1978).

Bruno, M. and Sussman, Z., 'Exchange Rate Flexibility, Inflation and Structural Change: Israel Under Alternative Regimes'. (Jerusalem, 1978). (Forthcoming in *Journal of Development Economics*.)

Cavallo, D. F., 'Stagflationary Effects of Monetarist Stabilization Policies'. (Unpublished Ph.D. thesis, Harvard University, 1977).

Díaz-Alejandro, C. F., 'A Note on the Impact of Devaluation and the Redistributive Effect', in *Journal of Political Economy*, LXXI (December, 1965), 577–80.

Eckaus, R. S., 'Is the IMF Guilty of Malpractice?' *Institutional Investor* (1977).

Krueger, Anne O., *Liberalization Attempts and Consequences*, National Bureau of Economic Research (1978).

Krugman, P. and Taylor, L., *Contractionary Effects of Devaluation*. (Department of Economics Working Paper No. 191.) (Cambridge, Mass.: MIT, 1976).

Little, I. M. D., Scitovsky, T. and Scott, M., *Industry and Trade in Some Developing Countries: A Comparative Study* (London: Oxford University Press, 1970).

Lundberg, E., *Problems of Economic Policy in Portugal* (Lisbon: Banco de Portugal, 1978).

Comments

Maurice Scott (UK)

Michael Bruno's interesting paper tackles an important question: are the conditions on which financial assistance is offered to less-developed countries (LDCs) in balance of payments difficulties by developed countries (DCs) or international organisations sensible? He asks, first, whether the measures which the creditors insist upon (such as devaluation and credit restrictions) are properly adapted to the structural features of LDCs or are appropriate only for DCs.

In tackling this first question, he does not, however, provide a list of relevant structural differences between LDCs and DCs, so I will attempt to fill this gap. Bearing in mind the difficulty of generalising about such a varied group of countries, I would nonetheless venture to suggest that the following are some of the more important differences.

(1) Agriculture is a more important sector, and both there and in small-scale manufacturing and services self-employment (including family workers) is the rule. Prices and incomes are rather flexible downwards. In short, the flex-price sector is more important in LDCs than in DCs.

(2) Price controls and rationing systems are less efficient in LDCs. In rural districts they are unenforceable, and in towns they are more open to corruption and evasion.

(3) Self-finance is more prevalent, and bank deposits are more important in relation to other privately held financial assets (such as government bonds, debentures, or shares). While I believe this is a relevant difference, it is not one which is properly made use of in the following comments, so I hope this deficiency will be made good by others, including Michael Bruno himself.

(4) Many LDCs are very small, and for them foreign trade is large in relation to national income, and exports are often concentrated in a few primary commodities whose prices fluctuate.

(5) A larger share of the gross domestic product consists of income belonging to foreigners. This was probably more important formerly than now. When mines and plantations were predominantly foreign-owned, a substantial part of the fluctuations in commodity prices was borne by foreigners. To an increasing extent (at least in some LDCs) residents and government revenue must now bear the brunt. Zambian copper is an example.

(6) The political situation is often more unstable. This is perhaps the most important relevant difference.

As Bruno points out, one cannot hope to change these (and other) structural features of LDCs quickly. Short-term stabilisation measures must largely take them for granted.

Bruno does not really say very much about the causes of balance-of-payment crises, and this leaves me unhappy, since I think one needs to bear them in mind when considering international measures to help deficit countries. It must surely make some difference whether, at one extreme, the main cause is a massive series of handouts before a presidential election, or whether, at the other extreme, the main cause is a quadrupling of oil or grain prices for an economy heavily dependent on imports of these commodities. I shall return to this point later.

Turning now to the efficacity of devaluation and credit restrictions, Bruno correctly shows that the former will not help if consequential adjustments in money wages offset it completely, and he asserts that a credit squeeze is likely to cause a big drop in output for a small drop in prices. It may even increase prices, he says, quoting evidence from the Argentine in support (although I would not class that country as a typical LDC). As Bruno points out one needs to distinguish between a devaluation which is combined with trade liberalisation, where the inflationary effects will be moderated, but so too will be the balance-of-payments improvement, and a devaluation whose main purpose is to improve the balance of payments, which is likely to raise prices much more.

If my list of structural differences between LDCs and DCs is anywhere near the mark, it is surely more, rather than less, likely that devaluation and credit restrictions will succeed in reducing real wages without (much) inflation, falls in output, or unemployment, in LDCs than in DCs. This is because the flex-price sector is bigger in LDCs. In the short run, agricultural output and employment, for example, will be scarcely affected by deflationary policies, while agricultural prices will be. Real wages will also be more flexible downwards, and it is not difficult to think of countries and occasions where very big real wage cuts have occurred—Brazil, the Philippines, South Korea and Taiwan, for example—and I am sure the list could be extended. The main consideration on the other side is the greater political instability of LDCs, which makes it risky for governments to take unpopular measures. It may be no accident that all the countries just mentioned had strong governments in power when the real wage-cuts were made. Outsiders are often insensitive to these political considerations. When one visits a country, one is too apt to think that reluctance to take this or that unpopular measure is mere shortsighted weakness. But when foreigners visit one's own country, and start talking in the same vein, one is horrified by their political naivety.

Strong governments may also be required to force through liberalisation measures (because of the powerful vested interests in controls), but, if this can be done, the resulting efficiency gains provide a handsome payoff in the not-so-long run. This applies both to import liberalisation, and to credit liberalisation, as McKinnon's stimulating book, *Money and Capital in Economic Development*, and his paper for this symposium (chapter 10) both testify. Hence, while the political risks of liberalisation measures are greater in LDCs than in DCs, the ultimate economic benefits are also probably greater. However, I would agree with Bruno that reforms of this kind should not be pushed through quickly. Our discussion of Giersch's paper on adjustment problems in DCs (chapter 7) shows that very clearly.

Bruno doubts whether a real devaluation provides sufficient stimulus to exports, and does not mention trade liberalisation as providing any stimulus at all. This leads him, in considering the second subdivision of his question (that is, the question of what should properly count as distortions in LDCs), to advocate export subsidies and other more direct measures to promote exports.

There is a great deal which could be said about this, but I will confine myself to the following points. First, while there is certainly a case for export subsidies to offset tariffs or quantitive import restrictions, it is much better still to reduce or eliminate the latter. Import liberalisation *does* stimulate exports (especially exports of manufactures made from imported materials), and does so more efficiently than a doubly bureaucratic system of restrictions offset by subsidies. It is doubly bureaucratic because you need one group of bureaucrats to administer the restrictions and another to administer the offsetting subsidies. There are examples (for example, Pakistan) of export subsidies which have *reduced* net foreign exchange earnings and so worsened the balance of payments. Secondly, one of Bruno's main arguments for special measures to promote exports seems to be the need to offset the extra costs of penetrating foreign markets. However, in so far as this is a real investment cost, it is not clear that the externality involved is greater than with most other forms of investment. Furthermore, marketing is often done by foreign firms who already have the requisite contacts and knowhow. Thirdly, while Bruno quotes the National Bureau of Economic Research studies as showing that export success in some countries resulted from special measures to promote their exports, one could quote, as counterexamples, the export success story of Hong Kong, without any export subsidies at all (but with complete import liberalisation) and Taiwan (with some export subsidies but not, in my judgement, enough to be an important explanation of success). Finally, Bruno raises the interesting question of the financing of export subsidies. I am not sure that this is really a short-term stabilisation issue, but I must protest against his summoning new income taxes to his aid as a relatively non-cost-raising source of finance. In so far as non-cost-raising income taxes can be increased in an LDC, they must, for the purposes of this analysis, have been increased *already*.

Turning to other so-called 'distortions', Bruno makes the point that, in the circumstances of some LDCs, food subsidies may be the best practicable way of helping the poor. Hence they should not be jettisoned in a crisis. He also advocates increased investment in housing because of its low import content and high employment-creating effect. Finally, as a general measure to induce foreign exchange saving in a crisis, he suggests that creditors might require debtor governments to operate a separate foreign exchange budget.

Both income redistribution measures and investment in housing seem to me to be mainly long-term measures, and not things to be switched on or off in a crisis. However, that does not mean that they should be altogether exempt in a period in which government expenditure is generally being cut. If, for example, the crisis is due to a large increase in government expenditure, including expenditure on food subsidies and housing, then it might well be reasonable to cut them back somewhat.

A separate foreign exchange budget might make sense as part of a strict system of rationing and controls, although even then its justification seems to be that one can indeed distinguish sharply between 'foreign exchange costs' and 'domestic currency costs'—a proposition which I am loathe to accept. But if rationing systems work especially badly in LDCs, do we want to insist upon them in a crisis?

There is one last general point I should like to make about this very interesting and stimulating paper. It is rather easy to draw attention to the difficulties and dangers of conventional policies to deal with balance-of-payments problems. In doing so one is implicitly comparing the situation *after* the measures have been adopted with the situation before. But that is not the right comparison to make. The right comparison is between the alternative situations *after* with different possible solutions to the crisis. It is very likely that the situation before the crisis will be a nice one. Incomes may have been growing rapidly thanks to an unusually favourable development of export prices or quantities, or government expenditure may have been high at the (for the moment painless) expense of foreign exchange reserves, or as a result of heavy borrowing from abroad. By contrast, the post-crisis situation is likely to be most unpleasant. But that may be true *whatever* set of measures is adopted. The real question is whether the best has been done in all the circumstances. Furthermore, and because of the point about different kinds of causes of crisis raised earlier, the international community may not always *want* all unpleasantness to be avoided. Precedents matter here as elsewhere, and it seems right that there should be rewards for prudence and punishments for being spendthrift. Of course, crises may confront even the most prudent of governments, people may not always get the government they deserve, and attempts to pursue very severe policies may simply make the situation much worse than would a more gradual and gentle approach. There are difficult issues here which certainly deserve to be discussed.

9 East, West, and South: the Role of the Centrally Planned Economies in the International Economy[1]

Richard Portes (UK)

I INTRODUCTION

Twenty-five years ago, the Eastern socialist countries had gone as far as they could to isolate themselves from the world economy and even from each other. Stalin's last year saw the full consequences of the autarchic policies and severe pressures he and his local administrators had imposed on the smaller countries of Eastern Europe as well as on the USSR. The strains proved excessive, the policies impossible to implement consistently, and a new political and economic leadership took a new course.

For different reasons, much the same may be said of the western embargo on sales of 'strategic' goods to the East, also at its height in the early 1950s. Thus while trade was rapidly expanding within each bloc, East and West gradually turned towards each other, then each pushed at a door which the other had already opened. Recently, both East and West have appeared to be trying to maximise the volume of trade between them, constrained only by limits on credit and a few residual strategic restrictions. One manifestation of this new climate is the East's hard currency debt to the West, up from a few billion dollars at the turn of the decade to over $50 billion at the end of 1977.

East–South economic relations have not been so dramatically transformed, and it is perhaps more difficult to discern the underlying forces shaping them. Both Western and Eastern analysts have devoted comparatively little attention to East–South trade and payments, and

319

even less to the reciprocal impacts of each of the major triangular relationships upon the others. Indeed, the terminological problem of deriving this triangle of First, Second and Third Worlds from North–South and East–West suggests a fundamental substantive issue: For what purposes, and in what contexts, is the East part of the North?

The East has itself been ambivalent, but it cannot long postpone taking positions as North–South negotiations proceed and Eastern involvement in the world economy deepens. Much of my discussion points towards the argument in Section VIII that the East's long-run interests and identification will be primarily with the North.

This overall identification partly arises from, partly determines Eastern attitudes towards the major separate issues: debt and the international financial system, trade preferences and restrictions cartels and stabilisation agreements for primary products, controls over multinational corporations, etc. It certainly does not preclude East – West conflict on these issues, but it defines the framework in which East – West disagreements can be handled. And if the argument is accepted, it implies that the long-run bargaining position of the South is weaker than it would otherwise be.

East or Eastern Europe means here the socialist, centrally planned economies of the USSR and the smaller countries of Eastern Europe (the Six), thus excluding Cuba, Yugoslavia, and the Asian CPEs. References to Comecon or CMEA (Council for Mutual Economic Assistance) will normally focus only on its East European members. The West is essentially OECD, the South all non-oil LDCs, and OPEC a separate fourth grouping. As indicated, constituents of the North are to be determined, mainly by reference to their relations with the South. Space constraints require that individual countries within these groups be distinguished only when necessary for the argument, but no bloc is monolithic. In particular, the position of some of the smaller Eastern countries may differ from those indicated in broad generalisations about CMEA.

I assume some fundamental geopolitical relationships, notably that the Warsaw Pact and Sino-Soviet hostility continue with little change for at least a generation. Soviet ideology remains Marxist, as do the Six, which stay in the Soviet sphere of influence, by armed force if necessary. East–West global strategic conflict and competition for economic and political influence continue without either East–West or Sino-Soviet War. That these restrictions still allow an extremely wide range of possible developments is suggested by the remarkable turnaround in East–West economic relations over the past twenty-five years.

The breadth of my topic will doubtless lead to superficiality, and I give a very personal and regrettably pessimistic view, with rather less diffidence than the actual uncertainties might justify. Some further detail may be found in Portes (1977a, 1977b), while a comprehensive recent book and extensive collections of papers offer diverse information and perspectives on some of the subjects covered here (Holzman, 1976, and Joint Economic Committee, 1976, 1977).

Section II provides an historical background and Section III a current picture of the role of Eastern Europe in the world economy, with special emphasis on East–West economic relations. Sections IV and V consider prospective developments within the CPEs of Eastern Europe and in their economic grouping, CMEA. Sections VI and VII separately discuss prospects for East–West and East–South relations, and Section VIII deals with the East–West–South triangle and the impact of the East on the international economic system.

II   HISTORICAL BACKGROUND

A brief historical survey will give background on some important issues: What have been the primary interests of the two superpowers conditioning their policies towards East–West economic interactions? In particular, should we see in the shift of the early 1970s a conscious policy decision by Soviet and East European planners and politicians?

East–West economic relations from 1948 to the mid-1950s were dominated by the consolidation of Soviet authority in the East and American efforts at 'containment'. Stalin could have imposed economic integration over the entire Warsaw Pact region but preferred to deal with each East European country separately. He therefore discouraged any plan of harmonisation or specialisation within the bloc and broke up initial attempts at economic co-operation between the Danubian states. CMEA was created but not really used, and bilateral agreements were the norm throughout the East. The USSR dissociated itself from Bretton Woods and the Havana World Trade Conference and stopped Czechoslovakia from accepting Marshall Plan aid. Meanwhile, the United States organised its allies to implement a comprehensive embargo on the export of strategic goods to the East (Adler-Karlsson, 1968, and Wolf, 1973).

The period from the mid-1950s to the late 1960s saw gradual relaxation on both sides, more diversity in motives and behaviour between individual countries in each alliance, and significant developments in both CMEA and Western economic integration. In the East, de-Stalinisation and political and economic strains within the smaller countries led them to question the pattern of their rapid economic growth. Arguments against self-sufficiency and import substitution gained force, especially in the resource-poor smaller countries, where the economists revived discussion of gains from trade and specialisation, and the planners discovered that autarchy was impossible (see Wiles, 1968). The rapid development of processing capacities forced increasing dependence on trade to import raw materials and export much of the output of the new factories. Thus the total trade of Eastern Europe rose from $4\frac{1}{2}$ per cent of world trade in 1948 to $7\frac{1}{2}$ per cent in 1953 and 11 per cent in 1962 (its peak share—recent figures are closer to 9 per cent, though perhaps somewhat underestimated because of price disparities).[2] The overall opening of the Eastern economies to trade is *not* a recent phenomenon, as distinct from the recent rapid expansion of *East–West* trade.

Meanwhile the USSR began to perceive increasing costs in maintaining the economic dependence of the Six on its raw materials and its willingness to absorb growing amounts of their low-quality manufacturing (especially engineering) output (Marer, in Joint Economic Committee, 1974). It reacted by attempting to reverse Stalin's policy and impose supranational control of national development plans in CMEA, so as to make the economies of the smaller countries more complementary to its own. In 1962 Romania blocked this effort, however, fearing that it would be relegated permanently to the role of supplying agricultural products to the more industrialised countries. The USSR then backed off, and there were no major initiatives in CMEA for several years (Kaser, 1967).

Also in 1962, Liberman's article on profits marked the beginning of public discussion of 'economic reform' in the USSR. The smaller, more trade-dependent countries were especially attracted to decentralisation, greater scope for the market and economic incentives, the acceptance of world market prices as opportunity costs, and an emphasis on technical progress and productivity. All this fitted in well with giving more autonomy in foreign trade to producing enterprises, especially in their dealings with the West. East–West industrial co-operation agreements started off in the mid-1960s, and Hungarian enterprises had concluded several dozen by the time of the major economic reforms in Hungary in 1968. Czechoslovakia was also a leader in reform, then in openness to the West, until August 1968.

Throughout this period, the Eastern countries were quite willing to accept export credits from the West to finance capital goods purchases; willingness to borrow from capitalists is *not* a new development (Wolf, 1975). Romania was the first to do so on a major scale, but competition between Western capital goods exporters spread, and terms were good for Eastern buyers. Even the USA was willing to trade with the East (but not to give Eximbank credits), though was still more restrained than other Western countries, and still maintained the strategic embargo. De-Stalinisation and the evident loosening up of the Eastern bloc made it politically more acceptable to deal with Eastern Europe and potentially more rewarding; it could be argued that trade might stimulate reforms (and 'convergence)' and some differentiation of the smaller countries' interests from those of the USSR. Important milestones were American grain sales to Poland, then the major sale of wheat to the USSR in 1963.

The main foreign economic concerns of both East and West were however within their respective groupings (this was also the time of progress from the Treaty of Rome to a functioning Common Market), and there was no drive from either side to expand East–West trade— just a greatly increased receptiveness. Moreover, the Six felt constrained to adhere to the unwritten rule that no more than one-third of their trade should be with countries outside CMEA. But East–West trade started at so low a base that its rate of growth during this period was quite high.

The Soviet invasion of Czechoslovakia in August 1968 marked a change of direction in CMEA and its relations with the rest of the world. First, it set explicit limits on how far internal liberalisation or approaches to the West could go without Soviet approval. Although the Hungarian economic reforms were not reversed, those in Czechoslovakia were, and elsewhere decentralisation was no longer a feasible option. The road to further growth became integration within CMEA—not on the basis of all adapting to Soviet priorities and needs, but rather through efforts to rationalise and integrate manufacturing production throughout the bloc. Emphasis turned to specialisation and modernisation through co-ordinated long-run planning in the CMEA framework.

This did not exclude industrial co-operation with Western firms, and the purchase of modern technology was to become a key element in the process. Nor was it intended to restrict East–West trade. But invest-ment and the restructuring of production were to be directed towards economic co-operation in the bloc, which would simultaneously work towards currency convertibility and multilateralisation. These far reaching, ambitious objectives were formalised in the CMEA 'Complex Programme' agreed and announced in the summer of 1971 (see NATO, 1977). To some extent, planned trade, specialisation and technical co-operation were to substitute for the decentralising reforms which seemed so difficult to control.

At the same time, the new Polish leadership which took over after the riots of December 1970 were deciding that the only way to break the economic constraints which had led to the discontent was to invest heavily in up-to-date technology for several years without reducing consumption. They embarked on massive purchases of Western plant and equipment on credit, encountering no serious obstacles in Western export restrictions, most of which had been relaxed at the end of the 1960s.

Events then brought the other Eastern countries into large hard currency import expenditures. The Polish decision, taken for special reasons in unique circumstances, was followed by the Soviet-American Trade Agreement discussions and the flowering of the *détente* atmosphere. The bad Soviet harvest of 1972 required the first round of large grain purchases. Then the commodity price boom of 1972–74, with the oil price increase, put great pressure on the smaller countris. But they could not have relieved this pressure with imports from the West, nor could the Polish strategy have been implemented, without Western willingness to provide finance. This necessary condition was satisfied for many reasons (Portes, 1977b): *détente*, the West German *Ostpolitik*, the accumulation of petrodollar deposits in Western banks, the recession beginning in 1974 which made both the banks and Western capital goods exporters seek customers—and find eager borrowers and buyers in the East.

Thus there was a sharp increase in Eastern hard currency imports in the early 1970s, with a lesser acceleration in Eastern exports to the West. To some extent, this sudden expansion of East–West economic relations reflects changes over the three postwar decades in the interests and motives of the various countries involved. The United States went from containment to linkage, the stick to the carrot, attempting with both to get political concessions using economic levers. But while the embargo, when observed, undoubtedly hindered East European economic and military development, it did not discernibly affect Eastern political behaviour. Nor have the inducements of trade and credit liberalisation been effective in achieving the political objectives foremost in American policy. The Federal Republic of Germany's political normalisation with the East likewise facilitated but was not itself brought about by its extensive trade with Eastern Europe. The interests of other Western countries in the East have been more narrowly mercantile, although Britain and France have retained some independent foreign policy aspirations.

The dominant Soviet interest throughout has been to maintain the economic dependence of its CMEA partners. Its strategy has, however, shifted somewhat from using simple dependence on its raw material supplies to integrating the other economies more deeply with that of the USSR, through specialisation of manufacturing output. This has allowed the smaller countries more freedom in their non-CMEA trade; indeed, desiring to sell more of its materials for hard currency, the USSR has in some cases encouraged the Six to seek alternative sources of supply. Recently Soviet interests have also turned towards obtaining from the West grain, technology and large capital imports for Soviet resource development, as well as seeking to establish some dependence of the West on Soviet raw materials. But these motives are secondary to maintaining the cohesion of CMEA. For the Six, on the other hand, the stability of Soviet raw material supplies and manufactures purchases is important, and there is no desire to buy any more raw materials for hard currency than necessary. But they feel more dependent on the West for technology imports and more constrained by the need to develop manufactures which can be sold for hard currency.

It has been argued that the sudden expansion of East European imports from the West beginning in the early 1970s was a conscious policy decision due to their perceived 'technological gap'. On this view, the East European countries concluded that massive Western imports were essential to modernise and that they would therefore accept the consequential burden of debt and technological dependence which they had previously avoided (Knirsch, 1978). This suggests more concerted policies and more strategic planning of trade with the West than I believe likely. Rather, except for the special cases of the USSR and Poland, it seems more plausible that the other countries' trade deficits with the West arose primarily from the general pressures discussed above. When they discovered that borrowing on a large scale was easy and relatively painless, the arguments for continuing were much stronger than those for self-discipline (see Section IV).

We turn finally to the relative importance of political and economic determinants of East–West economic relations in the past. Some judge that political factors have gradually lost weight as the economic dependence of each side on the other has increased (Knirsch, 1978); others maintain that with increasing interdependence, the international economy becomes more politicised (Brzezinski, 1976). I suggest a third hypothesis: that neither side has perceived their economic interdependence as having more than marginal significance, so that as Cold War tensions eased, political and economic forces *internal* to individual countries or to the two blocs became the primary determinant of their economic relations with each other. This seems the best explanation of events since the late 1950s, including of course the American attempt to attach political condition to trade and credits (the Jackson Amendment) and the negative East European response to it (Kaser, 1977).

But the growth of trade, technology transfer and debt has now established a significant though limited economic dependence of each side on the other which will affect their future political relations. In my view, the economic interaction of East and West will continue to reflect the fundamental economic forces underlying their respective patterns of growth, so I now turn to the present economic situation of Eastern Europe and its prospects.

III   THE CURRENT ROLE OF EASTERN EUROPE IN THE WORLD ECONOMY

The peculiarities of East European price systems invalidate the standard measures of foreign trade dependence (value of trade per capita, share of trade in GNP, etc.). It is however generally accepted that the East's trade participation is still relatively low, although in recent years their trade has been growing as fas as that of the rest of the world.

The structure of East European trade reflects the distribution of raw material supplies and manufacturing capacities (and the relative quality of manufactured output) between the seven countries. Within CMEA, there has been persistent excess demand for most foodstuffs and raw materials ('hard goods') and excess supply of low-quality machinery ('soft goods'), in part because it has been much easier to sell the former for hard currency. The USSR has supplied materials in exchange for machinery (taking an especially high proportion of the better East German products), some semifabricates, industrial consumer goods and food (primarily from Bulgaria and Romania), whereas the Six mainly trade machinery among themselves.

East–West trade, however, is primarily an exchange of raw materials and some simple manufactures from the East for more advanced manufactured goods and materials from the West. And East–South trade is similar to West–South trade: manufactures (including armaments) from the East in exchange for raw materials from the South. Thus in its relations with the West, the East is in a position rather like the South, while in its relations with the South, the East appears like the West. From another perspective, trade within the Six is in substitutable goods, as is most trade between the advanced industrial countries of the West; but trade between the USSR and the Six, between East and West, and between East and South is complementary. There are alternative hypotheses to explain these different patterns: natural resource endowments, or comparative advantage more broadly interpreted; differences in economic systems; or the relative levels of economic development of the regions. The likely evolution of trade patterns is discussed in Section VII.

Since the East's own use of raw materials is high, corresponding to its large manufacturing output, even Soviet supplies do not make the region important in world markets for very many commodities. Outside the bloc the USSR is a major supplier of oil, gas, coal, timber, chrome, cotton, diamonds, and gold, and Poland of coal, copper and sulphur. But otherwise the East holds no strong supplier positions.

Although since the early 1960s the total volume of East European trade has not grown more rapidly than world trade, East–West trade has grown much faster. About 30 per cent of East European exports now go to Western industrial countries, while about 37 to 38 per cent of East European imports come from the West (up from 23 per cent and 25 per cent respectively in 1965). Of total OECD exports, 5 per cent went to Eastern Europe in 1975, compared with 3 per cent in 1965. Eastern trade with the South has also been rising somewhat faster than intrabloc trade, the share of which has been falling for all seven countries. Even for the Six, which have always had a higher share of their trade within the bloc than the USSR, this share fell to 54 per cent in 1974 (rising to 59 per cent in 1975, but still well below the old 'two-thirds rule').[3]

The most striking figures are of course the East European hard currency trade deficits, at $1 billion in 1971, $2 billion in 1972, $4 billion in 1973, $6 billion in 1974, $12 billion in 1975, $10 billion in 1976, and about $8 billion in 1977.[4] Eastern Europe (mainly the USSR, but also Romania and Bulgaria) runs surpluses with the LDCs, not negligible at $1 to 2 billion annually, but little help in redressing the very large deficits with the West. Much of the surplus with the South is in inconvertible currencies or covered by long-term credits (economic aid) which may in the long run be unredeemable.

In other hard currency flows, Eastern Europe has a surplus of about $500 million annually on tourism and roughly the same on transfers (mainly emigrant remittances), but larger and rapidly growing interest payments (estimated at $1.8 billion in 1976) on its debt to the West. Thus overall, there have been large current account deficits for the past several years reflecting large real capital flows from West to East (with some from East to South) and creating a correspondingly large accumulation of East European debt (Portes, 1977b). Almost two-thirds of this debt has been financed by Western commercial banks without government guarantees; such lending is a phenomenon new in the 1970s.

These capital flows contrast with virtually negligible labour flows. Although several Eastern countries find themselves labour-short, there has been no attempt to import workers. An arrangement with Yugoslavia, for example, might make considerable sense for Hungary or East Germany, but nothing of this kind has been tried. Emigration is of course carefully controlled.

IV   PROSPECTIVE DEVELOPMENTS IN THE ECONOMIES OF EASTERN EUROPE

Although the East European economies are centrally planned, there are no plans of any practical significance for any period longer than five years. The current Five-year Plans carry us no further than 1980. This section is therefore a subjective assessment of the forces and trends likely to dominate economic growth and institutional change in Eastern Europe in the next two decades.

For resources, the picture is fairly clear, except for one point on which there has been considerable recent controversy, Soviet oil supplies. The labour force will grow more slowly throughout Eastern Europe than it did in the three postwar decades. Birth rates have been low since the 1950s (though rising somewhat recently); male participation rates have long been at their feasible maxima, and female participation rates cannot increase significantly; statutory work week lengths and formal retirement ages will probably fall in most countries, and pension entitlements will become more generous; and the transfer of labour out of agriculture to industry and services has already been excessive (except perhaps in Bulgaria and Romania), in so far as the composition of the remaining agricultural labour force has deteriorated and productivity has suffered. There is however considerable underemployment of labour in industry and construction, so that improvements in organisation and mechanisation of some processes (such as handling of materials) could release substantial labour reserves for redeployment. But this might require either major improvements in the structure of managerial incentives ('economic reforms') or capital investment, or both.

The existing capital stock reflected until recently emphasis on capital widening, building new factories to accommodate the influx of workers into industry and equipping them with low quality machinery, while scrapping very little. The shares of investment going to housing and transport were relatively low, while agricultural investment emphasised machinery to replace labour (tractors) to the neglect of irrigation, storage, etc. Thus there will be heavy investment requirements for housing (the shortage most deeply felt by the East European population), transport, agriculture, and mechanisation of the construction sector, as well as modernising the industrial capital stock.

Except for the Soviet Union and Poland, Eastern Europe is poor in raw materials. Romania has already passed the peak of its oil production and is now a net oil importer. Hungary has substantial bauxite reserves and potentially significant newly discovered copper. The German Democratic Republic has large amounts of low-grade coal. But among the Six, only Poland has a substantial resource base.

Soviet raw material supplies are varied and extensive, but an increasing proportion of production will have to come from the Eastern part of the country. Extraction in harsh natural conditions and transport to Western regions and the Six will raise costs. According to some analysts, the most serious medium and long-run economic problem for the USSR will be the rapid depletion of oil in the Western part of the country and inability to increase the output of Siberian oil enough to compensate. A detailed study by the CIA (1977a) argues that Soviet output may peak as early as 1978–79 at 550 to 600 million tonnes per annum (the Soviet plan is 640 million tonnes in 1980) and fall to 400 to 500 million tonnes by 1985. Although natural gas production will continue to rise rapidly, reaching (they estimate) the equivalent of 475 million tonnes of oil by 1985, the implications for the net East European oil balance would be very serious. The CIA 'baseline' estimates for 1985 project that the USSR will be a net importer of oil, in the amount of 55 million tonnes, while the import needs of the Six will be 130 million tonnes, the total coming to about $16 to 17 billion in 1977 prices. This contrasts with 1975 Soviet exports of 65 million tonnes to Eastern Europe (which then had to import only 20 million tonnes from elsewhere) and 55 million tonnes for hard currency, generating over 40 per cent of Soviet hard currency earnings (although this was only 5 per cent of total Western oil imports). But these are the most pessimistic forecasts at present. Much closer to a conventional view is Russell (1976), who projects net East European oil import requirements at anywhere between 50 and 120 million tonnes in 1985.[5] If undertaken soon, however, massive imports of Western energy technology and machinery, pipeline and pumping equipment (financed on credit) could make a significant difference to Soviet production capability from 1985 onwards.

There will be other sources, both foreign and domestic, of pressures on the economies of Eastern Europe. Although Poland and the USSR have benefited from improvements in their terms of trade outside CMEA since 1970, the other countries have faced deteriorating dollar terms of trade, to the extent of about 20 per cent for Czechoslovakia, the GDR and Hungary in 1970–75 (but with some improvement in 1976). Now that CMEA trade prices are set on the basis of a five-year moving average of world market prices, these terms of trade changes are being translated into a corresponding shift *within* the bloc to the benefit of the USSR. Consumer aspirations for a greater share of the fruits of economic growth pose severe problems in Poland, the German Democratic Republic, Hungary and Czechoslovakia, and cannot be neglected elsewhere. Agriculture will continue to be highly vulnerable to climatic conditions and suffer from incentive problems. On our assumption that East–West strategic conflict will continue, the planners cannot expect to reduce the share of output going to defence. And finally, the major weakness of all the East European economies will continue to be the 'technology gap' (outside of some military production): failure to generate and diffuse innovations in the industrial sector, poor product quality, low utilisation of computer technology, and generally inefficient use of resources (all relatively to the West).

This suggests some decline in overall growth rates for Eastern Europe. Contrary to the conventional wisdom of the 1960s, that East European growth performance would fall off in comparison with the 1950s unless radical economic reforms were implemented, the trend path of growth rates for the Six was gently but quite steadily upwards from the early 1960s to 1975.[6] Now, however, the resource constraints and other problems sketched above will take over—regardless of institutional change or immobility—and this trend will reverse. The 1976–80 plans in fact already show slight declines in growth rates compared to 1971–75 (except in Bulgaria). The Soviet growth rate has fallen fairly steadily since the 1950s (Bergson, 1978), and it would be surprising if this did not continue somewhat further.

These developments will therefore bring severe pressures on the East European economies, especially the more industrialised countries. I would in fact argue against conventional wisdom, that for all except Poland and the USSR, the hard currency deficits of the past several years have already been more a manifestation of excessive pressure at the macroeconomic level (excess real demand) than a policy response to the 'technology gap'.[7] For if there had been a decision to substitute Western for CMEA-produced machinery, this could have been accompanied by cutbacks of other imports from the West. But the composition of East–West trade did *not* change accordingly. In 1970, the East European hard currency trade deficit was less than $1 billion, and the share of engineering products in OECD exports to Eastern Europe was 35 per cent. In 1975, the figures were $12 billion and 36 per cent. The aggregate share of engineering, motor vehicles and other manufactures (mainly industrial consumer goods) in OECD exports to the East was unchanged at 47 per cent in both 1970 and 1975. The Western export categories which did rise faster than total East–West trade were food and ferrous metals.

Poland did buy substantial quantities of Western plant and equipment, and the USSR made major purchases of large-diameter pipe and grain, but East European machinery and equipment imports from OECD rose somewhat *less* rapidly than their total imports from OECD. And imports of machinery and equipment from the West came to less than 4 per cent of total machinery and equipment investment in the USSR in 1971–75 (about 25 per cent in Poland, much the highest in Eastern Europe). ECE data (Economic Bulletin for Europe, 1976) show the share of 'technology intensive' imports in total imports from ten industrialised Western countries *falling* from 51 per cent in 1965–68 to 46 per cent in 1971–74 for the East European Six, and from 54 per cent in 1965–68 to 43 per cent in 1971–74 for the USSR. Using a different definition of 'high technology' goods, Zaleski (1978) finds that their share in total Soviet machinery imports from OECD countries fell from 48 per cent in 1972 to 45 per cent in 1974 and 33 per cent in 1976. He

explains this tendency in terms of the general needs of the Soviet economy. The recent increase of machinery imports by the USSR would constitute more a source of capital imports, on credit, as much as possible, and also a safety valve against the failures of Soviet machinery industries. The objective of catching up to the Western technological level would then only be of secondary importance.

As this suggests, one reason for the conventional view is that the big credits go for the major machinery deals, turnkey plants, etc.; but these tied credits then free hard currency export earnings for the purchase of raw materials. These deals also get publicity, partly because they confirm our prejudices that the centrally planned systems simply cannot cope without Western help. And this interpretation of recent Eastern behaviour does follow the pattern of Russian economic relations with the West in the past—periodic moves into Western markets to obtain advanced technology, then withdrawal into self-sufficiency.

But the evidence indicates that the Eastern economies are actually becoming more like the rest of the world in their macro-economic behaviour: aggregate excess demand results in an import surplus. What happened in the 1970s was that the East European countries raised investment ratios without holding back consumption correspondingly, while in most cases their terms of trade were falling. The $6 billion hard currency deficit for the USSR in 1975 was slightly less than 1 per cent of GNP, but the $6 billion for the rest of Eastern Europe was over 2 per cent of GNP; and for Poland, Hungary and Bulgaria, total trade deficits were at least 5 per cent of GNP. The excess real demand came out in the foreign trade sector to this extent only when the Eastern countries realised they could allow it, because the West was willing to lend to finance the deficits. Except in Poland, there was no major conscious decision at the beginning of the 1970 to accept more dependence on the West for technological advance.

Given the pressures now facing the planners, the only effective limit on their hard currency current account deficits will be the perception of imminent credit constraints. The relative emphasis they then give to import restriction and export promotion will be determined in part by the external environment (in particular, the receptiveness of hard currency markets to their exports) and in part by the repercussions of each policy on internal economic and political equilibrium. If import restriction means food and industrial consumer goods, domestic political tensions will increase; if materials, there may be immediate bottleneck effects in production; and if capital goods, longer-run effects on technical progress, competitiveness, and growth. Export promotion, on the other hand, would require a serious drive to penetrate hard currency markets with manufactured goods. There would have to be institutional changes of a fairly radical nature: decentralisation in foreign trade to a degree that would have to entail some decentralisation in decision-making in production; much greater scope for industrial co-operation with Western firms, involving some institutional equivalent of equity participation, and a role in Eastern Europe for the multi-national corporations similar to their activities in the rest of the world.

I find such institutional changes highly improbable. Increased East–West trade in the 1970s has been in part a *substitute* for economic reforms (see Bornstein, 1977), as has the effort to increase specialisation and integration in CMEA. There may be some limited decentralisation in foreign trade itself, but not with a significant feedback on domestic economic organisation (always excepting Hungary).[8] The East European economies will remain centrally planned economies, and the logic of central planning suggests if anything that the increased trade dependence on unstable Western economies will motivate somewhat *greater* centralisation. Indeed, perhaps the only internally consistent way of mounting a successful drive to increase exports of manufactures would be to treat this as a high priority activity like military production: to separate it from the rest of the economy, creating enterprises (or divisions within them) specialising in production for export to hard currency markets and according them priority in allocations of materials, skilled manpower, etc. This approach would also fit in well with the effort to specialise and go for long production runs within CMEA, and it could then have the desired side-effect of raising the quality of manufactured goods exports to all destinations, including intra-CMEA (the Hungarian specialisation in bus production might be an example).

Immobilism in the structure of internal political control will rule out any radical changes in economic organisation. In the 1960s, it was often maintained that a 'managerial revolution' was in progress in Eastern Europe, that the technocratic, meritocratic élite would find its interests conflicting with those of the Party *apparat*, and that economic necessity would force the latter to yield. This proved incorrect, but now a similar argument is often heard in terms of 'generational change'—that a new, younger generation of political leaders will bring the flexibility lacking in those who have so far governed Eastern Europe in the postwar period. I believe this version to be equally unfounded.

Whatever combination of import restriction, export promotion, and trade reorientation is chosen to meet the pressures of the coming decades will have to be consistent with the basic structure of a political and economic system which has been remarkably stable since its inception. This stability has been maintained despite tremendous efforts and sacrifices for economic growth, and in the face of consequent political tensions which have occasionally been manifested openly. We must exclude any hypotheses about future developments in Eastern

Europe's external relations which derive from or entail farreaching internal systemic change.

V   PROSPECTIVE DEVELOPMENTS IN CMEA

Although the Soviet Union is the dominant partner in CMEA and can *in extremis* resort to overwhelming force to attain its objectives, it cannot treat the Six as constituent republics of the USSR. Its basic interest is to maintain the economic dependence of the Six on the USSR, given the costs of using force. A secondary objective is to increase the economic strength of all the countries of the bloc, both to improve the Eastern position in East–West conflict and to facilitate domestic political control in each country. Economic difficulties generate political tensions and can directly threaten internal stability (see, for example, Poland, 1970 and 1976) or can motivate policies which ultimately do so (Czechoslovakia 1965–68). Thus there are limits to the extent to which the Soviet Union can 'exploit' its partners.

From the mid-1950s to the late 1960s, in fact, the Soviet Union was willing to bear significant economic costs in its trade with the Six. Its terms of trade in CMEA were poorer than with the rest of the world, and it was accepting for its raw materials machinery of inferior quality. Over the past several years, however, the picture has changed. The USSR still supplies most of the Six's oil, coal, coke, phosphates, ferrous metals, timber, cotton, and other important materials. But around the turn of the decade, the USSR told its partners that they could not expect deliveries to continue to rise in proportion to their needs. Although Soviet shipments would increase, a higher proportion of incremental supplies would have to come from the West and the South. Moreover, the other Eastern countries would be expected to contribute to the capital costs of expanding supplies of the most capital-intensive materials. Such joint investment in Soviet raw material extraction and transport has now been underway for some time, and the costs to the Six in the 1976–80 Five-year Plan period have been estimated at as much as $9 billion (though some put the net cost significantly lower—see Snell, 1977). The major project so far is the Orenburg gas pipeline, which will bring large quantities of Soviet gas to Eastern Europe.

These Soviet initiatives preceded the commodity price boom of 1972–74. At first the USSR did not react to the sharp rise in commodity prices, not even to that of oil. The practice had been to set CMEA prices at the beginning of a Five-year Plan period for the whole of the Plan, on the basis of average world market prices for years immediately preceding the period. But by late 1974, the USSR could no longer accept selling oil to the Six at a quarter of the price it would bring in hard currency. A first stage of CMEA price increases was implemented at the beginning of 1975, and it was agreed that prices would be adjusted annually to follow a five-year moving average of world market prices. The result has been a substantial shift to the benefit of the Soviet Union and Poland within CMEA.

In addition, the USSR has been requiring since the late 1960s that the Six take higher proportions of Soviet machinery in their imports and export more materials and semifabricates in return. Thus the USSR is moving closer to the norm for trade between the Six, that 'hard' goods are exchanged for 'hard' goods and 'soft' goods accepted only to the extent that one's partner will accept one's own 'soft' exports. The ratio of Soviet machinery exports to machinery imports has for several years been rising fairly steadily with all but Bulgaria and Romania, although the USSR does still take about half of its partner's total machinery exports.

The overall effect has been to squeeze the smaller countries between their deteriorating position on Western markets and similarly disadvantageous trends in their trade with the USSR. Events weakened their bargaining position with the Soviet Union, and this may explain why they appear to have welcomed the parallel Soviet initiative for more specialisation and integration in industry through supranational planning in CMEA. Concerned over the future of their manufactured goods exports to the USSR, and lacking confidence that they could sell these goods in the West, they may have seen this process as a way of committing the USSR to take their output over the long run.[9]

Thus the Soviet Union has discovered that it can maintain, perhaps even strengthen, its economic hold over the others while reducing the cost of doing so. At a time when its own growth has been slowing, this has doubtless been an attractive policy, but the USSR is evidently running up now against the constraint that its partners' economies should not experience destabilising crises. Recent political difficulties in Poland, Czechoslovakia and East Germany suggest that if economic problems were to cause a serious retrenchment in consumption, latent dissatisfaction could surface and threaten the stability of the entire 'northern tier' of the Warsaw Pact. Until recently, the USSR had not realised the full magnitude of the strain its policies, taken as a whole, imposed on the economies of the Six: The 1976–80 plans showed a several billion dollar export surplus of the Six with the USSR, a resource transfer they could ill afford.

The Soviet Union must relax this pressure and reduce its demands. It is not likely to compromise on the principles of CMEA price formation or 'co-operative' investment in raw material production, but rather will allow its partners to run trade deficits with it. This would amount to extending credit on a large scale, and it does appear that the Soviet Union gave Poland a substantial formal Union (in commodities) at the end of 1976. The USSR will probably become a major long-term creditor in CMEA.[10]

This would be a very significant departure from what has been the invariable practice of short-term (over at most two years) bilateral balancing of trade in CMEA. Bilateralism itself will however remain the rule, and it is unlikely that much of the debts will be incurred in the form of borrowing by the Six from the CMEA banks (IBEC, the International Bank for Economic Co-operation, which finances intra-CMEA trade, and IIB, the International Investment Bank). Bilateralism increases the degree of dependence of each individual smaller country on its giant partner, and there are monetary obstacles to any meaningful multilateralism which will be insurmountable so long as central planning continues in its present form (see below).

But long-term lending by the USSR to its CMEA partners would be one manifestation of what I foresee as strong centripetal tendencies in CMEA (see also Marer, 1976, and Smith, 1977). These will be a response to forces impinging on the bloc from outside: the growth problems of Western economies and consequent weakness of Western markets for East European manufacturers, as well as the competition which the East can expect from some of the more advanced LDCs; integration in the EEC, and its insistence that Eastern countries deal in trade negotiations with the Community rather than individual members, which makes it in the interest of the East to respond as a bloc; and the increasing instability of the world economy, in prices and in overall cyclical behaviour, which central planners dislike and will, *ceteris paribus*, induce them to orient their trade more towards their centrally planned bloc partners. Similarly, increased cartelisation of primary product trade and 'market-sharing' in manufactures might also be met best by concerted CMEA responses.

Within the bloc itself, mutual desires for higher quality machinery deliveries and longer production runs will promote further integration of manufacturing production through specialisation agreements.

Perhaps the strongest centripetal force, however, will be exerted by the East European hard currency debt, which will require increased reliance of East European countries on imports from their CMEA partners. The proportion of manufactures in intra-bloc trade will rise, while the resource-poor countries will be forced to obtain an increasing share of their materials from outside CMEA.

Finally, we turn to the monetary framework within which intra-CMEA trade is conducted. The IBEC was established in 1963 to act as a clearing bank, and the 'transferable rouble' was introduced then. This is the unit in which intrabloc prices are set and transactions are denominated. It was an ostensibly important part of the 'Complex Programme' of 1971 to work towards multilateralism, in particular by making the transferable rouble into a true international currency, at least within CMEA. It was intended that a surplus of transferable roubles accumulated in one bilateral relation could be used for purchases elsewhere in the bloc, so the transferable rouble would become a proper medium of exchange and store of value in CMEA trade.

But currency convertibility in commodity trade is fundamentally incompatible with central allocation of resources in physical terms at the level of each national economy. Alternatively, convertibility would require central planning of the production and distribution of goods at the bloc level, that is, *complete* integration of the national economies.[11] For central plans cannot accommodate the uncertainty associated with giving agents outside the scope of regulation by the plan free access to goods produced and allocated under the plan. This is why Hungary advocated intrabloc convertibility, because it would have required that the other countries allow decentralisation of short-run production and allocation decisions, as Hungary had done in 1968. This would have given Hungarian enterprises the freedom to trade within CMEA, which was a natural complement to their freedom to deal with each other and with Western firms. But the other countries were predictably unwilling to decentralise in this way.

I argued above that central allocation will continue for the foreseeable future. Monetary institutions in CMEA will reflect this fundamental datum. This means bilateral negotiation of trade plans in detail and the associated bilateral accounting and balancing in monetary terms. The transferable rouble will remain only a unit of account, having indeed a different effective average value in each bilateral relation.

A recent development which has attracted attention is the practice of denominating payments for *above-plan* shipments of 'hard' goods (raw materials) in hard currency. Thus Hungary negotiated with the USSR a schedule of planned oil deliveries from 1976 to 1980. Additional amounts have however been agreed, to be charged at current world market prices in dollars. Such procedures may now extend to 5 to 10 per cent of total intra-CMEA trade (Brainard, 1978). But we cannot expect them ever to play any more than a marginal role (see also Kohn and Lang, 1977)—there will be no introduction of convertibility by the back door, as long as central allocation persists in Eastern Europe.[12]

VI   ECONOMIC RELATIONS BETWEEN EAST AND WEST

Although there was a steady relaxation of restrictions and expansion of East–West trade from the mid-1950s, the picture has been transformed by the rapid growth of Western exports and Eastern hard currency debt over the past five years. Another widespread phenomenon is industrial co-operation between Western and Eastern firms. Will these recent trends continue?

Our first conjecture is that even if Western governments remain unconcerned about the resource and technology transfer mirrored by the accumulation of debt, Western private financial institutions will not continue with substantial new net lending. The real rate of return on Western investment in Eastern Europe may be high, especially for raw material extraction, but the maturity structure of the credits being extended is much too short-term for such capital-intensive undertakings, and a significant part of the borrowing has in fact been for general balance of payments support.

Thus although 'world welfare' (with fairly egalitarian distributional weights) might be well served by substantial further Western investment in the East, new credit is likely to dry up in a few years. Because of the short average maturity of the debt, service will by then represent such a large fraction of hard currency earnings that Western lenders will be unwilling to do more than refinance existing debt. Without strong Western governmental action at that time to increase credits, there will have to be a stop in the growth of Eastern imports from the West, perhaps even a reduction from the late 1970s levels. Thus, for example, the CIA (1977b) estimates that Soviet hard currency import capacity will peak at £3 to 11 billion by 1985 (both figures in 1977 dollars). This probably exaggerates the Soviet problem, but similar figures would if anything understate that of the Six, whose debt servicing difficulties will restrict their credit and hard currency import capacity by 1980.[13]

Eastern Europe's plans up to 1980 incorporate hard currency export increases averaging 11 to 12 per cent per annum, with import increases of only about 3 per cent per annum (both in volume terms). I regard these figures as unrealistic and the plans on which they are based as infeasible; as long as further credit is available, the East will take it. Long-run quantitative projections of East–West trade are unreliable because it will be so heavily dependent on credit availability (but see Levcik and Stankovsky, 1977). Changes in the structure of Eastern imports and exports are more predictable, however. The range of Eastern capital goods imports is likely to narrow fairly rapidly down to rather specialised machinery unobtainable within CMEA (for example, the Soviet imports of high-capacity submersible pumps for oil production); the luxury of buying Western equipment on credit merely because it is of higher quality or technologically more advanced than its Eastern substitute will be shortlived. The East will also find it necessary to import from the West some materials and foodstuffs which are in short supply in the bloc and cannot be obtained from the South in exchange for Eastern manufactures. Overall, the share of materials in Eastern hard currency imports will probably rise.

There are two extreme alternative scenarios. One is that the credit constraint will bite suddenly and deeply. A jolt to market confidence, for whatever reason, could precipitate a serious breakdown in East–West trade. The overall effects on Western economies from the fall in exports would be comparatively small, given the low share of the East in total Western exports, but the damage to the smaller East European economies would be severe. Serious material supply bottlenecks would be unavoidable in the shortrun, and production would suffer. Czechoslovakia managed with great strains to cope with a balance-of-payments crisis of this kind in the early 1960s (Wiles, 1968), but the economies of the Six are now much more trade-dependent and especially vulnerable to an enforced cutoff of Western material supplies.

Western governments might well fear the consequent political instability in Eastern Europe, as well as the potential threat to Western financial markets if East European debt servicing capacity or willingness were called into question. Moreover, they might regard the continued expansion of East–West trade as desirable on foreign policy grounds, or because of strong lobbying from domestic exporters. Even subsidised export credits may be cheaper than unemployment. Such considerations could motivate governmental support for large increases in export credits.[14] This would seem to be the only way to maintain any significant increase in East–West trade beyond 1980. Reducing barriers to East European exports would be useful in permitting the East to meet its debt-servicing obligations, but unlikely to expand these exports enough to allow Eastern Europe to continue increasing its imports from the West (see Lenz and Kravalis, 1977, and Raffel, *et al.*, 1977).

In practice it is more likely that determined Eastern efforts to export manufactures will encounter market resistance in the West and claims of market disruption. Given the difficulty of establishing figures for 'costs' or 'domestic selling prices' in East European economies, we can expect a wide variety of antidumping and similar actions, which may even extend to the product repayment under 'buy-back' agreements. This could easily cause a great deal of conflict in East–West relations, especially since there is at present no institutional context within which such grievances might be negotiated. There is also substantial ignorance on both sides, in the East over which industries and products are likely to be sensitive and the domestic political problems of Western governments, in the West of how Eastern price systems work.

I have discussed elsewhere in some detail the interdependence between Eastern and Western economies created by the accumulation of East European hard currency debt (Portes, 1977b). The West is otherwise not at present significantly dependent economically on the East (although as noted, exports are in certain cases enough to create domestic political pressures), nor is it likely to become so unless there were large-scale Western participation in Soviet raw material extraction on a product payback basis. So far, the major instance is the contracted repayment for West German large-diameter pipe with Soviet natural gas, which is projected to amount to 16 per cent of Federal Republic of Germany gas supplies by the early 1980s. Japan too could potentially reach this level of dependence if the Siberian gas agreements on which it has sporadically negotiated were to be concluded. But only the United States would be capable of providing the capital for the largest projects,[15] and the output payback could not amount to any significant share of total American oil or gas consumption. Conversely, Western dependence on Eastern markets is likely to remain limited to particular products, with localised (though perhaps strong) domestic political impact but no large-scale economic importance (American grain is a possible exception).

East European dependence on Western technology is often cited as a benefit to the West from the growth of East–West trade and an argument against the embargo policy (Holzman, 1973). The embargo policy failed to win any political concessions from the East, although it was clearly economically damaging to them and presumably perceived to be so. Thus there is no evidence that the threat of cutting off or reducing Western technology exports would induce more co-operative Eastern political behaviour. The positive case for fostering dependence *per se* must instead rest on the supposed longer-term weakening of the independent innovating capacities of the Eastern economies. Here again, however, there is little evidence that either imitation or the importing of foreign-made equipment are economically debilitating as such.

The Soviet Union will not allow itself or its allies to become so dependent on Western technology or Western imports more generally as to make this a lever which could be used by the West to obtain significant political concessions. The transfer of technology and the provision of hard currency credits do reduce the pressure on the East to reallocate resources away from defence and to consider serious systemic 'reform'. But it cannot be demonstrated that without access to Western help, Poland would have tried thoroughgoing economic decentralisation instead of Gierek's 'dash for growth', or that without massive Western credits in the early 1980s, the USSR will be forced to weaken its military posture in order to keep the civilian economy going. There are alternatives—in particular, sacrificing consumption growth, with obvious but probably sustainable domestic political costs (on the economics of technology transfer and the use of technology exports as a bargaining counter with the East, see Holzman and Portes, 1978).

This does, however, define the tradeoff confronting both Eastern and Western policy-makers. The economic pressures on Eastern Europe will be severe and the centripetal forces in CMEA strong. Central planning can in all likelihood cope with the strains, but probably only by increasing centralisation (both within each economy and in CMEA planning) and holding down consumption increases. Further Western credits could ease these pressures and maintain the growth of East–West trade, but it is not clear that a halt to the expansion of credit would cause any disastrous breakdown in East–West economic and political relations. As we argue in Section VIII, there are strong common interests of East and West which will persist even if Eastern economic development does become more inward-oriented and East–West trade does not continue its recent rapid growth.

One form of East–West economic interdependence which is not so dependent on large credits is East–West industrial co-operation (McMillan, 1977). Agreements of this kind began in the mid-1960s and peaked in volume in the early 1970s. Then the recession in the West turned firms away from such activities, which are typically marginal in size and profitability; and at the same time, the East seems to have reassessed their benefits. The agreements have ranged from the mere purchase of licences or subcontracting to joint production or even the formation of jointly owned enterprises (typically to operate in third countries). Romania and Hungary now allow foreign equity participation in a domestic enterprise, but the constraints and limitations on the exercise of ownership rights are so restrictive that no significant response from Western firms is likely. Nor will these or any other East European countries allow direct investment under the same ground rules as the West or LDCs. The ideological barriers to a foreign capitalist ownership presence in the Eastern countries will in practice prove impassable.

The East European countries now take a more balanced view of industrial co-operation. Earlier they were enthusiastic about this apparently low-cost means of getting Western technology and access to Western markets. But they have found that often their Western partners are merely trying to recoup some of the development costs of a product or process which is already on its way out in the West, or possibly seeking access to Eastern markets with simple commodity exports which can cheaply be given a final stage of processing in the East. Frequently very little technology of value has actually been transferred, or the 'co-operation' in production and marketing has been minimal. But there are also impressive examples—a new and highly successful tractor design in Hungary, sophisticated optical equipment in Romania—of substantial mutual benefit. This is hardly surprising, since Eastern Europe has a large pool of skilled labour available at significantly lower real wages than its Western counterpart, but the region is still capital-poor relative to the West, and its major comparative disadvantages are in technological innovation and in marketing.

Industrial co-operation is likely to resume its earlier rate of expansion, especially if the East European planners can reduce the bureaucratic impediments which are often a serious hindrance even when policy is officially hospitable. There are institutional obstacles to co-operation in the industrial organisation and management structure of East European economies, especially the lack of incentive for individual enterprises and their managers to seek potentially fruitful projects and pursue them. The risks are relatively high, the effort often considerably greater than their routine tasks, and the rewards to them small. But these problems are now recognised and may be partially remediable even within the context of a centralised economy.

Industrial co-operation offers Eastern Europe a route of entry into a rapidly increasing component of commodity trade, the transnational transfers between units of multinational corporations. The 'liberalising' impact of contacts with Western businessmen on the domestic political and economic structure is minimal and easily contained. For the West, just as lending to the East and commodity trade, industrial co-operation creates substantial Western vested interests in avoiding any future difficulties in East–West economic relations. This may constrain policy options, but it may be sensible to promote a counterweight to the forces which threaten to disrupt relations.

The expansion of Western dealings with the East is likely to have some effects on the conduct of Western trade. The high degree of centralisation of economic decision-making in the East does in some cases put Western firms or governments at a disadvantage which might best be remedied by introducing more co-ordination on the Western side. An obvious example is the 'great grain raid', when Soviet buyers used their monopsonistic position brilliantly against dispersed and secretive American sellers and a Department of Agriculture which had little knowledge and less control over what was happening (Goldman, 1975). The subsequent reaction was indeed to bring some centralisation into American grain sales.

VII ECONOMIC RELATIONS BETWEEN EAST AND SOUTH

East–South trade is small relative to East–West trade and West–South trade, and East–South aid is small relative to West–South aid. But there are aspects of East–South economic relations which will clearly affect the development of the world economy and relations between West and South.

One example from postwar experience is in overall aid policy. When Soviet and East European economic assistance to selected LDCs began in the late 1950s, the competition it presented to Western donors contributed to important changes in the attitudes behind Western aid policy and the way in which aid was given. Thus neutrality or 'non-alignment' became acceptable, and recipients were no longer expected to show immediate appreciation for aid in their foreign policies. The East initiated accepting repayment in kind, an early form of linking aid and trade; they were also naturally biased towards large public sector projects and heavy industry, which then influenced the pattern of Western aid as well.

Eastern Europe does of course perceive a strategic competition with the West in the Third World. But the economic aspect of that competition, as distinct from the geopolitical, the East sees as socialism *vs.* capitalism. This view is to be contrasted, for example, with that of China (and perhaps the other Asian CPEs and Cuba), that the fundamental conflict is poor *vs.* rich. Thus the East is less inclined to see 'development' *per se* as a priority, and when it labels Western trade and economic relations with the South as 'imperialist' and 'neo-colonialist', it conveniently ignores the similar commodity composition of East – South trade.

It is understandable that the East should take this view, since if a line be drawn between rich and poor, they are clearly on the former side. And the South so views the East, on the whole. This may explain why even those countries of the South which are receptive to Marxist ideology are not generally disposed to take the standard Soviet-type economy as an economic system model (although Allande's Chile was moving in this direction, rather than toward the Cuban model). Another important reason, of course, is the persistent weakness of the East in agricultural performance, an objective which is relatively much more important in most countries of the South.

Eastern aid to the South is smaller even as a percentage of GNP than that of the West (on the order of 0.1 per cent of GNP). Though total new commitments in 1971–75 of $12.3 billion are not negligible, OECD estimates that in recent years actual Eastern aid has averaged only 5 per cent of total world official development assistance, and the trend seems to have been downwards.[16] The Eastern aid programme is perhaps more noticeable because it is highly concentrated geographically; seven out of the forty-two recipient countries have received two-thirds of the total amount. Visibility is also enhanced by putting assistance primarily into major industrial projects and undertakings like the Aswan Dam.

As agriculture has gradually become more important in development priorities, and some scepticism has been expressed about projects like the Bokaro steel complex in India, the image of East European aid has suffered somewhat, and they will in the future be handicapped in the non-oil LDCs by their focus on large industrial plants. And although the technical performance of their machinery is generally seen by the LDCs as acceptable, they have been widely criticised on its economic performance, their weak backup facilities (service and spares), and their inability to adapt to local conditions. A very high proportion of their aid is tied to procurement from donors, but this is considerably mitigated by their willingness, indeed preference, to accept repayment in commodities. This practice is naturally congenial to the East European barter-oriented approach to trade, and it is especially useful to them for projects in raw material extraction or first-stage processing. As the LDCs move into producing basic manufactures, however, Eastern Europe will be no more receptive than the West—indeed, probably less. The East has never seriously considered concessions to such exports from the LDCs.

The structure of East–South–West trade does seem to follow short-run comparative advantage, broadly interpreted. Recent empirical studies (surveyed by Donges, 1978) use a threefold categorisation of exports: Ricardo goods (some primary products), for which production functions differ between countries because of differing resource endowments; Heckscher–Ohlin goods, for which production functions are identical but capital–labour ratios differ across countries; and 'product cycle' goods, new commodities produced with new techniques which are not equally available to all countries. The Eastern countries appear to have current comparative advantages in some labour-intensive and some capital-intensive Heckscher–Ohlin goods, but they have been shifting fairly rapidly towards the latter (food, beverages and tobacco; non-metallic minerals; non-ferrous metal processing; pulp and paper; petroleum refining). The industrially advanced LDCs do seem to have their main comparative advantages in Ricardo goods (still) and some labour-intensive Heckscher–Ohlin goods (textiles, furniture, etc.), as well as some mature product cycle goods (such as electronics assembly). But they are likely to move towards capital-intensive exports and compete with Eastern countries in selling high income-elasticity items to the West. The East will also try to send more of its capital-intensive goods to the less advanced LDCs in exchange for Ricardo goods. Whether it can succeed and thereby substitute for some of its current hard currency expenditure on raw materials is a fundamental open question in the evolution of world trade patterns.

The most striking overall characteristic of Eastern trade with the South now, however, is its relative unimportance. Oddly, the Six, much more in need of the raw materials which the South could supply, do much less of their trade with the South than does the USSR (roughly 8 per cent as compared to 17 per cent).[17] Again surprisingly, Romania and Bulgaria have been considerably more successful than the other Eastern countries in expanding exports of manufactures to the South. Both the commodity composition and the geographical structure of the Eastern trade with the South are highly concentrated. Most of the trade is with West and South Asia and North Africa (excluding Cuba and the Asian CPEs), apparently reflecting Eastern strategic priorities.

All this suggests relatively little economic content or rationale behind

East–South Trade and aid. It seems likely that East–South economic relations will in good part 'continue to be a residuum in intention, a consequence of both parties not finding adequate markets in the West (Kidron, 1972, p. 14).'

Neither armaments nor oil fits this picture, however. Soviet arms exports to the South have been estimated at anywhere between two and four billion dollars annually over the past several years (the SIPRI Yearbook gives the lower figure).[18] These exports are likely to increase rapidly. For the East, the economic basis for this trade is at least as strong as the strategic and political rationale, since military equipment represents the Eastern comparative advantage *par excellence*: the only type of machinery in which the East can claim a rough technical parity with the West, and even superior quality or performance for cost in some areas.

Raising armaments exports would also fit well with the East's projected growing needs for oil imports. If we follow Russell (1976), the East will need to spend $5 to 10 billion (at 1977 prices) on oil imports by 1985. Already they have given substantial aid for oil production and refining (for example, Iraq), the payback to be in crude and product. But most of the East European technical capacities in exploration and production will doubtless be tied up in Siberia for many years to come (except for Romania, where a declining oil industry has already allowed the export of technical services in significant quantities). The logic of arms for oil should be irresistible both to the East and to those oil producers who have no strong political grounds for purchasing their arms from the West.

VIII   EAST, WEST, AND SOUTH: THE EAST AND THE NEW INTERNATIONAL ECONOMIC ORDER

In the past, Western analysts have focused primarily on East—West competition in the LDCs when looking at the relations between the First, Second and Third Worlds. In recent discussions of proposals for a 'new international economic order', the East has simply avoided taking positions on issues such as debt relief, primary product market 'stabilisation' (cartelisation), trade preferences for LDC-manufactured goods exports, etc. In the long run, however, the East is likely to find itself more Northern than Southern in its interests, and hence allied with the West on basic economic issues. This of course does not entail radically increased East–West economic co-operation, in the sense of trade, investment, etc. Rather, Eastern inability to penetrate Western markets for manufactures will impose tight constraints on such direct economic relations, despite a basic community of interest on the structure and operation of the international economic system.

There are reasons why the East might instead find it appealing to make common cause with the South in its demands on the West. First, there are ideological and geopolitical considerations—the East might naturally feel drawn to stand by the South in the battle against what both might see as exploitation by capitalist imperialism. Second, East and South are currently both primary product exporters to the West who seek access to Western markets for their basic manufactures, and they are also both borrowers in international (Western) capital markets. There might be mutual advantage in jointly seeking better treatment from the West.

These arguments can, however, be taken the other way. The East is in fact more rich than poor (with the low birth rates characteristic of rich and conservative societies). It cannot identify with the South except in opposition to capitalist exploitation, but (a) only a small part of the South is socialist, not capitalist, (b) the pattern of the East's trade relations with the South is also 'exploitative', and (c) China, a truly poor and also socialist country, will certainly be with the South, and it will be impossible to match China's anti-amperialist *bona fides*. It would, in fact, be demeaning as well as unconvincing for the East to act as if it were poor. Eastern Europe is and will be seen to be fundamentally con- servative, not revolutionary, with a considerable stake in the existing world order and its place in the world economy (from a different perspective, Adler-Karlsson, 1976, reaches some similar conclusions).

Moreover, the East will in fact be *competitors* with the South on Western markets for simple manufactures, for credit, for foodstuffs, and for technology transfer and the favourable attentions of the Western multinational corporations. Although the East might want whatever concessions the West may grant to the South, it will probably judge that it is unlikely to get much benefit this way and would be better off (because initially stronger) competing without the West giving anyone preferential treatment.

On food, for example, the Soviet agreement to buy at least six million tonnes of grain annually from the United States for several years is the action of a desirable customer whose credit is good and who can make this sort of arrangement to secure supplies, ahead of others (in the South) who cannot afford to take such a long-term view. The initial Soviet resistance to this arrangement reflected their reluctance to acknowledge formally a long-term inability to be self-sufficient in grain.

But the US–USSR grain agreement did not improve the overall stability of the world food market, to which a world food reserve might contribute. And although they will clearly have to continue feed grain imports indefinitely, in amounts varying widely with harvest vicissitudes, the USSR has so far shown no interest in such a co-operative undertaking. This is an example of the Soviet preference to operate bilaterally, unless there is a clear and strong balance of advantage to them in multilateralism. Hosoya *et al.* (1977) are therefore correct in judging that the USSR will not participate unless the West proceeds regardless, stressing that unless the Soviets joint in, they will find themselves at the end of the queue when the current bilateral agreement expires.

In exports of simple manufactures, the East currently competes with the South in selling clothing, furniture, shoes and similar items in the West. But only Romania, with its own distinctive strategy, has gone into the Group of 77 and the World Bank as an LDC and has qualified for the Generalised System of Preferences. None of the others would even try, and in any case, only Bulgaria would be a plausible candidate. In the longer run, the East should not wish to specialise in such goods. The opportunities on Western markets will be limited, given the extent of the competition (which will have the advantage of cheaper labour), and anyway these are not really highly profitable activities. The Eastern countries will be better off trying to sell in the West the engineering goods in which each will be specialising for export to other CMEA countries (the capital-intensive exports they have already developed will also face increasing competition from the more advanced LDCs).

This approach will need the sort of adaptation to Western market requirements which has so far been difficult for the East, but in which co-operation with Western firms could be very helpful.[19] Here also, with no special concessions, the East may have more to offer the multinationals than the South: political stability, relatively high income and growing markets, well-trained labour whose unions are oriented towards production rather than wage bargaining—all except equity participation, which may progressively become unsustainable in many Southern countries too.

The borrowing problem is complex. The Eastern countries have so far had better terms in the Euromarket than almost all LDCs except oil producers. In the Western 'gentlemen's agreement' on export credit terms (June 1976), however, the East Europeans were not to be treated as generously as most of the LDCs. The minimum interest rates and down payments and maximum maturities prescribed for the Eastern countries were those applying to the richest LDCs, while most of the South got preferential terms.

This is another example of the general proposition that the East cannot expect to be dealt with by the West on the same terms as the South, so it is sensible for them to stand with the West and keep concessions to the South down to a minimum. The East have a vital interest in keeping the flow of credit going, and they are doubtless as afraid as the betteroff LDCs that a few defaults by poorer or less responsible countries could endanger access to credit for all. On the other hand, if the West were to offer debt relief to the South, the East would probably seek similar treatment unless the scheme were carefully drawn up to limit relief to the 'most seriously affected' LDCs. If relief were only for official aid loans, the East would not benefit and would indeed then itself be approached by the South requesting the same deal on East–South credits. On balance, the East are probably best served by the *status quo*, except in so far as some way might be found to 'fund' some of the existing debt (refinance it with much longer maturities).[20]

Soviet concern with repayment of LDC debts to the USSR should motivate co-operation with the West in rescheduling exercises, with one strong reservation: the Soviet Union will not agree to reschedule official debt if the effect will merely be to allow an LDC to meet its obligations to Western commercial banks. They see no reason why they should bail out the banks, even if Western governments choose to do so.

Thus one can assume a continued East–West strategic opposition and specific economic conflicts but still suppose the East will seek a predominantly Northern identification in the international economy. The West is likely to see the East in this way as well and to find trade, investment and monetary relations with the East easier as time passes. And as the world moves away from liberal, non-interventionist trade and monetary rules, dealing with CMEA countries becomes less a departure from the norm.

It might be argued that the strategic and economic incentives in arms for oil trade will come to dominate East European interests in the world economy and push the East closer to the South, while the West too is driven into competition with the East by the same goals. But to the extent that this aspect of East–West competition does intensify, it will focus on the OPEC countries, not the non-oil LDCs we have called the South, and our view of the Eastern positions on international economic order issues is not affected.

Alternatively, there might be an apparent inconsistency between closer East–West identification and our projection of a slowdown or halt in the expansion of East–West trade. More co-operaton with the West is unlikely to loosen significantly the basic long-run constraint on East–West trade, the Eastern hard currency export capacity. Since the East will therefore find little payoff in increased hard currency imports from acting as part of the North, might it not turn instead towards the South? Indeed it may, in *trade*. My view of East–West identification does not mean much closer economic ties, in the sense of further substantial expansion of East–West economic relations and interdependence. Rather, I see arms-length, often tacit agreement and co-operation on the organisation of the world economy and the relations of both East and West with the non-oil LDCs. In this sense our institutional interdependence with the East will increase, and overall, I cannot help but see such cooperation as inimical to the interests of the South. East–West joint positions will generally be defensive, against the desires and demands of the South, save for exceptional instances of improved East–West management of world problems which may benefit the South.

Publicly expressed Soviet views of what the New International Economic Order is and should be about do not appear to contradict this assessment. Here we can quote O. Bogomolov (1978), the Director of the Institute for the Socialist World Economic System:

Any restructuring of the world economy cannot be confined to the relations between the industrialised capitalist countries and the Third World. The democratisation of the world economic system also requires complete normalisation of East–West relations, and elimination of things like artificial restrictions on economic ties between states with different social systems, discrimination in trade for political and ideological motives, and distortion of the international division of labour under the impact of the policies pursued by the Western powers or their economic groupings. Those are the requirements the CMEA countries seek to add to the conceptions of a new international economic order. The unfair international economic order does much to harm the socialist countries . . .

The CMEA countries support the developing countries on the new world economic order, but emphasise the need for progressive social transformations and the mustering of internal potentialities for economic growth as the chief means for changing their economic conditions. The Soviet Union and many other socialist countries resolutely oppose the diverse utopian projects for a world-wide redistribution of wealth . . . [They] cannot accept similar claims on all the industrialised countries, regardless of their social system, and the demand that the socialist countries should accord to the Third World countries unilateral advantages on the non-reciprocity principle.

Bogomolov's stress on Soviet interests, the emptiness of his 'support' for the South, and his perception of dangers for the East in the existing Southern NIEO proposals are all evident here. The East has indeed already reacted as an injured party, unjustly accused by the demands of the Group of 77 in the Manila Declaration (February 1976) for more aid and trade preferences, and the Eastern countries did not participate in the Paris Conference on International Economic Co-operation (December 1976–June 1977).

The Soviet Union has shown some concrete willingness to consider becoming involved in commodity price stabilisation schemes (sugar, for example), when financed on an entirely voluntary basis. On the other hand, Eastern Europe has so far taken no clear position of either support for or opposition to producer cartels for primary products. This is somewhat surprising since it would seem on balance to benefit the USSR in particular that such cartels be successfully organised. Clearly the oil cartel has brought substantial gains to the USSR. A very sophisticated calculation might have suggested that the consequent damage to the Western economies could in the long run bring a net loss to the East, or perhaps their temporising simply reflects a more diffuse consciousness of their 'Northern interests.' It is on the other hand quite likely that the East will find very congenial the current trend towards 'market sharing' discussions among industrialised countries, provided they are not excluded at the outset.

It might seem sensible to institutionalise the East's increased role in the world economy, both in trade and capital markets, with the accession of East European countries to GATT, the IMF, and other international organisations. Some framework will be needed for negotiating detailed economic conflicts and problems, which are likely to increase in number. But Eastern participation in these organisations could be disruptive, and the USSR will certainly not play unless the rules treat her as the equal of the USA. The Soviets still seem to think they can do as well bilaterally as multilaterally, without restricting their freedom of action. They may be right for themselves, but clearly not for the smaller Eastern countries, and they do appear to realise this. They are consequently somewhat more complaisant now about approaches by their partners to multilateral organisations, perhaps also because they recognise that the centripetal forces in CMEA will be so strong that they need not fear any reduction of Eastern dependence on the USSR. The EEC too might be sensible to acknowledge this and give up its ineffective attempt to avoid dealing with CMEA as a bloc.[21]

GATT has become more attractive to the Eastern countries because of its increasing focus on non-tariff barriers to trade. Despite the Soviet Union's historical non-participation, GATT does now include Czechoslovakia,[22] Poland (accession in 1967), Romania (1971), and Hungary (1973), so there is no insuperable ideological or practical barrier for the others.

Only Romania, however, belongs to the IMF, and it joined the Fund and World Bank as an LDC, primarily to obtain Bank loans (currently amounting to over $600 million). Here there are no great practical obstacles—many Fund members have currencies which are to some degree inconvertible—but East European leaders resist the infringement of sovereignty which they see as inherent in the IMF rules and the obligations of membership, as well as the weighting of votes. There would be no advantage in access to IMF loans if one were unprepared to accept the surveillance which might accompany them, and most East European countries (particularly the USSR) do not wish to give the IMF even the routine information on balance of payments, reserves, etc., which members must supply. They are very sensitive about such data, and Romania in fact reached a compromise with the Fund and Bank whereby the data it submits are kept confidential.

One can easily see Hungary acceding to the requirements of IMF membership, but only with full prior approval by the USSR; Poland is another potential candidate. But the other countries will remain aloof without a major Western initiative. In view of the recent accumulation of East European hard currency debt, this might well be advisable. A crude approach making further loans conditional on IMF membership would be rejected, but a more diplomatic line suggesting that this would be a likely outcome might be effective—though it would have to be credible. Alternatively, the BIS could be a useful context for monetary co-operation.

Currency convertibility will not be implemented within CMEA (Section 6), and the same arguments apply *a fortiori* to convertibllity for hard currency of any East European currency or of the transferable rouble. The external convertibility of the transferable rouble introduced with much initial excitement at the end of 1976 was a non-event. It gives non-CMEA transactors the dubious privilege of holding balances denominated in transferable roubles—but not of using such balances accumulated in trade with one Eastern country to purchase goods from another, nor of freely choosing which goods to purchase from the country where the balances were initially generated. The strong Soviet preference for a gold-based international monetary system will certainly not lead the USSR to tie either its own currency or the transferable rouble to gold in any operational way.

It should now be clear that I find relatively unimportant the role of political considerations—in particular, *détente* and its vicissitudes—in determining both past and future Eastern economic relations with the rest of the world, barring extreme contingencies like armed conflict (even Vietnam had little effect). This makes the task of projection easier and more congenial to the economist, and I have indicated some likely future trends. In particular, although I see various aspects of East–West economic co-operation as likely, I do not see East–West trade continuing to grow rapidly. Thus the economic dependence of each side on the other is likely to remain limited, except for the financial interdependence arising from the East European debt to the West. In its relations with the South, too, the East's role is likely to be limited, for the South cannot expect the East to support its proposals for a New International Economic Order.

ENDNOTES

1. Professor of Economics, Birkbeck College, University of London. A first version of this paper was prepared for OECD Project Interfutures, and I have received detailed and thoughtful comments from many sources. I take sole responsibility, however, for the views expressed here. I am grateful for support from the Institute for International Economic Studies of the University of Stockholm while revising the paper for publication.
2. Unless otherwise indicated, trade data are from OECD sources.
3. Only Bulgaria, Czechoslovakia and the GDR still do at least two-thirds of their trade with other CMEA countries.
4. These are not OECD figures, but rather derived directly from CMEA data.
5. The projections most favourable to the East are those of the Deutsche Institut für Wirtschaftsforschung (Wochenbericht 50/1977), which expects Soviet output of 640 million tonnes in 1980 and 780 million tonnes in 1985, allowing 1985 deliveries of 114–117 million tonnes to CMEA and 24 to 51 million tonnes for hard currency.
6. As Snell (1977, p. 25) put it, 'The East European countries have all taken in stride the enormous increase in complexity involved in planning and managing economies in rapid technological change, with increased involvement in foreign trade, while making minimal changes in institutions and doctrines . . . In 1960, hardly anyone expected such great changes with so little basic adaptation.'
7. This view does get some support from Zaleski (1978, see below) and Snell

(1977, p. 14), who suggests that 'as government credits and private bank loans became more readily available, running hard currency deficits became the chief—because the easiest—way of compensating for mischance and miscalculation'.

8. See Portes (1977a), where I suggest that Hungary is likely to maintain its (strongly) 'guided market system' for some time with fairly little change. But the other Eastern countries are unlikely to adopt the Hungarian model.

9. For a recent assessment of the progress in intra-CMEA co-operation and specialisation, see *Economic Survey of Europe in 1976, Part II*.

10. It has now run large surpluses with the Six for three consecutive years—the equivalent of $750 million in 1975, $1.5 billion in 1976, and perhaps $2 billion in 1977. It has been reported that the USSR is automatically transforming these surpluses into ten-year credits, but we have as yet no firm evidence of this.

11. There is an instructive analogy with the domestic implications of 'economic and monetary union' (and resistance to it) in the EEC.

12. It has in fact been reported that holders of the resulting balances cannot actually spend them outside the country from which they were earned—much less in Western markets. Such 'hard currency' is not convertible at all, but rather just represents the exchange of hard goods for hard goods, with the refinement that transactions are at current world prices.

13. On present indications, hard currency debt problems will be most severe for Poland, Bulgaria, the GDR and Hungary (in that order), and at least Poland will probably have to arrange a formal rescheduling with its Western creditors (Portes, 1977b, and Snell, 1977).

14. As they have so far weakened attempts to co-ordinate Western policies in this area. The Federal Republic of Germany for example, does after all export more to Eastern Europe than to North America: a £150 million Polish order means a great deal to the British shipbuilding industry, etc.

15. Which we are therefore unlikely to see in the medium-term future, because they would require official export credit guarantees which Congress will not permit.

16. Development Co-operation, 1977 Review. Appropriate concepts of aid and the numbers themselves are disputed. The commitments figure is from the UN World Economic Survey, Economic Bulletin for Europe, vol. 29; it gives UNCTAD figures for disbursements, with the 1975 level at $803 million. Note however that in the same year, amortisation and interest on past loans was $663 million, so the *net* flow was only $140 million.

17. In 1975–76, $18\frac{1}{2}$ per cent of Soviet exports went to LDCs and 16 per cent of Soviet imports came from them; the corresponding figures for the East European Six were $9\frac{1}{2}$ per cent and 7 per cent (ranging from $19\frac{1}{2}$ per cent and 17 per cent for Romania, to 9 per cent and 8 per cent for Hungary, and only 6 per cent and $4\frac{1}{2}$ per cent for Poland, $4\frac{1}{2}$ per cent and 6 per cent for the GDR). Imports from LDCs were 20 per cent of imports from the West for the Six, 38 per cent of imports from the West for the USSR.

18. It is not clear how much of this is reported in the Soviet trade statistics. Using CMEA trade data, Economic Bulletion for Europe (vol. 29, 1977) reports about $2.7 billion total exports from Eastern Europe to oil-producing LDCs in 1976 (about 23 per cent of all East European exports to

LDCs) and $2.0 billion imports from these countries.
19. Marer (1978) argues that the Western multinationals could also play a role in the development of intra-CMEA specialisation.
20. For further details on East–South competition for credit from the West, see Portes (1978a).
21. The Six do have different interests from the USSR in the EEC–CMEA context: the former want concessions on their manufactured exports and the Common Agricultural Policy, while the latter is most interested in large credits (with Western governmental support) for big projects in the Soviet Union. But any Western fears of enhancing Soviet influence over the smaller countries by dealing with CMEA as a bloc are probably misplaced – this shift in power is taking place regardless of what we do.
22. Czechoslovakia was a founding member but does not participate. Bulgaria has been an observer since 1967.

REFERENCES

Adler-Karlsson, G., *Western Economic Warfare 1947–1967* (Stockholm: Almqvist & Wiksell, 1968).

Adler-Karlsson, G., *Political Economy of East–West–South Cooperation* (Vienna: Springer-Verlag, 1976).

Bergson, A., 'The Soviet economic slowdown', Challenge (January–February, 1978).

Bogomolov, O., 'The CMEA countries in the changing international economic climate', paper for conference at Montebello, Canada (1978).

Bornstein, M., 'Economic reform in Eastern Europe'. In: *Joint Economic Committee* (1977) 102–134.

Brainard, L., 'The CMEA financial system and integration'. In: Marer and Montias (1978, forthcoming).

Brzezinski, Z., 'America in a hostile world', *Foreign Policy* (1976) 23, 65–96.

Central Intelligence Agency (US), *Prospects for Soviet Oil Production* (Washington, DC, 1977a).

Central Intelligence Agency (US), *Soviet Economic Problems and Prospects* (Washington, DC, 1977b).

Donges, J., 'North–South–East competition in the market for industrial products', paper for conference in Paris (1978).

Goldman, M., *Détente and Dollars* (New York: Basic Books, 1975).

Hardt, J. and Holliday G., *Western investment in Communist Economies* (Washington, DC, USGPO, 1974).

Holzman, F., 'East–West trade and investment policy issues', Joint Economic Committee (1973) 660–689.

Holzman, F., *International Trade under Communism* (London: Macmillan, 1976).

Holzman, F. and Portes, R., 'The economics of technology transfer to the Soviet Union and Eastern Europe', *Foreign Policy* (September, 1978).

Hosoya, C., *et al.*, 'Collaboration with Communist countries in managing global problems', Triangle Paper no. 13, Trilateral Commission (1977).

Joint Economic Committee (US Congress), *Soviet Economic Prospects for the Seventies* (Washington, DC: USGPO, 1973).

Joint Economic Committee (US Congress), *Reorientation and Commercial Relations of the Economies of Eastern Europe* (Washington, DC, USGPO, 1974).

Joint Economic Committee (US Congress), *Soviet Economy in a New Perspective* (Washington, DC, USGPO, 1976).

Joint Economic Committee (US Congress), *East European Economies Post-Helsinki* (Washington, DC, USGPO, 1977).

Kaser, M., *Comecon* (London, Oxford University Press for RIIA, 1967).

Kaser, M., 'American credits for Soviet development', *British Journal of International Studies* (1977).

Kidron, M., *Pakistan's Trade with Eastern Bloc Countries* (New York: Praeger, 1972).

Knirsch, P., Interdependence in East–West economic relations. In: *From Marshall Plan to Global Interdependence* (Paris: OECD, 1978).

Kohn, M. and Lang, N., 'The intra-CMEA foreign trade system: major price changes, little reform'. In: *Joint Economic Committee* (1977), 135–151.

Lenz, A. and Kravalis, H., 'An analysis of recent and potential Soviet and East European exports to fifteen industrialized Western countries'. In: *Joint Economic Committee* (1977) 1055–1131.

Levcik, F. and Stankovsky, J., 'Kredite des Westens und Osterreichs an Osteuropa und die UdSSR', Monatsbericht des Osterreichischen Institutes fur Wirtschaftsforschung, 5 (1977).

Marer, P., (ed.), *US Financing of East–West Trade* (Bloomington, Ind.: International Development Research Center, 1975).

Marer, P., 'Prospects for integration in the Council for Mutual Economic Assistance', *International Organization*, 30 (1976) 631–648.

Marer, P., 'Western multinational corporations in Eastern Europe and

CMEA integration', paper for conference at Montebello, Canada (1978).

Marer, P. and Montias, J. M., (eds.), *East European Integration and East–West Trade* (forthcoming).

McMillan, C., 1977, 'East–West industrial cooperation'. In: *Joint Economic Committee* (1974) 135–163.

NATO (Economic Directorate), *Comecon: Progress and Prospects* (Brussels: NATO, 1977).

Portes, R., 'Hungary: economic performance, policy, and prospects'. In: *Joint Economic Committee* (1977a), 766–815.

Portes, R., 'East Europe's debt to the West', *Foreign Affairs* (1977b), 55, 751–782.

Portes, R., 'East–South competition in international capital markets', presented to Conference on The Future of North–South–East Economic Relations, held by GERPI, Paris, and forthcoming in conference proceedings (1978a).

Portes, R., 'Western investment in Eastern Europe'. In: A. Shlaim and G. Yannopoulos, *The EEC and Eastern Europe* (Cambridge: Cambridge University Press, 1978b) 161–175.

Raffel, H., *et al.*, 1977, 'The MFN impact on U.S. imports from Eastern Europe'. In: *Joint Economic Committee* (1977) 1396–1427.

Russell, J., *Energy as a Factor in Soviet Foreign Policy* (London: Saxon House, 1976).

Smith, A., 'Soviet economic influence in Comecon'. In: NATO (Economic Directorate, 1977) 237–258.

Snell, E., 'East European economies between the Soviets and the capitalists' in *Joint Economic Committee* (1977) 12–53.

Stockholm International Peace Research Institute, *World Armaments and Disarmament*, SIPRI Yearbook (Cambridge, Mass.: MIT Press, 1977).

Wiles, P., *Communist International Economics* (Oxford: Blackwell, 1968).

Wolf, T., *U.S. East–West Trade Policy* (Lexington, Mass.: D. C. Heath, 1973).

Wolf, T., 'East–West trade credit policy: a comparative analysis'. In: Marer (1975) 149–199.

Zaleski, E., 'Les techniques de pointe et les choix des partenaires commerciaux de l'Union Sovietique', paper for conference at Montebello, Canada (1978).

Comments[1]

Rolf Eidem (Sweden)

All in all this paper is an excellent introduction into the fundamentals of the role of the centrally planned economies (CPEs) in the world economy. I have, however some criticisms.

(1) My first remark concerns the way in which Professor Portes characterises the background of the increased *Eastern indebtedness* since the beginning of 1970s. He takes here the 'heretic' view that—except for the special cases of Poland and the Soviet Union — the soaring Eastern debt was *not* the result of a concerted, *conscious* strategy in the East to increase dramatically technology imports. Rather, it was the outcome of a series of *events*, that, surprisingly enough, made borrowing in capitalist banks the cheapest way of adjustment! Professor Portes talks of 'excess real demand' almost as if it were market-type economies.

I think Professor Portes' 'westernised' explanation is somewhat misleading. Everybody knows that the process of procuring and distributing hard currency—not to mention hard currency in excess of plans—is a matter of great delicacy in a CPE. It is also well known that for a long time the East has been ideologically set against capital imports (of any importance) from capitalist nations. As a result each foreign trade transaction involving hard currency will be a matter of discussion in a CPE. Therefore 'events' do not affect a CPE in the way suggested by the capitalist term 'excess real demand'. Of course foreign trade planners in a CPE, too, can be up against unforeseen contingencies; but their type of freedom of action will be very different from that of the trading companies of the market economy. In think, with Knirsch and others, that the scheme *ex ante* for the 1970s was to use available hard currency credits to expand technology imports. It is quite another matter that *ex post* it was found out that the politically prepared credits had been used for somewhat different purposes. But it did not happen by chance.

(2) My second remark concerns Professor Portes' projection for *the*

future of East–West trade. To me they seem overly pessimistic. To begin
with, when business activity picks up in the West the East will surely
benefit on the export side. This should strengthen their credit capacity,
which I would not expect to be ruined as quickly as the author seems to
think. After all, bankers do not only look at the *stock* position of their
debtor clients, but also at their future net income *flows.* Of course, if
bankers in different banks in different countries really joined to trace the
exact debtor position of individual CPEs they might discover something
to give them cold feet. But they will not join for such purposes, for they
compete for Eastern clients. And governments will *not* urge them to do
it—along old Cold War lines. If anything the governments will do the
opposite, for employment purposes and others.

Also I think Professor Portes is perhaps taking a too stationary view
of what might become of Eastern *industrial goods exports* to the West;
though I am in basic agreement with him that this is a tremendous
problem it may not be insoluble. At this moment Russians are marketing
cars in our country not without success, and with repair shops
established around the country; and Polish and Rumanian ham is not
much different from Danish ham in price and quality, for instance.

But there is room for imaginative thinking here. Professor Portes
suggests that 'the only internally consistent way to increase exports
would be to treat this as a high priority activity, like military production:
to separate it from the rest of the economy'.

I myself have a different interpretation of which are the main
problems of the Eastern CPEs when selling manufactures in the West.
In my view the main problem is not to establish production units in the
East that can produce to any specification (like spaceships). Instead, the
main problem is to find the specification or product that can become
successful in the market in the West. This requires that the seller-
producer be close to the buyer-user in the Western economy (as in
scattered repair shops, mentioned above), and close long enough to
become really knowledgeable about many aspects (delivery conditions,
rebates of competitors, etc.). This means that the traditional attempts to
launch products through agents in the West and try a new one each year
is doomed to failure. Instead Eastern producers-sellers must literally get
on to the Western market *and* more or less simulate the same kind of
incentive structure, required returns on capital invested, etc., as their
competitors. This is the only way in which they can be forced to pay
attention to all the *million* little things to which that any successful
exporter must pay attention! If there is anything the capitalist system of
production has proved capable of it is to identify the minutest

requirements in the market and satisfy them. It is inconceivable that the East should ever be able to compete in this area without acting (at least temporarily) *as if* they were capitalist managers—and stockholders—themselves.

Instead of buying so much machine technology, the East should buy more export-promoting, organisational technology. They should buy themselves into *existing* capitalist companies where this technology is available. Industrial co-operation should be more in this area and deal less with technological transfer to the East.

(3) This brings me to my third remark which concerns Professor Portes' prophecy that the Eastern economies will again become the subject of *centripetal forces*. Clearly, this rather brave prophecy presupposes that the East will largely fail in their export-promoting activities. And this they need not do, neither will it require deep institutional change inside the CPEs, only in the way CPEs organise their activities in the market-type economies. Also, it is one thing to speak of a new and improved *programme* for specialisation among CMEA countries. It is not the first time that this has been done. But experiences of specialisation are not so good, and so all Eastern economies may not become party to the centripetal tendencies suggested by Professor Portes. Indeed, if individual Eastern economies succeed in Western markets, the centripetal tendencies may well be overshadowed by centrifugal tendencies.

To sum up: the centripetal tendencies among the East may not materialise, or will be modified by new export-promoting institutional change. Portes foresees 'immobilisms' in internal structures, but institutions may change gradually to improve trading potentials of the East. For example, in Poland, Hungary, Bulgaria and Romania greater rights for independent foreign trade decisions have been granted to individual firms. Marginal system's change is important in the long run!

(4) My fourth remark has to do with the relations *East–South*. Even if the South is divided into oil-producing and non-oil-producing countries, any such grand classification is misleading. For the Eastern economies (in fact, the Soviet Union) it has been—and will continue to be—natural to concentrate their cares on certain selected friendly countries (bilateralism). Therefore it is a little out of place to speak of 'Eastern attitudes to LDCs', etc., as if the Soviet Union had a specific attitude toward all the LDCs. It has not.

(5) Reforming the *international monetary system*—and, indeed, the Eastern monetary system to multilateralise trade—to include the East will be a very slow process. In the foreseeable future the East will not

openly join forces either with the South or with the Wast. I think they will continue their careful bilateral-style positioning from day to day as political ambitions suggest.

(6) Peter Knirsch begins his Marshall-fund article by pointing out that 'it is no simple matter . . . to develop any particularly *new thoughts on East–West economic relations*'.

To do this we would need many *more* statistics—on balance of payments, for example, and *better* statistics—on intra-CMEA trade prices, for example.

More than anything else, however, we need more information about the formal—and informal!—workings of the CPE. It remains hard to understand why so little basic institutional research has been done so far: 'how, and where are decisions made', etc. If we had more knowledge about this, it would not nearly have been so difficult to tell whether the upsurge in East–West trade – and Eastern indebtedness – since 1970 was the result of unforeseen 'events' or of conscious strategies to re-equip domestic factories.

ENDNOTE

1. In the preparation of this comment I have benefited from a conversation with Vilhelm Rappe, M.B.A.

Part IV

Finance and Foreign Exchange

10 Financial Repression and the Liberalisation Problem within Less-Developed Countries

Ronald McKinnon (USA)

In less-developed countries, open markets for common stocks, bonds, mortgages, or even commercial bills are insignificant. This does not constitute a 'distortion', but merely reflects low per capita income and the resulting small scale of individual acts of saving and investment. Information is insufficient to have small farmers or merchants issue their own notes or shares that are publicly traded.

The absence of open markets in primary securities implies that private financial savings in LDCs are largely currency and deposits: claims on central banks, commercial banks, and near banks such as savings and loan associations, *financieras* (development banks), postal savings depositories, and so on. These banking intermediaries issue liquid short-term deposits whose nominal value is virtually guaranteed by the state, a great advantage to small savers. If the banking system were free to manage its real loan portfolio on the principle of profit maximisation, high-yield loans, balanced against the risk of default, would be actively sought according to the ordinary canons of bank management. If the system were otherwise unrestricted, depositors would see the net proceeds from these loans after subtracting bank costs.

In practice, however, depositors usually fail to receive a real return accurately reflecting the scarcity value of capital in the economy. Some favoured bank borrowers—often in urban areas—are allocated very low-cost finance, whereas in rural areas others with potentially high-yield projects are often completely excluded. This is a consequence of an elaborate maze of interest restrictions on both deposits and loans, 'reserve' requirements, special loan tranches, and so forth that are imposed by the government on the deposit banks. In the face of these restrictions and ongoing price inflation, real yields to depositors and to holders of coin and currency can be highly negative. Not surprisingly, firms and households respond to such 'financial repression' by reducing saving or rechannelling investments outside of the organised financial sector, a process that turns out to be expensive and inefficient.

Hence, small farms and urban enterprises in LDCs are often financially isolated, being neither borrowers nor lenders. Instead they rely mainly on self-finance. While non-liquid for savers, such self-financed capital accumulation offers no assurance that funds will flow to high-yield uses in the economy. Instead, capital may be trapped in small-scale and obsolete technologies (McKinnon, 1973, Chapter 2).

Worse still, financial repression may make voluntary private savings *seem* inadequate to support even limited enclave industrialisation. LDCs become more prone to appeal for grants in aid from abroad or to rely on investments by multinational corporations. Domestically, authorities are often induced to use more coercive techniques for generating an economic 'surplus'—particularly from agriculture. The domestic terms of trade have commonly been turned against agriculture through protective tariffs for industry, unfavourable exchange rates for agricultural goods, the mandatory use of government marketing boards that depress crop prices, and so forth.

But it forced saving and the impoverishment of agriculture as a means of industrial finance is to be ended, voluntary financial saving by firms and households must replace it. Hence, the liberalisation of the foreign trade and financial sectors are two aspects of the same problem for many countries. In rather sharp contrast to the plethora of studies of repressed foreign trade in LDCs,[1] however, the equally common restraints on *financial* processes within these same LDCs now receive only sporadic attention from academics and from official agencies.[2]

The reader is forewarned that only important microeconomic aspects of the invent-saving problem and of financial repression are taken up in this paper. Although ongoing price inflation is an important aspect of the repression syndrome, a full macroeconomic model for ending inflation and achieving monetary control is reserved for another time. Nevertheless, the institutional reforms necessary for financial liberalisation to be successfully sustained are analysed in some detail.

I THE BANKING SYSTEM AND LOANABLE FUNDS

The study of financial repression and liberalisation in LDCs is best done by making a 'loanable funds' approach to the banking system as a whole (Tsiang 1978).[3] Initially, I ignore the liquidity distinctions among currency where the central bank could act as an intermediary, demand deposits that are liabilities of commercial banks, and less liquid one or two-year time deposits issued by some savings banks or *financieras*. All are potentially capable of mobilising saving for investment finance with high returns and one or all are equally vulnerable to being tapped by the government for fiscal support or to supply seigniorage at less than market rates of interest.

To begin with, let us consolidate the balance sheets of all the organised banking units in the economy into 'Monobank'. Monobank collects all checking (demand) and interest-bearing time deposits from, as well as issues coin and currency to, the non-bank public of private households and firms. Monobank's balance sheet, where all interbank claims and liabilities are netted out, is reported in Table 1 below:

TABLE 1
MONOBANK

Assets	*Liabilities*
Loans to private borrowers	Coin and currency
Government bonds	Demand deposits
Net claims on foreigners	Time deposits (interest bearing)
	Net worth (capital subscription)

Total assets = Total liabilities

Let M_2 be this broad definition of the banking system's liabilities, as represented by the right-hand side of Monobank's balance sheet (less the net worth of private banks).

To what extent can data on the *stock* of money, as measured by the ratio of M_2 to GNP, be an adequate measure of the *flow* of loanable funds in a typical less developed country? First, the M_2/GNP ratio is indicative of the absolute size of the banking system that reinvests funds, in potentially new directions, from old loans as they mature.

Secondly, the flow of current saving of households and firms, in part, shows up as changes in the assets and liabilities of Monobank. In particular, the percentage increase in the *real* stock of money measures *realised net private financial saving* (RNPFS) in our prototype LDC without open markets in primary securities. If M_2 is nominal money held by the private sector, and P is some broadly defined price index, the real stock of money is M_2/P. By definition

$$\text{Realised net private financial saving} = d\left(\frac{M_2}{P}\right)\bigg/ dt \qquad (1)$$

Note that by 'realised' saving I am referring only to the successful net accumulation of real financial assets by the private sector. That flow of private saving in monetary form that is eroded by inflation—part of the inflation tax collected by the government—is omitted from equation (1). However, equation (1) better measures real additions to the loanable funds capacity of the banking system.

The propensity to save is typically measured as a proportion of GNP, if only to provide a common scale factor for cross-country comparison. Let Y denote 'real' GNP, and PY be its current undeflated money flow. Then the economy's propensity to save in financial form is:

$$\frac{RNPFS}{Y} = \frac{M_2}{PY} \cdot \frac{dY/dt}{Y} + d\left(\frac{M_2}{PY}\right)\bigg/ dt \qquad (2)$$

The rate at which a country is saving in financial form depends on the rate of growth in GNP itself weighted by the money/income ratio, *and* on the growth of money/income ratio through time. With these interpretations in mind, some representative M_2/GNP ratios are reported in Tables 2, 3, and 4 below for three financially distinct groups of countries.

By conforming to the International Monetary Fund's definition of money (currency and demand deposits) plus quasi-money (time deposits in commercial banks) plus saving deposits in other financial institutions, the measured ratios of M_2 to GNP may be unduly narrow for some countries. Depository claims on certain kinds of rural savings co-operatives and industrial *financieras* could be missing—even though these latter kinds of deposits conform to our conceptually broad definition of M_2. Nevertheless, Tables 2, 3, and 4 give a reasonably comprehensive measure of the real size of, and growth in, the banking systems of:

(1) *Semi-Industrial LDCs* (Table 2) that are quite typical in not being able to sustain a high-level of economic growth in the postwar period.

(2) *Financially Mature Industrial Economies* (Table 3) with open capital markets in addition to the banking system.

TABLE 2
BANK LOANABLE FUNDS IN TYPICAL SEMI-INDUSTRIAL LDCs
(THE RATIO OF M_2 TO GNP)

	1960	*1965*	*1970*	*1975*	*Mean* *1960–75*
Argentina	0.245	0.209	0.267	0.168	*0.222*
Brazil	0.148	0.156	0.205	0.164	*0.168*
Chile	0.123	0.130	0.183	0.099	*0.134*
Colombia	0.191	0.204	0.235	—	*0.210*
Mean ratio of M_2/GNP for four Latin American countries:					*0.184*
India	0.283	0.262	0.264	0.295	*0.276*
Philippines	0.186	0.214	0.235	0.186	*0.205*
Sri Lanka	0.284	0.330	0.275	0.255	*0.286*
Turkey	0.202	0.223	0.237	0.222	*0.221*
Mean ratio of M_2/GNP for four Asian countries:					*0.247*

Source: *International Financial Statistics* (various issues), published by the International Monetary Fund, in which M_2 is defined as money (line 34) + quasi-money (line 35) + deposits outside commercial banks (line 45). M_2 is a stock tabulated as of 30 June for each calendar year, whereas GNP is the flow of output for that year.

(3) *Rapidly Growing Economies* (Table 4) that have recently undergone substantial capital accumulation.

Because of high and variable price inflation in some of the countries portrayed, it is not obvious at what point during the calendar year the stock of money should be measured. If M_2 is tabulated at the end of the year (31 December), while nominal GNP is an average of money income throughout the year, then high inflation countries (and those with high growth in real income) will show M_2/GNP ratios that are too high: the numerator is inflated relative to the denominator. Choosing mid-year (30 June) to measure M_2 is approximately correct for countries with modest or zero inflation, and modest growth in real income. However, choosing 30 June will discriminate (slightly) against those countries with high growth in their nominal GNPs, whatever the reason. In Tables 2, 3, and 4 below, M_2 is measured at mid-year, but readers should keep in mind the resulting biases in this rough measure of the availability of loanable funds.

TABLE 3
BANK LOANABLE FUNDS IN MATURE INDUSTRIAL ECONOMIES
(THE RATIO OF M_2 TO GNP)

	1960	1965	1970	1975	Mean 1960–75
Belgium	0.591	0.578	0.566	0.558	0.573
France	0.385	0.532	0.538	0.675	0.533
Sweden	0.678	0.632	0.604	——[a]	0.638
United Kingdom	0.493	0.509	0.510	0.558	0.518
United States	0.633	0.666	0.636	0.726	0.665

Mean ratio of M_2/GNP for industrial countries: 0.585

Source: *International Financial Statistics* (various issues), published by the International Monetary Fund, in which M_2 is defined as money (line 34) + quasi-money (line 35) + deposits outside commercial banks (line 45). M_2 is a stock tabulated as of 30 June for each calendar year, whereas GNP is the flow of output for that year.

[a] Data on time and savings deposits in special financial institutions (line 45) was not collected after 1971.

TABLE 4
BANK LOANABLE FUNDS IN RAPIDLY GROWING ECONOMIES
(THE RATIO OF M_2 TO GNP)

	1955	1960	1965	1970	1975	1977
German[a]	0.331	0.394	0.488	0.583	0.727	0.777
Japan	0.554[b]	0.737[b]	0.701[b]	0.863	1.026	1.087
Korea	0.069	0.114	0.102	0.325	0.323	0.334
Taiwan	0.115	0.166	0.331	0.462	0.588	0.702
Singapore	—	—	0.542[b]	0.701	0.668	0.750

Source: *International Financial Statistics* (various issues), published by the International Monetary Fund, in which M_2 is defined as money (line 34) + quasi-money (line 35) + deposits outside commercial banks (line 45). M_2 is a stock tabulated as of 30 June for each calendar year, whereas GNP is the flow of output for that year.

[a] In addition to deposits and currency, the German series includes bank bonds sold directly to the public.
[b] Downward bias because deposit information on specialised credit institutions (line 45) was not collected.

The eight semi-industrial less developed countries in Table 2 have made some substantial attempt to industrialise by import-substitution policies but they have not yet achieved balanced and rapid growth in real GNP. Their financial profiles are typical, with banking sectors quite attenuated for their levels of per capita income. Their ratios of M_2/GNP average less than 0.2 for the Latin American countries, and about 0.25 for the Asian ones. In each group, these low ratios fluctuate with no sustained tendency to increase. From both terms in equation (2), therefore, the flow of loanable funds through their banking systems is quite limited. Indeed, in a chronically high-inflation country like Chile, the real lending capacity of the banking system was only one-tenth of GNP in 1975.

Table 3 portrays the other end of the spectrum: mature industrial economies with broadly based capital markets within which the banking sector plays on important role. Their M_2/GNP ratios are about 0.6. Hence, relative to their national incomes, their banking systems are about two to three times as large as those of the semi-industrial LDCs! Moreover, many of these industrial economies have developed primary securities markets and/or non-bank financial intermediaries such as pension funds or insurance companies. The overall size of their capital markets relative to GNP is larger than a simple comparison of M_2/GNP ratios would suggest.

Standardising for levels of per capita income, the wide gap in financial development between semi-industrial LDCs and western industrial economies is more striking than differences in their performances in foreign trade. My hypothesis is that, rather than passively reflecting underdevelopment itself, misguided financial policies have actively repressed the flow of loanable fund in the eight LDCs depicted above— and in most other LDCs.

Before getting into the microeconomic specifics of financial repression and the testing of this hypothesis, let us first assure ourselves that better financial development is at least possible in countries that are not yet wealthy. Consider the five rapidly growing economies—West Germany, Japan, Korea, Taiwan, and Singapore—portrayed in Table 5. All developed a sophisticated banking system—and high or sharply rising M_2/GNP ratios—at fairly early stages in their growth in per capita income. To make their rapid rates of growth clearer, I have stretched out the time horizon from 1955 to 1977—about as far as International Monetary Fund's statistics permit.

In particular, *Japan* in 1955 had a per capita real income that was lower than that of many of the semi-industrial LDCs (Table 3) as of 1975.

Yet Japan's M_2/GNP ratio in 1955 was more than twice as large as that now prevailing in the semi-industrial LDCs. And Japan's financial growth continues apace. As of 1977, its M_2/GNP ratio of 1.087 is much higher than the mean M_2/GNP ratio of 0.6 for the 'mature' industrial economies, although Japan's per capita real income is still somewhat lower than the average of other industrial economies.

After the monetary turmoil and high inflation in the early 1950s, which sharply reduced the 'real' size of its monetary system where M_2/GNP was only 0.115, *Taiwan's* banking sector has grown rapidly through time to surpass that of the semi-industrial LDCs at comparable stages of per capita income. By 1970, its banking system was about twice as large as the average semi-industrial LDC. By 1977, its M_2/GNP ratio of 0.702 was comparable to that of the mature industrial economies, although Taiwan's per capita income is still substantially lower. Again, remarkably rapid financial growth apparently led, or was necessary for the achievement of, higher ratios of physical capital to labour.

Remembering that the monetary reform of 1948–49 drastically scaled down both bank assets and liabilities, West Germany's subsequent high and sustained growth in M_2/GNP has been remarkable.

In *Korea*, development languished prior to 1964, with little or no sustained growth in per capita income. Then major financial reforms in 1964–65 sharply increased the intermediary role of banks in private capital markets over the next five years to provide domestic finance for a major spurt of industrialisation. M_2/GNP rose from 0.102 in 1965 to 0.325 in 1970. Subsequently, Koreans have depended more on taxation and on foreign borrowing; domestic financial growth has been sustained less well than Taiwan's.

Singapore, another Asian success story, has largely internally financed its economic development by maintaining a money/GNP ratio at 'European' levels.

From equation (2), remember that growth itself increases the flow of realised private financial saving even further when M_2/GNP is high. Thus, these five countries have successfully completed a virtual financial circle. Financial development stimulates growth, and growth naturally increases the flow of loanable funds when financial development is robust. My main task, therefore, is to contrast the repression of flows of loanable funds in the slow-growth Asian and Latin American LDCs portrayed in Table 2 with the policy of financial liberalisation followed by the high-growth economies portrayed in Table 4.

II   INTEREST CEILINGS, RESERVE REQUIREMENTS, AND THE ORIGINS OF FINANCIAL REPRESSION

Using credit subsidies to promote the immediate goals of the development plan is a seductive idea in LDCs. The Minister of Finance is usually hard pressed to raise revenue to directly subsidise this or that production activity by outright grants. Tariffs and other restrictions on foreign trade to protect such industries have been effectively criticised on grounds of economic inefficiency. Moreover, in LDCs the central bank is often under the direct control of the minister of finance or other important economics ministries in the cabinet.[4] Thus selective credit subsidies to favoured borrowers on an industry-by-industry or firm-by-firm basis are easy to administer.

This mode of intervention, quite typical of the semi-industrial LDCs, is well illustrated by the case of Colombia in 1972. Breaking down Monobank into its components parts, Figure 1 provides an over-simplified sketch of the flow of funds from savers to investors: how banks collect deposits and make loans. Three characteristics of the Colombian banking system stand out: high reserve requirements, specialised credit agencies, and interest ceilings on deposits and loans.

HIGH RESERVE REQUIREMENTS

The commercial banks must keep 31 per cent of their deposits as non-interest-bearing reserves with the central bank, and another 26 per cent of their loan portfolio is directly specified by the central authorities. Similarly, the savings banks keep 25 per cent of their deposits in non-interest-bearing reserves, whereas another 44 per cent of their deposits must be placed in low yield (6 per cent) housing bonds.

SPECIALISED CREDIT AGENCIES

With this very substantial resource flow at its disposal, the central bank channels cheap credits to various specialised banking agencies (A, B, C, E, etc. in Figure 1) who in turn lend at low disequilibrium rates of interest for export promotion, credit for small farmers, industrial projects the government wishes to subsidise, and so forth. Because the government may have very detailed credit allocations in mind, these agencies decentralise the potentially huge administrative burden. Or, central bank credits can flow directly to the ministry of finance—shown in Figure 1—to cover current-account deficits in the government's budget.

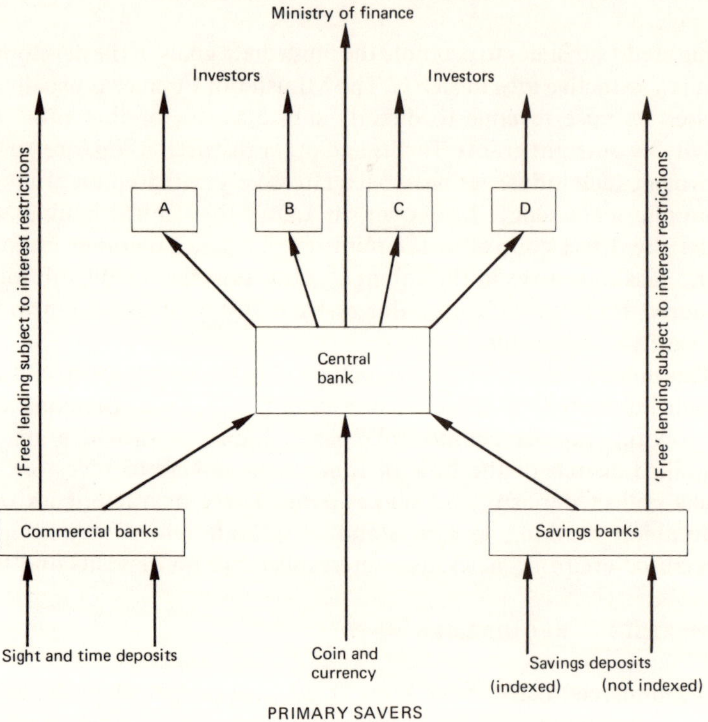

Note: A, B, C, D, E and so on are specialised credit agencies (banks) that get cheap finance from the central bank. A could be the export promotion fund; B the agricultural bank; C the central mortgage bank; and D the industrial development bank.

Fig. 1   Bank intermediation in a typical semi-industrial LDC.

INTEREST CEILINGS ON DEPOSITS AND LOANS

The standard commercial lending rate of interest on the 'free' part of the bank's portfolio had a 14 to 16 per cent official ceiling, with interest ceilings on loans as high as 22 per cent if banks obtained funds by selling certificates of deposit to firms and households. On the other hand, the specialised credit agencies (A, B, C, D, and so on) were required to lend for predesignated uses with interest rates starting as low as 2 or 4 per cent.

For the holders of monetary assets, the nominal yield on sight (demand) deposits was kept at zero and savings deposits for small depositors carried a low 5 to 8 per cent interest coupon. A few firms and households could buy certificates of deposit at much higher nominal rates of interest if they met the extremely large minimum deposit requirements.

Between 1970 and 1973 in Colombia, the annual rate of inflation in the wholesale price index was of the order of 18 per cent. Thus in terms of maintaining the capital value of their savings, those households receiving an 8 per cent nominal yield would be getting -10 per cent as the 'real' yield. Those savers holding sight deposits or non-interest-bearing coin and currency would be receiving -18 per cent as their 'real' yield. Moreover, recipients of credit from the subsidised special agencies would receive an unrequited gift in so far as the rate of inflation exceeded their low nominal borrowing costs.

In a repressed and therefore small financial system (as measured by M_2/GNP), the paradoxical proliferation of specialised credit agencies is worth further examination. As of 1972, Colombia had seven of these specialised credit institutions directly under the control of the central bank. In addition, many industrial *financieras* and specially designated institutions for buying home mortgages were authorised to borrow from deposit-collecting banks at less-than-market rates of interest. Chile in the late 1960s had many similar institutions, but the government also owned a large 'commercial' bank, Banco del Estado, that had unlimited discount privileges with the central bank in order to finance politically designated credits in agriculture, industry, or housing. Besides being expensive to administer, this elaborate institutional structure—in an otherwise constricted financial system—can make control over the monetary base next to impossible. At the margin, however, there is continual pressure on the government to create even more such agencies. Why?

As we have seen, commercial bankers are prevented from making an adequate capital market for channelling funds into socially profitable investments. There is always a queue of 'worthy' unsatisfied borrowers. Thus, serious new gaps in the provision of credit continually develop, from the leasing of industrial equipment to fertiliser distribution. Politically sensitive authorities respond by commissioning additional specialised credit agencies to satisfy these new needs. But these new agencies drain even more resources from the regulated commercial banks and savings institutions either by borrowing from them directly, or indirectly by having automatic rediscount privilege with the central bank (see Figure 1). Repression in the rest of the financial system is thereby worsened even as monetary control is further undermined. Nevertheless, *at the margin*, the social cost of creating one more agency may be worthwhile if the perceived gap to be filled is sufficiently important at the microeconomic level. Hence, financial repression feeds on itself.

Last but not least in contributing to financial repression, the state of the government's regular budget and its need for debt finance should also be considered.[5] Having no recourse to organised open markets in primary securities, the government often imposes heavy 'reserve' requirements against deposits in commercial and savings banks to force these institutions to buy low interest government bond in a non-inflationary manner. If reserve requirements are already high, the failure of the government in an LDC to cover its expenditures by taxation often means that government bonds must be sold to the central bank and directly monetised.[6] The resulting inflation reduces real rates of interest perceived by potential depositors (savers) in Monobank. Realised private financial saving falls, contracting the flow of loanable funds so as to reduce investment and employment. All of this substantially inhibits the proper functioning of capital markets in LDCs, as will become clearer when the response of commercial banks to inflation is analysed more formally below.

III INFLATION AND THE RESERVE REQUIREMENTS OF COMMERCIAL BANKS: A PARTIAL-EQUILIBRIUM ANALYSIS

Instead of continuing the highly aggregated analysis of Monobank necessary for understanding the macroeconomic problems of monetary control, let us now focus on the key role of the commercial banks in the microeconomics of liberalisation. Even when usury restrictions are absent, I will show that there exists a strong and positive relationship between the *real* lending rate of interest and the *nominal* rate of inflation, and a negative relationship between inflation and the real deposit rate of interest.

After correcting for inflation, Figure 2 portrays the flow of loans through commercial banks over one year, which is time enough for most outstanding bank loans to mature. It shows only partial equilibrium in the market for loanable funds because the level of income Y, its percentage rate of growth $\dot{Y}$, and the expected percentage rate of price inflation $\dot{P}^e$ are all given exogeneously. The notional or *ex ante* demand for real bank

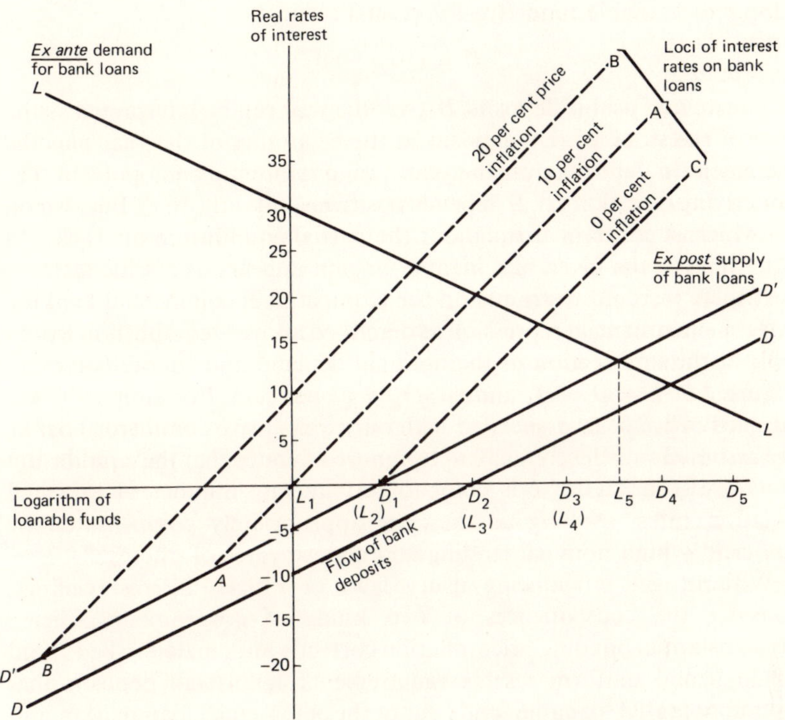

Fig. 2 Deposits and loans with a 50 per cent reserve requirement on commercial banks and varying rates of inflation

loans, L, is portrayed by the LL curve. Borrowers from the commercial banks are sensitive to the real loan rate of interest r_1, where

$$r_1 = i_1 - \dot{P}^e \text{ and } r_d = i_d - \dot{P}^e \tag{3}$$

i_1 is the nominal lending rate and i_d is the nominal deposit rate of interest. Algebraically the notional demand for loanable funds is:

$$L = L(r_1; \dot{Y}) \, Y \tag{4}$$

On the deposit side, savers respond to the real deposit rate of interest r_d along the notional supply curve DD in Figure 2; r_d is derived from i_d, which is the average nominal rate of interest (inclusive of chequing services) provided on all the commercial banks' liabilities—demand deposits, savings account, time deposits, and so forth. Then the notional supply of loanable funds (real deposits) is

$$D = D(r_d; \dot{Y})Y \qquad (5)$$

The flow of usable deposits, D, over the year can be interpreted as the sum of the stock of real deposits at the beginning of the year *plus* the increment in deposits over the year. Using reasoning analogous to that underlying equation (2), D depends positively not only on r_d, but also on $\dot{Y}$—which is constant throughout the partial-equilibrium analysis.[7] In equation (5), the given real income Y again appears as a scale factor.

If there were no restraints on the (competitive) commercial banking system—no financial repression as described above—equilibrium would exist at the intersection of the notional demand and supply curves: in Figure 2 at $L = D = D_4$ and $r_1 = r_d = 10$ per cent. For simplicity, the administrative costs associated with our competitive commercial banks are assumed sufficiently small to be ignored. Notice that the equilibrium at $(D_4, 10)$ in Figure 2 is compatible with any number of expected inflation rates, as long as they are appropriately compensated by sufficiently high nominal lending and deposit rates of interest.[8]

Without yet introducing usury laws or official interest ceilings, consider the consequences of two kinds of government policies: (1) substantial ongoing price inflation correctly anticipated to be $\dot{P}^e$; and (2) high and uniform reserve requirements against all deposits that siphon potential loanable funds out of the commercial loan market into 'consumption'.[9] A reserve requirement of k per cent is imposed on all deposits. Because loanable funds in Figure 2 are plotted on the horizontal logarithmic scale, this uniform, reserve requirement—say, a modest 50 per cent in the LDC context—linearly displaces the notional supply of deposits DD to the left by a uniform amount. $D'D'$ now represents the net loanable funds available after this flow of government seigniorage is taken out. In equilibrium (and out) deposits and loans are not equal:

$$L = (1 - k)D \qquad (6)$$

At first glance, the new equilibrium seems to be simply the intersection of $D'D'$ and LL at a flow of loanable funds equal to L_5 at an interest rate of 12.5 per cent on both deposits and loans. With a 50 per cent reserve requirement, however, this conclusion is incorrect if one constrains the commercial banks to operate with at least zero profits. Because $k = 0.5$, half the assets of the commercial banks are not interest-bearing. Their earnings are insufficient to support such a flow of deposits when $D > L$. Even with no official interest ceilings or other usury restrictions, the reserve requirement forces the commercial banks to substantially reduce deposit rates of interest, and raise loans rates, thus contracting the flow of loanable funds. But how much of each? Somewhat surprisingly to the author, the amount of contraction depends heavily on the rate of *price inflation*—even when nominal rates of interest can be freely adjusted to take inflation into account!

This fundamental nexus among reserve requirements, interest rates, and the rate of price inflation is best illustrated with an example. With $k = 0.5$, suppose $\dot{P}^e = 0.1$: that is, the expected percentage rate of price inflation is 10 per cent per annum. With these two parameters, the locus of *real* deposit and lending rates of interest just sufficient to satisfy the zero profit condition (on the commercial banks) is the curve AA in Figure 2; AA is derived numerically from Table 5 below, which in turn was constructed from the following equations that reflect the zero profit condition:

TABLE 5
**RATES OF INTEREST WITH A 50 PER CENT RESERVE
REQUIREMENT ON COMMERCIAL BANKS**

On deposits				*On loans*	
i_d	r_d			i_1	r_1
0	−10			0	−10
5	−5			10	0
10	0	10 per cent expected inflation		20	10
15	5			30	20
20	10			40	40
0	−20			0	−20
5	−15			10	−10
10	−10			20	0
15	−5	20 per cent expected inflation		30	10
20	0			40	20
25	+5			50	30

Note: i_d and i_1 are nominal rates of interest, r_d and r_1 are real rates that are calculated by subtracting the expected rate of inflation from the respective nominal rates of interest. The calculations assume the banks are making zero profits.

$$i_1 = \frac{i_d}{1-k} \quad \text{Nominal interest rates} \tag{7}$$

Then subtract $\dot{P}^e$ from each side of equation (7), and substitute $r_d + \dot{P}^e$ for i_d to get

$$r_1 = \frac{r_d}{1-k} + \dot{P}^e \left(\frac{k}{1-k} \right) \quad \text{Real interest rates} \tag{8}$$

Equations (7) and (8) indicate that the amount by which the real loan rate exceeds the real deposit rate is an increasing function of k, $\dot{P}$ and r_d or i_d. Real and nominal rates of interest are tabulated in Table 5.

The upper part of Table 5 with expected inflation of 10 per cent corresponds to the AA locus in Figure 2. The reserve requirement of 0.5 forces an otherwise unconstrained banking system to an equilibrium where the real deposit rate of interest is 5 per cent but the real loan rate is 20 per cent—a spread of 15 percentage points! With the commercial banks just breaking even, the flow of deposits is D_3, and of loans is half that at L_3. Notice that if the inflation rate were 20 per cent as tabulated in the lower half of Table 5, equilibrium in Figure 2 must be where the BB locus intersects LL. Here the real loan rate would be approximately 23 per cent, while the real deposit rate is about 2 per cent—a spread of 21 percentage points leading to a further contraction of the banking system. By similar reasoning, in the zero inflation case, equilibrium is where the curve CC cuts LL: the spread is only about 8.5 percentage points and the real deposit rate of interest is kept sufficiently large—also 8.5 per cent— that the flow of loanable funds is much more robust.

The moral of our story is clear. The burden of a given reserve requirement k on the flow of loanable funds depends *directly* on the rate of price inflation even when no other interest restrictions exist. If k is high and inflation is high, the gap between deposit and loan rates must be enormous, reflecting the proportionately greater seigniorage that is being extracted from the banking system. The high non-interest-bearing reserves of the commercial banks are essentially the base on which the inflation tax is levied, and the system of intermediation by commercial bank in LDCs is very sensitive to the rate of inflation that the authorities select.

A rather extreme example of this point is provided by the Chilean attempts to liberalise their banking system during 1976 and 1977 (McKinnon, 1978). In 1976 conventional usury restrictions on time deposits and loans were completely abolished, but high reserve require-ments were retained on the deposit banks and *financieras*, and price inflation continued out of control at over 100 per cent per annum. Although the banking system was reasonably competitive, the spread between real deposit and lending rates was 4 percentage points per month for most of 1976. Because real deposit rates of interest were close to zero during the period, the *real* bank lending rate of interest was of the order of 60 to 70 per cent per annum—a level so high that it astonished all outside observers! Needless to say, the real flow of bank loans made during this period was a mere trickle, despite the fact that the banking system was virtually the only domestic source of loanable funds in the economy.

Subsequently, by 1978 the Chileans had made good progress in reducing price inflation to close to 30 per cent on the one hand, and drastically lowering reserve requirements against commercial banks and *financieras* on the other. By early 1978, *real* lending rates on loans were 2 per cent per month (still fairly high), and the real deposit rate was positive at approximately 1 per cent per month for a spread of only 1 percentage point. The real flow of loanable funds is growing rapidly and the Chilean M_2/GNP ratio is finally increasing after decades of being repressed at unusually low levels (Table 2). Needless to say, the reduced volume of seigniorage being extracted by the Chilean government from the banking system, which makes the liberalisation possible, has important fiscal aspects that are not being analysed in this paper.

Finally, one should say a word about the other class of distortions: direct ceilings or usury restrictions on deposit and/or loan rates of interest. From our analysis of the Colombian economy above, these are as repressive as reserve requirements—but the two interact. One example should suffice.

From AA in Figure 2, a 50 per cent reserve requirement in the presence of 10 per cent inflation—and no formal interest ceilings—led to a 5 per cent real deposit rate and a 20 per cent real loan rate (third row in Table 5) when the supply and demand for loanable funds are balanced at D_3 and L_3 respectively. Suppose now a ceiling on *nominal* deposit rates of interest of just 5 per cent is imposed. For simplicity, the nominal loan rate is also regulated to keep bank profits close to zero. From the second row in Table 5, therefore, the new nominal loan rate is just 10 per cent. Now, real interest rates are fixed below market clearing levels; $\bar{r}_d$ is -5 per cent and the flow of deposits is limited to D_1; $\bar{r}_l$ is zero per cent with the flow of loans restricted to half of D_1 at L_1 (the $^-$ reflects the official interest ceilings). The real notional 'open-market' lending rate at L_1 is 30 per cent. However, with $\bar{r}_l = 0$ and a great excess demand for loans, the actual opportunity costs of lucky borrowers could be anything down to zero. No longer do we have assurance that the trickle of loanable funds flows to high-yield uses.

Suppose reserve requirements are close to zero rather than 50 per cent with some usury restrictions on i_d of 5 per cent again with $P^e = 10$ per cent. I leave the reader to figure out that I_2 will be the newly expanded flow of loans, whose notional opportunity costs are reduced form 30 to 25 per cent. So effective interest ceilings are more damaging in the presence of reserve requirements and vice versa. More than reserve requirements, usury ceilings can fragment the whole structure of interest rates—as Colombia's experience would attest.

Clearly, the co-ordinated removal of both interest ceilings and substantial reserve requirements are essential in overcoming financial repression—particularly in the face of significant price inflation.

IV   INSTITUTIONAL ASPECTS OF LIBERALISATION: A DILEMMA FOR FINANCIAL POLICY

A rather acute dilemma between second-best and first-best policies faces government authorities eager to eliminate financial repression and promote rapid growth in the flow of loanable funds in the semi-industrial LDCs.

If one takes the general character of the repressed financial system (including high and variable inflation) as given, then various second-best microeconomic policies, as were implicit in the above analysis, suggest themselves. New credit agencies—perhaps with special discount privileges—may be necessary to cover obvious credit gaps not being served by the regular banking system. The authorities may have to work with independently wealthy private capitalists or foreign firms in promoting new projects. A certain tolerance for possible extra-legal activities in the inevitable black market for loans might seem wise. A variety of other *ad hoc* decisions by the planning authorities to divert funds from the rather constipated financial system to support this or that enterprise may have some chance of improving resource allocation when considered one at a time. But savers in the deposit banks would be left with low or negative real yields.

Against this, a first-best policy would move to a completely open capital market where borrowing and lending take place at high equilibrium rates of interest. The M_2/GNP ratio would rise as depositors received the higher yield earned on bank loans. The real credit flow through the banking system would increase in the mode of the rapidly growing economies portrayed in Table 4. But success here requires the government to move on a broad front in the *opposite* direction from the second-best strategy. The authorities must be prepared to withdraw the hundreds of subventions, interest regulations, and special credit facilities that already influence the microeconomic allocation of investment resources in the economy.

In particular, the high reserve requirements against the commercial banks—which are an important source of subsidised finance for the special credit agencies and the government (Figure 1)—would have to be terminated. So too would direct discounting with the central bank by the special credit agencies, or by government itself, need to be ended to bring inflation under control. Thus major fiscal reforms to close a government budgetary deficit, currently covered by tapping seigniorage from the banking system, may well be necessary to support full liberalisation.[10] Chile's experience with partial liberalisation—where usury restrictions on interest rates were removed but reserve requirements and inflation remained high—suggest that interest decontrol by itself is not enough.

An important element in a successful reform, therefore, is to have commercial banks and related institutions move aggressively to provide high-interest loans to all comers as their reserve requirements are reduced and their interest ceilings are removed. For small borrowers, these real loan rates need be of the order of 18 to 24 per cent in order for the banks to cover their administrative costs and still pay depositors an attractive return that properly reflects the opportunity cost of scarce capital in the economy (Donald, 1976, page 32). The deposit-collecting banks may have little experience in aggressively seeking out borrowers who can pay high real yields on their loans, yields that accurately reflect high social productivity of the investments they are undertaking. Indeed, the whole process of seeking out small and innovative entrepreneurs in industry and agriculture outside the urban enclaves may be quite foreign to the banking system's recent experience.

In the transition to a more competitive banking system, another rather acute short-run problem may arise. As interest ceilings on deposits and loans are lifted and new commercial banks are allowed to begin operations, the older commercial banks may face a serious bankruptcy threat. 'Old' loans will bear rates of interest that had been artificially depressed (Mathieson, 1978) and the term to maturity of the banks' loan portfolio is typically longer than that of their deposits. New entrants would have an artificial competitive advantage in not having such an overhang of old low-yield loans. However, the liberalising monetary authority can take offsetting administrative action: until they mature, old low-yield loans can be assumed by the state, or they can be used for credit against the (declining) reserve requirements of the bank that owns them.

As a competitive bank-based capital market develops—but only then—the subsidised clienteles of the specialised credit agencies with the central bank would be terminated, allowing the latter to secure its control over the monetary base. Undoubtedly, the authorities would find that many hitherto favoured borrowers would be traumatised; others getting credit on an organised market for the first time would thrive in the mode of rapidly growing economies such as Taiwan or Korea. Once the price level is stabilised and the banking system grows rapidly to take care of short and intermediate-term credit needs, experiments in selling longer-term securities such as mortgages, industrial bonds, and equities to non-bank firms and households could begin.

Besides the important technical issues of monetary control not discussed here, the transitional fiscal problems of converting a repressed banking system to a leading sector in economic development should not be underestimated. But the social cost of leaving the domestic financial systems of LDCs in a repressed state may well be unacceptable. And the problem is primarily domestic, although the resulting shortage of capital in many LDCs is often incorrectly diagnosed as a deficiency in the international economic order.

ENDNOTES

1. Little, Scitovsky and Scott (1971); Balassa (1971); Bhagwati (1978); Krueger (1978).
2. S. C. Tsiang of Cornell University, and E. S. Shaw of Stanford University were influential advisers in Taiwan (1950s) and Korea (1960s), repectively, when the *modus operandi* of both countries' highly successful financial systems were established. However, academic treatises on the subject appeared surprisingly late in the postwar development game (see E. S. Shaw, 1973, and R. I. McKinnon, 1973).
3. Neither a monetarist nor a Keynesian theoretical framework is appropriate because in neither does the monetary system intermediate between savers and investors (McKinnon 1973, Chapter 5).
4. Unlike the United States where enabling statutes give the Federal Reserve autonomy from the day-to-day political and economic decisions of the government.
5. In many countries, it is useful to think of government spending as having two facets: (1) the 'regular' budget financed from raising taxes, which usually requires parliamentary approval; and (2) the 'monetary' budget where low-cost credits flow through the banking system, usually by official administrative action rather than being voted on by some legislature.
6. Unless the government is capable of borrowing from foreigners in one way

or another, and then allowing that borrowing to immediately widen the deficit on current account in foreign trade.

7. For an interesting statistical study of the sensitivity of private saving in LDCs to real interest and growth rates, see M. J. Fry (1978).

8. No allowance for the riskiness of the inflation process will be introduced in this paper. Uncertain inflation is obviously an important pratical consideration, particularly as it affects the term structure of lending and borrowing.

9. Reserve requirements can direct funds from the commercial banks to the central bank to the ministry of finance to cover a current deficit in the public budget; or by regulation the central bank can specify certain low or negative-yield loans that flow mainly for consumption—say, a special credit tranche for small farmers that are outside the market for commercial loans. The macroeconomic consequences of this seigniorage flow are important in a general-equilibrium model, but are ignored in the partial-equilibrium approach taken here.

10. This is not the place to analyse the rather difficult technical problems of monetary control that accompany any such broadly based reforms of the banking system. The authorities would have to co-ordinate a programme of first raising nominal rates of interest, then securing firm control over the monetary base, and then—when inflation wanes—eventually lowering nominal rates of interest in such a way as to keep the real rate of interest high and constant. Some aspects of these important issues have already been addressed by several authors: Shaw (1973), McKinnon (1973), Kapur (1976), and Mathieson (1978).

REFERENCES

Balassa, *et al.*, *The Structure of Protection in Developing Countries* (Johns Hopkins Press, 1971).

Bhagwati, J., *Anatomy and Consequences of Exchange Control Regimes* (National Bureau of Economic Research, 1978).

Donald, G., *Credit for Small Farmers in Developing Countries* (Westview Press, 1976).

Fry, M. S., 'Money and Capital or Financial Deepening in Economic Development?' *Journal of Money, Credit and Banking* (1978).

Kapur, B., 'Alternative Stabilisation Policies for Less Developed Economies', *Journal of Political Economy,* vol. 84, no. 4, part I (August, 1976).

Krueger, Anne, *Liberalisation Attempts and Consequences* (National Bureau of Economic Research, 1978).

Little, I., Scitovsky, T. and Scott, M., *The Structure of Protection in Developing Countries* (Johns Hopkins Press for the IRBD, 1971).

Mathieson, D. J., 'Financial Reform and Stabilisation Policy in a Developing Economy', Research Department of International Monetary Fund (mimeo) (March 1978).

McKinnon, R. I., *Money and Capital in Economic Development* (The Brookings Institution: Washington, DC, 1973).

McKinnon, R. I., 'La Intermediacion Financiera y el Control Monetario en Chile', *Cuadernos de Economia* (December 1977).

Shaw, E. S., *Financial Deepening in Economic Development* (Oxford University Press, 1973).

Tsiang, S. C., 'Exchange Rate, Interest Rate, and Economic Development,' in *Essays in Honor of T. C. Liu* (1978).

Comments

Sven Grassman (Sweden)

In my opinion, the basic message of McKinnon's paper is correct, powerful, and widely underestimated. It is that the financial 'superstructure' is of immense importance for the real performance of any economy and that inconsistencies—or even absence of—vital financial flows, prices and co-ordinating signals may reduce the performance of an economy to a fraction of its potential. McKinnon's paper describes in detail how usury laws and reserve requirements in combination with ongoing inflation make real yields on savings highly negative, and how firms and households respond by reducing or diverting savings to non-productive uses. While financial regression in various forms is crucial in explaining the low economic performance of many LDCs it is a more general problem, plaguing and distorting some of the mature industrialised economies as well.

Sweden is an interesting and paradoxical case in point. I mention Sweden not only because we are here now, but because its quick development to the highest income per capita in the world—in the 1960s—and its subsequent downturn is an interesting lesson. With the slowest growth in the OECD during the 1970s, Sweden now asymptotically approaches LDC income levels—so that our development experience can be studied in both directions, as it were. The industrialisation process over the last hundred years was made possible through efficient, competitive investment within a narrow, but 'clean' and uniform, domestic credit market, and through the access to almost unlimited portfolio capital from London and Paris. Since the Second World War, however, exchange restrictions—and a rigid goal of current-account balance—have effectively cut us off from the (long-term) international capital market. At the same time the domestic credit market was 'enriched' by a host of specialised institutions and misguided central bank regulations, fragmenting and distorting our credit market in much the same way as McKinnon's LDC caricature. Ironically, balance-of-payments problems in the depression of the 1970s have forced the Swedish monetary authorities to allow large-scale capital movements, which tend to swamp some of the domestic labyrinths and impediments to an efficient financial mechanism. I do not want to exaggerate the significance of financial deficiencies in the recent decline, but I think it was decisive in the earlier growth process.

I   THE NEED FOR INTERNAL FINANCIAL REFORM

If we agree with McKinnon's thesis that financial repression is a major obstacle to economic growth, then we have one more internal cause of reform within LDCs, one which is largely independent of the shape or deficiencies of the international economic order. In my view financial repression deserved a prominent place in Gunnar Myrdal's paper (Chapter 14) which scrutinises internal reform needs within the LDCs. So much better, then, that we here have a whole paper on one of the most important aspects of the internal reforms—reforms that, if carried through, might obliterate some of the need for a new international system.

While agreeing with the basic message of the paper, I shall confine myself to a few minor points in McKinnon's exposition: his *empirical evidence* on financial repression in countries at different levels of industrial development, and what I would like to call McKinnon's *magnification effect*. The latter is the mechanism through which reserve requirements in combination with inflation exponentially increase the gap between nominal and real interest rates, specifically between banks' lending and borrowing rates.

A more fundamental problem is the identification of cause and effect in McKinnon's comparisons of the broadness of money markets and income growth. I would like to ask McKinnon to elaborate on this; it suffices to note here that through equation (2) in his paper we automatically get an expansion of money markets through the income scale factor.

How should we know that the impressive increases in net real financial savings accompanying growth in Japan, Germany, etc., are a cause, and not an effect, of growth? Or rather: what are the proportions of these two components? Here the paper faces a serious identification problem.

II   THE MEASURE OF FINANCIAL REPRESSION

McKinnon has chosen the M_2/GNP ratio as an index of monetary development, interpreting a low money numerator as a sign of financial repression and a high one as a sign of a developed monetary system. In the paper countries are grouped into one of three sets

(1) *Semi-industrial LDCs* (Table 2)
(2) *Mature industrial economies* (Table 3)
(3) *Rapidly growing economies* (Table 4)

It is shown that the M_2/GNP ratio rises from around 0.2 for the first group up to 0.6 in the mature group—that is, two or three times higher than the semi-industrial LDCs. Finally, it is shown that the rapidly growing economies—Germany, Japan, Korea, Taiwan, Singapore— display very high M_2/GNP ratios, which in addition have risen quickly in pattern with the growth performance of these countries.

The M_2/GNP ratio may catch some of the vital differences between well and badly developed national credit markets. But one feels uneasy with this crude measure, and I think that one major objection is readily implied by McKinnon's own exposition in other parts of his paper. For instance, he argues that the LDCs suffer from the lack of markets for a lot of assets and credit instruments *other* than currency and deposits (that is, roughly what is included in M_2), and then he empirically demonstrates precisely how low the currency plus deposits (M_2) are in LDCs and explains their inefficiency in terms of the low M_2. This points to an obvious bias in using the M_2/GNP ratio in comparing financial markets of LDCs and developed countries—in the sense that financial repression in the LDCs is underestimated by the measure used.

As a measure of the inefficiency described in the paper, one would rather have, as an index of monetary sophistication, the total credit volume somehow weighted for the homogeneity of financial instruments and the uniformity or dispersion of their interest rates.

In general, I am more in sympathy with the general reasoning than with the empirical illustrations on this point. Still, McKinnon's tables do contain striking regularities between his narrow M_2/GNP measure and stage of development. But the 'burden of proof' for showing the nature of this correlation should rest with the author.

III   THE WEDGE BETWEEN REAL AND NOMINAL RATES

McKinnon's derivation and numerical illustrations of how inflation magnifies the gap between borrowing and lending rates for banks required to hold cash reserves is fascinating. Again, like the whole repression theme, this 'magnification effect' is not limited to LDCs. It is an interesting, general piece of analysis of monetary control and inflationary banking. I have no objections to McKinnon's analysis here. What makes his analysis particularly relevant in describing financial repression and distortion in LDCs (or Sweden!) is the fact that the two determinants of the distorting wedge—the levels of reserve, or placement, quotas and the speed of inflation—are both so high in these countries as to virtually destroy parts of the financial system, hampering savings and making efficient overall investment patterns impossible.

In summary, this paper makes a convincing *a priori* case both for the difficulties of calling forth financial savings in a fragmented credit market where savers have to *pay* heavy penalties for abstaining from their funds, and for the failure to channel these limited funds to their best use. Thus the paper has two major cornerstones: the *repression* of savings or supply of funds and the *discrimination* between borrowers and thus investors ruin much of the limited savings available in poor countries. While the M_2/GNP measure and the wedge between lending and borrowing rates may shed some light on the deficient supply of financial savings, they say little about the discrimination between uses and investors. Since the discrimination in lending is at least as important as the repression of financial savings in McKinnon's general argument, it would be interesting to have a further discussion of the possibilities of measuring empirically, and correcting by policy measures, the financial disincentives he describes.

Through its simplicity and intuitive insight this contribution may prove to be one of the most important of the interesting approaches to fostering LDC growth that have been discussed at this conference. It is an anticlimax in terms of spectacular or revolutionary implications, but in terms of operational relevance I feel that McKinnon's horse may again be a winner. Three years ago we had a conference in this same room—on the asset approach to exchange-rate determination—which in vital parts represented a breakthrough and elaboration of some early theorising of McKinnon's. Today's paper is highly unfashionable, but may prove equally influential for development theory in the years to come.

11 Exchange Rate Policy for Developing Countries

William Branson
and
Louka Katseli-Papaefstratiou (USA)

I INTRODUCTION

In his Per Jacobsson lecture, Arthur Lewis (1972 p. 33) said: 'It is now the conventional wisdom that the currencies of the developed countries should float, but the currencies of the less-developed (LDCs) should not; that is to say that each LDC should choose a more developed country (MDC) as a partner—or the SDR—and tie itself in a fixed relationship.'

This statement led us to think about the meaning of fixing the exchange rate in a world where the major currencies are floating, and about the implications for domestic policy targets of pegging to one or a combination of these major currencies. Under the Bretton Woods System and in the absence of major currency readjustments, the choice of a *numeraire* was only of minor importance: pegging to any one of the major currencies was equivalent to maintaining a fixed parity with all others. In a world of floating rates, however, pegging to any one of the major currencies implies floating *vis-a-vis* all others. It is precisely for this reason that in their effort to avoid large fluctuations in their exchanges rates, an increasing number of developing countries have abandoned single-peg policies and have started experimenting with composite pegs; and it is exactly this trend that poses new and interesting analytical questions regarding the choice of a numeraire of the choice of weights for a composite peg. These are the issues with which we are concerned in this paper.

In our discussion of choice of exchange rate regimes, we begin by separating considerations of feasibility and optimality in the floats *vs.* peg decision. In Section II we introduce two major feasibility conditions for floating: incomplete openness and internationally integrated capital markets. We argue that in general developing countries are not feasible floaters.

The question of pegging to a single currency or a 'currency basket' is raised in Section III. The degree of geographical concentration of trade becomes important for that choice. Countries which opt for a basket peg in turn must decide on weights for the currencies in the basket. These can be chosen to eliminate the effects of third-country exchange-rate fluctuations on any of a number of policy targets.

In Section IV we explicitly derive the weighting schemes for basket pegs that would eliminate the effects of third-country exchange-rate variation alternatively on the home country's terms of trade, relative price of traded *vs.* non-traded goods, or balance of trade. These weighting schemes are given in equations (28), (32), and (37), respectively. Thus, Section IV presents a menu of weighting schemes, one for each policy target. The choice among policy targets is discussed in Section V. Fluctuations in relative prices are related to fluctuations in real income. This gives us the contribution of each weighting scheme to reduction in real-income variations stemming from variations in third-country exchange rates. It also gives us the residual income instability that would remain in each case. Finally, we note cases in which the choice of a policy target is clearly dictated by the structure of the economy.

In that sense this paper is the beginning of a larger project where structural characteristics of the economy are explicitly introduced in the analysis of macroeconomic policy. Such an approach is especially relevant to the comparative study of policy choices for developing *vs.* developed economies.

II   FLOATING VS: PEGGING: FEASIBILITY CONSIDERATIONS

In choosing an exchange-rate policy, the first decision a country faces is whether to permit the rate to float, with its value being determined by the 'market'. In this section we provide some arguments and evidence suggesting that floating is not feasible for most developing countries. Thus the real policy choices are what to peg to, in a world in which most major currencies are floating, and how to adjust the peg. These are topics taken up in succeeding sections of the paper.

Our discussion will be cast in the framework set by Corden in *Monetary Integration* (1972). There Corden separated into two sets factors or considerations bearing on the dual questions of (a) choice of exchange rate regime, and (b) optimal size of currency areas. First we consider factors determining whether it is *feasible* for a country to decide to be a currency area and to float its exchange rate. Only after we make a determination on feasibility is it reasonable to move ahead to considerations bearing on the *optimal* choice of regime.

Most of the arguments concerning optimum currency areas and choice of exchange rate regime are well known, and will be mentioned only briefly below. Ishiyama (1975) has recently surveyed the literature on optimal currency areas; Black (1976a and b) and Crockett and Nsouli (1977) have focused on exchange-rate policies for less developed countries; Heller (1976) has provided some empirical evidence on actual choice of regimes. The new considerations, or twists on old considerations, in our discussion involve mainly (a) the role of asset markets in determining feasibility of floating, and (b) the role of market power in determining the currency basket to use when pegging.

Our discussion of exchange rate policy is illustrated by Figure 1, which

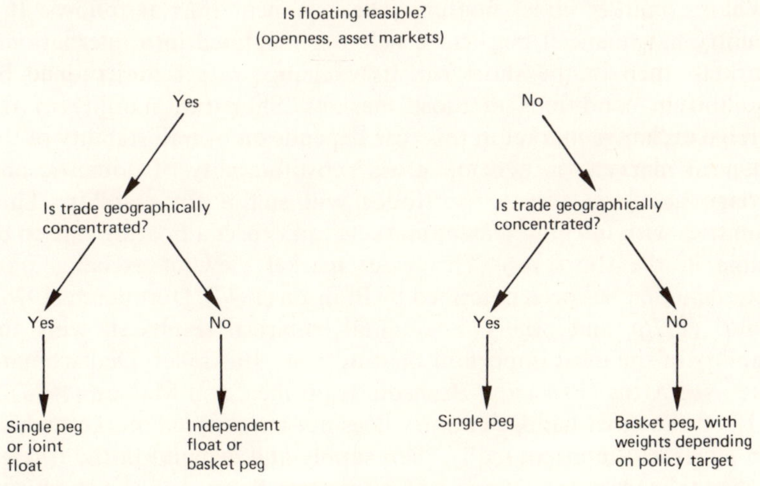

Fig. 1   Choice of exchange rate regimes

organises Sections II and III of the paper. It differs from a similar figure in Heller (1976, p. 24a) in that our structure separates feasibility and optimality considerations. Countries must first decide whether floating is feasible. Those for whom it is *not* feasible go on to consider various types of peg. This is the usual case for developing countries. Those who *can* float must then decide whether it is optimal to float independently or jointly as in the European 'snake', to peg to a currency basket. These are mainly the industrial OECD countries. Since our discussion concentrates on policy choices for developing countries, we will discuss mainly the right half of Figure 1.

The two major feasibility conditions are (a) degree of openness, and (b) existence of asset markets integrated into the international system. The openness criterion was introduced into the literature by McKinnon (1963), who noted that an economy can be so open that if the exchange rate were to float, domestic citizens would want contracts effectively denominated in foreign exchange. In that case, there would be no basis for demand for home currency, except for artificial legal constraints such as the requirement that taxes be paid in local currency. On the McKinnon argument, the more open an economy, the less likely it is that floating is feasible. This argument is supported by Heller's results, which show that relatively closed economies tend to float, alone or jointly, while relatively open economies tend to peg (Heller, 1976, p. 5).

The asset market argument involves the likely stability of the foreign exchange market under floating. The argument runs as follows. If a country has financial markets which are integrated into international markets, then in the short run its exchange rate is determined by equilibrium conditions in those markets. Short-run stability of the foreign exchange market in this case depends on overall stability of the financial markets; in general, gross substitutability of domestic and foreign assets in private portfolios will suffice for stability. Thus countries with integrated asset markets can expect a floating rate to be stable in the short run. This asset market view of exchange rate determination has been described by Branson (1977), Dornbusch (1976), Kouri (1976), and others. For initial empirical results showing the stability of the most important floating rate—the dollar–Deutschmark rate—see Artus (1976) and Branson, Halttunen, and Masson (1977).

If, on the other hand, a country does not have capital markets which are integrated internationally, then supply and demand in the foreign exchange market are determined by current flows, and the short-run stability conditions are the Marshall–Lerner conditions on trade elasticities. This is the model recently elaborated by Black (1976a). The feasibility problem appearing here is that for countries with any market power, the Marshall–Lerner elasticity conditions probably do not hold in the shortest of runs. A cursory review of the trade models surveyed by Stern, Francis, and Schumacher (1976) shows that many of the trade equations do not even have contemporaneous price terms, and that in general short-run price elasticities are low. This is such a strong empirical regularity that it is part of the conventional wisdom about J-curves, etc. (see, for example, Klein's (1972) comment on Branson, or Dornbusch and Krugman (1976).

If the Marshall–Lerner conditions do not hold in the short run and financial market separation prevents stabilising speculation, then the floating rate will be unstable.[1] Essentially, the argument is that if the financial markets, including the banking system, do not make a stable market in foreign exchange, the central bank must make the market, eliminating floating as a feasible policy. If, on the other hand, a country has well-integrated capital markets, it can expect a floating rate to be stable.

This argument could clarify an anomaly in Heller's (1976) results. There he argued that capital market integration should result in pegging, since external adjustment could be achieved easily through capital flows. But when he looked at the data, he found that countries with integrated capital markets tend to be floaters.[2] This is consistent with our argument that countries with integrated asset markets are feasible stable floaters.

One apparent difficulty with the asset-market argument is that countries that are small in the strict sense of being price-takers on international markets meet the Marshall–Lerner conditions for stability of a flow-determined exchange rate, and thus on this argument *could* float even without integrated asset markets. However, these small countries are likely to be sufficiently open that they fail the feasibility test on the openness ground.

The feasibility arguments can be summarised as follows: Countries (or groups of countries) which are relatively closed *and* have internationally integrated asset markets are feasible floaters, singly or jointly. Other countries are not feasible floaters and will choose one form of peg or another. In general, we would expect the set of feasible floaters to be the developed OECD countries, while the developing countries would peg their currencies either to one of the major currencies or to a basket. This conclusion is supported by Heller's discriminant analysis of floating *vs.* pegging, and by the data in Table 1.

Using the *World Bank Atlas* (1976), we calculated the average levels of real GDP and real GDP per capita in 1975 for the countries following

TABLE 1
INCOME LEVEL AND EXCHANGE RATE REGIME

		Mean GDP per capita (1975) ($ thousand)	Mean GDP (1975) ($ billion)	Number of countries
I.	Floaters	4.4	156.4	22
	A. Independent	3.3 (0.7)[1]	184.6 (100.5)	15
	B. Joint	6.5 (2.8)	96.1 (53.9)	7
II.	Managed flexibility	1.6	35.1	11
	A. Announced indicators	1.4 (0.4)	28.2 (14.4)	7
	B. Others	2.0 (1.3)	47.3 (16.2)	4
III.	Basket peg	1.7 (0.6)	17.8 (8.1)	11
IV.	Single currency peg	0.5	3.4	64
	A. Non-unified rates	0.5 (0.1)	5.1 (1.3)	32
	B. Others	0.5 (0.1)	1.5 (0.4)	32

[1] Standard errors of the means are in parentheses.

the exchange-rate regimes indicated in Table 1. These are reported along with their standard errors and the number of countries in each type of regime. Countries not in the *Atlas* were excluded from the computation: Guinea-Bissau, the Khmer Republic, the Peoples Democratic Republic of Laos, Lebanon, Malta, and the Yemen Arab Republic. We also excluded OPEC members and Bahrein from the calculations on the ground that their recent jump in income was not matched by an equally rapid development of industry and financial markets.

In Table 1, the twenty-two countries that are classified by the IMF as having floating exchange rates, either independent or joint, have a mean income of $4.4 thousand per capita, as compared with about $1.6 thousand for the twenty-two countries that have managed flexibility or peg to a currency basket, and $0.5 thousand for the 64 countries that peg to a single currency (as of 1975). Thus, in general, it is the high-income countries with internationally integrated capital markets that float, while the developing countries peg.

III   OPTIONS AND TARGETS FOR PEGGING

One floating is excluded on feasibility grounds, the next question is what to peg the currency to. The problem can be broken down into two steps. First, should the currency be pegged to a single major currency, and if so, which one? Second, if the single peg is rejected in favour of a currency basket, what can be achieved by a weighting scheme, and how should the weights be chosen for the basket? We see below and in Section IV that there exist optimal weighting schemes for currency baskets that eliminate the effects of third-country exchange rates on variables such as the terms of trade, the relative price of traded and non-traded goods, or the balance on current account. The basket peg can then be adjusted to meet other targets. But first we look at the determinants of the choice of a single currency peg.

PEGGING TO A SINGLE CURRENCY

Countries with trade that is highly concentrated in one currency area can gain from pegging to that currency area for two related reasons. First, pegging to the dominant trade currency will tend to minimise fluctuations in traded-good prices.[3] Second, the single peg achieves this stability with a minimum administrative cost and difficulty with public acceptance. Thus we expect small open economies, trade oriented to one major currency area, to peg to that currency.

The smaller ex-colonial countries with relatively undiversified economies and geographically concentrated trade are likely candidates for single-currency pegs. These are likely to be also relatively low-income countries. This presumption is supported by the data of Table 1, where we saw that the average GDP per capita of the countries with single-currency pegs is $0.5 thousand (1975), the lowest of the groups of countries given there.

To perform a preliminary test of the hypothesis that countries with concentrated trade who peg to a single currency, peg to that of the major trading partner, we have calculated the proportions of these countries' exports and imports allocated to each currency area. Countries were divided into groups according to the exchange rate regimes reported to the IMF in 1974. The five groups included countries pegging to the US dollar, the pound sterling, or the French franc; countries in the European snake; and countries allowing their exchange rate to float.

Using 1974 data from the *UN Yearbook of International Trade Statistics*, 1976, it was possible to calculate the percentage of exports to and imports from each of the five currency areas for a representative sample of countries. These are shown in Tables 2 and 3. To simplify calculations, 1974 data for the ten historically predominant export partners were used.[4] To the extent that the pattern of exports fluctuated during the 1970s, the percentage distribution of exports by currency area may be slightly understated. Currency areas which provided less than 5 per cent of the export market for a given country were excluded from the tables. This accounts for the large number of blanks.

TABLE 2
PERCENTAGE EXPORT SHARES BY CURRENCY BLOC IN 1974

Exporter	$	£	FFR	Snake	Float
$ peg					
Argentina	22.1	—	—	10.9	22.3
Bahamas	92.8	—	—	—	—
Burundi	32.5	—	—	42.8	5.5
Columbia	45.5	—	—	18.8	6.4
Costa Rica	57.9	—	—	21.1	6.5
Ethiopia	30.6	—	—	15.7	15.8
Guatemala	61.4	—	—	14.5	7.0
Haiti	68.6	—	8.3	12.5	7.3
Indonesia	22.6	—	—	—	62.2
Jordan	38.1	14.6	—	—	17.2
Kenya	10.1	11.3	—	25.6	8.0
Liberia	23.6	—	7.8	42.6	17.4
Nicaragua	43.4	—	—	19.8	13.7
Panama	73.3	—	—	12.3	6.5
Romania	—	—	—	9.7	5.3
Syrian Arab Republic	—	9.8	—	17.1	31.2
Thailand	12.5	—	—	10.8	38.5
Uganda	26.5	18.2	—	8.3	17.2
Venezuela	48.1	—	—	—	12.6
Western Samoa	13.9	6.0	—	33.0	43.5
£ peg					
Barbados	31.2	23.2	—	—	5.6
Ireland	9.1	56.4	—	14.4	—
Mauritius	18.4	35.3	—	—	37.2
Sierra Leone	5.7	63.9	—	20.1	6.8
FFR peg					
Central African Empire	11.5	—	45.4	10.3	19.8
Congo	—	—	49.0	9.9	26.8

TABLE 2 (*Continued*)

Exporter	$	£	*FFR*	*Snake*	*Float*
Ivory Coast	—	—	30.8	27.4	13.1
Niger	—	—	59.3	7.4	28.8
Togo	—	—	46.6	42.7	6.3
Snake					
Denmark	5.8	17.1	—	38.2	6.9
Germany	7.5	—	11.9	21.2	12.5
Netherlands	—	9.1	9.8	48.2	6.7
Sweden	5.3	13.2	5.2	36.3	10.1
Floaters					
Austria	—	6.4	—	26.6	14.7
Finland	—	18.9	—	36.3	—
Iceland	22.5	8.5	—	14.6	17.8
Japan	38.5	—	—	—	—
Malaysia	16.2	6.6	—	9.4	40.9
New Zealand	24.5	20.2	—	6.8	15.6
Singapore	25.8	—	—	—	28.0
Spain	11.7	9.1	12.6	19.2	10.6
Tunisia	16.3	—	21.7	6.6	36.6

TABLE 3
PERCENTAGE IMPORT SHARES BY CURRENCY BLOC IN 1974

Importer	$	£	*FFR*	*Snake*	*Float*
$ peg					
Argentina	39.5	—	—	10.8	16.3
Bahamas	64.5	—	—	—	16.8
Burundi	13.2	—	10.6	36.9	6.8
Columbia	41.6	—	—	9.1	17.0
Costa Rica	59.5	—	—	6.1	12.4
Ethiopia	13.8	7.8	—	14.3	28.5
Guatemala	63.1	—	—	8.2	9.0
Haiti	45.5	—	5.7	10.5	15.7
Indonesia	21.5	—	—	10.9	36.2
Jordan	22.2	7.7	—	9.3	15.8
Kenya	23.0	18.0	—	16.2	15.0
Liberia	46.8	9.4	—	17.6	5.4

TABLE 3 (*Continued*)

Importer	$	£	FFR	Snake	Float
Nicaragua	66.8	—	—	7.0	7.4
Panama	67.2	—	—	—	7.4
Romania	—	5.6	—	15.3	—
Syrian Arab Republic	6.3	—	8.8	12.1	20.1
Thailand	32.7	—	—	7.3	33.1
Uganda	—	30.9	—	16.0	17.4
Venezuela	49.5	—	—	11.5	19.4
Western Samoa	37.3	5.3	—	—	45.7
£ peg					
Barbados	32.1	32.3	—	5.2	13.5
Ireland	9.0	46.6	—	15.8	3.4
Mauritius	18.2	14.4	7.6	6.3	14.9
Sierra Leone	14.3	21.5	—	10.8	17.6
FFR peg					
Central African Empire	7.5	—	55.3	13.4	6.0
Congo	6.3	—	59.1	13.4	5.2
Ivory Coast	17.7	—	38.6	12.3	12.7
Niger	12.8	—	41.5	11.1	13.4
Togo	10.4	8.7	33.5	15.0	5.8
Snake					
Denmark	6.4	9.8	—	48.8	5.8
Germany	7.8	—	11.8	25.5	12.4
Netherlands	19.5	5.4	7.2	41.6	7.1
Sweden	6.6	11.1	—	42.2	8.5
Floaters					
Austria	6.7	—	—	45.8	—
Finland	5.1	8.5	—	39.8	—
Iceland	13.2	10.9	—	43.6	—
Japan	59.7	—	—	—	—
Malaysia	25.4	9.4	—	6.3	30.6
New Zealand	39.3	17.9	—	—	20.0
Singapore	33.7	—	—	—	31.1
Spain	31.5	—	8.5	14.0	7.6
Tunisia	14.9	—	31.0	13.1	12.6

As Tables 2 and 3 indicate, the trade data tend to support the hypothesis that the choice of a key currency is influenced by the geographical concentration of trade. Countries pegged to a key currency generally traded more with members of their own currency area than with members of other single-currency areas. Countries within the European Snake also concentrated their trade within their own currency area.

Nevertheless, there are some notable exceptions to the hypothesis of exchange rate regime choice. Although Romania and the Syrian Arab Republic have little trade with countries pegged to the US dollar, they have substantial export markets among the centrally planned economies that independently declare parties *vis-à-vis* the dollar; this would account for their pegs to the dollar.

It is difficult to rationalise membership in the dollar currency area for several Asian countries on the basis of export distribution. Indonesia, Thailand, and Western Samoa trade more heavily with Japan alone than with the US dollar area. However, in these cases political alliances and historical antipathies probably take precedence in the choice of a key currency.

A number of exchange rate regime changes which have occurred since 1974 are explained by previous trade patterns. In 1974 Barbados traded more with the dollar area than with the sterling area; by 1977 Barbados had switched to the US dollar as a key currency. In 1974 Argentina had a diversified export market in several currency areas with imports more concentrated on the dollar area; by 1977 Argentina had dropped the dollar standard and was maintaining a flexible exchange rate. Countries adopting the Special Drawing Right (SDR) as a currency peg since 1974 may have been motivated by trade factors. In 1974 the trade of Kenya and Western Samoa was not particularly concentratedd in the dollar area; by 1977 both countries had switched to a SDR peg. Although closely related to the dollar before 1971, the SDR exchange rate has since been determined by the basket of currencies pegged to it.

As expected, the trade of countries with flexible rates did not follow a pattern based on currency areas. It is also not surprising that exports for key currency countries were not concentrated in 'their' currency areas, since key currencies have flexible market-determined parities.

The data of Tables 2 and 3 are roughly consistent with the story of Figure 1 in Section II, that is, that geographical concentration of trade matters for the choice between (a) a joint or independent float, and (b) a single or composite peg. Countries with concentrated trade tend to choose a single peg or a joint float; these are in effect identical policy choices, since with the major currencies floating, a country that pegs to one of them joins the float with all other currencies pegging to that one.

The single-currency peg can be either fixed with $r = \bar{r}$, where r is the exchange rate in units of home currency per unit of the chosen *numeraire*, or adjustable. If movements in tastes, technology, etc., relative to the other members of the currency area, move the equilibrium value of r through time, then the single-currency peg could be moved gradually following a rule such as

$$\dot{r} = F(B); F' > 0; F(0) = 0, \tag{1}$$

where B is the relevant balance, perhaps current account or basic balance. This is a 'gliding parity' formula, as recently discussed by Kenen (1975). Some such managed adjustment relative to a single-currency peg has been chosen by many of the middle-income developing countries of Table 1.

PEGGING TO A CURRENCY BASKET

Countries which choose to (or must) peg, and have sufficiently diversified trade so that a single-currency peg is not appropriate, are left with the choice of a currency basket for the peg. Since 1973 a number of countries have turned to this option in the face of generalised floating of the major currencies. Pegging to a currency basket means stabilising the own-currency price of an arbitrarily chosen *numeraire* relative to an average of other currency prices of the *numeraire*. More formally, a fixed peg by country j to a currency basket defined over all other currencies $(i = 1, \ldots, J; i \neq j)$ is defined as

$$\dot{r}_j = - \sum_{i \neq j} w_i \dot{J}_i, \tag{2}$$

where:

$r_j = j$ currency units per unit of *numeraire* (assumed
here to be the US dollar);
$J_i = \$$ per unit of i currency;
$w_i = $ weight to be assigned to the i'th currency;
$\dot{x} = dx/x$, the proportional change in x, for any variable x.

The weights w_i are the weights assigned to movements in non-j currencies in terms of the *numeraire* in forming the currency basket. The rest of this paper is basically about how to choose the w_i. Since J_i is defined as dollars per i currency, while r_j is j currency per dollar, a minus sign enters equation (2). The integral of equation (2) gives the level of the exchange rate:

$$r_j = r_j^o \prod_{i \neq j} J_i^{-w_i} \tag{3}$$

The value r_j^o is the initial value of the index, or in mathematical terms the constant of integration from equation (2).

The fixed currency-basket peg rule in equation (2) gives the movement in the j currency price of the *numeraire* which holds the j currency constant against an average of all non-j currencies at the value given by r_j^o. Intervention to make r_j follow equation (2) could be in any of the non-j currencies if the markets maintain consistent cross-rates, but the natural intervention procedure would be to use the *numeraire*. Indeed, choice of *numeraire* might be dictated by which currency is most natural for intervention.

As in the case of the single-currency peg, the basket peg could be adjusted by a formula reflecting movement in the underlying equilibrium rate. A gliding basket peg, for example, could be defined by:

$$\dot{r} = -\sum w_i \dot{J}_i + G(B); \quad G' > 0; \quad G(0) = 0. \tag{4}$$

Here the home currency value of the *numeraire* is moved relative to the basket by a rule defined on the relevant balance.

POLICY TARGETS AND CHOICE OF WEIGHTS

For the country which does not float or peg to a single currency, choice of exchange-rate regime reduces to choice of the weights w_i (implicitly or explicitly) for the basket peg. On what principles can this choice be made?

The w_i will determine the effects of third country (non-j and non-*numeraire*) exchange-rate movements $\dot{J}_i$ on important variables such as the terms of trade (p_x/p_m), the relative price of traded and non-traded goods (p_T/p_N), and the balance of trade (BT) of country j. As the Deutschmark–dollar rate moves, for example, p_x/p_m, p_T/p_N, and BT of, say, Argentina will all normally be influenced. As we see in the next section of the paper, weights can be chosen that minimise the influence of $\dot{J}_i$ on each of these, and other, policy targets.

More precisely, we can solve for the sets of weights for a basket peg that will eliminate the effects of third-country exchange-rate changes J_i on each of the policy variables. To each target variable corresponds a different set of weights. Of course, if we use the weights eliminating the influence of $\dot{J}_i$ on p_T/p_N, for example, this will imply a predictable effect on p_x/p_m and on BT, and symmetrically for the choice of ay other particular set of weights. So the choice of weights will come down to the choice of policy targets.

We should point out explicitly here that in choosing weights we are eliminating the influence of $\dot{J}_i$ on the policy target chosen, *not* stabilising that variable altogether. There will be other influences than $\dot{J}_i$ on those variables, in general; choice of weights for the basket peg eliminates just one source of instability.

In Section IV we lay out the menu, deriving the weighting scheme for each of the three targets mentioned, and showing the general method for deriving weights, given a target. Then in Section V we discuss choice among targets as their instability generates instability in income; this suggests one way to choose among the menu items.

IV WEIGHTS FOR CURRENCY BASKETS

In the previous two sections of the paper, we have narrowed the questions of choice of exchange-rate regimes for an important class of developing countries down to the question of the choice of weights for a basket peg. The next step is to show the derivation of different optimal sets of weights corresponding to different policy targets, minimising the effects of third-country exchange-rate variation on (a) the terms of trade, (b) the relative price of traded *vs.* non-traded goods, (c) the balance of trade. To do this we decompose fluctuations in export and import prices into their components, namely fluctuations in (a) world-market demand prices for exports and supply prices for imports, (b) home supply prices for exports and demand prices for imports, and (c) exchange rates. We do the decomposition in a log-linear supply-and-demand model for one country j in a many-country ($i = 1, \ldots, I$) world, allowing for the possibility of the existence of market power. The small country facing infinite demand elasticity for its exports and supply elasticity for its imports will be treated as a special case. We begin with a model in which there is one export good and one import good, and the country j faces a unified world market. Disaggregation by commodity or trading partners should follow easily. Then we extend this model to include variations in all exchange rates in the system. This model can then be solved for the weighting schemes that meet our alternative policy targets.

A LOG-LINEAR MODEL OF MOVEMENTS IN TRADE PRICES AND QUANTITIES

To relate exchange-rate changes to movements in export and import prices and quantities, we use a simple log-linear supply-and-demand model that includes the exchange rate as the translator between prices in home currency p and prices in foreign exchange q. The model follows, for example, Sohmen (1969, Chapter 4). A listing of symbols and definitions used in this section is given in Table 4.

TABLE 4
SYMBOLS AND DEFINITIONS IN THE TRADE MODEL OF SECTION IV

i = index over I countries, $i = 1, \ldots I$. we study the jth country.

p_x, p_m = home (jth) country prices of exports and imports.

q_x, q_m = foreign exchange (\$) prices of jth country exports and imports

d_x, s_x = price-elasticities of export demand and supply in j.

$k = d_x/(d_x - s_x)$, an inverse index of export market power of j.

d_m, s_m = price-elasticities of import demand and supply of j.

$k' = s_m/(s_m - d_m)$, and inverse index of import market power of j.

π = terms of trade of j: $\pi \equiv p_x/p_m$

e = exchange rate of j in aggregate model: units of j currency per unit of foreign exchange; $p = eq$.

X, M = export and import quantities of j.

T_i = units of j currency per unit of i currency

J_i = units of *numeraire* (\$) per unit of i currency

r = units of j currency per unit of *numeraire* (\$); $T_i = J_i - r$.

α_i, β_i = j's export and import weights.

w_i = weights for j's basket peg.

$\dot{Z} = dZ/Z$, for any variable Z.

Export price movements

We assume that export supply prices are stated in home currency units, p_x, while demand prices are stated in foreign exchange units q_x. The exchange rate e links p_x to q_x. The supply function is written as

$$\ln p_x = \ln p_x^o + s_x^{-1} \ln X \tag{5}$$

Here p_x^o is a vertical shift parameter which can represent changes in domestic supply conditions, s_x is the price elasticity of supply, and X is the quantity exported. The demand function for exports, priced in foreign exchange units, is

$$\ln q_x = \ln q_x^o + d_x^{-1} \ln X \tag{6}$$

q_x^o is a vertical shift parameter which can represent changes in world market conditions, and d_x is the price elasticity of demand. To translate demand into home currency units, we use the relationship

$$p_x = eq_x, \text{ or } \ln p_x = \ln e + \ln q_x, \tag{7}$$

where e is the exchange rate in units of home currency per unit of foreign exchange. Substitution of $(\ln p_x - \ln e)$ for $\ln q_x$ in equation (7) gives export demand in home currency units,

$$\ln p_x = \ln q_x^o + d_x^{-1} \ln X + \ln e \tag{8}$$

We can now combine the supply function in equation (5)—and the demand function (8)—to solve for market equilibrium p_x and X, and then use equation (7) to get q. The total differentials of equation (5) and (8) are

$$\dot{p}_x - s_x^{-1} \dot{X} = \dot{p}_x^o, \text{ and} \tag{5'}$$

$$\dot{p}_x - d_x^{-1} \dot{X} = \dot{q}_x^o + \dot{e}. \tag{8'}$$

In matrix form we have

$$\begin{bmatrix} 1 & -s_x^{-1} \\ 1 & -d_x^{-1} \end{bmatrix} \begin{pmatrix} \dot{p}_x \\ \dot{X} \end{pmatrix} = \begin{bmatrix} 1 & 0 & 0 \\ 0 & 1 & 1 \end{bmatrix} \begin{pmatrix} \dot{p}_x^o \\ \dot{q}_x^o \\ \dot{e} \end{pmatrix} \tag{9}$$

The solutions for $\dot{X}$ and $\dot{p}_x$ are given by

$$\dot{p}_x = \frac{d_x}{d_x - s_x} (\dot{q}_x^o + \dot{e}) - \frac{s}{d_x - s_x} \dot{p}_x^o; \tag{10}$$

$$\dot{X} = \frac{s_x d_x}{d_x - s_x} \{ (\dot{q}_x^o + \dot{e}) - \dot{p}_x^o \} \tag{11}$$

We will write the equation for $\dot{p}_x$ as

$$\dot{p}_x = k(\dot{q}_x^o + \dot{e}) + (1 - k)\dot{p}_x^o. \tag{12}$$

Here k is defined as

$$k = \frac{d_x}{d_x - s_x} = \frac{1}{1 - \dfrac{s_x}{d_x}}; \quad 0 < k \le 1.$$

In equation (12) $\dot{p}_x$ is expressed as a weighted average of external and internal disturbances, with the weights given by k. We can use k as an index of market power on the export side. In the small-country case where $d_x \to -\infty$, k approaches unity. As d_x rises from $-\infty$ (demand becomes less than perfectly elastic), k falls from unity.

In the small-country case where $d_x = -\infty$ and $k = 1$, equation (12) reduces to:

$$\dot{p}_x = \dot{q}_x^o + \dot{e} \qquad (13)$$

Export prices are affected only by shifts in world market prices q_x^o and the exchange rate e. With market power, fluctuations in home-currency export prices are smaller than movements in q_x^o or e, by the factor of k.

Import price movements

Since the model for movements in the import price $\dot{p}_m$ is analogous to the model of the export market, we can develop the import side more briefly. Import supply is given in terms of foreign exchange prices:

$$\ln q_m = \ln q_m^o + s_m^{-1} \ln M. \qquad (14)$$

The translation between p_m and q_m is $p_m = eq_m$, so in home currency prices import supply is:

$$\ln p_m = \ln q_m^o + s_m^{-1} \ln M + \ln e. \qquad (15)$$

Import demand, in home-currency terms, is:

$$\ln p_m = \ln p_m^o + d_m^{-1} \ln M. \qquad (16)$$

Total differentiation of equations (15) and (16) gives us the matrix equation:

$$\begin{bmatrix} 1 & -s_m^{-1} \\ 1 & -d_m^{-1} \end{bmatrix} \begin{pmatrix} \dot{p}_m \\ \dot{M} \end{pmatrix} = \begin{bmatrix} 0 & 1 & 1 \\ 1 & 0 & 0 \end{bmatrix} \begin{pmatrix} \dot{p}_m^o \\ \dot{q}_m^o \\ \dot{e} \end{pmatrix}. \qquad (17)$$

The solutions for $\dot{p}_m$ and $\dot{M}$ are:

$$\dot{p}_m = \frac{s_m}{s_m - d_m}(\dot{q}_m^o + \dot{e}) - \frac{d_m}{s_m - d_m}\dot{p}_m^o; \qquad (18)$$

$$\dot{M} = \frac{s_m d_m}{s_m - d_m}\{(\dot{q}_m^o + \dot{e}) - p_m^o\}. \qquad (19)$$

We will write the equation for $\dot{p}_m$ as

$$\dot{p}_m = k'(\dot{q}_m^o + \dot{e}) + (1 - k')\dot{p}_m^o. \qquad (20)$$

On the import side, we define k' as:

$$k' \equiv \frac{s_m}{s_m - d_m} = \frac{1}{1 - \dfrac{d_m}{s_m}}; \quad 0 < k' \leq 1.$$

We can use k' as an index of market power on the import side. In the small-country case where $s_m \to \infty$, k' goes to unity. To the extent that the country has market power, s_m and k' become smaller. Thus k' is an inverse index of market power on the import side.

Again, in the small-country case where $s_m = \infty$ and $k' = 1$, equation (18) reduces to:

$$\dot{p}_m = \dot{q}_m^o + \dot{e}. \tag{21}$$

DISAGGREGATION TO MANY COUNTRIES $(i = 1, \ldots, I)$

In a world of floating exchange rates, movements in any rate will influence trade prices of all countries. Thus to study the effects of exchange rate changes on p_x and p_m, we should expand the model to include many countries, each defined as a separate currency unit. The extension will allow us to study exchange rate policies that minimise the effects of fluctuations in exchange rates on the terms of trade, relative prices of traded and non-traded goods, or the balance of trade.

In disaggregating the model, we will consider a world of I countries, $i = 1, \ldots, I$, and focus on the terms of trade of the j'th country, which we will call the 'home country'. The home country faces $I - 1$ exchange rates T_i ($=$ units of j currency per unit of i currency). It will be convenient to single out a *numeraire*, which we will call the dollar, and to define J_i as the dollar price of each ith currency, and r as the jth currency price of the dollar. Then we can decompose movements of T_i as follows:

$$T_i = J_i r, \quad \text{or} \quad \ln T_i = \ln J_i + \ln r,$$

and

$$\dot{T}_i = \dot{J}_i + \dot{r}. \tag{22}$$

Now in place of the single $\dot{e}$, $\dot{q}_x^o$, and $\dot{q}_m^o$ in equations (12) and (20) for $\dot{p}_x$ and $\dot{p}_m$, we have weighted averages of movements in all the exchange rates $\dot{T}_i$ and weighted averages of the shift factors $\dot{q}_{xi}^o$ and $\dot{q}_{mi}^o$.

On the export side, in place of equation (12), we have the weighted average equation:

$$\dot{p}_x = k \sum_{i \neq j} \alpha_i \ \dot{T}_i + k \sum_{\neq j} \alpha_i \ \dot{q}^o_{xi} + (1-k)\dot{p}^o_x. \tag{23}$$

Here α_i are export-share weights with the properties $\alpha_i \geq 0$; $\Sigma\alpha = 1$. In place of the single $\dot{e}$ of equation (12) we have a weighted average $\Sigma\alpha_i \dot{T}_i$, and in place of $\dot{q}^o_x$ we have $\Sigma\alpha_i\dot{q}^0_{xi}$ in equation (23).

Similarly, in place of equation (20) for $\dot{p}_m$ we now have

$$\dot{p}_m = k' \sum_{i \neq j} \beta_i\dot{T}_i + k' \sum_{i \neq j} \beta_i \dot{q}^o_{mi} + (1-k)\dot{p}^o_m \tag{24}$$

On the import side the single $\dot{e}$ of equation (20) is replaced by an import-weighted average $\Sigma\beta_i \dot{T}_i$, and similarly for $\dot{q}^o_m$. Equations (23) and (24) assume that d_x and s_m are the same for all trading partners. We could further disaggregate by making the market-power terms k and k' weighted averages combining country-by-country d_x and s_m elasticities. How to do this further extension is clear, but would unnecessarily complicate the story here.

Thus far, equations (23) and (24) are simply the weighted-average versions of equations (12) and (18). The more interesting step is to break $\dot{T}_i$ in these equations into $\dot{J}_i$ and $\dot{r}$. This will be the key to our solutions for optimal basket weights. Replacing $\dot{T}_i$ by $(\dot{J}_i + \dot{r})$ in equation (23) and noting that $\Sigma\alpha_i = 1$, we have for $\dot{p}_x$,

$$\dot{p}_x = k\dot{r} + k \sum_{i \neq j} \alpha_i \dot{J}_i + k \sum_{i \neq j} \alpha_i\dot{q}^o_{xi} + (1-k)\dot{p}^o_x. \tag{25}$$

Similarly for $\dot{p}_m$ we have

$$\dot{p}_m = k'\dot{r} + k' \sum_{i \neq j} \alpha_i \dot{J}_i + k' \sum_{i \neq j} \alpha_i\dot{q}^o_{mi} + (1-k')\dot{p}^o_m. \tag{26}$$

The first terms in equations (25) and (26) give the effect of the home-currency price of the *numeraire*, the second the effect of other countries' exchange rates, the third the effect of world market price disturbances, and the fourth the effect of home price disturbances, in moving export and import prices of the home-country j.

TERMS-OF-TRADE WEIGHTS

The terms of trade is defined as $\pi = p_x/p_m$. Thus we can combine equations (25) and (26) to obtain the expression for $\dot{\pi}$.

$$\dot{\pi} = \left\{ (k - k')\dot{r} + k \sum_{i \neq j} \alpha_i \dot{J}_i - k' \sum_{i \neq j} \beta_i \dot{J}_i \right\} \tag{27}$$

$$+ \left\{ k \sum_{i \neq j} \alpha_i \dot{q}^o_{xi} k' \sum_{i \neq j} \beta_i \dot{q}^o_{mi} \right\}$$

$$+ \left\{ (1 - k)\dot{p}^o_x - (1 - k')\dot{p}^o_m \right\}$$

The first bracketed term gives the influence of exchange-rate movements on the terms of trade broken into changes in the home currency price of the dollar $\dot{r}$ and the dollar prices of the other currencies $\dot{J}$. The second bracketed term gives the effects of shifts in export demand or import supply conditions in all the non-j countries. The last term gives effects of changes in domestic market conditions.

It is worth noting two properties of equation (27) for $\dot{\pi}$:

(1) Pegging to the dollar, or to any other *numeraire*, would eliminate $\dot{r}$ from equation (27), but fluctuations in the dollar price of other (non-j) currencies would still move π through J.

(2) For the small country, (27) reduces to

$$\dot{\pi} = \Sigma \alpha_i (\dot{J}_i + \dot{q}^o_{xi}) - \Sigma \beta_i (\dot{J}_i + \dot{q}^o_{mi}).$$

Fluctuations in the jth currency price of the *numeraire* disappear since $k = k'$ but π is still moved by J, q^o_x, and q^o_m.

The first bracketed term in equation (27) gives the effect of variations in exchange rates on the terms of trade. Choosing weights for a basket peg means selecting the weights w_i with the minimal property that $\Sigma w_i = 1$ for the formula $\dot{r} = -\Sigma w_i \dot{J}_i$, which makes $\Sigma \dot{T}_i = 0$.[5] Clearly from equation (27) the choice of a formula for $\dot{r}$ intending to minimise $\dot{\pi}$ is relevant only for countries with asymmetric market power. If $k = k'$, $\dot{r}$ falls out of the π equation. So the question of optimal choice of weights to minimise variations in the terms of trade arises only for countries with asymmetric market power.

Two obvious possibilities for weights are export shares α_i or import shares β_i.[6] If we set $\dot{r} = -\Sigma \alpha_i \dot{J}_i$ using export weights, the first term in equation (27) reduces to $k'\Sigma (\alpha_i - \beta_i)\dot{J}_i$. If we set $\dot{r} = -\Sigma \beta_i \dot{J}_i$ using import weights the same term reduces to $k\Sigma (\alpha_i - \beta_i)\dot{J}_i$. Thus if $k < k'$, that is market power is greater on the export side, import weights will reduce terms-of-trade fluctuations better than would export weights, and vice versa. Market power in the form of a small value for k or k' dampens the effect of disturbances onto the terms of trade, so the weights that eliminate disturbances where market power is smallest ($k \to 1$) are more effective. In Table 1 we saw that it is the middle-income countries that manage their rates or use basket pegs. Further, in Branson and Papaefstratiou (1978) we present evidence that many of these countries have market power on the export side, and that asymmetric market power and pegging to a currency basket are positively correlated. We are not limited to export or import weights, however. Assume for the moment that the $\dot{q}^o$ and $\dot{p}^o$ terms in equation (27) are zero. Then for $\dot{\pi}$ we have

$$\dot{\pi} = (k - k')\dot{r} + k \sum_{i \neq j} \alpha_i \dot{J}_i - k' \sum_{i \neq j} \beta_i \dot{J}_i \qquad (27')$$

Setting $\dot{r} = -\Sigma w_i \dot{J}_i$, with w_i to be determined, makes this expression

$$\dot{\pi} = (k' - k) \sum_{i \neq j} w_i \dot{J}_i + k \sum_{i \neq j} \alpha_i \dot{J}_i - k' \sum_{i \neq j} \beta_i \dot{J}_i \qquad (27'')$$

$$= \sum_{i \neq j} \left\{ (k' - k)w_i + k\alpha_i - k'\beta_i \right\} \dot{J}_i.$$

Changes in the terms of trade now are a weighted average of $\dot{J}_i$, with weights given by the bracketed term in equation (27''). To eliminate the effect of changes in exchange rates on the terms of trade, choose the weights w_i that make the total weights in equation (27'') zero;

$$0 = \left\{ (k' - k)w_i + k\alpha_i - k'\beta_i \right\}.$$

The solution is[7]

$$w_i = \frac{k\alpha_i - k'\beta_i}{k - k'}. \qquad (28)$$

Since $\Sigma \alpha_i = \Sigma \beta_i = 1$, $\Sigma w_i = 1$. But there is no constraint that all $w_i > 0$. In a 'typical' case of market power on the export side only, so $k < 1$, $k' = 1$, the weighting formula reduces to

$$w_i = \frac{\beta_i - k\alpha_i}{1 - k}.$$

Currencies with relatively large export shares α_i might have negative weights!

We emphasise that the weighting scheme—equation (28)—depends on three assumptions: (a) the country in question has asymmetric market power so that exchange policy can influence the terms of trade, (b) the objective of pegging is to minimise fluctuations in the terms of trade, and

(c) a decision has been made to peg to a basket. Violation of any of these assumptions makes the weighting scheme—equation (28)—irrelevant.

WEIGHTS STABILISING THE PRICE OF TRADED GOODS

An alternative weighting scheme would be one eliminating the effects of $\dot{J}_i$ on the domestic price of traded goods p_T or its ratio to the price of non-traded goods p_N. This is the weighting criterion suggested by Black (1976a) and Crockett and Nsouli (1977), among others.

Movements in the home-currency prices of traded goods are given by:

$$\dot{p}_T = z_x \dot{p}_x + z_m \dot{p}_m$$

where z_x is the proportion of exportable goods and z_m is the proportion of importables in tradeable output.[8] We are, again, searching for weghts for $\dot{r}$ that eliminate the effects of $\dot{J}_i$ on p_T, not attempting to stabilise p_T in the face of shifts in world market prices or domestic market conditions. So we substitute the first two terms in equations (25) and (26) for $\dot{p}_x$ and $\dot{p}_m$ into equation (29) to obtain

$$\dot{p}_T = (z_x k + z_m k')\dot{r} + z_x k \sum \alpha_i \dot{J}_i + z_m k' \sum \beta_i \dot{J}_i. \tag{30}$$

In general, we assume that the objective is to maintain $\dot{p}_T = \dot{p}_N$, with an exogenous factor moving $\dot{p}_N$. We will see that the solution for $\dot{p}_T = 0$ is a special case. Set $\dot{p}_T$ in equation (30) equal to the exogenous $\dot{p}_N$ and solve for $\dot{r}$:

$$\dot{r} = -\sum w_i \dot{J}_i + \frac{1}{z_x k + z_m k'} \dot{p}_N, \tag{31}$$

where the weights w_i are given by

$$w_i = \frac{z_x k \alpha_i + z_m k' \beta_i}{z_x k + z_m k'}. \tag{32}$$

These are the weights which eliminate the effect of $\dot{J}_i$ on p_T.

In the small-country case, the weights become

$$w_i = z_x \alpha_i + z_m \beta_i,$$

and the formula for $\dot{r}$ reduces to

$$\dot{r} = -\sum w_i \dot{J}_i + \dot{p}_N. \tag{33}$$

This is Black's (1976a) preferred weighting scheme.

Equations (31) and (32) give the weights for a currency basket on the assumption that the objective of the choice of weights is to eliminate the effects of $\dot{J}_i$ on the relative price of traded *vs.* non-traded goods.

BALANCE OF TRADE WEIGHTS

The third weighting objective we consider is elimination of third-country exchange rate fluctuations $\dot{J}_i$ on the current-account balance. This will give us a set of weights similar to the IMF MERM weights.[9]
The trade balance (or, at this level of generality, the balance on current account) in home currency is given by

$$BT = p_x X - p_m M. \tag{34}$$

If we set $q_x = p_m = 1$ initially, differentiation of equation (34) yields

$$dBT = (\dot{p}_x + \dot{X})X_o - (\dot{p}_m + \dot{M})M_o,$$

where X_o and M_o are initial values. Substitution for $\dot{p}_x$, $\dot{X}$, $\dot{p}_m$, $\dot{M}$ from equations (10), (11), (18) and (19) yields

$$dBT = \left\{ \frac{d_x(1+s_x)}{d_x - s_x}X_o - \frac{s_m(1+d_m)}{s_m - d_m}M_o \right\} \dot{e}$$

for the effect of a change in the exchange rate on the trade balance. The bracketed term is simply the Marshall–Lerner condition, which we will write more compactly as

$$dBT = \{k(1+s_x)X_o - k'(1+d_m)M_o\}\dot{e}, \tag{35}$$

where k and k' are the market-power indices developed earlier.
We now disaggregate $\dot{e}$ into the weighted averages of $\dot{T}_i$, and decompose $\dot{T}_i$ into $(\dot{J}_i + \dot{r})$. This yields the disaggregated equation for the change in the trade balance,

$$dBT = \{k(1+s_x)X_o - k'(1+d_m)M_o\}\dot{r} + k(1+s_x)X_o\sum \alpha_i \dot{J}_i$$

$$- k'(1+d_m)M_o\sum \beta_i \dot{J}_i. \tag{36}$$

It is worth noting that, in equation (36), movements in the exchange rate $\dot{r}$ influence the balance of trade even in the case of symmetric market power when $k = k'$. This occurs because of quantity effects, expressed by $(1+s_x)$ and $(1+d_m)$ in equation (36). If we now let $\dot{r} = -\sum w_i \dot{J}_i$, and solve for the weights w_i that set $dBT = 0$, we obtain for the balance of trade weights

$$w_i = \frac{X_o k(1+s_x)\alpha_i - M_o k'(1+d_m)\beta_i}{X_o k(1+s_x) - M_o k'(1+d_m)}. \tag{37}$$

These are analogous to the MERM weights. If trade is roughly balanced so $X_o = M_o$, and quantity effects are removed by setting s_x and d_m equal to zero, the weights of equation (37) are identical to the terms-of-trade weights of equation (28). This could be the case, for example, of a developing country exporting perishable agricultural goods and importing non-substitutable intermediate goods.

ADJUSTMENT OF THE BASKET PEG

It is important to remember the limited, if important, role of the weighting schemes just discussed. They only eliminate the effects of fluctuations of third-currency exchange rates, $\dot{J}_i$, on the relevant target variables for the home country. Simply pegging the price of the *numeraire* to any of these currency baskets will clearly not maintain external balance in almost all cases. Only in countries that are very open, so that movement of the nominal exchange rate does not affect the real rate, but have diversified trade, so pegging to a single currency is inappropriate, will simply pegging to a currency basket suffice for external balance.

In most countries, maintenance of external balance will require movement of the exchange rate relative to the currency basket from time to time. This adjustment could be achieved by a gliding parity of the form

$$\dot{r} = -\sum w_i \dot{J}_i + G(B),$$

suggested in Section III. We re-emphasise this point here in order not to leave the impression that the basket pegs described here can do more than eliminate the effects of variation in J_i on the chosen policy target.

V   CHOICE OF TARGETS

In the previous sections we looked at a number of alternative targets for exchange rate policy and derived weights for basket pegs which eliminate the effects of third-country exchange-rate movements (J_i) on the home country's terms of trade, on the price ratio of its non-traded *vs.* its traded goods or on its balance of trade.

Up to now attainment of each of the above targets has been considered in isolation with no regard paid to the possible tradeoffs or costs associated with each policy; yet, to give an example, a policy to eliminate the effects of J_i movements on a country's terms of trade through the appropriate choice of weights for its basket peg will probably be inconsistent with stabilisation of the relative price ratio of traded to non-traded goods. It is thus important to consider the possible tradeoffs associated with the pursuit of each of the targets described above as well as to attempt to isolate those structural characteristics of the economy, such as the degree of openness, which will dictate the target choice.

Since relative price fluctuations contribute significantly to income instability, we can use the latter as the ultimate objective of target choice. This has also been prompted by a number of additional factors. It has been shown (Mathieson and McKinnon, 1974, Branson and Papaefstratiou, 1978) that less-developed countries have traditionally experienced greater fluctuations in their real GNP than developed countries have, and that the properly measured welfare loss from a given degree of instability is expected to be greater the lower is the level of per capita income (Branson and Papaefstratiou 1978). In addition, terms-of-trade fluctuations have been shown to be more significant in the case of countries with low income per capita (Branson and Papaefstratiou, 1978) and thus an important source of income instability.

Let us assume then that, in the simplest of cases, domestic production in the economy consists of production of exportables (X^s), importables (M^s) and non-traded goods (H^s). Then, in the absence of intermediate goods, the total value of production will be equal to consumption plus saving or,

$$p_h H^s + p_x X^s + p_m M^s = Y = C + S = p_h H^d + p_x X^d$$
$$+ p_m M^d + p_m M + p_x{}^X - p_m^M \tag{38}$$

It is assumed here that some of the domestic production of exportables is consumed domestically ($p_x X^d$) and some is exported ($p_x X$) while the demand for importables is partly satisfied through domestic production ($p_m M^d = \mathrm{p}_m M^s$) and partly through imports ($p_m M$). It follows that total domestic consumption (C) is equal to,

$$C = p_h H^d + p_x X^d + p_m (M^d + M), \tag{39}$$

and that the consumer price index (p_c) can be defined as a weighted average of p_h, p_x and p_m. Thus

$$p_c = p_h \frac{H^d}{C} + p_x \frac{X^d}{C} + p_m \frac{M^d + M}{C}, \text{ and} \tag{40}$$

$$\dot{p}_c = w_1 \dot{p}_h + w_2 \dot{p}_x + w_3 \dot{p}_m; \sum w_i = 1. \tag{40'}$$

The weights in (40'), which represent the ratio of expenditures on each type of good to total consumption expenditures, are assumed constant in the short run.

Given equations (38) and (40), real income can be defined as the total value of production deflated by the CPI and thus is given by

$$\dot{Y} = \frac{Y}{p_c} = \frac{p_h}{p_c}H^s + \frac{p_x}{p_c}X^s + \frac{p_m}{p_c}M^s. \tag{41}$$

Differentiating (41) totally and making the appropriate substitutions using (40′) in the process, we can express the percentage change in income as a weighted average of relative price fluctuations:

$$\dot{y} = (\dot{p}_h - \dot{p}_x)\{w_2 . Eyh - w_1 . Eyx\} \tag{42}$$

$$+ (\dot{p}_h - \dot{p}_m)\{w_3 . Eyh - w_1 . Eym\}$$

$$+ (\dot{p}_x - \dot{p}_m)\{w_3 . Eyx - w_1 . Eym\}$$

In equation (42) the terms in parentheses are elasticity weights where Eyi, $i = x, m, h$ is the elasticity of total output (y) with respect to the relevant relative price change.

$$Eyi = \frac{dy/y}{d(p_i/p_c)/p_i/p_c}, \; Eyi \geq 0.[10]$$

From equation (42) we can weigh and evaluate the effects of different stabilisation schemes on income instability. If the aim of exchange rate policy is to eliminate the effects of third-country exchange rate movements on the terms of trade so that in the absence of other disturbances, $p_x = p_m$, then income fluctuations can be attributed to fluctuations in the price of traded commodities relative to those of non-traded goods.

In that case,

$$\dot{y} = (\dot{p}_h - \dot{p}_T)\{Eyh - w_1(Eyh + Eyx + Eym)\}. \tag{43}$$

If, on the other hand, the aim of policy is to eliminate the effects of $\dot{J}_i$ on average prices of traded goods, then income fluctuations will partly depend on terms-of-trade fluctuations weighted again by different elasticities. Thus, in the absence of other disturbances, if $\dot{p}_h = \dot{p}_x$,

$$\dot{y} = (\dot{p}_x - \dot{p}_m)\{-Eym + w_3(Eyh + Eyx + Eym)\}, \tag{44}$$

while if $\dot{p}_h = \dot{p}_m$,

$$\dot{y} = (\dot{p}_x - \dot{p}_m)\{Eyx - w_2(Eyh + Eyx + Eym)\}. \tag{45}$$

Thus policy which eliminates the effects of exchange-rate instability on one of the target variables will not eliminate income instability. The magnitude of the residual instability depends on the elasticity parameters and the effects of exchange rate instability on the other relative prices.

As far as the actual target choice is concerned, the following general observations can be made:

(1) If $\dot{p}_h$ is either small or independent of $\dot{p}_x$ and $\dot{p}_m$, then, *ceteris paribus*, the natural target for policy is terms-of-trade stabilisation. The same would hold true if the non-traded good sector itself is small.

(2) In the case where the composition of a country's exports and imports is similar so that fluctuations in the price of exportables as a result of exchange rate instability is roughly equal to that of importables, policies that minimise the fluctuations in p_h/p_T will also tend to minimise the fluctuations in real income.

(3) If, on the other hand, trade composition on the export and import sides is dissimilar, then exchange rate policy can focus on either $\dfrac{p_h}{p_x}$ or $\dfrac{p_h}{p_m}$. In that case, and if the overall objective of policy is the reduction of real income instability, the choice of target will be based on the relative magnitudes of w_2 and w_3, that is the degree of openness of the economy on the export and import side as well as the relative magnitudes of the income elasticities Eyx and Eym.

In conclusion, it is important to stress that what has been attempted in this paper is to sort out the policies that insulate an economy from random variations in third-country exchange rates. Even in the pursuit of this limited objective, one can see how important are the structural characteristics of the economy as determinants both of the target choice as well as of actual policy design. These results confirm, for us, the importance of consideration of differing structural characteristics across countries in analysis and design of macroeconomic policy in general.

ENDNOTES

1. In Black's model, for example, the external balance (TT) curve will become steeper than the internal balance (NN) curve as the short-run price elasticity of the excess demand goes toward zero, and the system becomes unstable.
2. See Heller (1976), Table 8 and p. 15.
3. In the basket-peg formula for PT below, equation (32), if at the limit α and β

for a particular i go to unity, the weight for that i is one, that is, a single-currency peg to i.
4. 1974 is the latest year directions of trade are available in UN statistics for all countries in the sample.
5. Note that since r is the home currency price of the *numeraire* and J_i is the numeraire price of the ith currency, we need the minus sign.
6. See Black (1976b), Crockett and Nsouli (1977), Artus and Rhomberg (1973) for discussion of choice of weights. Note that the discussion of weights for measuring changes in effective exchange rates has a different objective from ours. There the purpose is to choose the weights that translate a vector of arbitrary changes J_i into the uniform change r that would have the same effect on the balance of payments. Here we are choosing w_i to minimise the effect of J_i on the terms of trade.
7. Originally we set up the choice of weight problem as minimising the variance of π, after integrating equation (27) to get the expression for π. In that problem the J_i were random variables. The solution, worked out by Dennis Warner, was exactly equation (28). It was only after we saw the solution and observed it makes variance (π) zero, that James Healy noted that the w_i solution comes by inspection from equation (27).
8. If x is exportables and m importables, $z_x = p_x x / p_T (x + m)$, and $z_m = p_m m / p_T (x + m)$.
9. See Artus and Rhomberg (1973) for a discussion of the Multilateral Exchange Rate Model (MERM).
10. Here we assume that the nominal wage is rigid in the short run.

REFERENCES

Artus, J. R., 'Foreign Exchange Rate Stability and Managed Floating: The Experience of the Federal Republic of Germany', International Monetary Fund Staff Papers 23, no. 2 (July 1976).

Artus, J. R. and Rhomberg, R. R., 'A Multilateral Exchange Rate Model', IMF Staff Papers 20 (1973).

Black, S. W., 'Exchange Rate Policies for Less Developed Countries in a World of Floating Rates', Princeton Essays in International Finance 119 (1976a).

Black, S. W., 'Multilateral and Bilateral Effect Exchange Rates in a World Model of Traded Goods', *Journal of Political Economy* 84, no. 3 (1976b).

Branson, W. H., 'Asset Markets and Relative Prices in Exchange Rate Determination', *Sozialwissenschaftliche Annalen*, Band 1 (1977).

Branson, W. H., Halttunen, H. and Masson, P., 'Exchange Rates in the Short-run: The Dollar–Deutschmark Rate', *European Economic Review* (December, 1977).

Branson, W. H. and Katseli-Papaefstratiou L., 'Income Instability, Terms of Trade, and the Choice of Exchange Rate Regime', mimeo (1978).

Corden, W. M., 'Monetary Integration', Princeton Essays in International Finance, no. 93 (1972).

Crockett, A. D., and Nsouli S. M., 'Exchange Rate Policies for Developing Countries', *Journal of Development Studies* 13, no. 2 (1977).

Dornbusch, R., 'Expectations and Exchange Rate Dynamics', *Journal of Political Economy* 84, no. 6 (1976).

Dornbusch, R. and Krugman, P., 'Flexible Exchange rates in the Short Run', Brookings Papers on Economic Activity 3 (1976).

Heller, H. R., 'The Choice of an Exchange Rate Regime: Theory and Practice', unpublished document (International Monetary Fund, 1976).

Intertnational Monetary Fund Annual Report (Washington DC, 1975, 1977).

Ishiyama, Y., 'The Theory of Optimum Currency Areas: A Survey', IMF Staff Papers 22 (1975).

Kenen, P. B., 'Floats, Glides, and Indicators: a Comparison of Methods for Changing Exchange Rates', *Journal of International Economics* 5, no. 2 (1975).

Klein, L. R., 'Comment', Brookings Papers on Economic Activity (1972).

Kouri, P. J. K., 'The Exchange Rate and the Balance of Payments in the Short Run and in the Long Run: A Monetary approach', *Scandinavian Journal of Economics* 2 (1976).

Lewis, W. A., 'The Less Developed Countries and Stable Exchange Rates', in the International Monetary System in Operation, International Monetary Fund Per Jacobsson lectures (1972).

Mathieson, D. J. and McKinnon, R. I., 'Instability in Underdeveloped Countries: The Impact of the International Economy', in David, P., and Reder, M. (eds.), *Nations and Households in Economic Growth* (Academic Press, 1974).

McKinnon, R. I., 'Optimum currency areas', *American Economic Review* 53 (1963).

Sohmen, E., *Flexible Exchange Rates* (University of Chicago Press, 1969).

Stern, R. M., Francis, J. and Schumacher, B., *Price Elasticities in International Trade, An Annotated Bibliography* (Trade Policy Research Centre, London, 1976).

United Nations, *International Compensation for Fluctuations in Commodity Trade* (1961).

World Bank, *Atlas* (Washington, DC, 1976).

Comments

Stanislaw Wellisz (USA)

The Branson and Papaefstratiou paper represents a serious attempt to provide economically sound advice in response to urgent policy needs. While it is my duty as commentator to point out weaknesses and inadequacies, such criticisms are not meant to belittle the importance of the initiative.

The authors' first concern is to categorise countries into those which may float their currencies and those which, for structural reasons, must peg. The second, and major concern is to devise optimal rules for those who must (or who choose to) peg.

According to Branson and Papaefstratiou, floating is a feasible exchange rate regime 'for countries (or groups of countries) which are relatively closed *and* have internationally integrated asset markets . . . Other countries are not feasible floaters and will choose one form of peg or another'. The authors do not give a formal proof of this proposition, and their statistical evidence is unconvincing. Table 1 (page 396) shows that countries which, as of 1974, claimed to be floaters tended, on the average, to have higher per capita GNPs than those which claimed to be peggers. The table gives no information on the degree of 'openness' or on the 'degree of asset integration'. The eight proclaimed floaters enumerated in Table 2 (page 398) include Singapore (perhaps the most open economy in the world), Malaysia (whose trade/GNP ratio is over 80 per cent), and Tunisia (trade to GNP ratio of over 50 per cent and weak asset integration). These examples do not prove that Branson and Papaefstratiou are wrong, because the actual currency regimes often deviate from the declared regimes; moreover, the dividing line between a 'dirty float' and a 'crawling peg' is arbitrary and almost invisible. On the other hand the proposed criteria might be overly restrictive: for instance, stocks of internationally traded commodities might play much the same stabilising role as the holdings of internationally transferable paper assets, so that float stability may be obtained without international paper asset integration. The whole issue of floating feasibility clearly calls for more theoretical and empirical work.

The Branson and Papaefstratiou argument for pegging is based entirely on considerations of short-run stability (incidentally, nothing is said about the choice of regime for countries which may either float or peg). There is no doubt that short-run stability considerations play a role in decisions to peg, but long-run considerations are no less important. By linking to a large currency bloc, an economically weak country improves foreign (and even domestic) acceptability of its currency and, by the same token, selects an inflation rate compatible with the linkage. The authors subsume the entire long-term policy problem under the term $G(B)$ which they interpret as a 'crawling peg'. It is not clear, however, how the long-term policy is related to short-term stabilisation measures. Does a country which trades, say, with the United States and with Argentina have to adopt a rate of inflation which is a weighted average of the two rates? If not, it is presumably free to choose its own inflation rate, but in this case the long-run linkage disappears. Thus the choice of the currency basket to which to link, based entirely on short-run considerations, may conflict with the long-run reasons for currency pegging.

The model which underlies the short-term stabilisation rules assumes that in the short-run exchange rates affect the terms of trade. Empirical evidence suggests that this assumption fits reasonably well-developed countries which trade mainly in 'fixprice' goods. It is not so clear how well this assumption applies to developing countries trading mainly in 'auction' goods, the price of many of which is set on one particular market and denominated in a specific currency. Here again is an area calling for more empirical research.

Even if one were willing to accept the model, the application of the proposed rules is likely to run into serious practical difficulties. Developing countries typically have some market power on the export side, but very little on the import side. It follows, as shown by the authors, that such countries should utilise import weights in calculating the optimal exchange basket. But if the relative import prices of goods from different currency areas fluctuate in response to the third currency fluctuations, there will be substitution of one import source for another, and the basket composition will shift, requiring frequent recalculation. Thus the developing country would have the choice of using relatively ineffectual export weights, or of pegging to a shifting basket.

Even more serious difficulties arise in connection with the decision on the frequency of exchange rate adjustments. If the adjustments are to be frequent (say daily, weekly or even monthly), then short-term import and export elasticity coefficients must be fed into the formulas. Such coefficients tend to be highly volatile, and their calculations are subject to wide margins of error. In so far as the coefficients enter the formulas in difference and in quotient form, the errors are likely to be compounded, and the calculations to be highly unreliable. Longer-run coefficients are more reliable, but predictable adjustments are substantial (say quarterly or semi-annual) intervals are an open invitation to speculation, the probable effects of which are not taken into account by the stabilisation formulas.

An international policy proposal must be judged, first and foremost, in terms of its consequences for the system as a whole. This issue is never adressed by Branson and Papaefstratiou who concentrate exclusively on individual countries' problems. Unfortunately it is questionable whether their remedy would help the world if its use became widespread. Branson and Papaefstratiou propose to insulate developing countries from third countries' exchange rate fluctuations. The proposal implies a multiplication of idiosyncratic exchange-rate regimes, and of currencies floating against each other in a highly complex and not readily predictable manner. Such a system would, inevitably, impede progress toward closer co-operation among developing countries and tie them closely to traditional trading partners. It is not clear, therefore, that if the proposals were to be successfully implemented, the cause of a New World Economic Order would be furthered thereby.

Part V

Income Distribution Issues

12 The Fundamental Determinants of the Terms of Trade

Ronald Findlay (USA)

The determination of the terms of trade is, at one and the same time, an esoteric technical problem in the pure theory of international trade and a highly charged emotional issue in world politics. The apparent incongruity is removed once we replace Marshall's England and Germany with the contemporary fashion of dividing the world economy into a rich, industrialised North and a poor, primary producing South. In this context the terms of trade between these regions is an integral part of the mechanism determining the global income distribution and it is therefore no longer surprising that the intersection of reciprocal supply and demand curves causes passions to rise. Within a national economy the effects of the operation of the price system on the allocation of resources and the distribution of incomes can be mitigated by labour mobility and redistributive fiscal measures, both of which are largely absent between nations. For the past three decades spokesmen for the developing countries have contended that there is a secular tendency for their terms of trade to move unfavourably and that there is a systematic bias in the distribution of the gains from trade that runs against them. The farreaching proposals for a New International Economic Order are often put forward as measures of restitution to the Third World for past exploitation through the mechanism of declining terms of trade.

This paper is divided into two sections. The first attempts to provide a succinct critical survey of the major theoretical approaches to the determination of the terms of trade and also of the empirical evidence on the secular deterioration alleged to have taken place. The second part is intended to be an original contribution, looking at the terms of trade as the variable that makes the growth rate of the South conform to the exogenously given growth rate of the North in a simple dynamic model of the world economy.

I

EVOLUTION OF NEOCLASSICAL DOCTRINE

The distinction of being the first economist to provide an explicit demonstration of the determination of the terms of trade belongs to John Stuart Mill (1844). This was a remarkable achievement, especially since it was prior to the development of the marginal utility analysis of demand of Jevons, Menger and Walras. Ricardo had of course established that the terms of trade must lie between the domestic cost ratios of England and Portugal in his celebrated example, but it was the reciprocal supply and demand analysis of Mill and its subsequent geometric refinement into the 'offer curves' of Marshall, Edgeworth, Viner, Haberler, Lerner and Meade that made an exact determination of the level of the terms of trade possible.

It has frequently been said that the theory of value (relative prices) in international trade differs from that appropriate to a closed economy. The basis for this statement is that in the Ricardian example the relative price of cloth and wine would simply be equal to the domestic cost ratio (labour theory of value) if either England or Portugal were in isolation, whereas if they engaged in trade and neither was sufficiently 'small' to have its terms of trade determined by the cost ratio of the other, then a 'subjective' theory of value had to be invoked to determine relative prices between the poles established by the operation of the labour theory of value in each country. Graham (1948) sought to overcome this duality by extending the number of countries and commodities, so as to produce a situation in which, except by chance, the terms of trade would coincide with the domestic cost ratio in some 'marginal' country. The modern positon is that there is no dichotomy between an internal and an external theory of value since in either case both blades of the scissors must cut if the full solution is to be determined, factor endowments and technology being relevant on the supply or cost side and tastes on the demand side. In Graham's examples demand has to be introduced in order to locate the 'marginal' country whose domestic cost ratio sets the terms of trade. The modern general equilibrium view is therefore that the fundamental determinants of the terms of trade are tastes, technology and factor endowments.

Mill was also the first economist to consider the effects of technical improvements on the terms of trade. Edgeworth (1894) showed that a country could be 'damnified' by a productivity increase in the sense that the consequent deterioration of the terms of trade makes it worse off than it was initially. He obtained this result in a very simple model where a country is completely specialised in the production of a single export good that it does not consume, so that total production equals total exports, and consumption consists exclusively of a single imported good. If the elasticity of foreign demand as a function of the terms of trade is less than unity then it follows immediately that an increase in the productivity of domestic factors will lower welfare since the decline in the terms of trade will more than offset the increase in the quantity of exports. In this case not only the commodity but also the single factoral terms of trade deteriorate for the home country, in the sense that the purchasing power over imports of a given bundle of domestic inputs declines.

Bhagwati (1958) was able to show that growth could be 'immiserising' *a la* Edgeworth in the context of a much more general model in which the country is not specialised in either production or consumption. The effects of alterations in factor endowment on the terms of trade were analysed by Rybczynski (1955) and of factor bias in technological progress by Findlay and Grubert (1959). These and other results were combined into a taxonomic synthesis by Johnson (1959) in which the effects on the terms of trade of capital accumulation, population growth and various types of technical progress in conjunction with different patterns of the income-elasticity of demand are worked out. The analytical framework is that of comparative statics of the two-factor, two-good, two-country neoclassical trade model. Sodersten (1964) gives a comprehensive review and some further results along related lines.

This model can be adapted to the North–South question by identifying the capital-abundant country with the North and the labour-abundant one with the South, with the former exporting the capital-intensive and the latter the labour-intensive good. An additional hypothesis could be that the income-elasticity of demand for the capital-intensive good is greater, and of the labour-intensive good less than unity, though both are positive. Capital accumulation in either country would then turn the terms of trade against the North while population growth in either country would turn them in favour of the South. Since capital accumulation tends to proceed faster than population growth in both regions the model would seem to indicate a presumption for the terms of trade to move in favour of the South. However, technological progress tends to turn the terms of trade against a country if it occurs in the export sector and in favour of it if it occurs in the import-competing sector, so that an export bias in the South and an import bias in the North could make them turn the other way. No strong conclusion therefore emerges from this analysis regarding the possible direction of any secular trend.

In this connection it is interesting to recall that there is a long English tradition, going back at least to the first chapter of the *Wealth of Nations*, and taken up by Torrens, Ricardo, D. H. Robertson, Keynes and E. A. G. Robinson that technical progress in manufacturing and diminishing returns in agriculture, forestry and mining would result in a secular tendency for the prices of primary products to *rise* relative to manufactures, a point of view that has become familiar again in our own time in connection with the Club of Rome and related 'doomsday' forecasts. It was Beveridge, in his *Economic Journal* controversy with Keynes, who challenged this view, both empirically and in terms of an intuitive grasp of some of the general equilibrium complexities to which we have just referred.

THE PREBISCH-SINGER THESIS

The thesis that there is a systematic bias in the distribution of the gains from trade against the developing countries, revealed by a secular adverse tendency in their terms of trade, is most closely associated with the names of Raul Prebisch (1950) and Hans Singer (1950). The empirical basis for this contention will be examined below on page 437. Here we concentrate on the theoretical arguments that they put forward. Assessment and criticism is not easy since neither author has presented any formal model of the trade relations between North and South. Three major strands in the argument can however be identified:

(1) The income-elasticity of demand for imports from the South is low in the North while it is high in the South for imports from the North.

(2) Technological progress in the North tends to reduce the demand for imports from the South, while technological progress in the South tends to occur in the export sector.

(3) The structure of product and factor markets tends to be much more monopolistic in the North than in the South, on account of the existence of large corporations and well-organised labour unions. This makes technological progress lead to a rise in incomes in the North,

whereas it leads to a decline in the relative prices of exportable products in the South.

The first of these arguments can be expressed succinctly by means of a formula derived by Johnson (1954). Letting $\hat{\theta}$ denote the rate of change of the terms of trade of the 'periphery', $\hat{y}_1$ and $\hat{y}_2$ the growth rates of real income, ε_1 and ε_2 the income-elasticities of demand for imports, η_1 and η_2 the price-elasticities of demand for imports, with subscripts 1 and 2 denoting 'centre' and 'periphery' respectively, we have:

$$\theta = \frac{\varepsilon_1 \hat{y}_1 - \varepsilon_2 \hat{y}_2}{(\eta_1 + \eta_2 - 1)}$$

Since the denominator is positive if the usual Marshall–Lerner stability condition holds, the terms of trade will deteriorate for the 'periphery' if $\varepsilon_1 \hat{y}_1 < \varepsilon_2 \hat{y}_2$. Since $\varepsilon_1 < \varepsilon_2$ by hypothesis, $\hat{\theta}$ must be negative unless

$$\hat{y}_2 \le \frac{\varepsilon_1}{\varepsilon_2} \hat{y}_1$$

in other words, the 'periphery' grows more slowly than the fraction $\dfrac{\varepsilon_1}{\varepsilon_2}$ of the growth rate of the 'centre'. How plausible is the hypothesis that $\varepsilon_1 < 1$ and $\varepsilon_2 > 1$? Reference is sometimes made to Engel's law about the income-elasticity of demand for food but critics can point out that the direction of trade in food is now the other way around and that the income-elasticity of demand for coffee, sugar, etc. may be rather high. In any case, even if the income-elasticities of import demands are equal, the formula shows that it is difficult for the 'periphery' to close the gap without encountering deterioration in the terms of trade.

The second line of argument is consistent with the neoclassical analysis of the previous section. It has been pointed out, however, that the substitution of synthetic for natural products, which Prebisch emphasises in this connection, is not independent of relative prices. Furthermore, technological progress in the manufacturing sector in either region, which undoubtedly takes place, should work in the opposite direction to improve the terms of trade of the 'periphery'.

A crucial role is therefore played by the third strand in the Prebisch–Singer thesis, which argues that there is an asymmetry in the distribution of the gains from productivity improvements, with the 'center' keeping its gains in the form of higher real incomes while the 'periphery' dissipates its gains in lower prices. Technological progress therefore seems to be a sort of 'heads you win, tails I lose' phenomenon for the 'periphery'. Unfortunately, just at this interesting point the argument becomes most *ad hoc* and obscure, with an odd mixture of considerations regarding monopolies, trade unions, business cycles and price rigidities. Critics have generally been least convinced about this aspect of the Prebisch–Singer thesis, perhaps because it is hardest to reconcile with orthodox theory. As we shall demonstrate in Section II, however, these contentions are quite consistent with a model in which the North has full employment and a variable real wage that clears the labour market while the South has a dual economy with a fixed real wage and a variable level of employment.

THE LEWIS MODEL

In his Wicksell Lectures delivered almost a decade ago Lewis (1969) presents a highly ingenious and remarkably simple framework for the determinants of the terms of trade between the products of the 'temperate' and 'tropic' zones, which we may identify as North and South or 'centre' and 'periphery' for the purposes of this paper. Unlike the Prebisch–Singer discussion Lewis puts forward a specific, determinate model which makes the task of interpretation and criticism much easier. However, he does not formulate hid model in explicit general equilibrium terms and readers within the neoclassical tradition may find themselves puzzled by several aspects of the analysis, particularly the apparent exclusion of demand factors. It may therefore be a useful if somewhat pedantic exercise to reformulate Lewis in explicit general equilibrium terms.

The North produces two goods, which Lewis calls *steel* and *food* and the South also produces two goods, *coffee* and *food*, while each region consumes all three goods. The North therefore must export steel to the South and import coffee, but the direction of trade in food is left open. Labour is the only input into production in either country and there is a fixed technical coefficient for the production of each good in each country, so that the North has a linear transformation curve between steel and food and the South a similar curve between coffee and food. The model is thus a special case of a Ricardian system with three goods and two countries, and is reminiscent of the numerous examples analysed by Graham (1948). Relative prices of steel and food, and of coffee and food, are determined purely by the slopes of the linear transformation curves in each region, assuming that some food is produced in each. Arbitrage therefore fixes the relative price of steel and coffee, which Lewis identifies with the terms of trade. There is a 'food theory of value' operating since steel and coffee are evaluated in international exchange at the domestic opportunity cost of each in terms of food. If a unit of labour can produce two food or six steel in the North, and one food or nine coffee in the South, then one steel must be worth three coffee in international exchange under perfect competition.

Is there a determinate equilibrium for the world economy in this model? A quick check will reveal that there is. There are four outputs to be determined, six consumption levels and two price-ratios, making twelve unknowns for the system as a whole. Given the labour supplies and technical coefficients there are two equations for the linear transformation curves; profit maximisation by competitive producers gives the two price-ratios by the slopes of these curves; there is a budget equation for each region with income from production equal to expenditure on consumption; if tastes are specified the demand by each region for each product is determined in conjunction with the price-ratios and budget equations, but one of these demand functions is redundant in each region, so that there are four independent demand functions; finally, there is a world demand equal world supply equilibrium condition that is required to hold in two of the markets, Walras' Law then assuring that it will hold in the third. This gives twelve independent equations in all to determine the twelve unknowns so the system is determinate.

It is convenient to make food the *numeraire* in terms of which the two price-ratios and real income in each region are measured. Because of the linearity of the transformation curves and the absence of 'corner' solutions real income can be identified with the maximum feasible production of food in each country. Letting X stand for either steel or coffee we can depict important properties of the solution in terms of Figure 1. The supply of X is then perfectly elastic at the price-ratio determined by the slope of the corresponding transformation curve up to the point of maximum feasible production, after which it becomes perfectly inelastic. Real incomes in both regions being known demand curves for X can be drawn as functions of the price-ratio between X and food, with the price-ratio of the other commodity held constant at the equilibrium level. The equilibrium output of X, and hence of food in each region by the transformation curve in the lower panel, is determined at the point where the horizontal supply curve is intersected by the world demand curve. The two analogous diagrams represented in Figure 1 therefore show directly the equilibrium values of both price-ratios, all four outputs and four consumption levels, the only variables excluded

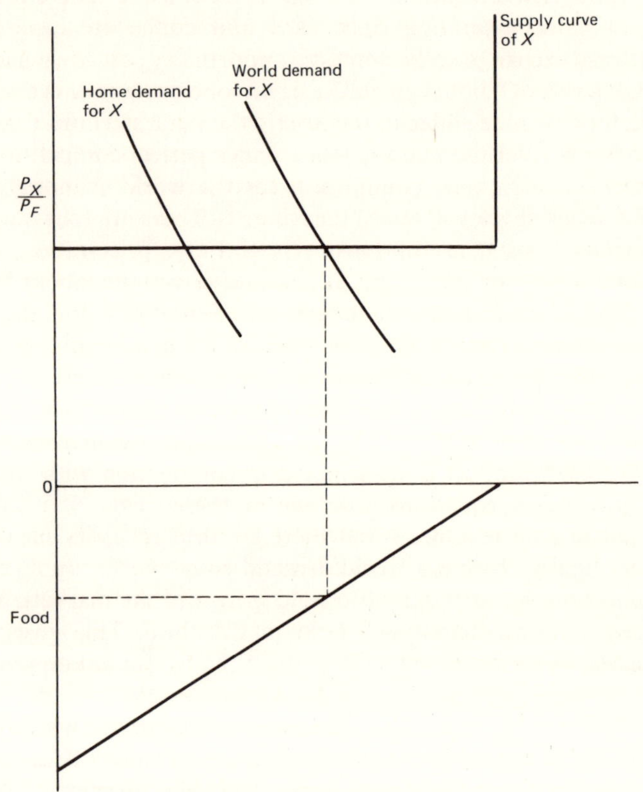

Fig. 1

being the consumption of food in each country. These, however, are residually determined by the budget equations and so are also represented in Figure 1, which thus provides a complete depiction of the general equilibrium of the system.

Comparative statics on the model can now be easily performed. Consider first the effects of a uniform increase in productivity in both sectors in the North. This shifts out the linear transformation curve of that region but leaves its slope unchanged. The relative price of coffee and steel is therefore left unchanged. With positive income-elasticities for both goods in both regions assumed (absence of inferior goods) the expansion of real income in the North leads to an increased demand for coffee, so that production and export of this commodity increase in the

South by the same amount, as Figure 1 reveals, with a consequent reduction in the output of food in the South. The export of steel by the North is unchanged, since relative prices and real income in the South are unchanged. The additional coffee imports of the North are matched either by an increase in food exports or a decline of food imports, depending upon the direction of trade in that commodity, so as to leave food consumption in the South unchanged. The North therefore does not lose any of the fruits of its expansion in a deterioration of its terms of trade, and welfare in the South is unaffected by the productivity increase in the North, that is, there is no 'spillover' effect on the South through better terms of trade. Exactly symmetrical conditions would hold if the uniform technical improvement were to have taken place in the South instead. This model therefore gives quite different predictions in comparison with the Johnson formula of the previous section, where the terms of trade must turn against the expanding region if its income-elasticity of demand for imports is positive. It is the presence of food production in the South *and* the assumption of the linearity of its transformation curve that prevents the Northern growth from raising the price of coffee relative to that of steel. This conclusion can be checked by noting that a sufficiently large expansion in the North would increase the demand for coffee to such an extent that the South completely specialised, after which point the price of coffee must rise to accommodate the higher demand. Also, it is clear that the South's terms of trade would be improved by growth in the North if the marginal cost of coffee were increasing instead of remaining constant in terms of food, that is, the transformation curve is concave to the origin instead of linear.

Lewis observes that the historical pattern of productivity improvement has been for it to increase faster in agriculture than in manufacturing in the developed regions of the temperate zone while the tropics are marked by some technical progress in exportable primary products but more or less complete technical stagnation in the production of subsistence crops. In the stylised model this means that the cost of a unit of food in terms of steel is falling in the North while it is rising in terms of coffee in the South. Thus more and more coffee exchanges for less and less steel as a result of the 'food theory of value', the logic of which is inexorable, given the assumptions. It is difficult to conceive of a more elegant and economical theory from which to derive the implication of an adverse secular trend in the terms of trade of the developing countries.

Lewis identifies the relative price of coffee and steel with the terms of trade. However, account must also be taken of trade in food and the proper expression for the terms of trade would be a suitably weighted average of the coffee–steel ratio and the coffee–food ratio, if food is imported by the South or the food–steel ratio if it is exported by the South. The Lewis result remains valid after this adjustment, whatever the direction of trade in food, since more coffee has to be given per unit of food if it is imported and less steel per unit of food is obtained if it is exported.

It is apparent that, other things being equal, an x per cent increase in productivity in coffee will cause an x per cent deterioration of the South's commodity terms of trade if food is imported and leave its single factoral terms of trade constant. It is easy to conclude from this that the South derives no gain whatsoever from such productivity increases that simply drive down the price in the same proportion and Lewis himself quite explicitly takes this view. This, however, would only be true if coffee were produced exclusively for export. If there is domestic consumption the South must be better off.

This proposition can be proved as follows. The price of both imports rises by x per cent in terms of coffee but the same labour that was previously paying for the quantities of these commodities imported is now x per cent more productive so that consumption of steel and food can be maintained at their previous levels if the same amount of labour is allocated to domestic food production as before. The proportion of the labour force engaged in producing coffee for domestic consumption is, however, also x per cent more efficient, making possible an x per cent increase in this component of consumption and thus an increase in welfare. It is of course likely that all of the gain will not be taken out in additional coffee consumption, since some of it could be exported for more steel or food or more labour could be allocated to domestic food production instead. If food is exported we observe that the price of steel in terms of food is constant, so that it is only the proportion of steel imports paid for by exports of coffee that costs x per cent more. The deterioration of the commodity terms of trade will be a weighted average of zero and x per cent, the weights being the shares of food and coffee in total exports. The proposition asserted then goes through by the same reasoning as before since coffee consumption can increase with food, and steel consumption hold constant. This example should be a warning against regarding the single factoral terms of trade on an unambiguous index of welfare even in a model where labour is the sole factor of production.

UNEQUAL EXCHANGE

This of course is the title of a now famous book by the Greek Marxist Arghiri Emmanuel (1972), now of the University of Paris. This work is notable as being the first serious attempt at a Marxian theory of international trade, as distinct from the familiar works of Lenin, Bukharin and Rosa Luxemburg on imperialism which concern themselves with macroeconomic aspects of foreign investment rather than with the determinants of the terms of trade. Like Marx, Emmanuel begins with Ricardo and displays an impressive knowledge of the orthodox trade theory literature up to about 1940. He knows Mill, Marshall, Edgeworth, Taussig, Viner, Ohlin and Haberler very well but references to subsequent work are thin and scattered. Particularly important omissions from the standpoint of his own approach and interests, are the extensive discussion since 1948 on the factor price equalisation theorem and the more recent literature by Kemp (1966) and Jones (1967) on trade with international capital mobility. Academic trade theorists, however, should welcome a fresh theoretical perspective, if only to divert them from their somewhat jaded pursuit of geometric and algebraic esoterica.

Marxian theorists themselves, however, have their own esoteric pursuits, in this case the arcane arithmetic of the 'transformation problem'. Emmanuel's analytical method largely consists of complicated numerical examples that are difficult to follow and evaluate. Fortunately, Bacha (1977) has performed the useful service of reducing the essential ideas to a particularly simple model that we shall use as the basis of our appraisal. Two fundamental assumptions of Emmanuel's work are that the real wage is exogenously determined in each country and that the rate of profit on capital is equalised across countries. The terms of trade are determined by these conditions in his model.

Suppose that both North and South are completely specialised, the former on steel and the latter on coffee. Let the real wage in each region initially be five units of steel, while a unit of labour in the North produces six units of steel and in the South twelve units of coffee. Capital consists solely of 'advances to labour', one period before the emergence of output of each commodity. The rate of profit is therefore 20 per cent in the North and by the assumption of perfect capital mobility must be 20 per cent in the South as well, which implies that the terms of trade must be two Coffee for one Steel or $\frac{1}{2}$ Steel for one Coffee. Since the real wage, the rate of profit and relative capital intensities are the same the double factoral terms of trade are unity, that is, the product of one unit of labour in the North exchanges for that of one unit of labour in the South. This is a situation of 'equal exchange'.

Let the productivity of labour in the North increase to eight units of steel and let the real wage remain initially at five units of steel. The profit rate in the North thus becomes 60 per cent and the terms of trade of the South improve to twelve Coffee for eight Steel or one Coffee for $\frac{2}{3}$ Steel, that is, in the same proportion that productivity in the North increases. The double factoral terms of trade remain at unity and we continue to have 'equal exchange'.

Suppose, however, that the workers in the North are able to obtain part of the increase in productivity for themselves in the form of a rise in the real wage to six units of steel, while it remains at five units in the South. The rate of profit now becomes $33\frac{1}{3}$ per cent and terms of trade become twelve Coffee for $6\frac{2}{3}$ Steel or $\frac{5}{9}$ Steel for one Coffee. The commodity terms of trade for the South are not as favourable as they would be if there were no increase of the real wage in the North but are still better than they were initially before the productivity increase in the North. The double factoral terms of trade have however turned against the South since it obtains less than a unit's worth of Northern labour in exchange for a unit's worth of their own. Emmanuel considers this as a situation of 'unequal exchange'. Trade between economies with different wage levels, in his conceptual scheme, must result in 'exploitation' of the one with the lower wage.

Our example shows, however, that becoming the victim of unequal exchange, in Emmanuel's definition, is consistent with substantial improvement in the commodity terms of trade and a rise in the absolute level of real income. It seems more than a little peculiar, particularly for someone on the 'left', to object to an increase in productivity that raises real wages in the North and improves the commodity terms of trade of the South and therefore its real income, on the grounds that it causes the double factoral terms of trade to diverge from unity. This doctrine implicitly specifies a social welfare function that is solely concerned with preventing disparities in income levels, regardless of the levels obtained, even of the least advantaged. It thus differs fundamentally from the position of John Rawls, for example, but I should leave these matters to the expert attention of Amartya Sen.

One question that intrigues me is whether or not factor price equalisation implies absence of unequal exchange. The double factoral terms of trade of labour are not equal to unity, even though the real wage and interest rate are equalised, since the labour content of the capital-abundant country's exports is less than that of its imports.

Emmanuel says, however, that he does not regard departures from the 'law of value' due to differences in capital intensity or 'organic composition of capital' as amounting to unequal exchange in the strict sense, only those based on differences in real wages. Therefore, whether there is unequal exchange or not in this case would seem to depend on whether it is the pre-trade or post-trade wage levels that are regarded as relevant. Emmanuel himself does not consider this question since for him real wages are fixed exogenously and are apparently not affected by trade.

Whatever may be the trend of the commodity terms of trade there is no doubt that the double factoral terms of trade for labour must have moved substantially in favour of the North, even though statistics are not easy to come by. This simply reflects the fact that technological progress has taken place much more rapidly in the North and is the main cause of the difference in relative income levels between the two regions. It is entirely false, however, to imply that this must reflect absolute impoverishment for the South through its trade relations with the North.

THE EMPIRICAL EVIDENCE

The empirical evidence on which the Prebisch–Singer hypothesis was advanced consisted of an index for the UK commodity terms of trade constructed by W. Schlote, which showed an improvement of over 40 per cent from 1870 to 1938. Taking the UK as representative of the industrial 'centre' as a whole and regarding the terms of trade of the 'periphery' as the reciprocal of this index, the case was regarded as established. In addition, later statements of this point of view pointed to direct evidence of sharp decline in the terms of trade of LDCs since 1950.

Both these pieces of evidence have been subjected to devestating criticism, without any effective reply, to the best of my knowledge. The criticism has not however prevented the maintenance of belief in the hypothesis as an article of faith in the folklore of the 'development' literature. The major objections have been:

(1) It is illegitimate to regard the terms of trade of the UK's trading partners as the reciprocal of her own since imports are measured c.i.f. and exports f.o.b. The period from 1870 to the early 1900s was one of dramatic decline in ocean freight rates, so that it is possible, and in fact likely, that the terms of trade moved favourably for *both* 'centre' and

'periphery' as a result of the fall in transport costs. This point was first made by Ellsworth (1956).

(2) Independent calculations of the terms of trade for the USA and continental industrial Europe do not reveal any long-run tendency in either direction. The index of the US terms of trade meticulously compiled by Robert Lipsey (1963) stood at 105.6 in 1960 with the base at 100 in 1913. For continental industrial Europe the index for 1952 was 104 with the same 1913 base of 100, according to the calculations of Kindleberger (1956). The UK data however do reveal quite a favourable movement from 100 in 1913 to 128 in 1960. All these figures are conveniently assembled in Appendix H of Lipsey's book.

(3) The terms of trade did drastically turn against the LDCs during the Great Depression of the 1930s. The US terms of trade improve from about 100 in 1927 to 141 in 1934 and 1935. The UK index moved from 118 in 1928 to 149 in 1933 and continental industrial Europe also shows an improvement from 98 in 1926 to 124 in 1934. It can therefore be seen that using the UK index for the period 1870 when it was about 90, to 1938 when it was about 140 produces a dramatic impression by combining favourable results of the fall in transport costs in the late nineteenth century with the effects of the Great Depression.

(4) In an interesting calculation which attempts to correct for all these biases by extending the coverage in the industrial world, adjusting for transport costs and choosing 1928 as the terminal year instead of 1938, Bairoch (1975) estimates an *improvement* of 0 to 20 per cent in the terms of trade of the developing world from 1872 to 1928.

(5) The second piece of evidence, showing decline in the terms of trade of LDCs since 1951 is easily disposed of, as that date represents a peak for commodity prices due to the Korean War. The UN index with 1963 at 100 stood at 119 in 1951 but was 95 in 1948 and 80 in 1938.

(6) Most significant of all is perhaps the point that none of these indices can capture the tremendous improvements in the quality and variety of manufactured imports of both consumer and capital goods that have taken place over the last century, including the introduction of wholly new classes of goods, such as electronics and aircraft and many major new products in the chemical and pharmaceutical fields. Exports of primary products and labour-intensive manufactures from the developing countries, on the other hand, have not changed very much in these respects, tending largely to be relatively homogeneous and standardised goods. It is difficult to imagine anyone preferring the manufactured goods obtainable in return for a given 'basket' of primary

products in 1878 to what would be obtainable by that same 'basket' today.

II

The objective of this second section of the paper is to develop a model of the terms of trade and equilibrium growth in the world economy. The final section presents a summary and the main conclusions of the analysis of the paper and also makes some general observations.

STRUCTURE OF THE MODEL

Imagine a world economy consisting of two regions, the North and the South. The North produces a single composite commodity, manufactures, which can be used for either consumption or investment. The technology for manufactures is represented by a neoclassical production function with constant returns to scale and with capital and labour as the inputs. Capital consists of a stock of manufactures. The size of the labour force is given at any instant and grows over time at a constant rate. There is also labour-augmenting technological progress at a fixed rate assumed to be going on. Under these assumptions, as is well known, the production function can be expressed in terms of capital and 'effective' labour, which grows over time at a fixed rate equal to the sum of the rate of natural increase and the rate of technological progress. A constant fraction of output is saved and invested. Markets are perfectly competitive and are cleared instantaneously so that there is always full employment of labour and full utilisation of capacity.

These assumptions of course correspond exactly to the Solow (1956) neoclassical growth model. The only change is that the portion of output in the North which is not saved is spent either on manufactures or on another homogeneous commodity, representing primary products, with the proportions depending upon the relative price of the two goods. Income-elasticities of demand for both goods are unity.

Primary products constitute the sole output of the South. There is again a neoclassical production function with capital and labour as the inputs governing the output of primary products. Capital consists of a stock of manufactures, just as in the North. Labour is in perfectly elastic supply from a 'hinterland', which is otherwise outside the model, at a fixed real wage in terms of primary products. There is perfect competition so labour is hired up to the point at which its marginal productivity is equal to the fixed real wage. Total employment at any instant will depend upon the quantity of capital available. The capital–labour ratio is uniquely determined by the fixed real wage and in turn determines the marginal product of capital and hence the amount of profit per unit of labour. The *rate* of profit, however, cannot be determined unless the relative price of manufactures and primary products is known, since capital consists of a stock of manufactures and profits of a flow of primary products.

It is assumed that a constant fraction of profits are saved and all wages are consumed. Consumption expenditure, whether out of wages or profits, is spend on manufactures and primary products with the proportions depending upon relative prices. Income-elasticities of demand for both goods are unity. Investment demand is thus purely for manufactures while consumption demand is divided between the two goods. The fraction of profits which is saved determines the increase in the stock of capital that propels the system forward.

It is apparent that this depiction of the South corresponds closely to the celebrated Lewis (1954) model of economic development with unlimited supplies of labour. The Solow economy of the North and the Lewis economy of the South are linked through international trade. It is assumed that there is no lending so that trade is always balanced. The demand for imports in each region depends upon the relative price of the two goods and real income. As we have seen, Johnson obtained a simple formula for the change in the terms of trade resulting from exogenously given growth rates of output in the two regions. In our model, however, there is a feedback from the terms of trade to the growth rate of output in the South. We will demonstrate how the terms of trade and the growth rate of the South have to adjust to the growth rate of the 'effective' labour force in the North that determines the steady state growth of the whole interdependent dynamic system that constitutes the specification of the world econonomy.

THE STEADY STATE SOLUTION

The constant returns to scale production function for primary products in the South is

$$\pi = \pi(k_s) \tag{1}$$

where π refers to the output of primary products per unit of labour and k_s to the capital–labour ratio. The profit maximisation condition is

$$\pi(k_s) - \pi'(k_s)k_s = \bar{w} \tag{2}$$

where $\bar{w}$ is the fixed real wage in terms of primary products. Nothing would be altered if the real wage were assumed to be fixed in terms of manufactures instead. Under the usual assumptions that $\pi'(k_s) > 0$ and $\pi''(k_s) < 0$ there will be a unique k_s^* that satisfies equation (2). Since output consists of a flow of primary products and capital of a stock of manufactures the rate of profit ρ in the South is

$$\rho = \theta\pi'(k_s^*) \tag{3}$$

where θ is the ratio of the price of primary products to the price of manufactures. The proportional relationship between ρ and θ is shown as the ray from the origin in Figure 2 with slope equal to $\pi'(k_s^*)$.

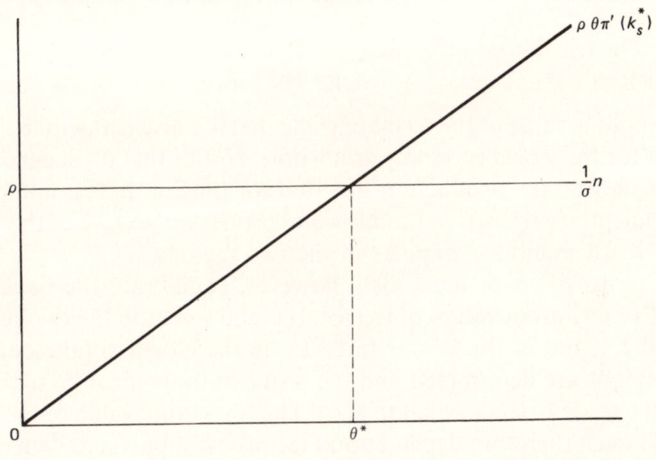

Fig. 2

The common growth rate of total capital, employment and output in the South, denoted g, is given by

$$g = \sigma\rho(\theta) \tag{4}$$

where σ is the proportion of profits that is saved. This is what Mrs Robinson has called the Anglo-Italian equation, which is familiar from her writings and those of Kaldor, Pasinetti and other members of the Cambridge school.

A necessary condition for a steady state equilibrium in the world economy is that the growth rates of manufactures and primary products, and hence of the North and the South, should be equal. Denoting the growth rate of 'effective' labour in the North by n we have the steady state condition

$$\rho(\theta) = \frac{1}{\sigma} n \tag{5}$$

The horizontal line in Figure 2 represents the fixed value $\frac{1}{\sigma} n$ to which the rate of profit in the South has to be equal for the steady state condition of equation (5) to be satisfied. The value θ^* of the terms of trade is determined by the intersection of the ray from the origin and this line, and represents the only value of the terms of trade consistent with (5). In conjunction with (3) this yields the remarkably simple expression

$$\theta^* = \frac{n}{\sigma \pi'(k_s^*)} \tag{6}$$

for the unique value of the terms of trade that is consistent with balanced growth for the world economy as a whole. Notice that θ^* depends only on n, σ, $\bar{w}$ and the production function for the South. It is completely independent of production function and propensity to save of the North and of the demand for imports in the two regions.

The terms of trade must also, however, equilibrate the balance of trade. For any given values of the total capital stocks in the two regions, K_N and K_S, and of the labour force L_N in the North, total incomes in both regions are determined and the terms of trade must be such as to make the trade balance equal to zero. The 'short run' value of the terms of trade must therefore depend upon reciprocal supply and demand for exports and imports in the usual manner. The short and long-run values of the terms of trade become reconciled when K_N and K_S, relative to L_N, take on their appropriate steady state values.

The import demand function of the North is

$$I_N = m[\theta, (1-s)f(k_N)]L_N \tag{7}$$

where m is the quantity of primary products demanded per capita. It is assumed that $m'(\theta) < 0$ and that the elasticity of import demand with respect to total consumption $(1-s)f(k_N^*)$ is equal to unity. The import demand function for the South is

$$I_s = \left[\theta \sigma \pi'(k_s^*)k_s^* + \mu\left(\frac{1}{\theta}, \bar{w} + (1-\sigma)\pi'(k_s^*)k_s^*\right)\right]L_s \tag{8}$$

The first term on the right-hand side of equation (8) is the investment demand for manufactured imports which is equal to the value in terms of manufactures of the propensity to save out of profits times the amount of profits in terms of primary products. The elasticity of investment demand for manufactures with respect to the terms of trade is therefore unity. The per capita consumption demand for manufactured imports is μ, with $\mu'\left(\dfrac{1}{\theta}\right) < 0$ and the elasticity of import demand with respect to total consumption $\bar{w} + (1 - \sigma)\pi'(k_s^*)k_s^*$ is equal to unity. It would be a trivial generalisation to permit different consumer import demands out of wages and profits net of savings.

In equations (7) and (8) we do not have s and σ depending upon θ, so that there is no Laursen–Metzler (1950) effect. The added generality does not seem to be worth the considerable complications that it would cause. An easy generalisation would be to permit s to depend upon the terms of trade expected to prevail in the long run, which with perfect foresight would be θ^*.

In the absence of international lending the trade balance must be zero so that

$$\theta I_N = I_s \tag{9}$$

Substituting for I_N and I_s from equations (7) and (8) and letting $\lambda = L_s/L_N$ denote the ratio of employment in the two regions equation (9) can be solved to obtain

$$\theta = \frac{\lambda\mu\left[\left(\dfrac{1}{\theta}\right),\bar{w} + (1 - \sigma)\pi'(k_s^*)k_s^*\right]}{\{m[\theta,\,(1 - s)f(k_N)] - \lambda\sigma\pi'(k_s^*)k_s^*\}} \tag{10}$$

where the numerator is the consumption imports of the South and the denominator is exports of primary products less the quantity of these exports spent on investment imports by the South. Corresponding to any given values of λ and k_N in the short run equation (10) determines the value of θ that keeps the trade balance in equilibrium. On the other hand if θ is at its long-run steady-state value θ^* as determined by equation (6) then for each k_N there is a unique value of λ such that equation (10) is satisfied.

If k_N is at the steady state value k_N^* given by

$$k_N^* = \frac{sf(k_N^*)}{n} \tag{11}$$

then equation (10) provides the corresponding unique steady-state value

$$\lambda^* = \frac{m(\theta^*, (1-s)f(k_N^*)]n}{\sigma\pi'(k_s^*)[\mu\left(\dfrac{1}{\theta^*}, \bar{w} + (1-\sigma)\pi'(k_s^*)k_s^*\right) + nk_s^*]} \qquad (12)$$

for λ, after using equation (6).

The ratio of total incomes Y_S and Y_N in the two regions in the steady state is

$$\frac{Y_S}{Y_N} = \frac{\theta^*\pi(k_S^*)\lambda^*}{f(k_N^*)} \qquad (13)$$

In interpreting equation (13) it should be remembered that $f(k_N^*)$ is output per unit of 'effective labour'. If n includes labour-augmenting technical progress then the ratio of 'effective' to actual labour will be continually increasing in the North so that the per capita income of the actual labour force will be continually increasing whereas it remains constant in the South because n is there the rate of growth of the actual labour force.

DYNAMICS OF CONVERGENCE

Having obtained the steady state solution of the model this section examines the question of convergence towards the steady state from arbitrary initial conditions. At any instant L_N, K_N and K_S are all given by past history and L_S is determined by the fixed wage $\bar{w}$ and the corresponding capital–labour ratio k_s^*. Dividing K_N and L_S by L_N one obtains the normalised variables k_N and λ which are the state variables of the dynamic system to be studied explicitly in this section. K_S is not a separate state variable since it is always strictly proportional to L_S by virtue of the fixed wage assumption. Under the assumptions about saving out of profits and wages the common growth rate of K_S and L_S is $\sigma\pi'$ $(k_S^*)\theta(\lambda, k_N)$. The relative rate of change of λ is therefore the difference between this rate and the fixed growth rate n of the labour force in the North. The rate of change of k_N is equal to the difference between per capita saving and the requirements for maintaining the capital per head of the growing labour force.

The basic dynamic system can therefore be formulated as

$$\dot{\lambda} = [\sigma\pi'(k_S^*)\theta(\lambda, k_N) - n]\lambda \qquad (14)$$

$$\dot{k}_N = sf(k_N) - nk_N \qquad (15)$$

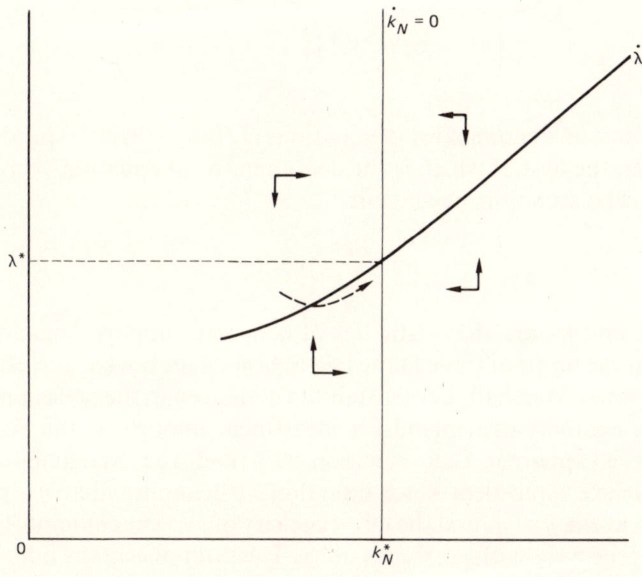

Fig. 3

The properties of this system can be conveniently seen by means of the phase diagram constructed in Figure 3. The $\dot{k}_N = 0$ locus is a vertical line at the value of k_N^* obtained in equation (11). It is independent of λ. The condition for $\dot{\lambda} = 0$ is that θ should be at the value θ^* obtained earlier in equation (6). The $\dot{\lambda} = 0$ locus is therefore one which shows the value of λ corresponding to any value of k_N such that $\theta = \theta^*$. The positive slope of the $\dot{\lambda} = 0$ locus is derived from the relation

$$\frac{d\lambda}{dk_N}\bigg|_{\theta=\theta^*} = -\frac{\dfrac{\partial\theta}{\partial k_N}}{\dfrac{\partial\theta}{\partial\lambda}} \tag{16}$$

which is obtained by total differentiation of equation (10) evaluated at θ^*, with

$$\frac{\partial\theta}{\partial k_N} = -\frac{(1-s)f'(k_N)\tilde{m}\theta}{[m-\lambda\sigma\pi'(k_s^*)k_s^*]\left(1-\eta_s-\dfrac{\theta m}{\lambda}\eta_N\right)} \tag{17}$$

$$\frac{\partial \theta}{\partial \lambda} = \frac{[\mu + \theta \sigma \pi'(k_s^*)k_s^*]}{[m - \lambda \sigma \pi'(k^*)k^*]\left(1 - \eta_s - \frac{\partial m}{\lambda \mu}\eta_N\right)} \tag{18}$$

The common denominator of equations (17) and (18) is the product of two terms, the first of which is the denominator of equation (10) and is positive. The second is negative if

$$\eta_S + \frac{\theta m}{\lambda \mu}\eta_N > 1 \tag{19}$$

where η_S and η_N are the elasticities of consumer import demand with respect to the terms of trade in the two regions. This is what corresponds to the familiar Marshall–Lerner stability condition in the present model, since the elasticity of demand for investment imports in the South is unity. It is apparent that equation (19) and the Marshall–Lerner condition are equivalent since equation (19) implies that η_N plus a weighted average of η_S and the unit elasticity of investment imports with $\lambda \mu / \theta m$ as the weight of η_S exceeds unity. The symbol $\bar{m}$ in the numerator of equation (17) is the marginal propensity to import out of total consumption expenditure and is the partial derivative of m with respect to total consumption expenditure $(1 - s)f(k_N)$ in equation (7). It follows that

$$\frac{\partial \theta}{\partial k_N} > 0, \; \frac{\partial \theta}{\partial \lambda} < 0$$

if equation (19) holds, which establishes the positive slope of the $\dot{\lambda} = 0$ locus from equation (16). The reason for this slope is clear since an increase in k_N improves the terms of trade of the South above θ^* so that an increase in λ is required to restore this value.

The intersection of the $\dot{\lambda} = 0$ and $\dot{k}_N = 0$ loci determines the steady state value λ^* of λ, already obtained in equation (12).

Examining the dynamic system in equations (14) and (15) the 'trace condition' for stability is seen to be satisfied since

$$\frac{\partial \dot{\lambda}}{\partial \lambda} = \lambda^* \sigma \pi'(k_S^*)\frac{\partial \theta}{\partial \lambda} < 0 \tag{20}$$

$$\frac{\partial \dot{k}_N}{\partial k_N} = sf'(k_N^*) - n < 0 \tag{21}$$

at the steady state point (λ^*, k_N^*) The condition in equation (21) is the same as the familiar stability condition for the Solow model of a closed economy.

The 'determinant condition' for stability is also fulfilled since

$$\frac{\partial \dot{\lambda}}{\partial k_N} = \lambda^* \sigma \pi'(k_S^*) \frac{\partial \theta}{\partial k_N} > 0 \tag{22}$$

$$\frac{\partial \dot{k}_N}{\partial \lambda} = 0 \tag{23}$$

These conditions imply that λ falls at any point above the $\dot{\lambda} = 0$ locus and rises at any point below it, while k_N increases at any point to the left of the $\dot{k}_N = 0$ locus and decreases at any point to the right. The motion of λ and k_N is indicated by the arrows in each of the quadrants. A possible trajectory from an arbitrary initial condition is indicated by the dashed curve in Figure 3. At the initial point θ is below θ^* so that the growth rate of the South is below n which means that λ falls and θ increases. When the $\dot{\lambda} = 0$ locus is reached $\theta = \theta^*$. The increase k_N raises the terms of trade above θ^* which means that λ must now start to increase together with k_N towards the steady state values λ^* and k_N^* while θ approaches θ^* from above. The terms of trade therefore overshoot the long-run value θ^* but then are pulled towards it. The intersection of the trajectory with the $\dot{\lambda} = 0$ locus divides the approach towards the steady state into two phases, the first in which the South grows more slowly than the North and the terms of trade continually improve and a second in which the South grows faster than the North and the terms of trade converge towards θ^* from above.

VARIATIONS IN PARAMETERS

This section investigates the impact and long-run effects of variations in the parameters. The initial position will in all cases be taken as the steady state point (λ^*, k_N^*). First, suppose that there is a shift of demand in the North towards primary products, so that m is larger for any given θ. The impact effect on θ is given by partial differentiation of equation (10) with respect to a shift parameter which reveals that θ would increase if the stability condition equation (19) holds. This raises the rate of profit in the South which causes λ to increase and θ to fall. It is clear from equation (6) that the long-run value of θ^* is independent of the import demand function of the North, so that θ converges back towards the original θ^*, while equation (12) indicates that λ^* increases in the same proportion as the increase in m. In terms of Figure 3 the effect is to shift the $\dot{\lambda} = 0$

schedule upwards, while leaving the $\dot{k}_N = 0$ schedule unchanged, so that λ^* rises and k_N^* remains constant.

The impact and long-run effects of the shift in import demand can be conveniently seen in terms of Figure 4. The BB curve shows the combinations of θ and λ that maintain equilibrium in the trade balance when the capital–labour ratio of the North is at its steady state value k_N^*. The negative slope follows from the assumption that the Marshall–Lerner stability condition in equation (19) holds. An increase in the propensity to import of the North shifts BB to the right to $B'B'$ since λ has to increase at constant θ for equation (10) to still hold. In the short run λ cannot change so it remains at the original value of λ^* while θ increases to the corresponding point on $B'B'$. This raises the rate of growth of the South so λ increases gradually while θ falls and the economy of the South moves down $B'B'$, approaching the point on it corresponding to the original terms of trade θ^*. The same line of

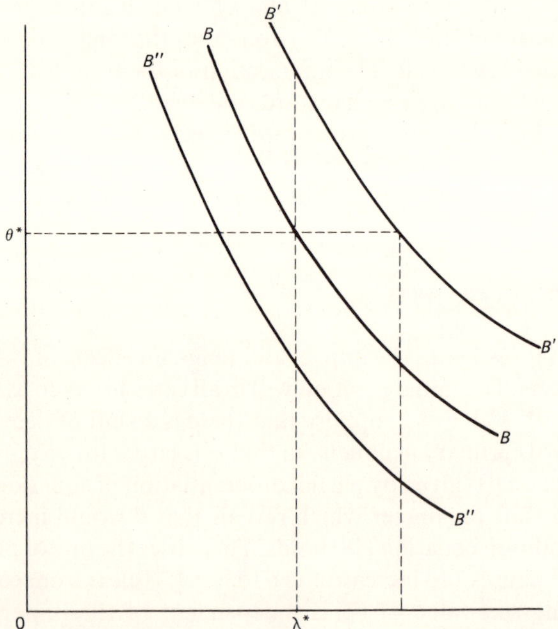

Fig. 4

reasoning indicates that a shift in the South's consumption demand towards manufactures eventually leaves θ^* unchanged but reduces λ^* by a proportion equal to the product of the increase in consumption demand and the share of imports for consumption to total imports in the South. The effects on relative income shares of these shifts in import demands are proportional to the changes in λ^*, as equation (13) indicates.

An increase in the propensity to save of the North raises k_N^* by virtue of equation (11) so that the $\dot{k}_N = 0$ schedule is shifted to the right, while equation (6) shows that θ^* is not affected by this change. An increase in s, for given values of θ and k_N, must lead by equation (10) to a reduction in λ, so that the $\dot{\lambda} = 0$ schedule is shifted downwards as a result. This is because a rise in s means a shift towards manufactures and away from primary products in the demand pattern of the North, so that λ must fall if there is to be equilibrium in the balance of trade with everything else held constant. The fact that the $\dot{\lambda} = 0$ locus shifts down while the $\dot{k}_N = 0$ locus shifts to the right might appear to render the effect of a rise in s on λ^* ambiguous. If the North is to the left of the Golden Rule point where $f'(k_N) = n$, however, a rise in s must raise total consumption per capita $(1 - s)f(k_N^*)$. It follows from equation (12) that λ^* must increase in the same proportion as steady-state per capita consumption in the North since the elasticity of demand for primary products with respect to consumption expenditure is unity. It is interesting to note, therefore, that λ^* is maximised, for given values of all other parameters, when the propensity to save in the North is at the level required by the Golden Rule. The disparity in per capita consumption and income levels between North and South are of course widened by the increase in s since the levels of these variables in the South are not affected by s. The ratio of *total* incomes shown in equation (13) worsens for the South in spite of the increase in λ^*, since the proportionate increase of this variable is equal to $(1 - s)f(k_N^*)$ which is less than that of $f(k_N^*)$ because of the rise in s. An increase in the North's propensity to save therefore raises relative employment in the South but it lowers its relative per capita income. The favourable effect on relative total income of the South of the improvement in relative employment is not sufficient to offset the decline in relative per capita incomes.

Technological change in the North can be introduced in the form of a once-and-for-all Hicks-neutral shift in the production function $f(k_N)$ or in the form of an increase in the rate of labour-augmenting Harrod-neutral progress that results in an increase in n, the growth rate of the effective labour force. Taking the case of the Hicks-neutral shift first, it is evident that the $\dot{k}_N = 0$ locus is shifted to the right and that k_N^* increases. For given values of θ and k_N equation (10) implies that λ must increase if $f(k_N)$ rises. The $\dot{\lambda} = 0$ locus is therefore shifted upward and so λ^* increases. The immediate impact of the Hicks-neutral shift in the production function of the North is for θ to increase with λ^* and k_N^* at their original steady-state values. The initial rise of θ raises the growth rate of the South above n, which causes λ to increase towards its new steady state value, while k_N also increases because savings in the North now exceed the steady state requirement. The fact that the South grows faster than the North means that θ falls after the initial jump in its level, and it eventually approaches its original level θ^* which, as may be seen from equation (6), is not affected by the shift in $f(k_N)$. It can be seen from equations (12) and (13) that the shift in $f(k_N)$ has no effect on the relative total incomes of the North and South since λ^* increases in the same proportion as $f(k_N)$ while θ^* remains unchanged. Relative per capita incomes of course move in favour of the North.

An increase in n shifts the $\dot{k}_N = 0$ locus to the left and reduces k_N^*. From equation (6) it is clear that θ^* must rise in the same proportion as n, so that there is a permanent improvement in the terms of trade of the South. For any given k_N it follows from equation (10) that a higher θ^* requires a lower λ to equilibrate the trade balance, so that the $\dot{\lambda} = 0$ schedule is shifted downward and λ^* falls.

A change in any of the South's parameters does not affect the $\dot{k}_N = 0$ locus and so leaves k_N^* unchanged. The welfare of the North, however, can be altered by these parameter shifts through their effects on the terms of trade. An increase in the fixed real wage $\bar{w}$ raises the capital–labour ratio k_S^* in the South and so reduces $\pi'(k_S^*)$, the marginal productivity of capital. This results by equation (6) in a rise in θ^* proportionately equal to the fall in $\pi'(k_S^*)$. The South is therefore able to improve its terms of trade in the long run by an exogenous increase in the fixed real wage. The price for this, however, will be a reduction in the relative employment ratio λ^*. This can be proved by showing that an increase in $\bar{w}$ must reduce λ^* if the terms of trade are held constant, so that the improvement in the South's terms of trade must reduce it even further by virtue of the fact

that $\dfrac{\partial \lambda}{\partial \theta} < 0$. The rise in k_S^* induced by the rise in $\bar{w}$, combined with the fact

that the South is to the left of the Golden Rule since $\sigma < 1$ means that total consumption expenditure $\bar{w} + (1 - \sigma)\pi'(k_S^*)k_S^*$ and investment nk_S^* both rise on a per capita basis. At constant terms of trade this means an increase in the demand for both consumption and investment purposes. Exports will however be constant, since the North's income is not affected, so that λ^* must fall as a result of the rise in $\bar{w}$ with θ^* held constant. But θ^* in fact rises, so that λ^* must fall even further since $\frac{\partial \lambda}{\partial \theta} < 0$.

An increase in σ, the propensity to save out of profits in the South, leads by equation (6) to a fall in θ^* in the same proportion. The effect on λ^* is obtained by logarithmic differentiation of equation (12) with respect to σ, using the fact that the elasticity of θ^* with respect to σ is minus unity. This establishes that

$$\frac{\sigma}{\lambda^*} \frac{d\lambda^*}{d\sigma} \gtreqless 0$$

depending upon whether

$$\frac{\theta^* m}{\lambda^* \mu} \eta_N + \eta_S \gtreqless 1 + \frac{(\theta^* - \tilde{\mu})\sigma \pi'(k_S^*)k_S^*}{\mu} \tag{24}$$

where $\tilde{\mu}$ is the additional import of manufactures for consumption resulting from an increase in total consumption expenditure in terms of primary products $\bar{w} + (1 - \sigma)\pi'(k_S^*)k_S^*$. The condition in equation (24) on the sum of the elasticities of import demands is more stringent than the stability condition in equation (19) since the marginal propensity to import when income in the South is measured in terms of manufactures is $\tilde{\mu}/\theta^*$, which is between zero and unity, making $(\theta^* - \tilde{\mu})$ positive.

The effect of a rise in σ on λ^* at constant terms of trade is for it to be reduced, since all of the increase in saving out of profits is spent in imports while only part of what was formerly being consumed was spent on imports, requiring λ^* to fall to equilibrate the trade balance. The terms of trade worsen, however, which, if equation (19) holds, leads to a rise in λ^*. The necessary and sufficient condition for the induced increase in λ^* to more than offset the fall at constant terms of trade is provided by equation (24).

In terms of Figure 4 the increase in σ shifts the BB curve to the left to $B''B''$. In the short run λ^* remains fixed so θ falls to the corresponding point on $B''B''$. This decline, however, may be smaller or greater than the long-run decline in θ^* which must be in the same proportion as the increase in σ. The new steady state value of λ^* will be at the point on $B''B''$ corresponding to this long-run decline in θ^* and the economy of the South moves along $B''B''$ in whichever direction is required to get to this point since $\dot{\lambda}$ will be positive or negative depending upon whether the impact effect on θ is less or more than the long-run effect.

The effect of the increase in σ is to *worsen* the relative per capita income of the South since θ^* falls while $\pi(k_S^*)$ and $f(k_N^*)$ are unchanged. The effect on relative total incomes depends in addition upon what happens to λ^*. So long as the total elasticity of λ^* with respect to σ, obtained earlier in connection with equation (24), does not exceed unity the relative total income of the South must also decline.

A simple way in which a once for all technological change in the South can be introduced is by an increase in the marginal productivity of capital with the capital–labour ratio and the marginal productivity of labour unchanged. This will lower θ^* in the same proportion as the rise in the marginal productivity of capital, as implied by equation (6). Denoting $\pi'(k_S^*)$ by r, the effect of this type of technical progress on λ^* is obtained by logarithmic differentiation of equation (12) with respect to r, using the fact that the elarticity of θ^* with respect to r is minus unity. This yields the result that

$$\frac{r}{\lambda^*}\frac{d\lambda^*}{dr} \gtrless 0$$

depending upon whether

$$\frac{\theta^* m}{\lambda^* \mu}\eta_N + \eta_S \gtrless 1 + \frac{[\theta^* - (1-\sigma)\tilde{\mu}]rk_S^*}{\mu} \tag{25}$$

The interpretation of equation (25) is analogous to that of equation (24). The impact and long-run effects on θ and λ can also be shown in terms of Figure 4 in a manner corresponding exactly to the preceding analysis of the increase in the propensity to save since the increase in the South's income at constant terms of trade requires λ to be reduced, thus shifting BB to the left.

The effect of this type of technological change is to *reduce* the relative per capita income of the South. The reason is that θ^* deteriorates in the same proportion as r increases while $\pi(k_S^*)$ increases only by the share of profit times this amount. Thus the relative total income of the South would also decline unless the total elasticity of λ^* with respect to r, obtained in connection with equation (25), were to exceed the share of wages times the proportionate increase in r resulting from the technological change.

POSSIBLE EXTENSIONS

The model presented here has been based upon some rather strong assumptions, which it would be desirable to relax in future work. The task is not attempted here due to limitations of both time and space but some possibilities can be sketched.

International capital mobility to equalise profit rates between North and South can be introduced into the model. Since the real wage and technology in the South are fixed the rate of profit for the world economy as a whole would be determined by these factors and therefore the capital–labour ratio in the manufacturing sector as well. The *ownership* of capital per capita in the North, however, would still be determined by the Solow steady-state condition and therefore also the amount of capital in the South owned by the North. The Anglo-Italian equation (4) would then only apply to the growth of domestically owned capital in the South. The balance-of-trade condition would be modified to permit an export surplus by the South necessary to pay interest on the Northern capital invested in primary production. There will thus continue to be a steady state with a growth rate equal to u, the only difference being that both North and South will each have a determinate constant share of capital used in the South and the long-run value of the terms of trade is whatever is necessary to generate the export surplus required to pay the interest on foreign capital.

Another significant possible extension is the introduction of a protected manufacturing sector into the economy of the South. The variable θ^* in equation (6) would now have to be interpreted as the tariff-inclusive domestic price ratio facing producers in the South, the necessary rate of protection being determined by the technological efficiency of the South in manufacturing relative to primary production. The model would then be qualitatively unchanged in most essentials but the overall capital–labour ratio and the allocation of capital between sectors in the South are further analytical problems that have to be solved.

The model was used only to obtain results of a positive or descriptive character but it can be used as a framework for optimal policy studies as well. For example the propensity to save out of profits may be regarded as a policy variable since it is subject to manipulation by taxation and other government instruments. This raises the question of what its optimal value might be. From equation (6) we see that θ^* varies inversely with σ so that the lower the σ the more favourable is θ^*. However equation (18) evaluated at $k_N = k_N^*$ shows that λ^* varies inversely with θ^* so that there is a tradeoff between favourable terms of trade and the level of employment in the South relative to that in the North in the steady state. An optimal value of σ would be one that appropriately balances these two considerations. For example if the objective is to maximise the level of income in the South evaluated in terms of manufactures which is $\theta^*\pi(h_S^*)\lambda^*(\theta^*)$ then σ should be set at a level where the corresponding value of θ^* from equation (6) is such that the elasticity of λ^* with respect to θ^* in the negatively sloped function in equation (12) is equal to unity.

While the focus of attention in Section II of the paper has been on the commodity terms of trade the single and double factoral terms of trade for both regions have also been determined. The single factoral terms of trade are $\theta^*\pi(k_S^*)$ for the South and $f(k_N^*)/\theta^*$ for the North, while the double factoral terms of trade are $\theta^*\pi(k_S^*)f(k_N^*)$ for the South and the reciprocal of this expression for the North. The effects of variations in the parameters on the factoral terms of trade of each region can readily be obtained by summation of the effects on θ^*, $\pi^*(k_N^*)$ and $f(k_N^*)$. The classic discussions of the meaning and significance of various alternative concepts of the terms of trade are still Viner (1937, pp. 558–64) and Haberler (1961, pp. 24–9) to which the interested reader is referred.

The most basic assumption of the model is of course that of 'unlimited supplies' of labour *a la* Lewis for the economy of the South. A desirable but not easy extension here would be to take the wage as fixed in terms of utility and not in terms of either good alone, since relative prices are changing when the system is not in the steady state. Eventually, of course, the Lewis supply curve must begin to turn up, at which point the system would change qualitatively to a fully neoclassical one for the world economy as a whole and structural differences between the North and the South would no longer exist. Hopefully that day will come, but it has not as yet.

III   CONCLUDING OBSERVATIONS

As we have seen the standard doctrine is that the fundamental determinants of the terms of trade are the tastes, technology and factor endowments of the trading partners. It is only in the short run, however, that factor endowments can be taken as given. In the long run factor endowments themselves must be determined by the propensities to save, as I state in Findlay (1973, Chapter 7) or more fundamentally by the rates of time preference as in the formulation of my 'Australian' model in Findlay (1978). Thus factor endowments are a reflection of tastes as regards the intertemporal pattern of consumption and so should not be considered as an independent variable in its own right.

This leaves tastes and technology as the sole determinants of the terms of trade. As we saw the special production structure of the Lewis model enabled technology alone to uniquely determine the terms of trade, the crucial assumption being the linearity of the transformation curves between food and steel in the North and food and coffee in the South. In Emmanuel's model the influence of tastes is also absent but the exogenously given wage levels of the trading partners are additional determinants of the terms of trade along with technology. This leaves room for socio-political factors such as the class struggle to be among the fundamental determinants of the terms of trade. It should not be forgotten, however, that although the South can improve its terms of trade simply by raising the level of real wages it will have to pay the price in terms of a lower volume of exports, with attendant repercussions on total income and employment. Thus demand factors cannot be ignored in any complete model of international trade. Lewis is only able to ignore demand factors, even on his own strong assumptions, only because he does not consider what determines the volume of steel and coffee exports and the direction and volume of trade in food in his model, as our general equilibrium formulation of it on pages 430–4 in Section I.

In our model of Section II the determinants of the terms of trade in the long-run steady state were the rate of growth of effective labour in the North, the technology of primary production and the real wage and propensity to save out of profits in the South. This set of fundamental determinants reflects the asymmetrical structure of the world economy specified in the model. Technology and tastes, in the form of the propensity to save out of profits in the South, are again the basic factors but they enter in an asymmetrical fashion, contrary to standard trade theory. Consumption demand patterns do not affect the long-run value of the terms of trade but they do determine another crucial variable, the relative employment ratio. The model shows that while trade is the 'engine of growth', in D. H. Robertson's famous phrase, the power that drives that engine is generated by the exogenously given natural growth rate of the North, the growth rate of the South adapting to that rate under the influence of changes in the terms of trade.

The structural difference in the determination of the growth rates of the two regions produce asymmetrical consequences on the terms of trade of changes in technology and the propensity to save. Singer's statement that '. . . technical progress in manufacturing industries showed in a rise in incomes while technical progress in the production of food and raw materials in underdeveloped countries showed in a fall of prices' is entirely consistent with the results of our model, for reasons quite independent of the rather fuzzy arguments put forward by him and Prebisch.

While our model is consistent with secular deterioration of the South's terms of trade, given appropriate initial conditions, there is a long-run equilibrium *level* to which they converge from either direction, so that the rate of deterioration must eventually diminish and approach zero, for any given set of values of the parameters. This theory is therefore also consistent with the empirical evidence of no significant variation over the long run in the terms of trade cited in on page 438 of Section I.

Uncritical belief in the secular deterioration thesis is widespread in the Third World and may have contributed substantially to the strong antitrade bias of government policy in many less developed countries, the costs of which have been amply documented in recent research, including the two separate series of country studies sponsored by the OECD and the NBER. As Moliere's *Le Malade Imaginaire* exemplifies, the medical expenses for a hypochondriac's disease are not only real but high.

REFERENCES

Bacha, E., 'An Interpretation of Unequal Exchange from Prebisch–Singer to Emmanuel', unpublished manuscript (June 1977) pp. 1–23.

Bairoch, P., *Economic Development in the Third World Since* 1900 (Methuen: London, 1975).

Bhagwati, J., 'Immiserizing Growth: A Geometric Note', *Review of Economic Studies* (June 1958).

Edgeworth, F. Y., 'The Theory of International Values', *Economic Journal* (1894).

Ellsworth, P. T., 'The Terms of Trade between Primary Producing and Industrial Countries', *Inter-American Economic Affairs* (Summer 1956).

Emmanuel, A., *Unequal Exchange* (New York: Monthly Review Press, 1972).

Findlay, R. and Grubert, H., 'Factor Intensities, Technological Progress and the Terms of Trade', *Oxford Economic Papers* (February 1959).

Findlay, R., *International Trade and Development Theory* (New York: Colombia University Press, 1973).

Findlay, R., 'An "Austrian" Model of International Trade and Interest Rate Equalization', *Journal of Political Economy* (forthcoming).

Graham, F. D., *The Theory of International Values* (Princeton, 1948).

Haberler, G., *A Survey of International Trade Theory* (Princeton, 1961).

Johnson, H. G., 'Increasing Productivity, Income-Price Trends and the

Trade Balance', *Economic Journal*, 64 (September 1954) 462–85.

Johnson, H. G., 'Economic Development and International Trade', *Nationalökonomisk Tidsskrift* (1959) pp. 253–72.

Jones, R. W., 'International Capital Movements and the Theory of Tariffs and Trade', *Quarterly Journal of Economics* (February 1967).

Kemp, M. C., 'The Gains from International Trade and Investment: A Neo-Heckscher–Ohlin Approach', *American Economic Review* (September 1966).

Kindleberger, C. P., *The Terms of Trade: A European Case Study* (New York: John Wiley, 1956).

Laursen, S. and Metzler, L. A., 'Flexible Exchange Rates and the Theory of Employment', *Review of Economics and Statistics*, 32 (November 1950), 281–99.

Lewis, W. A., 'Economic Development with Unlimited Supplies of Labour', *Manchester School*, 22 (May 1954) 139–91.

Lewis, W. A., *Aspects of Tropical Trade*, 1883–1965 (Stockholm: Almquist & Wiksell, 1969).

Lipsey, R. E., *Price and Quantity Trends in the Foreign Trade of the United States* (Princeton University Press, 1963).

Mill, J. S., *Essays on Some Unsettled Questions of Political Economy* (London, 1844).

Prebisch, R., *The Economic Development of Latin America and its Principal Problems* (New York: United Nations, 1950).

Rybczynski, T. M., 'Factory Endowment and Relative Commodity Prices', *Economica* (November 1955).

Singer, H., 'The Distribution of Gains between Borrowing and Investing Countries', *American Economic Review*, 40 (May 1950), 473–85.

Södersten, B., *A Study of Economic Growth and International Trade* (Stockholm: Almquist and Wiksell, 1964).

Solow, R. M., 'A Contribution to the Theory of Economic Growth', *Quarterly Journal of Economics*, 70 (February 1966), 65–94.

Viner, J., *Studies in the Theory of International Trade* (New York: Harper & Row, 1937).

Comments

Bo Södersten (Sweden)

Professor Findlay has produced an admirable paper on the fundamental determinants of terms of trade. The paper consists of two parts, The first is a survey of the most important approaches that have been made in analysing the problem. The second presents a new dynamic two-country model, where elements of a Solow-type growth model are combined with an approach based on the Lewis-type model with unlimited supplies of labour. The model presented in the latter part of the paper represents an interesting step forward and adds some new insights of a dynamic kind into a problem that previously has been studied primarily with the help of comparative statics.

It is the second part of Professor Findlay's paper which is most original. Here the author developes a dynamic model for the determination of terms of trade. There are two countries, the North and the South, and the economy of the North is depicted by a Solow-type of growth model with labour and capital, where one good, manufactures, is produced and where the capital stock consists of a stock of manufactures. The labour force grows over time at a constant rate and labour-augmenting technical progress is also taking place. The South produces only primary goods, again with a stock of capital that consists of manufactures and with labour. Here labour is to be found in unlimited supply at the given wage. What propels the economy of the South forward is the rate of profits and the savings ratio. In the South the so-called Anglo-Italian equation prevails and the growth rate of the Southern economy depends on how large a part of profits are saved and profits themselves are a function of the terms of trade.

The two economies are linked together by trade and in steady equilibrium the growth rates of the two outputs, manufactures and primary products should be equal.

Ronald Findlay starts by studying the steady state characteristics of the economies. The author derives a remarkably simple expression for the steady state solution to the terms of trade which is depicted in equation (6) on p. 442. It turns out that the equilibrium solution to the terms of trade depends on only four factors: the growth rate of the labour force in the North, on the savings rate, the given wage in the South, and the production function for the South. If regard is paid to the fact that the terms of trade do not only have to equilibrate the growth of the two outputs but also the fact that the trade between the two countries has to be balanced, the expression of the equilibrium value of the terms of trade becomes somewhat more involved as shown by equation (10) on p. 443.

The author then studies the dynamics of convergence in the model and finds that the model has the same kind of stability conditions as the Solow-model for instance. The dynamic characteristics of the model are also illustrated by a phase diagram in Figure 3.

The dynamic formulation of the model affords new and added insights into the fundamental determinants of the terms of trade. One interesting aspect of the model is that it shows how productivity increases may influence national incomes and per capita incomes asymmetrically in the two countries. We recall that this was one of the assertions of the Prebisch–Singer thesis.

Technical progress in the North will lead to an improvement in both the total income and the per capita income in the North. It will also lead to an increase in the total income in the South; as a matter of fact, the relation between total incomes in North and South will be unchanged because of technical progress in the North. This depends on the fact that the impact effect of such growth will be to improve the terms of trade of the South which will trigger off a dynamic development in the South leading to increased profits and capital accumulation and with expansion of employment; a process that will eventually lead to new steady states with relative incomes between North and South being the same as at the starting point. The North, however, will be able to keep its entire productivity gain.

Technological improvement in the South in the form of an increase in the productivity of capital will have a somewhat different effect. This will lead to a fall in the per capita income of the South. Total income in the South may either fall or it may increase. The explanation for this outcome is that technical progress of this type in the South will lead to deteriorating terms of trade. The model may then help to explain why the South may have a much dimmer view of the prospects for productivity increases than do spokesmen for the North. In fact, the best strategy may be for the South to sit back and wait for progress in the

North that will spill over to the South through the dynamic linkages existing between the two economies.

The Findlay model thus yields some new and unexpected results. As in most dynamic formulations there will be a difference between the impact effects and the steady state solutions.

Summing up, we may therefore say that in the neoclassic models of a comparative-static kind the fundamental determinants of the terms of trade are tastes, technology and factor endowments. In the dynamic model that Professor Findlay presents it is the growth of effective labour in the North which is the moving factor, together with the technology in the South, its real wage and its propensity to save out of profits.

This gives rise to an asymmetry as it is the growth rate of the labour force in the North, including labour-augmenting technical progress, which is the true engine of growth. The economy of the South may also grow but as a response to the impact effect of improved terms of trade. In this sense the North is the active, while the South is the passive partner in the 'dialogue' between the North and the South portrayed in Professor Findlay's model. As in most dynamic models, however, in the long run the variables in the model will settle down to equilibrium values, with a given equalibrium value also for the terms of trade.

Let me then add a few comments to Professor Findlay's paper. In the first part of his paper the author provides a good, but very brief review of the theory of growth and trade that was developed during the 1950s and clearly 1960s. This theory did not only propose to be a theory on the development of relative prices in international trade. It studied the interrelationships of two trading economies from a general equilibrium perspective. It demonstrated how different variables hang together and it showed the importance of adjustment on both the demand and supply side for the development of the terms of trade.

By the brevity of the exposition, Professor Findlay, it seems, tends to give a somewhat narrow picture of the theory of growth and trade, which still occupies a fairly central position in trade theory.

One of the results that one tended to loss sight of was the importance of the adaptability of the trading economies for the development of the terms of trade. This adaptability was usually measured by an elasticity factor as depicted in the denominator of the algebraic expressions for the terms of trade that this type of theory derived.

The growth and trade theory of the early 1960s was also a very supple theory, as neoclassic theory often is. A wide variety of hypotheses regarding the development of the terms of trade could be generated by various combinations of factor growth and technical progress. Perhaps the author could have been a little bit more explicit in his exposition at this point.

Returning to the Lewis model from Arthur Lewis' 1969 paper on tropical trade, it seems to me that the Lewis model represents an interesting special case but cannot claim the same generality as the growth and trade models of the early 60s. It may well be that it is not the more general approaches but the special cases which are of the greatest interest to study. Presumably the Lewis model studies the determination of the long-run terms of trade. If this be true then one may doubt whether it is realistic to assume that both goods in both countries are produced with fixed technical coefficients. It would have been interesting to view a somewhat closer comparison of these various models by Professor Findlay.

When it comes to the exposition of the Emmanuel model I feel some slight apprehension even though I cannot be very precise in my remarks. I share the same prejudices as professor Findlay does so I have no direct faults that I can point to. Still we have to remember that Emmanuel's model is the only antagonistic model to mainstream theory that the author deals with. Therefore it is important to give as fair a representation of the model as possible. Perhaps it is mostly a matter of the tone in which the model is presented.

Turning to the Findlay model in Section II it seems to be a contradiction between the results of the model and the empirical results reported in Section I. As we know the Findlay model predicts that the North will keep its productivity gains while the South will have to export away its productivity gains by decreasing terms of trade. This seems to be the most interesting proposition emanating from the model.

The basic empirical result that Professor Findlay reports in the first part of this paper is, however, that there is no secular tendency for adverse terms of trade for the South. The impression one gets is that the author started to construct his model and reached an interesting result, but that, alas, he later found that reality differed from the hypothesis generated by his model. Professor Findlay may defend himself by saying that in the steady state situation the terms of trade will settle down to an equilibrium value but then there will be no technical progress in the South either.

Another observation regarding the model is whether the dynamic properties of the model are really possible to reconcile with the assumption of unlimited supply of labour. In the steady state situation capital will accumulate in the South and labour will be sucked into primary production. This can presumably not go on forever. Sooner or later the 'hinterland' will have no more labour to supply. We may then ask: what will happen then? Is not the assumption of unlimited supply of labour unnecessarily restrictive? Would it not be more interesting to have two Solow-type economies trading with each other instead?

Another of Professor Findlay's points that is dubious is the contention that 'factor endowments are a reflection of tastes' and 'should not be considered as an independent variable in its own right'. What are exogenous factors and what are dependent variables vary from model to model. They depend on what type of problem is to be studied. It is easy to understand the author's proposal in terms of his own work, especially in connection with his 'Austrian' model. It seems, however, that Professor Findlay has been carried away by his own specific formulation of the problem. From a broader point of view factor endowments certainly should be taken as a *datum* for the analysis. To give an example: the most important influence in the world economy in the 1970s has been the availability of factor endowments in the form of oilfields and the possibility of greatly increasing the land rents accruing from these deposits. Oilfields are a very tangible type of factor endowment; they are not created or destroyed by changes in tastes or savings behaviour. Had the author scrutinised various models more closely he would probably have become aware of the fact that his own 'Austrian' approach only can be regarded as one of several interesting special cases.

As I have already stated, I think that Professor Findlay has presented us with a most valuable paper. My major criticism would be that he has been too ambitious, that in fact he has tried to roll two papers into one, where the survey in section I has really no strong logical connection with the dynamic model in Section II.

Once we know of the existence of his model he can then use it for comparative purposes in Section I, which, as it now stands, is too thin. It should be expanded and given a' stronger comparative emphasis. It is important to get a firm grasp of the nature of the assumptions of the various models and to closely compare the results. More emphasis could also be given to the empirical side. It may be useful to divide the historical development into somewhat shorter periods of say, ten, fifteen or twenty years' duration, somewhat like Professor Lewis did in his paper, and then compare these periods and see what models best fit as explanations. Professor Findlay may want to defend himself by saying that international trade theory is a field that is already well surveyed. What I had in mind, however, is a close scrutiny of the various models comparing in detailed form assumptions and results and evaluating various hypotheses generated by the models in an empirical setting; and this has not been done.

There is a great need for a good comparative synthesis in this area. Professor Findlay has shown that he is very well equipped to do this job. If he were to elaborate his paper in direction that I have suggested he may present us not only with one but with two very interesting papers.

13 Ethical Issues in Income Distribution: National and International

Amartya Sen (UK)

There is an old Jewish story about why British Jews have been less successful than Jews in America. They all left from Russia in a ship holding tickets to New York. When the ship stopped to refuel in Liverpool, the stupid ones got off.

I have, I fear, got off at 'ethical issues, etc.' It may well be that in view of that choice, this is indeed what I deserve, but it is much less clear whether I can at all deliver. While delivery here does not require one to assert, with John of Gaunt: 'methinks I am a prophet new inspired,' even the limited task of sorting out the complex issues involved is not an easy one. There will be gaps and rough corners; but no further apologies.

In Section I, there is an attempt to discuss the main moral principles involved—these are general and do not deal *only* with income distribution. Applications to income-distributional problems are systematised in Section 2. That discussion will not, however, bring in national boundaries; these will raise their heads—ugly or not—in Section 3. Concluding remarks are made in Section 4.

I   THE PRINCIPLES INVOLVED

UTILITARIANISM FACTORISED

Utilitarianism provides a convenient point of departure in examining moral issues. Utilitarianism can be factorised into the following constituent parts.

(1) *Consequentialism*: The rightness of actions—and (more generally)

of the choice of all control variables—must be judged entirely by the goodness of the consequent state of affairs.[1]

(2) *Welfarism*: The goodness of states of affairs must be judged entirely by the goodness of the set of individual utilities in the respective states of affairs.[2]

(3) *Sum-ranking*: The goodness of any set of individual utilities must be judged entirely by their sum total.[3]

Each of these features have much appeal and have received many defences. But they remain eminently controversial, and rival theories of morality have argued for the replacement of one or more of these features. A number of such rivals are considered next, with comments on how they differ from the axioms underlying utilitarianism.

MAXIMIN AND LEXIMIN

In the 'maximin' approach, the axiom of sum-ranking is replaced by the requirement that the goodness of any set of individual utilities must be judged entirely by the value of its least member, that is, by the utility level of the worst-off individual. This theory is identified with John Rawls' (1971) 'difference principle,' and it certainly came to prominence in that context, even though this interpretation of the 'difference principle' is strictly speaking apocryphal. While Rawls motivated his difference principle in terms of individual utilities and seemed to be pointing towards the maximin criterion, in fact he defined the principle formally not in terms of utilities at all but through an index of 'primary goods.'[4] This approach will be discussed in the next subsection, but the maximin approach—whether Rawlsian or not—has some claim to be considered on its own as an appealing moral approach, taking a particular view of 'economic justice.'

Furthermore, it can be made consistent with the strong Pareto principle—and other dominance-based criteria such as Suppes' (1966) 'grading principles'—by being defined in the lexicographic form (see Sen, 1970). In this form, if the worst-off utility levels happen to be the same in a pairwise comparison, then the pair can be ranked by the utility level of the second worst off; if they too tie, then by the utility level of the third worst off; and so on.[5] This 'leximin' approach, like maximin, satisfies welfarism, and can be combined with consequentialism,[6] but violate sum-ranking.

THE DIFFERENCE PRINCIPLE

In John Rawls' (1971, 1975) version of 'a Kantian concept of morality,' moral judgements of states of affairs take particular note of the conditions of the most deprived group of persons, deprivation being defined in terms of the availability of 'primary goods,' or 'things it is supposed a rational man wants whatever else he wants' (Rawls, 1971, p. 92). Despite the 'priority' given by Rawls to liberty, this difference principle is central to the Rawlsian notion of justice.

Since the list of primary goods is diverse (one list by Rawls includes 'rights, liberties and opportunities, income and wealth, and the social basis of self-respect'), to identify the least advantaged is—to put it mildly—a non-trivial task, and requires the construction of an overall index of vectors of different goods. Such a construction poses daunting problems, unless there are strong similarities of tastes and quasi-homotheticity of shared preferences.[7] But nevertheless the exercise may be relatively easier than operating on utilities, and avoid difficulties of identifying the efficiency of different persons as pleasure machines.[8]

But the contrast of the 'primary goods' version of the difference principle and utility-based leximin (or maximin) lies not merely—or even primarily—in these tactical advantages, but in the different basis of moral judgement. In leximin, a person's claim to more goods arises from his being worse off in terms of welfare, whereas in the pure Rawlsian version it originates in his having less primary goods than others. The latter avoids what many find the morally unattractive possibility of having to give a lot more income to people with expensive tastes (for example, to 'gourmets'—who are very unhappy in the absence of culinary extravaganza), and Rawls has emphasised the importance of recognising a person's responsibility for his own ends.

On the other hand, this Rawlsian version of the difference principle is insensitive to special needs, such as, of the disabled, the old, or the ill. Having the same supply of primary goods leaves them clearly worse off, and the difference may not be due to anything for which they can be held responsible. Rawls (1975, p. 96) may be right that 'problems of special health care and how to treat the mentally defective' and other 'hard cases' can 'distract our moral perception by leading us to think of people distant from us whose fate arouses pity and anxiety', but our moral approach must deal with these cases as well. Such handicaps may not be very rare either, since neither illness nor old age are unusual predicaments of human beings.

Differences of needs can also arise from climatic conditions (such as clothing, shelter, food), urbanisation (such as transport, pollution effects), work performed (such as calories or other nutrients), or even body size (such as food and clothing). To judge advantage in terms of availability of primary goods only leads to the loss of these important parameters. Thus Rawls' own version of the difference principle seems to have serious difficulties. Its possibly superior ability to handle the man with the expensive taste, through justice by neglect, is achieved at a high cost.

EQUITY, NEEDS AND POWERS

Utilitarianism is sensitive to *total* benefits of different persons; the difference principle, leximin or maximin is not. On the other hand, the latter is sensitive to interpersonal utility *distribution*, which utilitarianism is not. It is tempting to combine total-sensitivity with distribution-sensitivity. Various equity criteria have tried to do this by incorporating considerations of distributive justice without forcing the extremism of leximin or maximin or the difference principle.[9] The Weak Equity Axiom (henceforth WEA) requires that if person 1 is worse off than person 2 whenever both have the same income, then in dividing a given total of income among a group including persons 1 and 2, the best division must give more income to person 1 and to 2.[10]

Utilitarianism will often violate WEA, but leximin always satisfies it.[11] While WEA was motivated by Rawlsian arguments against utilitarianism, Rawls' own version of the difference principle can violate WEA. This is because the difference principle operates on the availability of primary goods as the indicator of advantage and is, therefore, unable to notice differences arising from other sources, in particular differences in needs. The appeal of WEA is certainly not unconditional, but in cases of obvious variation of recognised primary needs arising from, say, the person being a cripple or having a back-breaking load of work (see Sen, 1973, pp. 16–9), WEA would reflect a moral intuition shared by many. On the other hand, in the case of the man who plunges into depression when deprived of champagne and caviar, WEA may not be all that attractive.

It is possible to consider a modification of WEA which will capture the rationale of Rawls' focus on 'primary goods' as opposed to utility, and at the same time avoid the pitfall of identifying everyone's needs irrespective of work load, location, physical fitness, climatic conditions, etc. It is possible to concentrate neither on *utility* as such, nor on the availability of primary *goods*, but on the realisation of certain primary *powers* (or 'basic abilities'), for example, the power to fulfil one's nutritional requirements or the necessities of clothing and shelter, or the ability to move about. The cripple's entitlement to more income arises in this view neither from his low utility level, nor from any lower availability of primary goods, but from the deprivation of his ability to move about unless he happens to have more income or more specialised goods (for example, vehicles for the disabled) at his command. Similarly, the greater needs of a higher workload lead to a greater entitlement not on the basis of utility deprivation as such but the deprivation of the power to meet the necessary calorie requirements *if* one had the same intake of food that would meet the calorie requirements of someone working much less.[12] The modified version of WEA would require that a person whose primary powers (or basic abilities) are less for the same level of income is entitled to get more income.

This general framework of judging advantage in terms neither of utilities nor of primary goods but in terms of primary powers has, of course, many problems of its own. There is the difficult problem of arriving at an index of primary power fulfilment since different types of powers are involved. (It is a problem comparable to Rawls' problem of getting an index of the availability of primary goods.) There is also the complicated issue of what powers count as primary (for example, why not the power to satisfy the requirements of one's cultivated palate?), and philistinism is not a negligible danger.[13] I have tried to go into these issues elsewhere (Sen, 1978a), and will not attempt here a facile answer to rather profound problems. Instead, I shall merely claim that the approach of primary powers provides an alternative framework for considerations of equity, distinct both from the framework of utilities and from that of availabilities of primary goods, but also note *each* of these three approaches has many problems.

PERSONAL LIBERTY AND RIGHTS

Utilitarianism involves consequentialism, welfarism, and sum-ranking. Leximin or maximin relaxes sum-ranking, but sticks to welfarism and is consistent with consequentialism. Rawls' difference principle based on primary goods, and equity principles based on primary powers, drop welfarism also, but remain consistent with consequentialism. I turn now to right-based moralities that focus on such issues as personal liberty, and these frequently involve the rejection of consequentialism as well.

Under the consequentialist approach actions, obligations and rights must be judged ultimately in terms of the 'outcome morality', that is, morality involved in judging states of affairs. But it is possible to defend a person's rights not in terms of the goodness of its consequences, but on the grounds that these rights have innate moral acceptability irrespective of the consequences of the exercise of these rights. Many libertarians and proponents of other right-based moralities take a non-consequentialist route to these morals. 'Rights', argues Nozick (1974, p. 166), 'do not determine the position of an alternative or the relative position of two alternatives in a social ordering; they operate upon a social ordering to constrain the choice it can yield'. Severing the discipline of consequentalism permits firm acceptance of rights in judgements of actions, for example, in rejecting interference in what Hayek (1960, p. 140) calls a person's 'protected sphere'.

An alternative way of dealing with liberty and other rights in the moral structure is to incorporate them in the outcome morality itself, judging the outcomes in terms of whether people get their entitlements as specified by a system of rights. The 'social ordering' of outcomes then incorporates attitudes towards the fulfilment or violation of rights, and the actions can then be judged taking note of rights even within a consequentialist framework. Outcome morality formulations of liberty and rights (see Sen (1970, 1976b), Gibbard (1974), Blau (1975), Farrell (1976), Suzumura (1978), among others) will violate welfarism, but may or may not be combined with full consequentialism.[14]

These formulations may, however, conflict with the Pareto principle, even when the rights are internally compatible with each other, and there are consistency problems for the 'Paretian libertarian' (see Sen, 1970; 1976b). While many economists seem to respond to any violation of the Pareto principle as if motherhood is under cruel attack, Paretianism is essentially a weak version of welfarism. Considerations of liberty and rights, which militate against an exclusive concern with utility values, can go against relying exclusively on utility magnitudes even in the Paretian special case ('everyone has more utility, ask no further questions'), and this becomes clear when *interpair* consistency of judgements is considered.

The alternative of leaving considerations of liberty and rights completely out of the outcome morality and using a vigorously non-consequentialist framework has problems of its own. First, there is the difficulty that an outcome involving gross violation of rights (such as, a person being roughed up by a gang of sadists) may have to be described as a good *outcome* (for example, under utilitarian outcome morality when the aggregate utility gain of the gang exceeds the utility loss of the solitary victim), even though the *action* of roughing up is taken to be unacceptable in view of the right of the victim not to be tortured. Apart from severely restricting the nature of moral judgements made, this makes it difficult to accomodate person 1's moral involvement when person 2 is roughed up by a strong-armed person, 3.[15] Second, by keeping considerations of liberty and rights outside outcome morality, and by downgrading the role of outcome morality to a lexicographically inferior position, this approach makes it difficult to accomodate 'tradeoffs' between competing moral claims,[16] involving those considerations that are incorporated in the outcome evaluation (for example, utility aggregates and distribution) and those that come in as constraints on actions (for example, rights and liberties). The weighing and balancing of conflicting consequences within an outcome morality provides a more flexible format than a hierarchy of priorities and constraints.

ENTITLEMENT THEORIES: LABOUR AND PROPERTY RIGHTS

The labour theory of value can be interpreted in many different ways, for example, descriptive, predictive or evaluative,[17] and while the descriptive interpretation can be thought to be the primary one, the evaluative interpretation has been important in social criticism using such Marxian concepts as 'exploitation'. In this approach welfarism is rejected, and the entitlements are related not to utilities but to labour contributions (or to corrected labour contributions in terms of 'socially necessary labour'). In a limited form the concept of labour entitlements also find expression in such demands as 'equal pay for equal work'. On a much wider canvas it lends critical weight to the diagnosis of 'unequal exchange' in international economic relations (see Emmanuel, 1972).

While labour rights have a wide moral appeal, property rights have also had much support for nearly three hundred years (see Locke, 1690). Recently Robert Nozick (1974) has provided an elegantly worked out entitlement theory covering property rights. He defines principles of justice in *acquisition* and *transfer*; a person acquiring holdings in accordance with these principles are entitled to them, and no one is entitled to a holding except by repeated applications of these two principles. The principles are so constructed that a person is not only entitled to what he himself produces with his own labour, but also to what is produced by resources owned by him and what he can acquire by free exchange of what he legitimately holds. Holdings also legitimately pass from one person to another through inheritance or gift. This structure of entitlements differs sharply from the labour-based entitlement system chiefly in three respects: (a) assigning to the owners of non-labour productive resources the fruits of using those resources; (b) accepting free exchange as just irrespective of the inequality in the distribution of means of production; and (c) accepting the legitimacy of inheritance (and gift).[18]

Most of the criticisms of these entitlement theories—whether of labour entitlements (and 'exploitation') or of property rights (and Nozick's structure)—have emphasised the arbitrariness of the chosen 'principles'.[19] In so far as the ethical framework is one of moral intuition, the question has to be whether these principles capture these moral intuitions deeply enough, or whether they build on immediate prejudices, which will be rejected on reflection. More structured tests will be used by those who choose a non-intuitionist framework, for example, by making use of the discipline of the language of morals (see Hare, 1976), or by attributing unique ethical relevance to acceptability in a hypothetical 'original position' with primordial equality without anyone knowing who is going to be who (see Rawls, 1971; and Harsanyi, 1977).

It is perhaps worth remarking that while Marx made considerable use of the notion of exploitation and undoubtedly gave it evaluative relevance, he also expressed scepticism about the moral depth of labour entitlements (see particularly Marx, 1844; 1875). Giving ultimate priority to distribution 'according to needs', he describes claims arising from labour as residing within 'the narrow horizon of bourgeois rights', viewing persons 'only as workers, and nothing more is seen in them, everything else being ignored' (Marx, 1875, pp. 22–3).

AGENT-RELATIVE ACTION MORALITIES

The special sense of responsibility that a person feels for his or her family or friends may influence his moral judgements. If that influence affects his judgements of goodness of outcomes, it may be argued that this partiality is a violation of the requirement of 'universalisability' which has characterised much of ethical theory at least since Kant (1785). While such partiality in judging states of affairs may be thought to be a moral weakness, the case is somewhat less clear when it comes to judging actions, since actions are agent-specific in a manner that states of affairs are not. A person conceding that the outcome in which he gives a toy to a child he meets in the street may be a better outcome than the one resulting from his giving this toy to his own child, may nevertheless argue that it is right that he should give the toy to his child for he owes a special duty to his own child. He could universalise this judgement by arguing that anyone in his circumstances should do the same. If this line is taken, then the morality in question has to be non-consequentialist, since agent-relativity would have to be introduced in evaluating actions but not outcomes.

Agent relativity is one of the most complex issues in ethics. It is possible to argue that the moral appeal of agent relativity is 'instrumental'. It is a rule which, if widely followed, might well serve non-agent-relative goals, even utilitarian ones. If agent-relative decisions are justified on these lines, that is, as fulfilling non-agent-relative goals, then the moral approach can satisfy consequentialism, properly defined, to take note of having rules rather than acts as 'control' variables.

Whether this captures all there is to capture in the moral appeal of agent-relative evaluation of actions is, however, less clear.[20] Arguments for taking a non-instrumental view of agent-relativity can be strong (see Williams, 1973). The vision of the good society of hard men doing agent-independent calculations not responding to demands of love and affection except instrumentally is perhaps also slightly depressing. Agent-relative duties can also be based on ties other than those of kinship and affection, and can even reflect economic or political relations, for example, what one citizen owes to another. I shall call this general class of agent-relative obligations as 'relational obligations'.

Agent-relative duties can also be based on past events, leading to a sense of 'duty owed'. In Tolstoy's *Resurrection*, when Katyusha is wrongly sentenced to Siberia, and Nekhlyudov, who was in the jury, recognises the girl as the one whom he had seduced leading to an abortive pregnancy and then abandoned, his response is unequivocal: 'Of course, it's a strange and striking coincidence, and it is absolutely necessary to do all in my power to lighten her fate, and to do it as soon as possible'.[21] I shall refer to this type of agent-relativity arising from events that have taken place as 'event obligation'.

II   DISTRIBUTIONAL CONFLICTS

MORAL CLAIMS TO INCOME

In what does the force of a person's moral claim to income rest? The answer would clearly depend on the moral approach chosen. On the basis of the principles discussed in the last section, at least the following different sources are potentially relevant:

(1) High marginal utility of personal income, for example, under utilitarianism (page 464).

(2) Low total personal utility, for example, under leximin or maximin (page 465).

(3) Low personal availability of primary goods, for example, under Rawlsian difference principle (p. 466).

(4) Low primary powers of the person, for example, under need-based equity axioms (page 467).

(5) Violation of personal liberty consequent on denial of income to the person, for example, under libertarian principles (page 468).

(6) High labour contribution (or necessary labour contribution) to production, for example, under labour entitlement theories (page 470).

(7) High entitlement under acknowledged principles of justice in acquisition and transfer, for example, under Nozick's entitlement theories (page 470).

(8) High relational obligation or event obligation of others *vis-à-vis* him on matters of income, for example, under agent-relative action moralities (page 471).

There is, of course, nothing contradictory in accepting more than one source of moral claim. Indeed, value judgements in this area typically tend to be 'non-compulsive' (see Sen, 1967), even though purist systems like utilitarianism or entitlement theories demand unqualified adherence. When more than one moral claim is accepted and there are several non-compulsive principles competing for attention, we have a complex moral structure. Since moral complexity, in this sense, is a commonly observed phenomenon, it is necessary to discuss how such complexities may be resolved. This question is taken up in the next two subsections.

WEIGHTING AND PARTIAL ORDERING

Faced with conflicts between different criteria, a common approach is to go by dominance, that is, make only those judgements that satisfy *all* the criteria. Dominance is a widely used approach in economics, for example, in 'efficiency' calculations based on vector dominance over commodity bundles, or in 'Pareto optimality' discussions based on vector dominance over interpersonal utility bundles. The approach can be more widely used without bringing in real numbers and vectors, and it is easy to establish that when one considers a group of criteria each yielding a complete ordering of a set, then the dominance ranking based on their intersection will be a partial ordering of that set, satisfying the property of transitivity fully.[22] For example, different criteria for outcome morality can be used to generate a dominance partial ordering of states of affairs, and then using consequentialism, the combinations of control variables can be partially ordered correspondingly, leading to some guidance to policy, even though not a complete determination of all policy choices. If a non-consequentialist approach is chosen, the different criteria can be applied directly or indirectly, to the control variables (that is, with or without invoking their consequences), and then the dominance partial ordering of controls can be identified from that.

Sometimes the partial ordering based on dominance may be quite extensive, and may be able to give much guidance to policy. In other cases, it may yield very little. Indeed, if two criteria yield two complete orderings that conflict with each other over every ranking, then the dominance partial ranking will yield nothing whatever (still radiating the glory of transitivity, but—alas—in vacuum). Something like this is, in fact, a very real possibility in dealing with distribution of income by invoking as diverse a set of criteria as we listed on page 473. In the field of income distribution much moral complacency is, I imagine, based on the failure of dominance reasoning to yield much.

An alternative is to go beyond the dominance reasoning by specifying a weighting procedure for different criteria. The weighting can be in the lexicographic form with no tradeoffs, for example, criteria 7 used first, and then criteria 1 'if there are any choices left to make',[23] and so on. Or else, tradeoffs may be specified, even though often such tradeoff mappings have to be very complex given the nature of the criteria in question. It is possible to specify tradeoffs *ranges*, if there are difficulties in choosing clear-cut values, and such ranges would typically yield partial orderings more extensive than the dominance ranking but less pervasive than a complete ordering.[24] The narrower the range of tradeoffs specified, the more extensive, in general, will be the derived partial ordering. There is a real conflict here between arbitrary articulation (making the ranges very narrow) and indecisive judgements (keeping them very wide).

PARTIAL INFORMATION AND PERMISSIVE DOMINANCE

So far nothing has been said about informational limitation that may make it difficult to apply one or more of the criteria in question. But moral arguments are often based on informational limitation that rule out the use of one criterion or another. Lionel Robbins' (1938) attack on utilitarianism based on the alleged absence of interpersonally comparable utility information is a well-known example. The informational limitation can be intrinsic (for example, in Robbins' claim about the impossibility of making factual statements about interpersonal comparisons of utility[25]), or it can be case-specific (for example, not knowing how well off a recipient of charity might be).

The dominance reasoning discussed in the last section proceeded on the 'affirmative' basis of asserting only those rankings that are endorsed by all the criteria. If instead one proceeds on the 'permissive' basis of asserting those rankings that are affirmed by some criteria and not contradicted by any,[26] then the silence induced by informational lacuna can help to make the dominance partial ordering more extensive. This approach is very often taken in practical moral decisions when one proceeds on the basis of an established case for some action and none established against, possibly due to informational limitation.

The point can be illustrated by considering the problem of a person who is asked by three boys to arbitrate who should get a flute made of bamboo about which the boys are quarrelling. Consider first three alternative scenarios. In the first case, it is known that boy A plays the flute well and with very great pleasure, while boys B and C are less musical. It is clear to the arbitrator that A will get more happiness out of the flute than the other two. The arbitrator knows nothing else about the three boys, and decides to give the flute to A, in conformity with utilitarianism. In the second case, the arbitrator knows that boy B is much more deprived than the other two and has very few toys and other sources of pleasure and that he is generally much less happy than the other two. Nothing else is known about the boys, including who plays the flute well; the arbitrator decides, in this case, to give the flute to B on grounds of leximin or difference principle. In the third case, the arbitrator gathers that boy C made the flute with his own labour starting from a bamboo belonging to no one, while the others not only did not contribute anything to this effort, but wanted to take the flute away from him. She knows nothing else about the boys, for example, who is how well off, or who enjoys playing the flute more. In this case, the arbitrator decides to give the flute to C because of his labour, or on libertarian grounds, or as part of an entitlement structure incorporating the right to what one has produced (see, for example, Nozick, 1974).

In each case the arbitrator may feel that an unambiguously correct decision has been made. On the other hand, the three sets of information on which the three different decisions are based happen to be consistent with each other. It could be the case that boy A will get more joy out of the flute, boy B is most deprived, and boy C in fact did make the flute. What makes the decision unambiguous in *each* case for an arbitrator having a complex moral structure involving the principle cited is the dual characteristic of the *presence* of some information *and* the *absence* of others.[27]

INSTRUMENTAL JUSTIFICATIONS AND INCENTIVES

So far we have been concerned only with a person's moral claim to income. But a person can be rightly given more income not only on grounds that he has a moral claim to have it, but also on grounds that giving more income would have the consequence of serving some other goal, for example, produce more income and make others happier. This type of 'instrumental' justification is quite important in income distributional policy, and indeed the whole of the incentive literature depends crucially on such instrumental reasoning.

Consider, for example, the case for wage differential in favour of the more productive. Though they are frequently confused, it is possible to make a clear distinction between entitlements arguments based on instrumental considerations. The distinction is brought out by considering cases in which one of the two arguments cannot operate while the other still will. If productive workers remain just as productive irrespective of what they are paid, then the incentive argument for paying them more does not hold, whereas the entitlement argument, if accepted, will still apply.[28]

On the other hand, if conspicuously high payment to the Joneses does not increase their own productivity much but increases remarkably the productivity of others in their effort to keep up with the aforementioned Joneses, then the case for such high payment to Joneses must be based on instrumental grounds of incentives rather than on entitlement arguments based on productivity. The two types of argument are quite distinct, even though they are typically not distinguished in 'the why and wherefore of differentials': 'a differential is defended because it is right and proper'.[29]

Similarly, the entitlement argument for rewards to ownership of non-labour resources (as in Nozick, 1974) must not be confused with the instrumental argument for such rewards (as in Friedman, 1962). In the first case the rewards reflect rights that are not to be violated irrespective of consequences, while in the second case they are justified on the basis of the consequences of these rights within the structure of competitive capitalism. Someone arguing against these rewards would have to take quite different routes depending on which of these two justifications he happens to be currently disputing.

III   INTERNATIONAL ISSUES

THE RICH AND THE POOR

The ethics of international income distribution have been much discussed recently in the context of proposals for the so-called 'New International Economic Order'. Two simple approaches to this thorny issue are so common that it may be just as well to get them out of the way.

The first approach is based in treating rich and poor nations as if they are rich and poor persons, and the moral case for income transfers from the rich to the poor nations is usually then based on some kind of a welfarist and consequentialist argument, such as, poor nations have a higher marginal utility of income (the utilitarian argument), or the poor nations have a lower total utility per head (the leximin argument). The question of distribution within each country does not arise in this formulation.

I shall call this approach the 'fiction of all nations throbbing as symbolic individuals in existence'—'fantasie' for short. The literature demanding New International Economic Order does show a touch of 'fantasie', and as Richard Cooper (1977, p. 355) has noted, 'much recent discussion on transfer of resources falls uncritically into the practice of what I would call anthropomorphising nations, of treating nations as though they are individuals and extrapolating to them on the basis of average per capita income the various ethical arguments that have been developed to apply to individuals'.

The question of distribution within each country is certainly an important consideration, and treating nations as persons is to lose this perspective altogether (see Sen, 1976a; 1976c). This is particularly limiting in the context of policy questions that arise in negotiations for a new economic order, since there is some evidence that 'the international bargaining process now under way, to the extent it results in fairer shares for the South, serves to strengthen Southern élites who in the main have little autonomy form antiequity class forces at home' Fishlow et al., (1978, p. 199). Given the 'power realities' of the prevailing political system in the developing countries, it may indeed be 'touchingly naive not to anticipate the failure of asset distribution policies or the appropriation by the rich of a disproportionate share of the benefits of public investment' (Bardhan, 1974, p. 261).

So much for one of the two simple approaches; I turn now to the other. The other is a conservative belief that the population of each country is entitled to what it happens to have currently, and while a change needs justification, the *status quo* does not. I shall call this approach that of 'entitlement valid for all substance I own now'—'evasion' for short. If demands for a new international order often reflect 'fantasie', the resistance to it in rich countries frequently reveals 'evasion'. In its stronger form 'evasion' leads to a hard-nosed dismissal of humanitarian arguments for transfer to, or a better deal for, the poor countries. In its milder form, the morality of such transfers or better deals are dismissed *unless* the case for them is 'clearly' or 'unequivocally' established. Given the difficulty of tracing cause-and-effect relations in the field of international policy, such clarity or unambiguity is often absent, and then even the milder version of 'evasion' leads to inaction, if not complacency.

The moral basis of 'evasion' may be thought to rest on some entitlement theory, for example, that of Nozick (1974). But in order to establish this, one would have to show that the existing holdings were derived exclusively from the 'principles of justice in acquisition and transfer' (see p. 470). Given the acknowledged lack of free and competitive exchange in the trade between nations, and given the documented records of colonial economic relations, this would be, to put it midly, no mean task. While Nozick's entitlement theory is not inimical to inequality as such, it is exacting in its own way.

CONSEQUENTIALIST REASONING

Among the three principles into which utilitarianism was factorised (page 464), consequentialism had the role of disciplining the assessment of actions, institutions, etc., by confining the assessment to the evaluation of the consequent states of affairs generated by those actions, institutions, etc. In judging intercountry transfers, or changes in the institutional features of international relations, the consequentialist approach will require that the relevant effects of these policies on states of affairs be identified as much as possible. The criterion of what effects are relevant will, of course, depend on the outcome morality chosen.

With the utilitarian outcome morality, the consequences that have to be pursued are the utility gains or losses incurred by people in different countries. While the ultimate focus has to be on utility, and not on other descriptive features, such as incomes, prices, distributional parameters, etc., it is quite natural that non-utility features may be studied either as 'intermediate products' in the causal chain from policies to utilities, or as 'surrogates' for utilities themselves. There are many tactical issues involved in this, but the main strategic one is to focus on *utility gains and losses*. In contrast, the leximin approach will lead to a strategic focus on *utility levels* as such, that is, not on whether there is a great deal of utility gain, but whether the gains go to the people who are relatively worse off in utility terms. These 'welfarist' approaches are, however, united in not giving more than a tactical role to non-utility consequences.

In contrast, the Rawlsian version of the difference principle will concentrate on the availability of primary goods not as surrogates to utility, but as the relevant focus in itself. Similarly, equity principles based on primary powers will have a non-utility focus. In the context of international policies, the difference introduced by concentrating on primary *powers* as opposed to primary *goods* (see page 467) is rather significant. Calorie and nutritional requirements as well as needs of clothing and shelter vary with climatic conditions. Social developments like urbanisation bring about additional needs, and thus a lowering of primary powers given the same availability of primary goods. These differences have to be seriously dealt with in moral judgements of international distribution of incomes, and a person in the rich country with a higher real income than a person in a poor country must not automatically be taken to be more advantaged.[30] Even after such adjustments the moral case for international redistributions based on equity considerations is likely to be quite strong, and there is little merit in spoiling a legitimate moral argument by arbitrary overstatement based on overlooking relevant differences.

In applying consequentialist reasoning to policy issue the task consists essentially of (a) determining the outcome morality to be used, and (b) identifying the consequences of alternative policies on factors relevant to the chosen outcome morality. In a universalised con-sequentialist moral structure, the population of the world has to be viewed together, and the outcome morality chosen has, in principle, to be applied to the world population as a whole. (Needless to say actual moral debates must be based on less exacting exercises in view of practical difficulties, but the general approach is the one against which practical shortcuts have to be judged.) The approach leads to the rejection not merely of the make-believe world of 'fantasie' and the unreasoned prejudice of 'evasion', but also of the tradition of viewing 'social welfare' *separately* for each country in nationalist terms.[31] The differences in circumstances depending on the country of one's residence must, of course, be reflected as part of the relevant data, not because social welfare is best thought of in national terms, but because consideration of social welfare in the world context requires one to be alive to these relevant distinctions. More than the mechanics of such calculations, there is in this a shift in the entire *outlook* to international policy affecting the way of viewing these problems; the mechanics are merely reflections of this fundamental departure.

AGENT-RELATIVITY AND OBLIGATIONS

The universalised consequentialist approaches discussed in the last section can, of course, be rejected if an agent-relative action morality is chosen (see page 471), asserting that the government of each country has an obligation to pursue the interests of its own members only (or pursuing these interests *more* than the interests of non-members). It is necessary in this context to make a distinction between an *instrumental* justification of such agent-relativity as opposed to a justification of it in terms of its own merits (see page 472). In the instrumental sense, the argument has to be that a system in which each government is responsible for its own members is an optimum feasible system for pursuing world welfare in terms of the chosen outcome morality. Support for such a position may be based on, say, the role of effective control in apportioning responsibility, or on the need for delineating spheres of obligation in line with informational availability. Assessment of such arguments will require complex cause-and-effect studies.

On the other hand, if a non-international justification is sought, it would have to be argued that irrespective of the consequences of such nationalist focus on world affairs, it is right that each national government should cofine itself to such a focus. This would then be treated as a fundamental 'relational obligation'.

As was mentioned earlier such relational obligations are difficult to assess, even when the relations involved have the simplicity of family ties. But it is also worth noting that consideration of 'event obligations' (see page 472) may require a somewhat different focus. While Harry Johnson (1977, p. 360) refers to the 'largely mythological view of past relations between advanced and less developed countries as "imperialism"', imperialism is hardly a unicorn.[32] For the rich countries of today to sink into the complacency of a nation-focused morality will leave something to be desired even *within* the structure of agent-relative moral reasoning.

There is also some evidence to indicate that the narrowness of the focus of relational obligations is not independent of the nature of the morality that is used within that focus. Erik Lundberg (1977, p. 370) has noted that the 'egalitarian spirit', once 'established *inside* a country like Sweden', seems to have had the effect 'In a very half-hearted way to extend beyond its boundaries'. There seem to exist forces of 'disequilibrium' even *within* these moral structures. This perhaps does bring out the *ad hoc* nature of these agent-relative moralities—based on a narrow national focus—which tend to dominate policy discussions today.

RIGHTS AND ENTITLEMENTS

It may be useful to distinguish between two types of obligations which might act as barriers to taxing the rich countries to benefit the poor ones. One, which was discussed in the last section, is the question of the relational obligation of taxing authorities of a rich country to serve the interests of the members of that country. The second, essentially unrelated to this, concerns the right of people not to be taxed, and the freedom to enjoy what one has legitimately come to hold. As was argued on page 478 (in the context of examining the approach that was called 'evasion'), it is difficult to find justification within the 'entitlement theories' for the exact inequalities that we happen to observe today. This does not, however, imply that the entitlement theories will not argue for any restriction whatever to redistributions, but only that the restrictions will not take the form of blanket prohibitions.

In so far as entitlement theories like those of Nozick will impose restrictions to redistribution, it is important to be clear whether one accepts such entitlements or not. Resistance to such acceptance will come not only from need-based or welfarist moralities (such as utilitarianism or leximin), but also from *rival* entitlement theories giving competing views of desert. Even ignoring such austere views of desert as Hamlet's: 'use every man after his desert, and who shall escape whipping?', there are entitlement theories focusing on other sources of right, in particular labour (page 470). For example, what is an application of 'the principle of justice in acquisition' for Nozick (1974) is patently 'unequal exchange' for Emmanuel (1972).[33]

Other concepts of rights discussed in Section I of the paper include the right to a minimal amount of primary goods (page 466), and that to a minimum amount of primary powers (page 467). While the force of Nozick's entitlement system is in the direction of recognising the moral case for inequalities, the force of labour-based rights as well as that of need-based rights would be usually in the opposite direction. It is, I think, a mistake to presume that a right-based morality must typically be conservative in contrast with, say, utilitarianism.

CONSEQUENCES AND ASYMMETRY

As was discussed earlier (pages 468–71), rights and entitlements can be incorporated in the outcome morality itself rather than being kept out of it for application only in judgements of action. This would have the effect of expanding the scope of consequentialist framework very substantially. This is particularly important since explicitly or implicitly various right-based considerations do enter people's moral values.

But the importance of studying consequences need not be based on the acceptance of consequentialism, since a denial of consequentialism is a denial of the *sufficiency* of consequences for moral judgements, not of their *necessity*. There are, in fact, very few moral theories that are fully consequence-independent. The necessity to check the *actual* consequences of international policies, thus, goes well beyond the rejection of 'fantasie' or 'evasion' (page 477).

In the context of the relevance of studying consequences, Richard Cooper (1977, p. 355) has referred to an important difficulty.

> Not to ask questions about these linkages would be morally obtuse. Yet to ask them involves peering inside the national shell, an activity that many developing countries view as a gross and unwarranted infringement of their national sovereignty. The current mood among developing countries resists strongly the notion that donor nations have a legitimate interest, much less (on the above argument) a moral obligation, to inquire closely into the use of resource transfers to be sure that their ethically based objectives are being served. A clear impass thus results.

The problem arises partly from the *asymmetry* in the position of the donor and recipient countries, in the sense that it is the 'national shell' of the recipient country that has to be 'peered inside' according to the quoted position, without the necessity of such a peering exercise the other way.

But is there a moral case for such an asymmetry? If the correctness of a policy would depend upon *all* its consequences, clearly there is the need for checking the consequence of such policies on donor nations *as well as* on recipient countries. Indeed, the donor country has no more a 'legitimate interest' or 'moral obligation' to peer inside the national shell of the recipient country than the recipient country has to peer inside the national shell of the donor country. As far as the judgement of outcomes is concerned, the moral requirement is direction neutral.

It can, of course, be argued that the asymmetry is legitimate since it is the disposition of the wealth of the donor countries that is being discussed. In practical terms, possession is indeed nine points of the law, but to argue that a corresponding *moral* asymmetry also exists will require some type of an entitlement reasoning, which is missing. Such a moral assertion can, of course, be easily made, for example, in the form of what was called 'evasion' (page 478), but a moral defence is less straightforward (page 481).

It may, however, be argued that the asymmetry arises from the fact that it is the donor country that is taking the *action* of transfer, and is thus peculiarly responsible. But, in fact, the actions will typically take the form of bilateral or multilateral agreements, and they are not only actions of the donor country. (The belief that he who pays the piper should call the tune, is not based on the idea that the *action* is only that of the payer and not of the piper, but on the notion that the payer has an *entitlement* based on the money he is offering.)

Nor can it be argued that the consequences on the donor countries are obvious in a manner that consequences on recipient countries are not. In fact, the effects of international policies on national economies can be very complicated indeed. Consider Richard Cooper's argument (1977, p. 356) that

> if we are to justify resource transfers on ethical grounds, then, it must be on the basis of knowledge that via one mechanism or another the transferred resources will benefit those residents of the recipient countries who are clearly worse off than the worst-off 'taxed' (including taxes levied implicitly through commodity prices) residents of the donor countries.

The wording might suggest implicit use of leximin or the difference principle as the relevant 'ethical grounds' (ignoring, for example, *how much* is gained or lost), but that is clearly not the intention of Cooper's remark; leximin if chosen is presumably chosen for illustration. What is more important in the current context is the asymmetry that would arise in comparing the *actual* gain in the recipient country with the *maximal* loss that the donor country can potentially sustain, that is, the loss to the worst-off taxed resident. It is quite legitimate for someone from the recipient country to ask: Is the *actual* effect of an additional unit of transfer in the donor country to increase the 'tax' on the *worst-off* 'taxed' resident in that country?[34] The moral search for consequences has to be even-handed.[35] The recipient country has no worse a case, on consequentialist reasoning, for 'peering inside' the donor country to decide how much aid it should demand, than the donor country has for 'peering inside' the recipient country to decide how much aid it should offer.

INFORMATION AND CONSEQUENCES

Richard Cooper is certainly right in emphasising the necessity of examining consequences; the need to universalise his recommendation does not distract from the merit of his criticism of consequence-independent policy prescriptions. The critique applies not merely to intergovernment transfers, but also to international agreements on schemes such as 'brain-drain taxation'.

The consequences to be examined are not merely of immediate effects on income distribution (important though they are), but also the overall effects on the respective societies. To tax Picasso, the drained brain, to pay General Franco, ruling poor Spain, need not have been morally blissful. To dissociate the analysis of consequences from political considerations is to leave the consequential analysis seriously deficient, and morality can hardly be based on half-blindness. Such justice, to borrow a phrase from Arthur Miller, 'would freeze beer'.

Partial information on consequences can have the effect of producing 'permissive dominance' in a pluralist morality (page 474). It is common to acknowledge the relevance of multiplicity of claims, and if some important ones are snuffed out by the absence of information, others— maybe less important ones—could dominate. For someone of a strongly conservative bent and somewhat attracted by 'evasion', the lack of definitive information as to who would benefit from transfers could lead to complacency about inaction. For apolitical income-redistributors, lack of information on precisely who would gain given the political mechanism, or how the political mechanism itself might be affected, could lead to simplistic policy analyses, not far removed from 'fantasie'. The sensitivity of moral judgements to information may be very great indeed.

Information also has an important role in changing people's focus from agent-relative moralities based on a narrow, nationalist conception of relational obligation. One may, with some justice, deny responsibility for inaction about matters the existence of which one does not know. In a small way, even the limited publicity given by OXFAM or UNICEF to human suffering, and to the relatively low cost of removal of some of these sufferings, have the effect of making many people face responsibility which they would not have otherwise acknowledged. The role of information in the ethics of international income distribution can hardly be overemphasised.

IV CONCLUDING REMARKS

There will be no attempt to summarise the arguments presented in this paper, but some general remarks will be made to put the discussion in perspective.

(1) Utilitarianism is an amalgam of (a) consequentialism, (b) welfarism, and (c) sum-ranking (page 464). Each of these characteristics can be and has been criticised, and can be eschewed, severally or jointly. For example, leximin violates sum-ranking but is welfarist and consequentialist (page 465); Rawls' difference principle is not even welfarist, but can be combined with consequentialism (page 466); agent-relative moralities based on relational obligation violate consequentialism, but not necessarily the other two characteristics (page 471).

(2) The moral claim to income can be seen as arising from many different factors (pages 464 to 473). For example (a) high marginal utility (utilitarianism), (b) low total utility (leximin), (c) low availability of primary goods (differences principle), (d) low primary powers (need-based equity principles), (e) labour contribution (labour entitlement theories), (f) holdings justified by principles of acquisition and transfer (Nozick's entitlement theory), (h) consistency with personal liberty (libertarian principles), and (i) relational obligations or event obligations (agent-relative moralities).

(3) When moral considerations conflict, one has to go either by dominance, yielding partial orderings, or by supplementation through weighting, or through no-tradeoff (lexicographic) priorities. If dominance is considered in the 'permissive' rather than the 'affirmative' form, the scope of the generated partial ordering may be very substantially expanded in a situation of incomplete information (page 474), a fact of some considerable relevance for judgements of international income distribution (page 484).

(4) It may be instrumentally right that a person receives a particular income even when he has no moral claim to it, *if* the consequence of his having that income is a greater fulfilment of some other goal. Incentive arguments for inequality rest on such reasoning, and must be distinguished from arguments based on entitlement or desert (page 476).

(5) While Rawls' formation of the difference principle in terms of primary goods rather than utility avoids some of the difficulties of a utility-based equity criterion (such as, leximin), it is exposed to difficulties of another kind (page 466). Both these types of problems are avoided in an approach based on 'primary powers', which is a version of a need-based approach, but it too has problems of its own (page 467). The differences between these alternative need-based approaches are acutely relevant in judging international distributions of income, because of systematic variation of needs (page 478).

(6) Considerations of rights can enter moral judgements in various contexts (such as, in judging outcomes or actions), and in various forms (such as labour entitlements, libertarian rights, or entitlements based on rules of acquisition and transfer). There are some advantages in incorporating them in the outcome morality in a consequence-dependent framework rather than only in judgements of action in a consequence-independent framework, even though this may require an eschewal of the unqualified acceptance of the Pareto principle (pages 468 and 470).

(7) Entitlement theories conflict not only with non-entitlement theories, but also with each other (page 470), and these conflicts are of considerable importance in judging the morality of international inequalities (page 481).

(8) The relevance of identifying consequences is not confined merely to consequentialist theories, and may be very great even for non-consequentialist approaches, since they need not be consequence-independent. In assessing consequences, certain asymmetries between the need to 'peer inside' donor and recipient countries may appear natural, but as it happens these alleged asymmetries have little moral force (page 482).

(9) While nation-focused, agent-relativity can have complex instrumental justification, there seems to be some considerable *ad hocism* in treating this to be valuable in itself. Relational obligations can also conflict with event obligations based on historical considerations (page 480).

(10) The importance of the role of information in moral judgements on international distribution can hardly be overemphasised.

Informational limitation restricts or distorts consequential judgements, encourages arbitrary agent-relativity, and even provides 'permissive' justification for the make-belief reasoning of 'fantasie' and the unreasoned prejudice of 'evasion' (page 484), despite the crippling limitation of both these approaches (page 477).

This paper was aimed at sorting out ethical issues in distributional judgement, and not at achieving a unique moral resolution. Apart from the complexity of the moral concepts involved, their abundance is really rather remarkable. There is also some evidence that the moralities people adopt often vary—in a most un-Kantian way—with their own position. This makes a moral consensus on these issues which are particularly difficult. I end with some discouraging words which Shakespeare put on the lips of Philip the Bastard, and only hope—but not expect—that he got it wrong:

> Well, whiles I am a beggar, I will rail,
> And say there is no sin but to be rich;
> And being rich, my virtue then shall be
> To say that there is no vice but beggary.

ENDNOTES

1. Various versions of utilitarianism, such as act utilitarianism, rule utilitarianism, motive utilitrararianism, differ on the nature of the control variable chosen for the consequentialist exercise.
2. In the collective choice literature, the condition of 'neutrality' or 'strong neutrality' is close to this (see Sen, 1977b).
3. If population is a variable, then there is need for further specification as to whether the maximand should be the simple sum ('classical utilitarianism'), or the sum per head ('average utilitarianism').
4. See Rawls (1975) for clarification of a possible ambiguity.
5. It is this leximin criterion that has recently been axiomatised elegantly by Hammond (1976), Strasnick (1976), d'Aspremont and Gevers (1977), Deschamps and Gevers (1977), and others. On related issues, see Arrow (1977), Roberts (1977) and Maskin (1978).
6. The use of consequentialism is implicitly—but very firmly—present in the applications of maximin and leximin to public finance and other policy issues; see Atkinson (1973), Phelps (1973), Dasgupta (1974), Meade (1976), Calvo (1978), Phelps and Riley (1978), among others.
7. See Gorman (1975) and Muellbauer (1976).
8. Some of the difficulties of utility theory in its 'static, descriptive interpretation' (see Kornai, 1971, Chapters 10 and 11) will, however, apply also to the Rawlsian use of primary goods index. But not all of them apply, especially since the index may not be based on the revealed preference interpretation of actual behaviour. In making effective use of leximin (or

maximin) also, there is a good case for going beyond the crude framework of revealed preference and modern utility theory (see Sen, 1977a).

9. This extremism comes out sharply in cases in which the interest of the worse-off person goes against that of everybody else, possibly millions or billions. Curiously enough it can be shown that the 2-person version of leximin (such that the worse-off person receives priority when all persons other than two are indifferent) logically entails leximin *in general* within the framework of social welfare functionals with unrestricted domain and independence of irrelevant alternatives (see Theorem 8, Sen, 1977b).

10. Proposed in Sen (1973). A requirement very similar to this was used much earlier by Ragnar Bentzel in his Inaugural Lecture at Uppsala University dealing with social insurance against being born an idiot.

11. Indeed, Hammond's (1976) axiomatisation of leximin is based on a generalised and more demanding version of WEA. See also d'Appremont and Gevers (1977) and Deschamps and Gevers (1977).

12. The generalisation involved in moving from primary goods to primary powers involves going beyond the framework of 'characteristics' explored by Gorman (1956), Lancaster (1966) and others. The 'characteristics' (for example, calories) are properties of goods on their own (for example, of bread) and not of the relationship of people to goods (for example, the power to meet one's calorie requirements).

13. Cf. Marx's (1844) warning about 'crude communism' and 'levelling-down proceeding from *preconcieved* minimum.' 'How little this annulment of private property is really an appropriation is in fact proved by the abstract negation of the entire world of culture and civilisation, the regression to the *unnatural* simplicity of the *poor* and crude man who has few needs and who has not only failed to go beyond private property, but has not yet even reached it' (p. 95).

14. Obviously for the outcome morality to have any muscle at all in judging actions, actions must be judged taking note of goodness of outcomes. But whether the moral structure will be *fully* consequentialist or not will depend on whether this is *all* that is taken into account. There can be alternative definitions of what counts as 'consequent' states of affairs, for example, whether the actions themselves could count as part of the states generated by them; this would be the case under a broad view of consequentialism. But even with such a broad view, consequentialism is not a trivial issue (on which see Williams, 1973, pp. 82–93).

15. I have tried to discuss this problem in Sen (1978a).

16. Cf. Hart's (1973) farreaching critique of Rawls' position on the 'priority' of liberty.

17. See Sen (1978b).

18. While Nozick's moral structure is not consequentialist, it is possible to construct a consequentialist version of it incorporating the principles of justice directly in a non-Paretian outcome morality (see Sen, 1978a).

19. For critiques of Nozick on these lines, see—among many other contributions—Nagel (1975) and Scanlon (1977).

20. Since duty relations can be mirror images of rights, a non-consequentialist structure of rights *vis-à-vis* others will involve an agent-relative structure of duties. (On these relationships, see Kanger (1971; 1972) and Lindahl

(1977).) If you have a non-consequentialist right irrespective of outcome that I do something for you (such as, feed you or work for you), then I have an agent-relative duty to do that thing for you, irrespective of outcome. This type of agent-relative duties relates closely to the issues discussed earlier, in the context of possible non-consequentialist formulations of rights.

21. L. Tolstoy, *Resurrection*, English translation by L. Maude (Progressive Publishers, Moscow, 1972), p. 117.

22. See Sen (1973), pp. 72–4. The dominance ranking will be a partial ordering even when the criteria themselves yield partial (rather than complete) orderings. The dominance partial ordering can be defined either *narrowly* to cover only those rankings that are strictly endorsed by all criteria, or *broadly* to cover those rankings that are strictly endorsed ('better than') by some criterion and weakly endorsed ('at least as good as') by all criteria.

23. Nozick (1974, p. 166). Nozick is specific on the one-step lexicographic priority of entitlement judgements on action over judgements derived from other criteria involved in the social ordering of states of affairs, but does not go on to outline a full lexicographic structure.

24. See Sen (1970, Chapter 7*), Blackorby (1975), Fine (1975), Basu (1976).

25. On the validity of this claim, see Little (1957).

26. Contrasted with the 'broad' version of the affirmative dominance ranking (see footnote 22 above), the permissive dominance ranking is more extensive in treating 'incompleteness' in the same way as 'indifference'. An alternative is ranked above another in the permissive dominance ranking if it is higher according to some criterion and not lower (covering both asserted indifference as well as no assertion at all) according to any.

27. The role of information in moral judgements raises many related issues, which I have tried to analyse elsewhere—Sen (1967, 1977c, 1978a).

28. It was indeed this case that Marx (1875, p. 23) considered in his vision of the good society in the 'higher phase' of socialism, 'after labour has become not only a means of life but life's prime want; after the productive forces have also increased with the all-round development of the individual, and all the springs of cooperative wealth flow more abundantly'. Marx's rejection of differentials based on work and productivity in this case—crossing 'the narrow horizon of bourgeois right' based on labour—shows that his support for payment according to labour in early socialism was largely based on instrumental grounds rather than on entitlement reasoning.

29. Phelps-Brown (1962, p. 147). Phelps-Brown argues that 'it may even be that instead of opinions about what is fair having shaped the pay structure, it is the structure that has shaped the opinions' (p. 151).

30. This consideration is quite distinct from (and, in a sense, additional to) the point that real income differences are often less acute than nominal money income contrasts, because of differences in the price structure (see, for example, Usher, 1969).

31. If the outcome morality satisfies certain conditions of 'separability' (see Gorman, 1975), it may be legitimate to think of world welfare as a function of national welfares, even when national welfares are of no innate interest in themselves. But the assumptions are exacting, and even when fulfilled, give

rather limited status to national welfares (based on 'representation' possibilities).

32. For examples of arguments leading to a very different diagnosis from Johnson's, see Frank (1967), Magdoff (1969), Sunkel (1973), and Amin (1974). See also Díaz-Alejandro (1978) and Fishlow (1978).

33. See also Amin (1974).

34. Or: is the *actual* effect of avoiding an international transfer to bring relief to the *poorest* 'taxed' resident?

35. Commenting on this paper, Richard Cooper has explained to me, in a private communication, that this was indeed what he wanted: 'I may have worded my sentence clumsily, but its intent is to compare the *actual* gain with the *actual* loss'.

REFERENCES

Amin, S., *Accumulation in a World Scale* (New York: Monthly Review Press, 1974).

Arrow, K. J., 'Extended Sympathy and the Possibility of Social Choice', *American Economic Review*, 67 (1977).

Atkinson, A. B., 'How Progressive Should Income Tax Be?', in M. Parkin (ed.), *Essays in Modern Economics* (London: Longmans, 1973).

Bardhan, P., 'Redistribution with Growth: Some Country Experiences: India', in Chenery *et al.* (1974).

Basu, K., 'Revealed Preference of Governments: Concept, Analysis, Evaluation' (London School of Economics Ph.D. dissertation; to be published by Cambridge University Press).

Bhagwati, J. N. (ed.) *The New International Economic Order: The North–South Debate* (Cambridge, Mass.: MIT Press, 1977).

Blackorby, C., 'Degrees of Cardinality and Aggregate Partial Ordering', *Econometrica*, 43 (1975).

Blau, J. H., 'Liberal Values and Independence', *Review of Economic Studies*, 42 (1975).

Calvo, G., 'Some Notes on Time Inconsistency and Rawls' Maximin Criterion', *Review of Economic Studies*, 45 (1978).

Chenery, H., Ahluwalia, M. S., Bell, C. L. G., Duloy, J. H., and Jolly, R. *Redistribution with Growth* (London: Oxford University Press, 1974).

Cooper, R. N., 'Panel Discussion on the New International Economic Order', in Bhagwati (ed.) (1977).

Dasgupta, P., 'Some Alternative Criteria for Justice between Generations', *Journal of Public Economics*, 3 (1974).

D'Aspremont, C. and Gevers, L., 'Equity and Informational Basis of

Collective Choice', *Review of Economic Studies*, 46 (1977).

Deschamps, R. and Gevers, L., 'Leximin and Utilitarian Rules: A Joint Characterization', *Journal of Economic Theory* (1977).

Díaz-Alejandro, C. F., 'Delinking North and South: Unshackled or Unhinged?', in Fishlow *et al.* (1978).

Emmanuel, A., *Unequal Exchange: A Study of the Imperialism of Trade* (New York: Monthly Review Press, and London: NLB, 1972).

Farrell, M. J., 'Liberalism in the Theory of Social Choice', *Review of Economic Studies*, 43 (1976).

Fine, B., 'A Note on "Interpersonal Comparisons and Partial Comparability"', *Econometrica*, 43 (1975).

Fishlow, A., 'A New International Order: What Kind?' in Fishlow *et al.* (1978).

Fishlow, A., Díaz-Alejandro, C. F., Fagen, R. R., and Hansen, R. D., *Rich and Poor Nations in the World Economy* (New York: McGraw-Hill, 1978).

Frank, A. G., *Capitalism and Underdevelopment in Latin America* (New York: Monthly Review Press, 1967).

Friedman, M., *Capitalism and Freedom* (Chicago: Chicago University Press, 1962).

Gibbard, A., 'A Pareto-Consistent Libertarian Claim', *Journal of Economic Theory*, 7 (1974).

Gorman, W. M., 'The Demand for Related Goods', *Journal Paper J 3129* (Iowa Agricultural Experimental Station, Ames, Iowa, 1956).

Gorman, W. M., 'Tricks with Utility Functions', in M. Artis and A. R. Nobay (eds.), *Essays in Economic Analysis* (Cambridge: Cambridge University Press, 1975).

Hammond, P. J., 'Equity, Arrow's Conditions and Rawls' Difference Principle', *Econometrica*, 44 (1976).

Hare, R. M., 'Ethical Theory and Utilitarianism', in H. D. Lewis (ed.), *Contemporary British Philosophy* (London: Allen and Unwin, 1976).

Harsanyi, J. C., 'Morality and the Theory of Rational Behaviour', *Social Research*, 44 (1977).

Hart, H. L. A., 'Rawls on Liberty and Its Priority', *University of Chicago Law Review*, 40 (1973); reprinted in N. Daniels (ed.) *Reading Rawls* (Oxford: Blackwell, 1975).

Hayek, F. A., *The Constitution of Liberty* (London: Routledge, 1960).

Johnson, H. G., 'Panel Discussion on the New International Economic Order', in Bhagwati (ed.) (1977).

Kanger, S., 'New Foundations for Ethical Theory', in R. Hilpinen (ed.)

Deontic Logic: Introductory and Systematic Readings (Dordrecht: Reidel, 1971).

Kanger, S., 'Law and Logic', *Theoria*, 38 (1972).

Kant, I., *Grundlegung zur Metaphysik der Sitten*. English translation by T. K. Abbott, *Fundamental Principles of the Metaphysics of Ethics*, 3rd ed. (London: Longmans, 1907).

Kornai, J., *Anti-Equilibrium* (Amsterdam: North-Holland, 1971).

Lancaster, K. J., 'A New Approach to Consumer Theory', *Journal of Political Economy*, 74 (1966).

Lindahl, L., *Position and Change: A Study in Law and Logic* (Dordrecht: Reidel, 1977).

Little, I. M. D., *A Critique of Welfare Economics* (Oxford: Clarendon Press, 1957).

Locke, J., *Two Treatises on Government*. (ed. P. Laslett), 2nd. edn. (Cambridge: Cambridge University Press, 1967).

Lundberg, E., 'Panel Discussion on the New International Economic Order', in Bhagwati (ed.) (1977).

Magdoff, H., *The Age of Imperialism* (New York: Monthly Review Press, 1969).

Marx, K., (1844). *Economic and Philosophic Manuscripts of 1844*, English translation (Moscow: Progress Publishers, 1977).

Marx, K., (1875). *Critique of the Gotha Programme* English translation in K. Marx and F. Engels, *Selected Works*, vol. II (Moscow: Foreign Language Publishing House, 1951).

Maskin, E., 'A Theorem on Utilitarianism', *Review of Economic Studies*, 45 (1978).

Meade, J. E., *The Just Economy* (London: Allen & Unwin, 1976).

Mirrlees, J. A., 'An Exploration in the Theory of Optimal Income Taxation', *Review of Economic Studies*, 38 (1971).

Muellbauer, J., 'Community Preferences and the Representative Consumer', *Econometrica*, 44 (1976).

Nagel, T., 'Libertarianism without Foundations', *Yale Law Review*, 85 (1975).

Nozick, R., *Anarchy, State and Utopia* (Oxford: Blackwell, 1974).

Phelps, E. S., (ed.) *Economic Justice* (Harmondsworth: Penguin, 1973).

Phelps, E. S. and Riley, J. G., 'Rawlsian Growth: Dynamic Programming for Capital and Wealth for Intergeneration "Maximin" Justice', *Review of Economic Studies*, 45 (1978).

Phelps-Brown, E. H., *The Economics of Labour* (New Haven, Conn.: Yale University Press, 1962).

Rawls, J., *A Theory of Justice* (Cambridge, Mass.: Harvard University Press, and Oxford: Clarendon Press, 1971).

Rawls, J., 'A Kantian Conception of Equality', *Cambridge Review* (February 1975).

Robbins, L., 'Interpersonal Comparisons of Utility', *Economic Journal*, 48 (1938).

Roberts, K., 'Interpersonal Comparability and Social Choice Theory', *Review of Economic Studies*, forthcoming.

Scanlon, T., 'Rights, Goals and Fairness', forthcoming in S. Hampshire (ed.), *Public and Private Morality* (Cambridge: Cambridge University Press).

Scitovsky, T., *The Joyless Economy* (London and New York: Oxford University Press, 1976).

Sen, A. K., 'The Nature and Classes of Prescriptive Judgments', *Philosophical Quarterly*, 17 (1967).

Sen, A. K., *Collective Choice and Social Welfare* (San Francisco: Holden-Day, and Edinburgh: Oliver and Boyd; distribution taken over by North-Holland, Amsterdam, 1970).

Sen, A. K., *On Economic Inequality* (Oxford: Clarendon Press, and New York: Norton, 1973).

Sen, A. K., 'Real National Income', *Review of Economic Studies*, 43 (1976a).

Sen, A. K., 'Liberty, Unanimity and Rights', *Economica*, 43 (1976b).

Sen, A. K., 'Poverty: An Ordinal Approach to Measurement', *Econometrica*, 44 (1976c).

Sen, A. K., 'Rational Fools: A Critique of the Behaviour Foundations of Economic Theory', *Philosophy and Public Affairs*, 6 (1977a).

Sen, A. K., 'On Weights and Measures: Informational Constraints in Social Welfare Analysis', *Econometrica*, 45 (1977b).

Sen, A. K., 'Informational Analysis of Moral Principles', presented at the Thyssen Philosophy Group meeting (September 1977), forthcoming in Ross Harrison (ed.), *Rational Action* (Cambridge: Cambridge University Press, 1977c).

Sen, A. K., 'Welfare and Rights', text of Hägerström Lectures given at Uppsala University (1978a).

Sen, A. K., 'On the Labour Theory of Value: Some Methodological Issues', *Cambridge Journal of Economics*, 2 (1978b).

Strasnick, S., 'Social Choice Theory and the Derivation of Rawls' Difference Principle', *Journal of Philosophy* (1976).

Sunkel, O., 'Transnational Capital and National Disintegration in Latin America', *Social and Economic Studies* (1973).

Suppes, P., 'Some Formal Models of Grading Principles', *Synthese*, 6 (1966).

Suzumura, K., 'On the Consistency of Libertarian Claims', *Review of Economic Studies*, 45 (1978).

Usher, D., *The Price Mechanism and the Meaning of National Income Statistics* (Oxford: Clarendon Press, 1969).

Williams, B., 'A Critique of Utilitarianism', in J. J. C. Smart and B. Williams, *Utilitarianism: For and Against* (Cambridge: Cambridge University Press, 1963).

Comments

János Kornai (Hungary)

The first section of Sen's paper is a brilliant summary of the alternative ethical principles of income distribution. The same questions are treated here as have been disputed in philosophy for hundreds of years, and have been the subject of thousands of books and articles. Sen succeeded in condensing his survey into nine pages, and in such a clear and easy style that it can be followed without difficulty even by the economist reader less well versed in philosophy.

In my opinion, one important alternative is missing from the list. Among consequentialists Sen mentions exclusively those who observe consequences affecting in some way the *individual*. It is useful to distinguish also the consequentialist approach in which a *collective* goal comes into prominence. Such ethics may appear, for example, in political-revolutionary, or in religious movements.

The second section throws light upon the conflicts that may arise between the different ethical principles, and points out the important role of information in selection. The fascinating story about which child should receive the flute brings close to every reader what conflicts between different ethical principles mean, and how the decision-maker's knowledge influences choice.

In the third section the international income distribution is analysed. A lot of valuable thoughts are contained there, too, and, for myself, I agree with the statements of this section. It is my impression, however, that the discussion here is not sufficiently systematic. The first part of the study builds up a powerful intellectual apparatus, and it is not used by the author efficiently enough in his inquiry into international income distribution. I hope that Amartya Sen will continue his very promising research in this direction.

There are four aspects from which we could approach the relationship between ethics and international income distribution. In the following explication I shall combine some of Sen's thoughts with my own ideas.

ASPECT 1: DESCRIPTIVE APPROACH

The analyst puts aside his own judgements. He observes objectively and describes the *actions* of persons, of governments, of political parties, and of movements, playing a role on the international stage. Analogously with the concept of 'revealed preference' we can talk about morality revealed in the conduct of individuals or institutions. Sen's categorisation can be applied in description of the 'revealed ethics'. In that case we do not study what persons or institutions say, but what they do.

The ethical problem may be reversed in a sense. We do not derive action from ethics, but start in our analyses in the opposite direction. A complete 'mapping' seems feasible. There belongs to every consistent line of conduct a set of ethical principles which morally support this conduct, and precisely this conduct. This may be some 'pure' set of principles—according to Sen's categorisation—or the combination of several 'pure' principles—'Tell me the action—and I shall provide for it the moral code that will justify the action'.

I would not undertake to appraise upon such grounds the ethics revealed in the question of international income distribution by governments and movements actually functioning in our times. My first guess would be that, in Sen's terminology, various combinations of the 'entitlement' ethics and 'agent-related' ethics prevail. This is indicated among other things by widespread nationalism.

ASPECT 2: COMPARISON OF DECLARED AND REVEALED ETHICS

Here we draw a comparison between what is *said* and what is *done* by the different political personalities, governments, parties, and movements. We distinguish between the various cases of 'single-talk' and 'double-talk'. We confront preaching with morals embodied in real action. For example declarations in the spirit of Rawl's principle are frequent, while 'ethics of entitlement according proper acquisition' is asserted.

ASPECT 3: CAUSAL ANALYSIS

Both declared and revealed ethics are observable facts of life. They appear as a consequence of definite causes. Which morality is generated by which social mechanism? What is the interdependence between a set of social conditions and political power structures and the international income distribution ethics generated by them? Such investigation is the common research subject of sociologist, historian and economist.

ASPECT 4: NORMATIVE JUDGEMENT

The economist may function as a consultant, whom some government or social or political movement expects to take sides and submit propositions. Can he refer to some *generally accepted* ethical principles in the question of international income distribution?

Rawls' theory is grounded upon the idea of 'social contract'. According to this, people are able, by virtue of their rationality, to agree upon the ethical principle of income distribution which happens to be the maximising principle.

My impression is that the idea of 'social contract' is incredibly naive. The truth is that usually even in one single individual's soul there is not a perfectly consistent inner harmony, but, facing any complicated problem, totally contrasting ethical principles confront each other again and again. If that were not so, writers of tragedies as well as neurologists could stop their trade. It holds even more for groups consisting of masses of people: nations, or international communities. No perfect ethical consensus may exist between different people and groups of people whose interests are not identical. Conflicts get solved in temporary compromises, so that later they can give way to the emergence of new conflicts. It is *impossible* to find a generally accepted ethical code. I think the impossibility of such an undertaking could also be proved deductively.

A number of our economist colleagues would gladly brush off this depressing recognition. They would be reassured by the thought that there exists some income distribution principle whose justness is plausible and generally accepted, and which they can take as a basis in their works without any particular considerations. Sen's paper renders a highly useful service by making it clear what a large variety there is of alternative systems of ethical principles, each of which seems at first sight very 'just', and easily acceptable—yet are sharply contradictory. In none of the really important social decisions—and international income distribution is one of them—does such an ethic exist on which everybody could rely without hesitation. We are left to ourselves in the freedom of choice among the alternatives of mutually contradictory income distribution principles. The choice can be based on nothing else but our own consciences, and political and ethical convictions.

Part VI

Reform Problems

14 Need for Reforms in Underdeveloped Countries

Gunnar Myrdal (Sweden)

To provide an end vignette to this symposium we are now in this last afternoon session also considering internal problems within the underdeveloped countries, and I have been asked to write a paper on their need for reforms at home.

By formulating the topic in this realistic and inclusive way, I am not free, as my colleagues here, to select a limited and special problem, that I could then isolate and circumscribe by abstract assumptions.[1] I have therefore to rely on very broad and summary generalizations and nevertheless try to convey a realistic view of conditions and spell out conclusions in regard to the political and practical problems formulated in the title given me. And in spite of my efforts the paper has become uncomfortably long.[2]

I restrict my observations to the non-Communist Third World – what not long ago even in scholary writings often was referred to as 'the Free World', though never by me. For practical reason this in the first hand implies exclusion of China.

I   THE COLONIAL THEORY AND THE POSTWAR REACTION AGAINST IT

There is a tendency for all knowledge, like all ignorance, to deviate from the truth in an opportunistic direction. The economic research on

501

conditions in underdeveloped countries has at all times lived under a heavy cloud of biases, distorting the facts, the analysis and the conclusions.

In colonial times not much work was done by economists on conditions in the 'backward regions'—mostly they were not countries at that time—least of all directed to the abject poverty of most of their inhabitants and what could be done about it. The colonial power system, in general, did not encourage intensive research on economic underdevelopment because it gave little political importance and public interest to such research.

Nevertheless one can distil from the scanty economic literature of that time a certain structure of thoughts which were also shared by educated people generally in the developed world—and also by higher class people in the regions themselves. I have called it 'the colonial theory'. It was apologetic and freed the colonial regimes from responsibility.

It was taken as established by experience and observation that the people in the backward regions were so constituted that they reacted differently from Europeans: normally they did not respond positively to opportunities for improving their incomes and levels of living. The supply curve was backward-sloping. Generally they were supposed to be racially inferior in these and other respects.

In more sophisticated writings, these traits were, however, understood to have roots in various elements in the entire system of social relations and institutions, with which the colonial governments, for good reasons, generally abstained from interfering too much. Occasionally it was also noted that malnutrition and generally inferior levels of living among the masses of people lowered stamina. The climate was also regularly seen as a crucial cause of impairing people's ability and willingness for sustained work.

The decolonisation hurricane that swept over the globe after the Second World War created an altogether new situation. Rather suddenly economists in steadily growing numbers began planning for development of underdeveloped countries, and I, in fact, was one of them. This was not an independent development of economics as a science, but clearly brought about by a radically changed political world environment for economic research.

In the cold war that developed simultaneously the communists unhesitatingly laid the blame for the underdevelopment of the underdeveloped countries on the colonial power system that was now ending. The educated and alert élites in the new independent countries that had fought for independence, or at least now identified themselves with that fight, wholeheartedly agreed with them, as this also supported their hopes that independence should make possible government policies ending relative stagnation.

In particular, they reacted against the colonial theory that people in the underdeveloped countries were different from the Europeans. Unfortunately, they then threw out not only the racist dogma, which undoubtedly was a clear advance, but also the stress in the more accomplished colonial theory on rigid and irrational institutions and attitudes and on the productivity consequences of very inferior levels of living. Nor did they wish to hear about the climate as a difficulty in development.

All this could strengthen their optimism as they now embarked upon development planning. In the new situation the Western economists rapidly gave up the colonial theory, together with those elements of it that had validity.

By sharing the optimism of the indigenous planners, Western economists could also hope for development without too much aid from the developed world. This optimism could appear the less unrealistic as not until around the censuses of 1960 did they have reason to fear to population explosion.

In the cold war situation there was also diplomacy in the writings of Western economists, demonstrated even in the terminology. And so the pendulum of biases in economic research had rapidly swung from one extreme to the other, the ultimate cause being a radical change of the political environment for research: the fact of decolonisation.

II INCONGRUENT MODELS AND CONCEPTS

A parallel and supporting cause was the natural tendency by economists to bring with them, and utilise, models they were accustomed to use for the analysis of the developed countries, without too many qualms about whether or not they fitted conditions in these very different countries. Actually, they do not. That approach abstracts from most of the conditions that are not only peculiar to the underdeveloped countries but are largely responsible for their underdevelopment, and for the specific difficulties they meet in trying to induce development.

Already the concepts used—income, consumption, savings, invest-ment, output, supply, demand and prices, all-in markets, and all-in aggregate or average terms—are not adequate to reality in the underde-veloped countries. An analysis in these terms had an appearance of realism because statistics that could fill the models with figures were prepared and presented in great abundance.

In regard to their dealing with figures, economists have never shown the same urge for clear and realistic concepts and the same concern for estimating uncertainty of measurements as, for instance, has been standard in demographic research. In studying underdeveloped countries, their carelessness with figures reached a climax, and this is still largely true about much of the economic literature on these problems.

The deficiency of the statistics being presented is not due merely to the inferior quality of the statistical services in underdeveloped countries, although that is important, but more fundamentally to the false categories under which facts are observed and recorded. Let me consider for a moment the hecatombs of statistics on unemployment.

Unemployment is properly defined as involuntary worklessness within a fluid labour market with standardised requirements, and where the unemployed are fully aware of work opportunities and are skilled for the type of work they are seeking. In underdeveloped countries there are only minor sections of the economy where such conditions exist, and even there only with important reservations. Labour utilisation has to be studied in terms of: who works at all, for how long a time during the day, the week, the month and the year, and with what effectiveness. On that there exist no overall statistics, and the trust in the carelessly assembled false statistics on unemployment and underemployment actually discourages the undertaking of more realistic and relevant research on worklessness.

The few economists in colonial times who bothered to study how the masses lived and worked did not think of producing statistics on unemployment but dealt with the problem of worklessness in institutional terms. We can also note that in the United States, where there is a large underclass in the urban and rural slums not in the mainstream of American economic life, it is now generally recognised that the ordinary unemployment statistics are helpless in measuring and characterising their worklessness. Let me add that if economists would venture to deal with the problems of labour utilisation in preindustrial Europe in terms of unemploylent and underemployment, they would risk a harsh denouncement from the economic and social historians.

The fact, observed in the economic literature in colonial times, that much of the underdevelopment in the stagnant regions was caused by rigid and irrational institutions and by attitudes caused by them at the same time as they were upholding them, can find no place in the concepts that in the Western approach were borrowed from the analysis of developed countries.

For my own part I think that institutional factors rightly should be given more interest even when discussing our own economic problems in developed countries, and that various developments in recent decades leading up to the stagflation crisis have made this even more important. But the difference between underdeveloped and developed countries in this respect is simply enormous. First, in an abstract way: generally in developed countries development itself has meant that institutions and attitudes have become more adjusted to changes and are thus less hampering for development, so that they also continuously and more rapidly adjust to allow for development. In underdeveloped countries they are frozen in traditions resisting accommodation. I return to this problem below.

The economists in colonial times also saw how poverty itself caused continued poverty. Again there is a fundamental difference between developed and underdeveloped countries. In the developed countries, where even the poorer classes have much higher levels of living, held up also by income transferences within systems of social security, it may be permissible to use, as an approximation, development models that do not include consumption as a determinant.

In underdeveloped countries with masses of people suffering from severe nutritional and other deficiencies, which bear on labour productivity, it is not permissible. This analytical error becomes accentuated when it is assumed, as often also in more recent writings, that increased savings even by the povertystricken masses would increase the possibility of development or be a condition for it. The productivity of consumption is a major explanation why egalitarian reforms particularly in the underdeveloped countries can be a condition for a more rapid and stable economic growth.

In the apologetic colonial theory climate was given an important role as restraining development, but has now almost disappeared from the economic literature. I mention this as an extreme example, demonstrating how unsparing was the postwar revolt against the colonial theory, helped by the economists' application of models borrowed from the analysis of developed countries. Even the word climate has almost disappeared from the literature except from occasional brief statements that 'climate is of no importance for development'.

In the developed countries, all located in the temperate zones, differences in climate have never had much economic significance and could therefore safely be left outside considerations. This is not true, however, in the tropical and subtropical zones where all the underdeveloped countries are situated.

It is a fact that extremes of heat and humidity in most underdeveloped countries contribute to deterioration of soil and many kinds of material goods, including buildings and machines; that they bear a partial responsibility for low productivity of certain crops, forests and animals; and that these climatic factors not only cause discomfort to workers but, by facilitating the spread of infectious and parasitical diseases, impair their health and so decrease the participation in, and the duration of, work and its efficiency. There is an extensive literature about this in all the special fields, but even the more general conclusions from this knowledge have not been incorporated in the postwar economic literature.

Almost all these unfavourable effects of climate can largely be avoided or counteracted by planned policies in the fields of husbandry, housing, sanitation, etc. But overcoming the negative effects of the climate—and occasionally turning them into advantages, which in regard to agriculture and forestry in several regions is quite feasible— requires planning and expenditures of the investment type.

III   THE PRODUCTIVITY OF GREATER EQUALITY

The remarkable thing is that, on the whole, this methodological approach to the problems of underdeveloped countries that was established by the revolt in the underdeveloped countries against the colonial theory, and accepted and then supported by the economists' natural tendency to use the tools they had developed for the study of developed countries, has persisted and largely persists today, particularly as presented in that core of the economic literature which is directed upon planning for development.

There are, indeed, many studies outside that core dealing with more specific 'non-economic' problems, such as health, education and housing, but they generally do not intrude upon the main economic analysis. Still less do the efforts of sociologists, psychologists and anthropologists, who as a matter of course came to deal with the type of problems I noted as falling outside the economists' interests, the more so as these studies are seldom focused on the general problem of planning for development.

Economists have always kept their distance from the other social sciences, and after the Second World War their isolation hardened. The fact that they exclusively dominate planning for development, being in fact traditionally the only ones among social scientists daring to raise that problem as an inclusive national issue, makes it easier to exclude knowledge from other disciplines.

Right from the beginning development was understood simply as growth, regularly accounted for in terms of very questionable statistics on aggregate gross product or income. This is still the dominant pattern in much economic literature. Social reforms to decrease inequality in these ordinarily very inegalitarian societies were reckoned as expensive and as hampering to development; it was best to wait for a rise in production.

Although in recent years there has been more emphasis on distribution of wealth and income, and then often the antagonism between growth and increased equality has been questioned and sometimes even denied, this has seldom led to more concrete proposals in national planning.

That as a general proposition policy measures leading to greater equality could lead to more rapid growth, I believe is unquestionable. In highly developed countries rationally planned and effective egalitarian reforms have proved to be investments in the quality of the people and their productivity. Sweden, which from this point of view was becoming an advanced welfare state, did not lose momentum in economic growth but surpassed the United States in the postwar period—until the stagflation crisis, which had other causes, arrived. If this holds true in highly developed countries which have already achieved so much higher levels of living even in the lower income brackets, it is even more true and of greater significance in underdeveloped countries where masses of people are suffering from very serious consumption deficiencies which keep down their productivity.

It should be stressed, however, that in underdeveloped countries, as opposed to developed countries, egalitarian reforms cannot in any measure be effectuated by transfers of money. Tax evasion by the well-to-do is colossal, but they are relatively few, while there are so many poor. Taxation becomes forced to rely on regressive indirect taxes. Spending money in cash transfers to the poor would only lead to a circle, because they would only have to pay for it themselves. Even small-scale attempts in this direction would spur inflation, which hurts the poor particularly.

What the poor need in order to raise their miserable living levels is not a little money but radical institutional reforms; I will exemplify the types of such reforms in the sections below, but at this point I want to stress that these reforms in underdeveloped countries regularly serve the double interest of greater equality and economic growth. The two goals are inextricably joined, although to a different extent from developed countries, where they can be, and often are, pursued separately.

IV LAND REFORM

About half the population in some underdeveloped countries, mainly in Latin America, but up to more than three-fourths in others, get their livelihood from agriculture. In addition, the mass of people in the urban slums can rightly be considered as rural refugees. Migration to cities, particularly very large ones, has been, and continues to be, proceeding at sometimes unprecedented speed and is generally caused by a push from agriculture more than a pull from existing needs for more labour in cities. Industry, in fact, could grow many times faster than it actually does without the need for more unskilled labour from agriculture.

The yields of land are in underdeveloped countries generally extremely low. At the same time the man/land ratio is very high; this means also that labour productivity is extremely low. India, with 70 per cent of its labour force in agriculture cannot feed its whole population to a proper nutritional standard. The constellation of low productivity of both land and labour would seem to constitute what Ragnar Nurkse called a 'disguised saving potential', as yields would be raised by a higher labour input. But this potential is not utilised. The situation in agriculture has mostly remained unchanged, or worsened in some countries.

Meanwhile land values are most often kept up or have been rising. In these countries, where landownership mostly also traditionally gives social status, buying and owning land has become a favoured way of holding wealth. The losers are the landless, whether tenants or unattached labourers. The increase in the labour force is in many ways pressing down opportunities for small landowners and increasing the proportion of landless. In many countries their living standard has become still more depressed in recent times.

Without going further in analysing the several vicious circles which cause the very low productivity of land at the same time as gross underutilisation of the labour force, let me only conclude that the obvious way to break these circles is a radical reform of landownership and tenancy, widely distributing the land to those who work on it. The labourers will then always have work to do, and they will have the opportunity and the incentive to work steadily, harder and more efficiently in order to raise the yield by improving the land.

Programmes for land reform—often expressed in the radical terms of a request for 'land to the tiller'—have been given the stamp of official commitment in a number of countries, and legislation has been passed to implement the programmes. The laws, however, have been weaker than the pronounced programmes, so the interests of the totally landless labourers have thus largely been neglected. And the new laws have not, in practice, been implemented.

The landowners have stood against land reform, often even those who own title land. They have not only exerted influence upwards, on government and on political parties and parliaments where such exist, but they have also very generally drawn into collusion local officials, who have declined to take action against the powerful landowners. In countries where landownership, often absentee, is common, particularly in higher strata, there is a very powerful pressure group against land reform, and the pressure from below has been weak and unorganised.

There are also obvious difficulties facing land reform, even where it is carried out honestly and effectively. The new owners of usually small plots need to co-operate in many ways, and this they are not accustomed to. A large part of the increased labour input should be directed towards sharing work for improving the land, building more and better roads, constructing wells, irrigation ditches and storage facilities, and generally ameliorating the conditions for life and work in the villages. This would assume the creation of entirely new attitudes, very different from the traditional rigid village culture.

For these last-mentioned needs of co-operation there has been much understanding in India and many other underdeveloped countries, manifested in community development schemes with attached extension services, co-operative arrangements for the provision of credits, seeds, fertilisers and other production implements, and improved market outlets, etc. often combined with subsidies. All these schemes, however, were bypassing the need for land reform, and they have nothing to offer landless labourers.

They were nevertheless argued and motivated as policy measures in the interest of the poorer sections of the villages. When studied more carefully, they turn out generally to have mostly aided the landholders, who were in a better position to make use of the new opportunities, and increased the inequalities that remain at the bottom of the agricultural problem.

In fact, though it has seldom been argued openly, the inherited inegalitarian system has a particular function from one point of view: to extract, with the help of the landlords, enough food for the rest of the population. Many of the new independent small landholders after an effective rural reform would be underfed from the start and would in the new situation appropriate more food for themselves and their families. To undertake a serious land reform, it would therefore be important to have a rapid result in higher yields; it would be reasonable to retain and increase the aid now provided by the various schemes referred to, but to direct it according to the new ownership situation.

Although the general rule is that land reform, even when legislated, has mostly been a sham, there are exceptions. Thus a small country like Taiwan has, to its great advantage, carried out a substantial land reform—like Japan, then under pressure from the United States, who immediately after the war for a brief time followed a radical line in regard to agriculture organisations.

In sub-Saharan Africa the agricultural problem is rather one of deciding upon whether to reorganise an inherited tribal system of collective ownership or to establish a new system of individual ownership. The fact that in so many of the now-independent countries Europeans had acquired land, and mostly the best land, raises problems of a particular kind, both when the Europeans stay on and when they prefer to, or are forced to, leave.

Many Latin American countries, with their *latifundia* and *minifundia* existing under their shadow, have, of course, a very different type of agriculture from an Asian country like India. Nevertheless there are fundamental similarities in regard to the problem with which I am dealing. In most of Latin America, too, land yields are very low, and everywhere there is a large class of underutilised landless people. In broad outline, the need for a land reform to give the land to the tiller is the same; and here too, and even more so, the spurious efforts in that direction have been a sham.

Under these circumstances the brave declarations of the need for a land reform have, on the whole, in recent years rather tended to disappear in public discussion of agricultural problems in most underdeveloped countries; in developed countries too there is a similar tendency to forget about the problem. In the food crisis of 1974 that brought about a World Food Conference the problem of land reform was by mutual agreement entirely bypassed.

Instead attention has increasingly been directed upon technical advance, the provision of remunerative prices on food products, and mobilising more capital for investment. Without new efforts in the direction of land reform it is to be feared that all efforts in these three directions will work only towards increased inequality.

The need for land reform is great and increasing. It is of tremendous importance for development, because the great majority of people depend for their livelihood on agriculture. But the prospects of this need being met by political action are not good in most underdeveloped countries.

V   POPULATION POLICY

Meanwhile population increase is relentlessly proceeding, in many ways intensifying the inequalities in agriculture at the same time as it spurs the flight of poor people to the urban slums. The need for a policy to spread birth control among the masses of people has in recent years, on the whole, become increasingly recognised in underdeveloped countries, although it labours under tremendous difficulties.

These difficulties are rooted in the poverty of the masses and the fact that their situation is unlikely to improve. It would be different if the many millions of individual couples could feel that they were living in a dynamic society where their working and living conditions were improving, and that they themselves could hope for further improvements in their social and economic situation. In that way the population problem is rooted in the general absence or slowness of reforms in all other fields. This theory is broadly confirmed by the fact that there has been more progress for the masses of people in the few, mostly small countries, where in recent decades the rate of population increases has more substantially been brought down.

For the large regions of Asia, Latin America and Africa nobody expects more than a continued and still very rapid increase in the population until the end of the century and beyond. There is a vicious circle inherent in the trend. A sustained relatively high rate of population increase must itself hamper both economic development, and certainly the effectiveness of egalitarian reforms to raise the levels of living among the poor people. This, in turn, makes the attempt at population policy less effective.

VI EDUCATION

The colonial era ended by leaving the poor people in the newly independent countries mostly untouched by any formal education. There are exceptions, of course. The United States, in its short time as a colonial power over the Philippines, unlike the English, the Dutch, and the French in other parts of South Asia, placed more emphasis on education of the people. Ceylon has had for some time more and better schools for children of the common people.

With that and other exceptions, the main objective was to train a small section of the population to serve as clerks, minor officials of all sorts, in certain colonies, even as higher administrative functionaries and, to some extent, as professionals. It is important to state that this bent of their interest was thoroughly shared by the upper strata in the colonies, who were eager to avail themselves of the opportunities to profit by serving their masters.

These élite schools were regularly of a 'literary' or 'academic' type— what is now called 'general'—even more than in the metropolitan countries themselves at that time. However, little attention was given to science and still less to technical subjects. Students commonly expected to be 'deskmen', and not soil their hands. Importance was given to passing examinations and acquiring status, while practical training for life and work was ignored.

Wherever there was much of a liberation movement, educational reform stood high on the agenda. And after independence, demands were often raised that the entire system of education should be 'revolutionised'. But this is exactly what did *not* happen—obviously the coming of independence did not cause great changes within the people or their society.

The educational establishment is part of the larger institutional system which includes the social and economic stratification, the distribution of property, and the power relations. It embodies strong vested interests on the part of the administrators, the teachers, the students and, above all, the families in the powerful upper strata who do not want to undermine the bolstering of their position provided by the inherited school system.

There was, however, one reform idea continually expressed with seemingly great determination: the extension of popular education and the elimination of illiteracy. This represents the main, and almost the only, break with the élite ideology from the colonial era. Literacy is needed for acquiring skill in all fields; it is a precondition for any attempt to create an integrated nation with wide participation of the poor.

The goal was limited, however, to making available schools for all children. Unfortunately this implied downgrading adult education, particularly literacy classes, which are needed to shorten the time-period before literacy becomes universal. For another thing, adult education, with an emphasis on literacy, could help to make the school education of children more effective. All the information we have suggests that children living in illiterate surroundings more easily lapse into illiteracy.

Some efforts to build up adult education have been made in some underdeveloped countries, but little has arisen from it. When a country 'goes communist', however, one of the first things which usually happens is that a vigorous literacy campaign is waged to make the whole population literate within a few years. There should be nothing sinisterly communistic about this particular policy line, which is an inheritance from Russia, where it orginated long before the communist revolution.

Meanwhile, in many underdeveloped countries graduates from high schools and universities crowd into the cities as 'educated unemployed', but it has proved impossible to get them out into the villages and the urban slums to teach the poor to read, write, and calculate figures. Many of the graduates are radical, but apparently they do not identify themselves with the huge underclass.

The efforts have thus been directed to enlarging the intake of children into the primary schools. These countries then start out with great difficulties. For one thing, children of school age form a much larger percentage of the population; and there is at the start less of everything needed to run schools—school buildings, teachers, textbooks, writing paper, etc.

But nevertheless there is a valid criticism to make. Although the declared purpose was to give priority to the increase of elementary schooling in order to raise the rate of literacy in the population, what has actually happened in most underdeveloped countries is that secondary and also tertiary schooling has increased still more rapidly. This has happened in spite of the fact that secondary schooling seems to be three to five times more expensive than primary schooling, and schooling at the tertiary level five to seven times more expensive than at the secondary level.

Even more remarkable is the fact that these tendencies seem rather more accentuated in the poorest countries, which start out with many fewer children in primary schools and which should have the strongest reasons to carry out the programme of giving primary schooling the highest priority.

When this happens, it implies that the school system has been allowed to let in a swelling stream of pupils through the established channels without interfering with it, except by trying to enlarge those channels were the pressure in society is the greatest. Those who can effectively exert pressure are parents in the middle and upper strata. Here again we see how the school system is determined by the inegalitarian economic and social stratification and the unequal distribution of power.

I should warn that most of the statistics on education in underdeveloped countries seriously exaggerate the accomplishments of the primary schools. The figures for literacy, gathered in the censuses, regularly overestimate the actual *spread* of any degree of literacy. If we mean by literacy that degree of functional literacy which enables a person to have any use of it in life and work, the figures are mostly valueless.

Another type of statistics often quoted by economists, if they happen to touch upon the problems of education, such as enrolment, does not give true information about whether children attend school, and still less whether they will complete the term of five years' primary schooling.

Important in that respect is what in South Asia is called 'wastage' and 'stagnation' but is prevalent everywhere in underdeveloped countries. Children who have enrolled drop out or do not attend school regularly. If they do not drop out of enrolment they then become repeaters, which is often a prelude to dropping out. In the every poor countries like India or Pakistan ordinarily less than half of those children who were enrolled originally complete primary school.

Irregular attendance, repeating, and dropping out represent a huge waste of resources. If the expenditure for primary schools were expressed in terms of cost per child who successfully completes primary school, the cost per pupil would be much greater than is commonly accounted for; it would be particularly high in the poorer countries and the rural districts. The wastage is greatest where it can least be afforded.

Still far too little attention is given to this problem. The legislation dealing with compulsory education is seldom enforced. A general lack of efficiency and of discipline permeates the whole primary school system, particularly in the poorer countries and the poorer districts.

The availability of adequate schoolrooms, textbooks, writing paper, and other kinds of teaching aids is usually very inadequate in primary schools, though more so in the poorest countries and the poorest regions. There is almost everywhere lack of properly trained teachers. In most underdeveloped countries the situation in primary schools, particularly in rural districts and the city slums where the poor live, is desperate. In line with an evil tradition from precolonial and colonial times, and under the other limiting conditions mentioned above, teaching becomes 'bookish', even though very few books and little writing paper are available to pupils.

The secondary schools are usually somewhat better. But the attempts made in some countries to orient teaching to practical life, to impart useful skills, and in particular to give more emphasis to vocational and technical education, have had relatively little success.

The increase in vocational and technical schools—though somewhat larger in percentage terms—has usually been very small, and almost nowhere has the curriculum of the general secondary schools, where the larger part of the expansion has taken place, been modernised in any appreciable manner.

This would seem astonishing as there has been agreement among political leaders and experts for a long time that a radical change was needed in this respect. Among the facts that can explain this conservatism are the scarcity of teachers of technical subjects, particularly as they are also needed in government and industry, where they can expect higher salaries and social status than in the schools. Moreover, instruction in sciences and other technical and vocational subjects often requires costly laboratories and other technical aids.

But most important is the heavy weight of tradition from colonial and precolonial times. The dominating upper strata who are 'educated' feel a vested interest in maintaining the cleft between the 'educated' and the poor illiterate masses. The fact that a more practical vocational orientation of the secondary schools would often require participation in manual work, which is despised, and that schools presumably prepare students for jobs where manual work is part of the routine, contribute to making such schools less popular than the traditional general ones.

At the tertiary level, even more than at the secondary, the schools should, of course, be job-oriented and directed towards preparing the students for particular professions. Nevertheless, they mostly continue to produce an oversupply of 'generalists' who have been trained in the humanities, law, social sciences, and a sort of 'academic' science, and who then often swell the ranks of underqualified administrators, clerks, and the 'educated unemployed'. At the same time more engineers, agricultural technicians, doctors, dentists, pharmacologists (and, not least, teachers) on all levels are needed. By far the most important industry in most underdeveloped countries, agriculture, is particularly disfavoured.

Underlying the difficulties in changing the structure of higher education as inherited from colonial times are again the traditional ideas of what upper class élite education should amount to.

The views I have expressed are not only my own but shared by competent observers. In India, in particular, there has been much honest and penetrating discussion of the problems, though little action. The excellent *Report of the Education Commission* (1966) is outspoken: the educational system 'is tending to widen the gulf between the classes and the masses'. And the Commission concludes: 'Indian education needs a drastic reconstruction, almost a revolution . . . This calls for determined and large-scale action. Tinkering with the existing situation, and moving forward with faltering steps and lack of faith can make things worse than before.' The situation is not any better in other countries in South Asia, except a few. Very little has been accomplished to improve it, in India as elsewhere.

I am particularly concerned with the huge region of underdeveloped countries in South Asia, whose development problems I have studied intensively, and I would refer to the last chapters in the *Asian Drama* and Chapter 6 in the *Challenge of World Poverty* for a fuller treatment. A more cursory study of the literature and personal visits have confirmed the impression that almost everywhere in the underdeveloped world the situation is rather similar. There are, it is true, important differences between countries elsewhere, as indeed in South-east Asia. But broadly the picture is very much the same.

The historical background and many other conditioning factors are very different in Latin America, in Western Asia, and in North Africa, and the considerable similarities are for this reason surprising. The one unifying common trait is the political domination by a small upper and middle class. The independent sub-Saharan African countries are still in an emerging situation, but there are obvious signs of the establishment of an élite class structure in many of these countries, too.

I will have to be brief in sketching the reforms needed. The goal to make literacy universal should be taken seriously. In the first place there is need for vigorous efforts in adult education. These efforts should be closely related to and, indeed, be an extension of the activity of the schools. The universities should also be engaged in this activity, to bring both professors and students nearer the people and their problems.

Major emphasis should be placed on elementary education, and relatively more resources should be devoted to education at this stage. Serious attention should be given to raising the qualitative standards of the primary schools, and decreasing the tremendous wastage on account of dropouts and repeaters.

A crucial task is to increase the number and qualifications of trained teachers. The schools for their training should be the 'power plants' that generate moral and intellectual energy among the students to prepare the people for development.

In most underdeveloped countries there should be a halt to the more rapid increase in enrolment in secondary and tertiary schools, or even a temporary decrease. There is no reason why technical, vocational, and professional training should not be increased substantially within the present or even somewhat smaller secondary and tertiary educational system—providing more and better trained teachers, agricultural extension workers, and medical and paramedical personnel, to cite only a few of the fields where more trained young people are urgently needed.

VII   HEALTH

In all underdeveloped countries, after the Second World War there was a drastic fall in mortality increasing average life expectancy, which, however, is still far lower than in developed countries. This fall in mortality has been the major cause of the population explosion, as fertility tended to remain high. We might note in passing that causing a rise in mortality, or even hampering its further decline, cannot be accepted as a population policy.

The instrumental factor in bringing down mortality has been the availability of an inexpensive new medical technology for preventing and partly curing infectious diseases like malaria. Further overall progress will be more difficult to attain and will probably be slower, as it would imply more costly remedial measures like sanitation of the water supply, more active co-operation of the people in raising the level of hygiene, and more availability of treatment for individual illnesses.

When health standards are accounted for in terms of mortality and life expectancy, this is partly due to the lack of equally reliable information about morbidity. This should be a reason for greater care when drawing conclusions from mortality rates to the general health conditions in a country. A large part of a population may become more diseased or at least lacking in vigour although rate of mortality are decreasing. This is, I believe, the situation among poverty-stricken people in many underdeveloped countries or regions of countries. And the health effects of increased undernutrition during the recent food crises cannot be measured by those who starved to death.

Figures for mortality and life expectancy are also usually given for whole countries or districts of countries. This is misleading as the differences are large between rich and poor and between urban and rural. Similarly the often-quoted figures for the number of doctors per 10,000 inhabitants are also simply misleading. It is a well-known fact that the majority of doctors are in the cities and there mostly cater to the rich. Likewise the urban districts are generally favoured because hospitals are located there.

In no other field is there a greater inequality in these countries than in in the availability of health facilities, being mostly monopolised by the upper strata. Even a government that tried to make medical aid available to the poor and, in particular, to those in the rural districts, meets tremendous resistance.

Reformers who see that one condition for bringing some more medical care to the poor in the villages would be to have a large number of health workers, with a lower and less expensive training behind them—such as the 'barefoot doctors' in China—meet mostly stiff resistance from the doctors as a body.

VIII   THE SOFT STATE

Underdeveloped countries are, though to a slightly different degree, soft states. By this I refer to all the various forms of lack of social discipline which manifest themselves by deficiencies in legislation and more particularly law observation and enforcement, a widespread disobedience by public officials on various levels to rules and directives handed down to them, and often their collusion with powerful persons and groups of persons, whose conduct they should regulate—and, in addition, the commonly shared knowledge that things are as they are and will remain so.

Though in one sense the soft state is systematically lenient towards people's wish to do what they please, there is usually much cruelty displayed in relations between individuals and groups, and by officials of governments. In that last respect this is particularly true in the military dictatorships, which have in recent times been increasing in number.

I will focus my observations here on corruption in particular as an important aspect of the soft state. Bascially it implies that while, on the one hand, it has proved difficult in underdeveloped countries to introduce rational profit motives and market behaviour into the sector of life where they commonly operate in developed countries—that is, the sphere of business—it has, on the other hand, proved difficult to eliminate motives of private gain in the sector where they have been largely suppressed in the developed countries—the sphere of public responsibility and power.

The historical background of this social pattern is widely different in South Asia, Western Asia, Latin America and the independent countries of Africa. Nevertheless the end result has been very much the same; and almost everywhere corruption has been increasing and is still continuing to increase.

An important role in this development has been played by Western business concerns, whose collective interests have been damaged. To the intellectuals in underdeveloped countries, Western business concerns have been seen as guilty of bribing their politicians and officials, which tends to create animosity towards developed countries in general. And it implies an element of unfair competition, which within all developed countries with common support has been legislated against.

Up till now, however, the tax authorities in Western developed countries have mostly been permitting the deduction of bribes as business expenditures. And while bribing politicians and officials at home is dealt with as a crime, it regularly goes unpunished if it is done abroad. The growing critical interest in the behaviour of transnational corporations and the recent explosion of scandals in the United States may activate a defence of the common interests of Western business concerns to keep out of corruption abroad.

Meanwhile, corruption has in most underdeveloped countries become a way of life and, as I said, it is mostly still on the increase. The small island state of Singapore is practically the single exception, and I have seen that effective measures have been taken by a government which itself apparently is incorrupt.

In the few underdeveloped countries where the press has been free, it has eagerly reported on cases of corruption. Some years ago in particular, legislative and administrative action had been taken in some countries, and some culprits prosecuted, but usually without much effect on the further spread of corruption.

Corruption is very seldom discussed in the economic literature, and never completely and exhaustively. When again some years ago a few American economists—other economists have remained completely silent on this issue—put the idea across that 'bribing . . . is a necessary and not harmful lubricant' for carrying on business under a cumbersome and arbitrary administration, they were wrong.

Corruption is part and parcel of underdeveloped countries being soft states. It is a major inhibition and raises serious obstacles against efforts to increase social discipline. Moreover, corruption introduces an element of irrationality into all planning and plan fulfilment. As the threat of obstruction and delay is the regular method of exploiting a position of public responsibility for private gain, corruption impedes the processes of decision-making and execution on all levels. Instead of lubricating these processes they are rendered more cumbersome and, at the same time, less effective for their purposes.

In a soft state the lack of social discipline spreads to all strata in society. Tolerance of corruption at the highest level of politics, administration and business has its counterpart in a similar tendency to extract a bribe by the lowly clerk for not stopping a paper on its way upwards or by a gatekeeper for opening the gate. Even if almost everybody gets his slice of irregular advantages in a soft state, there is no question that only those with political, social and economic power have the opportunity for large-scale exploitation. Corruption is not only hampering to growth and developement, as I pointed out, but, at the same time, is a built-in cause of inequality in underdeveloped countries.

I might end this exemplification of reforms needed in underdeveloped countries by stressing again that greater equality cannot be effectuated simply by redistributed transferences of money, but requires fundamental changes in deeply rooted institutions and attitudes. In such reforms the two goals of growth and greater equality are inextricably joined and the needed reforms are all causally interrelated as exemplified in regard to population and health.

IX   THE CONSPIRACY OF THE UPPER STRATA

A further generalisation can be concluded from my exemplification of reforms that are needed,—that almost all of them have met resistance from those in power. These upper strata are a very diversified crowd, stretching from landowners and moneylenders in the villages and local officials in collusion with them, to industrialists, higher officials, members of legislative assemblies, and teachers in secondary, and particularly tertiary schools, etc. In fact, they are best defined as people who are in a position to hinder the acceptance of reforms, or to twist them, and in the end, obstruct their implementation.

Because of their influence there has been little progress in land reform and none in stamping out corruption. Greater democracy in the fields of education and health services is for the most part not effectively realised to any degree. In addition to this, a more rapid fall in the population increase, that in many ways leads to increased pressure upon opportunities and living levels of the poor, cannot be expected in the majority of underdeveloped countries. The breaking distance is so long with their skewed age distribution, itself a result of high fertility up till now. However, in the absence of other reforms, the societies cannot make individual couples among the poverty-stricken masses very receptive to family planning, even were it forcefully propagated from above.

It is the equalisation element implied in the reforms that makes the upper strata unwilling to accept them and causes their failure. They are not willing to give up advantages they enjoy. This is often a shortsighted view, because of the productivity gains that can also be expected from the reforms. There are, therefore, certain improved opportunities even, and not least for the upper strata, but they are unaware of these.

We now see that when reforms in the fields I have discussed in sections above and in other fields are legislated, the new laws are already provided with loopholes, and their administration becomes ineffective. Regarding income taxation, for instance, the authorities responsible for tax assessment and tax collection are often intentionally given very small staffs, and such low salaries that the temptation is great to become corrupted. Even various reforms explicitly motivated to aid the poorest sections actually turn out in reality to subsidise the already well-off and thus to increase inequality. No public activity in most underdeveloped countries is so drenched in hypocrisy as the work on needed reforms.

Their hearts are divided. It was the more intellectual of these upper strata that after independence carried over the modernisation ideals and among them prominently the egalitarian one. In general proclamations these ideals are ordinarily given a conspicuous place. India and many other underdeveloped countries declared themselves as wanting to establish a classless, socialist society. And I know of no underdeveloped country where policy has been explained as leaving the masses of people impoverished while favouring the upper strata.

The power situation being what it is, the actual development confirms, however, the historical experience that no upper-class group has ever climbed down from its privileges and opened up its monopolies simply because of its good intentions or ideals. Pressure from below is needed to give force to the ideals, and such a pressure is mostly missing or ineffective in underdeveloped countries.

I should here review the predominant pattern of mass passivity in underdeveloped countries, broken here and there by more or less widespread attempts at revolts, usually not well organised and unclear about either goals or effective means of reaching them. I believe that one of the common weaknesses is the lack of identification between reform-minded people in the upper strata and the poor people in the villages and the slums. But for the purpose of writing this paper, here I draw the borderline.

X   THE NEOCOLONIAL MECHANISM

The needed reforms in underdeveloped countries as broadly exemplified and analysed in the preceding section are all in line with Western ideals, and they have all to a varying extent and in somewhat different forms been carried out, and this has for a hundred years and sometimes much longer constituted an important part of the political, social and and economic history of all developed countries. Even in a country like the United States, which for various historical reasons does not belong to the more advanced Western countries in this respect, I believe that every Congressman would heartily welcome hearing that an underdeveloped country was carrying out an effective land reform, was democratising its educational and health services, and had become adamant in stamping out corruption. But little or no influence by developed countries is exerted in this direction. This needs explanation.

In colonial times there was a built-in mechanism that almost automatically led a metropolitan power to ally itself with the privileged group in a colony and often to create new such groups. To support its reign, the colonial government would thus feel an interest in upholding and even strengthening the inherited inegalitarian social and economic structure there. Without a doubt, there is similar mechanism at work after the liberation of the colonies, in relation to Latin America, and now on the part of all Western developed countries (and not only the old colonial powers), a mechanism which tends to operate automatically whether wanted or not.

All transaction with underdeveloped countries have to be conducted with the ruling upper-class élite, who prevent or subvert the institutional reforms at home needed for the promotion of more equality and, at the same time, in a longer perspective make possible a more rapid and stable economic growth.

It is their representatives who turn up at intergovernmental meetings, such as those where they have pressed for a New Economic World Order. They certainly did not find it opportune to stress or even mention the need for a New Economic Order at home. Unfortunately it is with people in this élite that all business has to be conducted. Even aid has to be negotiated through them. When they have insisted on the principle, and had it recognised, not only by the United Nations aid agencies but more generally, that the use of aid and its direction should be determined by the aid-receiving country and fit into its planning, the power of the ruling élites is then backed up.

In all these ways developed countries, without even wanting it, have undoubtedly strengthened the inegalitarian social and economic power structure in underdeveloped countries that stands as the main impediment to institutional reforms. Even those developed countries which cannot be suspected of willingly wanting to exert that type of influence on them are caught up in this mechanism of neocolonialism.

Meanwhile, and in line with this automatic mechanism, in the developed countries very little attention is being paid to the prevailing inegalitarian power structure in most underdeveloped countries and, in particular, to the need for radical institutional reform to make possible not only greater equality but economic development. The tardiness of developed countries in giving substantial aid to underdeveloped countries must cause a creeping feeling of guilt. And quite generally, those who feel warmest towards people in the underdeveloped countries are often least willing to discuss those countries' faults and policy failures.

The regular run of economists have incorporated their work on conditions in underdeveloped countries in the neocolonial mechanism. As the needed reforms all call for institutional changes their accommodation has been the more easy, as from the very beginning of their research on underdeveloped countries at the end of the Second World War their approach, as I noted in Section II, commonly excluded considerations of 'non-economic' factors.

Hundreds of books and articles on conditions in underdeveloped countries have been published, and are published today, where there is no mention of such crucially important facts as the soft state and corruption. Problems of land reform or the needed redirection of health administration and the educational system are seldom central to their analysis or dealt with in realistic terms from the point of view of equality and growth. Indeed, they are seldom mentioned—most of the time these crucial problems are pushed under the table. This is a flagrant bias, inherent in the neocolonial mechanism.

Journalists have, as often also in other fields, been more eager to give an unbiased picture of the situation in underdeveloped countries. And under the official silence on the part of politicians, bureaucrats and economists, there is a widespread and growing awareness of these problems among ordinary people in the developed countries. Unfortunately this has, in fact, meant a lack of popular support for the aid programmes in many developed countries, and raised doubt in others. The ordinary person is apt to ask why underdeveloped countries do not see to it that they can effectively tax their own rich people and reform their own societies before they come begging for aid.

I believe this is a most unfortunate situation. Those of us who ardently support not only the few enlightened and courageous individuals to be found among their élites vainly arguing for reforms, but also the poor in underdeveloped countries, should not be silent on these awkward problems. We should be prepared to explore the grossly inegalitarian social and economic situation in most underdeveloped countries and give rational reasons for institutional reforms, thereby strengthening those who are fighting for reforms against heavy odds.

A special duty should fall, of course, upon economists who continuously carry the main responsibility for overall national planning. Their duty should be to lay bare the facts and on that basis outline an economic policy that is realistic and can bear fruit. The idea that we should be 'diplomatic' in our research on underdeveloped countries means being exculpating towards the ruling upper strata, and that is merely playing our role in what I defined as the neocolonialist mechanism, which implies heavy biases in our research.

I have been dealing above with the internal situation in underdeveloped countries. But no realistic and truthful discussion of their international relations can be carried out, when abstracting from conditions and developments at home. A study of the effects of transnational corporations becomes defective without consideration of the power relations and the propensity to corruption among the rulers in the underdeveloped countries where they operate. And the same is true all round. The bias of our closing our eyes to what goes on within underdeveloped countries lays a heavy fog of lack of realism and truth over the whole literature about underdeveloped countries and their existence in the world.

To end on a positive note, I would emphasise the crucial importance it would have in the world if the huge establishment of economists working on the problems of underdeveloped countries would break out of the neoclassical mechanism and base their studies on an attempt to record and analyse the actual situation in these countries and the political, social and economic forces that operate there. With what probability such a fundamental change of approach can be expected, I will leave without comment at this point.

ENDNOTES

1. In the writings of ordinary economists there are also assumptions with respect to conditions and determinants in the economic and social process that are not accounted for and most of the time not consciously perceived. This absence often conceals systematic biases, as I will touch upon at the end of my paper. For a condensed critique see Myrdal (1978).
2. For a fuller but still highly compressed statement of my views I can refer to the first eight chapters of my book *The Challenge of World Poverty*, which contains a summary of the political conclusions scattered in various parts of *Asian Drama*, where also sources and documentation are provided.

    I might add that the thereafter following chapters in the first mentioned book contain in summary form my views on what is now referred to as 'A New International Economic World Order'. The demand has already been raised by the underdeveloped countries and resulted in the establishment of UNCTAD. There the demand had then had a history not unlike what has happened after the Special Assembly of the United Nations 1974, when the slogan was coined.

REFERENCES

Mydral, G., *Asian Drama*, (New York: Twentieth Century Fund/Pantheon Books, 1968).

Myrdal, G. *The Challenge of World Poverty* (New York: Pantheon Books, 1970).

Myrdal, G. "Institutional Economics", *Journal of Economic Issues*, 12 (1978) no. 4.

Comments

Jagdish Bhagwati (USA)

This is a vintage Gunnar Myrdal piece: broad in canvas, rich in insights, unabashed in its statement of the follies of countries and their élites, confident about what needs to be done, and apparently optimistic despite his acute perceptions of obstacles and barriers that indeed it can be done.

In a splendid overview of the developmental problems and associated reforms that the LDCs must undertake, Gunnar Myrdal (a) traces the evolution of developmental theory from its early origins in colonial thought to its postwar transformation into the allegedly inadequate doctrines that we came to accept fairly generally; (b) emphasises how there are fundamental asymmetries between LDCs and DCs, a principal one being that greater equality in the LDCs will produce rather than compromise growth; (c) argues that radical land reform, 'widely distributing the land to those who work on it' is the manner in which this equality and induced growth must be brought about; (d) emphasises the importance of population control and again its source in 'the general absence or slowness of reforms in all other fields'; (e) stresses the need to increase adult and elementary education and to reorient education towards vocational and technical needs rather than the liberal arts degrees conferred in higher-educational institutions; and (f) underlines the urban bias in availability of medical facilities and the need to correct it for the benefit of the poor.

From these rather stylised factual contentions, Gunnar Myrdal proceeds then to argue that:

(1) The LDCs are soft states, characterised by corruption and associated forms of lack of social discipline, with these bad habits often reinforced significantly by the bribing activities of Western MNCs and condoned by Western governments; and this corruption harms both growth and equality;

(2) There is a 'conspiracy of the upper strata': 'almost all of [the

needed reforms] have met resistance from those in power'; indeed 'because of the influence of [these upper strata groups] there has been little progress in land reform and none in stamping out corruption . . . . No public activity in most underdeveloped countries is so drenched in hypocrisy as the work on needed reforms';

(3) There is a 'neocolonial mechanism' at work, leading to a conspiracy of silence on these follies and failures between the DCs and the LDC élites: 'all transactions with underdeveloped countries have to be conducted with the ruling upper-class élite, who participate in preventing or subverting the institutional reforms at home that would be needed for the promotion of more equality and, at the same time, in a little longer perspective making possible a more rapid and stable growth';

(4) Aid without strings, as demanded nowadays, would only mean that 'it is the power of the ruling élites which is then backed up';

(5) Therefore, all 'diplomatic' silence on this question should be broken and that

a change in economic research in public opinion in developed countries towards [such] truthful realism is a necessary precondition for making possible the transference of funds raised to more substantial levels. We are either boosting the selfish and shortsighted interests of the ruling élites or trying to influence them to take broader considerations. In selecting the countries to be aided, preference can be given to those who have governments prepared to enter upon the road to reforms. And aid can be given on such conditions that move them in that direction.

Faced with the task of commenting on this sweepingly panoramic and stimulating paper, I feel quite inadequate and gladly take refuge behind the time-limit imposed by the Chairman and mainly concentrate on some major themes.

Let me begin first with Gunnar Myrdal's basic argument. In essence, it proceeds on four major, underlying steps: (1) that the LDCs have basically failed to provide benefits to the poor; (2) that there is in fact a set of remedies or reforms which can be identified fairly readily as those necessary for changing this situation; (3) that the progress in this direction is held up by the élites in LDCs; and (4) the DCs, presumably *their* élites and·their electorates, can recognise the desirability of these reforms and be easily persuaded to utilise aid programmes to bring pressure on the LDC élites to undertake the necessary reforms. I am afraid that I have my doubts on each of these arguments, and I express them here largely in the hope that Gunnar Myrdal can lay the worst of them at rest, in his response.

ARGUMENT 1

There is indeed little doubt that our early optimism about the removal of poverty with the developmental programmes of the 1950s and 1960s was to prove unjustified. But we need to be cautious in our interpretation of what happened.[1] For one thing, there has been considerable diversity of experience. There *are* LDCs that have experienced a decline in inequality, however defined, and in the percentage of people below the poverty line, whether defined by reference to a budget constraint or calorie requirements. Moreover, the data on income distribution, however weak and tenuous they are, suggest that, despite the enormous pressure from population growth, even some of the poorly performing LDCs such as India seem to have managed to prevent relative inequality, and the relative numbers below a poverty line, from increasing.

Thus, for India, the data recently processed by Ahluwalia of the World Bank show that, in rural areas, where nearly 80 per cent of India's population lives, the proportion of the population below a normatively defined poverty line fluctuated substantially over the period 1956–57 to 1973–74, and there was no evidence of a significant trend in these fluctuations over time. Moreover, the fluctuations in the incidence of poverty in individual states largely follow the all-India pattern, showing no clear trend (with a statistically significant positive time trend, that is, the proportion of people below the poverty line steadily increasing, in three states and a negative trend in one state). Next, the relative inequality, as measured by Gini coefficients, of the distribution of per capita household consumption has noticeably declined in eight states out of thirteen, while the remaining five show no trend. Thus Ahluwalia finds no significant increase in the proportion of poor in India, and relative inequality appears to have decreased. Indirect evidence, such as the rising expectation of life at birth, and declining mortality (including infant mortality) and fertility rates would seem to corroborate the conclusion that there could not have been a serious decline in the living standards of the poor.

For Brazil, the evidence is mixed. And for South Korea and Taiwan (mentioned by Myrdal himself), the rapid growth in real income has been indeed shared by those at the bottom end of the income distribution. And so on.

It is therefore a little harsh on the LDC elites to argue that the record of the last three decades is so totally poor as one might perhaps infer from Gunnar Myrdal's paper. Moreover, the stark example, India, that is chosen often to illustrate the failure of the growth strategy in the past to trickle down to the poor, is not merely not so sorry a picture, as already argued above; it is also a bad example because growth was *not* so good in India anyway: there was little there to trickle down, thanks to *external* trade and payments policies—excluded from Myrdal's paper— which were seriously counterproductive of growth.[2]

ARGUMENT 2

Turning to the mix of desirable reforms, then, I have doubts also as to the underlying view in the paper that we really have a reasonable professional consensus on what needs to be done in regard to land reforms, population policy, educational policy, etc. Here, I mean only *partly* the objectives and *mostly* the means and the knowhow to implement them.

Thus, land reform in the sense of land to the tiller seems to me to be a thoroughly desirable objective and one which, not merely on egalitarian but also efficiency grounds, should be implemented. But here, again, note that Dr Amin argues in his paper (Chapter 15) that rural collectivisation is necessary instead, a position that I do not share at all but which I quote merely to show divergent opinions even in the progressive ranks.

Again, on land-to-the-tiller reform, the conditions regarding land/man ratio can lead to serious difficulties in some countries. In India, this prescription could mean, if taken literally, extensive re- distribution and fragmentation of land, and the attendant need to organise co-operative farming, marketing, etc. The difficulties with co- operation have led frustrated planners to think of instituting 'com- pulsory co-operation', which, much like 'open marriage', is easy to conceive but difficult to sustain!

Where I find myself in total sympathy with Gunnar Myrdal is on the need to reorient education away from its frequent emphasis on higher education. Whether this can be done, however, is a question that admits of no simple answer, with the best will in the world. Let me explain. We are all familiar with the human capital approach to education, as also the radical 'socialisation' theory of education which both, for different reasons, assign a positive and equal social and private marginal product to education. In contrast, the Arrow–Spence screening theory views education as merely a certification device that conveys to prospective employers *information* about ability, so that education provides a more able means to secure higher wages and hence a private return. However a divergence between social and private marginal products can follow. The theory that applies to liberal arts education, which has over-expanded in some LDCs such as India, is however none of these three but rather the one recently developed by myself, Srinivasan and Fields and which I have christened the 'fairness-in-hiring' theory.[3] Here, education becomes an instrument of job competition. With few jobs available in an economy that I call a 'job ladder' economy, the market is cleared for them, not by reducing salaries but by rationing, with preference being given to those who have higher education over those who have less for jobs which require objectively no education! This is evidently a socially unproductive role for education; and while there is a positive *marginal* product here, the social product is negative. From the viewpoint of shutting off the demand for such socially unproductive education, however, the situation is politically untenable in a democratic society. For, not merely will there be pressure to increase the amount of university places, for those who wish to acquire more degrees, but politically, this process will often also lead to demands for subsidisation of university education. The result is a situation that is all too often observed in LDCs such as India and Pakistan. In the light of these realities, the planners have often had to give in, rather than successfully deflect educational expansion in favour of other forms of education; this is not because they are perverse in their preferences but because they often feel that they have practically no other realistic options open to them.[4]

ARGUMENT 3

This leads me directly into the question of whether progress in reforms has been delayed by LDC élites.

While undoubtedly this argument is valid for issues such as land reform, one has to admit that even difficult land reforms have sometimes been carried out, within the democratic framework, in certain areas (for instance, the state of Gujerat in India) and that experience, as always, is rather diverse on this issue.

Besides, it is not evident to me that in matters of economics, where even the economists are generally not clear about the distributional impact of different economic policies, specific groups, whether described as 'élites' or not, can readily identify their own interest and militate against efficient and/or progressive policies that run contrary to their interests. By sheer laws of chance, the élites must allow for some desirable policies to follow through, even if they ultimately, and unintentionally, result in harm to their own interests.

Moreover, I would like to stress again that, even with goodwill on the part of benign élites, certain problems may defy solution. Myrdal's example of bias in the supply of medical services to the urban areas is a good case in point. Admittedly, the élites have not done much in many LDCs to supply medical services to the rural areas. But how much *can* be done? How are doctors, in a relatively free labour market, to be 'sent to the countryside'? There is obviously *some* price, a Chicago economist will say, at which doctors would even go to Siberia. But the resulting cost of extending medical services on an extensive scale to the rural areas in, say, India, could impose an extremely severe cost on the budget and then impinge on other programmes. The constraint would seem then to be better described as a resource constraint rather than one imposed by a conspiracy of self-serving élite groups! The example of 'barefoot doctors' in China is probably an example of success in this regard. But much that we were told about China has now been revealed as exaggerated, and the glories of their technological capability under a policy of self-reliance, which were attested to by occasional visitors, are now revealed as untrue, and the new Chinese leadership is desperately seeking to train students almost anywhere abroad (including small colleges of no distinction). Perhaps then one may be allowed to entertain some scepticism about the successes of the barefoot doctors and to imagine that the bulk of their time is spent in bending over to remove the thorns from their feet as they roam the countryside?

None of this is to deny that LDC élites, like élites everywhere else, generally tend to promote their own interests and try to slow down reforms that are *clearly* to their own disadvantage. At this very Conference, an LDC economist has described the proposal to tax the brain drain for raising developmental resources for LDCs as 'morally obtuse' because Picasso, for example, would be taxed to support Franco's regime! Such a reaction is ridiculous because it shows ignorance of the proposal in its fundamentals and also because it contrasts ill with the revealed willingness to pay taxes to DCs whose policies in Rhodesia and South Africa, for example, have not been exactly virtuous. But the reaction is exactly what is to be expected from members of the LDC élite groups who would rather exhort DC governments to undertake foreign aid programmes than tax themselves! Therefore, Gunnar Myrdal is evidently on firm ground in his complaints against the LDC élites. It is just that I think that one should not lean on this insight as much as he seems to.

ARGUMENT 4

On the other hand, Myrdal argues that the élites in the DCs, as also the DC electorates, will act in an enlightened fashion and will recognise the need for reforms in LDCs, if only these were honestly pointed out, and that aid pressure in this regard will produce the desired results.

These arguments are the least likely to command agreement, I am afraid. Are the DC élites and the LDC élites so far apart in their interests or is there a mutuality of interests among them, *à la* radical analyses? Indeed, even if one does not take the radical theses too literally, one may still not go to the other extreme and embrace Myrdal's views. After the assassination of Chile's President Allende, who was indeed implementing redistributive policies after a fashion, I find it difficult to accept the statement that no United States Congressman will object to the Myrdal programme of LDC reforms, for example!

Again, one must at least ask whether aid pressure, once we admit its legitimacy, is not likely to be applied for reactionary rather than progressive policies. Can we rule out altogether the possibility, often raised in the aid literature, that DCs push for conservative options and LDCs for socialist options: for example, Nehru's India versus World Bank and USA? Thus, may there not be a case for relatively stringless transfers of aid to several recipients, based on the best-likelihood estimate of what may happen with the aid flows?

Again, if Myrdal believes in the soft state thesis, he should have doubts about even the feasibility of successful exercise of pressure by aid donors. The arm-twisting surely would be ineffective when applied to a soft and flabby arm!

Paul Streeten has described Myrdal, the author of the *Asian Drama*, as the cheerful pessimist. Today, he seems to me to come across rather as the despondent optimist. For, he seems to believe, despite all the obstacles that he identifies in getting the needed reforms through, that DCs can nudge and push them in the right direction. I wish I could share his optimism.

However, I am more than glad to go along with his call to shed the hypocrisy that has often led to our looking the other way in our analyses of LDCs. Several of the developmental research institutes and aid agencies of the DCs seem to have come to regard the 'genuine' Third World voices to be those that are distinguished by their stridency rather than by pragmatic and thoughtful analysis of the problems facing the LDCs. This is precisely the type of patronising double standard that Myrdal's observations address so beautifully.

ENDNOTES

1. For a detailed analysis, from which I have benefited, see T. N. Srinivasan (1978).
2. For detailed analysis of the failures of these policies, see Bhagwati and Desai (1970) and Bhagwati and Srinivasan (1977).
3. Cf. Bhagwati and Srinivasan (1977a) and Fields (1974).
4. I have proposed some remedies such as elimination of such a preferential rule by hiring (at least in the public sector) by lottery from a pool of both just-qualified and 'overqualified' applicants, which would eliminate the incentive to become overqualified. See my (1973) Shastri Lectures.

REFERENCES

Bhagwati, J., and Desai, P., *India: Planning for Industrialization* (London: Oxford University Press, 1970).

Bhagwati, J., *India in the International Economy*, Lal Bahadur Shastri Lectures (Hyderabad, India: Osmania University Press, 1973).

Bhagwati, J., and Srinivasan, T. N., 'Education in a "Job Ladder" Model and the Fairness-in-Hiring Rule', *Journal of Public Economics*, 7 (February 1977) 1–22.

Bhagwati, J., and Srinivasan, T. N., *Foreign Exchange Regimes and Economic Development* (India, New York: NBER, Columbia University Press, 1977).

Fields, G., 'The Private Demand for Education in Relation to Labour Market Conditions in Less-Developed Countries', *Economic Journal* 84, 906–25.

Srinivasan, T. N., 'Development, Poverty and Basic Human Needs: Some Issues', *Food Research Institute Studies* (Stanford) 16, no. 2 (1977).

15 Some Thoughts of Self-reliant Development, Collective Self-reliance and the New International Economic Order

Samir Amin (Senegal)

I

The decades following the Second World War were marked by the rise of the liberation movement in the three continents, the main goals of which, in Asia and in Africa, were the reconquest of national independence and its defence by refusing the military alliances through which the United States sought to dominate the policy of the Third World states. But in general, the goals and methods of economic development pursued did not challenge the main features of the international division of labour shaped during the last century. Hence, an externally oriented and dependent development model was usually accepted. The objective failure of this model and the increasingly difficult problems gradually induced the Third World countries to embark upon a new strategy with the aim of consolidating their reconquered political independence by strengthening their economic independence.

The new development strategy is asserted in three complementary aspects: (1) the choice of a 'self-reliant' development based on the principle of relying on one's own resources, (2) the priority given to co-operation and economic integration between the countries of the Third

World ('collective self-reliance'), and (3) the demand for a New International Economic Order based on higher prices for raw materials and the control of natural resources, access of the manufactures of the Third World to the markets of the developed countries, and the acceleration of the transfer of technologies.

It is easy to understand that such general slogans—even if they are sound—lend themselves to different interpretations. Apart from commonplace demagogic attempts by local circles, which cannot envisage development as other than dependent, to take up the slogans, and apart from their verbal and opportunistic acceptance by certain of the external forces who are in practice hostile to the goals of the New International Economic Order, some serious divergences remain both as to the ultimate goals and as to the means of a self-reliant development within the context of an effective attempt to impose a new world order.

Actually, the real issue is whether the alternatives can be defined as we have just done, that is, irrespective of the ultimate goals, the choice of socialism or capitalism. In other words, is the goal of *autonomous* capitalist development in the Third World countries realistic? For the developed capitalist economies are indeed self-reliant, although not economically self-sufficient. In this case, it makes sense to speak of interdependence—even among unequals (French capitalism, for instance, is not the equal of German or American capitalism). But the peripheral capitalist economies have so far been externally oriented and dependent, not 'interdependent'. Could they become 'self-reliant' without withdrawing from the world system of exchange of commodities, technologies and capital? Could they do it by forcing the world system to readjust, by imposing an equal, and no longer unequal, division of labour? Could they attain this goal by the means which define the programme for the New International Economic Order? These issues cannot be evaded.

To sum up, does this recent evolution of the Third World call into question our theory of peripheral capitalism? I would recall that this theory asserts that there is a fundamental difference between the model of self-reliant accumulation and the model that describes the peripheral capitalist system, thus rejecting any linear theory of 'stages' of development. It excludes the prospect of a mature, autonomous, capitalism in the periphery. It asserts that a socialist break with this system is here objectively necessary. Thus, in this very precise sense, it claims that the national liberation movement constitutes a period in the socialist transformation of the world and not a stage of the development of capitalism on the world scale. This is a permanent question, but which arises continually in new terms. And it is these new terms that we propose to consider in this article.

II

The determining interrelation in a self-reliant capitalist system is that which links the sector producing mass-consumption goods with the sector producing capital goods. This determining interrelation has been the characteristic feature of the historical development of capitalism in the centre of the system (in Europe, North America and Japan). Thus, it provides an abstract definition of the 'pure' capitalist mode of production and has been analysed as such in Marx's *Das Kapital*. Marx, in fact, shows that in the capitalist mode of production, there is an *objective* (that is, *necessary*) relation between the rate of surplus value and the level of development of the productive forces. The rate of surplus value is the main determinant of the pattern of social distribution of the national income (its distribution between wages and profit), and hence that of demand (wages being the main source of demand for mass-consumption goods and profits being wholly or partly 'saved' for 'investment' purposes). The level of development of the productive forces is expressed through the social division of labour: the allocation of the labour force, in suitable proportions, to each of the two sectors.

Despite the schematic nature of this model, it nevertheless describes the core of the system. External relations are left out of the model, meaning not that the development of capitalism took place within a framework of national autarchy, but that the main relations within the system can be understood without including such relations. More precisely, external relations are subject to the logic and the requirements of self-reliant internal accumulation. Furthermore, the model clearly brings out the historically *relative* nature of the distinction between the mass-consumption good and the luxury good. In the strict sense of the term, 'luxury' goods are those for which the demand originates from that part of profit which is consumed, whereas the demand which stems from wages increases with the progress of the productive forces. However, the historical sequence in the type of mass-consumption goods is of decisive importance for an understanding of the problem in hand. The structure of demand in the early history of the system speeded the agricultural revolution by providing a *domestic market* for food products. Hence, agrarian capitalism came before the expansion and maturity of the capitalist mode in industry.

So, from the lessons of this model, we will derive three important conclusions:

(1) The emergence of the capitalist mode of production in the regions which are to become the centres of the world capitalist system stems from an internal process of breaking-up of the precapitalist (here feudal) modes. This breaking-up of the feudal relations of production in the European rural world constitutes the social framework conducive to the famous 'agricultural revolution' which precedes—and makes possible—the subsequent 'industrial revolution'. The prior increase of productivity in agriculture makes it possible to drive out of the rural world a 'surplus' (proletarianised) population and simultaneously gives rise to a surplus of marketed foodstuffs necessary for the reproduction of this proletariat.

(2) The interrelation in time and space of class alliances which enable new capitalist relations to flourish in industry, while it takes various forms, always expresses the same principal condition: the alliance between the new dominant class (the industrial bourgeoisie) and the landowners (either peasants—after a French-type revolution—of *latif-undiaries*, when the former feudal landowners are transformed and integrated into the market, as in England or Germany) in the context of a mature and powerful national State.

(3) Thus the subjection of external relations (economic and political) to the requirements of internal accumulation gradually shapes the world capitalist system. The latter emerges as a series of central formations, self-reliant and interdependent (even if they are unequally advanced) and of peripheral formations subjected to the logic of accumulation in the centres that dominate them.

So we conclude that, although the vision of a development by 'stages' (with some simply lagging historically behind others) is roughly valid as regards the gradual constitution of the centres, it is not valid as regards the peripheries.

It is precisely this conclusion which is the real object of the explicit or implicit divergences in all the debates about the future of the 'Third World'. Hence, we must now consider the stages in the formation and evolution of the peripheries, and the likely prospects in front of them. For the opposite view maintains (explicitly or implicitly) that, despite their externally propelled origin, the underdeveloped economies are progressing, through the specific stages of their evolution, towards the constitution of mature self-reliant economies. These could be either 'capitalist' or 'socialist' for reasons related to a sphere which lies outside the one which defines our analytical method.

III

Let us now consider the stages in the evolution of the peripheries of the world capitalist system, at least since the middle of last century. This model of accumulation at the periphery of the world system begins under an impetus from the centre, with the creation of an export sector which will play the determining role in the creation and shaping of the market. The underlying *reason* which rendered possible the creation of this export sector must be sought in the answer to the question pertaining to the conditions which make its establishment 'profitable'. There is no pressure for central national capital to emigrate because of insufficient possible outlets at the centre; but it will emigrate to the periphery if it can obtain a better return there. The equalisation of the rate of profit will redistribute the advantages of this higher return and use the export of capital as a means to fight the trend of a falling profit rate. The *reason* for creating an export sector therefore lies in obtaining, from the periphery, products which are constituents of constant capital (raw materials) or of variable capital (food products) at production costs lower than those at the centre for similar products (or for substitutes in the case of specific products).

This is therefore the framework for the *essential* theory of *unequal exchange*. The products exported by the periphery are important to the extent that the difference between the returns to labour is greater than the differences between the productivities. And this can be so because the society will, by every means—economic and non-economic—be made subject to this new function: to provide relatively cheap labour to the export sector.

Here, then, the main link which characterises the process of capital accumulation at the centre—expressed by the objective relation between wage rate and the level of development of the productive forces—disappears completely. The wage rate in the export sector will, in this case, be as low as the economic, social and *political* conditions allow it to be. As regards the level of development of the productive forces, it will, in this case, be heterogeneous (whereas in the self-reliant model, it was homogeneous), advanced (and sometimes very advanced) in the export sector and backward in 'the rest of the economy'. This backwardness (maintained by the system) is the condition which allows the export sector to benefit from cheap labour.

Under these conditions, the domestic market generated by the development of the export sector, will be limited and distorted. The smallness of the internal market explains the fact that the periphery attracts only a limited alount of capital from the centre although it offers it a better return. The contradiction between the consumption and production capacities is overcome at the level of the world system as a whole (centre and periphery) by a widening of the market at the centre, the periphery—fully deserving its name—merely fulfilling a sub-ordinate and limited function. This leads to an increasing polarisation of wealth at the centre.

However, once the export sector has expanded to a certain size, a domestic market emerges. As compared with the market generated in the central process, this one is (relatively) in favour of the demand for 'luxury' goods. If all the capital invested in the export sector were foreign, and if all the returns to this capital were re-exported to the centre, the domestic market would, in fact, be confined to a demand for mass-consumption goods, and the lower the wage rate, the smaller the demand would be. But a part of this capital is locally owned. In addition, the methods used to ensure a low return to labour are based on the strengthening of the various local social classes which serve as conveyor-belts: *latifundiaries* in some places, *kulaks* in others, *comprador* commercial bourgeoisie, state bureaucracy, etc. The domestic market will thus be *mainly* based on the demand for 'luxury goods' from these social strata.

This picture actually corresponds to the historical reality of the *first phase of the imperialist system*. No doubt this phase had its golden age between 1880 and 1914, but it started earlier for Latin America, and it has sometimes lasted much longer (up to the 1950s) elsewhere, such as in tropical Africa. It is the age of the 'colonial pact', the colonial and semi-colonial form of domination exerted over the periphery.

As opposed to the central model, this model has three qualitatively different features:

(1) Here, the capitalist model is 'introduced from outside', by political domination. There is no breaking-up of precapitalist rural relations, but (this is quite different) they are distorted because they are subjected to the laws of accumulation of the central capitalist mode which dominates them. This is shown in the absence of a prior 'agricultural revolution', that is the stagnation of productivity in agriculture.

(2) The class alliances which provide the political framework for the

reproduction of the system are not principally internal class alliances, but an international alliance between the capital of the dominant monopolies and its (subordinate) 'allies', to use an all-embracing term: the 'feudal lords' (meaning the varied range of dominant classes in the precapitalist rural systems) and the '*comprador* bourgeoisie'. There is no really mature independent national state serving these local classes, but only administrations serving monopoly capital, directly (colonial case) or indirectly (semi-colonial case).

(3) In this case, external relations are not subject to the logic of an internal development, but are on the contrary the driving force of development and determine its direction and pace.

IV

This first phase of imperialism is now over. What forces led to this and what type of evolution is taking place?

The engine of change is constituted by the *anti-imperialist national liberation movement*. This movement comprises three social forces: (a) the (still emerging) super-exploited proletariat, (b) the mass of the peasantry doubly exploited by the local classes which dominate it (the 'feudal lords') and by monopoly capital on account of which the 'feudal lords' have entered the 'world market', and (c) the national bourgeoisie, at this stage a 'potential' class rather than a 'real' one, which aspires to alter the terms of the international division of labour so as to acquire an economic base. For the international division of labour of the 'colonial pact' is simple: the periphery exports only primary commodities, with which it has to buy all the manufactured goods necessary to satisfy its needs, mainly for luxury consumption; it is not allowed any industry. The national bourgeoisie and the proletariat compete for the leadership of the national liberation movement, that is, the leadership of the peasant revolt.

On the whole, this first phase ended in the victory of the national liberation movement under bourgeois leadership. This victory forced imperialism to revise the terms of the division of labour, and so enabled the Third World to start industrialising. We can even put a date to this victory: it is earlier in some places—for example in Mexico with the revolution of the 1910s, in Turkey with Kemal Atatürk, in Egypt with the Wafd, in Brazil and in Argentina in the 'populist' form, and later in others—in South Asia after the Second World War, in Africa with the independence of the 1960s, etc. Except for East Asia and Cuba, where the national liberation movement operated at that stage a withdrawal from the world imperialist system, everywhere else the triumphant national bourgeoisie has embarked upon a strategy of industrialisation which now has a name: the strategy of import substitution.

Since the peripheral model is characterised by the specific interconnection expressed by the link between the export sector and luxury goods consumptions, import-substitution industrialisation will start from 'the end', in other words, the manufacture of products corresponding to the more advanced stages of development of the centre, or consumer durables. These products are highly capital-intensive and users of scarce resources (skilled labour, etc.). The result will necessarily be a *distortion* in the allocation of resources in favour of these products and to the detriment of the production of mass-consumption goods. The latter sector will be systematically handicapped: it will not give rise to any 'demand' for its products and will not attract any capital or labour to ensure its modernisation. This explains the stagnation in 'subsistence agriculture' whose potential products attract little demand and which does not acquire enough share in the allocation of scarce resources to enable any serious changes to be made. Any 'development strategy' based on 'profitability' (the structure of income distribution, the structures of relative prices and demand being what they are), necessarily leads to this type of systematic distortion.

From the 'social' angle, this model leads to a specific phenomenon—the *marginalisation* of the masses. By this we mean a series of mechanisms of various kinds which impoverish the masses: proletarisation, semi-proletarisation and impoverishment without proletarisation of the peasants, urbanisation and massive increase of urban unemployment and underemployment, etc. Unemployment and underemployment thus have a function which is different from their function in the central model: the high level of unemployment ensures a minimum wage rate which is relatively rigid and frozen both in the export sector and in the luxury goods sector; wages do not emerge both as a cost and an income which creates a demand, vital to the model, but on the contrary only as a cost, demand itself originating elsewhere (from abroad or out of the income of the privileged social classes).

The 'externally propelled' nature of this type of development which is perpetuating itself in spite of the increasing diversification of the economy, its industrialisation, etc., is not *original sin*, a *deus ex machina* foreign to the dependent peripheral model of capital accumulation, since it is a model of *reproduction* of its functional social and economic conditions. The marginalisation of the masses is the very condition underlying the integration of the minority within the world system, the guarantee of an increasing income for this minority, which conditions the adoption, by this minority, of 'European' patterns of consumption. The extension of this pattern of consumption ensures the 'profitability' of the luxury goods sector and confirms the social, cultural, ideological and political integration of the privileged classes.

At this stage of diversification and reinforcement of underdevelopment, there appear new mechanisms of domination/dependence. Cultural and political mechanisms, but also economic ones: technological dependence and the domination by transnational companies. The luxury goods sector, in fact, calls for capital-intensive investments which only the big transnational oilgopoly firms are in a position to embark upon and which constitute the material support for technological dependence. But also, at this stage, more complex forms of the structure of ownership and economic management also make their appearance. Experience shows that the participation of private or public local capital—however subservient—in the process of import-substitution industrialisation, is quite common. It also shows—at least in the big countries—that a large enough market created by the development of the export and luxury goods sectors may make it possible to create a sector producing capital goods. The latter is frequently brought into being by the state. But the development of a basic industry and a public sector does not in any way mean that the system is evolving towards a mature self-reliant form, since the capital goods sector is here used, not for the development of mass consumption, but to serve the growth of export and luxury goods production.

So this second phase of imperialism is by no means a 'stage' towards the constitution of a self-reliant economy. It does not reproduce a previous phase of central development, but on the contrary extends the first externally propelled phase. In fact:

(1) The 'agricultural revolution' has still not taken place. We must, however, qualify this a little. The national bourgeoisie in power has often eliminated some former allies of imperialism and has, among other things, carried out some land reforms on the basis of which a development of capitalism in agriculture has sometimes been launched (the 'green revolution'). Can this development 'wipe out' the original backwardness of agriculture and bring the peripheral model closer to the central model? This question must be settled not in 'theory', but in 'fact'. What we note is that the relative backwardness of agriculture has been increasing to the paradoxical point where the Third World

countries, the majority to whose population is rural, have become importers of food. The reason for this failure is not mysterious, it is political: in our era the bourgeoisie has to be supported by classes capable of dominating the peasants, even if these are more broadly based (*kulaks* instead of large landowners); it cannot be supported by the peasant masses whose interests are in conflict with its own. While the central bourgeoisies had the 'necessary time' for a slow primitive accumulation based on alliance with the peasants, those of the periphery face the dual constraint of external pressure from the monopolies and the internal threat of socialism.

(2) The dominant class alliances remain international; the bourgeoisie is substituted for the former 'feudal lords' and the *compradors* as the subordinate ally of imperialism. Because of this, the bourgeoisie, from the second phase, loses its former national character: it is 'compradorised'. The 'national' state it dominates therefore remains weak and poorly integrated.

(3) The continuation of the development process is still dependent on exports which still consist essentially of raw materials. This main source of finance for the necessary imports of capital equipment ultimately determines the rates of growth, and in this sense growth still externally propelled.

The crisis of this second phase of imperialism was opened by the demand for a New International Economic Order.

Reduced to its bare outlines, this demand seems to be the following: to impose a real rise in the prices of raw materials exported by the Third World countries in order to acquire further resources which, with the importing of advanced technologies, could finance a new stage of industrialisation involving large-scale exports, to the centres, of products manufactured by those peripheries which have the advantage of favourable natural resources and abundant cheap labour (hence the demand for access to the markets of developed countries for these industrial products).

Since 1973, this demand has constituted the clear common objective of all the Third World countries. It is put forward as the necessary and sufficient condition for completing political independence by giving it an economic basis. It is also presented as a possible joint demand of all the Third World states irrespective of their social options and their international sympathies.

This new situation raises some essential issues on which there is a need for the most open-ended debate.

The first issue is whether the local bourgeoisie—which generally dominates these States—can 'combat imperialism' to impose its point of view. There are those who argue that the new international division of labour is the strategic goal of imperialism itself, and that this demand is therefore manipulated by the monopolies, particularly the North American ones, and that it does not express a specific goal of the Third World states in conflict with the strategy of imperialism. These people usually give priority to the interimperialist conflicts (United States, Europe, Japan) over the apparent North–South conflict. We know that this 'theory' was abundantly formulated in connection with the raising of the price of petroleum by OPEC in 1973, both in right-wing and left-wing, even ultra-left-wing, versions. But the facts do not bear out this interpretation. In fact the theory only reflects the naive views of an ultra-left-wing which, with wishful thinking, would like the bloc of bourgeoisies to appear without 'cracks' on the world scene so as to 'simplify' (on paper) the tasks of the proletariat which, they assume, are everywhere the same, because the proletariat would not have to take account of the contradictions between the bourgeoisies.

In the past, the bourgeoisie of the peripheries had clashed with imperialism. The transition from the first to the second phase of imperialism had not been 'planned' by the monopolies: it had been imposed by the national liberation movement when the bourgeoisie of the peripheries had won, against imperialism, the right to an industry. But, as we have said, the industrialisation strategy pursued during this second phase transformed the relations between the bourgoisie of the peripheries and the monopolies. The peripheral bourgeoisie ceased to be national and became the subordinate ally of imperialism by joining in the new division of labour. The ally is now rebelling and demanding new terms of the division of labour. It does not thereby become 'national', since its demand is located right at the heart of the system, but it is rebelling all the same. If that rebellion were to succeed, it would simply inaugurate a new phase of imperialism characterised by a new division of labour. For there is no doubt that in 'theory' this new division can be 'absorbed', 'co-opted'. But only 'in theory', because what counts in history are the unexpected accidents, and there can be some here and there in the peripheries and in the centres (and serieous ones for capitalism) during the transition, laden with contradictions, from the second to the third 'theoretical' phase of imperialism.

The second issue is whether this third possible phase would, or would not, be a stage towards the autonomy of the peripheries. The bourgeoisies of the Third World argue that it would be, just as they asserted at the beginning of the second phase that *it* would be. But the facts have belied these illusions, which were shared at the time by a large proportion of the left-wing in the Third World.

My own view is that if the demand in question were to succeed, it would not by any means constitute a new stage along a line of development leading gradually to the flourishing of mature capitalist formations similar to those of the developed centres. Once again, the vision of a linear development by stages will inevitably be disproved.

The reason, a quite fundamental one, is that the new division of labour will be based on the export by the periphery of cheap manufactured goods, that is, for which the advantage of low wages (bearing in mind comparative productivities) makes it possible to raise the rate of profit in the world system as a whole. The worldwide equalisation of profit would then modify the relative prices and hence would conceal this extra transfer of value from the periphery to the centre. In other words, the new division of labour would perpetuate and worsen unequal exchange. Furthermore, this unequal division of labour would perpetuate the distorted pattern of demand in the peripheries to the detriment of mass consumption, just as in the previous phases. Therefore, the development of the world system would remain fundamentally unequal. So external demand would still be the main motive force propelling this still dependent type of development.

Need we add that, in this context of renovated dependence, the backwardness of agriculture would also be perpetuated. No doubt some nuances must be introduced here, because after all, capitalism would continue its progress in agriculture, which it started in the second phase of imperialism, but certainly at rates far lower than its progress in the traditional and new export sectors and in that of luxury production for the domestic market, since those sectors benefit from massive importing of the most advanced world-scale technologies.

In this general context, we may well wonder what would be the real significance of the slogans about 'self-reliant development' and 'collective self-reliance' which accompany the demand for this new international division of labour.

Actually, the first of these slogans would be devoid of all content. It would mean nothing more than the ideological justification of the (impossible) claim that a development 'by progressive stages' within the world system of (unequal) division of labour ought to lead to economic independence.

On the other hand, the second slogan does acquire a meaning, albeit a particular one, in this perspective. The first phases of imperialism did not imply any 'co-operation' between countries and regions of the periphery. Being exclusively outward-oriented and limited in their industrialisation to the satisfaction of their domestic market, the peripheral economies had nothing to exchange with each other. In theory, the third phase of the unequal division of labour does not call for any more positive co-operation between the Third World countries, apart from conducting a joint struggle for a rise in the prices of their primary exports (through producers' associations), since the 'second wind' of peripheral industrialisation would derive its momentum from exports to the centres. The fact remains that the Third World countries are highly unequal candidates for taking advantage of this new division of labour. Those who are best placed as regards their economic potential (abundant natural resources, more advanced proletarisation, etc.) and their political solidity ('legitimisation' of the power of the weak local bourgeoisie, military strength, etc.) could advance faster on the path of the new dependence if they also had the markets of the less developed countries and if they could have direct and cheap access to their supplies of raw materials and food. Naturally, the problematics of the so-called 'sub-imperialism' is relevant here.

A good example will illustrate this vision of the interlinking of the 'Third' and 'Fourth' World in the new global perspective. Together, the countries of the Persian Gulf, Egypt and Sudan constitute—if the political conditions were favourable, which is far from being the case today—a 'good candidate'. The Gulf would provide the capital, the export industry would be concentrated in Egypt, and Sudan would export food to the latter. Let us look more closely at the mechanism of this interlinking. Even if Sudanese agriculture were to be 'modernised' so as to supply the necessary exportable surplus, its productivity would still for a long time to come be lower than that of the advanced countries. But Sudanese foodstuffs will have to be competitive with those of North America on the Egyptian market, so as to ensure the lowest possible wages in Egypt. This is only possible because the Sudanese peasant would be super-exploited (rewards to labour more uneuqal than the differential productivities). In its turn, the Egyptian proletarian would be super-exploited, since his starvation wage together with his relatively high productivity would make it possible to export his product to the centres. A double and interlinked unequal exchange would operate in favour of the centre; the Sudan would cease to be directly dependent on the centre and would become the partner of the first-rank periphery in which the export industry is concentrated.

V

But if this is the content of the organisation of the new phase of imperialism, cannot the triple demand for national autonomy, collective self-reliance and a new world order have quite a different meaning? Aim at different goals? And under what conditions?

While the pivot of the neoimperialist interpretation of the programme in question is constituted by the new unequal international division of labour, which conditions both the internal strategies and the objectives of intra-Third World co-operation, this same programme assumes quite a different meaning when one does the opposite operation, that is, when one first defines the internal objectives of a really self-reliant and 'popular' development and then considers the ways in which the world order must be acted on in order to promote the achievement of these objectives.

A genuinely self-reliant development is necessarily that of the people, because externally propelled development in all the phases of evolution of the imperialist system effectively benefits the privileged dominant classes which make an alliance with the monopolies. Conversely and as a corollary, a 'popular' development can only be national and self-reliant. For in order to serve the mass of the peasantry, industrialisation must first be made to concentrate on improving rural productivity. Similarly, in order to serve the urban masses, it is necessary to give up luxury production for the local market and give up exporting, since they are both based on the reproduction of a cheap labour force. Let us consider more closely this authentic strategy aimed both at national independence and social progress.

So far, the industrialisation of the Third World has not been contemplated as aiding the progress of agriculture. Unlike the countries of the centre, where the 'agricultural revolution' preceded the 'industrial revolution', the countries of the periphery have imported the latter without having started the former stage. That is the source of the distortions typical of these countries, and of the renewed dependence which fetters them. First, we must go into reverse gear. Up to now, industry in the Third World has been parasitic, in the sense that it has built up its accumulation by extortions from the rural world in real terms (it gets its labour from the rural–urban migration) and financial terms (heavy taxation, internal terms of trade unfavourable to the peasants, etc.) with no counterpart provided in return to sustain the takeoff of agriculture. How can we alter our course? Clearly all cost-benefit criteria, which are necessarily based on reproducing price and income distribution patterns, must be entirely abandoned and replaced by other fundamental criteria of resource allocation. Two essential issues are involved here, which we will simply point out: (1) how a 'modern' industrial sector, with its basic guidelines renovated, is to be linked up with the sector of small-scale rural industries which can directly mobilise the latent forces of progress, (2) why the social form required here is that of rural collectivisation, even at a low level of development of the productive forces, and not the form of 'private' agriculture even if remodelled by a radical land reform. It is only on these conditions that agriculture—which must first make up its historical time-lag—will be able to finance a healthy industrialisation and provide a food surplus sufficient to ensure national independence.

Similarly, industry must be made to serve the poor urban masses and no longer be guided by the 'profitability' criteria which favour the privileged local market and exports to the developed centres.

In any case, this kind of remodelled industry cannot find its technological models readymade in the developed countries. Nor can it find them in the technological past of the centres, borrowing their production techniques of yesterday, as the theme of 'intermediate technologies' suggests. This is because the problem here is different, since in this case industrialisation has to enable the agricultural revolution to take place, whereas in the centre it was based on that revolution. So the real issue is not the conditions of 'transfer of technology', but the creation of conditions conducive to creativity in this field, not for motives of 'cultural nationalism', but for objective reasons. Furthermore, there is another problem to be pointed out: the borrowed technologies are necessarily vectors of capitalist relations of production, whereas the social framework required by the agrarian revolution and urban mobilisation must be socialist. This is a fundamental question, which reflects the fact that socialism is necessary in the periphery since it is an essential condition of progress and independence and not, therefore, the result of an ideological or moral motivation which could be 'free'. We simply raise this question in passing; it is the reason why we shall continue to assert that the national liberation movement of the periphery mainly constitutes a stage in the socialist transformation of the world and only secondarily a phase in the development of capitalism.

Although a self-reliant development model is not in theory synonymous with autarchy (economic self-sufficiency), it may lead to it whether we like it or not, for obvious internal and external political reasons. This may be the case, not only for vast countries—witness the experiences of the USSR and China—but even for small countries (such as Korea, Vietnam, Cambodia, Cuba, Albania). So, although autarchy in itself is not synonymous with self-reliant development (think of Burma), it may be the condition for it under certain historical circumstances.

But imposed autarchy may also, if it is too drastic or total, hamper self-reliant development by involving extra costs which could in some cases be very heavy. For the point is not to reject any theory of comparative advantages, but only to note that if the international division of labour is unequal, the argument of comparative advantages loses its validity. A country choosing the self-reliant and 'popular' path may find itself in a situation where it is relatively cheaper to import certain inputs needed to accelerate its development (such as energy in some cases, or certain raw materials or capital goods) than to do without them.

To deal with this type of problem, the liberated states of the Third World could act collectively in two directions:

(1) The first is that of mutual assistance. For the Third World countries, rich in natural resources which are usually exploited for the sole benefit of the developed countries, could exchange with each other the raw materials that will be useful for their national projects of self-reliant development. At present, these imports nearly always transit through the developed centres which control the raw materials 'markets' and centralise the payment facilities. By agreements for mutual assistance (trade agreements and multilaterial payments agreements), the liberated countries of the Third World could short-circuit these middlemen. Moreover, exchanges of technology could accelerate the development of appropriate production techniques, since the problems that the Third World countries have to solve are often similar. We can see that this type of co-operation among the Third World is very different from what was envisaged in the neoimperialist context. We are no longer talking of 'common markets' which can only reproduce and aggravate the inequalities of development. We have proposed the guidelines for a 'package deal' in the spirit of co-operation in the service of an autonomous national development.

(2) The second direction of collective action is aimed at modifying the international division of labour between developed countries and Third World countries in the direction of a reduction of inequality, and no longer that of a 'renovation' with no reduction of inequality. At present, a large number of Third World countries have already been

won over to the idea of confronting the veritable monopoly of the 'consumers' with associations of raw materials producers, and of strengthening these associations by establishing collective support funds. A self-reliant development strategy involves more than this. It requires as a first step the national (state) control of the exploitation of its natural resources. By this we mean not only the formal national-isation of that exploitation, but *also* and *above all* the regulation of the flow of exports and the *reduction* of the flow of imports required by the internal strategy of self-reliant development. For at present the externally oriented strategy is based on exactly the opposite relation: exports are first pushed to the maximum, solely as a function of the 'demand' (of the centres), and then the question arises of how to use the export earnings. The unequal international division of labour is based on this strategy. Reducing inequality in the division of labour most certainly implies reducing the flow of raw materials exports. The incredible resistance of the developed world to this reduction is evidence that the centre, despite so many misleading speeches, cannot do without the pillage of the Third World. If that pillage were to stop, the centres would be forced to modify their structures accordingly, in order to adjust to a new, less unequal international division of labour. Then, and only then, could we begin to speak of a genuine new world order, and no longer merely of new terms of the unequal international division of labour.

These two general lines—that of a new imperialist order and that of an order which would really start off progress in the liberation of the peoples of the Third World—are not just two verbal themes, two possible theoretical alternatives. They are already actually clashing, and are the subject of daily conflicts.

The main reason for this is the contradictory nature of the national liberation movement. This reflects both the development of capitalism and its crisis. Hence, the trends of capitalism and those of socialism are constantly clashing within the movement itself, precisely because the forces of capitalism here are still those of a weak, peripheral, dependent capitalism, which objectively cannot attain the goals of a mature capitalism. These forces are clashing in all the regimes of the Third World. We know very well that these bourgeois trends still persist in those countries that have broken with capitalism. But, conversely, the capitalist states of the Third World do not have the complete and unilateral nature of the central capitalist States. Hence, the volatility of their regimes and the wide range of situations, from that of triumphant neocolonialism to that of nationalism in conflict with imperialism, via that of shamefaced or crisis-ridden neocolonialisms.

For the conflict with imperailism has well and truly begun. So far the themes of the new international order have been totally rejected, as witness the failure of UNCTAD IV and of the North–South negotiations. At the ideological level itself, the Club of Rome is endeavouring to oppose a substitute construct to these themes. The fact is that the themes of the new order involve the aspiration to control the natural resources and to strengthen the national states, which imperialism does not accept.

In theory, the new unequal division of labour would suit everybody, the bourgeoisies of the peripheries and the monopolies of the centres. For the transfer of industries would make it possible to recreate in the centre a reserve army of unemployed which a quarter of a century of growth has reduced to such an extent that the system has lost its 'normal' flexibility. And this unemployment would raise the rate of surplus value in the centre itself. In the longer run, the centre would develop the new activities that control the whole system—the 'quaternary' (software, research and development, etc.), the new leading industries, the military sector—thereby renewing and extending the conditions of the social-democrat hegemony in the centre.

But in the long run, as we know, we are all dead. At present resistance to the transfer of industries still largely prevails. And this resistance frustrates the Third World bourgeoisies who, being the weaker partners, would have to bear the whole brunt of the crisis. It then becomes impossible to attenuate the violent social contradictions in the Third World: the food deficit gets larger, the establishment of export industries is postponed *sine die*, etc. Hence, the political conditions may evolve in a direction favourable to the beginning of a self-reliant development. This is the reality: the struggle of the Third World against the dominant imperialist hegemony. For many reasons, this struggle is still today the main force for the transformation of the world.

ENDNOTES

1. My general thesis concerning the opposition between central capitalism and peripheral capitalism was formulated in the following publications:

   Le développement inégal (Minuit, 1973), *L'impérialisme et le développement inégal* (Minuit, 1975), especially the chapters on the links between agriculture and industry (Chapter 2), the opposition between socialism and capitalism (Chapter 3), the problem of the environment (Chapter 7) and those of technology (Chapters 9 and 10); *Impérialisme et sous-développement en Afrique* (Anthropos, 1976) particularly the introduction. A reply to my critics was published in *L'Homme et la Société*, No. 39–40 (*À propos de la critique*).

2. For the debate on unequal exchange, see also: *L'échange inégal et la loi de la valeur* (Anthropos, 1973) — English version IDEP/ET/R/2558); *L'impérialisme et le développement inégal*, Chapter 6.

3. Concerning the current crisis of imperialism, the nature of the national liberation movement and the prospects it opens up, see also:

L'impérialisme et le développement inégal, Chapter 5, Amin, Faire, Hussein and Massiah, *La crise de l'impérialisme* (Minuit, 1975), *Introduction to* book by Beaud, Bellon and Francois, *Lire le capitalisme* (Antropos, 1976) *La nation arabe* (Minuit, 1976), Chapter VI; *Les perspectives de la localisation internationale des activités industrielles, un point de vue arabo africain* (GRESI, Paris, 1976, mimeographed, to be published by Anthropos); *Après nairobi, préparer le Sommet des Non-Alignés à Colombo, bilan de la CNUCED IV* (I.D.E.P., Dakar, 1976, mimeographed, to be published by Anthropos); *Impérialisme et sous-développement en Afrique*, Chapters III–IX (concerning Eurafrica) and III–X (Some notes on petroleum and Afro-Arab relations); The future of Southern Africa (Introduction to a book to be published in English, Tanzanian Publishing House); *Quale 1984?* in collaboration with Frank and Jaffe, Jace Book, Milan, 1975).

4. Concerning some more specific aspects of the formation of the world system and African underdevelopment, see also:

Impérialisme et sous-développement en Afrique, Chapters I–I (Sous développement et dépendance en Afrique), I–II (la formation due systéme mondial), I–III (le développement du capitalisme en Africque), II–II (CNUCED III–Un bilan), II–III (les problèmes de la transition en Afrique), II–IV (les migrations contemporaines en Afrique de l'Ouest), II–V (Le commerce inter-africain), II–VI et VII (La révolution verte), III–III et IV (L'Afrique du Sud et l'Angola) III–VI (aspects économiques de l'unité africaine).

5. Lastly, as regards the debate on the transition to socialism and the role of the link between agriculture and industry in that transition, the reader should refer at least to the books by C. Bettleheim (*Las lutte des classes en Union Soviétique*, Seuil, 1973); M. Liebman (*Le Léninisme sous Lénine*, Seuil, 2 vols., 1973) et S. Grosshopf (*L'alliance ouvrière et paysanne on U.R.S.S. 1921–28*, Maspero, 1976).

Comments

Assar Lindbeck (Sweden)

It would seem that the main thesis in Samir Amin's paper is the assertion of what he calls 'the objective failure' of 'an externally oriented and dependent development model' for the LDCs. I understand that this rather categorical statement is based both on certain alleged *empirical generalisations* and on some kind of (implicit) *theory* that is said to exclude 'the prospect of a mature, autonomous capitalism in the periphery' (p. 535).

I GROWTH POSSIBILITIES OF THE PERIPHERY

One conceivable interpretation of Amin's position would be that capitalist economic development cannot spread from centre to periphery countries. In fact, Amin says in one place that the dynamics of the world economy 'leads to an increasing polarisation of wealth at the centre' (p. 539), which indeed suggests a view of the world according to which centres always grow faster than peripheries, and where a country on the periphery can never wind up in the centre.

To me, this view of the world is impossible to reconcile with historical facts. Firstly, the various highly developed capitalist countries of today embarked upon a process of modern economic growth at quite different points of time in history; in other words, *all of them*, except England, were at some time periphery to some centre countries; nevertheless they sooner or later became 'centre' countries.

Secondly, the post-Second World War period has witnessed a large number of LDCs—which in Samir's terminology are the periphery countries of today—embarking upon a rather impressive process of per capita economic growth and industrialisation. This means that Amin's assertion is certainly not consistent with the experience of *all* LDCs during the post-Second World War period, when we look at per capita income growth. It is also difficult to argue that 'outward-oriented' LDCs have been *less* successful in economic growth during the last decades than 'inward-oriented' countries—either those countries following an import-substitution strategy, or those following even more pronounced autarchic patterns.[1] The opposite statement is probably closer to the truth. It is rather paradoxical that the industrial revolution has been accelerating in a great number of externally oriented LDCs at about the same time as Amin, and some other authors, are declaring 'the objective failure' of 'an externally oriented and dependent developing model' for the LDCs.

Moreover, if this process proceeds at the same remarkable speed as during the last two decades in a number of LDCs, this will probably depend more on the future *policies* in the developed and less developed countries—in particular on the degree of protectionism in the DCs—than on the organisation of international markets.

II   DEPENDENCE

An alternative interpretation of Amin's position might be that externally oriented growth paths along capitalist lines in the periphery countries of today, though not impossible in terms of per capita GNP, would make these countries excessively 'dependent' on the developed countries—in contrast to the developed countries themselves which are asserted to be 'self-reliant' and 'interdependent'. However, to a large extent such 'dependence' is largely a logical consequence of being a *latecomer* and/or being a *small* country with strong external relations. For instance, was not Sweden during its first half-century of modern economic growth heavily 'dependent' on the centre countries of those days—as an *importer* of capital and technology, and an *exporter* of primary products and labour? And are not also today *all* small countries 'dependent' on, rather than interdependent with, the outside world—in the sense that outside conditions have strong effects on the national economy whereas domestic events have only insignificant effects on the outside world?

III   DOMESTIC PECULIARITIES OF THE LDCs

We know, of course, that sustained growth of per capita GNP does not necessarily give the poorest part of the population more decent living conditions, not even after several decades of growth. We also know that the latecomers among nations today to a large extent experience domestic problems different from those of the latecomers a hundred years ago. Maybe Amin's statement about 'the objective failure' of 'an externally oriented and dependent development model' should be understood in the context of these distributional and other problems *within* the LDCs?

It would seem that Amin emphasises three such problems. *The first* one is related to the lack of previous developments in agriculture; *the second* to the inequalities and therewith related composition of domestic demand; and *the third* to the lack of domestic institutions and the capacity to administer relations with the outside world, for instance as regards the impact of trade and foreign technology.

On these three issues, I do not think that Amin's position is very controversial in *substance*. It is a commonplace that a modernisation of agriculture to a large extent preceded the industrial revolution in the present developed capitalist countries, and that the absence of such a development in the LDCs of today often generates severe problems—because it provides only small domestic markets for manufacturing products and it creates difficulties in generating a surplus of food and savings in the agricultural sector.

Amin's point about the inequalities of the LDCs, and therewith connected peculiarities of the composition of domestic demand in these countries (the relative importance of 'luxury goods'), is also a commonplace. In fact, Amin's analysis of the causes of the composition of domestic demand in the LDCs is quite 'neoclassical' in nature—that is, expressed in terms of income and relative price effects. And Amin's points about the lack of institutions to deal effectively with the external relations—such as intenational transport and marketing, and the handling of technology transfer—are also rather conventional observations.

In other words, all three points made by Amin about domestic peculiarities of the LDCs are clearly rather generally accepted by development economists, and it is possible to handle them analytically by conventional methods of analysis, provided appropriate consideration is given to institutional factors in specific countries. I cannot see that Amin gets out anything 'extra' by his Marxist terminology—except a leap to premature policy conclusions and assertions about the future, to be discussed below.

IV POLICY CONCLUSIONS

I assume that Amin's main policy recommendations are that the LDCs should turn to national autarchy and to some (authoritarian?) version of socialism. By contrast, the conventional recommendation based on the same empirical observations would probably be that it is important that *institutional reforms, changes in attitudes* and *redistribution of assets* precede, or at least run parallel with per capita growth of GNP. The potential usefulness of this strategy is illustrated, I believe, by countries like Japan, South Korea and Taiwan, where both institutional changes and redistribution of assets—such as land and human capital—came quite early in the modernisation process. As a consequence, these countries have been able to combine a rapid growth with a rather even distribution of income and wealth. As these countries also happen to be rather outward-looking—in particular South Korea and Taiwan— perhaps it is reasonable to hypothesise that it is the lack of *domestic* institutional reforms and *domestic* redistribution of assets, rather than an externally oriented strategy, that often results in an unequal distribution of the gains of per capita growth in a great number of LDCs.

V ASSERTIONS ABOUT THE FUTURE

However, what makes a conventional economist, like myself, particularly dissatisfied with Amin's discussion is not his policy conclusions, but rather the self-confident assertions about the future of the world. Amin obviously wants to give the impression that he *knows* what the rest of us think can only be guessed about the far distant future. For instance, Amin states not only that a capitalist development in the LDCs is impossible, but also that the LDCs are bound for some (undefined) socialism (pp. 535 and 540), and that only a collectivisation of agriculture can solve the problems of the farm sector in the LDCs—in *all* of the LDCs, I imagine. (I assume that it is not the experiences of Soviet agriculture that lie behind this last assertion.) It is a puzzle to me how such assertions can be made without even presenting the assumptions and mechanisms that would generate the asserted conclusions. The conclusions and the assumptions seem to coincide!

Moreover, I do not know how Amin's deterministic philosophy of history can be reconciled with his statement, at another place in the paper (p. 544), that what counts in history are the 'unexpected accidents'!

VI   GENERAL COMMENTS

In general Samir Amin is, in my judgement, a victim of the temptation to make *premature generalisations* about 'grand' aspects of the development process in the LDCs, that is by making generalisations before enough theoretical and empirical knowledge has been generated. This deficiency, which plagues much of the literature on LDCs, is particularly striking in Amin's case as he, contrary to some other 'overgeneralisers', does not in his paper even present a model from which the conclusions can be derived by generally accepted rules of deduction, and as some of his assertions are so obviously inconsistent with the development of a number of LDCs during the last two decades. At least, it would have been useful if Amin had told the reader on what points his (implicit) model deviates from some well-known analyses of the LDCs, such as the analyses by Arthur Lewis and Gunnar Myrdal. As Amin's paper stands, it has to be characterised as an exercise in political rhetoric rather than economic and social research.

However, to end on a positive note, I think that Amin's paper—unintentionally no doubt—makes a strong case for relying on more analytical research methods—empirical work as well as explicit theoretical model-building. In recent years many economists, including myself, have been complaining about 'overformalisation' by some model-building economists. However, Amin's paper certainly (indirectly) illustrates the importance of using explicit and possibly formalised models—if these models catch relevant factors and if they can be, and *are* subject to empirical confrontations.

ENDNOTE

1. It looks, occasionally, as if Amin in his criticism of outward-looking strategies is in fact criticising import-substitution policies, which economists usually call 'inward-looking', rather than export-oriented strategies which by conventional standards are regarded as 'outward-looking'.

16 Mutual Interests and the Implications for Reform of the International Economic Order[1]

Richard Jolly (UK)

I INTRODUCTION

There has been a decided shift in the last two or three years from confrontation to co-operation as the fulcrum on which a point of purchase for the reform of international economic relationships between developed and developing countries is to be found. The emphasis on co-operation has led to a stress on 'mutual interests', the search for areas of specific action and general policy where the interests of North and South, or at least of major groups of countries within the North and the South, overlap.

In some important respects this emphasis on mutual interests in North–South relationships differs from earlier approaches. The post-war approaches to developing countries—or at least the public presentation of such approaches—almost always built on the moral obligations of the rich to assist the poor, though usually recognising a broad enlightened self-interest in doing so. As Kennedy put it in 1960: 'If a free society cannot save the many who are poor, it cannot save the few who are rich'. A decade or so later, Kissinger shifted the emphasis to interdependence, but within a paternalistic frame of broad political-economic interests and US hegemony. The emphasis on mutual interests now stresses common concerns for and common benefits from action at a much more specific level: the South will benefit from X and Y and Z being done, and the North from W, X and Y^1; X is common to both and there is an important subset of common interests between Y

and Y^1. This is something new. It goes beyond but does not replace the former *general* interest which the North is said to have had in the development of the South or the *moral* obligation to aid the process through programmes of development assistance, now renamed development co-operation.

Of the many reasons which may underlie this shift of emphasis, two in particular may be mentioned. First, the frustration and weariness with previous international approaches to development, especially given the apparently miniscule growth of real aid transfers (about 0.7 per cent per year in real terms over the decade until 1976, compared with an increase of two-and-a-half times in private overseas investment) has inevitably led to a search for new ideas and approaches. Part of this has been the search for a new rationale, and hopefully one which will be more effective in convincing governments to act and not merely to make public pledges. Although there is no logical need for the search for a new rationale to imply also a search for new means, or *vice versa*, in fact development assistance, both as the expression of an obligation between rich and poor nations and as a specific means for carrying it out, is tending to be downplayed at the moment in favour of an emphasis on a broader range of actions based on mutual interests.

The second reason for a shift of emphasis to mutual interests is more objective. This relates to the recession and continuing economic problems within the industrial countries and to the greater interdependence within the global economy, particularly growing links between the developed and the developing countries. Taken together, and contrasted with the 1950s or the 1960s, these two features of the 1970s are alleged to lead to a new situation in which North and South have a mutual interest in recovery, of which economic development in the South is a vital component. As President Carter recently put it: 'The industrial nations cannot by themselves bring about world economic recovery. Strong growth and expansion in the developing countries are essential.'[2] Mutual interests in recovery are not merely said to be conjunctural and short-term, but also to relate to a number of structural changes over the medium and longer run, which both North and South will find necessary to seek and promote if their individual economies are to continue to develop and prosper.

II   WHAT DEFINES MUTUAL INTERESTS?

Before turning to specific areas of mutual interest, it is necessary to identify the nature of the interests which concern us and to indicate how the strength of these can be measured, if at all. In what follows, we will primarily concentrate on economic interests and economic measures of them. It is, however, a mistake to imply that these can be rigidly separated from the political and social dimensions of the same issues, with which they are closely intertwined in ways which orthodox economics too readily ignores.

For a mutual interest to exist one needs evidence of more than just a link or an involvement between two countries. One needs evidence of a positive gain to each party from the involvement, in the form of either a benefit shared or of a cost avoided. These define mutual interests in some given situation—but as regards future action, mutual interests refer to the potential of additional benefits or costs avoided, over and above what would otherwise take place.

Defined so generally, mutual interests could cover the whole range of economic activities and transactions, from the completion of an individual economic transaction to the establishment of new international institutions. Although in principle the benefits to each side might be measured in conventional economic terms, the interaction with geo-political factors in practice makes this both difficult and a far from complete representation of the total costs and benefits. Moreover, the net 'additionality' implied by the definition, ('over and above what would otherwise have taken place'), will usually make it impossible to produce any unambiguous measure *ex post*, let alone *ex ante*.

Ambiguity and uncertainty are likely to remain for a more fundamental reason. In the analysis of any particular situation, the results seem to depend as much on the frame of analysis used – the paradigm in the eye of the analyst – as on the facts of the case. For example, neoclassical economists find an element of mutual interest or benefit in virtually all market transactions, providing each party is free to act voluntarily and correctly interprets the broad effect of the transaction on his own interests.[3] In the ideal circumstances of the free market these may seem to be mild conditions, but given world market imperfections they are, in fact, strong and restrictive, as Helleiner has recently shown.[4]

In contrast, Hobson, and later Lenin, saw the search for raw materials, markets and investment opportunities in developing countries as imperialist exploitation, the highest stage of monopoly capitalism. Marxist and neo-Marxist analysts continue in this tradition, in which virtually all relationships between capitalist developed and developing countries must involve an element of exploitation: mutual interests, by definition, cannot exist across class boundaries and, by contrast, exist fundamentally, if not always in recognized form, between labour in different countries. (This, of course, has not prevented much of the trade between socialist countries and the Third World taking place on terms remarkably similar to those of trade between capitalist countries and the Third World – but this, like exceptions to the neo-classical model, is usually considered an empirical point not a theoretical one.)

Somewhat in between these two paradigms is the structuralist school, less formalised, more eclectic but tending to stress structural factors and relationships rather than flexibility and price responsiveness on the one hand or systematic and inevitable exploitation and the power of capital on the other.[5] Its weakness is its lack of general, overarching theory – which makes it too easy to fit the facts of any particular situation.

For both practical and theoretical reasons it is a mistake to ignore these several and different paradigms, as so often is done when analysing issues of international policy. Practically, it is a mistake because these frameworks of thought exercise an important influence on how policy issues and their likely outcome are perceived and analysed – particularly in North/South matters where different paradigms are often dominant among the different regional or national groups involved.[6] Theoretically, it is also a mistake, because, whether one likes it or not, economics is a subject (like crystallography) in which several paradigms co-exist and contrasting but seriously-studied theoretical work and insights are provided by the different major approaches.[7] Especially in matters of international policy-making where these different intellectual traditions and national experiences are also involved, it is highly misleading to ignore these alternative viewpoints, which often have a very direct impact on the decision-makers closely involved in practical negotiation and policy-making, especially when time and data are limited and one must appeal to general principles rather than engage in a direct detailed evaluation of the issue.

Two further points about mutual interests should be made, even if more briefly. The first concerns the choice of time-frame. Our analysis will primarily be concerned with medium- and long-term interests, not short-term. This is obviously desirable if one is concerned with reform over the longer term, and especially with change of institutions and institutional arrangements. However desirable this may be in principle, in practice it involves enormous difficulties in practical policy-making. The conflict between what is desirable in the medium and longer term and the immediate pressures of the short run, whether for action or simply inaction, may frequently be a more important conflict than conflicts of medium-term interest between the different parties concerned. Economists tend to analyse these issues by discounting future costs and benefits as a technical exercise. The issues are much broader, encompassing (as economists have recognised) conflicts between the present and future generations on the one hand, and on the other (as orthodox economists have tended to ignore) defects in the *imaginative* faculty and in the political process of societies, all of which may lead to much greater discounting of the future than concern with the general interest would justify.

The second point is that mutual interests, even over the long term, are rarely unmixed. A number of countries are likely to be involved and, within each country, a number of different parties. There will usually be conflicts of interest as well as mutual gains and benefits. Netting the gains and losses in this situation into a single aggregate for each block of countries or each individual country tends to hide the crucial problems, for several reasons. First, the allocation of gains and losses may in situations of market imperfection be in part determined by access to information and the exercise of bargaining skill and power. Second, the gains and losses may often fall upon different parties, making the question of compensation a vital component for realising potential gains. Compensation then enters into the bargaining process as an additional and highly visible variable influencing the outcome. Third, some of the important costs and benefits are likely to be very difficult to quantify, and almost certainly must be omitted or treated qualitatively. In these circumstances, the existence of quantified welfare gains to both (or all) parties may not be sufficient to produce agreement on a joint move, since any one party may judge that even greater welfare gains may be obtained if he holds out for a settlement on terms that are even more favourable than those at present on offer.

III   SPECIFIC AREAS OF MUTUAL INTERESTS

Sewell, in his pioneering paper 'Can the Rich Prosper Without the Progress of the Poor?'[8] identifies six major areas of contemporary mutual interest between North and South, all concerned with the medium or the long run.[9] In the medium run, over the next decade, he sees three major areas:

  - *liberalisation of international trade,*

- *stabilisation of commodity prices,* and
- *maintenance of a growing transfer of financial resources* from a variety of sources to developing countries in order to continue to service the rising debt-service ratios and avoid any risk of default by major developing countries and thus ensure the stability of the international financial system.

As regards the liberalisation of trade, a recent Brookings study by Cline[10] suggests that the annual welfare gains in the developed countries from a 60 per cent cut in their tariffs would amount to some $8\frac{1}{2}$ billion if both direct and indirect benefits were included. Discounted, the total welfare benefits over time are estimated to be $170 billion, of which $50 billion would accrue to the United States. The indirect economic benefits in this calculation, estimated in value to be about four times larger than the direct benefits, include benefits from (1) economies of scale made possible by larger markets, (2) increased investment and faster growth rates resulting from increased exports, (3) cost-cutting technological change and increased efficiency encouraged by import competition, and (4) lower domestic price inflation resulting from cheaper imports and increased competition. A 60 per cent reduction in existing tariffs in the United States would directly lower the consumer price index by a quarter of one per cent and, depending on secondary effects, could lead to greater reductions or (more probably) a more significant slowing in the rate of price inflation. In other industrial countries where imports form a larger share of consumption, the beneficial price effects could of course be several times greater.

Such positive assessments of the gains from trade are not new, indeed they might be described as the stock-in-trade of neo-classical economists. Giersch's paper in this volume quotes studies by Glisman on the positive gains to Germany if both MFN tariffs and non-tariff barriers to imports of textiles and apparel were eliminated. Static welfare gains for these two measures would total about 0.2 of 1 per cent of GNP. Although 'minor', as Giersch describes them, these gains are positive – indeed almost inevitably so, given a methodology in which greater access to cheaper imports can only increase welfare, not reduce it.

Stabilisation of world commodity prices offers, in principle, some of the same benefits as trade liberalisation: steadier prices could lower inflationary pressures, especially in situations when "ratchet" mechanisms are operating. But quantification is difficult and hazardous, primarily because so central to the calculation are the links assumed, on the one hand between the change in import prices and changes in the general level of consumer or wholesale prices and, on the other hand, the links between these changes in the general level of prices and potential gains in output. Behrman[11] has simulated the effects of buffer stock programmes designed to keep commodity prices within a 15 per cent range of market-determined trend prices over the last quarter century. This has led to estimates that in the United States the gains from lowering inflationary pressure and thus making possible increased employment and higher output over the period 1963–72 could have been as much as 0.1 to 0.9 per cent of GNP for two or three years of the decade, or taking the middle value of the range, a gain of $9 billion (in 1975 prices) for the years in question and a discounted total value of $15 billion over the decade. The gains from price stabilisation to the developed countries in this calculation were three times the size of the $5 billion *direct* gains to the developing countries. Once more, it is possible to argue that in other industrial countries, where consumer prices are more directly affected by import prices than in the United States, the gains from commodity price stabilisation could have been even greater.

The third area of mutual advantage—ensuring a growing transfer of financial resources—is more difficult to quantify. Yet financial instability is undoubtedly a significant risk at present, and the reduction of this risk and the avoidance of major financial difficulties could be of substantial benefit, given the considerable exposure of some of the major banks and their dependence on Third World countries for an important share of earnings, especially in the United States.

As regards the longer run, Sewell identifies three crucial areas for action offering 'potential for mutual gains from global efficiency' if both rich and poor countries could together tackle certain systemic global problems: food, energy and population.

As regards *food production*, Sewell follows the earlier argument of Grant[12] that the industrial countries of the Northern Hemisphere have a direct interest in increasing food production in developing countries in order to offset somewhat their present extreme dependence on food exports and food aid from the North, 90 per cent of which comes from the United States and Canada. By 1990, it is estimated that the demand for foodgrains in developing countries will increase by some 350 million tons (over 1970; nearly one-and-a-half times current US production). Over the same period, demand in the developed countries is likely to increase by some 200 million tons. Without offsetting measures, these two developments are likely to add greatly to US export demand, exerting a strong upward pressure on prices, which are already projected to increase because of the rising costs of key inputs like fertiliser and the levelling off of yields on account of marginal land being brought into cultivation.

The mutual interest of the industrial countries in seeing the developing countries become more self-sufficient lies, according to this line of thinking, in the avoidance of sharp increases in grain prices, by increasing production relatively more in developing countries where marginal returns to fertiliser and other energy-intensive inputs are often four or five times higher than in the industrial countries. Although it is difficult to quantify the gains from such an approach, Grant has suggested that without such measures cost increases in US grain production and distribution could be as high as 50 to 100 per cent within a decade.[13] Although the direct effect on retail prices would be much smaller than that, the benefit, if inflation were reduced and employment raised, could be considerable.

As regards *energy*, the industrial countries have for several years clearly recognised the competing demands on energy rerources, and the risk that if nothing is done to promote a global co-operative effort, the combined needs of the developing and developed countries will lead to severe shortages of supply and to further increases in the price of petroleum. A mutual interest can be identified in an alternative approach which would entail the developed countries assisting the developing countries to develop their own sources of energy and in adopting energy strategies that do not rely exclusively on petroleum and, indeed, that help them to move directly to the post-petroleum energy technologies of the future. Technologies relying on renewable sources of energy, including solar, would be particularly relevant for developing countries because these countries do not for the most part have the massive investments in petroleum-oriented energy infrastructures that mark the industrial nations; many of them have more sunlight than the industrial countries, making solar energy a more reliable source; their climatic conditions permit faster growth of vegetation for firewood and biogasification; and the decentralised nature of renewable energy makes it an ideal energy source for programmes of small-scale rural development.

This argument can usefully be expanded to take account of the differing interests of the OPEC and NOPEC (non-oil-exporting) developing countries. The former have a clear long-run interest in using their oil revenues over a transition period to diversify their economies, in the meantime generating oil revenues sufficient to meet the cost of imports and build up some external assets, but not past the point when their prospective returns on oil in the ground exceed their returns on external assets. This gives them an interest in supporting measures to discover and diversify energy sources in other developing countries— though not an unmixed one since they also have a monopolistic interest in limiting the number of oil exporters. In this, their interests clearly overlap with the interests of the NOPEC countries themselves, as well with those of the developed countries. In the same way, all these groups of countries have overlapping though not identical interests with respect to conservation measures.

Although interests may overlap with respect to the broad lines of production and diversification, they can and do diverge with respect to prices, especially in the short run. With inelastic elasticities, revenue can be raised by reducing oil supply, a desirable combination from an OPEC point of view since, *ceteris paribus*, it would add both to revenue and preserve oil reserves in the ground for the longer term. But from the viewpoint of oil importing countries, such price increases are clearly not in their general interest.[14]

Finally, Sewell recognizes a third area of long-run mutual interest in *population* and migration, in which both poor and rich countries have direct concerns: poor countries, in order to limit the claims on the resources needed to meet the basic human needs of their growing populations; rich countries for reasons of 'both global justice and equality' and because 'the resulting stresses and strains on the globe's political, economic, social and physical environment are likely to pose a number of almost insurmountable difficulties before the end of the century and beyond'. Illegal immigration into the United States, Western Europe or the Middle East is identified as one immediate manifestation of just such problems, the long-run solution to which requires active rural development programmes within the countries concerned, which offer to potential emigrants the prospect of achieving a decent life in their own countries.

Other areas of mutual interests between developing and developed countries can be identified and have been by other analysts, for example:

(1) To develop new sources and ensure regular supplies of raw materials from developing countries.

(2) To expand research on and ensure the free flow of technology, especially of technologies which are 'appropriate' to Third World development.

(3) To maintain co-operation in management of the 'global commons' such as the oceans and seabeds.

(4) To expand private investment in developing countries.

(5) To formulate international measures for more effective 'positive' social regulation of multinational enterprises.

(6) To protect the environment and introduce positive measures to move towards environmentally self-sustaining patterns of development.

(7) To introduce various measures for the more effective macro-management of the world economy.

Rather than elaborate on these here, it may be helpful to attempt to set all the potential areas of mutual interest in a broader framework, in order to clarify the analytical issues involved, to assess their validity and to consider how the framework might be used to generate further specific examples of mutual interest. One must also ask: why, if mutual interests are so clear, are they so often not realised?

Essentially, the seven areas of mutual interest identified are all cases where the allocation or use of resources is inefficient within the world economy, considered as a single, global unit. The gains are those which could follow from the following factors.

GREATER GLOBAL EFFICIENCY

This is in the sense of moving over time to a position of increased production and incomes through greater efficiency in the allocation of world economic resources, by expanding production in countries where marginal returns are higher. This argument is perhaps clearest in the case of food production where the expansion of Third World output is argued expressly on the grounds that the marginal returns to additional fertiliser and other inputs are four or five times higher in food-importing developing countries than in the food-exporting industrial ones. But the argument of greater global efficiency also underlies at least part of the case for trade liberalisation, which would lead to greater efficiency in the allocation of industry, for greater investment in energy production in developing countries, and presumably also for other areas of investment in developing countries.

GREATER STABILITY OF PRICES

There is expressly the gain to be obtained from commodity price stabilisation, the benefits of which come from both lower prices in the short run and the moderation of inflationary pressures over the longer run, which—it is argued—make it possible for governments to pursue policies resulting in lower levels of unemployment and higher levels of output and income. Greater stability, in addition, reduces risk and uncertainty, thus also encouraging investment and higher output. This argument is also relevant in the cases of agriculture, energy and the argument for maintaining the flow of finance to avoid monetary instability in the Third World financial markets.

GREATER SECURITY OR LESS VULNERABILITY IN SUPPLY

This covers two types of vulnerability. There is first a vulnerability from natural causes, for instance from weather affecting food production, in which excessive dependence on North American production in world trade makes all food-importing countries disproportionately dependent on and vulnerable to weather conditions in the North American continent. A broader distribution of supplies would introduce an ecological diversification spreading the risk and greatly reducing instability from natural causes. Less risk and greater stability have an economic value, in making possible a better allocation of resources on a more continuous basis and in saving resources which consumers and producers may otherwise use to guard against or offset risk and uncertainty.

There is also a political component underlying potential vulnerability. This appears particularly in the case of energy, in which diversification of sources of supply makes importing nations less vulnerable to monopolistic or oligopolistic action by a limited group of exporters.

SLOWING POPULATION GROWTH

This, *ceteris paribus*, ensures a higher ratio of resources to population, thereby making possible higher income per capita and less demand for key scarce resources. In the long run, the case for moderating the growth of population in the Third World must be recognised to be in part related to political vulnerability.

The above four changes would, over the longer run, all affect the structure of the world economy, though the second and third would also influence its functioning and management in the shorter term. It may, however, be useful to identify more efficient management of the global economy as a separate area of mutual interests, in which both

North and South have overlapping interests in seeing improvements. Thus we have a fifth area.

INSTITUTIONS AND MECHANISMS FOR IMPROVED
MACRO-MANAGEMENT OF THE WORLD ECONOMY

This would cover particular matters related to the maintenance of full employment demand and steady growth but also to a potentially broader set of concerns with harmonisation of national policy in ways which would increase national benefits. It could also cover issues of equity, resource transfers and more balanced representation in the management of international institutions, argued on the grounds that these would be conditions for obtaining effective worldwide support for any form of management in which the richer countries could reasonably meet their own objectives.

IV   CRITICAL ASSUMPTIONS UNDERLYING THE MUTUAL INTEREST OF NORTH AND SOUTH IN STRUCTURAL CHANGE

The main underlying assumption in each of the points above is that certain basic elements of a single interdependent global economy already exist but the potential benefits of these have yet to be realised. Too little production of food or energy or industrial goods takes place in the developing countries as a group (or in some subgroups of them, as for the non-oil-exporting countries), where marginal returns are higher or where further production could reduce risks and vulnerabilities. Population is also growing too fast in the poorer parts of the globe, giving all countries a long-run interest in seeing the rate moderated.

It is assumed that the developing countries have an interest in righting these imbalances, since they imply greater production, more stable prices or additional resources for developing countries as a group. The interest of the developed countries is via the higher returns, the lower prices, the savings on risk and vulnerabilities and the higher resource and capital-labour ratios which such structural changes would make possible in the longer run.

Put in this general form, it becomes clear that a number of critical assumptions underlie the argument, and that even when specific sectors have been identified some additional conditions must be met before implementation can be assumed to lead necessarily to the benefits envisaged.

Most important, distributional issues between and within countries of both North and South must be explicitly considered and measures to ensure an acceptable outcome incorporated. Within the North, major losing groups within countries must be compensated or encouraged and enabled to move into new activities more effectively than at present, if the global structural changes are to be politically feasible. Within the South, more effective distributional policies will be needed within many developing countries if increases of production are to lead to rising real incomes and living standards for the mass of the population and not merely for a limited stratum at the top. But unlike the adjustment mechanisms in the North, the existence of adequate distributional mechanisms *within* countries of the South is unlikely to be a condition for implementation of the structural changes. In contrast, some mechanisms for ensuring at least a minimum of control on the allocation of increased production of, say, food or energy, between countries of the South may be necessary, particularly if international agreement on the measures is needed.

The emphasis on the distribution of the benefits of these structural changes between different countries of the South (or the North) can scarcely be overstressed. Neither South nor North is a homogeneous group and, as experience with oil has shown, the incidence of important changes of price or production level can vary enormously, with strongly negative effects to some countries flowing from positive gains from others. Some distributional mechanisms and international commitments used in clear support of international measures of structural change would be desirable, to encourage general support of the measures. Packages of policies would also help to diversify the effects and expand the groups of gaining countries.

At the same time, one can note that in the examples of food and energy, some potential distributional conflicts are avoided, since the mutual interest identified implies expansion of production in the South but not necessarily contraction in the North.

Minimal influences on allocation and distribution between countries exist already, of course, to the extent that countries exercise control over imports and exports across their borders and over national production. At the very least, measures to encourage structural change in favour of greater production within developing countries must assume that participating countries will use such influences and controls to their own advantage. But there are limits to the effectiveness of such national measures and there are potential gains from pursuing a more co-ordinated approach among some or all countries within the North or South.

This, however, is a key point on which both analysts and policy-makers diverge in their judgements about the possibilities and probable effectiveness of policy. Their judgements are likely to be closely related to the analytical paradigms mentioned earlier in Section II, in which some analysts will assume that with few exceptions market outcomes are acceptable, and others will see a major need for strengthening the bargaining capacity and sources of information available to developing countries. A critical question for policy will therefore be appropriate measures to strengthen the capacity of individual countries to bargain more effectively internationally to ensure that they obtain a reasonable share of the benefits of additional production or additional flows of investment or other resources. Although much depends on the internal organisation and economic capacity of each country individually, international action can help to strengthen the capacity of individual countries or groups of countries.

Helleiner in his earlier-quoted study has identified a number of the respects in which the present international economic system operates inadequately, resulting in consistently biased outcomes in relation to the interests and needs of the developing countries. International and national action to deal with such points is needed.

A further issue concerns the identification and agreement on specific measures of international structural change. Many, of course, have taken place and will continue to do so, with or without specific measures of national and international policy to encourage them. With respect to practical policy formulation, I see no alternative to a pragmatic approach: an assessment, perhaps a more formal monitoring, of the broad process of international structural change with the specific study and identification of potential area of further change which might be in the mutual interests of North and South if the costs to injured countries could be compensated. This underlines the importance of devising acceptable and effective measures of international as well as national compensation.

Finally, structural change cannot only be concerned with geographical shifts in the existing pattern of production but also of changes within this pattern which a more international approach might make possible. The most important example of such changes at present—perhaps better described as 'the most flagrant example of current failure of international co-operation'—is the nuclear arms race and the vast sums of money devoted each year to armaments and military expenditures. Each year this activity absorbs some 5 per cent of global GNP (some $400 billion in 1978) as well as contributing a measure of vulnerability which could literally destroy the whole world economy. The gains from at least a measure of reduction in this excessive and dangerous use of resources represent only part of the broader gains from a more harmonious and co-ordinated approach to global interests. Measures of disarmament should be a specific goal incorporated within an international framework of *economic* structural change.

V MORE EFFICIENT MACRO-MANAGEMENT OF THE WORLD ECONOMY

Greater measures of price stabilisation and security in supplies and some reduction in vulnerability are potentially important goals for the better short- to medium-term management of the global economy. It is important to stress *potential*, because two key assumptions underlying the argument are that policy options exist which would in fact be successful in reducing price fluctuations and vulnerabilities and, secondly, that such reductions would not be offset by increases in supply fluctuations or other elements adding to vulnerabilities of the international economic system. Put in terms of the conditions for successfully realising the potential benefits, this means that some mechanisms or institutions will be needed to ensure that these possible offsetting outcomes would not occur.

Central to an evaluation of the benefits to the North of stabilisation of commodity (and possibly other) prices is the question: how much would a reduction in inflationary pressures enable governments to follow more expansionary policies leading to higher levels of employment and thus of output and incomes? It is useful to distinguish two polar answers to this question. The first is that it would have no effect, on the grounds that the level of unemployment is set as a basic target by governments' macro-policies in relation to major political and economic considerations and would not be affected by rather small changes in the level of prices and inflation rates. The second answer would imply some important effect, on the grounds that the rate of unemployment is the resultant of a sensitive tradeoff by governments between unemployment and inflation and that any reduction in the latter would affect the former. The second approach is, in fact, the one taken by Behrman in calculating the economic benefits of stabilising commodity prices: he applies an estimated reduction in prices to an assumed Philip's curve relationship in order to obtain a potential increment of employment consistent with maintaining the original rate of price increase. This increment in employment is then used to estimate the associated increase in output, assuming an 'Okun's Law' relationship. The estimated benefits are thus highly sensitive to the existence of unemployment at the base period.

There need be no doubt about the widespread existence of unemployment and underutilised capacity within the OECD economies at present (though some have doubted whether this is true of the export industries for which demand would be stimulated if expansionary measures were to be set in train).

More debatable is the extent to which a reduction of prices and inflationary pressures from the side of imports would lead governments to adopt more expansionary measures. Clearly the situation differs among the various OECD countries, both in terms of government priorities and responsiveness and in terms of the economic and political context, especially the extent to which import prices are, and are seen as, an important factor in influencing inflationary pressures.

The existence of unemployment, however, introduces a much more important measure of potential gain from the better macro-management of the world economy. Underutilisation of capacity within the OECD area was estimated in mid-1978 to be some $200 billion per year. The gain from measures for reducing this margin could be very considerable. Measures which would expand economic activity in developing countries could thereby act as an important stimulus to activity within the developed countries themselves.

Lindbeck, in his important and broad-ranging article on 'economic dependence and interdependence in the industrialised world' (Lindbeck 1978) has identified some of the major ways in which increased international interdependence has altered the effectiveness of national economic policy instruments: changes in domestic aggregate demand would as a rule be expected to have smaller effects on the domestic economy than before, while changes in relative prices between countries and changes in aggregate demand in other countries would as a rule have greater effects than before. At the same time, uncertainty about the effects of changes in domestic and foreign policy instruments would be expected to increase, as will uncertainty about the effects of non-policy shocks and about the character (distribution) of such disturbances. These changes enhance the potential gains from policy co-ordination with other countries, as well as raising the effectiveness of policy instruments relying on relative price changes and of 'packages' of policy instruments which make possible some pooling of risks.

Although Lindbeck applied these conclusions to the co-ordination of policy among the industrialised countries, the same arguments can also be applied to the coordination of policy between the industrialised and developing countries, where for similar and perhaps additional reasons, linkages have also increased.[15] From the viewpoint of the developed countries, co-ordination of policy with the developing countries is still of less significance than co-ordination of policy among the developed countries, yet in particular sectors—as experience with oil or in sectors like textiles or footwear clearly shows—and even in overall policy, the developing countries as a group now can have a significant impact on the economies of the developed countries.

Recent calculations have illustrated the extent to which an increase in the growth of the developing countries might at the present time stimulate expansion in the industrialised countries. A 1976 UNCTAD report, based on the Link model, estimated that an increase of 1 per cent in LDC growth would raise OECD country GNP by about one-third of 1 per cent and that additional capital transfers of about $40 billion to the developing countries would be required to stimulate this.

This may somewhat overestimate the immediate effects, since time-lags are ignored and the Link model has no significant supply constraints. At the same time, it may overestimate the extent to which additional capital transfers are required to stimulate additional growth in the developing countries. In some developing countries, foreign exchange is not the bottleneck to expansion. Moreover, if such transfers were concentrated on the non-oil developing countries, 3 per cent growth might involve no more than $8 to $12 billion of additional imports requiring financing from abroad. Assuming an OECD multiplier of two-and-a-half and that 80 per cent of such imports came from the OECD area, this would generate an additional $16 to $24 billion of economic activity within the OECD area, or some 0.35 to 0.5 of 1 per cent of GNP of which some 0.2 to 0.3 of 1 per cent might be expected to result in the first year.[16]

Discussion of such calculations has often been polarised around the issue of whether or not they demonstrate that the developing countries have or could become the 'engine of growth', sufficient by itself to take the developed countries out of recession. This is unfortunate and misleading, since with underutilisation of resources equivalent to some $200 billion, the calculations clearly indicate that expanding growth within the developing countries by itself will be a far from sufficient solution to the problems of recession in the OECD area. But the calculations provide at least an order of magnitude of the extent to which measures leading to expansion in the developing countries could provide a useful stimulus to the developed countries. In quantitative terms, the benefits to the OECD countries from such measures could well be two or three times the estimated welfare gains from either trade liberalisation or commodity price stabilisation.[17]

Yet in quantitative terms, a 5 per cent measure of disarmament would release each year resources valued at $20 billion, of which $17 billion would be released in the developed countries (including Eastern Europe). This would be comparable to the potential gains from a major stimulus to third world growth and far exceeding the estimated gains from trade liberalisation or commodity price stabilisation.

It may be helpful in summary to put together the figures quoted:

Estimated welfare gains per year to developed countries from:

—5 per cent measure of disarmament	$17 billion, including Eastern Europe
—increase in **OECD GNP** consequent upon additional transfer of about $10 billion to LDCs	$20 billion
—60 per cent liberalisation in trade tariffs	$1.7 billion, but a possible total of $8½ billion including indirect effects
—measures for greater commodity price stabilisation	averaging $2–$3 billion

Leibenstein, in his celebrated article in 1966 on "X Efficiency versus Allocative Efficiency"[18] showed how greater X efficiency in the use of inputs in production would usually increase output substantially more than the estimated gains from greater allocative efficiency. It might be helpful to generalise the point by considering three types of efficiency, X, Y and Z, in addition to allocative efficiency:

X efficiency—greater output from existing quantum of inputs
Y efficiency—greater output by reducing Keynesian deficiency of demand

Z efficiency—greater welfare by changes in the pattern of output (for example, in such areas as armaments).

In the examples given, movements towards greater Y and Z efficiency would each offer welfare gains of some \$20 billion, an order of magnitude greater than the gains offered from international improvements in allocative efficiency. The economics profession might itself make a bigger contribution to an improved economic world order if more of its time and effort was devoted to issues of Y and Z rather than allocative efficiency.

VI POLICY-MAKING FRAME FOR A NORTH–SOUTH APPROACH BASED ON MUTUAL INTERESTS

Greater interdependence within the world economy has indicated a number of areas for substantial gains from changes in the economic relationships between developed and developing countries. But for such changes to be realised, substantial improvements in the management of interdependence within the world economy will be needed, particularly with respect to measures enabling and encouraging developing countries to play a fuller and more supportive role within the international economic system.

Three areas of policy can be identified which together may provide a framework in which specific measures can be set.

(1) Measures for the more effective *management of interdependence* in the short to medium term.

(2) Measures of *structural change* over the medium to longer term, particularly with respect to sectors of production where both industrial and developing countries recognise a mutual interest in achieving a better balance in the pattern of world production.

(3) A commitment from the developed countries to some new programme of *development co-operation* which would go beyond the strict needs of economic interdependence (a) to strengthen the capacity of developing countries to participate more equitably within the world economy, and (b) to provide for accelerated development in poorer parts of the world, if possible, with some broad frame of objectives for the next decade or two.

This would provide a pragmatic frame for working out specific policies, building on areas of mutual interests identified in this paper—and possibly others. It would provide a practical approach for pursuing more effective management of interdependence and of structural change, but recognising—as in item (3)—that certain additional measures would be necessary as a condition for obtaining support for the broad approach. These measures would be needed to strengthen the capacity of developing countries to participate less inequitably within the world economy and also to ensure that all the poorer countries have at least the minimum international resources required for accelerated development. This would openly and in a further way deal with the distributional problem earlier identified as critical.

Item (3) is much broader than the 'old aid approach'. Although it acknowledges that mutual interests alone will be an insufficient basis on which to build a set of international policies adequate to provide for accelerated development within all developing countries, it is complementary to and an integral part of the mutual interests approach, not a contradiction to it. The broad framework proposed rests directly on the mutual interests which North and South have in the better management of interdependence and measures of structural change. Development co-operation on a new basis would be a supplement where needed, a recognition of the long-term interest in an economically more balanced global economy, as well as a recognition that the avoidance of negative-sum outcomes may be as important as the achievement of positive-sum ones.

If fully worked out with imagination and vision, such an approach could—and ought to—go far beyond the narrow calculation of immediate benefits from exploiting obvious imperfections in the existing economic order. It may not be rigorous cost-benefit economics—but it is well within the great tradition of human discovery and leadership to realise that mankind's affairs can be organised on a larger canvas and in a more effective manner than has been achieved so far. In this respect, the calculations summarised in this paper and the specific benefits identified are on the larger horizon, a pale glimpse of the gains which mankind might realise if international economic affairs could be ordered on a more harmonious basis than has so far been achieved. Technology has provided the capacity. Limited vision, nationalistic attitudes and the lack of political will hold us back. It is not for economists alone to chart the way forward—but as a profession, we must be wary lest our professional concerns prevent ourselves or others from indicating what might be possible and the costs of not realising it.

Towards the end of the Second World War, Keynes in barely fifteen pages outlined the framework for what might then have become—and even in the form adopted became in part—a new international economic order. It contrasted sharply with the order of the 1930s and provided the international framework in which the most sustained economic expansion in the history of the world subsequently took place. This framework has now collapsed, inadequate not only in terms of developments within the industrial countries but outmoded in terms of the political and economic context, in which more than seventy additional countries have joined the international community, exceeding in number and with markedly differing characteristics from those existing at the time when the Bretton Woods system was inaugurated. These goals and requirements need to be expressly and specifically incorporated into a new international system. Ultimately the gains to the industrial countries, to the North, in doing so must be assessed in terms of the gains from human solidarity within a global context, within a dynamic and not a static perspective. The consequences could be much larger than those of the Marshall Plan or the ending of colonial empires. Ultimately, the mutual interests of North and South can only be assessed against a perspective as broad as this.

ENDNOTES

1. This paper leans heavily on work and ideas developed during six months with the OECD in Paris. It owes much to many stimulating experiences and discussions with Secretariat members and government representatives—but the views and interpretations of the paper are those of the author and not necessarily those of the Organisation itself. I am also grateful for comments made at the Saltsjöbaden seminar, especially from Professor Komiya, and for written comments from Göran Ohlin.
2. In his speech in Caracas, Venezuela (March 1978).
3. Note that the neoclassical conditions for a transaction offering positive benefit to each party are less restrictive than those for avoiding exploitation. See Cooper (1977). For a broad-ranging critique from a structuralist position of neoclassical approaches to international policy, see Balogh and Balacs (1974).
4. Helleiner (1978).
5. I have elaborated more systematically on these three paradigms in relating to development issues in Jolly (forthcoming) and more briefly in H. Chenery et al. (1974). Jagdish Bhagwati (1977) in his introduction distinguishes four "ideologies": benign neglect, malign neglect, benign intent and malign intent. The first and third of these closely correspond to neoclassical doctrine, the second to structuralist and the fourth to Marxist or neo-Marxist. I prefer the term 'paradigm' to 'ideology', since it relates the views more clearly to analytical frameworks which tend to dominate academic research and teaching. I also think it a mistake to distinguish

sharply between benign neglect and benign intent ideologies, since intellectually they have many analytical points in common. In contrast, the difference between the malign neglect and malign intent ideologies is not in their distinction between neglect and intent, but in the variables and structural assumptions which they assume are central.

6. Although in some cases this is related to the different intellectual traditions of the nations involved, this is clearly inadequate to explain the differences of position and rationale one observes. It is noteworthy that many of the key analysts and leaders on North/South matters attended the same universities, often at the same time, and with the same teachers. Yet, in many cases, they have since developed systematically different views and positions on economic matters—perhaps a point worthy of more thought and attention than it often seems to receive.

7. In this respect Kuhn (1962) tended to overstate the generality of scientific experience by concentrating on those branches of science in which the co-existence of different mainstream paradigms is rare.

8. Sewell (1978) and (forthcoming).

9. This point deserves emphasis because a good part of the criticisms which an earlier version of the paper attracted relate to the argument whether action along the lines proposed will by itself be sufficient to reflate the rich countries out of their current recession, an argument which was never central to the paper nor even, in this oversimple and unqualified form, part of it.

10. Cline, et al. (1978).

11. Behrman (1977).

12. Grant (1977), drawing on the study by the US National Academy of Sciences, 1977, and thinking of the World Food Conference, 1974.

13. Between 1972 and 1974–75 a 3 per cent shortfall in grain production led to more than a 300 per cent increase in prices, a result reflecting not only the elasticities of the basic demand and supply functions but the fact that the 'self-sufficiency' agricultural policies of many countries make the world market a marginal one which has to bear the brunt of the adjustment. Simantov (personal communication) has suggested that, for various reasons, future demand for food and future price increases are unlikely to be as large as those estimated but does not disagree with the direction of the argument, except to stress that increases in agricultural output in developing countries ought to be supported as much for their own sake as for the self-interest of the OECD countries.

14. The fact that this option has not been taken since the major initial oil price increases would appear to reflect both political pressure and some degree of broader self-interest among oil producers not to create economic problems for the industrial countries which may have undesirable economic and political repercussions on the world economy and thus on themselves as oil producers. It may also reflect uncertainty about the longer-term repercussions of higher real oil prices. The net effect is that the price of oil in terms of industrial goods has fallen—as have the surpluses of the major OPED producers.

15. Most of the reasons for increased international integration also apply to the links between many of the industrialised and a number of developing

countries: the greater integration of markets made possible by re-volutionary developments of technology in the communication of me-ssages; the internationalization of entrepreneurship and technology and hence the expansion of direct foreign investment; an increase in the trade shares within practically all private production sectors; the fact that the most important *external effects* of production and consumption today are, like air and ocean pollution, external to nations, including increased international 'demonstration' effects. There is also within developing countries, as in the developed, a greater general awareness of international interdependence and of the 'tension between international economic forces and domestic policy ambitions, because domestic political objectives have become so much more numerous, detailed and ambitious'. In one respect, that of the moves towards *political* independence, whether *de jure* or *de facto*, policy-making and attitudes in the Third World may in certain respects be less effectively co-ordinated with that of the metropolitan powers than two or three decades earlier. But one suspects that this measure of greater independence is far outweighed by the increased links of interdependence, following upon the substantial growth of the economies of developing countries along patterns characterised by the factors identified by Lindbeck.

At the same time the impact of these factors is far from uniform, particularly across the wide spectrum of different developing countries. It could well be that the differences between different countries in these respects has made interdependence a new source of inequality of income and power between countries.

16. These calculations draw on a personal communication from Guy Erb and make use of OECD Secretariat calculations.
17. Note that this conclusion is not so dependent on the existence of high levels of unemployment in the OECD area as might first appear. Three quarters of the benefits of trade liberalisation and most of the benefits earlier estimated from commodity price stabilisation also result from reducing unemploy-ment. Only if unemployment were to be effectively abolished would trade liberalisation offer the largest potential welfare gains – and even then, far less than a measure of disarmament.
18. Leibenstein (1966).

REFERENCES

Balogh, T. and Balacs, P., 'Fact and Fancy in International Economic Relations', *World Development*, vol. 1, nos 1 and 2 (1974) pp. 76–92.
Behrman, J. E., *International Commodity Agreements: an Evaluation of the UNCTAD Integrated Commodity Programme*, Monograph No. 9, N.I.E.O. Series (Washington D.C.: Overseas Development Council, 1977).
Bhagwati, J., Introduction to *The New International Economic Order: The North–South Debate* (Cambridge, Mass.: M.I.T. Press, 1977).

Chenery, H. et al., *Redistribution with Growth*, (Oxford: Oxford University Press, 1974).

Cline, W. R., Kwanabe, N., Kronsjo, T. O. M. and Williams, T., *Trade Negotiations in the Tokyo Round: A Quantitative Assessment* (Washington, D.C.: The Brookings Institution, 1978).

Cooper, R. N., 'A New International Economic Order for Mutual Gain', *Foreign Policy*, no. 26 (1977), pp. 60–120.

Grant, J. P., 'Rural Development in the Third World and the Impact on Fertilizer Demand', (mimeo), drawing on the National Academy of Sciences, *World Food & Nutrition Study* (1977) and the World Food Conference (1974).

Helleiner, G. K., *World Market Imperfections and the Developing Countries*, Occasional Paper No. 11 (Washington D.C.: Overseas Development Council, 1978).

Jolly, R., 'Restructuring the Industrialized Economies: A Positive Sum Game?', ISS 25th Anniversary Conference Papers (The Hague: forthcoming).

Kuhn, T. S., in *The Structure of Scientific Revolutions*, Encyclopedia of Unified Science 2:2 (Chicago: 1962).

Leibenstein, H., 'X Efficiency versus Allocative Efficiency', *American Economic Review* (1966).

Lindbeck, A., 'Economic Dependence and Interdependence in the Industrial World', in *Marshall Plan to Global Interdependence. New Challenges for the Industrialized Nations* (Paris: OECD, 1978).

Sewell, D. O., 'Can the Rich Prosper without the Progress of the Poor?', (mimeo) (Washington: Overseas Development Council, July 1978).

Sewell, D. O., *Agenda for Action 1979* (forthcoming), earlier version presented to the North South Roundtable of the Society for International Development, Rome, May 1978.

Comments

Ryutaro Komiya (Japan)

Professor Jolly's paper deals with a very important policy issue, and appears highly relevant and reasonable. It seems difficult to argue against what is proposed. Yet, the paper lacks persuasiveness, at least to me. It is partly because my own view, or it might be better to say my prejudice, on the North–South problem is perhaps fundamentally different from Professor Jolly's. The paper is somewhat like some documents prepared by the Secretariat of an international organisation: although what is stated appears reasonable and desirable from an international point of view, after reading it those who must be persuaded remain unconvinced and do not begin to take the action proposed by the documents. The question to be asked in such a situation is why the readers are not persuaded and do not begin to take the action proposed.

When looking at a national economy, especially one in which political democracy prevails, the image of an economy in which the overall efficiency is to be maximised and income distributed in an equitable way is not entirely unrealistic. It is a fiction, but that fiction has a certain force in public discussion of economic policy and in politics. But such an image is not applicable, in my view, to the world economy consisting of a large number of very jealous sovereign states.

For example, Professor Jolly says that the mutual interest of the North and the South points to increasing food production relatively more in the South, where marginal returns to fertiliser and other inputs are much higher than in the North. But, it is important, from the mutual interests point of view, that the gains from such a programme are distributed. equitably among the participants of the programme. Otherwise the countries concerned will not be motivated to participate in the programme. It is, however, much more difficult to work out a programme which ensures an equitable distribution of gains from it when many sovereign states are involved, than in cases within a national economy. To begin with, the views on what is equitable and what is not differ very much among countries, and especially so between the North and the South. What is considered a very desirable and equitable co-operation programme from the Northern point of view may be totally unacceptable from the Southern one.

Taking up another example, Professor Jolly identifies financial instability as one of the policy areas of mutual interest between the North and the South, and states that the reduction of the risk of financial instability is a substantial benefit, given the considerable exposure of some of the major banks and their dependence on the Southern countries for an important share of profits. I do not feel that such a possibility of major financial difficulties is now very high, but assuming that the North and the South have common interests in reducing the financial instability, a crucial question is: how should the cost of such a programme be borne? If the chief beneficiaries are the American banks, is it not fair that United States or American banks themselves bear a large part of the cost of such a programme? Would it not be unfair to let taxpayers in other countries bear the cost of bailing out American major banks from excessive exposure, from which they have been deriving an important share of profits?

In order to analyse the policy issues such as those taken up in this paper, it is not unimportant, in my view, to understand the political power relationships or the power structure underlying economic policy making. This is true in cases of national economic policies as well, but it is more so when considering international economic issues. In a national case, the above-mentioned fiction that economic efficiency is to be maximised and income distributed most equitably within the economy can be useful in overcoming the resistance or inertia of the power structure, but on the international scene such a fiction is far more unrealistic and its appeal is largely lost.

It is useful in this connection to consider why the growth of real aid transfer from the North to the South has been so small, as Professor Jolly points out. I think there is a trend of diminishing enthusiasm for development aids among OECD countries, especially during the recent deep depression following the oil crisis. In the case of my own country, Japan, for example, I would say that recently the political support for developing aids has probably been diminishing. I would not be surprised if the aid transfers in real terms from the OECD countries will not be increasing in the coming five years as fast as they did in the 1960s.

The shift of the emphasis to mutual interests from moral obligations in the North–South relationship, which is the main theme of Professor Jolly's paper, may be viewed as a response on the part of opinion leaders and international organisations to this trend of diminishing enthusiasm for development programmes.

Undoubtedly the primary reason for this trend of diminishing enthusiasm is stagflation, high unemployment and the large government budget deficits which most OECD governments are confronted with. Most of those in key positions in the policy-making process within OECD countries now feel it difficult to increase appropriation for development aids or co-operation programmes, when heavy demands for public expenditures and for tax reduction from all sorts of domestic pressure groups are making the budget deficit larger and larger. But, I think there are other reasons also.

In OECD countries the policy-makers and politicians must win popular support for policies they propose. Politicians need to win the election and for that purpose they do what the average voters and influential public opinion leaders want them to do. It is not easy for a politician to pursuade the public that development aid is necessary and/or desirable from a world economic point of view.

The power structure within any country has a tendency of maintaining the *status quo*. Whether good or bad, this tendency of behavioural inertia is very strong, not only in OECD countries, but also in the South and even in the communist countries. Those who hold the political power and wealth, whether a dictator or voters in a democracy, want to maintain it and expand it if possible. This comes from the very nature of the power itself and the setup of the power structure. Also, major policy decisions are being made largely on a country-by-country basis. There is a very high barrier or wall of national sovereignty, which stands in the way of international co-operation. Even in the limited area of macro-economic policy, international co-ordination of policies among a small number of major OCED countries has so far proved very difficult.

Professor Jolly proposes an across-the-board 5 per cent reduction in military expenditures which would release resources amounting to 20 billion dollars annually for development purposes. This is very desirable from economic and humanistic points of view. But why just 5 per cent? It would be wonderful if not only a 5 per cent but 20 per cent, 50 per cent or 100 per cent across-the-board reduction in military expenditures could somehow be achieved. I do not think, however, that disarmament can be achieved easily, however desirable it is from an economic welfare point of view.

The international power structure on the one hand, and the

political power relationships within each country, especially in a dictatorial regime, on the other, is such that a dangerously high level of military expenditure is maintained in order to bolster up the *status quo*. At least those in key power positions appear to think that they need to maintain heavy military expenditure, and it is very difficult to change this *status quo*.

One of the reasons why the voters in developed countries are now less enthusiastic than sometime ago about the development aid or the North–South co-operation is that they feel the development programmes in the past have not achieved much of the objectives envisaged in the beginning.

Talking again about Japan, the largest flows of official development aids on a bilateral basis have gone to Indonesia, South Korea and perhaps the Philippines. I think the average Japanese are sceptical about the usefulness of these aids in raising the welfare of common people in recipient countries. On the other hand they feel that the dictatorial regimes and a certain part of the élite class in the recipient countries, and also some Japanese big businesses would have benefited much from the aid programmes. I am here not talking about what actually happened, which almost nobody knows, but about a deep-rooted feeling, prejudice or suspicion among the average Japanese.

Newspapers report from time to time cases of bribing and kickbacks in the South and in Japan which are related to development programmes. Sometimes a part of proceeds of Japanese exports under a development programme was reported to have been used to finance lobbying and other dubious political activity within Japan. This could happen whether the aid is tied or not. The Lockheed scandal in 1975 and the arrest of the former Prime Minister Tanaka shocked the public, and a strong public suspicion was aroused about international transactions involving politics, and the development programme become one of the focuses of such a suspicion.

It is difficult to embark upon an ambitious international development or co-operation programme, unless politicians and policy-makers in major countries can persuade the general public that it is worth while. Politically, the present time does not appear to be very opportune for large-scale, North–South co-operation programmes.

I agree with Professor Jolly that potential gains from co-operation between the North and the South in many of the areas identified in this paper could be very substantial. It is very difficult, however, to turn the potential gains into actual ones. It is easy merely to compute, for example, the tremendous potential gains from raising the per hectare yield of rice in South-east Asia to the present Japanese or Formosan level.

Great difficulty is involved in preparing a programme which is really workable both economically and politically. For that purpose, economists must take into consideration the political power relationships as well, which underlie the policy decision-making processes within and among countries concerned.

Index